2006

Caravan
Camping
Britain & Ireland

CREDITS

This 38th edition published 2006 © Automobile Association Developments Limited 2005 Automobile Association Developments Limited retains the copyright in the current edition ©2005 and in all subsequent editions, reprints and amendments to editions. The information contained in this directory is sourced entirely from the AA's establishment database, Information Research, Hotel Services. All rights reserved. No part of this publication may be reproduced, stored in a retrieval system, or transmitted in any form or by any means - electronic, photocopying, recording or otherwise - unless the written permission of the publishers has been obtained beforehand. This book may not be sold, resold, hired out or otherwise disposed of by way of trade in any form of binding or cover other than that with which it is published, without the prior consent of all relevant publishers. The contents of this publication are believed correct at the time of printing. Nevertheless, the publishers cannot be held responsible for any errors or omissions or for changes in the details given in this guide or for the consequences of any reliance on the information provided by the same. This does not affect your statutory rights. Assessments of the campsites are based on the experience of the AA Caravan & Camping Inspectors on the occasion of their visit(s) and therefore descriptions given in this guide necessarily contain an element of subjective opinion which may not reflect or dictate a reader's own opinion on another occasion. The AA strives to ensure accuracy in this guide at the time of printing. Due to the constantly evolving nature of the subject matter the information is subject to change. The AA will gratefully receive any advice from our readers of any necessary updated information.

To contact us:
Advertisement Sales: advertisingsales@theAA.com
Editorial: lifestyleguides@theAA.com

Picture credits; Front cover, AA World Travel Library/D Forss; Back cover top, AA World Travel Library/E A Bowness; Back cover bottom, AA World Travel Library/R Moss.

Editor: Denise Laing
Feature 'What shall we do today?' by Kate Trew

Typeset and colour organisation by Keenes Repro, Andover
Printed and bound by Printer Trento srl, Italy

Published by AA Publishing, a trading name of Automobile Association Developments Limited, whose registered office is Fanum House, Basing View, Basingstoke, Hampshire RG21 4EA. Registered number 1878835
A CIP catalogue record for this book is available from the British Library
ISBN-10: 0-7495-4711-1
ISBN-13: 978-0-7495-4711-0
A02539

Maps prepared by the Cartography Department of The Automobile Association. Maps © Automobile Association Developments Limited 2005.

This product includes mapping data licensed from Ordnance Survey® with the permission of the Controller of Her Majesty's Stationery Office. © Crown copyright 2005. All rights reserved. Licence number 399221.

This product includes mapping based upon data licensed from Ordnance Survey of Northern Ireland® reproduced by permission of the Chief Executive, acting on behalf of the Controller of Her Majesty's Stationery Office. © Crown copyright 2005. Permit No. 40468.

Republic of Ireland mapping based on Ordnance Survey Ireland Permit No. MP000105 © Ordnance Survey Ireland and Government of Ireland.

CONTENTS

What shall we do today?

By Kate Trew

Waterside Holiday Park, Weymouth

IT'S A QUESTION THAT IS FAMILIAR TO ALL PARENTS HOLIDAYING WITH THEIR CHILDREN, AND ONE THAT IS NOT ALWAYS ANSWERED EASILY. WARM, SUNNY DAYS MIGHT FLOAT BY IN A HAZE OF PLEASURE, BUT COLD, WET ONES CAN SEEM TO GO ON FOR EVER. LUCKY ARE THOSE CHILDREN WHOSE HOBBIES AND TASTES ARE CATERED FOR ON HOLIDAY, AND ARRANGING SUCH A VACATION IS EASIER THAN YOU MIGHT EXPECT. THIS YEAR WE ASKED ALL THE PARKS FEATURED IN THIS GUIDE TO TELL US ABOUT THE ACTIVITIES THEY ORGANISE FOR CHILDREN, ESPECIALLY DURING THE LONG SUMMER BREAK. WE WERE SURPRISED AT THE HUGE RANGE OF ACTIVITIES THAT ARE OFFERED, FROM TRADITIONAL CRAFTS RIGHT THROUGH TO ADVENTURE SPORTS. HERE ARE A FEW IDEAS TO WHET YOUR APPETITE AND HELP YOU CHOOSE THE RIGHT PARK FOR YOUR CHILDREN, WHATEVER THEIR AGES.

Organised activities

If it's an all singing and dancing leisure and entertainment holiday you're after, there are around 80 Holiday Centres listed in this guide. They provide a great variety of facilities, including, perhaps several swimming pools (one park has ten pools!) with water flumes, water cannons or river rapid features. They probably also have extensive indoor and outdoor play areas and multi-sport facilities for all the family to enjoy. Many of these centres offer a full programme of organised activities, sometimes with clubs for children of different ages. It's not just the holiday centres that offer these programmes either; many of the parks who responded to our survey offer fantastic programmes to keep the children entertained. In some cases parents can join in the fun and accompany younger children, while elsewhere adults can relax by the pool or enjoy a well-earned rest while someone else entertains the children for a morning, afternoon or whole day.

With the Olympic Games coming to London in 2012, parks can provide a unique chance for more children to get involved in different sports. Some parks even offer specialist coaching during the school holidays, with the chance to try a new sport like sailing or beach volleyball, or improve in a familiar sport such as table tennis or swimming. Football remains one of the most popular activities, and most parks provide some facility whether it's an informal playing field or a choice of proper pitches. One park in our survey has really taken the initiative. At Waterside Holiday Park, Weymouth (Dorset) two enterprising barmen set up a football coaching programme after taking their coaching qualifications. The skills-based training, open to girls and boys aged 7-11, three times a week, is very popular, and participants receive a certificate at the end of the course.

Many other parks offer football-oriented activities, and there is a very popular 5-a-side tournament held on August Bank Holiday each year at Ranch Caravan Park, Honeybourne (Worcestershire). The park also hosts a swimming gala at the same time, and many people come back year after year to take part in these activities.

Anyone for tennis?

Tennis is another popular sport, and if your child wants to take it up or improve their skills it might be worth choosing a park with good facilities or even a coaching programme. One such park is Silverbow Park, Goonhaven (Cornwall). Here children can enjoy free coaching three times weekly with a qualified coach (one hour for beginners and one hour for players, rackets and balls supplied). Facilities include two grass tennis courts and two all weather tennis courts, with three grass courts for badminton.

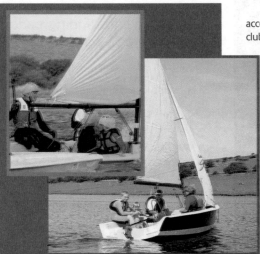
South West Lakes Trust

Messing about on the Water

Playing on and in the water is often a big part of camping holidays, with so many parks offering fantastic pools or lake and seaside locations. Several parks offer organised watersport activities to children of all ages (and adults!). Those parks making up the South West Lakes Trust also offer scenic camping pitches overlooking inland waters.

At three of these Trust sites – Tamar Lake, Kilkhampton (Cornwall), Wimbleball Lake, Dulverton (Somerset), and Roadford Lake, Broadwoodwidger, (Devon), visitors have the opportunity to learn and enjoy dinghy sailing, windsurfing or kayaking. Each centre is a Royal Yachting Association Training Centre and holds an Adventure Activities Licensing Authority License, to provide tuition, equipment hire and self-launch for all its activities. Other exciting watersport activities for all age groups include raft building, banana boating and powerboating. Taster sessions are designed to give you a feel for the sport, and the trust runs RYA and BCU courses for those wanting to gain qualifications, with 'Kids Krazy' Saturday morning clubs to encourage youngsters aged 8-16 to take part in watersports.

Looking for a bit of adventure?

Some parks offer activities for the adventurous-minded, along with more traditional ones for younger children. Golden Coast Holiday Village, Woolacombe (Devon) runs the 'Billy Beachball Kids Club' for 5-12 year olds (under 5s must be accompanied by an adult), plus an adventure club, and activities like quad biking and diving.

At Warner Farm Touring Park, Selsey (West Sussex) children can enjoy a Go-Kart grand prix or snorkelling alongside sports like football, basketball, volleyball, tennis and bowling, The FunkyTz is a club for 11-16 year olds whose activities include a playstation challenge and line dancing lessons. For the younger children the Bunni Club (5-10 year olds) provides discos, magic shows, drawing and painting.

Making the most of the area

For some parks location is the key to some great activities for all the family. Whether there's a theme park next door or a great beach or lake on the doorstep, you can really get something extra as part of your holiday. At Trevornick Holiday Park, Holywell Bay (Cornwall), The Kanga Club provides on-site fun, games, competitions and an opportunity to meet new friends. Golf, a bowling alley and an 18-hole pitch and putt course extend the range of activities. As if all that weren't enough, next door is Holywell Bay Fun Park with special arrangements for those staying at Trevornick.

If it's the great outdoors you're after, at Park Foot Caravan and Camping Park, Pooley Bridge (Cumbria) the Children's Club offers an action-packed programme for 4-12 year olds. Activities include games, football, tennis, archery, pool and table tennis. The park also offers local activities to take advantage of its unique location, with pony trekking onto Barton Fell, mountain bike hire to explore the area, and direct access onto the lake for watersports such as sailing, windsurfing, canoeing, boat hire or fishing.

If you'd like to explore the New Forest, Sandy Balls Holiday Centre, Fordingbridge (Hampshire) offers activities for the whole family, from hiring mountain bikes, children's trailers or trailer bikes (there are even tandems available for double the fun), to horse riding from their own Arniss Stables, fishing on the River Avon and a nature trail. A full programme of organised activities is bookable each morning, including pottery, painting or clay modelling, laser clay pigeon shooting, archery or orienteering.

continued

Fun for all the family

We haven't been able to mention all the activities provided by our parks, but here are a few highlights: the holiday prince and princess competition for 3-10 year olds, and storytime with Sidney the Sealion at Searles of Hunstanton, Hunstanton (Norfolk); beach rambles and treasure hunts at Stanwix Park Holiday Centre, Silloth (Cumbria); diving lessons, pillow fights, pony trekking and donkey derby at Freshwater Beach Holiday Park, Bridport (Dorset); and twice weekly free instruction in archery and climbing at Warren Farm Holiday Park, Brean (Somerset), plus tractor rides and donkey racing nights at a nearby park.

South West Lakes Trust

Handy hints for finding parks with children's activities:

Ask for details of children's activities before you book. Most parks can send you a brochure and entertainment guide or an example of their weekly programme of activities. Before you book make sure you know about the following:

- Age restrictions
- Whether parents are asked to accompany children
- Are there separate clubs for different ages?
- Are there bad weather options?
- Are clubs or activities free?
- Are there free or paid attractions nearby?
- What times do the activities run?
- Is any food included?
- Are clubs/activities/facilities limited to certain dates?
- Is there any specialist sports coaching?
- Are there any courses leading to qualifications e.g. sailing?

The AA Campsite Classification Scheme

AA Pennant Rating and Holiday Centres
AA parks are classified on a 5-point scale according to their style and the range of facilities they offer. As the number of pennants increases, so the quality and variety of facilities is generally greater. There is also a separate category for Holiday Centres which provide full day and night holiday entertainment as well as offering complete touring facilities for campers and caravanners.

What can you expect at an AA-rated park?
All AA parks must meet a minimum standard: they should be clean, well maintained and welcoming. In addition they should have a local authority site licence (unless specially exempted), and satisfy local authority fire regulations.

ABOUT THE AA INSPECTION
Every year one of a team of highly-qualified inspectors pays an unannounced visit to each campsite in Great Britain in the guide to make a thorough check on its facilities, services and hospitality. Establishments pay an annual fee for the inspection, recognition and rating, and receive a free basic text entry in the AA Caravan and Camping Guide. AA inspectors pay when they stay overnight on a park. The criteria used by AA inspectors in awarding the AA pennant rating are given on page 8.

AA Quality % Score

AA Rated Parks and Holiday Centres are awarded a percentage alongside their pennant rating or holiday centre status. This is a qualitative assessment of various factors including customer care and hospitality, toilet facilities and park landscaping. The % score runs from 50% to 100% and indicates the relative quality of parks with the same number of pennants. For example, one 3 pennant park may score 60%, while another 3 pennant park may achieve 70%. Holiday Centres also receive a % score between 50% and 100% to differentiate between quality levels within this grading. Like the pennant rating, the percentage is reassessed annually.

Holiday Centres

In this category we distinguish parks which cater for all holiday needs. Anyone staying on one of these parks will have no need to go elsewhere for meals or entertainment. They provide:

- A wide range of on-site sports, leisure and recreational facilities
- Supervision and security of a very high level
- A choice of eating outlets
- Touring facilities of equal importance to statics
- A maximum density of 30 pitches per acre
- Clubhouse with entertainment provided
- Automatic laundry

▶ One Pennant Parks

These parks offer a fairly simple standard of facilities including:

- No more than 30 pitches per acre
- At least 6 pitches or 10% of total allocated to tourers
- An adequate drinking water supply and reasonable drainage
- Washroom with flush toilets and toilet paper provided, unless no sanitary facilities provided in which case this should be clearly stated
- Chemical disposal arrangements, ideally with running water, unless tents only
- Adequate refuse disposal arrangements, clearly signed
- Well-drained ground, and some level pitches
- Entrance and access roads of adequate width and surface
- Whereabouts of emergency telephone displayed
- Urgent telephone numbers signed

 ## ▶▶ Two Pennant Parks

Parks in this category should meet all of the above requirements, but offer a better level of facilities, services, customer care, security and ground maintenance. They should include the following:

- Separate washrooms, including at least 2 WCs and 2 washbasins per sex per 30 pitches
- Hot and cold water direct to each basin
- Externally-lit toilet blocks
- Warden to be available during day, times to be indicated
- Whereabouts of shop/chemist clearly signed
- Dish-washing facilities, covered and lit
- Reception area

 ## ▶▶▶ Three Pennant Parks

Many parks come within this rating, and the range of facilities is quite wide. All parks will be of a very good standard meeting the following criteria:

- Facilities, services and park grounds very clean and well maintained, buildings in good repair, and attention paid to customer care and park security
- Evenly-surfaced roads and paths
- Decent modern or modernised toilet blocks, all-night lit, containing:

  Mirrors, shelves and hooks   Shaver/hairdryer points
  Lidded waste bins in ladies toilets   Uncracked toilet seats
  Soap and hand dryer/towels

- A reasonable number of modern shower cubicles with hot water, 1 per 35 pitches per sex. Privacy whilst changing and showering is essential.
- Electric hook-ups
- Some hardstandings/wheel runs/firm, level ground
- Laundry with automatic washing and drying facilities, separate from toilets
- Children's playground with some equipment
- Public telephone on site or nearby, available 24 hours
- Warden's hours and 24-hour contact number clearly signed

 ## ▶▶▶▶ Four Pennant Parks

These parks have achieved an extremely high standard in all areas, including landscaping of grounds, natural screening and attractive park buildings, and also customer care and park security.

Toilets are smartly modern and immaculately maintained, and offer the following:

- Spacious vanitory-style washbasins or similar, including some in lockable cubicles, at least 2 per 25 pitches per sex
- Fully-tiled shower cubicles with doors, dry areas, shelves and hooks, at least 1 per 30 pitches per sex
- Some combined toilet/washing cubicles, or shower/toilet/washing cubicles

Other requirements are:

- Shop on site, or within reasonable distance
- Warden available 24 hours
- Reception area open during the day, with tourist information available
- Internal roads, paths and toilet blocks lit at night
- Maximum 25 pitches per campable acre
- Toilet blocks heated October to Easter
- Minimum 50% electric hook-ups
- Minimum 10% hardstandings where necessary
- Late arrivals enclosure

 ## ▶▶▶▶▶ Five Pennant Premier Parks

Premier parks are of an excellent standard, set in attractive surroundings with superb mature landscaping. Facilities, security and customer care are of an exceptional quality. As well as the above they will offer:

- Some fully-serviced 'super' pitches
- Electricity to most pitches
- First-class toilet facilities including several designated self-contained cubicles ideally with WC, washbasin and shower.

Many Premier Parks will also provide:

- Heated swimming pool
- Well-equipped shop
- Café or restaurant and bar
- Serious catering indoors and outdoors for young people
- A designated walking area for dogs (if accepted)

Useful Information

Chemical Closet Disposal Point (CDP)
You will usually find one on every park, except those catering only for tents. It must be a specially constructed unit, or a WC permanently set aside for the purpose with adjacent rinsing facilities. However, some local authorities are concerned about the effect of chemicals on bacteria in septic tanks etc, and may prohibit or restrict provision of CDPs in their areas.

Cold Storage
A fridge and/or freezer or icepacks for the use of holidaymakers.

Booking Information
It is advisable to book in advance during peak holiday seasons and in school or public holidays. Where an individual park requires advance booking, 'advance bookings accepted' or 'booking advisable' (followed by dates) appears in the entry. It is also wise to check whether a reservation entitles you to a particular pitch. It does not necessarily follow that an early booking will get you the best pitch; you may just have the choice of what is available at the time you check in.

The words 'Advance bookings not accepted' indicate that a park does not accept reservations. Some parks may require a deposit on booking which may well be non-returnable if you have to cancel your holiday. If you have to cancel, notify the proprietor at once because you may be held legally responsible for partial or full payment unless the pitch can be re-let. Do consider taking out insurance such as AA Travel Insurance (telephone 0870 606 1612 or consult the AA website www.theAA.com for details) to cover a lost deposit or compensation. Some parks will not accept overnight bookings unless payment for a full minimum period (e.g. two or three days) is made. If you are not sure whether your camping or caravanning equipment can be used at a park, check beforehand.

Please note: The AA does not undertake to find accommodation or to make reservations.

Last Arrival – Unless otherwise stated, parks will usually accept arrivals at any time of the day or night but some have a special 'late arrivals' enclosure where you have to make temporary camp so as not to disturb other people on site. Please note that on some parks access to the toilet block is by key or pass card only, so if you know you will be late, do check with the park.

Last Departure – As with hotel rooms and self-catering accommodation, most parks will specify their overnight period – e.g. noon to noon. If you overstay the departure time you can be charged for an extra day. Do make sure you know what the regulations are.

Complaints
Speak to the park proprietor or supervisor immediately if you have any complaints, so that the matter can be sorted out on the spot. If this personal approach fails, you may decide, if the matter is serious, to approach the local authority or tourist board. AA guide users may write to:

The Editor, The AA Caravan
& Camping Guide,
AA Lifestyle Guides,
Fanum House, Basing View,
Basingstoke, Hants RG21 4EA

The AA may at its sole discretion investigate any complaints received from guide users for the purpose of making any necessary amendments to the guide. The AA will not in any circumstances act as representative or negotiator or undertake to obtain compensation or enter into further correspondence or deal with the matter in any other way whatsoever. The AA will not guarantee to take any specific action.

Electric Hook-Up
This is becoming more generally available at parks with three or more pennants, but if it is important to you, you should check before booking. The voltage is generally 240v AC, 50 cycles, although variations between 200v and 250v may still be found. All parks in the AA scheme which provide electric hook-ups do so in accordance with International Electrotechnical Commission regulations. Outlets are coloured blue and take the form of a lidded plug with recessed contacts, making it impossible to touch a live point by accident. They are also waterproof. A similar plug, but with protruding contacts which hook into the recessed plug, is on the end of the cable which connects the caravan to the source of supply, and is dead. These cables can usually be hired on site, or a plug supplied to fit your own cable. You should ask for the male plug; the female plug is the one already fixed to the power supply.

continued

This supply is rated for either 5, 10 or 16 amps and this is usually displayed on a triangular yellow plate attached to source of supply. If it is not, be sure to ask at Reception. This is important because if you overload the circuit, the trip switch will operate to cut off the power supply. The trip switch can only be reset by a park official, who will first have to go round all the hook-ups on park to find the cause of the trip. This can take a long time and will make the culprit distinctly unpopular with all the other caravanners deprived of power, to say nothing of the park official. Tents and trailer tents are recommended to have a Residual Circuit Device (RCD) for safety reasons and to avoid overloading the circuit.

It is a relatively simple matter to calculate whether your appliances will overload the circuit. The amperage used by an appliance depends on its wattage and the total amperage used is the total of all the appliances in use at any one time. See the table below.

Portable black & white TV 50 watts approx.	0.2 amp
Small colour TV 90 watts approx.	0.4 amp
Small fan heater 1000 watts (1kW) approx.	4.2 amp
One-bar electric fire NB each extra bar rates 1000 watts (1kW)	4.2 amp
60 watt table lamp approx.	0.25 amp
100 watt light bulb approx.	0.4 amp
Battery charger 100 watts approx.	0.4 amp
Small refrigerator 125 watts approx.	0.4 amp
Domestic microwave 600 watts approx.	2.5 amp

Motor Caravans
At some parks motor caravans are only accepted if they remain static throughout the stay. Also check that there are suitable level pitches at the parks where you plan to stay.

Parking
Some park operators insist that cars be put in a parking area separate from the pitches; others will not allow more than one car for each caravan or tent.

Park Rules
Most parks display a set of rules which you should read on your arrival. Dogs may or may not be accepted on parks, and this is entirely at the owners' or wardens' discretion. Even when parks say they accept dogs, it is still discretionary and we most strongly advise that you check when you book. Dogs should always be kept on a lead and under control. Dogs sleeping in cars is not encouraged.

Pitches
Campsites are legally entitled to use an overflow field which is not a normal part of their camping area for up to 28 days in any one year as an emergency method of coping with additional numbers at busy periods.

When this 28 day rule is being invoked site owners should increase the numbers of sanitary facilities accordingly when the permanent facilities become insufficient to cope with extra numbers. In these circumstances the extra facilities are sometimes no more than temporary portacabins.

Shops
The range of food and equipment in shops is usually in proportion to the size of the park. As far as our pennant requirements are concerned, a mobile shop calling several times a week, or a general store within easy walking distance of the park entrance is acceptable.

Importing Animals
The importation of animals into the UK is subject to strict controls. Penalties for trying to avoid these controls are severe. However, the Pet Travel Scheme (PETS) allows cats, dogs and ferrets and certain other pets coming from the EU and certain other countries to enter the UK without quarantine provided the appropriate conditions are met. Visitors intending to bring pets into the UK should consult DEFRA at least 7 months in advance of their proposed date of travel. Details of other qualifying countries and further information are available on the Department for Environment, Food & Rural Affairs (DEFRA) website: www.defra.gov.uk/animalh/quarantine/index.htm PETS HELPLINE on 0870 241 1710 (08.30-17.00 Mon-Fri). E-mail: pets.helpline@defra.gsi.gov.uk

Pets resident in the British Isles (UK, Republic of Ireland, Isle of Man and Channel Islands) are not subject to any quarantine or PETS rules when travelling within the British Isles.

Important Note on Restrictions
Many parks in our guide are selective about the categories of people they will accept on their parks. In the caravan and camping world there are many restrictions and some categories of visitor are banned altogether.

On many parks in this guide, unaccompanied young people, single-sex groups, single adults, and motorcycle groups will not be accepted. The AA takes no stance in this matter, basing its pennant classification on facilities, quality and maintenance.

On the other hand, some parks cater well for teenagers and offer magnificent sporting and leisure facilities as well as discos; others have only very simple amenities.

Most parks accept dogs, but some have no suitable areas for exercise, and some will refuse to accept certain breeds, so you should always check with the park before you set out. A small number of parks in our guide have decided to concentrate on the adults-only market, aiming to attract holiday makers who are in search of total peace and quiet. (See p.19) Always telephone the park before you travel.

How do I find the perfect place?

Island Camping

Scotland

The Shetland Islands There are four official campsites on the Shetlands, but visitors can camp anywhere with prior permission. Caravans and motor caravans must stick to the main roads. Camping 'böds' offer budget accommodation in unisex dormitories for campers with their own bed rolls and sleeping bags. There is no camping or caravanning on Noss and Fair Isle, and the Tresta Links in Fetlar.

The Orkney Isles There are no camping and caravanning restrictions, and plenty of beauty spots in which to pitch camp.

The Western Isles (Outer Hebrides) There are official campsites on these islands, but 'wild' camping is allowed within reason, and with the landowner's prior permission.

The Inner Isles and other Scottish Islands Skye is accessible to caravans and motor caravans, and has official camping sites, but its sister isles of Rhum and Eigg have no car ferries, and take only backpackers. Official camping only is allowed at Rothsay on the Isle of Bute. The islands of Mull, Islay, Coll and Arran have official campsites, and welcome caravans, motor caravans and tenters. Offsite camping is also allowed with the usual permission. Iona is car free, and a backpacker's paradise, while Tiree does not accept caravans or motor caravans, and has no official sites. Colonsay and Cumbrae allow no caravanning or camping, although organized groups such as the Guides or Scouts may stay with official permission. Jura and Gigha allow neither camping nor caravanning, and Lismore bans caravans but permits camping, although there are no official sites and few suitable places.

The Channel Islands

Tight controls are operated because of the narrowness of the mainly rural roads. On all of the islands tents can be hired on recognized campsites.

Jersey
Visiting caravans are now allowed into Jersey, provided they are to be used as holiday accommodation only. Caravans will require a permit for travelling to and from the port and campsite on their arrival and departure days only. Motorvans may travel around the island on a daily basis, but must return to the campsite each night. Bookings should be made through the chosen campsite, who will also arrange for a permit. Booking is strongly recommended during July and August.

Guernsey
Only islanders may own and use towed caravans, though motor caravans are allowed under strict conditions. A permit must be sought and received in advance, the vehicle must not be used for sleeping, and when not in use for transport the van must be left under cover at a camping park with prior permission. Tents and trailer tents are allowed provided you stay on official campsites; booking is strongly recommended during July and August.

Herm and Sark
These two small islands are traffic free. Herm has a small campsite for tents, and these can also be hired. Sark has three campsites. New arrivals are met off the boat by a tractor which carries people and luggage up the steep hill from the harbour. All travel is by foot, on bicycle, or by horse and cart.

Alderney
Neither caravans nor motor caravans are allowed, and campers must have a confirmed booking on the one official camp site before they arrive.

Isle of Man

Motor caravans may enter with prior permission. Trailer caravans are generally only allowed in connection with trade shows and exhibitions, or for demonstration purposes, not for living accommodation. Written application for permission should be made to the Secretary, Planning Committee, Isle of Man Local Government Board, Murray House, Mount Havelock. The shipping line cannot accept caravans without this written permission.

Isles of Scilly

Caravans and motor caravans are not allowed, and campers must stay at official sites. Booking is advisable on all sites, especially during school holidays. Please note that strict control is kept on the landing of animals on these islands.

AA Campsite of the Year Awards 2006

AA Campsite of the Year for England, and Overall Winner of the Best Campsite of the Year 2006

Oxon Hall Touring Park, Shrewsbury, Shropshire

Although Oxon Hall is only seven years old, it has matured into a first class park with facilities to suit a wide range of customers. The reception staff are efficient and friendly, and their influence pervades the whole park. The spacious grounds are divided into several attractive areas by trees, shrubs and hedges, with different interest groups given their own separate areas. Adults, for example, can choose the adult-only section, giving them peace and freedom from boisterous games. Families are also well catered for, with an exciting play area for children. Super pitches with everything from electricity to TV point are available along with grassy pitches and extra-long ones for large motor homes. The conservatory coffee house overlooking the attractive lake is the perfect spot for relaxing and getting to know your neighbours, and outside the park gates is the Park and Ride bus for Shrewsbury. And with top-class security in place, you can leave all your worries outside.

AA Campsite of the Year for Scotland 2006

Glen Nevis Caravan & Camping Park, Fort William, Highlands

The stunning mountain scenery all around this park is both awe-inspiring and an invitation to explore. It sits at the foot of Ben Nevis, Britain's highest peak, in an area rich in history and wildlife. Outdoor lovers will relish the space and opportunity for walking, climbing and mountain biking, whilst enjoying the comfort and security of a well-managed and supervised site. Pitches are sited in small enclosures allowing for privacy and peace, with plenty of mature trees and hedges to provide shelter. The five amenity blocks are housed at strategic points around the park, so you don't have to walk far to find the quality showers and washing facilities which are a feature here. The park also boasts a lounge bar and restaurant, where drinks and meals are popular with locals as well as campers. With 30 acres of immediate park, a 1000-acre estate to enjoy and the whole of the Western Highlands to discover, this park is perfect for anyone wanting to holiday in the heart of Britain's wildest countryside.

AA Campsite of the Year for Wales 2006

Pencelli Castle Caravan & Camping Park, Brecon, Powys

For the second time in four years this attractive campsite in the heart of the Brecon Beacons has won this coveted award. The Rees family who own the park and run it to impeccably high standards have left nothing to chance when it comes to providing holidays and breaks for the discerning family. Campers have the use of a large landscaped field where they can commune with nature safe in the knowledge that all the latest mod cons are a short walk away. A drying room with lockers, a machine dispensing hot drinks, and an information room packed with maps and tourist brochures are some of the perks they can access in the main amenity block. Nearer to hand are the bike and boot wash, which come into their own after a day out in the hills. Caravanners can book a well-maintained 'super' pitch if they wish, or go for an ordinary hardstanding with electric hook-up. Parents will appreciate the family rooms in the toilet block, where they can shower their children together, and see to their needs in one large cubicle. Everything is beautifully designed and carefully looked after. And it goes without saying that the Rees family welcome extends right to the last day of your holiday.

Premier Parks & Holiday Centres

▶▶▶▶▶

Premier Parks

ENGLAND

CAMBRIDGESHIRE
ST IVES
Stroud Hill Park
CORNWALL
& ISLES OF SCILLY
BOSWINGER
Sea View International
BUDE
Wooda Farm Park
PENTEWAN
Sun Valley Holiday Park
ST IVES
Polmanter Tourist Park
CUMBRIA
APPLEBY-IN WESTMORLAND
Wild Rose Park
WINDERMERE
Fallbarrow Park
Limefitt Park
DEVON
NEWTON ABBOT
Ross Park
Dornafield
DORSET
BRIDPORT
Highlands End Farm
Holiday Park
WIMBORNE MINSTER
Wilksworth Farm Caravan Park
Merley Court Touring Park
LANCASHIRE
SILVERDALE
Holgate's Caravan Park
LINCOLNSHIRE
WOODHALL SPA
Bainland Country Park
NORTHUMBERLAND
BERWICK-UPON-TWEED
Ord House Country Park
OXFORDSHIRE
STANDLAKE
Lincoln Farm Park
SHROPSHIRE
SHREWSBURY
Beaconsfield Farm Caravan Park
SOMERSET
CHEDDAR
Broadway House Holiday Caravan
& Camping Park
GLASTONBURY
The Old Oaks Touring Park

SUFFOLK
WOODBRIDGE
Moon & Sixpence
WIGHT, ISLE OF
NEWBRIDGE
Orchards Holiday Caravan Park
NEWCHURCH
Southland Camping Park
SANDOWN
Camping & Caravanning
Club Site
YORKSHIRE, NORTH
HARROGATE
Rudding Holiday Park
Ripley Caravan Park

CHANNEL ISLANDS

JERSEY
ST MARTIN
Beuvelande Camp Site

SCOTLAND

DUMFRIES & GALLOWAY
BRIGHOUSE BAY
Brighouse Bay Holiday Park
CREETOWN
Castle Cary Holiday Park
ECCLEFECHAN
Hoddom Castle Caravan Park
EAST LOTHIAN
DUNBAR
Thurston Manor Holiday
Home Park
FIFE
ST ANDREWS
Craigtoun Meadows Holiday Park
HIGHLAND
CORPACH
Linnhe Lochside Holidays
INVERNESS
Torvean Caravan Park
PERTH & KINROSS
BLAIR ATHOLL
Blair Castle Caravan Park
River Tilt Caravan Park
STIRLING
LUIB
Glendochart Caravan Park

WALES

CARMARTHENSHIRE
NEWCASTLE EMLYN
Cenarth Falls Holiday Park
WREXHAM
EYTON
The Plassey Leisure Park

Holiday Centres

ENGLAND

CORNWALL
& ISLES OF SCILLY
BUDE
Sandymouth Bay Holiday Park
HAYLE
St Ives Bay Holiday Park
HOLYWELL BAY
Holywell Bay Holiday Park
Trevornick Holiday Park
LOOE
Tencreek Holiday Park
MULLION
Mullion Holiday Park
NEWQUAY
Hendra Holiday Park
Newquay Holiday Park
PENTEWAN
Pentewan Sands Holiday Park
PERRANPORTH
Perran Sands Holiday Park
POLPERRO
Killigarth Manor Holiday Centre

REJERRAH
Monkey Tree Holiday Park
ST MERRYN
Harlyn Sands Holiday Park
ST MINVER
St Minver Holiday Park
TORPOINT
Whitsand Bay Holiday Park
WHITECROSS
White Acres Holiday Park
WIDEMOUTH BAY
Widemouth Bay Caravan Parc
CUMBRIA
FLOOKBURGH
Lakeland Leisure Park
SILLOTH
Stanwix Park Holiday Centre
DEVON
CROYDE BAY
Ruda Holiday Park
DAWLISH
Golden Sands Holiday Park
Lady's Mile Touring & Caravan
Park
Peppermint Park
EXMOUTH
Devon Cliffs Holiday Park
LADRAM BAY
Ladram Bay Holiday Centre
MORTEHOE
Twitchen Parc
PAIGNTON
Beverley Parks
Caravan & Camping Centre
SHALDON
Coast View Holiday Park
WOOLACOMBE
Golden Coast Holiday Village
Woolacombe Bay Holiday Village
Woolacombe Sands Holiday Park
DORSET
BRIDPORT
Freshwater Beach Holiday Park
West Bay Holiday Park
HOLTON HEATH
Sandford Holiday Park
POOLE
Rockley Park
ST LEONARDS
Oakdene Forest Park
WEYMOUTH
Littlesea Holiday Park
Seaview Holiday Park
Waterside Holiday Park
ESSEX
MERSEA ISLAND
Waldegraves Holiday Park
HAMPSHIRE
FORDINGBRIDGE
Sandy Balls Holiday Centre

LANCASHIRE
BLACKPOOL
Marton Mere Holiday Village
HEYSHAM
Ocean Edge Caravan Park
LINCOLNSHIRE
CLEETHORPES
Thorpe Park Holiday Centre
MABLETHORPE
Golden Sands Holiday Park
NORFOLK
BELTON
Wild Duck Holiday Park
GREAT YARMOUTH
Vauxhall Holiday Park
HUNSTANTON
Searles of Hunstanton
NORTHUMBERLAND
BERWICK-UPON-TWEED
Haggerston Castle
SOMERSET
BREAN
Warren Farm Holiday Park
BURNHAM-ON-SEA
Burnham-on-Sea Holiday Centre
WATCHET
Doniford Bay Holiday Park
SUFFOLK
KESSINGLAND
Kessingland Beach Holiday Park
SUSSEX, WEST
SELSEY
Warner Farm Touring Park
WIGHT, ISLE OF
ST HELENS
Nodes Point Holiday Park
SHANKLIN
Lower Hyde Holiday Park
THORNESS
Thorness Bay Holiday Park
WHITECLIFF BAY
Whitecliff Bay Holiday Park
YORKSHIRE, EAST RIDING
SKIPSEA
Low Skirlington Leisure Park
YORKSHIRE, NORTH
FILEY
Blue Dolphin Holiday Park
Flower of May Holiday Park
Primrose Valley
Reighton Sands Holiday Park

SCOTLAND
DUMFRIES & GALLOWAY
GATEHOUSE-OF-FLEET
Auchenlarie Holiday Park
SOUTHERNESS
Southerness Holiday Village

EAST LOTHIAN
LONGNIDDRY
Seton Sands Holiday Village
HIGHLAND
DORNOCH
Grannie's Heilan
  Hame Holiday Park
PERTH & KINROSS
TUMMEL BRIDGE
Tummel Valley Holiday Park
SOUTH AYRSHIRE
AYR
Craig Tara Holiday Park
COYLTON
Sandrum Castle
  Holiday Park

WALES
CEREDIGION
ABERYSTWYTH
Brynowen Holiday Park
CONWY
TOWYN
Ty Mawr Holiday Park
DENBIGHSHIRE
PRESTATYN
Presthaven Sands
GWYNEDD
PORTHMADOG
Greenacres
PEMBROKESHIRE
TENBY
Kiln Park Holiday Centre
SWANSEA
SWANSEA
Riverside Caravan Park

REPUBLIC OF IRELAND
CO KERRY
KILLARNEY
Fossa Caravan Park

Before You Go

This is the checklist compiled by one of our campsite inspectors to ensure that he leaves nothing behind when he sets off either from home or from park visits with a towed caravan. We thought you might like to share his handy hints, and save yourself from embarrassment ... or worse.

- Check that all interior caravan items are safely stored, cupboards are closed, loos not full of moveable objects, all interior electrics set correctly. Remember that vase of flowers!

- Check roof lights are closed and windows secure.

- Corner steadies should be up tightly, blocks cleared away, steps stowed.

- Disconnect electric hook-ups to site and check that gas bottles are turned off.

- Make sure electrics to car are secure.

- Check that the tow-hook safety wire is clipped on, and, if used, that the anti-snake device is fitted correctly.

- Visually check that caravan number plate is secure - and that it reads the same as the one on the car.

- Using a second person to stand behind the caravan, check that all lights and indicators are working correctly.

- Move forward about 15 metres, then stop, get out and inspect your pitch for any items which have been left under the caravan.

- If you use Calor Gas, they issue a free directory of stockists and dealers. Simply call free on 0800 626 626

- Another useful and potentially life-saving tip is to always travel with a small fire extinguisher, fire blanket or both. Fires in caravans and tents are all too commonplace, and once started can take hold very quickly. By the time help has come, or you have gone to find the site's fire-fighting equipment, a tent in particular can already have burned down completely. Never treat fire lightly.

- Check that the caravan door is locked and secure.

Adult Only Parks

Over 30 of the parks in the AA pennant rating scheme have opted to provide facilities for adults only, and do not accept children. The minimum age for individual parks may be 18, or 21, while one or two pitch the limit even higher. For more information please contact the individual parks.

ENGLAND

Cambridgeshire
Stroud Hill Park, St Ives

Cheshire
Lamb Cottage Caravan Park, Whitegate

Cornwall
Killiwerris Touring Park, Truro

Wayfarers Caravan & Camping Park, St Hilary

Cumbria
Larches Caravan Park, Mealsgate

Derbyshire
Thornheyes, Buxton

Devon
Zeacombe House Caravan Park, East Anstey

Woodland Springs, Drewsteignton

Moor View, Modbury

Dorset
Back of Beyond Touring Park, St Leonards

Warmwell Country Touring Park, Warmwell

Greater Manchester
Gelder Wood Country Park, Rochdale

Lincolnshire
Orchard Park, Boston

Pilgrims Way, Boston

Delph Bank, Fleet Hargate

The Fisheries, Saltfleetby St Peter

Norfolk
Little Haven Camping &

   Caravanning Park, Erpingham

Two Mills Touring Park, North Walsham

Bank Farm, Saddlebow

Breckland Meadows Touring Park, Swaffham

Nottinghamshire
New Hall Farm Touring Park, Southwell

Shropshire
Beaconsfield Farm Caravan Park, Shrewsbury

Somerset
Exe Valley Caravan Site, Bridgetown

Cheddar Bridge Touring Park, Cheddar

Old Oaks Touring Park, Glastonbury

Homestead Caravan & Camping Park, Wells

Waterrow, Wiveliscombe

Suffolk
Polstead Touring Park, Polstead

Wiltshire
Greenhill Farm C & Camping Park, Landford

Yorkshire, East Riding of
Croft Park, Beverley

Yorkshire, North
Shaws Trailer Park, Harrogate

Foxholme Caravan & Camping Park, Helmsley

Willow House Caravan Park, York

Yorkshire, West
Moor Lodge Park, Bardsey

St Helena's Caravan Park, Horsforth

SCOTLAND

Highland
Faichemard Caravan & Camping Park,

Invergarry

WALES

Denbighshire
Penddol Caravan Park, Llangollen

Pembrokeshire
Rosebush Caravan & Camping Park, Rosebush

Powys
Riverside Caravan & Camping Park, Crickhowell

Dalmore Camping & Caravanning Park,

Llandrindod Wells

Useful Addresses

British Holiday & HomesParks Association Ltd
6 Pullman CourtGreat Western Rd Gloucester, GL1 3ND Tel: 01452 526911

Camping and Caravanning Club
Greenfields House Coventry, CV4 8JH
Tel: 02476 694995

Caravan Club
East Grinstead House East Grinstead West Sussex RH19 1UA Tel: 01342 326944

National Caravan Council Ltd
Catherine House Victoria Road Aldershot Hampshire, GU11 1SS Tel: 01252 318251

The Best of British Touring & Holiday Parks
PO Box 28249 Edinburgh, EH9 2YZ

How to use the Guide

This guide aims to give you a great choice of over 1,000 quality caravan and camping parks across Great Britain and Ireland. To give you the most accurate information, the AA inspects and rates the parks in its scheme and updates the information in the guide annually. Please read the information on the Pennant Classification Scheme (page 7) so that you know what the classification symbols used in this guide mean.

Whether you are travelling around in a motorhome, camping at weekends or looking for somewhere to take your caravan for a two week holiday, this guide will help you find something to suit you. The AA pennant rating or holiday centre classification means that you can quickly find a park in the guide with the kind of facilities you are looking for. If you are looking for a park while you are on the road, the AA signs showing the pennants or holiday centre will point you in the right direction.

1 — ANY TOWN   Map 10 SW87

2 — NEW ▶ ▶ ▶73% Name Caravan Park
(SW862728) PL28 8PN ☎ 01841 520230
📠 01841 520231
4 — 📧 camping@somewhere.co.uk
4 — 🌐 www.campingsomewhere.com
5 — *Dir: Off B376 Padstow-Newquay road 2m SW of village.*
6 — ★ 🚐 £5-£8 🚐 £5-£8 ⛺ £5-£8

3 —

13 —

7 — Open Apr-Oct 1st Apr-Whit & mid Sep-Oct shop closed Booking advisable Jul-Aug. Last arrival 23.00hrs. Last departure noon
8 — *A working farm site with better than average facilities. The very well converted farm buildings look purpose built. A 3-acre site with 40 touring pitches, 6 hardstandings.*
9 — Sports field & pitch 'n' putt
Leisure: 🏊♣⚲🏠   Facilities: ↔🚿🚻♿🏪⛲🐾 — 10
Services: 🚽🚿🔌⚡🛒→∪🔩 🔧
11 — 🚮🚏🚗🚕🚌 Notes: Dogs on leads at all times — 12

Directory Entries

If the name of a park is printed in italics this indicates that we have not been able to get current details or prices confirmed by the owners. A star (★) in front of the prices means that we only have information about the previous year's prices.

1 **Map Reference** Each location in the directory has a map reference, starting with the map page number and followed by a number based on the National Grid and can be used in conjunction with the 24-page atlas at the back of the guide. To find a location, read the first figure horizontally and the second figure vertically within a lettered square. In order to find the precise location of a site, each entry in the directory has a 6-figure map reference also based on the National Grid.

2 **AA Pennant Rating** Parks are rated from 1-5 pennants. They are also awarded a Quality Assessment Score ranging from 50% to 100% according to how they compare with other parks within the same pennant rating. For a fuller explanation of the AA Scheme see page 7. NEW identifies parks new to the guide this year.

3 **David Bellamy Awards:** 🏅
Many AA recognised parks are also recipients of a David Bellamy Award for Conservation. The awards are graded Bronze, Silver and Gold. Beside each relevant park's entry we show a symbol to indicate the 2004/5 winners, the latest information at the time of going to press. For 2005/6 winners please contact: British Holiday & Homes Parks Association direct on: 01452 526911.

Best of British: 🏅
A group of just over 40 parks, both large and small, which focus on high quality facilities and amenities.

Countryside Discovery: 🏅
A group of over 30 family-run parks with fewer than 150 pitches, each sharing a common theme of tranquillity.

4 **Web Addresses** Web Site addresses are included where they have been supplied and specified by the respective establishment. Such Web Sites are not under the control of The Automobile Association Developments Limited and as

such The Automobile Association Developments Limited has no control over them and will not accept any responsibility or liability in respect of any and all matters whatsoever relating to such Web Sites including access, content, material and functionality. By including the addresses of third party Web Sites the AA does not intend to solicit business or offer any security to any person in any country, directly or indirectly.

5 **Directions** We give route directions as supplied by the park, but as space in the directory is limited we cannot go into great detail.

6 **Charges** Charges given immediately after the appropriate symbol (caravan ⬛, tent ▲, motorvan ⬛) are the overnight cost for one tent or caravan, one car and two adults, or one motor caravan and two adults. The price may vary according to the number of people in your party, but some parks have a fixed fee per pitch regardless of the number of people. Please note that some parks may charge separately for some of the park's facilities, including the showers. Some parks charge a different rate for pitches with or without electricity.

In the Republic of Ireland section of the guide the prices are given in Euros - €.
Prices have been supplied to us in good faith by the park operators and are as accurate as possible. They are, however, only a guide and are subject to change at any time during the currency of this book.

7 **Booking Information** - see Useful Information section on page 9.

8 **Pitches** The brief description of the park includes the number of touring pitches and hardstandings. We give the number of static van pitches available in the entries in our guide in order to give a picture of the nature and size of the park. The AA pennant classification is based on an inspection of the touring pitches and facilities only. AA inspectors do not visit or report on static accommodation. The AA takes no responsibility for the condition of rented caravans or chalets and can take no action whatsoever about complaints relating to them.

9 **Additional Information** We include in the entry any further or more specific information about facilities, supplied by the campsite, that is not represented by a symbol.

10 **Symbols & Abbreviations** See pages in the directory for explanation of symbols and abbreviations used in entries. Please note that any symbol appearing after the arrow symbol ➔ represents facilities found within 3 miles of the site.

11 **Credit/Debit Cards** Most of the larger parks accept payment by credit or charge card. We use the following symbols at the end of the entry to show which cards are accepted

	Access/Mastercard
	Barclaycard/Visa
	Connect
	Maestro (Switch)
	Delta

12 **Notes** These are the restrictions the park has told us about (see also Useful Information p.9)

13 Establishments may choose to include a photograph or map extract with their entry.

Facilities for Disabled Visitors
The final stage (Part III) of the Disability Discrimination Act (access to Goods and Services) came into force in October 2004. This means that service providers may have to consider making permanent physical adjustments to their premises. For further information, see the government website www.disability.gov.uk/dda

We indicate in the guide entries if a campsite has told us that they provide facilities for disabled visitors, and this is indicated by this symbol: ♿

The establishments in this guide should all be aware of their responsibilities under the Act. We recommend that you always telephone in advance to ensure that the establishment you have chosen has appropriate facilities.

Whatever, wherever, whenever...

...there's a superb
Caravan Club Site
that's perfect for you!

With around 200 top class
Sites to choose from in
fabulous locations
throughout the British
Isles, finding your
perfect holiday location
has never been easier.

You don't
have to be a
member to stay on
many Club Sites but
members save up
to £7 per night
on pitch fees

Whatever holiday experience you're looking for
there's a Club Site to suit you, including
40 Sites open all-year-round.

Whichever Site you choose, you can be
assured of excellent facilities, a friendly
welcome from our Resident Wardens, and
consistently high standards.

THE CARAVAN CLUB

The Caravan Club, East Grinstead House,
East Grinstead, West Sussex RH19 1UA

England

ENGLAND

ISLE OF Places incorporating the words `Isle of' or `Isle' will be found under the actual name, eg Isle of Wight is listed under Wight, Isle of. Channel Islands and Isle of Man, however, are between England and Scotland and there is a section containing Scottish Islands at the end of the Scotland gazetteer.

BERKSHIRE

FINCHAMPSTEAD   Map 05 SU76

▶ ▶ ▶ **73% California Chalet & Touring Park (SU788651)**
Nine Mile Ride RG40 4HU
☎ 0118 973 3928
▤ 0118 932 8720
✆ california.dodd@virgin.net
ⓦ www.californiapark.co.uk
Dir: From A321 S of Wokingham, turn right onto B3016 to Finchampstead, and follow Country Park signs along Nine Mile Ride to site
★ ⬛ £11-£13 ⬛ £11-£13 ⚑ £8-£16

Open Mar-Dec Booking advisable Jul & Aug Last arrival 20.00hrs Last departure noon
A peaceful woodland site with secluded pitches among the trees, adjacent to the country park. Several pitches have a prime position beside the lake with their own fishing area. A 5.5-acre site with 30 touring pitches, 30 hardstandings.
Facilities: �
Services: ⬛▤⊤→∪▶◉♦

HURLEY   Map 05 SU88

▶ ▶ ▶ **77% Hurley Riverside Park (SU826839)**
Park Office SL6 5NE
☎ 01628 823501 & 824493 Bookings
▤ 01628 825533
✆ info@hurleyriversidepark.co.uk
ⓦ www.hurleyriversidepark.co.uk
Dir: Signed off A4130 Henley to Maidenhead road, just W of Hurley village
★ ⬛ £9.25-£15.25 ⬛ £9.25-£15.25 ⚑ £8-£14
Open Mar-Oct Booking advisable bank hols, school hols & Henley Regatta Last arrival 20.00hrs Last departure noon
Large Thames-side site with good touring area

HURLEY
RIVERSIDE PARK

Park Office, Hurley Riverside Park, Hurley, Maidenhead, Berks SL6 5NE
Tel: 01628 824493 Fax: 01628 825533
Website: www.hurleyriversidepark.co.uk
Email: info@hurleyriversidepark.co.uk

Our family run park is situated in the picturesque Thames Valley surrounded by farmland with access to the Thames Path. We are an ideal location for visiting Windsor, (Legoland), Oxford & London. Multi-service and electric hook-ups – Launderette – Free hot showers – Shop – Slipway – Fishing in Season. Also fully serviced Caravan Holiday Homes for hire. Open 1 March – 31 October.

close to river. Level grassy pitches in small, sectioned areas, and a generally peaceful setting. A 15-acre site with 200 touring pitches and 290 statics. Fishing in season, slipway
Facilities: ⬛◉♦✖⚷⬛⬛⚓
Services: ⬛⚑▤⬛⬛⊤→∪▶◉♦⚑▤ **Notes:** No unsupervised children, dogs must be kept on leads ⬛ ▤ ⬛ ⬛ ⬛

NEWBURY   Map 05 SU46

▶ ▶ **75% Bishops Green Farm Camp Site (SU502630)**
Bishops Green RG20 4JP ☎ 01635 268365
Dir: Turn off A339 (opp New Greenham Park) towards Bishops Green & Ecchinswell. Site on left, approx 0.5m by barn
⬛⬛⚓
Open Apr-Oct Booking advisable Last arrival 21.30hrs
A sheltered and secluded meadowland park close to the Hampshire/Berkshire border, offering very clean and well-maintained facilities. There are woodland and riverside walks to be enjoyed around the farm, and coarse fishing is also available. A 1.5-acre site with 30 touring pitches.
Facilities: ⬛◉⚓⚷
Services: ⬛⚑▤⬛→▶♦

contd.

Services: ⊤ Toilet Fluid ✖ Café/ Restaurant ⬛ Fast Food/Takeaway ⬤ Baby Care ⬛ Electric Hook Up ⚑ Motorvan Service Point ◉ Launderette ⚷ Licensed Bar ⬛ Calor Gaz ⬛ Camping Gaz ⬛ Battery Charging

England

RISELEY   Map 05 SU76

► ► ► 76% **Wellington Country Park** (SU728628)
RG7 1SP ☎ 0118 932 6444 📠 0118 932 6445
🅔 info@wellington-country-park.co.uk
🆆 www.wellington-country-park.co.uk
*Dir: Signed off A33 between Reading and Basingstoke,
4m S of M4 junct 11*
★ 🚐 £16-£22 🚍 £16-£22 ▲ £13-£18

Open Mar-Nov Booking advisable peak periods Last
arrival 17.30hrs Last departure 13.00hrs
*A peaceful woodland site set within an extensive
country park, which comes complete with lakes,
nature trails, deer farm and boating. Ideal for M4
travellers. An 80-acre site with 72 touring pitches,
10 hardstandings.*
Boating, fishing, miniature railway, crazy golf
Leisure: 🅜 **Facilities:** 🏽⊙🍽⚡🔌🚿🛁🚻 🐾
Services: 🔌🅑🛢🚿✕ →🅤⊚♨🔆 🦯 **Notes:** No open
fires ☎ 🎴 🎴 🎴 🎴

BRISTOL

BRISTOL
See **Redhill (Somerset)**

CAMBRIDGESHIRE

BURWELL   Map 12 TL56

► ► ► 69% **Stanford Park** (TL578675)
Weirs Drove CB5 0BP
☎ 01638 741547 & 07802 439997
🆆 www.stanfordcaravanpark.co.uk
Dir: Signed from B1102
★ 🚐 £12-£14 🚍 £12-£14 ▲ £12
Open all year Booking advisable bank hols Last
arrival 20.00hrs Last departure 11.00hrs
*A secluded site on the outskirts of Burwell with
modern amenities. A 20-acre site with 100 touring
pitches, 10 hardstandings.*
Leisure: 🅜 **Facilities:** 🏽⊙🍽❄🔌🚿🚻
Services: 🔌🛒🛢🚿🅑🚾 →🅤▶🔆🦯🅑🛁

CAMBRIDGE
See **Burwell & Comberton**

COMBERTON   Map 12 TL35

► ► ► ► 90% **Highfield Farm
Touring Park** (TL389572)
Long Rd CB3 7DG
☎ 01223 262308
📠 01223 262308
🅔 enquiries@highfieldfarmtouringpark.co.uk
🆆 www.highfieldfarmtouringpark.co.uk
*Dir: From M11 junct 12, take A603 (Sandy) for 0.5m,
then right onto B1046 to Comberton*
★ 🚐 £9.25-£13 🚍 £9.25-£13 ▲ £9-£13

Best of British

Open Apr-Oct Booking advisable bank hols wknds
Last arrival 22.00hrs Last departure 14.00hrs
*Run by a very efficient and friendly family, the park
is on a well-sheltered hilltop, with spacious pitches
including a cosy backpackers/cyclists area, and
separate sections for couples and families. There is
a 1.5m marked walk around the family farm, with*

contd.

stunning views. An 8-acre site with 120 touring pitches, 52 hardstandings.
Postbox, farm walk

Leisure: ⚲ Facilities: 𝄞⊙☜※ﭖ☕⬛🐾
Services: 🐕🛒🚻🍴∅🔌💷→∪▶♨

GRAFHAM   Map 12 TL16

▶ ▶ ▶ ▶ 80% **Old Manor Caravan Park (TL160269)**
Church Rd PE28 0BB
☎ 01480 810264 📠 01480 819099
🖃 camping@old-manor.co.uk
🌐 www.old-manor.co.uk
Dir: Signed off A1, S of Huntingdon at Buckden and from A14, W of Huntingdon at Ellington
★ 🚐 £15-£18 🚐 £15-£18 ▲ £13-£16
Open all year (rs Nov-Feb on site shop closed)
Booking advisable wknds & peak times Last arrival 21.30hrs Last departure 18.00hrs
A secluded, well screened park in attractive gardens surrounding a 17th-century cottage. Pitches have lovely views of the countryside and Grafham Water is only a mile away. The enthusiastic owners continue to upgrade every area of the park.
A 6.5-acre site with 84 touring pitches, 7 hardstandings.
Leisure: ⚲ ⚲ Facilities: 𝄞⊙☜※ﭖ☕ﭖ
Services: 🐕🛒🍴∅🔌💷♨→∪▶♨♨
Notes: Dogs on leads 🐕 🚭 🏴

GREAT SHELFORD   Map 12 TL45

▶ ▶ ▶ 72% **Camping & Caravanning Club Site (TL455539)**
19 Cabbage Moor CB2 5NB ☎ 01223 841185
🌐 www.campingandcaravanningclub.co.uk
Dir: M11 junct 11 onto B1309 signed Cambridge. At 1st lights turn right. After 0.5m follow site sign on left
★ 🚐 £13.60-£17.80 🚐 £13.60-£17.80 ▲ £13.60-£17.80
Open Mar-Oct Booking advisable bank hols & peak periods Last arrival 21.00hrs Last departure noon
A popular, open site close to Cambridge and the M11, surrounded by high hedging and trees, with well-maintained toilet facilities. The large rally field is well used. Please see advertisement on page 11 for information on Club sites and membership.
An 11-acre site with 120 touring pitches.
Leisure: ⚲ Facilities: 𝄞⊙☜※ﭖ☕⬛🐾
Services: 🐕🛒∅🔌💷→▶♨♨♨
🐕 🚭 🏴 🏴 🏴

HEMINGFORD ABBOTS   Map 12 TL27

▶ ▶ ▶ 77% **Quiet Waters Caravan Park (TL283712)**
PE28 9AJ ☎ 01480 463405 📠 01480 463405
🖃 quietwaters.park@btopenworld.com
🌐 www.quietwaterscaravanpark.co.uk
Dir: Follow village signs off A14 junct 25, E of Huntingdon, site in village centre
★ 🚐 £11.50-£14.50 🚐 £11.50-£14.50 ▲ £11.50-£14.50
Open Apr-Oct Booking advisable high season Last arrival 20.00hrs Last departure noon
This attractive little riverside site is found in a most charming village just 1m from the A14 making an

ideal centre to tour the Cambridgeshire area. A 1-acre site with 20 touring pitches, 18 hardstandings and 40 statics.
Fishing & boating.
Facilities: 𝄞⊙☜※ﭖ☕
Services: 🐕🛒∅→∪▶♨♨♨♨♨
Notes: Pets on leads 🐕 🚭 🚭 🏴 🏴

HUNTINGDON   Map 12 TL27

▶ ▶ ▶ 80% **Huntingdon Boathaven & Caravan Park (TL249706)**
The Avenue, Godmanchester PE29 2AF
☎ 01480 411977 📠 01480 411977
🖃 boathaven.hunts@virgin.net
Dir: S of town off B1043 or leave A14 at Godmanchester junct, through Godmanchester on B1043 to site on left side by River Ouse
★ 🚐 £14-£15 🚐 £14-£15 ▲ £10-£14
Open all year open in winter only when weather permits Booking advisable Last arrival 21.00hrs
Small, well laid out site overlooking a boat marina and the River Ouse, set close to the A14 and within walking distance of Huntingdon town centre. Clean, well kept toilets. A pretty area has been created for tents beside the marina, with wide views across the Ouse Valley. Weekend family activities organized throughout the season. A 2-acre site with 24 touring pitches, 4 hardstandings.
Facilities: 𝄞⊙☜※ﭖ☕🎏🐾
Services: 🐕💷→▶♨♨♨♨♨
Notes: No cars by tents

▶ ▶ ▶ 75% **The Willows Caravan Park (TL224708)**
Bromholme Ln, Brampton PE28 4NE
☎ 01480 437566 📠 01480 437566
🖃 willows@willows33.freeserve.co.uk
Dir: Leave A14/A1 signed Brampton, follow signs for Huntingdon. Site on right close to Brampton Mill pub
★ 🚐 £14-£16 🚐 £14-£16 ▲ £12-£16
Open all year (rs 31 Oct-1 Mar 10 pitches only plus 6 storage spaces) Booking advisable all bank hols & school hols Last arrival 22.00hrs Last departure noon
A small, friendly site in a pleasant setting beside the River Ouse, on the Ouse Valley Walk. Bay areas have been provided for caravans and motorhomes, and planting for screening is gradually maturing. There are launching facilities, and free river fishing. A 4-acre site with 50 touring pitches.
Free book lending
Leisure: ⚲ Facilities: 𝄞⊙※ﭖ🎏
Services: 🐕🛒💷→▶♨♨♨ Notes: No cars by tents, dogs must be on leads, ball games on field provided, no generators, one-way system 5mph, no groundsheets

contd.

An increasing number of parks do not accept children. There is a list of adult-only sites on page 19.

England

ST IVES   Map 12 TL37

PREMIER PARK

▶ ▶ ▶ ▶ ▶ 88% **Stroud Hill Park (TL335787)**
Fen Rd PE28 3DE ☎ 01487 741333
🖹 01487 741365
✉ stroudhillpark@btconnect.com
⊕ www.stroudhillpark.co.uk
Dir: Off B1040 in Pidley follow signs for Lakeside Lodge Complex, down Fen Road site on right
🚐 £20 🚙 £20 ⚑ £15

Open all year Booking advisable At all times
A superb adults only caravan park built to a very high specification in a secluded and sheltered spot not far from St Ives. A traditional timber-framed bar houses the exceptional facilities, including beautifully tiled toilets with spacious cubicles containing combined showers, washbasins and toilets. A bar and café, restaurant, small licensed shop, tennis court and coarse fishing are among the attractions, and there are three pay-as-you-go golf courses and a ten-pin bowling alley nearby. A 6-acre site with 54 touring pitches, 44 hardstandings.
Leisure: ৭ Facilities: ⋒⊙৭⋇ᗱ℀🐕🔭
Services: ⬚🔌⬚ⓘ∅🔟✕→∪▶⊙⏏♨🍴
Notes: Adult only park, no large motorhomes
💳 💳 💳 📶 🔊

ST NEOTS   Map 12 TL16

▶ ▶ ▶ 79% **Camping & Caravanning Club Site (TL182598)**
Hardwick Rd, Eynesbury PE19 2PR
☎ 01480 474404
⊕ www.campingandcaravanningclub.co.uk
Dir: From A1 take A428 to Cambridge, 2nd rdbt left to Tesco's, past Sports Centre. International Camping signs to site
⚑ 🚐 £13.60-£19.80 🚙 £13.60-£19.80 ⚑ £13.60-£19.80
Open Mar-Oct Booking advisable BH's & peak periods Last arrival 21.00hrs Last departure noon
A level meadowland site adjacent to the River Ouse on the outskirts of St Neots, with well maintained and modern facilities, and helpful, attentive staff. A proposal by the town council to construct a landing stage and provide an electric boat to ferry campers into town should prove popular. Please see the advertisement on page 11 for information on Club sites and membership. An 11-acre site with 180 touring pitches, 33 hardstandings.
contd.

WISBECH   Map 12 TF40

NEW ▶ ▶ ▶ 79% **Little Ranch Leisure (TF456062)**
Begdale, Elm PE14 0AZ ☎ 01945 860066
Dir: From rdbt on A47 (SW of Wisbech) take Redmoor Lane to Begdale
Set in an apple orchard, with 25 fully-serviced pitches and a beautifully designed, spacious toilet block. The site overlooks a large fishing lake, and the famous horticultural auctions at Wisbech are nearby.

CHESHIRE

CHESTER   Map 15 SJ46

▶ ▶ ▶ 68% **Chester Southerly Caravan Park (SJ385624)**
Balderton Ln, Marlston-Cum-Lache CH4 9LF
☎ 07976 743888 & 01244 671308 🖹 01244 659804
⊕ www.chestersoutherlytouringpark.co.uk
Dir: Just off A55/A483 rdbt
⚑ 🚐 £14-£18 🚙 £14-£18 ⚑ £14-£18
Open Etr-Nov Booking advisable bank hols essential
Last arrival 21.00hrs Last departure noon
Set amidst very attractive and informal landscaping, the park is located on the rural south side of the Roman city of Chester, close to the bypass. An 8-acre site with 90 touring pitches, 70 hardstandings.
Leisure: ⚠ Facilities: ⋒⊙৭⋇ᗱ℀🐕🔭🐕
Services: ⬚ⓘ🔟→∪▶⊙♨☘♨🍴
Notes: No commercial vehicles, no dogs in tents, no skate boards or cycles, no ball games.

CODDINGTON   Map 15 SJ45

NEW ▶ ▶ ▶ 84% **Manor Wood Country Caravan Park (SJ453553)**
Manor Wood CH3 9EN ☎ 01829 782990 & 782442
🖹 01829 782990
✉ info@manorwoodcaravans.co.uk
⊕ www.cheshire-caravan-sites.co.uk
Dir: From A534 at Barton, turn opposite Cock O'Barton pub signed Coddington. Left in 100yds. Site 0.5m on left
⚑ 🚐 £13-£15 🚙 £13-£15 ⚑ £13-£15
Open all year (rs Oct-May Swimming pool closed)
Booking advisable Last arrival 20.30hrs Last departure 11.00hrs
A secluded landscaped park in a tranquil country setting with extensive views towards the Welsh Hills across the Cheshire Plain. This newly developed park offers fully serviced pitches, modern facilities, a heated outdoor pool and tennis courts. Wildlife is encouraged, and lake fishing with country walks and pubs are added attractions. An 8-acre site with 45 touring pitches, 38 hardstandings. Fishing
Leisure: ৲ ৭ ⚠ Facilities: ⋒⊙৭⋇ᗱ℀🐕
Services: ⬚⬚ⓘ∅→▶☘♨ Notes: No cars by caravans, no cars by tents

---

Facilities: 🛁 Bath ⋒ Shower ⊙ Electric Shaver ৭ Hairdryer ⋇ Ice Pack Facility ᗱ Disabled Facilities ℀ Public Telephone
🏪 Shop on Site or within 200yds 📱 Mobile Shop (calls at least 5 days a week) 🍴 BBQ Area ⏍ Picnic Area 🐕 Dog Exercise Area

England

KNUTSFORD   Map 15 SJ77

► ► ► 74% **Woodlands Park (SJ743710)**
Wash Ln, Allostock WA16 9LG
☎ 01565 723429 & 07976 702490 ▤ 01332 810818
*Dir: From Holmes Chapel take A50 N for 3m, turn into
Wash Lane by Boundary Water Park. Site 0.25m on left*
★ ₩ £9-£11 ₩ £9-£11 ▲ £9-£11
Open Mar-6 Jan Booking advisable bank hols Last
arrival 21.00hrs Last departure 11.00hrs
*A very attractive park in the heart of rural Cheshire,
and set in 16 acres of mature woodland. 3m from
Jodrell Bank. A 16-acre site with 50 touring pitches
and 140 statics.*
Facilities: ╟⊙& Services: ❄▤î→▶◢⚓

MACCLESFIELD   Map 16 SJ97

► ► ► 75% **Capesthorne Hall (SJ840727)**
Siddington SK11 9JY ☎ 01625 861779 & 861221
▤ 01625 861619
➌ info@capesthorne.com
Ⓦ www.capesthorne.com
Dir: On A34, 1m S of A537
★ ₩ £15-£18 ₩ £15-£18
Open Mar-Oct Booking advisable public hols Last
arrival 16.30hrs Last departure noon
*Set in the magnificent grounds of the historic
Capesthorpe Hall, with access to the lakes, gardens
and woodland walks free to site users. Pitches in
the open parkland are spacious and can take the
larger motorhomes, and the clean toilet facilities are
housed in the old stable block. The beautiful
Cheshire countryside is easily explored. No tents or
trailer tents. A 5.5-acre site with 30 touring pitches.*
Capesthorne Hall & gardens
Facilities: ╟⊙╰♣ Services: ❄→∪▶⚓

MIDDLEWICH   Map 15 SJ76

► ► 70% *Yatehouse Farm Caravan Park
(SJ702685)*
Yatehouse Ln, Byley CW10 9NS ☎ 01606 833125
➌ bookings@yatehouse.co.uk
Ⓦ www.yatehouse.co.uk
*Dir: M6 junct 18, A533 to Middlewich. Take B5309, turn
right for site*
❄ Open all year
*A pleasant farm site with good level pitches, electric
hook-ups and simple toilet facilities. It is close to
Jodrell Bank, and the Anderton Boat Lift at
Northwich, and an ideal stopover site. A 3-acre site
with 25 touring pitches.*
Leisure: ⚲ Facilities: ╟ Services: ❄

WARRINGTON   Map 15 SJ68

► ► ► 73% **Holly Bank Caravan Park (SJ693904)**
Warburton Bridge Rd WA3 6HU ☎ 0161 775 2842
*Dir: 2m E of M6 junct 21 on A57 (Irlam). Turn right at 1st
lights, site 30yds on left*
★ ₩ £15 ₩ £15 ▲ £13
Open all year Booking advisable bank hols & wknds
Apr-Oct Last arrival 20.00hrs Last departure noon
*A well-run and attractive park in a rural setting with
mature trees. The spotless toilets are located in the
main block, with a good portakabin facility on the
touring field. A good base for access to Warrington
Retail Parks, Manchester, and the Trafford Centre
shopping complex. An 8.75-acre site with 75 touring
pitches, 2 hardstandings.*
Lending library.
Leisure: ⚲ Facilities: ╟⊙ℚ❋&╰⚓♣
Services: ❄▤î⊘▣▣→∪▶△♨◢
Notes: No cars by tents, no groups

WHITEGATE   Map 15 SJ66

► ► ► ► 86% **Lamb Cottage Caravan
Park (SJ613692)**
Dalefords Ln CW8 2BN ☎ 01606 882302
▤ 01606 888491
➌ lynn@lccp.fsworld.co.uk
Ⓦ www.lambcottage.co.uk
*Dir: From A556, turn at Sandiway lights into Dalefords
Lane, signed Winsford. Site 1m on right*
₩ £17-£20 ₩ £17-£20
Open Mar-Oct Booking advisable All season Last
arrival 20.00hrs Last departure noon
*A secluded and attractively landscaped adults-only
park with the emphasis on peace and relaxation. The
serviced pitches are spacious with wide grass borders
for sitting out. A good central base for exploring the
surrounding countryside, with access to nearby
woodland walks and cycle trails. A 6-acre site with
60 touring pitches, 28 hardstandings and 12 statics.*
Facilities: ╟⊙ℚ&╰♣
Services: ❄î→∪▶◢⚓
Notes: Adult only park, no tents ex trailer tents,
no commercial vehicles ⬤ ▬ ▨ ▨ ⬚

CORNWALL & ISLES OF SCILLY

ASHTON   Map 02 SW62

▶ ▶ ▶ 70% **Boscrege Caravan & Camping Park** (SW595305) TR13 9TG ☎ 01736 762231
✉ enquiries@caravanparkcornwall.com
ⓦ www.caravanparkcornwall.com
Dir: Follow signs from B3202, Hayle to Helston road, to Godolphin Cross. Turn right at pub to site
⚏ £6.75-£13.75 ⚏ £6.75-£13.75 ▲ £6.75-£13.75
Open Mar-Nov Booking advisable Jul-Aug Last arrival 22.00hrs Last departure 11.00hrs
A quiet and bright little touring park divided into small paddocks with hedges, and offering plenty of open spaces for children to play in. The family-owned park offers clean, well-painted toilet facilities and neatly trimmed grass. In an Area of Outstanding Natural Beauty at the foot of Tregonning Hill. A 12-acre site with 50 touring pitches and 26 statics.
Recreation fields, Microwave, Nature trail.
Leisure: ⚓ ⚑ ⏁ Facilities: ⬡⊙⚒❋⚓⛶⛱⛩
Services: ⬚⬚⬚⬚⬚⬚ → ∪ ▶ ⊙ ⬚⬚ ⬚⬚ ⬚
⬚⬚ ⬚⬚ ⬚⬚ ⬚⬚ ⬚

See advertisement on page 40

BLACKWATER   Map 02 SW74

▶ ▶ ▶ 90% **Chiverton Caravan & Touring Park** (SW743468)
East Hill TR4 8HS ☎ 01872 560667 🖷 01872 560667
✉ chivertonpark@btopenworld.com
ⓦ www.chivertonpark.co.uk
Dir: Leave A30 at Chiverton rdbt (Little Chef) onto unclass road signed Blackwater (3rd exit). Take 1st right. Park 300mtrs on right
★ ⚏ £8-£17 ⚏ £8-£22 ▲ £6-£17

Open 8 Feb-6 Jan (rs Feb-May & mid Sep-Jan limited stock kept in shop) Booking advisable mid Jul-Aug Last arrival 21.00hrs Last departure noon
A small, well-maintained site with some mature hedges dividing pitches, sited midway between Truro and St Agnes, and an ideal touring centre. A new toilet block and a steam room, sauna and gym are welcome additions. A 4-acre site with 12 touring pitches, 10 hardstandings and 50 statics.
Drying lines, Sauna, Steam room, Gym
Leisure: ⚓ ⚑ Facilities: ⬡⊙⚒❋⚓⛶⛱⛩
Services: ⬚⬚⬚⬚ → ∪ ▶ ⬚ ⬚ ⬚

▶ ▶ ▶ 76% *Trevarth Holiday Park* (SW744468)
TR4 8HR ☎ 01872 560266 🖷 01872 560379
✉ trevarth@lineone.net
Dir: Leave A30 at Chiverton rdbt onto unclass rd signed Blackwater. Site on right in 200mtrs
⚏ ⚏ ▲

Open Etr or Apr-Oct Booking advisable Jul-Aug Last arrival 22.00hrs Last departure noon
A neat and compact park with touring pitches laid out on attractive, well-screened high ground adjacent to A30/A39 junction. This pleasant little park is centrally located for touring, and is maintained to a very good standard. A 4-acre site with 30 touring pitches, 2 hardstandings and 21 statics.
Baby changing facilities
Leisure: ⚓ ⚑ Facilities: ⬡⊙⚒❋⚓⛱
Services: ⬚⬚⬚⬚⬚ → ∪ ⬚ ⬚ ⬚⬚ ⬚⬚ ⬚

BLISLAND   Map 02 SX17

▶ 78% **South Penquite Farm** (SX108751)
South Penquite PL30 4LH ☎ 01208 850491
🖷 0870 1367926
✉ thefarm@bodminmoor.co.uk
ⓦ www.southpenquite.co.uk
Dir: Leave A30 at 1st sign to St Breward on right from Exeter, 2nd sign on left from Bodmin. Follow narrow road across Bodmin Moor. Ignore left & right turns until South Penquite Farm Lane on right in 2m
★ ▲ £8
Open 14 May-Oct Booking advisable Aug Last departure 14.00hrs
Located on a working organic farm on Bodmin Moor, this fairly simple, mainly tenting site is sheltered by mature trees and hedges. The two fields afford plenty of space, and the friendly conservation-conscious owners will give details of a lovely riverside walk past a Bronze Age settlement. A 4-acre site with 40 touring pitches.
Organic produce available
Leisure: ⚑
Facilities: ⬡⊙⚒❋♿⛶→∪▶⬚⬚⬚⬚
Notes: ⌀

> Remember to check your tent or caravan thoroughly before leaving home to ensure everything is in good order.

Leisure: 🏊 Indoor swimming pool   🏊 Outdoor swimming pool   🎾 Tennis court   ⚓ Games room   ⚑ Children's playground   ∪ Stables
▶ 9/18 hole golf course   ⚓ Boats for hire   🎦 Cinema   🎣 Fishing   ⊚ Mini golf   △ Watersports   ⬚ Separate TV room

England

BODMIN
Map 02 SX06

See also **Lanivet**

▶ ▶ ▶ 70% Camping & Caravanning Club Site (SX081676)
Old Callywith Rd PL31 2DZ ☎ 01208 73834
Ⓦ www.campingandcaravanningclub.co.uk
Dir: A30 from N, at sign for Bodmin turn right crossing dual carriageway in front of industrial estate, turn left at international sign, site left
★ 🚐 £12.40-£16.70 🚐 £12.40-£16.70 ▲ £12.40-£16.70
Open Mar-Oct Booking advisable bank hols & peak periods Last arrival 21.00hrs Last departure noon
Undulating grassy site with trees and bushes set in meadowland close to the town of Bodmin with all its attractions. The site is close to the A30 and makes a very good touring base. Please see the advertisement on page 11 for information on Club sites and membership. An 11-acre site with 130 touring pitches, 12 hardstandings.
Leisure: ⚤ Facilities: 🏪⊙🔍✳🕹🛁🚻
Services: 🔌♨🚰🔋⊘🔲🛗→🛆🔧💺
📶 💳 🏧 📡 🦮

BOLVENTOR
Map 02 SX17

▶ ▶ ▶ ▶ 68% *Colliford Tavern Campsite* (SX171740)
Colliford Lake, St Neot PL14 6PZ ☎ 01208 821335
🖨 01208 821335
Ⓔ info@colliford.com
Ⓦ www.colliford.com
Dir: Leave A30 1.25m W of Bolventor onto unclass rd signed Colliford Lake. Site 0.25m on left
🚐 🚐 ▲
Open Etr-Sep Booking advisable bank hols & Jul-Aug Last arrival 22.30hrs Last departure 11.00hrs
An oasis on Bodmin Moor, a small site with spacious grassy pitches and very good quality facilities. The park is surrounded by mature trees and very sheltered in the centre of Bodmin Moor. Fly fishing is available at nearby Colliford Lake. A 3.5-acre site with 40 touring pitches.
Leisure: ⚤ Facilities: 🏪⊙🔍✳🕹🛁🚻
Services: 🔌♨🔋⊘✗🛗→ 🔧 Notes: Dogs must be kept on leads 📶 💳 🏧 📡 🦮

BOSCASTLE
Map 02 SX09

▶ 75% **Lower Pennycrocker Farm** (SX125927)
PL35 0BY ☎ 01840 250257 🖨 01840 250613
Ⓔ holidays@pennycrocker.fsnet.co.uk
Ⓦ www.pennycrockerinternet.co.uk
Dir: Leave A39 at Marshgate onto B3263 towards Boscastle, site signed in 2m
🚐 🚐 ▲
Open Etr-Sep Booking advisable
Mature Cornish hedges provide shelter for this small, family-run site on a dairy farm. Spectacular scenery and the nearby coastal footpath are among the many attractions, along with fresh eggs, milk and home-made clotted cream for sale. The small toilet block is very clean if quite basic. A 6-acre site with 40 touring pitches.
Facilities: 🏪⊙✳🛉🚻
Services: 🔌♨🔲→🛆🔧 ⬛

BOSWINGER
Map 02 SW94

PREMIER PARK

▶ ▶ ▶ ▶ ▶ 93% **Sea View International Caravan & Camping Park** (SW990412)
PL26 6LL ☎ 01726 843425
🖨 01726 843358

Ⓔ holidays@seaviewinternational.com
Ⓦ www.seaviewinternational.com
Dir: From St Austell take B3273 signed Mevagissey. Turn right before entering village. Follow brown tourist signs to site
🚐 £7-£25 🚐 £7-£25 ▲ £7-£25
Open Mar-Oct Booking advisable Jul-Sep Last arrival 21.00hrs Last departure 11.00hrs
This attractive holiday park is set in a beautiful environment overlooking Veryan Bay, with colourful landscaping including attractive flowers and shrubs. It continues to offer an outstanding holiday experience, with its luxury family pitches, superb toilet facilities and beautiful grounds. The beach and sea are just half a mile away. A 28-acre site with 189 touring pitches, 13 hardstandings and 38 statics.
Crazy golf, volleyball, badminton, cycle hire
Leisure: 🎾 ⚽ 🎱 ⚤
Facilities: 🚿🏪⊙🔍✳🛁🚻🛉🏪🍴🚻
Services: 🔌♨🚰🔋⊘🛗→⊙🛆🔧🔧
Notes: Restrictions on certain breeds of dog
📶 💳 🏧 📡 🦮

See advertisement on opposite page

BRYHER
Map 02 SV81

See **Scilly, Isles**

BUDE
Map 02 SS20

See also **Kilkhampton & Bridgerule (Devon)**

 68% **Sandymouth Bay Holiday Park** (SS214104)
Sandymouth Bay EX23 9HW
☎ 01288 352563 🖨 01288 354822
Ⓔ sandymouthbay@aol.com
Ⓦ www.sandymouthbay.co.uk
Dir: Signed off A39 approx 0.5m S of Kilkhampton, 4m N of Bude
★ 🚐 £7.90-£16 🚐 £7.90-£16 ▲ £7.90-£16
Open Apr-Oct Booking advisable Jul & Aug Last arrival 22.00hrs Last departure 10.00hrs
A friendly holiday park with glorious and extensive sea views. Many on-site facilities, and an extensive entertainment programme for all ages. A 4-acre site with 100 touring pitches and 158 statics.
Sauna, solarium, crazy golf
Leisure: 🎾 ⚽ ⚤
Facilities: 🏪⊙✳🛁🚻🏪🍴
Services: 🔌♨🚰🔋⊘🔲🛗✗🛗→⊙🛆🔧🔧
📶 💳 🏧 📡 🦮

See advertisement on opposite page

England

are a short drive away. A 15-acre site with 200 touring pitches, 60 hardstandings and 55 statics. Coarse fishing, clay pigeon shooting, pets corner

Leisure: ♥ ♣ ⚠ 🖵 **Facilities:** ⇥ ♠ ⊙ ♣ ✳ ⚓ ⟨ ⚑ ⩎ ♒

Services: 🔌 💶 🍴 ♨ ⌀ 🚻 🎦 ✗ 🛁 ➪ → ∪ ⌲ ☺ ⚠ ✚

🐾 ✦ **Notes:** Restrictions on certain breeds of dogs ● 💳 ▒ ▒ 🗺 𝄞

See advertisement below

▶ ▶ ▶ ▶ **81% Budemeadows Touring Holiday Park (SS215012)**
EX23 0NA ☎ 01288 361646
✉ holiday@budemeadows.com
ⓦ www.budemeadows.com
Dir: 3m S of Bude on A39. Park entered via layby
★ 🚐 £7.80-£18 🚐 £7.80-£18 ▲ £7.80-£18
Open all year (rs Sep-Spring BH shop, bar & pool closed) Booking advisable Jul-Aug Last arrival
contd.

A real Cornish welcome awaits you from the Colwill family. Enjoy a farm and seaside holiday with us overlooking Bude Bay and countryside with its safe, sandy beaches. The Splash Indoor Pool is nearby. We offer luxury holiday homes and excellent facilities for touring and camping with individual screened pitches. Our activities include: Children's playground, coarse fishing, short golf course, woodland walks, farmyard friends. In main season archery. Clay pigeon shooting – licensed farm restaurant.
Please write or telephone for a brochure to:
Mrs A. Colwill, Wooda Farm Park, Poughill, Bude, Cornwall EX23 9HJ.
Tel: 01288 352069 Fax: 01288 355258
www.wooda.co.uk

Surfers at Widemouth Bay

Budemeadows Touring Holiday Park
21.00hrs Last departure 11.00hrs
A very well kept site of distinction, with good quality facilities. Budemeadows is set on a gentle sheltered slope in nine acres of naturally landscaped parkland, surrounded by mature hedges. Just one mile from Widemouth Bay, and three miles from the unspoilt resort of Bude. A 9-acre site with 144 touring pitches, 24 hardstandings. Table tennis, giant chess, baby changing facility

Leisure: ♥ ♣ ⚠ 🖵
Facilities: ⇥ ♠ ⊙ ♣ ✳ ⚓ ⟨ 🎦 ⚑ ♒
Services: 🔌 💶 🍴 ♨ ⌀ 🚻 🛁 → ∪ ⌲ ☺ ⚠ ✚ 🐾 ✦
● 💳 ▒ ▒ 🗺 𝄞

See advertisement on opposite page

▶ ▶ ▶ ▶ **81% Penstowe Caravan & Camping Park (SS230100)**
Stibb Rd, Kilkhampton EX23 9QY
☎ 01288 321601 📠 01288 321601
✉ camping@penstowecaravans.wanadoo.co.uk
ⓦ www.penstoweleisure.co.uk
Dir: A39 4m N of Bude, turn left to Sandymouth site, 200yds on right
🚐 🚐 ▲

Open all year Booking advisable Aug Last arrival 22.00hrs Last departure 10.00hrs
An all-touring park with quality facilities located about 2 miles from Sandymouth Bay with its beaches and surf. The mixture of grass and hardstanding are all level. Visitors can take advantage of the adjoining Penstowe Leisure Club, accessed via a private road on the estate. Some of the amenities require a small membership charge. A 6-acre site with 140 touring pitches, 80 hardstandings.
Sports facilities, tenpin bowling, green bowls
Leisure: ♥ ✦ ♥ ♣ ⚠ **Facilities:** ♠ ⊙ ♣ ✳ ⚓ ⟨ ⚑ ⩎ ♒
Services: 🔌 💶 🍴 ♨ ⌀ ✗ 🛁 → ∪ ⌲ ✦
● 💳 ▒ ▒ 🗺 𝄞

England

▶ ▶ ▶ 73% **Upper Lynstone Caravan Park**
(SS205053)
Lynstone EX23 0LP ☎ 01288 352017 ▤ 01288 359034
✉ reception@upperlynstone.co.uk
ⓦ www.upperlynstone.co.uk
Dir: 0.75m S of Bude on coastal road to Widemouth Bay
★ ⚌ £7.50-£14.50 ⚌ £7.50-£14.50 ⚊ £7.50-£14.50

Open Apr-Oct Booking advisable Last arrival
22.00hrs Last departure 10.00hrs
There are extensive views over Bude to be enjoyed
from this quiet family-run park set on sheltered
ground. There is a small shop selling camping
spares, and a children's playground. A path leads
directly to the coastal footpath with its stunning sea
views, and the old Bude Canal is a stroll away.
A 6-acre site with 65 touring pitches and 41 statics.
Baby changing room
Leisure: ⚑ Facilities: ↖⊙♋⚹⅋⚓⚐⚑
Services: ⊟⊞⊘⊟⎁→ ∪⟜⊙⚐⚹⚌⚒
Notes: No groups 💳 💳 🔊

▶ ▶ ▶ 75% **Willow Valley Holiday Park**
(SS236078)
Bush EX23 9LB ☎ 01288 353104
✉ willowvalley@talk21.com
ⓦ www.willowvalley.co.uk
Dir: On A39, 0.5m N of junct with A3072 at Stratton
⚌ £8-£11 ⚌ £8-£11 ⚊ £8-£11

Open Mar-Dec Booking advisable Jul & Aug Last
arrival 21.00hrs Last departure noon
A small sheltered park in Strat Valley with a stream
running through and level grassy pitches. The
friendly new owners have improved all areas of this
attractive park, which has direct access off the A39,
and is only 2 miles from the sandy beaches at Bude.
A 3-acre site with 41 touring pitches and 4 statics.
Leisure: ⚑ Facilities: ↖⊙♋⚹⅋⚓⚐⚑
Services: ⊟⊞⊘⊟⎁→ ∪⟜⊙⚐⚹⚒
💳 💳 🔊

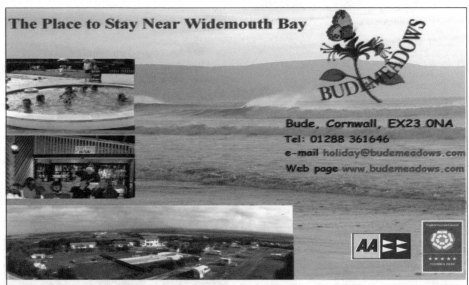
Leisure: 🏊 Indoor swimming pool 🏊 Outdoor swimming pool 🎾 Tennis court 🎱 Games room ⚑ Children's playground ∪ Stables
▶ 9/18 hole golf course 🚤 Boats for hire 🎬 Cinema 🎣 Fishing ◎ Mini golf ⚓ Watersports ⊟ Separate TV room

England

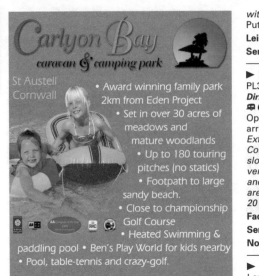

Carlyon Bay caravan & camping park

St Austell
Cornwall

- Award winning family park 2km from Eden Project
- Set in over 30 acres of meadows and mature woodlands
- Up to 180 touring pitches (no statics)
- Footpath to large sandy beach.
- Close to championship Golf Course
- Heated Swimming & paddling pool • Ben's Play World for kids nearby
- Pool, table-tennis and crazy-golf.

For colour brochure call:
01726 812735
www.carlyonbay.net
e-mail:holidays@carlyonbay.net

CAMELFORD   **Map 02 SX18**

▶ ▶ ▶ 73% **Juliot's Well Holiday Park** (SX095829)
PL32 9RF ☎ 01840 213302
🖹 01840 212700
🟢 juliotswell@travelsmith.co.uk
ⓦ www.holidaysincornwall.net
Dir: Through Camelford, A39 at Valley Truckle turn right onto B3266, then 1st left signed Lanteglos, site 300yds on right
★ ₽ £8-£12 ₽ £8-£12 Å £8-£12

Open all year (rs Nov-Feb bar/restaurant not open daily) Booking advisable All year Last arrival 20.00hrs Last departure 11.00hrs
Set in the wooded grounds of an old manor house, this quiet site enjoys lovely and extensive views across the countryside. A rustic inn on site offers occasional entertainment, and there is plenty to do both on the park and in the vicinity. A 31-acre site
contd.

---

with 60 touring pitches, 16 hardstandings. Putting green
Leisure: ⊰ ⚲ ◗ ⚲ Facilities: ⊷ ⋔ ⊙ ⚲ ※ Ⴝ ⅃ ⋒ ↑
Services: ⊠ 🖭 ⚲ ✕ ⬥ → ∪ ▶ 🍴 ▨

▶ ▶ ▶ 77% **Kings Acre** (SX090850)
PL32 9UR ☎ 01840 213561 🖹 01840 213561
Dir: On B3266, towards Boscastle, on right
₽ ₽ Å
Open Mar-Oct Booking advisable Jul-Aug Last arrival 22.00hrs Last departure noon
Extensive rural views towards the rugged north Cornish coast can be enjoyed from this slightly sloping and sheltered park. Toilet facilities are to a very good standard. The site is handy for the ancient town of Camelford, while various beaches are within a 6-mile drive. A 1.5-acre site with 20 touring pitches and 1 static.
Facilities: ⋔ ※ Ⴝ ⅃ ⋒
Services: ⊠ 🖭 ⚲ ⊞ ⊡ ✕ ⬥ → ∪ ▶ ◭ ⅃
Notes: No pets

▶ ▶ ▶ 70% **Lakefield Caravan Park** (SX095853)
Lower Pendavey Farm PL32 9TX ☎ 01840 213279
🟢 lakefield@pendavey.fsnet.co.uk
ⓦ www.lakefieldcaravanpark.co.uk
Dir: From A39 in Camelford turn right onto B3266, then right at T-junct and site 1.5m on left
₽ ₽ Å
Open Etr or Apr-Oct Booking advisable Jul-Aug Last arrival 22.00hrs Last departure noon
Set in a rural location, this friendly park is part of a specialist equestrian centre, and offers good quality services. Riding lessons and hacks always available, with BHS qualified instructor. A 5-acre site with 40 touring pitches.
Own lake & full equestrian centre.
Facilities: ⋔ ⊙ ⚲ ※ Ⴝ ⋒
Services: ⊠ 🖭 ⅃ ⊞ ⊡ ✕ → ∪ ▶ ◭ ⅃

CARLYON BAY   **Map 02 SX05**

▶ ▶ ▶ ▶ 83% **Carlyon Bay Caravan & Camping Park** (SX052526)
Bethesda, Cypress Av PL25 3RE ☎ 01726 812735
🖹 01726 815496
🟢 holidays@carlyonbay.net
ⓦ www.carlyonbay.net
Dir: Off A390 W of St Blazey, turn left on A3092 for Par, right in 0.5m. On private road to Carlyon Bay
₽ ₽ Å

contd.

Open Etr-3 Oct (rs Etr-mid May & mid Sep-3 Oct swimming pool, take-away & shop closed) Booking advisable mid Jul-mid Aug Last arrival 21.00hrs Last departure 11.00hrs
An attractive, secluded site set amongst a belt of trees with background woodland. The spacious grassy park offers plenty of on-site attractions, with occasional family entertainment, and it is less than 0.5m from a sandy beach. The Eden Project is only 2m away. A 35-acre site with 180 touring pitches, 6 hardstandings.
Crazy golf, children's entertainment in Jul & Aug.

Leisure: ⚡ ৭ ✦ ⚠ ❑
Facilities: ⛷ ☉ ৭ ※ ↻ ⚑ ☎ ⤧ ⚲
Services: ⚙ ☷ 🛈 ⌀ ⊟ ⊡ 🚻 ♺→ ∪ ▶ ◎ ♨ ⚺ ⚑ ♩
🍴 ▭ ▱ ⊠ ⬘

See advertisement on previous page

▶ ▶ ▶ **70% East Crinnis Camping & Caravan Park (SX062528)**
Lantyan, East Crinnis PL24 2SQ ☎ 01726 813023
🖷 01726 813023
📧 eastcrinnis@btconnect.com
🌐 www.crinniscamping.co.uk
Dir: From A390, Lostwithiel to St Austell, take A3082 signed Fowey at rdbt by Britannia Inn, site on left
⚘ £8-£15 ⚙ £8-£15 ⚑ £7-£15

Open Etr-Oct Booking advisable Jul & Aug Last arrival 21.00hrs Last departure 11.00hrs
A small rural park with spacious pitches set in individual bays about one mile from the beaches at Carlyon Bay. The friendly owners keep the site very clean, and the Eden Project is just 2m away. A 2-acre site with 25 touring pitches, 6 hardstandings.

Leisure: ⚠ Facilities: ⛷ ☉ ※ ⚹ ⚑
Services: ⚙ → ∪ ▶ ⊹ ⚺ ♩ ⊟ ⚔
Notes: Dogs must be kept on leads at all times
🍴 ▭ ▱ ⊠ ⬘

COVERACK	Map 02 SW71

▶ ▶ ▶ **70% Little Trevothan Caravan & Camping Park (SW772179)**
Trevothan TR12 6SD ☎ 01326 280260
🖷 01326 280260
📧 mmita@btopenworld.com
🌐 www.littletrevothan.com
Dir: From A3083 turn left onto B3293 signed Coverack, approx 2m after Goonhilly ESS right at Zoar Garage on unclass rd. Take 3rd on left, site 0.5m on right
★ ⚘ £9.50-£12 ⚙ £9.50-£12 ⚑ £9.50-£12

Open May-Sep Booking advisable Aug Last arrival 21.00hrs Last departure noon
A secluded site near the unspoilt fishing village of Coverack, with a large recreation area. The nearby sandy beach has lots of rock pools for children to play in, and the many walks both from the park and the village offer stunning scenery. A 10.5-acre site with 65 touring pitches and 21 statics.

Leisure: ✦ ⚠ ❑ Facilities: ⛷ ☉ ৭ ※ ↻ ⚑ ☎ ⤧ ⚑
Services: ⚙ 🛈 ⌀ ⊟ ⊡ → ⊹ ♩ ⬘ Notes: No groups

CRACKINGTON HAVEN	Map 02 SX19

▶ ▶ ▶ **71% Hentervene Holiday Park (SX155944)**
EX23 0LF ☎ 01840 230365
📧 contact@hentervene.co.uk
🌐 www.hentervene.co.uk
Dir: Leave A39 approx 10m SW of Bude and 1.5m beyond Wainhouse Corner onto B3263 signed Boscastle & Crackington Haven. After 0.75m, at Tresparret Posts junct, right signed for Hentervene. Site 0.75 on right
★ ⚘ £8-£12 ⚙ £8-£12 ⚑ £8-£12
Open Mar-Oct (rs Nov-Feb statics only) Booking advisable Bank and school holidays Last arrival 21.00hrs Last departure 11.00hrs
This much improved park is set in a rural location a short drive from a golden sandy beach. It is in an Area of Outstanding Natural Beauty, and pitches are in paddocks which are bordered by mature hedges, with a small stream running past. Some pitches are on level terraces, and there are also hardstandings. A 4.5-acre site with 43 touring pitches, 9 hardstandings and 24 statics.
Caravan storage, baby bathroom, microwave

Leisure: ✦ ⚠ ❑
Facilities: ⛷ ☉ ৭ ※ ↻ ⚑ ☎ ⤧
Services: ⚙ ☷ 🛈 → ⊹ ♩ ⚴ 🍴 ▭ ⬘

CRANTOCK (NEAR NEWQUAY)	Map 02 SW76

▶ ▶ ▶ ▶ **77% Trevella Tourist Park (SW801599)**
TR8 5EW ☎ 01637 830308
🖷 01637 830155
📧 trevellapark@aol.com
🌐 www.trevella.co.uk
Dir: Between Crantock and A3075
★ ⚘ £8.20-£14 ⚙ £7.20-£13 ⚑ £8.20-£14
Open Etr-Oct Booking advisable BH's & Jul-Aug
A well established and very well run family site, with outstanding floral displays. Set in a rural area close to Newquay, this attractive park boasts three teeming fishing lakes for the experienced and novice angler, and a superb outdoor swimming pool and paddling area. All areas are neat and clean. A 15-acre site with 313 touring pitches, 53 hardstandings and 76 statics.
Crazy golf, fishing & badminton.

Leisure: ⚡ ✦ ⚠ ❑
Facilities: ⛷ ☉ ৭ ※ ⚹ ↻ ⚑ ☎ ⤧
Services: ⚙ 🖳 ☷ 🛈 ⌀ ⊟ ⊡ ✗ ⬚→ ∪ ▶ ◎ ♨ ⚺ ⚑ ♩
🍴 ▭ ▱ ⚙ ⊠ ⬘

See advertisement on page 49

contd.

► ► ► 76%**Crantock Plains Touring Park**
(SW805589)
TR8 5PH ☎ 01637 830955 & 831273
ⓦ www.crantock-plains.co.uk
*Dir: Leave Newquay on A3075, take 3rd turn on right
signed to park and Crantock. Park on left in 0.75m, on
narrow road*
♨ ♨ ▲
Open all year Booking advisable Jul-Aug Last
arrival 22.00hrs Last departure noon
*A small rural park with pitches on either side of a
narrow lane, surrounded by mature trees for
shelter. The family-run park has newly modernised
toilet facilities created to a good standard. A 6-acre
site with 60 touring pitches.*
Leisure: ♠ ⚙ Facilities: ⌂ ⊙ ৭ ☀ ╰ ☎ ⅋
Services: 🖭 🖺 🗓 ⌀ ⊞ →∪ ► ♨ ♪

NEW ► ► ► 80%**Higher Moor (SW782600)**
Treago Rd TR8 5QS ☎ 01637 830928
*Dir: Turn off A3075 (Newquay to Redruth road) for
Crantock. Follow brown signs for Treago. Site 200mtrs
beyond Treago Farm*
★ ♨ £8-£12 ▲ £8-£12
Open Apr-Oct Booking advisable Jul-Aug Last
arrival 23.00hrs Last departure 11.00hrs
*On the edge of the extensive NT Cubert Common,
this site is one of Cornwall's best kept secrets. It is
tucked away from the main tourist areas, and has
new toilet facilities. Lovely beaches nearby. A 2-acre
site with 22 touring pitches.*
Leisure: ⚙ Facilities: ⌂ ⊙ ☀ ╰ ☎ ⅋
Services: ⊞ ↯ →∪ ► ⊙ ♨ ♪ 🖺

► ► ► 76% *Treago Farm Caravan Site
(SW782601)*
TR8 5QS ☎ 01637 830277 & 830522 🖺 01637 830277
*Dir: From A3075 W of Newquay turn right for Crantock.
Site signed beyond village*
♨ ♨ ▲
Open mid May-mid Sep (rs Apr-mid May & Oct no
shop or bar) Booking advisable Jun-Aug Last arrival
22.00hrs Last departure 18.00hrs
*A grass site in open farmland in a south-facing
sheltered valley. This friendly family park has direct
access to Crantock and Polly Joke beaches, National
Trust land and many natural beauty spots. A 5-acre
site with 90 touring pitches and 10 statics.*
Leisure: ♠ 🖵 Facilities: ⌂ ⊙ ৭ ☀ ╰ ☎ ⍟ ⍟ ⅋
Services: 🖭 🖺 ⅌ ⌀ ⊞ Ⓣ →∪ ► ⊙ ♨ ♪
💳 📇 💳 Ⓓ 💳 🖾 🗓

CUBERT	Map 02 SW75

► ► ► 76%**Cottage Farm Touring Park**
(SW786589)
Treworgans TR8 5HH ☎ 01637 831083
*Dir: From A392 towards Newquay, left onto A3075
towards Redruth. In 2m turn right signed for Cubert,
right again in 1.5m signed Crantock and left in 0.5m*
★ ♨ £9-£11 ♨ £9-£11 ▲ £9-£11
Open Apr-Sep Booking advisable late Jul-Aug Last
arrival 22.30hrs Last departure noon
A small grassy touring park nestling in the tiny
contd.

*hamlet of Treworgans, in sheltered open
countryside close to a lovely beach at Holywell Bay.
This quiet family-run park boasts very good quality
facilities. A 2-acre site with 45 touring pitches, 2
hardstandings and 1 static.*
Facilities: ⌂ ⊙ ৭ ☀ ╰ ☎
Services: 🖭 🖺 🗓 ⌀ ⊞ ↯ →∪ ► ⊙ ♨ ╇ ☎ ♪
Notes: 🐾

EDGCUMBE	Map 02 SW73

► ► ► 70%**Retanna Holiday Park (SW711327)**
TR13 OEJ ☎ 01326 340643 🖺 01326 340643
Ⓔ retannaholpark@lineone.net
ⓦ www.retanna.co.uk
Dir: 100mtrs off A394, signed
♨ £11-£15 ♨ £11-£15 ▲ £11-£15
Open Apr-Oct Booking advisable Jul & Aug Last
arrival 21.00hrs Last departure noon
*A small family-owned and run park in a rural
location midway between Falmouth and Helston. Its
well-sheltered grassy pitches make this an ideal
location for visiting the lovely beaches and towns
nearby. An 8-acre site with 24 touring pitches, 2
hardstandings and 29 statics.*
Leisure: ♠ ⚙ 🖵 Facilities: ⌂ ⊙ ৭ ☀ ໒ ╰ ☎ ⍟ ⅋
Services: 🖭 🖺 🗓 ⌀ ⊞ Ⓣ ⬥ →∪ ► ⊙ ♨ ╇ ♪
Notes: No dogs allowed during school holidays
💳 💳 📇 🖾 🗓

FALMOUTH	Map 02 SW83

► ► ► 74% *Pennance Mill Farm Touring Park
(SW792307)*
Maenporth TR11 5HJ ☎ 01326 317431 & 312616
🖺 01326 317431
ⓦ www.pennancemill.co.uk
*Dir: From A39 (Truro-Falmouth) follow brown camping
signs towards Maenporth Beach*
♨ ♨ ▲
Open Etr-Xmas (rs Jan-Etr) Booking advisable Jan-
Etr Last arrival 22.00hrs Last departure 10.00hrs
*Set approximately half a mile from the safe, sandy
Bay of Maenporth this is a mainly level, grassy park
in a rural location sheltered by mature trees and
shrubs and divided into three meadows. It has a
modern toilet block. A 6-acre site with 75 touring
pitches, 3 hardstandings and 4 statics.*
Leisure: ◠ ♠ ⚙ Facilities: ⌂ ⊙ ৭ ☀ ╰ ☎ ⅋
Services: 🖭 🖺 🗓 ⌀ ⊞ ⬥ →∪ ► ⊙ ♨ ╇ ☎ ♪

► ► 73%**Tregedna Farm Touring Caravan & Tent
Park (SW785305)**
Maenporth TR11 5HL ☎ 01326 250529
Ⓔ enquiries@tregednafarmholidays.co.uk
ⓦ www.tregednafarmholidays.co.uk
*Dir: Take A39 from Truro to Falmouth. Turn right at Hill
Head rdbt. Site 2.5m on right*
★ ♨ £9-£10 ♨ £9-£10 ▲ £9-£10
Open Apr-Sep Booking advisable Last arrival
23.00hrs Last departure 13.00hrs
*Set in the picturesque Maen Valley, this gently-
sloping, south-facing park is part of a 100-acre farm.
It is surrounded by beautiful wooded countryside*
contd.

---

just minutes from the beach, with spacious pitches and well-kept facilities. A 12-acre site with 40 touring pitches.

Leisure: /Λ **Facilities:** 𝄢 ☉ ✳ ✆ 💺 ⍩

Services: 🖾 🛢 🖊 → 🏳 ☉ ⚓ 🍴 🗑

Notes: One dog only per pitch

FOWEY   Map 02 SX15

▶ ▶ ▶ 70% **Penhale Caravan & Camping Park (SX104526)**
PL23 1JU ☎ 01726 833425 🖹 01726 833425
BRONZE
❸ info@penhale-fowey.co.uk
Ⓦ www.penhale-fowey.co.uk
Dir: Off A3082, 0.5m before junct with B3269
🚐 🚐 Å

Open Etr/Apr-Oct Booking advisable
Set on a working farm 1.5m from a sandy beach and the town of Fowey, this grassy park has stunning coastal and country views. Pitches are well spaced, and there is an indoor room for wet weather. A 4.5-acre site with 56 touring pitches and 15 statics.

Leisure: ⚘ **Facilities:** 𝄢 ☉ ☜ ✆ 💺

Services: 🖾 🖾 🛢 🖊 → ∪ 🏳 ⚓ 🍴 🗑

▶ ▶ ▶ 77% **Penmarlam Caravan & Camping Park (SX134526)**
Bodinnick PL23 1LZ ☎ 01726 870088
🖹 01726 870082
❸ info@penmarlampark.co.uk
Ⓦ www.penmarlampark.co.uk
Dir: From A390 at East Taphouse take B3359 signed Looe & Polperro. Follow signs for Bodinnick & Fowey, via ferry. Site on right at entrance to Bodinnick.
★ 🚐 £8-£13.50 🚐 £8-£13.50 Å £7-£13.50

Open Apr-Oct Booking advisable Jul-Aug, bank holidays
A tranquil park set above the Fowey Estuary in an
contd.

Area of Outstanding Natural Beauty, with access to the water. Pitches are level, and sheltered by trees and bushes in two paddocks, while the toilets are well maintained. A 4-acre site with 65 touring pitches and 1 static.
Private slipway/quay, storage of small boats.

Facilities: 𝄢 ☉ ☜ ✳ ⚓ 💺 🗚 ⍩

Services: 🖾 🖾 🛢 🖊 🖉 🖵 🕥 → ∪ 🏳 ⚓ 🍴 🗑

🖾 🖾 🖾 🖾 🖾 🖾

GOONHAVERN   Map 02 SW75
See also **Rejerrah**

▶ ▶ ▶ ▶ 80% **Penrose Farm Touring Park (SW795534)**
TR4 9QF ☎ 01872 573185 🖹 01872 571972
Ⓦ www.penrosefarm.co.uk
Dir: From Exeter take A30, past Bodmin and Indian Queens. Just after Wind Farm take B3285 towards Perranporth, site on left on entering Goonhavern
🚐 🚐 Å
Open Apr-Oct Booking advisable Jul & Aug Last arrival 21.30hrs
A quiet sheltered park set in five paddocks divided by hedges and shrubs, only a short walk from the village. Lovely floral displays enhance the park's appearance, and the grass and hedges are neatly trimmed. Four cubicled family rooms are very popular, and there is a good laundry. A 9-acre site with 100 touring pitches, 8 hardstandings.

Leisure: /Λ **Facilities:** 𝄢 ☉ ☜ ✳ ⚓ ✆ 💺 🖦 🗚 ⍩

Services: 🖾 🛢 🖊 🖉 🖵 🕥 → ∪ 🏳 🍴

🖾 🖾 🖾 Ⓓ 🖾 🖾 🖾

See advertisement under PERRANPORTH

▶ ▶ ▶ ▶ 80% **Silverbow Park (SW782531)**
Perranwell TR4 9NX
☎ 01872 572347 🖹 01872 572347
GOLD
Ⓦ www.chycor.co.uk/parks/silverbow
Dir: Adjacent to A3075, 0.5m S of village
★ 🚐 £8-£17 🚐 £8-£17 Å £8-£17
Open May-mid Sep (rs mid Sep-Oct & Etr-mid May swimming pool & shop closed) Booking advisable Jun-Sep Last arrival 22.00hrs Last departure noon
This park has a quiet garden atmosphere, and appeals to families with young children. The landscaped grounds and good quality toilet facilities - including four family rooms - are maintained to a very high standard with attention paid to detail. A 14-acre site with 100 touring pitches, 2 hardstandings and 15 statics. Badminton courts, short mat bowls rink

Leisure: ⸖ ☜ ⚘ /Λ

Facilities: ➜ 𝄢 ☉ ☜ ✳ ⚓ ✆ 💺 🗚 ⍩

Services: 🖾 🖾 🛢 🖊 🖉 🕥 → ∪ 🏳 🍴

See advertisement under PERRANPORTH

Leisure: ⸖ Indoor swimming pool ☜ Outdoor swimming pool ☌ Tennis court ⚘ Games room /Λ Children's playground ∪ Stables
🏳 9/18 hole golf course ⚓ Boats for hire 💺 Cinema 🍴 Fishing ◎ Mini golf ⚕ Watersports 🖵 Separate TV room

England

▶ ▶ ▶ 69% **Roseville Holiday Park (SW787540)**
TR4 9LA ☎ 01872 572448 📠 01872 572448
🕲 www.rosevilleholidaypark.co.uk
*Dir: From mini rdbt in Goonhavern follow B3285
towards Perranporth, site 0.5m on right*
★ 🚇 £8.50-£14 🚐 £8.50-£14 ▲ £8.50-£14
Open Whit-Oct (rs Apr-Jul, Sep-Oct Shop closed)
Booking advisable Jul-Aug Last arrival 21.30hrs Last
departure 11.00hrs
*A family park set in a rural location with sheltered
grassy pitches, some gently sloping. The toilet
facilities are modern, and there is an attractive
outdoor swimming pool complex. Approx 2 miles
from the long sandy beach at Perranporth. A 7-acre
site with 95 touring pitches and 5 statics.
Off-licence in shop.*
Leisure: ♠ /Λ Facilities: 𝄆 ⊙ ♋ ※ & 💄 ⴕ
Services: 🖵 🛢 🛈 🗑 🖩 🔟 → ∪ 🖡 ◎ ♨ ♪

▶ ▶ ▶ 73% *Sunny Meadows Tourist Park
(SW782542)*
Rosehill TR4 9JT ☎ 01872 572548 & 571333
📠 01872 571491
*Dir: From A30 onto B3285 signed Perranporth. At
Goonhavern turn left at T-junct, then right at rdbt to
Perranporth. Site on left*
🚇 🚐 ▲
Open Etr-Oct Booking advisable mid Jul-Aug
*A gently-sloping park with mostly level pitches set
into three small hedge-lined paddocks. Run in its
peaceful rural location by a friendly family, the park
is just 2 miles from the long sandy beach at
Perranporth. A 14.5-acre site with 52 touring
pitches, 1 hardstanding.
Pool table & TV family room*
Leisure: /Λ Facilities: 𝄆 ⊙ ※ & 💄 ⴕ
Services: 🖵 ⌀ 🖩 🔟 → ∪ 🖡 ♪ 🖩 💄
Notes: Dogs must be kept on leads
See advertisement under PERRANPORTH

▶ ▶ ▶ 76% **Little Treamble Farm Touring Park
(SW785560)**
Rose TR4 9PR ☎ 01872 573823 & 0797 1070760
🄴 info@treamble.co.uk
🕲 www.treamble.co.uk
*Dir: A30 onto B3285 signed Perranporth. Approx 0.5m
right into Scotland Rd signed Newquay. Approx 2m to
T-junct, right onto A3075 signed Newquay. 0.25m left at
Rejerrah sign. Site signed 0.75m on right*
★ 🚇 fr £9 🚐 fr £9
Open all year Booking advisable Jun-Aug & BHs
Last departure noon
*This site set in a quiet rural location with extensive
countryside views across an undulating valley.
There is a small new toilet block, and this working
farm is next to a Caravan Club site. A 1.5-acre site
with 20 touring pitches.*
Facilities: 𝄆 💄
Services: 🖵 🔟 → ∪ 🖡 ◎ ♪

GORRAN	Map 02 SW94

▶ ▶ ▶ 75% **Treveague Farm Caravan & Camping
Site (SX002410)**
PL26 6NY ☎ 01726 842295 📠 01726 842295
🄴 treveague@btconnect.com
*Dir: From St Austell take B3273 towards Mevagissey,
past Pentewan at top of hill, turn right signed Gorran.
Past Heligan Gardens towards Gorran Churchtown.
Follow brown tourist signs from fork in road*
★ 🚇 £10-£12 🚐 £10-£12 ▲ £5-£10

Open Apr-Sep Booking advisable at all times Last
arrival 21.00hrs Last departure noon
*Spectacular panoramic coastal views are a fine
feature of this rural park, which is well equipped
with modern facilities. A stone-faced toilet block
with a Cornish slate roof is an attractive and
welcome feature of the park. A footpath leads to the
fishing village of Gorran Haven in one direction,
and the secluded sandy Vault Beach in the other.
A 4-acre site with 30 touring pitches.*
Leisure: ♋ Facilities: 𝄆 ⊙ ※ & 🎋 ⴕ
Services: 🖵 🛢 ⌀ 🖩 → ♨ ⌲ ♪ 💄

▶ ▶ ▶ 69% **Treveor Farm Caravan & Camping
Site (SW988418)**
PL26 6LW ☎ 01726 842387
📠 01726 842387
🄴 info@treveorfarm.co.uk
🕲 www.treveorfarm.co.uk
*Dir: From St Austell bypass left onto B3273 for
Mevagissey. On hilltop before descent to village turn
right on unclass road for Gorran. Right in 3.5m, site on
right*
★ 🚇 £6.50-£14 🚐 £6.50-£14 ▲ £5-£12

Open Apr-Oct Booking advisable Last arrival
20.00hrs Last departure noon
*A small family-run camping park set on a working
farm, with grassy pitches backing onto mature*

contd.

---

hedging. This quiet park with good facilities is close to beaches, and it offers a large coarse fishing lake. A 4-acre site with 50 touring pitches.

Leisure: △ Facilities: ↑⊙℧☀♦
Services: ➡▣→↲↳ℤ

GORRAN HAVEN   Map 02 SX04

▶ ▶ ▶ 67% **Trelispen Caravan & Camping Park** (SX008421)
PL26 6HT ☎ 01726 843501 🖹 01726 843501
✉ trelispen@care4free.net
Dir: B3273 from St Austell towards Mevagissey, on hilltop at x-roads before descent into Mevagissey right on unclass road to Gorran. Through village, 2nd right towards Gorran Haven, site signed on left in 250mtrs
★ ➡ £10-£12 ➡ £10-£12 ▲ £10-£12
Open Etr & Apr-Oct Booking advisable Last arrival 22.00hrs Last departure noon
A very simple site in a beautiful quiet location within easy reach of beaches. The dated toilets have plenty of hot water, and there is a small laundry. A 2-acre site with 40 touring pitches. A 30-acre nature reserve may be visited.

Leisure: △ Facilities: ↑⊙☀
Services: ➡▣→↲↳ℤ

GWITHIAN   Map 02 SW54

▶ ▶ ▶ 78% **Gwithian Farm Campsite** (SW586412)
Gwithian Farm TR27 5BX ☎ 01736 753127
🌐 www.gwithianfarm.co.uk
Dir: Exit A30 at Hayle rdbt, take 4th exit signed Hayle, 100mtrs. At 1st mini-rdbt turn right onto B3301 signed Portreath. Site 2m on left on entering village
★ ➡ £9-£14.50 ➡ ▲ £7-£12.50
Open 1 week before Good Fri-Sep Booking advisable Jul-Aug Last arrival 21.00hrs Last departure 17.00hrs
An unspoilt site located behind the sand dunes of Gwithian's golden beach, which can be reached directly by footpath. The site boasts a superb new toilet block with excellent facilities including a bathroom and baby changing unit. There is a good pub opposite. A 7.5-acre site with 87 touring pitches.
Surf board & wet suit hire

Leisure: ⬜ Facilities: ➡↑⊙℧☀♿ℤ▣▦🐕
Services: ➡👤🛒🗑▣⊞✕➡→∪▶◎♦↲▣
Notes: No cars by caravans

HAYLE   Map 02 SW53

 75% *St Ives Bay Holiday Park* (SW577398)
73 Loggans Rd,
Upton Towans TR27 5BH
☎ 01736 752274 🖹 01736 754523
✉ stivesbay@btconnect.com
🌐 www.stivesbay.co.uk
Dir: Exit A30 at Hayle. Immediate right at mini-rdbts. Park entrance 0.5m on left
➡➡▲
Open May-1 Oct (rs Etr-1 May & 25 Sep-25 Oct no entertainment, food & bar service) Booking
contd.

advisable Jan-Mar Last arrival 23.00hrs Last departure 09.00hrs
An extremely well maintained holiday park with a relaxed atmosphere, built on sand dunes adjacent to a 3-mile-long beach. The touring section forms a number of separate locations in amongst the statics. The park is specially geared for families and couples, and as well as the large indoor swimming pool there are two pubs with seasonal entertainment. Dogs are not allowed. A 90-acre site with 240 touring pitches and 250 statics.
Crazy golf, video room.

Leisure: ≈ ⚲ ♣ △ ⬜ Facilities: ↑⊙℧☀♦ℤ
Services: ➡▣👤🛒▣⊞▣✕➡→∪▶↲
Notes: ⊗ 💳 💳 💳 ◪ ▥

▶ ▶ ▶ 74% **Higher Trevaskis Caravan Park** (SW611381)
Gwinear Rd, Connor Downs TR27 5JQ
☎ 01209 831736
Dir: At Hayle rdbt on A30 take 1st exit signed Connor Downs, in 1m turn right signed Carnhell Green. Site 0.75m just past level crossing
★ ➡ £8-£16 ➡ £8-£16 ▲ £8-£16
Open mid Apr-Sep Booking advisable May-Sep Last arrival 20.00hrs Last departure 11.00hrs
An attractive paddocked park in a sheltered rural position with views towards St Ives. This secluded park is personally run by owners who keep it quiet and welcoming. Three unisex showers are a great hit with visitors. Fluent German spoken. A 6.5-acre site with 82 touring pitches, 3 hardstandings.

Leisure: △ Facilities: ↑⊙℧☀♦ℤ🐕
Services: ➡▣👤🗑▣⊞▣→▶◎♦↲

▶ ▶ ▶ 68% **Parbola Holiday Park** (SW612366)
Wall, Gwinear TR27 5LE ☎ 01209 831503
🖹 01209 831503
✉ bookings@parbola.co.uk
🌐 www.parbola.co.uk
Dir: At Hayle rdbt on A30 take Connor Downs exit. In 1m turn right signed Carnhell Green. In village right to Wall and site in village on left
➡➡▲
Open Etr-Sep (rs Etr-Spring bank hol & Sep shop closed) Booking advisable Jul-Aug Last arrival 21.00hrs Last departure noon
Pitches are provided in both woodland and open areas in this well-maintained park in Cornish downland. The spacious park is centrally located for touring the seaside resorts and towns in the area, especially nearby Hayle with its three miles of golden sands. A 16.5-acre site with 110 touring pitches and 28 statics.
Crazy golf & table tennis

Leisure: ⚲ ♣ △ ⬜
Facilities: ↑⊙℧☀♿ℤ▦
Services: ➡▣👤🗑▣⊞▣→∪▶◎↲
Notes: ⊗ Dogs not allowed Jul-Aug
💳 💳 💳 ◪ ▥

England

Boscrege Caravan & Camping Park

Aston, Cornwall

"A breath of fresh air"

Set in 14 acres of peaceful, tranquil surroundings including the special scientific interest of Tregonning Hill. It is centrally situated for exploring West Cornwall a land famous for its myths and legends as well as its rugged beauty, coves and fishing villages. The Park has been extensively landscaped and refurbished and specialises in holiday for families & couples.

Tel: 01736 762231
www.caravanparkcornwall.com
enquiries@caravanparkcornwall.com

▶ ▶ ▶ 71% **Treglisson Camping & Caravan Park** (SW581367)
Wheal Alfred Rd TR27 5JT ☎ 01736 753141
🅱 enquiries@treglisson.co.uk
🆆 www.treglisson.co.uk
Dir: 4th exit off rdbt on A30 at Hayle. 100mtrs, turn left at 1st mini-rdbt.1.5km past golf course, site sign on left
★ 🚐 £8-£12.50 🚐 £8-£12.50 ▲ £8-£12.50
Open Etr-Oct Booking advisable Jul-Aug Last arrival 20.00hrs Last departure 11.00hrs
A small secluded site in a peaceful wooded meadow, a former apple and pear orchard. This quiet rural site has a well-planned modern toilet block and level grass pitches, and is just 2 miles from the glorious beach at Hayle with its vast stretch of golden sand. A 3-acre site with 30 touring pitches. Tourist information available. Milk deliveries
Leisure: ९ ⁄M Facilities: ৲⊙९⋇६६⊡⊞★
Services: ⊕⊡⊟→ ▶⚫🍴🛎️ Notes: Max 6 people to a pitch, dogs must be on lead at all times

HELSTON	Map 02 SW62

▶ ▶ ▶ 74% **Lower Polladras Touring Park** (SW617308)
Carleen, Breage TR13 9NX
☎ 01736 762220 🖨 01736 762220
🅱 lowerpolladras@btinternet.com
🆆 www.lower-polladras.co.uk
Dir: From Helston take A394 then B3302 (Hayle road) at Hilltop Garage, 2nd left to Carleen, site 2m on right
🚐 🚐 ▲

contd.

Lower Polladras Touring Park
Open Apr-Oct Booking advisable Jul-Aug Last arrival 22.00hrs Last departure noon
A rural park with extensive views of surrounding fields, appealing to families who enjoy the countryside. The trees and shrubs are maturing, and help to divide the area into paddocks with spacious grassy pitches. A 4-acre site with 60 touring pitches.
Caravan and boat storage area
Leisure: ⁄M
Facilities: ৲⊙९⋇🛒🚿★★
Services: ⊕📍⊟🛒⊘⊞⊡→⊍▶⊙△⋇🛎️⚫

▶ ▶ ▶ 67% **Poldown Caravan Park** (SW629298)
Poldown, Carleen TR13 9NN ☎ 01326 574560
🅱 Poldown@poldown.co.uk
🆆 www.poldown.co.uk
Dir: From Helston follow Penzance signs for 1m then right onto B3302 to Hayle, 2nd left to Carleen, 0.5m to site.
★ 🚐 £7.75-£10.75 🚐 £7.75-£10.75 ▲ £7.75-£10.75
Open Apr-Sep Booking advisable Jul-Aug Last arrival 22.00hrs Last departure noon
A small, quiet site set in attractive countryside with bright toilet facilities. All of the level grass pitches have electricity, and the sunny park is sheltered by mature trees and shrubs. A 2-acre site with 13 touring pitches and 7 statics.
Leisure: ⁄M
Facilities: ৲⊙९⋇६🚿★★
Services: ⊕📍⊟→⊍▶△⋇🛎️⚫🛒

▶ 78% **Skyburriowe Farm** (SW698227)
Garras TR12 6LR ☎ 01326 221646
🅱 brenda.benney@amserve.com
Dir: From Helston on A3083 towards Lizard. Left in 1.5m after rdbt at sign for farmhouse/B&B & campsite. Follow for 0.5m
★ 🚐 £6-£9 🚐 £6-£9 ▲ £6-£9
Open Apr-Oct Booking advisable Last arrival 22.00hrs Last departure 11.00hrs
A leafy no-through road leads to this picturesque farm park in a rural location on the Lizard Peninsula. The facilities are fairly basic, but most pitches have electricity. There are some beautiful coves and beaches nearby. A 1.75-acre site with 15 touring pitches.
Facilities: ৲⊙⋇★
Services: ⊕⊟→⊍▶🛎️⚫🛒⊡🛒

England

HOLYWELL BAY   Map 02 SW75

  70% Holywell Bay Holiday Park (SW773582)
TR8 5PR ☎ 01637 871111 &
0870 420 2991 ▤ 01637 850818
❸ enquiries@parkdeanholidays.co.uk
ⓦ www.parkdeanholidays.co.uk
Dir: Leave A30 onto A392, take A3075 signed Redruth, then left in 2m signed Holywell/Cubert. Follow road through Cubert past Trevornick to park on right
★ ⊞ £7-£24 ⊞ £9-£27 Å £7-£24
Open Mar-Oct Booking advisable Jun-Aug Last arrival 21.00hrs Last departure 10.00hrs
Close to lovely beaches in a rural location, this level grassy park borders on National Trust land, and is only a short distance from the Cornish Coastal Path. The park provides a popular entertainment programme for the whole family. A 40-acre site with 56 touring pitches and 144 statics.
Live family entertainment & children's club
Leisure: ⏅ ⋀ Facilities: ⋒ ⊙ & ⛨ ⅏ ⋔ ⋒
Services: ⊡ ⊞ ⅋ ⅋ ⊞ ⊡ ⅏ → ∪ ☀ ⊙ ⋀ ⅃
Notes: ⊗ ⊟ ⊡ ⊠ ⑤

 90% Trevornick Holiday Park (SW776586)
TR8 5PW ☎ 01637 830531
▤ 01637 831000
❸ info@trevornick.co.uk
ⓦ www.trevornick.co.uk
Dir: 3m from Newquay off A3075 towards Redruth. Follow Cubert & Holywell Bay signs
★ ⊞ £9.90-£16.50 ⊞ Å
Open Etr & mid May-mid Sep Booking advisable Jul-Aug Last arrival 21.00hrs Last departure 10.00hrs
A large seaside holiday complex with excellent facilities and amenities. There is plenty of entertainment including a children's club and an evening cabaret, adding up to a full holiday experience for all the family. A sandy beach is a 15-minute footpath walk away. The park has ready-erected tents for hire. A 20-acre site 593 touring pitches, 6 hardstandings.
Fishing, golf course, entertainment.
Leisure: ⏅ ⋇ ⋀ Facilities: ⅏ ⋒ ⊙ ⅏ ⋇ & ⅊ ⅏ ⋔
Services: ⊡ ⊞ ⅋ ⅋ ⅋ ⊞ ⊡ ✕ ⅏ → ∪ ☀ ⊙ ⋀ ⅍
Notes: Families and couples only ⊟ ⊡ ⊟ ⑤

See advertisement on page 49

INDIAN QUEENS   Map 02 SW95

▶ ▶ ▶ **70% Gnome World Caravan & Camping Site (SW890599)**
Moorland Rd TR9 6HN ☎ 01726 860812
▤ 01726 860812
Dir: Signed from slip road at A30 & A39 rdbt in village of Indian Queens - park on old A30, now unclass rd
★ ⊞ £7-£9 ⊞ £7-£9 Å £7-£9
Open all year (rs Nov-Mar Statics closed) Booking advisable Jul-Aug Last arrival 22.00hrs Last departure noon
Set in open countryside, this spacious park is set on level grassy land only 0.5m from the A30 (Cornwall's main artery route), in a central holiday
contd.

Gnome World Caravan & Camping Site *location for touring the county. There are no narrow lanes to negotiate. A 4.5-acre site with 50 touring pitches and 60 statics.*
Nature trail.
Leisure: ⋀ Facilities: ⋒ ⊙ ⅏ & ⅏ ⋔
Services: ⊡ ⊞ ⊞ → ∪ ☀ ⅌
Notes: Dogs must be kept on leads
⊟ ⊟ ⊟ ⊠ ⑤

JACOBSTOW   Map 02 SX19

▶ ▶ ▶ **70% Edmore Tourist Park (SX184955)**
Edgar Rd, Wainhouse Corner EX23 0BJ
☎ 01840 230467 ▤ 01840 230467
❸ edmorepark@aol.com
ⓦ www.cornwallvisited.co.uk
Dir: Leave A39 at Wainhouse Corner onto Edgar Rd, site signed on right in 200yds
★ ⊞ £7.50-£9.50 ⊞ £7.50-£9.50 Å £6-£9.50
Open 1 wk before Etr-Oct Booking advisable Bank & school holidays Last arrival 21.00hrs Last dep noon
A quiet family-owned site in a rural location with extensive views, set close to the sandy surfing beaches of Bude, and the unspoilt sandy beach and rock pools at Crackington Haven. Friendly owners keep all facilities in a very good condition. A 3-acre site with 28 touring pitches.
Leisure: ⋀ Facilities: ⋒ ⊙ ⅊ ⅏ ⅌ ⅊ Services: ⊡ ⅋ ⊞

KENNACK SANDS   Map 02 SW71

▶ ▶ ▶ **69% Chy-Carne Holiday Park (SW725164)**
Kuggar, Ruan Minor TR12 7LX ☎ 01326 290200
❸ enquiries@chy-carne.co.uk
ⓦ www.chy-carne.co.uk
Dir: From A3083 turn left on B3293 after Culdrose Naval Air Station. At Goonhilly ESS right onto unclass road signed Kennack Sands. Left in 3m at junct
★ ⊞ £14-£16 ⊞ £14-£16 Å £5-£6

contd.

Leisure: ⏅ Indoor swimming pool   ⏇ Outdoor swimming pool   ⋇ Tennis court   ⋇ Games room   ⋀ Children's playground   ∪ Stables
▶ 9/18 hole golf course   ⅃ Boats for hire   ⅏ Cinema   ⅃ Fishing   ◉ Mini golf   ⅍ Watersports   ⊟ Separate TV room

England

Open Etr-Oct Booking advisable Aug Last arrival dusk
Small but spacious park in quiet, sheltered spot,
with extensive sea and coastal views from the
grassy touring area. A village pub with restaurant is
a short walk by footpath from the touring area, and
a sandy beach is less than 0.5 miles away. A 6-acre
site with 14 touring pitches and 18 statics.
Leisure: ♦ ⚠ Facilities: ⬚⊙🍴※♿⛤ ⛱ 🏇
Services: 🖵⬚🅱⬚⬚⬚→∪▶⊙🥤⬚ ⬚⬚ ⬚⬚ ⬚ ⬚

▶ ▶ ▶ 72% Gwendreath Farm Holiday Park
(SW738168)
TR12 7LZ ☎ 01326 290666
🅰 tom.gibson@virgin.net
🌐 www.tomandlinda.co.uk
Dir: From A3083 turn left past Culdrose Naval Air
Station onto B3293. Right past Goonhilly ESS signed
Kennack Sands, left in 1m
★ 🚐 fr £9 🅰 fr £7
Open Etr-Oct Booking advisable all times Last
arrival 21.00hrs Last departure 10.00hrs
A grassy park in an elevated position with extensive
sea and coastal views, and the beach just a short
walk through the woods. Campers can use the bar
and takeaway at an adjoining site. A 5-acre site with
10 touring pitches and 21 statics.
Leisure: ⚠ Facilities: ⬚⊙※♿⛤⛱🏇
Services: 🖵⬚🅱⬚⬚→∪▶⊙♿🥤

▶ ▶ ▶ 74% Silver Sands
Holiday Park (SW727166)
Gwendreath TR12 7LZ
☎ 01326 290631 🖶 01326 290631
🅰 enquiries@silversandsholidaypark.co.uk
🌐 www.silversandsholidaypark.co.uk
Dir: From Helston follow signs to Goonhilly. 300yds after
Goonhilly Earth Station turn right at x-roads signed
Kennack Sands, 1.5m, left at Gwendreath sign, park 1m
★ 🚐 £11-£16.50 🚐 £11-£16.50 🅰 £9.50-£13.70
Open Etr-Sep Booking advisable Jul-Aug Last
arrival 21.00hrs Last departure 11.00hrs
A small park in a remote location, with individually
screened pitches providing sheltered suntraps. A
footpath through the woods from the family-owned
park leads to the beach and the local pub. A 9-acre
site with 34 touring pitches and 14 statics.
Leisure: ⚠ Facilities: ⬚⊙※♿⛤⛱🏇
Services: 🖵⬚🅱⬚⬚→∪🥤🍴⛤ Notes: No groups
⬚ ⬚ ⬚ ⬚ ⬚

KILKHAMPTON   Map 02 SS21

▶ ▶ 71% Tamar Lake (SS288118)
Upper Tamar Lake ☎ 01288 321712
🌐 www.swlakestrust.org.uk
Dir: From A39 at Kilkhampton onto B3254, left in 0.5m
onto unclass road, follow signs approx 4m to site
🅰
Open 31 Mar-Oct Booking advisable
A well-trimmed, slightly sloping site overlooking
the lake and countryside, with several signed walks.
The site benefits from the excellent facilities
provided for the watersports centre and coarse
anglers, with a rescue launch on the lake when the
flags are flying. A good family site, with Bude's
contd.

Tamar Lake

beaches and surfing waves only 8m away.
A 2-acre site with 36 touring pitches.
Watersports centre, canoeing, sailing, windsurfing
Leisure: ⚠ Facilities: ⬚⬚♿⛤⛱🏇
Services: ✕ ⬚→∪♿🥤🍴⛤ Notes: Dogs must be
kept on a lead ⬚ ⬚ ⬚ ⬚ ⬚

LANDRAKE   Map 03 SX36

▶ ▶ ▶ 81% Dolbeare Caravan & Camping Park
(SX363616)
St Ive Rd PL12 5AF ☎ 01752 851332 🖶 01752 851332
🅰 dolbeare@btopenworld.com
🌐 www.dolbeare.co.uk
Dir: A38 to Landrake, 4m W of Saltash. At footbridge
over A38 turn N following signs to site (0.75m from A38)
★ 🚐 £11-£15.50 🚐 £11-£15.50 🅰 £3-£15.50

Open all year Booking advisable peak periods only
Last arrival 23.00hrs Last departure noon
A mainly level grass site with trees and bushes set
in meadowland. The keen and friendly owners set
high standards, and the park is always neat and
clean. A 4-acre site with 60 touring pitches, 54
hardstandings.
Info centre, licensed off sales, internet access
Leisure: ⚠ Facilities: ⬚⊙🍴※♿⛤⛱🏇
Services: 🖵⬚🅱⬚⬚⬚→▶🥤🍴⬚ ⬚ ⬚

LAND'S END   Map 02 SW32

▶ ▶ ▶ 78% Sea View Holiday Park (SW357254)
TR19 7AD ☎ 01736 871266 🖶 01736 871190
🌐 www.seaview.org.uk
Dir: At Penzance take road signed A30 Land's End.
Proceed to Sennen, through village until First & Last
pub, site on left
★ 🚐 fr £12 🚐 fr £12 🅰 fr £9
Open all year (rs Sep-Mar coffee shop closed, pool
unheated) Booking advisable Last arrival 18.30hrs
contd.

England

Last departure 10.00hrs
On the outskirts of Sennen and close to Land's End, this park is set in unspoilt countryside with views of the sea. There are lots of local attractions to visit from this park which is only minutes away from the golden sandy beach of Whitsand Bay. An 11.5-acre site with 180 touring pitches, 6 hardstandings and 95 statics.

Leisure: ⟡ ⟡ ⚲   Facilities: ⟊ ⊙ ⟦ ⁂ ⏦ ⅃ ⎀ ⊞ ⟙
Services: ⚱ ⛫ ⊟ ⓘ ⌀ ⊞ ⟩ ✕ ⚐ → ∪ ⏵ ⊚ △ ⤨ ⟋
Notes: Dogs only with permission

⬤ ⬛ ⬛ ⬛ ⬛ ⬛

LANIVET   Map 02 SX06

▶ ▶ ▶ **77% Mena Caravan & Camping Site (SW041626)**
Mena Farm PL30 5HW ☎ 01208 831845
✉ mena@campsitesincornwall.co.uk
ⓦ www.campsitesincornwall.co.uk
Dir: Exit A30 at Innes Downs rdbt onto A391 signed St Austell. 0.5m 1st left, then 0.75m turn right (before bridge) signed Fowey/Lanhydrock. 0.5m to staggered junct and monument stone, sharp right, 0.5m down hill, right into site
★ ⚍ £7-£11 ⚌ £7-£11 ▲ £7-£11
Open May-Sep Booking advisable Jul-Aug Last arrival 22.00hrs Last departure noon
Set in a secluded, elevated location with high hedges for shelter, and plenty of peace. This grassy site is about 4 miles from the Eden Project, and midway between N and S coasts. On site is a small coarse fishing lake. A 4-acre site with 25 touring pitches and 2 statics.

Leisure: ⚬ ⚲   Facilities: ⟊ ⊙ ⁂ ⏦ ⟙ ⟒
Services: ⚱ ⊟ ⊞ → ∪ ⏵ ⟋ ⚘

LAUNCELLS   Map 02 SS20

▶ ▶ **81% Red Post Inn & Holiday Park (SS264052)**
EX23 9NW ☎ 01288 381305 ⊟ 01288 381305
✉ gsharp@redpostinn1.wanadoo.co.uk
ⓦ www.redpostinn.co.uk
Dir: At junct of A3072/B3254, 4m from Bude, entered by side of Red Post Inn
★ ⚍ £9-£12.50 ⚌ £9-£12.50 ▲ £9-£12.50
Open all year Booking advisable Jul & Aug Last arrival 21.00hrs Last departure 11.00hrs
Set in rolling countryside just 4 miles from the seaside town of Bude, this park has benefited from a major upgrading programme, and the facilities are fresh and clean. The 16th-century Red Post Inn is next door. A 4-acre site with 33 touring pitches, 33 hardstandings and 13 statics.

Leisure: ⚲   Facilities: ⟊ ⊙ ⁂ ⏦ ⎀ ⟙
Services: ⚱ ⊟ ⊞ ⓘ ⟩ ✕ ⚐ → ∪ ⏵ ⊚ △ ⟋

⬤ ⬛ ⬛ ⬛ ⬛

THE PERCENTAGE RATING
FOR ALL PARKS RANGES FROM
50% - 100%.

LEEDSTOWN (NEAR HAYLE)   Map 02 SW63

▶ ▶ ▶ **77% Calloose Caravan & Camping Park (SW597352)**
TR27 5ET ☎ 01736 850431 ⊟ 01736 850431
✉ calloose@hotmail.com
ⓦ www.calloose.co.uk
Dir: From Hayle take B3302 to Leedstown, turn left opposite village hall, before entering village, park 0.5m on left at bottom of hill
⚍ ⚌ ▲
Open Mar-Nov, Xmas & New Year (rs Mar-mid May & late Sep-Nov swimming pool closed) Booking advisable Etr, May bank hols & Jun-Aug Last arrival 22.00hrs Last departure 11.00hrs
A comprehensively equipped leisure park in a remote rural setting in a small river valley. This very good park is busy and bustling, and offers bright and clean facilities. A 12.5-acre site with 120 touring pitches and 17 statics.
Crazy golf, skittle alley

Leisure: ⟡ ⟡ ⚬ ⚲ ⟓
Facilities: ⟊ ⊙ ⟦ ⏦ ⅃ ⎀ ⟙ ⟒
Services: ⚱ ⊟ ⓘ ⌀ ⊞ ⟩ ✕ ⚐ → ⟋

⬤ ⬛ ⬛ ⬛ ⬛   See advertisement on page 44

LOOE   Map 02 SX25

68% Tencreek Holiday Park (SX233525)
Polperro Rd PL13 2JR
☎ 01503 262447 ⊟ 01503 262760
✉ reception@tencreek.co.uk
ⓦ www.dolphinholidays.co.uk
Dir: Take A387 1.25m from Looe. Site on left
★ ⚍ £8.90-£17 ⚌ £8.90-£17 ▲ £8.90-£17
Open all year Booking advisable Jul & Aug Last arrival 23.00hrs Last departure 10.00hrs
Occupying a lovely position with extensive countryside and sea views, this holiday centre is in a rural spot but close to Looe and Polperro. There is a full family entertainment programme, with indoor and outdoor swimming pools and an adventure playground, and an exciting children's club. A 14-acre site with 254 touring pitches and 101 statics.
Nightly entertainment, solarium, 45mtr pool flume

Leisure: ⟓ ⟡ ⚬ ⚲   Facilities: ⟊ ⊙ ⟦ ⁂ ⏦ ⎀ ⟒
Services: ⚱ ⊟ ⓘ ⌀ ⊞ ⟩ ✕ ⚐ → ∪ ⏵ ⊚ △ ⤨ ⚘ ⟋
Notes: Families & couples only

⬤ ⬛ ⬛ ⬛ ⬛

▶ ▶ ▶ **67% Camping Caradon Touring Park (SX218539)**
Trelawne PL13 2NA ☎ 01503 272388
✉ stephen.cox2@virgin.net
ⓦ www.campingcaradon.co.uk
Dir: Signed off B3359 near junct with A387, between Looe and Polperro
★ ⚍ £6-£17 ⚌ £6-£17 ▲ £6-£17
Open Etr-Oct Booking advisable Jul-Aug Last arrival 22.00hrs Last departure noon
Set in a quiet rural location between the popular coastal resorts of Looe and Polperro, this family-run park is just 1.5m from the beach at Talland Bay.
contd.

The new owners have upgraded the bar and restaurant, and all facilities are very clean. A 3.5-acre site with 85 touring pitches.
Leisure: ♠ Facilities: ♪⊙◯⋇☎♫
Services: ♀♀⋯⊞①⋇→∪♨↯◢⬚
▣▦▦▨ ⑤

▶ ▶ ▶ 77% **Polborder House Caravan & Camping Park (SX283557)**
Bucklawren Rd, St Martins PL13 1NZ
☎ 01503 240265
✆ reception@peaceful-polborder.co.uk
✇ www.peaceful-polborder.co.uk
Dir: Approach Looe from E on A387, follow B3253 for 1m, left at Polborder & Monkey Sanctuary sign. Site 0.5m on right
★ ⚏ £8.60-£12 ⚏ £8.60-£12 ⚑ £8.60-£12
Open 25 Mar-4 Nov Booking advisable Jul-Aug Last arrival 22.00hrs Last departure 11.00hrs
A very neat and well-kept small grassy site on high ground above Looe in a peaceful rural setting. Friendly and enthusiastic owners. A 3-acre site with 31 touring pitches, 15 hardstandings and 5 statics. Washing/food prep sinks, information centre
Leisure: ♒ Facilities: ♪⊙◯⋇♨♿☎
Services: ♀⑤⋯⊞①⛟→∪↯♨↯◢
Notes: No trade vehicles, dogs allowed on touring pitches only ▣ ▦ ▨ ⑤

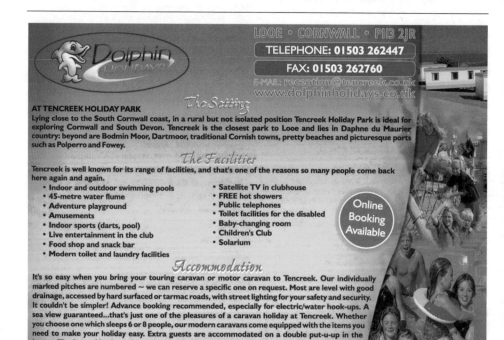
Services: ⊤ Toilet Fluid   ✗ Café/ Restaurant   ⇮ Fast Food/Takeaway   ⇝ Baby Care   ☺ Electric Hook Up
🔧 Motorvan Service Point   ⑤ Launderette   ⚲ Licensed Bar   ⬤ Calor Gaz   ⌀ Camping Gaz   ⊞ Battery Charging

▶ ▶ ▶ 72% *Talland Caravan Park (SX230516)*
Talland Bay PL13 2JA
☎ 01503 272715 ▤ 01503 272224
🖃 tallandcaravan@btconnect.com
🌐 www.tallandcaravanpark.co.uk
Dir: 1m from A387 on unclass road to Talland Bay
🚐🚙⚠
Open Apr-Oct Booking advisable School hols Last
arrival 20.00hrs Last departure noon
*Overlooking the sea just 300 yards from Talland
Bay's two beaches, this quiet park has an elevated
touring area with sea views. Surrounded by
unspoilt countryside and with direct access to the
coastal footpath, it is approximately halfway
between Looe and Polperro. A 4-acre site with 80
touring pitches and 46 statics.*

Leisure: ⚠
Facilities: ⬔⊙🏸⚑※🕭🍴🎣🏪👣
Services: 🖳🖴🛒🔌🧴🖃🔲✗ 🖕→▶♨❄✔🖉
💳 💳 📶 🗞

▶ ▶ ▶ 75% *Tregoad Park (SX272560)*
St Martin's PL13 1PB
☎ 01503 262718 ▤ 01503 264777
🖃 tregoadfarmccp@aol.com
🌐 www.cornwall-online.co.uk/tregoad
*Dir: Signed with direct access from B3253, or from E on
A387 follow B3253 for 1.75m towards Looe and site on
left*
★ 🚐 £13.50-£21.50 🚙 £13.50-£21.50 ⚠ £7.50-£14.50

Open Etr-Jan Bistro open in high and mid season
Booking advisable Jul & Aug Last arrival 21.00hrs
Last departure 11.00hrs
*A terraced grassy park with extensive sea and rural
views, about 1.5m from Looe. All pitches are level,
and the facilities are well maintained. There is a
new licensed bar, and bar meals served in the
conservatory. A 55-acre site with 150 touring
pitches and 3 statics.*
Fishing lake, crazy golf
Leisure: ⟨ ⚓ ⚠ 🖵
Facilities: 🛁⬔⊙🏸⚑※🍴🕭🎣🏪🎾👣
Services: 🖳🖴🛒🔌🧴🖃🔲✗ 🖕→♨▶◉♨❄🎪✔🖉
💳 💳 🅾 📶 🗞

> The number of touring pitches listed for
> each site includes tents, caravans and
> motorvans.

▶ ▶ ▶ 78% *Trelay Farmpark (SX210544)*
Pelynt PL13 2JX ☎ 01503 220900 ▤ 01503 220900
🖃 stay@trelay.co.uk
🌐 www.trelay.co.uk
*Dir: From A390 at East Taphouse, take B3359 S towards
Looe. After Pelynt, site 0.5m on left*
★ 🚐 £7.50-£11 🚙 £7.50-£11 ⚠ £7-£11
Open Apr-Oct Booking advisable Jul & Aug Last
arrival 21.00hrs Last departure noon
*A small site with a friendly atmosphere set in a
pretty rural area with extensive views. The good
size grass pitches are on slightly sloping ground,
and the toilets are immaculately kept. Looe and
Polperro are just 3 miles away. A 4.5-acre site with
55 touring pitches and 20 statics.*
Baby bath & mat, fridge, freezer
Facilities: 🛁⊙🏸⚑⚑🕭🍴🎣
Services: 🖳🖴🛒🔌🧴🖃🔲↯→♨◉♨✔🖉🍴

LOSTWITHIEL   **Map 02 SX15**

▶ ▶ ▶ 74% **Powderham Castle Tourist Park**
(SX083593)
PL30 5BU ☎ 01208 872277
🖃 powderhamcastletp@tiscali.co.uk
🌐 www.powderhamcastletouristpark.co.uk
*Dir: 1.5m SW of Lostwithiel on A390 turn right at
brown/white sign in 400mtrs*
★ 🚐 £10-£14 🚙 £10-£14 ⚠ £10-£14
Open Etr or Apr-Oct Booking advisable Jul-Aug Last
arrival 22.00hrs Last departure 11.30hrs
*A grassy park set in paddocks with mature trees.
New owners have embarked on a gradual
upgrading of facilities. This park is ideally located
for visiting the Eden Project, the nearby golden
beaches and sailing at Fowey. A 12-acre site with
75 touring pitches, 12 hardstandings and 38 statics.*
Badminton & soft tennis, putting green.
Leisure: ⟨ ⚠ 🖵 Facilities: 🛁⊙🏸⚑※🍴🎣👣
Services: 🖳🖴🛒🔌🧴🖃→♨▶◉♨❄✔🖉🍴
💳 💳 📶 🗞

LUXULYAN   **Map 02 SX05**

▶ ▶ ▶ 73% **Croft Farm Holiday Park**
(SX044568)
PL30 5EQ ☎ 01726 850228 ▤ 01726 850498
🖃 lynpick@ukonline.co.uk
🌐 www.croftfarm.co.uk
*Dir: Leave A30 at Bodmin for A391 towards St Austell.
In 7m left at double rdbt onto unclass road towards
Luxulyan/Eden Project, continue to T-junct, turn left
signed Luxulyan. Croft Farm 1m on left. Do not
approach any other way as roads are very narrow*
🚐 £9.40-£13.50 🚙 £9.40-£13.50 ⚠ £6.50-£13.50
Open 21 Mar-21 Jan (rs Nov-21 Jan Shower block
closed, bathroom available) Booking advisable Jul
& Aug Last arrival 18.00hrs Last departure noon
*A peaceful, picturesque setting at the edge of a
wooded valley, and only 1m from The Eden Project,
Cornwall's biodomes. A 5-acre site with 52 touring
pitches, 10 hardstandings and 35 statics.*
Mother & baby room, info centre, microwave
Leisure: ⟨ ⚠ Facilities: 🛁⊙🏸⚑※🍴🕭🎣👣
Services: 🖳🖴🛒🔌🧴🖃🔲→♨✔
Notes: Dogs must be kept on leads, no smoking in
buildings/caravans/cottages 💳 💳 📶 🗞

England

MARAZION   Map 02 SW53
See also **St Hilary**

▶ ▶ ▶ 73% **Wheal Rodney Holiday Park**
(SW525315)
Gwallon Ln TR17 0HL ☎ 01736 710605
✉ reception@whealrodney.co.uk
Ⓦ www.whealrodney.co.uk
Dir: Turn off A30 at Crowlas, signed Rospeath. Site 1.5m on right. From Marazion centre turn opposite Fire Engine Inn, site 500mtrs on left.
★ ⊞ £8-£14 ⊞ £8-£14 ▲ £7-£12
Open all year Booking advisable Xmas & Etr-Oct Last arrival 20.00hrs Last departure 11.00hrs
Set in a quiet rural location surrounded by farmland, with level grass pitches and well-kept facilities. Just half a mile away are the beach at Marazion and the causeway or ferry to St Michael's Mount. A cycle route is just 400yds away. A 2.5-acre site with 30 touring pitches.
Sauna room
Leisure: ⚐ Facilities: 🛝⊙⚲⚹🌣🔌
Services: 🔲🔳🔲→∪▶⊙♨🔧⚙🔴 ▦ 🔲 🔳

MAWGAN PORTH   Map 02 SW86

▶ ▶ ▶ ▶ 72% **Sun Haven Valley Holiday Park**
(SW861669)
TR8 4BQ ☎ 01637 860373 🗐 01637 860373
✉ sunhaven@hotmail.co.uk
Ⓦ www.sunhavenvalley.co.uk
Dir: From B3276 in Newquay take Padstow road. Right onto unclass road just after petrol station complex. Park in 1.75m
★ ⊞ £9.50-£16 ⊞ £9.50-£16 ▲ £9.50-£16
Open Apr-Oct (rs Oct-Mar Chalets only) Booking advisable Jul-Aug Last arrival 22.00hrs Last departure 10.30hrs
An attractive site with level pitches on the side of a river valley. The very high quality facilities include a TV lounge and a games room in a Swedish-style chalet, and a well-kept adventure playground. Trees and hedges fringe the park, and the ground is well drained. A 5-acre site with 118 touring pitches and 36 statics.
Leisure: ⚫ 🔺 ⎓ ▢
Facilities: 🛝🛝⊙⚲⚹🔵🔌🌊🚿
Services: 🔲🔳🔲⚙⊡→∪▶⊙⚙
Notes: Families and couples only
🔴 ▦ 🔲 🔳 🔳

▶ ▶ ▶ 74% *Trevarrian Holiday Park*
(SW853661)
TR8 4AQ ☎ 01637 860381 & 0845 2255910
✉ holiday@trevarrian.co.uk
Ⓦ www.trevarrian.co.uk
Dir: From A39 at St Columb rdbt turn right onto A3059 towards Newquay. Fork right in approx 2m for St Mawgan onto B3276. Turn right and site on left
⊞ ⊞ ▲
Open Etr-Sep Booking advisable Jun-Aug Last arrival 22.00hrs Last departure 11.00hrs
A well-established and well-run holiday park overlooking Mawgan Porth beach. This park has a wide range of attractions including a free

contd.

Trevarrian Holiday Park

entertainment programme in peak season. A 7-acre site with 185 touring pitches.
Sports field & pitch 'n' putt.
Leisure: ⚐⚫⚪🔺⎓▢ Facilities: 🛝🛝⊙⚲🌣🔌🌊
Services: 🔲🔳🔲⚙⚫⊡⊞⊡✗→∪▶⊙♨🔧→⚙ ▦ 🔳

MEVAGISSEY
See **Boswinger, Gorran & Pentewan**

MULLION   Map 02 SW61

72% **Mullion Holiday Park**
(SW699182)
Ruan Minor TR12 7LJ
☎ 01326 240428 & 0870 444 5344
🗐 01326 241141
✉ bookings@weststarholidays.co.uk
Ⓦ www.weststarholidays.co.uk
Dir: A30 onto A39 through Truro towards Falmouth. A394 to Helston then A3083 for Lizard. Park 7m on left opposite Mullion turning
★ ⊞ £12.50-£30 ⊞ £12.50-£30 ▲ £12.50-£30
Open 21 May-10 Sep (rs 24 Mar-20 May & 11 Sep-Oct No camping or caravans) Booking advisable Jul-Aug & bank holidays Last arrival 22.00hrs Last departure 10.00hrs
A comprehensively-equipped leisure park geared mainly for self-catering holidays, and set close to the sandy beaches, coves and fishing villages on the Lizard Peninsula. There is plenty of on-site entertainment for all ages, with indoor and outdoor swimming pools. A 49-acre site with 150 touring pitches, 8 hardstandings and 347 statics.
Adventure playground, scuba diving, football pitch
Leisure: ⚐⚫⚪🔺⎓▢
Facilities: 🛝⊙⚲⚹🔵🔌🌊🚿🎣🎇
Services: 🔲🔳🔲⚙⚫✗ 🍺→∪▶⊙🔧⚙
🔴 ▦ 🔳 🔳

See advertisement on opposite page

▶ ▶ ▶ 70% **'Franchis' Holiday Park** (SW698203)
Cury Cross Lanes TR12 7AZ ☎ 01326 240301
✉ enquiries@franchis.co.uk
Ⓦ www.franchis.co.uk
Dir: Off A3083 on left 0.5m past Wheal Inn PH, between Helston & The Lizard
★ ⊞ £10-£12 ⊞ £8-£12 ▲ £8-£10
Open Apr-Oct Booking advisable end Jul-Aug Last arrival 22.00hrs Last departure 11.00hrs
A grassy site surrounded by hedges and coppices,

contd.

---

and divided into two paddocks for tourers, in an ideal position for exploring the Lizard peninsula. Pitches are a mixture of level and slightly sloping. A 4-acre site with 70 touring pitches and 12 statics. Woodland walks

Facilities: ⬟⊙🍴⚡☂💺✖

Services: 🔧🍴🚿📶🚽🚮→∪🏪✂🌳◎

NEWQUAY   Map 02 SW86
See also **Rejerrah**

 75% **Hendra Holiday Park**
(SW833601)
TR8 4NY ☎ 01637 875778
📖 01637 879017
🅴 enquiries@hendra-holidays.com
🆆 www.hendra-holidays.com
Dir: A30 onto A392 signed Newquay. At Quintrell Downs over rdbt, signed Lane, 0.5m on left
★ 🚐 £9.35-£15.40 🚗 £9.35-£15.40 ▲ £9.35-£15.40
Open Apr-Oct (rs Apr-Spring bank hol outdoor pool closed) Booking advisable Jul-Aug Last arrival dusk Last departure 10.00hrs
A large complex with superb facilities including an indoor fun pool and an outdoor pool. There is a children's club for the over 6s, and evening entertainment during high season. The touring pitches are set amongst mature trees and shrubs, and some have fully-serviced facilities. All amenities are open to the public. A 46-acre site with 600 touring pitches and 283 statics. Solarium, fish bar, kids' club, train rides.

contd.

Leisure: 🏊 🏊 🎾 ⛰ 🎱

Facilities: ⬟⊙🍴☂⚡💺🛁📶✖🌳

Services: 🔧🚿🍴🍽→∪🏪✂🌳

Notes: Families and couples only 💳 💳 💳 🅖

See advertisement on page 48

 73% **Newquay Holiday Park**
(SW853626)
TR8 4HS ☎ 01637 871111 & 0870 420 2991 📖 01637 850818
🅴 enquiries@parkdeanholidays.co.uk
🆆 www.parkdeanholidays.co.uk
Dir: From Bodmin on A30, under low bridge, turn right towards RAF St Mawgan. Take A3059 towards Newquay, site past Treloy Golf Club
★ 🚐 £9-£27 🚗 £7-£27 ▲ £7-£24.50
Open Mar-Oct Booking advisable At all times Last arrival 21.00hrs Last departure 10.00hrs
A well-maintained park with a wide range of indoor and outdoor activities. A children's playground and café/take-away have enhanced the facilities, and the club and bars have been extended, offering quality entertainment. A 60-acre site with 196 touring pitches, hardstandings and 262 statics. Snooker, 9 hole pitch & putt, family entertainment

Leisure: 🏊 🎱 ⛰ 🎱

Facilities: ⬟⊙🍴☂⚡💺🛁📶

Services: 🔧📶🍽🚿📶🚽🚮✖💺→∪🏪✂🌳
💳 💳 🅖

Facilities: ➡ Bath 🍴 Shower ⊙ Electric Shaver ⚡ Hairdryer ☀ Ice Pack Facility ⚡ Disabled Facilities 📞 Public Telephone
🛒 Shop on Site or within 200yds 📱 Mobile Shop (calls at least 5 days a week) 🍖 BBQ Area 🌳 Picnic Area 🐕 Dog Exercise Area

England

Services: T Toilet Fluid   ✗ Café/ Restaurant   Fast Food/Takeaway   Baby Care   Electric Hook Up   Motorvan Service Point   Launderette   Licensed Bar   Calor Gaz   Camping Gaz   Battery Charging

Leisure: 🏊 Indoor swimming pool 🏊 Outdoor swimming pool 🎾 Tennis court 🎱 Games room 🛝 Children's playground ∪ Stables
▶ 9/18 hole golf course ⚓ Boats for hire 🎬 Cinema 🎣 Fishing ◎ Mini golf ⛵ Watersports 📺 Separate TV room

► ► ► ► 75% **Trencreek Holiday Park**
(SW828609)
Hillcrest, Higher Trencreek TR8 4NS
☎ 01637 874210 🖨 01637 874210
✆ trencreek@btconnect.com
Ⓦ www.trencreekholidaypark.co.uk
*Dir: A392 to Quintrell Downs, turn right towards
Newquay, turn left at 2 mini rdbts into Trevenson Road
to park*
★ 🚐 £9.70-£13.90 🚐 £9.70-£13.90 ⚑ £9.70-£13.90

Open Whit-mid Sep (rs Etr, Apr-May & late Sep
swimming pool, cafe & bar closed) Booking
advisable Jul-Aug Last arrival 22.00hrs Last
departure noon
*An attractively landscaped park in the village of
Trencreek, with modern toilet facilities of a very
high standard. Two well-stocked fishing lakes, and
evening entertainment in the licensed clubhouse,*

contd.

*are extra draws. Located about 2 miles from
Newquay with its beaches and surfing. A 10-acre
site with 194 touring pitches,
8 hardstandings and 6 statics.*
Free coarse fishing on site
Leisure: ₹ ♣ ⚁ ▱
Facilities: ℕ ⊙ ✳ ⚲ & ⚘ ⚑ ⌨ ☰
Services: ♨ 🔋 ⚑ ⊠ 🍴 ⊘ ⊞ ⊤ ✗ 🖤 → ∪ ▶ ⊙ ⚠ ⚥ 🚐
Notes: ⚑ Couples & families only

► ► ► 81% *Porth Beach Tourist Park*
(SW834629)
Porth TR7 3NH ☎ 01637 876531 🖨 01637 871227
✆ info@porthbeach.co.uk
Ⓦ www.porthbeach.co.uk
Dir: 1m NE off B3276 towards Padstow
🚐 🚐 ⚑
Open Mar-Nov Booking advisable Jul-Aug Last
arrival 18.00hrs Last departure 10.00hrs
*This attractive, popular park offers level, grassy
pitches in neat and tidy surroundings. A well-run
site set in meadowland and adjacent to sea and a
fine sandy beach. A 6-acre site with 201 touring
pitches, 19 hardstandings.*
Leisure: ⚁ Facilities: ℕ ⊙ & ⚘ ⚚
Services: ♨ 🔋 ⊠ 🍴 ⊘ ⊞ → ∪ ▶ ⊙ ⚥ 🚐
Notes: Families and couples only
⊛ ▭ ▬ ▭ ▢

See advertisement on page 49

Abbreviations: BH/bank hols-bank holidays   Etr-Easter   Whit-Whitsun   dep-departure   fr-from   hrs-hours   m-mile   mdnt-midnight   rdbt-roundabout   rs-restricted service   wk-week   wknd-weekend   ⚑-no dogs

▶ ▶ ▶ 68% **Riverside Holiday Park (SW829592)**
Ln TR8 4PE ☎ 01637 873617 🖷 01637 877051
🔂 info@riversideholidaypark.co.uk
🔊 www.riversideholidaypark.co.uk
*Dir: A30 onto A392 signed Newquay. At Quintrell
Downs cross rdbt signed Lane. 2nd left in 0.5m onto
unclass road signed Gwills. Park in 400yds*
🚐🚙▲

Open Mar-Dec Booking advisable Jul-Aug Last
departure 10.00hrs
*A sheltered valley beside a river in a quiet location
is the idyllic setting for this lightly wooded park.
The fairly simple facilities are being gradually
upgraded, and the park caters for families and
couples only. The site is close to the wide variety of
attractions offered by this major resort. An 11-acre
site with 100 touring pitches and 65 statics.
Fishing.*
Leisure: 🜄 ♦ � symbols **Facilities:** 🜁⊙🜂☀🜃🜄🜅
Services: 🜆🜇🜈🜉🜊🜋🜌 🜍→∪▶◎🜎🜏 🜐
Notes: Families and couples only 🔲 🔳 🔳 🔳

▶ ▶ ▶ 70% **Trebellan Park (SW790571)**
Cubert TR8 5PY ☎ 01637 830522 🖷 01637 830277
🔂 treagofarm@aol.com
🔊 www.treagofarm.co.uk
*Dir: 4m S of Newquay, turn W off A3075 at Cubert sign
and turn left in 0.75m onto unclass road*
★ 🚐 £12.50-£16.50 🚙 £12.50-£16.50 ▲ £10-£14
Open May-Oct Booking advisable Jul-Aug Last
arrival 21.00hrs Last departure 11.00hrs
*A terraced grassy rural park within a picturesque
valley with views of Cubert Common, and adjacent
to the Smuggler's Den, a 16th-century thatched inn.
This park has some excellent coarse fishing on site.
An 8-acre site with 150 touring pitches and 6 statics.
Three well stocked coarse fishing lakes.*
Leisure: 🜄 symbols **Facilities:** 🜁⊙🜂☀🜃🜅
Services: 🜆🜇🜈🜉→∪▶◎🜎🜏🜐
Notes: Families & couples only 🔲 🔳 🔳 🔳

▶ ▶ ▶ 78% **Treloy Touring Park (SW858625)**
TR8 4JN ☎ 01637 872063 & 876279 🖷 01637 872063
🔂 holidays@treloy.co.uk
🔊 www.treloy.co.uk
Dir: Off A3059 (St Columb Major-Newquay road)
★ 🚐 £10-£16 🚙 £10-£16 ▲ £10-£16
Open Apr-Sep (rs Apr & Sep swimming pool & bar
closed) Booking advisable Jul-Aug Last arrival
21.00hrs Last departure 10.00hrs
Attractive site with fine countryside views, within

*easy reach of resorts and beaches. The pitches are
set in four paddocks with mainly level but some
slightly sloping grassy areas. Maintenance and
cleanliness are very high. A 12-acre site with 175
touring pitches, 24 hardstandings.
Concessionary green fees for golf, entertainment*
Leisure: 🜄 ♦ symbols
Facilities: 🜁⊙🜂☀🜃🜅
Services: 🜆🜇🜈🜉🜊🜋🗙 🜍→∪▶🜎🜏🜐
🔲 🔳 🔳 🔳

See advertisement on page 48

▶ ▶ ▶ 70% **Trenance Holiday Park (SW818612)**
Edgcumbe Av TR7 2JY ☎ 01637 873447
🖷 01637 852677
🔂 enquiries@trenanceholidaypark.co.uk
🔊 www.trenanceholidaypark.co.uk
Dir: Off A3075 near viaduct. Site by boating lake rdbt
★ 🚐 £10-£13 🚙 £10-£13 ▲ £10-£13

contd.

contd.

England

Open 26 May-Oct. Booking advisable Jul-Aug Last arrival 22.00hrs Last departure 10.00hrs
A mainly static park popular with tenters, close to Newquay's vibrant nightlife, and serving excellent breakfasts and takeaways. Set on high ground in an urban area of town, with cheerful owners and clean facilities. A 12-acre site with 50 touring pitches and 190 statics.
Leisure: ♦ Facilities: ♠ Services: Notes:

▶ ▶ ▶ 75% **Trethiggey Touring Park**
(SW846596)
Quintrell Downs TR8 4QR
☎ 01637 877672 ▤ 01637 879706
✉ enquiries@trethiggey.co.uk
ⓦ www.trethiggey.co.uk
Dir: From A30 take A392 signed Newquay at Quintrell Downs rdbt, turn left onto A3058 past pearl centre to site 0.5m on left
★ ⊕ £12.15-£16.25 ⊕ £11.15-£15.25 ▲ £8.40-£12.50

Open Mar-Dec Booking advisable Jul-Aug Last arrival 22.00hrs Last departure 10.30hrs
A family-owned park in a rural setting that is ideal for touring this part of Cornwall. Pleasantly divided into paddocks with maturing trees and shrubs, and offering coarse fishing and tackle hire. A 15-acre site with 145 touring pitches, 35 hardstandings and 12 statics.
Off licence, recreation field, fishing
Leisure: ♦ ⚲ ⊡
Facilities:
Services:

NOTTER BRIDGE   Map 03 SX36

▶ ▶ ▶ 82% **Notter Bridge Caravan & Camping Park** (SX384608)
PL12 4RW ☎ 01752 842318
✉ holidays@notterbridge.co.uk
ⓦ www.notterbridge.co.uk
Dir: On A38, 3.5m W of Tamar Bridge (do not enter Saltash)
★ ⊕ £8-£11 ⊕ £8-£11 ▲ £8-£9
Open Etr-Sep Booking advisable Jul-Aug Last arrival 20.30hrs Last departure 11.00hrs
A sheltered valley park surrounded by woodland, and flanked on one side by the River Lynher. The friendly owners maintain the facilities to a high

contd.

standard, and there are plenty of hard pitches with electric and TV hook-up. A good base for visiting nearby beaches, with a country pub close by. A 6.25-acre site with 30 touring pitches, 24 hardstandings and 24 statics.
Games field, river frontage & fishing

Leisure: 🄐 Facilities: ⛏⊙❄♿🏪

Services: 🖃🖬⊟→▶🛆🍴🛒 Notes: Groups & commercial vehicles only by arrangement

---

OTTERHAM Map 02 SX19

▶ ▶ ▶ 71% St Tinney Farm Holidays (SX169906)
PL32 9TA ☎ 01840 261274
🖷 01840 261575
🕲 info@st-tinney.co.uk
🕏 www.st-tinney.co.uk
Dir: Signed 1m off A39 via unclass road signed Otterham
★ 🚐 £8-£12 🛆 £8-£12
Open Etr-Oct (rs Nov-Etr self catering lodges/static caravan only) Booking advisable Spring BH & Jul-Aug Last arrival 21.00hrs Last departure 11.00hrs
A family-run farm site in a rural area, with nature trails, lakes, valleys and complete seclusion. Visitors are free to walk around the farmland lakes and lose themselves in the countryside. A 34-acre site with 20 touring pitches and 15 statics.
Coarse fishing, horse/donkey rides, pony trekking

Leisure: ♦ 🄐 Facilities: ⛏⊙❄🍴🛒🏪

Services: 🖃🖬🍴⊘⊟✗ 🛆→U🍴🍽 🎮 📺 📶 ⬤

PADSTOW Map 02 SW97

▶ ▶ ▶ 70% Dennis Cove Camping (SW920744)
Dennis Ln PL28 8DR ☎ 01841 532349
🕲 denniscove@freeuk.com
🕏 www.denniscove.co.uk
Dir: Approach Padstow on A389, turn right at Tesco into Sarah's Lane, 2nd right to Dennis Lane, follow lane to site at end
★ 🚐 £11-£14.50 🛞 £11-£14.50 🛆 £11-£14.50
Open Apr-Sep Booking advisable throughout season Last arrival 22.00hrs Last departure 11.00hrs
Set in meadowland with mature trees, this site overlooks Padstow Bay, with access to the Camel Estuary and the nearby beach. The centre of town is just a 10 minute walk away, and bike hire is available on site, with the famous Camel Trail beginning right outside. A 3-acre site with 42 touring pitches.
Facilities: ⛏⊙❄❄

Services: 🖃🍴⊘⊟→U🍴⊚🛆🍽🛒

▶ ▶ ▶ 79% *Padstow Touring Park (SW913738)*
PL28 8LE ☎ 01841 532061 🖷 01841 532061
🕲 mail@padstowtouringpark.co.uk
🕏 www.padstowtouringpark.co.uk
Dir: 1m S of Padstow, on E side of A389 (Padstow to Wadebridge road)
🚐🛞🛆
Open Apr-mid Oct Booking advisable Jul-Aug Last arrival 19.00hrs Last departure 16.00hrs
Set in open countryside above the quaint fishing

contd.

town of Padstow which can be approached by footpath directly from the park. This level grassy site is divided into paddocks by maturing bushes and hedges to create a peaceful and relaxing holiday atmosphere. A 13.5-acre site with 100 touring pitches, 9 hardstandings.

Leisure: 🄐

Facilities: ⛏⊙❄❄🛒🏪

Services: 🖃🖵🖬🍴⊘⊟⊟→U🍴🛆🍽🛒⊚

▶ ▶ 72% Padstow Holiday Park (SW009073)
Cliffdowne PL28 8LB ☎ 01841 532289
🖷 01841 532289
🕲 alex@cliffdowne.freeserve.co.uk
🕏 www.padstowholidaypark.co.uk
Dir: On B3274/A389 into Padstow. Signed 1.5m before Padstow
★ 🚐 £9.50-£13 🛞 £9.50-£13 🛆 £9.50-£13
Open Mar-Dec Booking advisable at all times Last arrival 17.00hrs Last departure noon
A mainly static park with some touring pitches in a small paddock and others in an open field. This quiet holiday site can be reached from Padstow (1m away) by a footpath. A 5.5-acre site with 27 touring pitches and 74 statics.

Leisure: 🄐

Facilities: ⛏⊙❄🍴🖿

Services: 🖃🖬🍴⊘⊟→U🍴⊚🛆🍽🛒

Notes: 🐾

PENTEWAN Map 02 SX04

78% Pentewan Sands Holiday Park (SX018468)
PL26 6BT ☎ 01726 843485
🖷 01726 844142
🕲 info@pentewan.co.uk
🕏 www.pentewan.co.uk
Dir: On B3273 4m S of St Austell
🚐 £10.65-£24.85 🛞 £10.65-£24.85
🛆 £10.65-£24.85
Open Apr-Oct (rs Apr-14 May & 15 Sep-Oct some facilities closed) Booking advisable Jul-Aug Last arrival 22.00hrs Last departure 10.30hrs
A large holiday park with a wide range of amenities, set on the dunes adjacent to a private beach where plenty of aquatic activities are available. A short stroll leads to the pretty village of Pentewan, and other attractions are a short drive away. A club on site offers evening entertainment. A 32-acre site with 500 touring pitches and 120 statics.
Cycles, boat launch, water sports, caravan store

Leisure: 🕿 ❄ ♦ 🄐

Facilities: ⛏⊙❄♿🖿

Services: 🖃🖵🖬🍴⊘⊟⊟✗ 🛆→U🍴⊚🛆🍽

Notes: 🐾 No jet skis
🎮 📺 📶 ⬤

England

PREMIER PARK

▶ ▶ ▶ ▶ ▶ 86% **Sun Valley Holiday Park (SX005486)**
Pentewan Rd PL26 6DJ
☎ 01726 843266 & 844393
🖺 01726 843266
🅴 reception@sunvalleyholidays.co.uk
🅦 www.sunvalleyholidays.co.uk
Dir: From St Austell take B3273 towards Mevagissey. Park is 2m on right
★ 🚐 £12.50-£28 🚐 £12.50-£28 ▲ £12.50-£28
Open Apr (or Etr if earlier)-Oct Booking advisable May-Sep Last arrival 22.00hrs Last departure noon
In a picturesque valley amongst woodland, this neat park is kept to an exceptionally high standard. The extensive amenities include tennis courts, indoor swimming pool, licensed clubhouse and restaurant. The sea is 1m away, and can be accessed via a footpath and cycle path along the river bank. A 20-acre site with 22 touring pitches and 75 statics.
Leisure: ❊ ❊ ◆ ⚑ Facilities: ⬛⊙❊✻❤◆❤⚑⚒
Services: ⬛⬚⬛⬛⬚⬚⬚✕ ⬛→⊙ ▶⬛✚⬛ ✦
⬛ ⬛ ⬛ ⬛ ⬚

▶ ▶ ▶ 71% *Heligan Woods (SW998470)*
PL26 6BT ☎ 01726 842714 🖺 01726 844142
🅴 info@pentewan.co.uk
🅦 www.pentewan.co.uk
Dir: From A390 take B3273 for Mevagissey at x-roads signed 'No caravans beyond this point'. Right onto unclass road towards Gorran, site 0.75m on left
🚐 £9.60-£21.50 🚐 £9.60-£21.50 ▲ £9.60-£21.50
Open 1 wk before Good Fri-Nov Booking advisable late July & Aug Last arrival 22.30hrs Last departure 10.30hrs
A pleasant peaceful park adjacent to the Lost Gardens of Heligan, with views over St Austell Bay, and well-maintained facilities. Guests can also use the extensive amenities at the sister park, Pentewan Sands. A 12-acre site with 89 touring pitches and 30 statics.
Leisure: ⚑ Facilities: ⬛⊙❊❤⚑⚒
Services: ⬛⬚⬛⬛⬚→⊙ ▶⬛✚⬛ ✦
⬛ ⬛ ⬛ ⬛ ⬚

▶ ▶ ▶ 67% *Penhaven Touring Park (SX008481)*
PL26 6DL ☎ 01726 843687 🖺 01726 843870
🅴 enquiries@penhaventouring.co.uk
🅦 www.penhaventouring.co.uk
Dir: S from St Austell on B3273 towards Mevagissey. Site on left 1m after village of London Apprentice
🚐 🚐 ▲
Open Apr-Oct Booking advisable public hols & end Jul-Aug Last arrival 21.00hrs Last departure 10.00hrs
An open park in a wooded valley with a river running past. The sandy beach at Pentewan is just a mile away, and can be accessed by a footpath and cycle path along the river bank directly from the park. A 13-acre site with 105 touring pitches, 12 hardstandings.

contd.

Penhaven Touring Park
Off-licence, motorvan service point
Leisure: ❊ ⚑ Facilities: ⬛⊙❊✻◆❤⚑⚒
Services: ⬛⬚⬛⬚⬚⬛⬚ ⬛→ ▶⬛✚⬛ ✦
⬛ ⬛ ⬛ ⬛ ⬚

| PENZANCE | Map 02 SW43 |
See also **Relubbus & Rosudgeon**

▶ ▶ ▶ 72% **Bone Valley Caravan & Camping Park (SW472316)**
Heamoor TR20 8UJ ☎ 01736 360313
🖺 01736 360313
🅴 enquiries@bonevalleycandcpark.co.uk
Dir: A30 to Penzance, then towards Land's End, at 2nd rdbt right into Heamoor, 300yds right into Josephs Lane, 1st left, site 500yds on left
★ 🚐 £8-£13 🚐 £8-£13 ▲ £8-£9.50

Open all year Booking advisable Jul-Aug Last arrival 22.00hrs Last departure 11.00hrs
A compact grassy park on the outskirts of Penzance, with well maintained facilities. It is divided into paddocks by mature hedges, and a small stream runs alongside. A 1-acre site with 17 touring pitches, 2 hardstandings and 5 statics.
Baby changing facilities, campers' kitchen
Leisure: ▢ Facilities: ⬛⊙❊✻◆❤⚑⚒
Services: ⬛⬚⬛⬛⬚⬛ ⬛→⊙◎◆✚⬛ ✦
⬛ ⬛ ⬛ ⬛ ⬛ ⬛ ⬚

NEW ▶ ▶ 84% **Higher Chellew Holiday Park (SW496353)**
Higher Trenowin, Nancledra TR20 8BD
☎ 01736 364532 🖺 01736 332380
🅴 higherchellew@btinternet.com
🅦 www.higherchellewcamping.co.uk
Dir: From A30 turn off towards St Ives, left at mini-rdbt towards Nancledra. Turn left at B3311 junct, through Nancledra, site 0.5m on left.
🚐 £6.80-£12.50 🚐 £6.80-£12.50 ▲ £6.80-£12.50

contd.

Higher Chellew Holiday Park

Open Fri before Etr-Oct Booking advisable mid Jul-Aug Last departure 10.30hrs
A small rural park quietly located just four miles from the golden beaches at St Ives, and a similar distance from Penzance. This well sheltered park occupies an elevated location, and all pitches are level. A 1.25-acre site with 30 touring pitches.
Facilities: ⚑ ☼ ⚘   Services: ⊟ ⓑ → ∪ ⚄

| PERRANPORTH | Map 02 SW75 |

 75% Perran Sands Holiday Park (SW767554)
TR6 0AQ ☎ 01872 573551
🖹 01872 571158
ⓦ www.havenholidays.com
Dir: A30 onto B3285 towards Perranporth. Park on right before descent on hill into Perranporth
🐕
Open mid Mar-Oct (rs mid Mar-May & Sep-Oct Some facilities may be reduced) Booking advisable school hols Last arrival 22.00hrs Last departure noon
Nestling amid 500 acres of protected dune grassland, and with a footpath through to the surf and 3 miles of golden sandy beach, this lively park is set in a large village-style complex. It offers a complete range of on-site facilities and entertainment for all the family which makes it an extremely popular park. A 550-acre site with 412 touring pitches and 395 statics.
Leisure: ⚓ ⚑   Facilities: 🔧 ⚅ ⚅ ⚄
Services: ⊟ ⚅ 🍴 ✕ 🛒 ⚄ ⚄ ⚄ ⚄ 🔵

▶ ▶ ▶ 69% *Perranporth Camping & Touring Park*
(SW768542)
Budnick Rd TR6 0DB ☎ 01872 572174
🖹 01872 572174
Dir: 0.5m E off B3285
🐕 🐕 Å
Open Whit-Sep (rs Etr-Whit & mid Sep-end Sep shop & club facilities closed) Booking advisable Jul-Aug Last arrival 23.00hrs Last departure noon
A mainly tenting site with few level pitches, located high above a fine sandy beach which is much-frequented by surfers. The park is attractive to young people, and is set in a lively town on a spectacular part of the coast. A 6-acre site with 120 touring pitches, 4 hardstandings and 9 statics.
Leisure: ⚓ ⚑ ⚑ ⊡   Facilities: ⚑ ⚄ ⊙ 🔧 ☼ ⚅ ⚄ ⚄ 🐕
Services: ⊟ ⚅ 🍴 ⚅ ⚄ ⊟ ⊤ ⚄ → ∪ ▶ ◎ ⚄ ☂ 🔵
🍴 ⚄ ⚄ 🔵

Discover River Valley

L ocated along the bank of a clear shallow stream, River Valley offers you a sense of utter peace and tranquillity.
● 100 Touring, Motorhome or Tent pitches
● Luxury Caravan Holiday Homes & Lodges Available
● 18 Acres of partly wooded countryside
● Shop & Launderette
● SEASONAL PITCHES FROM £630.00

River Valley Country Park, Relubbus, Penzance, Cornwall, TR20 9ER
Tel 0845 60 12 516   Fax 01736 763398
www.rivervalley.co.uk   rivervalley@surfbay.dircon.co.uk

Perranporth ▶▶▶ Camping & Touring Park

The park, within easy walking distance (approx. 5 minutes) of beach and town, comprises seven acres of well drained sheltered grass land with tarmacadam access roads and all modern facilities.

Mini Supermarket • Swimming Pool • Launderette • Showers and Washrooms • Six berth luxury vans • Adjacent 'Failte Club' with licensed bar, overlooking heated swimming pool and children's paddling pool • Take away.

Budnick Road, Perranporth, Cornwall Tel: Perranporth (0187257) 2174

AA, Camping Club, Caravan Club British Tourist Authority listed site

► ► ► 83% **Tollgate Farm Caravan & Camping Park** (SW768547)
Budnick Hill TR6 0AD
☎ 01872 572130 & 0845 1662126
✉ enquiries@tollgatefarm.co.uk
⊕ www.tollgatefarm.co.uk
Dir: Off A30 onto B3285 to Perranporth. Site on right 1.5m after Goonhavern
★ ⊕ £9.50-£14 ⊕ £9.50-£14 ⚑ £9.50-£14

Open Etr-Oct Booking advisable Jul-Aug Last arrival 21.00hrs Last departure 11.00hrs
A quiet site in a rural location with spectacular coastal views. Pitches are divided into four paddocks sheltered and screened by mature hedges. Children will enjoy the play equipment and pets' corner. The three miles of sand at Perran Bay are just a walk away through the sand dunes, or a 0.75m drive. A 10-acre site with 102 touring pitches, 10 hardstandings. Animal area

Leisure: ⚑

Facilities: ⬕⊙⬑⚙✳⬕⬕⬕⬕⬕⬕

Services: ⬕⬕⬕⬕⬕⬕⬕⬕→∪▸⬕⬕⬕⬕⬕

Notes: No large groups

See advertisement on opposite page

► 84% *Higher Golla Touring & Caravan Park* (SW756514)
Penhallow TR4 9LZ ☎ 01872 573963 & 572116
▤ 01872 572116
✉ trevor@cornishhair.fsnet.com.uk
Dir: A30 onto B3248 towards Perranporth. (Straight on at junct with A3075). Approx 2m. Site signed on right
⊕ ⊕
Open Etr- mid Oct Booking advisable Jul-Aug Last arrival 20.00hrs Last departure 10.30hrs
Extensive country views can be enjoyed from all pitches on this quietly located site. The facilities are very simple (2 WCs and 1 cold washbasin) but there are plans to upgrade. Every pitch has electricity and water tap. A 1.5-acre site with 12 touring pitches and 2 statics.

Facilities: ⬕⬕

Services: ⬕→∪▸⬕⬕⬕⬕⬕
⬕⬕⬕⬕⬕

The number of touring pitches listed for each site includes tents, caravans and motorvans.

POLPERRO   Map 02 SX25

69% *Killigarth Manor Holiday
Centre (SX214519)*
PL13 2JQ ☎ 01503 272216 & 272409
📠 01503 272065
📧 killigarthmanor@breathemail.net
🌐 www.killigarth.co.uk
*Dir: From A38 at Trerulefoot rdbt onto A387,
through Looe, over bridge signed Polperro. In 3.5m
left past shelter/phone box. Park 400yds on left*
🐾🐾👤
Open Etr-Oct Booking advisable 3rd wk Jul-Aug
Last arrival 20.00hrs Last departure noon
*Set on high ground at the approach to the
historic fishing village, this large holiday centre
offers a wide variety of leisure activities based
around the indoor complex. In the evening the
entertainment centres around the lively Harbour
Lights Club. A 7-acre site with 202 touring
pitches and 147 statics.*
Amusement arcade, pool table & table tennis.
Leisure: 🏊 🎾 🎱 🎠 📺
Facilities: 🚿☉🍴⚡❄️👶🔧♨️🐕👤
Services: 🔌🛢🚰🔥🚽🔵✕ 🛒→♻️▶✂️♨️🚐↗
Notes: 🐾 💳 💳 💳 💳 🔲

POLRUAN   Map 02 SX15

► ► ► 78% Polruan Holidays-
Camping & Caravanning (SX133509)
Polruan-by-Fowey PL23 1QH
☎ 01726 870263 📠 01726 870263
📧 polholiday@aol.com
*Dir: A38 to Dobwalls, left onto A390 to East Taphouse.
Left onto B3359. Right in 4.5m signed Polruan*
★ 🚐 £9.50-£13.50 🚐 £9.50-£13.50 ⛺ £7-£13.50
Open Etr-Sep Booking advisable Jul, Aug & bank
hols Last arrival 21.00hrs Last departure noon
*A very rural and quiet site in a lovely elevated
position above the village, with good views of the
sea. The River Fowey passenger ferry is close by,
and the site has a good shop, and barbecues to
borrow. A 3-acre site with 47 touring pitches,
7 hardstandings and 11 statics.*
Tourist information.
Leisure: 🎠
Facilities: 🚿☉🍴❄️⚡♨️🐕🔲
Services: 🔌🛢🚰🔥🚽🔵→♻️🔺✂️♨️

POLZEATH   Map 02 SW97

► ► ► 74% South Winds Caravan & Camping
Park (SW948790)
Polzeath Rd PL27 6QU ☎ 01208 863267
📠 01208 862080
📧 paul@tristramf/s.co.uk
🌐 www.rockinfo.co.uk
*Dir: Leave B3314 on unclass road signed Polzeath, park
on right just past turn to New Polzeath*
★ 🚐 £25-£35 🚐 £25-£35 ⛺ £20-£35
Open Mar-Oct Booking advisable Jul & Aug &
school hols Last arrival 21.00hrs Last departure
11.00hrs
A peaceful site with beautiful sea and panoramic

contd.

England

Abbreviations: BH/bank hols-bank holidays   Etr-Easter   Whit-Whitsun   dep-departure   fr-from   hrs-hours   m-mile   mdnt-midnight   rdbt-roundabout   rs-restricted service   wk-week   wknd-weekend   🐕-no dogs

England

rural views, within walking distance of a new golf complex, and 0.75m from beach and village. A 16-acre site with 100 touring pitches.

Facilities: 👣☉🌑❄🔌🖳🍴📷🐾

Services: 🔌🗓🚽🛢🌐🔲→U🅿☉⛽✚♨🍴🛒

Notes: No disposable barbecues, no noise 11pm-7am & dogs must be on leads at all times

💳 🔳 🔲 ⑤   See advertisement on opposite page

► ► ► 75% **Tristram Caravan & Camping Park** (SW936790)
PL27 6UG ☎ 01208 862215 📠 01208 862080
🄴 paul@tristramf/s.co.uk
Ⓦ www.rockinfo.co.uk
Dir: From B3314 take unclass road signed Polzeath. Through village, up hill, site 2nd turn on right
★ 🚐 £25-£40 🚍 £25-£40 ▲ £20-£40
Open Mar-Nov Booking advisable Jul, Aug & school hols Last arrival 21.00hrs Last departure 10.00hrs
An ideal family site, positioned on a gently sloping cliff with grassy pitches and glorious sea views. There is direct gated access to the beach, where surfing is very popular. The local amenities of the village are only a few hundred yards away. A 10-acre site with 100 touring pitches.
Private footpath onto beach

Facilities: 👣☉🌑❄🔌🖳🍴📷🐾

Services: 🔌🖐🔌🗓🛢🌐🔲✕🚿→U🅿☉⛽✚♨🍴

Notes: No ball games, no disposable BBQs, no noise between 11pm-7am, dogs on leads at all times 💳 🔳 🔲 🔳 ⑤

See advertisement on opposite page

PORTHTOWAN	Map 02 SW64

► ► ► ► 78% **Porthtowan Tourist Park** (SW693473)
Mile Hill TR4 8TY ☎ 01209 890256
🄴 admin@porthtowantouristpark.co.uk
Ⓦ www.porthtowantouristpark.co.uk
Dir: Exit A30 at junct signed Redruth/Porthtowan. 3rd exit from rdbt, 2m. Right at T-junct. Park at top of hill
★ 🚐 £7-£11.75 🚍 £7-£11.75 ▲ £7-£11.75

SILVER

Open Etr-Oct Booking advisable Jul-Aug Last arrival 21.30hrs Last departure 11.00hrs
A neat, level grassy site on high ground above Porthtowan, with plenty of shelter from mature trees and shrubs. The superb toilet facilities considerably enhance the appeal of this peaceful rural park, which is almost midway between the small seaside resorts of Portreath and Porthtowan,
contd.

---

with their beaches and surfing. A 5-acre site with 50 touring pitches, 4 hardstandings.

Leisure: 🏊 ⛰ **Facilities:** 👣☉🌑❄🔌🖳🍴📷🐾

Services: 🔌🗓🛢🌐🔲→U🅿☉⛽✚♨🍴🛢

► ► ► ► 80% **Rose Hill Touring Park** (SW693466)
TR4 8AR ☎ 01209 890802
🄴 reception@rosehillcamping.co.uk
Ⓦ www.rosehillcamping.co.uk
Dir: A30 onto B3277 signed St Agnes. In 1m turn left signed Porthtowan. Site 100yds past beach road
★ 🚐 £12-£18 🚍 £12-£18 ▲ £12-£18
Open end Mar-end Oct Booking advisable Jun-Aug/bank hols Last arrival 20.00hrs Last departure 10.30hrs
A small, well-kept park in an attractive position, set into the hillside and terraced. The park is quiet and sheltered, hidden away in a wooded valley, with some hardstandings among many level pitches. Only a short distance from a popular sandy beach and surf centre, plus village pubs and restaurants. A 2.5-acre site with 50 touring pitches, 10 hardstandings.
Tourist information, wet suit wash, bakery

Facilities: 👣☉🌑❄🔌🖳🍴📷

Services: 🔌🗓🛢🌐🔲✕🖐🚿→U🅿☉⛽✚♨🍴

💳 🔳 🔲 🅞 🔳 🔳 ⑤

► ► ► 78% **Wheal Rose Caravan & Camping Park** (SW717449)
Wheal Rose TR16 5DD ☎ 01209 891496
🄴 les@whealrosecaravanpark.co.uk
Ⓦ www.whealrosecaravanpark.co.uk
Dir: Leave A30 at Scorrier sign and follow signs on unclass road to Wheal Rose. Park 0.5m on left
★ 🚐 £7-£11 🚍 £7-£11 ▲ £7-£11

Open Mar-Dec Booking advisable Aug Last arrival 23.00hrs Last departure 11.00hrs
A quiet, peaceful park in a secluded valley setting, central for beaches and countryside, and 2m from the surfing beaches of Porthtowan. The friendly owners work hard to keep this park immaculate, with a bright toilet block and well-trimmed pitches. A 6-acre site with 50 touring pitches, 6 hardstandings and 2 statics.

Leisure: 🏌 🏊 ⛰ **Facilities:** 👣☉🌑❄🔌🖳🍴📷

Services: 🔌🗓🛢🌐🔲→U🅿♨🍴

Notes: 5mph speed limit, dogs on leads, minimum noise after 11pm, gates locked 11pm.

PORTSCATHO	Map 02 SW83

▶ ▶ ▶ **74% Trewince Farm Touring Park** (SW868339)
TR2 5ET ☎ 01872 580430 🖷 01872 580430
✉ info@trewincefarm.co.uk
🌐 www.trewincefarm.co.uk
Dir: From St Austell take A390 towards Truro. Left on B3287 to Tregony, following signs to St Mawes. At Trewithian, turn left to St Anthony. Trewince Manor 0.75m past church
★ 🚉 £9-£15 🚐 £9-£15 ▲ £9-£15

Open May-Sep Booking advisable high season Last arrival 23.00hrs Last departure noon
A recently-developed site on a working farm with spectacular sea views from its elevated position. The facilities on adjacent Trewince Manor are open to visitors, including a bar and a restaurant specialising in seafood. Dinghies can also be launched from the manor's own slipway.
A 3-acre site with 25 touring pitches.
Private quay & moorings
Facilities: 🏕⊙🔦✻🛱🏕🏇
Services: 🖭🖥🎛→∪⅄🗡

▶ ▶ **72%** *Treloan Coastal Farm Holidays* (SW876348)
Treloan Ln TR2 5EF ☎ 01872 580888 & 580899
🖷 01872 580989
✉ holidays@treloan.freeserve.co.uk
🌐 www.coastalfarmholidays.co.uk
Dir: Take unclass road to Gerrans off A3078 (Tregony to St Mawes road). Immediately after Gerrans church road divides - take Treloan Ln (by Royal Standard pub) to park
🚉 🚐 ▲

Open all year Booking advisable High Season Last departure 11.00hrs
A quiet, well-screened coastal park with mature

contd.

---

trees and bushes, and three nearby secluded beaches. All pitches offer sea views, and there is a camping barn for walkers on the South West Coastal Footpath. A 7-acre site with 49 touring pitches, 8 hardstandings and 8 statics.
Coastal footpath on site
Facilities: 🏕⊙✻🔦🛱🐾🏇
Services: 🖭🖥🛢🎛→∪⅄⅄🗡🖲 🖳🖳 🖳 🖳

See advertisement under TRURO

REDRUTH	Map 02 SW64

▶ ▶ ▶ **71% Cambrose Touring Park (SW684453)**
Portreath Rd TR16 4HT ☎ 01209 890747
✉ cambrosetouringpark@supanet.com
🌐 www.cambrosetouringpark.co.uk
Dir: A30 onto B3300 towards Portreath. Approx 0.75m at 1st rdbt right onto B3300. Take unclass road on right signed Porthtowan. Site 200yds on left
★ 🚉 £7.50-£12.50 🚐 £7.50-£12.50 ▲ £7.50-£12.50

Open Apr-Oct Booking advisable Jul-Aug Last arrival 22.00hrs Last departure 11.30hrs
Situated in a rural setting surrounded by trees and shrubs, this park is divided into grassy paddocks. About two miles from the harbour village of Portreath. A 6-acre site with 60 touring pitches.
Mini football pitch
Leisure: ⅄ ♦ ⚲ **Facilities:** 🏕⊙✻🔦🐾🛱🏇
Services: 🖭🖥🛢✎🎛🖽 🖳→∪▶◉♨🗡

▶ ▶ ▶ **71% Lanyon Holiday Park (SW684387)**
Loscombe Ln, Four Lanes TR16 6LP
☎ 01209 313474
✉ jamierielly@btconnect.com
🌐 www.lanyonholidaypark.co.uk
Dir: Signed 0.5m off B2397 on Helston side of Four Lanes village
★ 🚉 £12-£16 🚐 £12-£16 ▲ £12-£16
Open Mar-Oct Booking advisable Jul & Aug Last arrival 21.00hrs Last departure noon
Small, friendly rural park in elevated position with fine views to distant St Ives Bay. This family owned and run park is being upgraded in all areas, and is close to a cycling trail. Stithian's Reservoir for fishing, sailing and windsurfing is two miles away. A 14-acre site with 25 touring pitches and 49 statics.
Take-away service, all-day games room
Leisure: ⅄ ♦ ⚲ 🖵
Facilities: 🛠🏕⊙🔦✻🛱🐾🏇
Services: 🖭🖥🍷🛢🎛🖽 🖳→∪▶◉△⅄♨🗡
🖳 🖳 🖳 🖳 🖳

Services: 🎛 Toilet Fluid ✖ Café/ Restaurant 🖽 Fast Food/Takeaway 🖳 Baby Care 🖭 Electric Hook Up
🖳 Motorvan Service Point 🖥 Launderette 🍷 Licensed Bar 🛢 Calor Gaz ✎ Camping Gaz 🎛 Battery Charging

▶ ▶ ▶ 80% **Tehidy Holiday Park (SW682432)**
Harris Mill, Illogan TR16 4JQ ☎ 01209 216489
📠 01209 216489
🅑 holiday@tehidy.co.uk
🅦 www.tehidy.co.uk
Dir: Exit A30 at Redruth/Portreath junct onto A3047 to 1st rdbt. Left onto B3300. At junct straight over signed Tehidy Holiday Park. Past Cornish Arms pub, 800yds bottom of hill on left.
★ 🚐 £7.50-£11 🚐 £7.50-£11 ▲ £7.50-£11

Open Apr-Oct Booking advisable Jul-Aug Last arrival 20.00hrs Last departure 10.00hrs
An attractive wooded location in a quiet rural area only 2.5m from popular beaches. Mostly level pitches on tiered ground, and the toilet facilities are bright and modern. A 4.5-acre site with 18 touring pitches, 2 hardstandings and 32 statics. Trampoline, off-licence.

Leisure: 🔍 🎢 🖵
Facilities: 🔔⊙🍴✳🔧🚿🧺🏊🌳🍴
Services: 🔌🎱🍴🧺🚽🗑→∪🛒♿✦🐕🍴
Notes: Dogs by arrangement 💳 💳 💳 💳 💳

REJERRAH   **Map 02 SW75**

 73% **Monkey Tree Holiday Park (SW803545)**
Scotland Rd TR8 5QR
☎ 01872 572032
📠 01872 573577
🅑 enquiries@monkeytreeholidaypark.co.uk
🅦 www.monkeytreeholidaypark.co.uk
Dir: Exit A30 onto B3285 to Perranporth, 0.25m right into Scotland Rd, site on left in 1.5m
★ 🚐 £7-£11.90 🚐 £7-£11.90 ▲ £7-£11.90
Open all year Booking advisable Jul & Aug Last arrival 22.00hrs Last departure from 10.00hrs
*A busy holiday park with plenty of activities and a jolly holiday atmosphere. Set close to lovely beaches between Newquay and Perranporth, it offers an outdoor swimming pool, children's playground, two bars with entertainment, and a good choice of eating outlets including a restaurant and a takeaway. A 56-acre site with 505 touring pitches and 80 statics.
Sauna, solarium, mountain bike hire & football pitch*

Leisure: ⭐ 🔍 🎢
Facilities: 🔔⊙✳🔧🚿🧺🏊🌳🍴
Services: 🔌🎱🍴🧺🗑🚽✖🧹→∪🛒◎♿✦🍴
Notes: Family park 💳 💳 💳 💳 💳

AWARD WINNING HOLIDAY PARK

Monkey Tree HOLIDAY PARK

For a great family holiday - minutes from Perranporth and Newquay and close to exciting visitor attractions!

FREE heated pool
FREE kids club
FREE family entertainment
Restaurant, bar and shop

Monkey Tree Holiday Park, Rejerrah, Newquay, Cornwall TR8 5QR
www.monkeytreeholidaypark.co.uk
enquiries@monkeytreeholidaypark.co.uk

Booking Hotline
01872 572032

▶ ▶ ▶ ▶ 82% **Newperran Holiday Park (SW801555)**
TR8 5QJ ☎ 01872 572407 📠 01872 571254
🅑 holidays@newperran.co.uk
🅦 www.newperran.co.uk
Dir: 4m SE of Newquay & 1m S of Rejerrah on A3075
★ 🚐 £8.90-£14 🚐 £8.90-£14 ▲ £8.90-£14
Open Etr-Oct Booking advisable Jul-Aug Last arrival mdnt Last departure 10.00hrs
*A family site in a lovely rural position near several beaches and bays. This airy park offers screening to some pitches, which are set in paddocks on level ground. High season entertainment is available in the park's country inn, and the café has an extensive menu. A 25-acre site with 270 touring pitches, 18 hardstandings and 5 statics.
Crazy golf, adventure playground & pool*

Leisure: ⭐ 🔍 🎢 **Facilities:** 🔔⊙🍴✳🔧🚿🧺🏊🌳🍴
Services: 🔌🎱🍴🧺🗑🚽✖🧹→∪🛒◎♿✦🐕🍴
💳 💳 💳 💳 💳

See advertisement under NEWQUAY

▶ ▶ ▶ 72% **Perran-Quay Tourist Park (SW800554)**
Hendra Croft TR8 5QP
☎ 01872 572561 📠 01872 575043
🅑 rose@perran-quay.co.uk
Dir: direct access off A3075 behind Braefel Inn
★ 🚐 £7-£19 🚐 £7-£19 ▲ £5-£17
Open all year Booking advisable Jul-Aug Last departure 10.00hrs
A friendly family-run site set in paddocks with mature trees and shrubs for shelter. The park has its
contd.

Leisure: 🔍 Indoor swimming pool 🔍 Outdoor swimming pool 🎾 Tennis court 🔍 Games room 🎢 Children's playground ∪ Stables
▶ 9/18 hole golf course 🧹 Boats for hire 🎬 Cinema 🍴 Fishing ◎ Mini golf ♿ Watersports 🖵 Separate TV room

own pub serving food and drink, and is close to the sandy beach at Holywell Bay. With its swimming pool and quiet surroundings midway between Newquay and Perranporth, it is well liked by families. A 7-acre site with 110 touring pitches, 2 hardstandings and 16 statics.

Leisure: 🎣 ⚓ ⚲ Facilities: 🚿🛁⚹🛒🔱🛎
Services: 🚽🔌🍴🎱✕→∪🅿◉△🗑🐕 ▦ 🔳 🔳 🔲

RELUBBUS   Map 02 SW53

▶ ▶ ▶ ▶ **77% River Valley Country Park (SW565326)**
TR20 9ER ☎ 01736 763398
📠 01736 763398
🅰 rivervalley@surfbay.dircon.co.uk
🌐 www.rivervalley.co.uk
Dir: From A30 follow sign for Helston A394. At next rbdt 1st left signed Relubbus
🚐 🚐 ⛺

Open Mar-Dec (rs Nov-4 Jan hardstanding & lodges only) Booking advisable Jul-Aug Last arrival 20.00hrs Last departure 11.00hrs
A quiet, attractive site of quality in a picturesque river valley with direct access to a shallow trout stream. This level park has a good mix of grass and hard pitches, and is partly wooded with pleasant walks. It is surrounded by farmland, and just a few miles from the sandy beaches of both the north and south coasts, as well as St Michael's Mount at Marazion. An 18-acre site with 119 touring pitches and 48 statics. Fishing, licensed shop.
Facilities: 🔱☉⚲⚹🛁⚵🛎🔨
Services: 🚽🔌🚿▦🅃→∪🅿◉△🗑
Notes: No pets in tents 🔲 ▦ 🔲

See advertisement under PENZANCE

ROSUDGEON   Map 02 SW52

▶ ▶ ▶ **77% Kenneggy Cove Holiday Park (SW562287)**
Higher Kenneggy TR20 9AU ☎ 01736 763453
🅰 enquiries@kenneggycove.co.uk
🌐 www.kenneggycove.co.uk
Dir: On A394 between Penzance & Helston, turn S into signed lane to site & Higher Kenneggy
★ 🚐 £8-£16 🚐 £8-£16 ⛺ £8-£16
Open Apr-Nov Booking advisable Jul-Aug Last arrival 21.00hrs Last departure 11.00hrs
Set in an Area of Outstanding Natural Beauty with spectacular sea views, this family-owned park is quiet and well kept. A short walk along a country footpath leads to the Cornish Coastal Path, and on
                                                              contd.

Kenneggy Cove Holiday Park
to the golden sandy beach at Kenneggy Cove.
A 4-acre site with 60 touring pitches and 9 statics.
Fresh bakery items
Leisure: ⚓ Facilities: 🔱🔨☉⚲⚹🛁⚵🛎🔲
Services: 🚽🔌🚿▦🅃 🛎→∪🅿△↘🗑
Notes: No large groups

RUTHERNBRIDGE   Map 02 SX06

▶ ▶ ▶ **76% Ruthern Valley Holidays (SX014665)**
PL30 5LU
☎ 01208 831395 📠 01208 831395
🅰 ruthern.valley@btconnect.com
🌐 www.self-catering-ruthern.co.uk
Dir: From A30 at Exeter, take A389 through Bodmin, signed St Austell. At top of hill turn right on unclass road signed Ruthernbridge. Follow signs
★ 🚐 £9-£13.50 🚐 £9-£13.50 ⛺ £9-£13.50
Open Fri before Etr or Apr-Oct Booking advisable high season & BHs Last arrival 20.30hrs Last departure noon
An attractive woodland site peacefully located in a small river valley west of Bodmin Moor. This away-from-it-all park is ideal for those wanting a quiet holiday, and the informal pitches are spread in four natural areas, with plenty of sheltered space. A 7.5-acre site with 29 touring pitches, 3 hardstandings and 18 statics.
Woodland area, children's play area
Leisure: ⚓ Facilities: 🔱☉⚹🛁⚵🛎🔲🔳
Services: 🚽🔌🚿▦🅃→∪🗑
Notes: No pets in Jul/Aug 🔲 ▦ 🔳 🔲

ST AGNES   Map 02 SW75

▶ ▶ ▶ **70% Beacon Cottage Farm Touring Park (SW705502)**
Beacon Dr TR5 0NU ☎ 01872 552347 & 553381
🅰 beaconcottagefarm@lineone.net
🌐 www.beaconcottagefarmholidays.co.uk
Dir: From A30 at Threeburrows rdbt, take B3277 to St Agnes, left into Goonvrea Rd & right into Beacon Drive
🚐 £10-£18 🚐 £10-£18 ⛺ £10-£18
Open Apr-Oct (rs Etr-Whit shop closed) Booking advisable Jul-Aug Last arrival 20.00hrs Last departure noon
A neat and compact site utilizing a cottage and outhouses, an old orchard and adjoining walled paddock. Unique location on a headland looking NE along the coast. A 5-acre site with 70 touring pitches.
Leisure: ⚓ Facilities: 🔱☉⚹🛁⚵🛎🔨
Services: 🚽🔌🚿▦🅃→∪🅿◉△↘🗑
Notes: No large groups 🔲 ▦ 🔳 🔲

▶ ▶ ▶ **70%** *Blue Hills Touring Park (SW832521)*
Cross Combe TR5 0XP ☎ 01872 552999
*Dir: Pass through St Agnes towards Perranporth, turn
left at Trevallas with brown sign to site in 1m*
🏠 🏠 ⚠
Open Etr-Oct Booking advisable Aug Last arrival
23.30hrs Last departure 16.00hrs
*Set in a beautiful rural position close to a coastal
footpath, a small site with good toilets. A pleasant
location for exploring nearby coves, beaches and
villages. A 2-acre site with 30 touring pitches.*
Facilities: 📶 ⚒ ✳ ⚫ 🐾
Services: 🔌 → ∪ ▶ 🔺 ✚ 🧺 ☕

▶ ▶ ▶ **71% Presingoll Farm Caravan & Camping
Park** (SW721494)
TR5 0PB ☎ 01872 552333 🖨 01872 552333
🅔 pam@presingollfarm.fsbusiness.co.uk
🅦 www.presingollfarm.fsbusiness.co.uk
*Dir: From A30 Chiverton rdbt (Little Chef) take B3277
towards St Agnes. Park 3m on right*
★ 🏠 fr £10 🏠 fr £10 ⚠ fr £10
Open Etr/Apr-Oct Booking advisable Jul & Aug Last
departure 10.00hrs
*An attractive rural park adjoining farmland, with
extensive views of the coast beyond. Family owned
and run, with level grass pitches, and modernised
toilet block in smart converted farm buildings.
A 5-acre site with 90 touring pitches.*
Microwave, coffee/tea making facilities
Leisure: ⚠
Facilities: 📶 ⊙ ⚒ ✳ ⚫ ⚫ 🛒 🔲 🎾 🐾
Services: 🔌 🖨 → ∪ 🌙

ST AUSTELL   **Map 02 SX05**
See also **Carlyon Bay**

▶ ▶ ▶ ▶ **78% River Valley Holiday
Park** (SX010503)
London Apprentice PL26 7AP
☎ 01726 73533 🖨 01726 73533
🅔 river.valley@tesco.net
🅦 www.cornwall-holidays.co.uk
*Dir: Direct access to park signed on B3273 from St
Austell at London Apprentice*
★ 🏠 £10-£20 🏠 £10-£20 ⚠ £10-£20

SILVER

Open end Mar-Sep Booking advisable Jul-Aug Last
arrival 22.00hrs Last departure 11.00hrs
*A neat, well-maintained family-run park set in a
pleasant river valley. The quality toilet block and
attractively landscaped grounds make this a
delightful base for a holiday. A 2-acre site with 45*
contd.

touring pitches and 40 statics.
Cycle trail to beach.
Leisure: 🎣 ⚫ ⚠ **Facilities:** 📶 ⊙ ⚒ ✳ ⚫ ⚫ 🛒 🐾
Services: 🔌 🖨 → ▶ 🔺 🔺 ✚ 🌙 ☕ 🖂 🍴

NEW ▶ ▶ ▶ **72% Old Kerrow Farm Holiday Park**
(SX020573)
Stenalees PL26 8TP ☎ 01726 851651
🖨 01726 852826
🅔 oldkerrowfarmholidaypark@hotmail.com
🅦 www.oldkerrowfarmholidaypark.co.uk
*Dir: exit A30 at Innis Downs rdbt onto A391 to Bugle.
Left at lights onto unclassified road. Site on right
approx 1m just after sign for Kerrow Moor*
★ 🏠 £10-£19 🏠 £10-£19 ⚠ £10-£19

Open all year Booking advisable At all times Last
departure 14.00hrs
*A recently opened park set on a former working
farm, with new toilet facilities. The touring area is
divided into two paddocks - one especially for dog
owners with an extensive dog walk. Cycle hire can
be arranged, and there is a cycle track to the Eden
Project 4 miles away. A 20-acre site with 50 touring
pitches, 11 hardstandings.*
Leisure: ⚠ **Facilities:** 📶 ⊙ ⚒ ✳ ⚫ ⚫ 🔲 🎾 🐾
Services: 🔌 🖨 🍴 🖊 🖨 🔲 ✕ 🧹 ✚ → ∪ ▶ 🧺 🌙
Notes: No noise as in quiet, peaceful location
💳 🖂 🖂 🔲 🖂

▶ ▶ ▶ **70% Trencreek Farm Country Holiday Park**
(SW966485)
Hewas Water PL26 7JG ☎ 01726 882540
🖨 01726 883254
🅔 reception@trencreek.co.uk
🅦 www.trencreek.co.uk
Dir: Off B3287, 1m from junct with A390
★ 🏠 £8.95-£15.50 🏠 £8.95-£15.50 ⚠ £7-£15.50
Open Etr-Oct Booking advisable Jul-Aug Last arrival
21.00hrs Last departure noon
*Set in a quiet rural area, this park is divided into
paddocks with mature hedges and trees, and with
its own coarse fishing lake. This friendly, family
park offers organised activities for children indoors
and out in the summer holidays, and at other times
caters for adult breaks. Some animals roam around
the park, and others are in pens which children can
enter. A 56-acre site with 184 touring pitches,
18 hardstandings and 37 statics.*
Fishing, fitness & agility course & mini golf.
Leisure: 🎣 🎣 ⚫ ⚠ 🔲 **Facilities:** ✚ 📶 ⊙ ✳ ⚫ ⚫ 🛒 🐾
Services: 🔌 🖨 🍴 🖊 🖨 🔲 ✕ 🧹 → ∪ ▶ 🔺 🧺 🌙
💳 🖂 🖂 🔲 🖂   See advertisement on next page

Facilities: ✚ Bath 📶 Shower ⊙ Electric Shaver ⚒ Hairdryer ✳ Ice Pack Facility ⚫ Disabled Facilities ⚫ Public Telephone
🛒 Shop on Site or within 200yds 🖂 Mobile Shop (calls at least 5 days a week) 🔲 BBQ Area 🎾 Picnic Area 🐾 Dog Exercise Area

▶ ▶ ▶ 65% **Trewhiddle Holiday Estate (SX010508)**
Pentewan Rd PL26 7AD ☎ 01726 879420
▤ 01726 879421
✉ dmcclelland@btconnect.com
ⓦ www.trewhiddle.co.uk
Dir: Take B3273 from St Austell towards Mevagissey.
Site 0.75m from rdbt on right
★ ⊞ £9-£18 ⊞ £9-£18 ▲ £9-£18
Open all year Booking advisable Jul & Aug
Secluded wooded site with well-kept gardens,
lawns and flower beds, set in the grounds of a
mature estate. The Trewhiddle Pub is right in the
centre of the park. A 16.5-acre site with 105 touring
pitches and 74 statics.
Beauty salon & fast tan sunbed

Leisure: ⚲ ♣ ⚠ Facilities: ↝ ♠ ☉ ⚛ ✳ ☾ ⛲ ♞
Services: ☱ ♀ ▤ ⊘ ✗ ⚏ → ∪ ▶ ☎ ♫ ⚑
⬤ ▭ ◉ ▩ ⚑

NEW ▶ ▶ 72% **Court Farm Holidays (SW953524)**
St Stephen PL26 7LE ☎ 01726 823684
▤ 01726 823684
✉ truscott@ctfarm.freeserve.co.uk
ⓦ www.courtfarmcornwall.co.uk
Dir: from St Austell take A3058 towards Newquay.
Through St Stephen (pass Peugeot garage). Turn right
at sign 'St Stephen/Coombe Hay/Langreth/Industrial
site'. 400yds, site on right
★ ⊞ £10-£12.50 ⊞ £12.50-£15 ▲ £7.50-£15
Open Apr-Sep Booking advisable Jul-mid Sep Last
departure 11.00hrs

contd.

Set in a peaceful rural location, this large camping
field offers plenty of space, and is handy for the
Eden Project and the Lost Gardens of Heligan.
Coarse fishing and use of a large telescope are
among the attractions. A 4-acre site with 20 touring
pitches, 5 hardstandings.
Astronomical lectures, fishing

Leisure: ⚠
Facilities: ♠ ☉ ✳ ☾ ♞
Services: ☱ ▤ ⚏ → ∪ ☎ ▤ ♫
Notes: No noisy behaviour after dark
⬤ ▭ ▭ ▩ ⚑

ST BLAZEY GATE	Map 02 SX05

▶ ▶ ▶ 81% **Doubletrees Farm (SX060540)**
Luxulyan Rd PL24 2EH ☎ 01726 812266
✉ doubletrees@eids.co.uk
ⓦ www.eids.co.uk/doubletrees
Dir: On A390 at Blazey Gate. Turn by Leek Seed Chapel,
almost opposite BP filling station. After approx 300yds
turn R by public bench into site.
⊞ £11-£12 ⊞ £11-£12 ▲ fr £10
Open all year Booking advisable Last arrival
22.30hrs Last departure 11.30hrs
A popular park with terraced pitches offering
superb sea and coastal views. Close to beaches,
and the nearest park to the Eden Project, it is very
well maintained by friendly owners. A 1.75-acre site
with 32 touring pitches, 6 hardstandings.

Facilities: ♠ ☉ ✳ ⚷ ⚏ ☾ ♞
Services: ☱ ▤ → ∪ ▶ ◉ ▤

Services: ⊤ Toilet Fluid　✗ Café/ Restaurant　⚏ Fast Food/Takeaway　⚏ Baby Care　⚏ Electric Hook Up
⚏ Motorvan Service Point　⚏ Launderette　♀ Licensed Bar　⚏ Calor Gas　⚏ Camping Gaz　⚏ Battery Charging

England

ST BURYAN   Map 02 SW42

▶ ▶ ▶ 70% **Camping & Caravanning Club Site** (SW378276)
Higher Tregiffian Farm TR19 6JB ☎ 01736 871588
Ⓦ www.campingandcaravanningclub.co.uk
Dir: A30 towards Land's End. Right onto A3306 St Just/Pendeen Rd. Site 50yds on left
★ 🏕 £12.40-£16.70 🚐 £12.40-£16.70 ▲ £12.40-£16.70
Open Apr-Oct Booking advisable bank hols & peak periods Last arrival 21.00hrs Last departure noon
Set in a rural area with distant views of Carn Brae and the coast just 2m from Land's End, this very good club site is well run with modern, clean facilities. It offers a children's playfield, late arrivals area and a dog-exercising paddock. Please see the advertisement on page 11 for information on Club sites and membership. A 4-acre site with 75 touring pitches, 6 hardstandings.
Leisure: 🅰 **Facilities:** 🏳️⊙🥤✳⚘&🔧🛁🏕
Services: 🔌 ⛽🛢️🖊️⭕🔛→▶🔥🛒🐕
🎫 🚰 📧 🔲 🌀

▶ ▶ ▶ 74% **Lower Treave Caravan & Camping Park** (SW388272)
Crows-an-Wra TR19 6HZ ☎ 01736 810559
📠 0870 0553647
🅔 camping@lowertreave.demon.co.uk
Ⓦ www.lowertreave.demon.co.uk
Dir: Just off A30 midway between Penzance & Land's End, after village of Crows-an-Wra. Site signed on left
★ 🏕 £8-£10 🚐 £8-£10 ▲ £8-£10
Open Apr-Oct Booking advisable Jul-Aug Last arrival 22.30hrs Last departure 11.00hrs
A terraced grass site sheltered by mature trees and bushes, but still enjoying extensive rural views. The popular blue-flag beaches at Whitesand Bay and Sennen Cove are just 2.5m away, and ideal for families and surfers. A 5-acre site with 80 touring pitches and 5 statics.
Facilities: 🏳️⊙🥤✳🛁
Services: 🔌🛢️🖊️⭕🔛→⭕▶🔥🛒🎫🚰📧📺🔲🌀

▶ ▶ ▶ 70% *Treverven Touring Caravan & Camping Park* (SW410237)
Treverven Farm TR19 6DL
☎ 01736 810200 & 810318 📠 01736 871977
Ⓦ www.chycor.co.uk/camping/treverven
Dir: Leave A30 onto B3283 1.5m after St Buryan, left onto B3315. Site on right in 1m
🏕🚐▲

contd.

Open Etr-Oct Booking advisable Jul-Aug Last departure noon
Situated in a quiet Area of Outstanding Natural Beauty with panoramic views, this family-owned site is off a traffic-free lane leading directly to the coastal path. Ideal for touring West Cornwall. Toilet facilities are very good. A 6-acre site with 115 touring pitches.
Leisure: 🅰 **Facilities:** 🏳️⊙🥤✳&🔧🛁🏕🐕
Services: 🔌⛽🛢️🖊️🔛🛒🛍️→⭕▶🔥🛒🚰🔲🌀

ST COLUMB MAJOR   Map 02 SW96

▶ ▶ ▶ 77% **Southleigh Manor Tourist Park** (SW918623)
TR9 6HY ☎ 01637 880938 📠 01637 881108
🅔 enquiries@southleigh-manor.com
Dir: Leave A30 at sign to RAF St Mawgan onto A3059. Park 3m on left
★ 🏕 £18-£21.50 🚐 £18-£21.50 ▲ £18-£21.50
Open Etr-Oct Shop open peak times only Booking advisable Jun-Aug Last arrival 20.00hrs Last departure 11.00hrs
A very well maintained naturist park in the heart of the Cornish countryside, catering for families and couples only. Seclusion and security are very well planned, and the lovely gardens provide a calm setting. A 2.5-acre site with 50 touring pitches. Sauna, spa bath, pool table, putting green
Leisure: ⚡🅰 **Facilities:** 🏳️⊙🥤✳🔥🛁🎋
Services: 🔌🛢️🖊️🔛🍺✖→⭕▶🔥

ST DAY   Map 02 SW74

▶ ▶ ▶ 62% **St Day Holiday Park** (SW733422)
Church Hill TR16 5LE ☎ 01209 820459
🅔 holiday@stday.co.uk
Ⓦ www.stday.co.uk
Dir: From A30 at Scorrier onto B3298 towards Falmouth. Site signed on right in 2m.
★ 🏕 £10-£12 🚐 £10-£12 ▲ £5-£12
Open Etr & Apr-Oct Booking advisable Jul-Aug
A tidy grass park, with friendly owners who keep it well maintained. Situated in a quiet spot in a rural area between Falmouth & Newquay, and within close walking distance of the attractive village of St Day. A 4-acre site with 35 touring pitches, 11 hardstandings and 23 statics.
Facilities: 🏳️⊙✳&🔧🛁
Services: 🔌🛢️🔛→⭕▶🍺🔥🛁

ST GENNYS   Map 02 SX19

▶ ▶ ▶ 70% **Camping & Caravanning Club Site** (SX176943)
Gillards Moor EX23 0BG ☎ 01840 230650
Ⓦ www.campingandcaravanningclub.co.uk
Dir: From N on A39 site on right in lay-by, 9m from Bude. From S on A39 site on left in lay-by 9m from Camelford. Approx 3m from B3262 junct.
★ 🏕 £13.60-£17.80 🚐 £13.60-£17.80 ▲ £13.60-£17.80
Open Apr-Oct Booking advisable bank hols & peak periods Last arrival 21.00hrs Last departure noon
A well-kept, level grass site with good quality facilities. Located midway between Bude and Camelford in an area full of sandy coves and

contd.

---

beaches with good surfing. Please see the advertisement on page 11 for information on Club sites and membership. A 6-acre site with 100 touring pitches, 9 hardstandings.

Leisure: /🄰 Facilities: 🏕⊙🥤⚹🔥🛁
Services: 🔋🗑🖊🛢🚽🖃→🚻 🚐 🍴📶▦ ▦ 🔌

ST GILES-ON-THE-HEATH
See Chapmans Well (Devon)

ST HILARY   Map 02 SW53
▶ ▶ ▶ ▶ 78% Wayfarers Caravan & Camping Park (SW558314)
Relubbus Ln TR20 9EF ☎ 01736 763326
🄴 wayfarers@eurobell.co.uk
🅦 www.wayfarerspark.co.uk
Dir: Turn left off A30 onto A394 towards Helston. Turn left at rdbt onto B3280 after 2m. Site 1.5m on left of main road
★ 🚐 £10-£16 🚐 £10-£16 🅐 £9-£13
Open 5 Mar-Nov Booking advisable Jun-Sep Last arrival 20.00hrs Last departure 11.00hrs
A quiet sheltered park in a peaceful rural setting within 2.5m of St Michael's Mount. It offers spacious, well-drained pitches and very well cared for facilities. A 4.75-acre site with 45 touring pitches, 23 hardstandings and 4 statics.
Tourist info room
Facilities: 🏕⊙🥤⚹🔥🛁🚿▦🔥
Services: 🔋🗑🖊🛢🖃→🚻🍴⊙🔥⚹🛢
Notes: Adults only

NEW ▶ ▶ ▶ 66% Trevair Touring Park (SW548326)
South Treveneague TR20 9BY ☎ 01736 740647
Dir: A30 onto A394 signed Helston. 2m to rdbt, left onto B3280. Through Goldsithney. Left at brown site sign. Through 20mph zone to site 1m on right
🚐 🅐
Open Etr-Nov
Set in a rural location adjacent to woodland, this park is level and secluded, with grassy pitches. Marazion's beaches and the famous St Michael's Mount are just three miles away. The friendly owners live at the farmhouse on the park. A 3.5-acre site with 40 touring pitches.

ST ISSEY   Map 02 SW97
▶ ▶ ▶ 78% Trewince Farm Holiday Park (SW937715)
PL27 7RL ☎ 01208 812830 🖷 01208 812835
Dir: From Wadebridge on A39 take A389 signed Padstow. Site 2m on left
🚐 🚐 🅐
Open Etr-Oct Booking advisable anytime Last departure 11.00hrs
Set amongst rolling farmland close to the coast, this park is part of a working farm, and set in well landscaped grounds. It offers good facilities in a comfortable and friendly atmosphere, and is only three miles from Padstow. A 6-acre site with 120 touring pitches and 35 statics.

contd.

Crazy golf, farm rides in summer, near Camel Trail
Leisure: ⚹🥤🔥/🄰 Facilities: 🏕🏕⊙🥤⚹🔥🛁🛁▦🔥🔥
Services: 🔋🗑🖊🛢🖃→🚻🍴⚹🛢🚽
🚐 🍴📶▦ ▦ 🔌

See advertisement under WADEBRIDGE

ST IVES   Map 02 SW54
PREMIER PARK
▶ ▶ ▶ ▶ ▶ 83% Polmanter Tourist Park (SW510388)
Halsetown TR26 3LX ☎ 01736 795640
🖷 01736 793607
🄴 reception@polmanter.com
🅦 www.polmanter.com
Dir: Signed off B3311 at Halsetown
★ 🚐 £12.50-£24 🚐 £12.50-£24 🅐 £10-£19
Open Whit-10 Sep (rs Mar-Whit & 12 Sep-Oct shop, pool, bar & takeaway food closed)
Booking advisable Jul-Aug Last arrival 21.00hrs Last departure 10.00hrs
A well-developed touring park on high ground, Polmanter offers high quality in all areas, from the immaculate modern toilet blocks to the outdoor swimming pool and hard tennis courts. Pitches are individually marked and sited in meadows, and the park has been tastefully landscaped. The fishing port and beaches of St Ives are just 1.5m away, and there is a bus service in high season. A 20-acre site with 240 touring pitches, 10 hardstandings. Putting, sports field, 7 family shower rooms.
Leisure: ⚹🥤🔥/🄰 Facilities: 🏕⊙🥤⚹🔥🛁🚿🔥
Services: 🔋🚿🔋⊙🛢🖊🖃🚽✕ 🍴🚽→🚻🍴⊙🔥⚹🛢
🚽🚐 🍴📶▦ ▦ 🔌

▶ ▶ ▶ ▶ 85% Ayr Holiday Park (SW509408)
TR26 1EJ ☎ 01736 795855
🖷 01736 798797
🄴 recept@ayrholidaypark.co.uk
🅦 www.ayrholidaypark.co.uk
Dir: From A30 follow St Ives 'large vehicles' route via B3311 through Halsetown onto B3306. Park signed towards St Ives town centre
🚐 🚐 🅐

Open all year Booking advisable Jun-Aug Last arrival 22.00hrs Last departure 10.00hrs
A well-established park on a cliffside overlooking St Ives Bay, with a heated toilet block making winter holidaying more attractive. There are stunning views from most pitches, and the town centre, harbour and

contd.

beach are only 0.5m away, with direct access to the coastal footpath. A 4-acre site with 40 touring pitches, 20 hardstandings and 50 statics.

Leisure: ◣ ⚲

Facilities: ⊷ ⋔ ⊙ 🏐 ✳ & ↳ ⊟ ⚑ ♉

Services: ▣ 🖤 🗑 🛢 ⌀ ⊞ ⊤ → ∪ ⌐ △ ⋎ 🛎 🥢

💳 ▤▥ 📇 ▧ 🔕

▶ ▶ ▶ 81% Little Trevarrack Tourist Park (SW525379)
Laity Ln, Carbis Bay TR26 3HW ☎ 01736 797580
✉ littletrevarrack@hotmail.com
ⓦ www.littletrevarrack.com
Dir: From A30 take A3074 signed 'Carbis Bay & St Ives', turn left opposite turning to beach. 150yds, over x-rds, site 2nd on right
★ 🚐 £9-£16 🚐 £9-£16 ▲ £9-£16
Open Etr-Oct (rs mid Sep-Oct Games room closed)
Booking advisable summer hols Last arrival 21.30hrs Last departure 10.00hrs
A pleasant grass park set in countryside but close to beaches and local amenities. Plenty of tree planting will result in more shelter and privacy in this landscaped park, and there are superb sea views. A private bus service runs to St Ives in high season. A 20-acre site with 234 touring pitches.
Sports area

Leisure: ◣ ⚲ **Facilities:** ⋔ ⊙ ✳ & ↳ ♉
Services: ▣ 🗑 🛢 ⌀ ⊤ → ∪ ⌐ ⊙ △ ⋎ 🛎 🥢

💳 ▤▥ 🔕

▶ ▶ ▶ 76% Penderleath Caravan & Camping Park (SW496375)
Towednack TR26 3AF ☎ 01736 798403   GOLD
✉ holidays@penderleath.co.uk
ⓦ www.penderleath.co.uk
Dir: From A30 take A3074 towards St Ives. At 2nd mini-rdbt turn left, approx 3m to T-junct. Left then immediately right, turn left at next fork
★ 🚐 £10.50-£15 🚐 £10.50-£15 ▲ £10.50-£15

Open Etr-Oct Booking advisable Jul-Aug Last arrival 21.30hrs Last departure 10.30hrs
Set in a rugged rural location, this tranquil park has extensive views towards St Ives Bay and the north coast. Facilities are all housed in modernised granite barns, and include a quiet licensed bar with beer garden, breakfast room and bar meals. The owners are welcoming and helpful. A 10-acre site with 75 touring pitches.
Leisure: ◣ ⚲ **Facilities:** ⋔ ⊙ 🏐 ✳ & ↳ 🛒
Services: ▣ 🗑 🖤 🛢 ⌀ ⊞ ⊤ ✕ ⬛ → ∪ ⌐ ⊙ △ ⋎ 🛎 🥢
Notes: Dogs must be well behaved & kept on a lead

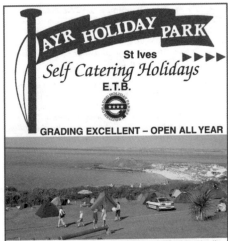

▶ ▶ ▶ 78% Trevalgan Touring Park (SW490402)   SILVER
Trevalgan TR26 3BJ
☎ 01736 796433 🖷 01736 798797
✉ recept@trevalgantouringpark.co.uk
ⓦ www.trevalgantouringpark.co.uk
Dir: From A30 follow holiday route to St Ives. B3311 through Halsetown to B3306. Left towards Land's End. Site signed 0.5m on right
★ 🚐 £10.50-£17.50 🚐 £10.50-£17.50
▲ £10.50-£17.50
Open Jun-Aug (rs Apr-May & Sep shop & takeaway closed) Booking advisable mid Jul-Aug Last arrival 22.00hrs Last departure 10.00hrs
An open park next to a working farm in a rural area on the coastal road from St Ives to Zennor. The park is surrounded by mature hedges, but there are extensive views out over the sea. There are very good toilet facilities including family rooms, and a large TV lounge and recreation room with drinks machine. A 4.75-acre site with 120 touring pitches.
Farm trail, crazy golf
Leisure: ◣ ⚲ 🎱
Facilities: ⋔ ⊙ 🏐 ✳ & ↳ ⊟ ♉
Services: ▣ 🖤 🗑 🛢 ⌀ ⊞ ⊤ ✕ ⬛ → ∪ ⌐ △ ⋎ 🛎 🥢
💳 ▤▥ 📇 ▧ 🔕

England

▶ ▶ 85% **Balnoon Camping Site** (SW509382)
Halsetown TR26 3JA ☎ 01736 795431
📧 nat@balnoon.fsnet.co.uk
*Dir: From A30 take A3074, at 2nd mini-rdbt take 1st left
signed St Ives. After 3m turn right after Balnoon Inn*
★ 🚐 £7-£12 🚐 £7-£12 ▲ £7-£12
Open Etr-Oct Booking advisable Jul-Aug
*Small, quiet and friendly, this sheltered site offers
superb views of the adjacent rolling hills. The three
paddocks are surrounded by mature hedges, and
the toilet facilities are kept spotlessly clean. The
beaches of Carbis Bay and St Ives are about 2 miles
away. A 1-acre site with 23 touring pitches.*
Facilities: ↑ ⊙ ❑ ✻ 🌡
Services: 🚐 🅿 🛢 ⊞ → ∪ ▶ ⊙ ✦ 🐾 🗑 🗄

ST JUST (NEAR LAND'S END)	Map 02 SW33

▶ ▶ ▶ 71% **Kelynack Caravan & Camping Park**
(SW374301)
Kelynack TR19 7RE ☎ 01736 787633
🖨 01736 787633
📧 kelynackholidays@tiscali.co.uk
Dir: 1m S of St Just, 5m N of Land's End on B3306
★ 🚐 £8-£10 🚐 £8-£10 ▲ £8-£10

Open Apr-Oct Booking advisable Jul-Aug Last
arrival 22.00hrs Last departure 10.00hrs
*A small secluded park nestling alongside a stream
in an unspoilt rural location. The level grass pitches
are in two areas, and the park is close to many
coves, beaches, and ancient villages. A 3-acre site
with 20 touring pitches, 4 hardstandings and 13
statics.*
Dining & cooking shelter
Leisure: ✦ ⚠ **Facilities:** ↑ ⊙ ❑ ✻ ⅃ ⚓ 🌡 🛁 🖐 🎣 🐎
Services: 🚐 ⚱ 🛢 ⊞ 🅣 → ∪ ▶ ⚓ 🗑 🗄

▶ ▶ ▶ 75% **Roselands Caravan Park** (SW387305)
Dowran TR19 7RS ☎ 01736 788571
📧 camping@roseland84.freeserve.co.uk
🌐 www.roselands.co.uk
*Dir: From A30 Penzance bypass turn right for St Just on
A3071. 5m, turn left after Tin Mine Chimney at sign,
follow signs to park*
★ 🚐 £9-£11.50 🚐 £9-£11.50 ▲ £7-£9
Open Etr-Oct Booking advisable Jun-Sep Last
arrival 21.00hrs Last departure 11.00hrs
*A small, friendly park in a sheltered rural setting,
an ideal location for a quiet family holiday. The
owners are continuing to upgrade the park, and in
addition to the attractive little bar there is an indoor*

Roselands Caravan Park

*games room, children's playground, and good toilet
facilities. A 3-acre site with 15 touring pitches and
15 statics.*
Cycle hire
Leisure: ✦ ⚠ **Facilities:** ↑ ⊙ ❑ ✻ ⅃ ⚓ 🌡 🛁 🖐 🎣 🐎
Services: 🚐 🅱 ⚱ 🛢 ⊞ 🅣 ✗ 🖐 → ∪ ▶ 🗑
Notes: No cars by caravans

▶ ▶ ▶ 75% **Secret Garden Caravan & Camping
Park** (SW370305)
Bosavern House TR19 7RD ☎ 01736 788301
🖨 01736 788301
📧 mail@bosavern.com
🌐 www.secretbosavern.com
*Dir: Turn off A3071 near St Just onto B3306 Land's End
road. Park 0.5m on left*
🚐 £11-£14.50 🚐 £11-£14.50 ▲ £11-£14.50
Open Mar-Oct Booking advisable Jul-Aug Last
arrival 22.00hrs Last departure noon
*A neat little site in a walled garden behind a guest
house, where visitors can enjoy breakfast, and
snacks in the bar in the evening. This site is in a
fairly sheltered location with all grassy pitches.
There is no children's playground. A 1.5-acre site
with 12 touring pitches.*
Leisure: ❑ **Facilities:** ↑ ⊙ ✻ ⚓ 🛁
Services: 🚐 ⚱ ⊞ 🖐 → ∪ ▶ ⚓ 🗑 🗄 🌡
Notes: ✗ 🍴 🚬 💳 🎋 🎐

▶ ▶ ▶ 70% **Trevaylor Caravan & Camping Park**
(SW368222)
Botallack TR19 7PU ☎ 01736 787016
📧 bookings@trevaylor.com
🌐 www.trevaylor.com
*Dir: On B3306 (St Just -St Ives road), site on right 0.75m
from St Just*
★ 🚐 £7-£11 🚐 £7-£11 ▲ £7-£11
Open Fri before Etr-Oct Booking advisable Jul &
Aug Last departure noon
*A sheltered grassy site located off the beaten track
in a peaceful location at the western tip of Cornwall.
The dramatic coastline and the pretty villages
nearby are truly unspoilt. Clean, well-maintained
facilities and a good shop are offered along with a
bar serving tasty bar meals. A 6-acre site with 50
touring pitches.*
Leisure: ✦ ⚠ **Facilities:** ↑ ⊙ ❑ ✻ 🌡 ⚓ 🛁 ⅃
Services: 🚐 🅱 ⚱ 🛢 ⊞ 🅣 ✗ 🖐 → ▶ ⊙ 🗑

contd.

ST JUST-IN-ROSELAND   Map 02 SW83

▶ ▶ ▶ 85% **Trethem Mill Touring Park**
(SW860365)
TR2 5JF ☎ 01872 580504 🖷 01872 580968
❸ reception@trethem.com
Ⓦ www.trethem.com
*Dir: From Tregony on A3078 to St Mawes. 2m after
Trewithian, follow signs to park*
★ 🏕 £11-£15 🚐 £11-£15 ⚑ £11-£15

Open Apr-Oct Booking advisable Jul-Aug Last
arrival 21.00hrs Last departure 11.00hrs
*A quality park in all areas, with upgraded amenities
including a reception, shop, laundry, and
disabled/family room. This carefully-tended and
sheltered park is in a lovely rural setting, with
spacious pitches separated by young trees and
shrubs. The very keen family who own it are
continually looking for ways to enhance its facilities.
An 11-acre site with 84 touring pitches,
15 hardstandings.*
Info centre

Leisure: 🎢 Facilities: 🏧⊙🍴✳&ꞇ🐾🖐
Services: 🖪🎛🗑🗋🎚🛈🍴➡🔧⊹♨🔌
🖿 🖿 🖿 🖿 🖿

ST MABYN   Map 02 SX07

▶ ▶ ▶ 79% **Glenmorris Park**
(SX055733)
Longstone Rd PL30 3BY
☎ 01208 841677 🖷 01208 841677
❸ info@glenmorris.co.uk
Ⓦ www.glenmorris.co.uk
*Dir: S of Camelford on A39, left after BP garage to
B3266 to Bodmin, 6m to Longstone, right at x-rds to St
Mabyn, site approx 400mtrs on right.*
★ 🏕 £7.50-£9.90 🚐 £7.50-£9.90 ⚑ £7.50-£9.90

Open Etr-Oct (rs Etr-mid May & mid Sep-Nov
Swimming pool closed) Booking advisable Jul-Aug,
all year for statics Last arrival 23.30hrs Last
departure 10.30hrs
*A very good, mainly level park in a peaceful rural
location offering clean and well-maintained facilities
- a small games room, heated outdoor swimming
pool and sunbathing area, and shop. An ideal
location for visiting this unspoilt area. An 11-acre
site with 80 touring pitches and 8 statics.*

Leisure: ⌁♠🎢 Facilities: 🏧⊙🍴✳&ꞇ🐾🎏
Services: 🖪🎛🗑🗋🎚➡∪▶🔧
Notes: Quiet after 10pm 🖿 🖿 🖿 🖿 🖿

ST MARY'S   Map 02 SV91
See Scilly, Isles

ST MERRYN (NEAR PADSTOW)   Map 02 SW87

76% *Harlyn Sands Holiday Park*
(SW873752)
Lighthouse Rd,
Trevose Head PL28 8SQ
☎ 01841 520720
*Dir: Leave B3276 in centre of St Merryn on
unclassified road towards Harlyn Sands & Trevose
Head. Follow brown park signs for approx 1m.
(NB Do not turn right to Harlyn Sands)*
🚐🚐 ⚑ Open Etr-Nov
*A family park for 'bucket and spade' holidays,
surrounded by seven bays each with its own
sandy beach. On site entertainment for children
and adults is extensive, and there is an indoor
swimming pool complex, excellent restaurant
and take-away, plus a quiet over-30s lounge bar.
A 21-acre site with 160 touring pitches,
6 hardstandings and 350 statics.*
Arcade, clubhouse

Leisure: ⌁🎢 Facilities: 🏧ꞇ Services: 🖪🗋🍴✕

Leisure: ⌁ Indoor swimming pool ⌁ Outdoor swimming pool 🎾 Tennis court ♠ Games room 🎢 Children's playground ∪ Stables
▶ 9/18 hole golf course 🛶 Boats for hire 🎦 Cinema 🎣 Fishing ⊙ Mini golf 🛆 Watersports 🖵 Separate TV room

▶ ▶ ▶ 88% **Carnevas Holiday Park & Farm Cottages (SW862728)**
Carnevas Farm PL28 8PN
☎ 01841 520230 & 521209 ▤ 01841 520230
✆ carnevascampsite@aol.com
Ⓦ www.carnevasholidaypark.co.uk
Dir: From St Merryn on B3276 towards Porthcothan Bay, approx 2m turn right at site sign onto unclass road opposite Tredrea Inn. Site 0.25m on right
★ ⊞ £7.50-£15 ⊞ £7.50-£15 ▲ £7.50-£15

Open Apr-Oct (rs Apr-Whit & mid Sep-Oct shop, bar & restaurant closed) Booking advisable Jul-Aug
A family-run park on a working farm, divided into four paddocks on slightly sloping grass. The toilets are central to all areas, and there is a small licensed bar serving bar meals. An 8-acre site with 195 touring pitches and 14 statics. 2 family bathrooms.

Leisure: ◕ ⚲
Facilities: 🛈 ⊙ ⚑ ✳ ⅃ ⚲ 🐾 ⊪
Services: ⊡ ⊟ ⚲ ⊘ ⊞ ⊤ ✕ → ∪ ▶ ▲ ┛

▶ ▶ ▶ 69% *Point Curlew Chalet & Touring Park (SW890717)*
St Merryn PL28 8PY ☎ 01841 520855
▤ 01841 521413
✆ pointcurlew@lineone.net
Ⓦ www.pointcurlew.co.uk
Dir: Take B3274 towards Padstow. In 3m turn left onto unclass road to St Merryn, follow brown signs to park
⊞ ⊞ ▲

Open Etr-Oct Booking advisable end Jun-early Sep Last arrival mdnt Last departure noon
This touring area, part of a larger chalet park set in a quiet rural spot yet only 2 miles from seven popular bays. Free entertainment is available in high season and there are children's fun nights, and a quiet bar. A 4.5-acre site with

contd.

70 touring pitches and 220 statics.
Leisure: ◕ ⚲ ⊡   Facilities: 🛈 ⊙ ⚑ ✳ ⅃ ⚲ 🐾 ⊞ 🝙
Services: ⊡ ⊟ ⚲ ✕ → ∪ ▶ ⊙ ▲ ⋄ 🌡 ┛
Notes: No pets ⊜⊜ ⊟ ⊟ ⊡ ⊟ 🝙 🄳

▶ ▶ 70% **Tregavone Touring Park (SW898732)**
Tregavone Farm PL28 8JZ ☎ 01841 520148
Dir: From A389 towards Padstow, turn right after Little Petherick, in 1m just beyond Padstow Holiday Park turn left into unclass road signed St Merryn. Site on left in approx 1m
★ ⊞ £6.50-£8 ⊞ £6.50-£8 ▲ £6.50-£8
Open Mar-Oct Booking advisable end Jul-beg Aug
This rather open grassy park on a working farm has good facilities in well-converted farm buildings. Run by friendly owners, and handy for the beaches and surfing areas on the North Cornish coast. A 3-acre site with 40 touring pitches.
Facilities: 🛈 ⊙ ✳ ⊪
Services: ⊡ ⊟ ⊟ → ∪ ▶ ⊙ ▲ ⋄ 🌡 ┛ ⊠

▶ ▶ 76% **Trevean Caravan & Camping Park (SW875724)**
Trevean Ln PL28 8PR ☎ 01841 520772
▤ 01841 520772
Dir: From St Merryn take B3276 to Newquay for 1m. Turn left for Rumford. Site 0.25m on right
⊞ £8-£10 ⊞ £8-£10 ▲ £8-£10

Open Apr-Oct Shop open Whit-Sep Booking advisable mid Jul-Aug Last arrival 22.00hrs Last departure 11.00hrs
A small working farm site with level grassy pitches in open countryside. The toilet facilities are clean and well kept, and there is a laundry and good children's playground. A 1.5-acre site with 36 touring pitches.
Leisure: ⚲   Facilities: 🛈 ⊙ ✳ ⚲ 🐾 ⊞ ⊪
Services: ⊡ ⊟ ⚲ ⊟ → ∪ ▶ ⊙ ⋄ 🌡 ┛
Notes: No teenage groups

ST MINVER	Map 02 SW97

68% **St Minver Holiday Park (SW965772)**
PL27 6RR ☎ 01208 862305 & 0870 420 2991 ▤ 01208 862265
✆ enquiries@parkdeanholidays.co.uk
Ⓦ www.parkdeanholidays.co.uk
Dir: From A39 N of Wadebridge take B3314 Port Isaac road. Site signed on left in 3m
★ ⊞ £7-£27 ⊞ £9-£27 ▲ £7-£24
Open Mar-Oct Booking advisable at all times

contd.

Last arrival 21.00hrs Last departure 10.00hrs
A large holiday park set around St Minver House in sylvan surroundings. The park offers a wide range of holiday activities, including crazy golf, table tennis, and large indoor fun pool and waterslide. A programme of family entertainment is offered during evenings in the high season. A 44-acre site with 33 touring pitches and 328 statics.
Crazy golf, live family entertainment, amusements.
Leisure: ♥ ♣ ⚲ **Facilities:** ↿⊙ ❑ ✳ ⬭ ⤸ ➤
Services: ⊞ ⬚ ♈ ⬥ ∅ ⊟ ⊤ ✗ ⬥ → ▶ ⬥ ♨
⬤ ▦ ⬚ ⬡

► ► ► ► **72% Gunvenna Caravan Park (SW969782)**
PL27 6QN ☎ 01208 862405
▤ 01208 869107
Dir: From A39 N of Wadebridge take B3314 (Port Isaac road), park 4m on right
★ ⬤ £7-£17 ⬤ £7-£17 ⚠ £7-£17

Open Etr-Oct Booking advisable Jul-Aug Last arrival 21.00hrs Last departure 11.00hrs
Attractive park with extensive rural views in a quiet country location, yet within three miles of Polzeath. This popular park is family owned and run, and provides good facilities in an ideal position for touring north Cornwall. A 10-acre site with 75 touring pitches, 5 hardstandings and 44 statics.
Leisure: ♥ ♣ ⚲ **Facilities:** ⬤↿⊙❑✳⬭⤸⊞⬡⛱➤
Services: ⊞ ⬚ ⬚ ♈ ⬥ ∅ ⊤ → ∪ ▶ ⬥ ✛ ♨ ⬥

SCILLY, ISLES

BRYHER   **Map 02 SV81**

► ► ► ► **76% Bryher Camp Site (SV880155)**
TR23 0PR ☎ 01720 422886 ▤ 01720 423092
⚠
Open Apr-Oct Booking advisable summer months
Set on the smallest Scilly Isle with spectacular scenery and white beaches, this tent-only site is in a sheltered valley surrounded by hedges. Pitches are located in paddocks at the northern end of the island, and easily reached from the quay. There is a good modern toilet block, and plenty of peace and quiet. A 2.25-acre site with 38 touring pitches.
Facilities: ↿⊙❑✳⬭
Services: ♈∅⊟→∪▶⊙⬥✛♨⬚
Notes: No pets ⬤ ▦ ⬚ ⬡

ST MARY'S   **Map 02 SV91**

► ► ► **74% Garrison Campsite (SV897104)**
Tower Cottage, The Garrison TR21 0LS
☎ 01720 422670 ▤ 01720 422670
✉ tedmoulson@aol.com
⊕ www.garrisonholidays.com
Dir: 10 mins walk from the quay to site
★ ⚠ £12-£15.90
Open Etr-Oct Booking advisable Jul & Aug Last arrival 20.00hrs Last departure 19.00hrs
Set on the top of an old fort with superb views, this park offers tent-only pitches in a choice of well-sheltered paddocks. There are modern toilet facilities and a good shop at this attractive site, which is only 10 mins from the town, the quay and the nearest beaches. A 9.5-acre site with 120 touring pitches.
Facilities: ↿⊙❑✳⬭⤸
Services: ⬚♈∅⊟→∪▶⬥✛♨
Notes: No pets, no open fires, no cars on site

SENNEN   **Map 02 SW32**

► ► ► *72% Trevedra Farm Caravan & Camping Site (SW368276)*
TR19 7BE ☎ 01736 871818 & 871835
▤ 01736 871835
✉ nicholastrevedra@farming.co.uk
⊕ www.sennen-cove.com/trevedra.htm
Dir: Take A30 towards Land's End. After junct with B3306 turn right into farm lane
⬤ ⬤ ⚠
Open Etr or Apr-Oct Booking advisable peak seasons Last arrival mdnt Last departure noon
A working farm with dramatic sea views over to the Scilly Isles, just a mile from Land's end. The popular campsite offers refurbished toilets, a well-stocked shop, and a cooked breakfast or evening meal from the food bar. There is direct access to the coastal footpath, and two beautiful beaches are a short walk away. An 8-acre site with 100 touring pitches.
Facilities: ↿⊙❑✳⬭⤸⊞⬭➤
Services: ⊞⬚♈∅⊟⊤⬥⬥→∪▶⬥♨⬥
Notes: Dogs must be kept on a lead at all times

TINTAGEL   **Map 02 SX08**
See also **Camelford**

► ► ► **70% Headland Caravan & Camping Park (SX056887)**
Atlantic Rd PL34 0DE ☎ 01840 770239
▤ 01840 770925
✉ headland.caravan@btconnect.com
⊕ www.headlandcaravanpark.co.uk
Dir: From B3263 follow brown tourist signs through village to Headland
★ ⬤ £11-£13 ⬤ £10-£12 ⚠ £10-£13
Open Etr-Oct Booking advisable Jul-Aug Last arrival 21.00hrs
A peaceful family-run site in the mystical village of Tintagel, close to the ruins of King Arthur's Castle. The Cornish coastal path and the spectacular scenery are just two of the attractions here, and

contd.

England

The Headland

Telephone: 01840 770239

CARAVAN & CAMPING PARK
TINTAGEL CORNWALL

Headland Caravan & Camping Park
there are safe bathing beaches nearby. A 5-acre site
with 62 touring pitches and 28 statics.

Leisure: ⚴ **Facilities:** ⛌⊙⛆⚹⚿⛬⛩⛫

Services: ⚡⚐⛴⛹⚽⚇⊞⛁→∪◭⚹⛏

Notes: Dogs must be kept on short leads &
exercised off park, quiet after 11pm

⛔ ⚏ ⚎ ⚌ 🏴

TORPOINT   Map 03 SX45

68% **Whitsand Bay Holiday Park**
(SX410515)
Millbrook PL10 1JZ ☎ 01752 822597
🗎 01752 823444
✉ enquiries@whitsandbayholidays.co.uk
Ⓦ www.whitsandbayholidays.co.uk
*Dir: From Torpoint take A374, turn left at Anthony
onto B3247 for 1.25m to T-junct. Turn left, 0.25m
then right onto Cliff Rd. Site 2m on left*
⛱⛺⚹
Open all year Booking advisable Jul-Sep Last
arrival midnight Last departure 10.00hrs
*A very well equipped park with panoramic views
from its terraced pitches, and plenty of on-site
entertainment including discos and children's
club in high season in the lively clubhouse.
A 27-acre site with 100 touring pitches,
50 hardstandings and 30 statics.
Sauna, sunbed, entertainment, putting, chapel,
library*
Leisure: ⚿ ◆ ⚴ ⛫
Facilities: ⛌⊙⛆⚹⚿⛬⛩⛲⛫⛩
Services: ⚡⛁⚐⛹⚇⊞⛁✗⛩⛒→∪◗⊙◭⚹⛏
Notes: Families & couples only
⛔ ⚏ ⚎ ⚌ 🏴

TREGURRIAN   Map 02 SW86

▶ ▶ ▶ 77% **Camping & Caravanning Club Site**
(SW853654)
TR8 4AE ☎ 01637 860448
Ⓦ www.campingandcaravanningclub.co.uk
*Dir: A30 onto A3059, 1.5m turn right signed Newquay
Airport. Left at junct after airport, then right at grass
triangle, follow signs to park*
★ ⛱ £13.60-£19.80 ⛺ £13.60-£19.80 ⚹ £13.60-£19.80
Open Apr-Oct Booking advisable bank hols & peak
periods Last arrival 21.00hrs Last departure noon
*A level grassy site close to the famous beaches of
Watergate Bay, with a modern amenity block. This
upgraded club site is an excellent touring centre for*

contd.

---

the Padstow-Newquay coast. Please see the
advertisement on page 11 for information on Club
sites and membership. A 4.25-acre site with
90 touring pitches, 8 hardstandings.

Facilities: ⛌⊙⛆⚹⚿⛬⛫⛲
Services: ⚡⛹⛴⛁⚽⚇⊞⛁→∪◗◭⚹⛏
⛔ ⚏ ⚎ ⚌ 🏴

TRURO   Map 02 SW84

▶ ▶ ▶ ▶ 83% **Carnon Downs
Caravan & Camping Park
(SW805406)**
Carnon Downs TR3 6JJ
☎ 01872 862283
✉ info@carnon-downs-caravanpark.co.uk
Ⓦ www.carnon-downs-caravanpark.co.uk
*Dir: Take A39 from Truro towards Falmouth. Site just off
main Carnon Downs rdbt, on left*
★ ⛱ £11-£18 ⛺ £11-£18 ⚹ £9-£16

The Best of British GOLD

Open all year Booking advisable Jul-Aug Last
arrival 22.00hrs Last departure 11.00hrs
*A mature park with a high standard of landscaping,
set in meadowland and woodland close to the
village amenities of Carnon Downs. The toilet
facilities provide quality and comfort in private
cubicles. A 33-acre site with 150 touring pitches,
67 hardstandings and 1 static.
Baby & child bathroom, 3 family bathrooms.*
Leisure: ⚴⛫⛏ **Facilities:** ⛨⛌⊙⛆⚹⚿⛬⛩⛫⛩
Services: ⚡⛹⛴⛁⚽⚇⊞⛁→∪◗◭⚹⛎⛏⛒
⛔ ⚏ ⚎ ⚌ 🏴

▶ ▶ ▶ ▶ 77% **Liskey Holiday Park (SW772452)**
Greenbottom TR4 8QN
☎ 01872 560274
🗎 01872 561413
✉ enquiries@liskeyholidaypark.co.uk
Ⓦ www.liskey.co.uk
*Dir: Exit A390 at Threemilestone rdbt onto unclass road
towards Chacewater. Site signed on right in 0.5m*
★ ⛱ £12.50-£17.50 ⛺ £12.50-£17.50 ⚹ £12.50-£17.50
Open all year Booking advisable Jul-Aug Last
arrival 21.00hrs Last departure 10.30hrs
*An attractive south facing park divided into
paddocks by mature hedging, and with quality
modern toilets. It is located on the fringes of an
urban area a few miles from the city, and almost
equidistant from both the rugged north coast and
the calmer south coastal areas. A nearby removals
company sometimes works at night, and the nearby
A390 is busy in the daytime. An 8.5-acre site with*

contd.

England

91 touring pitches, 30 hardstandings and 23 statics.
Serviced pitches, undercover playbarn.
Leisure: ᗃ⊓ Facilities: ⇥Ւ☺۞⁂ᵫᏝ⫞ᵺ
Services: ⊟⬚ᵻᵼ⊞Ṭ→∪Ṗ☺ᵸⱼ
Notes: No bicycles or skateboards
▢ ▢ ▢ ▢ ▢

▶ ▶ ▶ 71% **Cosawes Caravan Park** (SW768376)
Perranarworthal TR3 7QS ☎ 01872 863724
🖥 01872 870268
✉ info@cosawes.com
🌐 www.cosawes.com
Dir: On A39 midway between Truro & Falmouth, with
direct access at park sign at Perranarworthal
★ ⊞ fr £10 ⊞ fr £10 Å fr £10

Open all year Booking advisable mid Jul-mid Aug
Last departure noon
*A small touring park in a peaceful wooded valley,
midway between Truro and Falmouth. Its stunning
location is ideal for visiting the many nearby
hamlets and villages on the Carrick Roads, a stretch
of tidal water which is a centre for sailing and other
boats. A 2-acre site with 40 touring pitches and
113 statics.*
Squash court.
Facilities: Ւ☺⁂ℓ▢⊞⊞ᵺ
Services: ⊟Ṽ⬚ᵻᵼ⊞Ṭ→∪Ṗ☺△ᴥⱼᏝ
Notes: Dogs must be kept on leads at all times
▢ ▢ ▢ ▢ ▢

▶ ▶ ▶ 74% **Summer Valley**
(SW800479)
Shortlanesend TR4 9DW
☎ 01872 277878
✉ res@summervalley.co.uk
🌐 www.summervalley.co.uk
Dir: 3m NW off B3284
★ ⊞ £9-£11.50 ⊞ £9-£11.50 Å £9-£11.50

Treloan Coastal Farm
Treloan Lane, Portscatho, The Roseland,
Truro, Cornwall TR2 5EF
Tel:/Fax: (01872) 580989
Tel:/Answerphone: (01872) 580899
E-mail: holidays@treloan.freeserve.co.uk
Website: www.coastalfarmholidays.co.uk

CORNWALL

Idyllic site with uninterrupted views on coastal footpath,
private access to three beautiful, clean and safe coves.
Traditional organic working farm of the 1930s with Shire
horses and Jersey milking cows. Facilities: Mobile homes
with telephone/modem points, touring and camping
pitches with electric hook-ups, superpitch options, hot
showers, laundry, basic onsite catering, sea fishing, river
moorings. Three minutes walk from Portscatho with
shops, pubs and churches. Half hour drive from Truro,
Eden Project, St Austell and Maritime Museum,
Falmouth. Pets welcome.

Open Apr-Oct Booking advisable Jul-Aug Last
arrival 22.00hrs Last departure noon
*A very attractive and secluded site in a rural setting
midway between the A30 and the cathedral city of
Truro. Keen owners maintain the facilities to a good
standard. A 3-acre site with 60 touring pitches.*
Campers' lounge.
Leisure: ᗃ
Facilities: Ւ☺ᵯ⁂ℓᏝᵺ
Services: ⊟⬚ᵻᵼ⊞Ṭ→∪Ṗᵸⱼ▢▢▢

▶ 78% **Tolcarne Campsite** (SW827511)
Tolcarne Bungalow, St Allen TR4 9QX
☎ 01872 540652 & 540416
✉ ianmcdonnell2@hotmail.com
Dir: Leave A30 approx 1m after rdbt at Carland Cross
and turn left into unclassified road signed St Allen.
Follow single track road for approx 1.5m to site signed
on left
★ ⊞ fr £6 ⊞ fr £6 Å fr £6
Open all year Booking advisable Last arrival
22.00hrs Last departure noon
*A large, slightly sloping field with touring pitches
on level terracing, sheltered by mature hedges, with
wide countryside views. This rural location is
approached along one of Cornwall's designated
"quiet lanes", and is handy for the golden beaches
of Perranporth and the city of Truro. A 1-acre site
with 5 touring pitches.*
Facilities: Ւ☺ᵯ⊞ᵺ
Services: Ṽ→∪ṖⱼᏝ

contd.

Leisure: ⚑ Indoor swimming pool ⚑ Outdoor swimming pool ℺ Tennis court ⚉ Games room ᗃ Children's playground ∪ Stables
▷ 9/18 hole golf course ⚓ Boats for hire 🎦 Cinema ⱼ Fishing ☺ Mini golf △ Watersports ⊟ Separate TV room

Open Apr/Etr-Oct Booking advisable Jul-Sep Last
arrival 20.00hrs Last departure 11.00hrs
*A very smart and well-equipped park with
individual pitches screened by hedges and young
shrubs. The dog walk is of great benefit to pet
owners, and the Camel cycle trail and Padstow are
not far away. A 2.25-acre site with 30 touring
pitches.*

Leisure: /Δ\ **Facilities:** ⋒⊙ℚ⋇⊞Ռ⊼ 𝄐
Services: ⏚⑤⊞→∪ ▶ ⋏ ⚌ ⤶ ⤶⚊
Notes: Dogs must be kept on leads

► ► ► **70%** *Little Bodieve Holiday Park*
(SW995734)
Bodieve Rd PL27 6EG ☎ 01208 812323
❸ berry@littlebodieveholidaypark.fsnet.co.uk
Ⓦ www.littlebodieve.co.uk
*Dir: From A39 rdbt on Wadebridge by-pass take B3314
signed Rock/Port Isaac, site 0.25m on right*
⏚⏚Å
Open Apr-Oct (rs early & late season pool, shop &
clubhouse closed) Booking advisable Jul-Aug Last
arrival 20.00hrs Last departure 11.00hrs
*Set in a rural area with pitches located in three large
paddocks of mostly level grass, this family park is
close to the Camel Estuary. The licensed clubhouse
provides bar meals, with an entertainment
programme in high season, and there is a
swimming pool with sun terrace, and a separate
waterslide and splash pool. A 20-acre site with
195 touring pitches and 75 statics.*
Crazy golf, water shute/splash pool & pets corner.

Leisure: ⋇ ⋐ /Δ\ **Facilities:** ⇥⋒⊙ℚ⋇⥁⚊⤶
Services: ⏚⑤⅌⌀⊞Ⓣ⋇ ⬥→∪▶⬟⚌⤶
⏺ ⌷⌷ ⎙⎙ Ⓖ

WATERGATE BAY   **Map 02 SW86**

► ► ► **76%** *Watergate Bay Tourist Park*
(SW850653)
Watergate Bay TR8 4AD ☎ 01637 860387
▤ 01637 860387
❸ email@watergatebaytouringpark.co.uk
Ⓦ www.watergatebaytouringpark.co.uk
Dir: 4m N of Newquay on B3276 coast road
★ 𝄐 £8.50-£14 𝄐 £8.50-£14 Å £8.50-£14
Open Mar-Oct (rs Mar-22 May & 13 Sep-Nov
restricted bar, cafe, shop & swimming pool)
Booking advisable Jul-Aug Last arrival 22.00hrs
Last departure noon
*A well-established park above Watergate Bay,
where acres of golden sand, rock pools and surf are
seen as a holidaymaker's paradise. Toilet facilities
are to a high standard, and there is a wide range of
activities including a regular entertainment
programme in the clubhouse. A 30-acre site with
171 touring pitches, 14 hardstandings.*
Entertainment, free minibus to beach.

Leisure: ⋇ ⋐ /Δ\ ⛄
Facilities: ⇥⋒⊙ℚ⋇⥁⚊⊞⤶
Services: ⏚⑤⅌⌀⊞Ⓣ⋇ ⬥→▶◉⬟⤶
⏺ ▬▬ ⌷⌷ ⎙⎙ Ⓖ

See advertisement under NEWQUAY

VERYAN   **Map 02 SW93**

► ► ► **74% Camping & Caravanning Club Site**
(SW934414)
Tretheake Manor TR2 5PP ☎ 01872 501658
Ⓦ www.campingandcaravanningclub.co.uk
*Dir: Left off A3078 at filling station signed
Veryan/Portloe on unclass road. Site signed on left*
★ 𝄐 £13.60-£17.80 𝄐 £13.60-£17.80 Å £13.60-£17.80
Open Mar-Oct Booking advisable BH's & peak
periods Last arrival 21.00hrs Last departure noon
*A quiet park on slightly undulating land with
pleasant views of the surrounding countryside.
A tranquil fishing lake holds appeal for anglers, and
the site is just 2.5 miles from one of Cornwall's
finest sandy beaches. Please see the advertisement
on page 11 for information on Club sites and
membership.*
A 9-acre site with 150 touring pitches, 14 hardstandings.

Leisure: ⋐ /Δ\ **Facilities:** ⋒⊙ℚ⋇⚊⋐⎙⊼𝄐
Services: ⏚⅌⊞⌀⊞Ⓣ→∪▶⬟⤶⚊
⏺ ⌷⌷ ▬▬ ⎙⎙ Ⓖ

WADEBRIDGE   **Map 02 SW97**

► ► ► **80% The Laurels Holiday Park (SW957715)**
Padstow Rd, Whitecross PL27 7JQ ☎ 01208 813341
& 07799 777715 ▤ 01208 816590
❸ anicholson@thelaurelsholidaypark.co.uk
Ⓦ www.thelaurelsholidaypark.co.uk
*Dir: Off A389 (Padstow road) near junct with A39,
W of Wadebridge*
★ 𝄐 £5-£13 𝄐 £5-£13 Å £5-£13

contd.

England

WHITE CROSS   Map 02 SW85

78% **White Acres Holiday Park (SW890599)**
TR8 4LW ☎ 01726 862100 & 0870 420 2991 🖹 01726 860777
🔵 enquiries@parkdeanholidays.co.uk
🌐 www.parkdeanholidays.co.uk
Dir: From A30 at Indian Queens take A392 signed Newquay. Site 2m on right
★ 🚐 £9-£28 🚐 £12.50-£32 ⚊ £9-£28
Open May-Oct Booking advisable high season Last arrival 21.00hrs Last departure 10.00hrs
A high quality holiday park with upmarket facilities and plenty of leisure activities and entertainment for the whole family. Boasting one of the best coarse fishing centres in the South West, it also offers a heated indoor swimming pool, sauna, jacuzzi and gym, coffee bar, restaurant and pub, and clubs for children. The touring area is partly terraced, and the setting of 100 rural acres is very attractive. A 167-acre site with 40 touring pitches, 6 hardstandings and 271 statics.
Entertainment, sauna, solarium, fishing, gym, bowling
Leisure: ₹ ◖ 🅰 Facilities: 🛈⊙🗨❄⚡⚿⚡🛒
Services: 🖭♀🛢⦻✕ 🖐→∪◎🌙🖭 🚮 🚛 🔧 🔲

▶ ▶ ▶ 69% *Summer Lodge Holiday Park (SW890597)*
TR8 4LW ☎ 01726 860415
🖹 01726 861490
🔵 summer.lodge@snootyfoxresorts.co.uk
🌐 www.snootyfoxresorts.co.uk
Dir: From Indian Queens on A30 take A392 to Newquay. Site on left at Whitecross in 2.5m
🚐🚐⚊
Open Mar-Oct (rs Etr-Whit & Sep-Oct shop cafe closed) Booking advisable Jul-Aug Last departure 10.00hrs
Small holiday complex offering use of good facilities. This park has a nightly cabaret in the licensed pub, plus other on-site entertainment including crazy golf. A 26-acre site with 100 touring pitches and 118 statics.
Leisure: ₹ ◖ 🅰 Facilities: 🛈⊙🗨❄⚡⚿⚡🛒
Services: 🖭♀🛢🛢⦻🖍🖭✕ 🖐→∪🌙
Notes: ⚘ 🖭 🚮 🚛 🔧 🔲
See advertisement on page 51

WIDEMOUTH BAY   Map 02 SS20

68% *Widemouth Bay Caravan Park (SS199008)*
EX23 0DF ☎ 01288 361208 & 01271 866766 🖹 01271 866791
🔵 bookings@jfhols.co.uk
🌐 www.johnfowlerholidays.com
Dir: Take Widemouth Bay coastal road off A39, turn left. Park on left
🚐🚐⚊
Open Mar-Oct Booking advisable Last dep 10.00hrs
A partly sloping rural site set in countryside overlooking the sea and one of Cornwall's finest beaches. Nightly entertainment in high season
contd.

---

with emphasis on children's and family club programmes. This park is located less than half a mile from the sandy beaches of Widemouth Bay. A 58-acre site with 220 touring pitches, 90 hardstandings and 200 statics.
Leisure: ₹ 🅰 Facilities: 🛈⊙🗨❄⚡⚿⚡🛒🐕
Services: 🖭🛢♀✕ 🖐→∪🌗◎🛆🌙🖭🍴
🖭 🚛 🚮 🚛 🔲
See advertisement under BUDE

▶ ▶ ▶ 68% **Cornish Coast Caravan & Camping (SS202981)**
Middle Penlean, Poundstock EX23 0EE
☎ 01288 361380
🔵 enquiries5@cornishcoasts.co.uk
🌐 www.cornishcoasts.co.uk
Dir: 5m S of Bude on A39, 0.5m S of Rebel Cinema
🚐🚐⚊
Open Apr-Oct Last arrival 22.00hrs Last departure 10.30hrs
A quiet family-run park, with terraced pitches making the most of the stunning views over the countryside to the sea at Widemouth Bay. Reception is in a 13th-century cottage, and the park is well equipped and tidy. A 3.5-acre site with 46 touring pitches, 2 hardstandings and 4 statics.
Leisure: 🅰 Facilities: 🛈⊙🗨❄⚿🛒
Services: 🖭🛢🛢🖍🖭🗓🖐→∪◎🌙🍴🌙

▶ ▶ ▶ 70% **Penhalt Farm Holiday Park (SS194003)**
EX23 0DG ☎ 01288 361210 🖹 01288 361210
🔵 denandjennie@penhaltfarm.fsnet.co.uk
🌐 www.holidaybank.co.uk/penhaltfarmholidaypark
Dir: From Bude take 2nd turn right to Widemouth Bay road off A39, left at end by Widemouth Manor signed Millook onto coastal road. Site 0.75m on left
★ 🚐 £7-£15 🚐 £7-£15 ⚊ £6-£12

Open Etr-Oct Booking advisable Jul & Aug
Splendid views of the sea and coast can be enjoyed from all pitches on this sloping but partly level site, set in a lovely rural area on a working farm. About a mile away is one of Cornwall's finest beaches which is popular with all the family as well as surfers. An 8-acre site with 100 touring pitches.
Pool table, netball & football posts
Leisure: ◖ 🅰
Facilities: 🛈⊙🗨❄⚿⚡🛒🐕
Services: 🖭🛢🖍🖭→∪🌗🛆🌙🍴🌙🖭 🚛 🚮 🔲

Facilities: ➽ Bath 🛈 Shower ⊙ Electric Shaver 🗨 Hairdryer ❄ Ice Pack Facility ⚿ Disabled Facilities ⚡ Public Telephone
🛒 Shop on Site or within 200yds 🖭 Mobile Shop (calls at least 5 days a week) 🔥 BBQ Area 🛒 Picnic Area 🐕 Dog Exercise Area

England

CUMBRIA

AMBLESIDE	Map 18 NY30

▶ ▶ ▶ ▶ 78% *Skelwith Fold Caravan Park (NY355029)*
LA22 0HX ☎ 015394 32277
📠 015394 34344
✉ info@skelwith.com
🌐 www.skelwith.com
Dir: Leave Ambleside on A593 towards Coniston, turn left at Clappersgate onto B5286 Hawkshead road. Park 1m on right
🐕 🐕
Open Mar-15 Nov Booking advisable public hols & Jul-Aug Last arrival dusk Last departure noon
In the grounds of a former mansion, this park is in a beautiful setting close to Lake Windermere. Touring areas are dotted in paddocks around the extensively wooded grounds, and the all-weather pitches are set close to the many facility buildings. There is a 5-acre family recreation area which has spectacular views of Loughrigg Fell. A 130-acre site with 150 touring pitches, 150 hardstandings and 300 statics.
Family recreation area.
Leisure: ⚙
Facilities: 🏕👁🍴☀🚿♿🛒🛁🔌🎣🐕
Services: 🚰🗑🔌🧺☎🚽→∪▶♿🔋🛢🍴
🍴 🚰 🗑 🔋 🚿

▶ ▶ ▶ 71% **Low Wray National Trust Campsite (NY372013)**
Low Wray LA22 0JA ☎ 015394 32810
📠 015394 32684
✉ lowwraycampsite@nationaltrust.org.uk
🌐 www.lowwraycampsite.org.uk
Dir: 3m SW of Ambleside on A593 to Clappersgate, then B5286. Approx 1m turn left at Wray sign. Site less than 1m on left
★ 🐕 fr £11.50 ⛺ £11.50-£16.50
Open wk before Etr-Oct Last arrival 20.00hrs Last departure 11.00hrs
Picturesquely set on the wooded shores of Lake Windermere, this site is a favourite with tenters and watersports enthusiasts. The well-maintained facilities are housed in wooden cabins, and tents can be pitched in wooded glades with lake views or open grassland. Off-road biking, walks and pub food are all nearby. A 10-acre site with 200 touring pitches.
Launching for sailing.
Leisure: ⚙ Facilities: 🏕👁☀♿🛒🛁
Services: 🛢🍴→◎♿🔋🛢🍴🗑
Notes: No cars by caravans or tents, No large groups 🍴 🚰 🗑 🔋 🚿

An increasing number of parks do not accept children. There is a list of adult-only sites on page 19.

APPLEBY-IN-WESTMORLAND   Map 18 NY62

PREMIER PARK

▶ ▶ ▶ ▶ ▶ 92% **Wild Rose
Park** (NY698165)
Ormside CA16 6EJ
☎ 017683 51077 📠 017683 52551

❸ reception@wildrose.co.uk
Ⓦ www.wildrose.co.uk
*Dir: Signed on unclass road to Great Ormside,
off B6260*
★ 🚐 £11-£18.60 🚐 £11-£18.60 ▲ £4-£18.60
Open all year (rs Nov-Mar shop & swimming
pool closed) Booking advisable bank & school
hols Last arrival 22.00hrs Last departure noon
*Situated in the Eden Valley, this large family-run
park has been carefully landscaped and offers
superb facilities maintained to an extremely
high standard. There are several individual
pitches, and extensive views from most areas of
the park. Traditional stone walls and the
planting of lots of indigenous trees help it to
blend into the environment, and wildlife is
actively encouraged. A 40-acre site with
240 touring pitches, 140 hardstandings and
273 statics.*
Tourist Information, pitch and putt.
Leisure: ⚲ ⚫ ⚠ ⛶
Facilities: ⚫⊙⚲✳⚒⚫⚒⛟
Services: ⚑⚐⚑⚑⚑⚑⚑✕ 🛒→▸⚒
Notes: No unaccompanied teenagers,
no dangerous dogs 🔳 🔳 🔳 🔳 🔳

*Family run park situated in the heart of the beautiful Eden Valley.
Ideal base for exploring the Lake District and Yorkshire Dales.
All facilities are maintained to an exceptionally high standard –
licensed restaurant and take-away, mini-market, laundrette, play
areas, TV and games rooms and heated outdoor pools.*
Luxury holiday homes for sale. Brochure with pleasure.

**Ormside, Appleby-in-Westmorland,
Cumbria CA16 6EJ**
Tel: Appleby (017683) 51077
E-Mail: broch@wildrose.co.uk
or visit our Website www.wildrose.co.uk

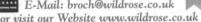

AYSIDE   Map 18 SD38

▶ ▶ ▶ 67% **Oak Head Caravan Park** (SD389839)
LA11 6JA ☎ 015395 31475
Ⓦ www.oakheadcaravanpark.co.uk
*Dir: M6 junct 36, A590 towards Newby Bridge, 14m.
Park sign on left, 1.25m past High Newton*
★ 🚐 £12 🚐 £12 ▲ £10
Open Mar-Oct Booking advisable bank hols Last
arrival anytime Last departure noon
*A pleasant terraced site with two separate areas -
grass for tents and all gravel pitches for caravans
and motorhomes. The site is enclosed within
mature woodland and surrounded by hills. A 3-acre
site with 60 touring pitches, 30 hardstandings and
71 statics.*
Facilities: ⚫⊙⚲✳⚫⚒⛟
Services: ⚑⚑⚑⚑⚑→⚑⚑⚒⚒⚒

South End Caravan Park

Open Mar-Oct Booking advisable Jul-Aug Last
arrival 22.00hrs Last departure noon
*Mainly level grass site adjacent to sea, and close to
a nature reserve, on southern end of Walney Island.
This friendly family-owned and run park offers an
extensive range of good quality amenities and high
standards of cleanliness and maintenance. A new
adult lounge extension is excellent. A 7-acre site
with 60 touring pitches and 100 statics.*
Bowling green, snooker table
Leisure: ⚲ ⚫ ⚠ ⛶
Facilities: ⚫⊙✳⚫⚒⚒⛟
Services: ⚑⚑⚑⚑⚑ 🛒→⚑▸⚒⚒⚒
🔳 🔳 🔳 🔳

BARROW-IN-FURNESS   Map 18 SD26

▶ ▶ ▶ 82% **South End Caravan Park**
(SD208628)
Walney Island LA14 3YQ
☎ 01229 472823 & 471556 📠 01229 472822
❸ kathmulgrew@aol.com
Ⓦ www.walney-island-caravan-park.co.uk
*Dir: A590 in Barrow follow signs for Walney Island.
Turn left after crossing bridge. 4m S*
★ 🚐 £12-£18 🚐 £12-£18 ▲ £12-£18

BASSENTHWAITE LAKE
See map for locations of sites in the vicinity

contd.

Leisure: ⚲ Indoor swimming pool ⚲ Outdoor swimming pool ⚲ Tennis court ⚫ Games room ⚠ Children's playground ⚲ Stables
▸ 9/18 hole golf course ⚒ Boats for hire ⚒ Cinema ⚒ Fishing ⚲ Mini golf ⚲ Watersports ⛶ Separate TV room

England

BOOT   Map 18 NY10

► ► ► 78% **Hollins Farm Campsite (NY178011)**
Hollins Farm CA19 1TH ☎ 019467 23253
✉ jim.bogg@btconnect.com
🌐 www.hollinsfarmcampsite.co.uk
*Dir: Leave A595 at Gosforth or Holmbrook to Eskdale
Green and on to Boot. Site on left towards Hardknott
Pass after railway*
★ **A** £12
Open Mar-Oct Booking advisable BH's & wk/ends
Last departure 18.30hrs
*A very pleasant farm site with a few hardstandings.
It is an ideal touring base with excellent hill walking,
and a popular site with backpackers/tenters. Only
0.25m from Boot station on the Ravenglas/Eskdale
railway ('Ratty'). There are no electric hook-ups or
chemical disposal points. A 2-acre site with 35
touring pitches, 4 hardstandings.*
Facilities: ♠ ⊙ ⚘ ※ → ⊡ ⚓ **Notes:** No under 18s
unless accompanied by mature adult, no groups of
4+ without notice, no open fires

BOWNESS-ON-WINDERMERE
Sites are listed under **Windermere**

BRAITHWAITE   Map 18 NY22

► ► ► 74% **Scotgate Holiday Park (NY235235)**
CA12 5TF ☎ 017687 78343 ▤ 017687 78099
✉ info@scotgateholidaypark.co.uk
🌐 www.scotgateholidaypark.co.uk
Dir: At junct of A66 and B5292, 2m from Keswick
★ 🚐 £14.50-£18.50 🚙 £11-£12.50 **A** £11-£12.50

Open Mar-Oct Last arrival 22.00hrs Last departure
11.00hrs
*Dramatic views of Skiddaw and the northern Fells
dominate this pleasant rural site, which is
frequented by tenters and close to the starting point
of several walking routes. A popular café serves
breakfast and other meals, and there is easy access
to Whinlatter Forest, Keswick, and Bassenthwaite
Lake. An 8-acre site with 165 touring pitches and
35 statics.*
Leisure: ♠ **Facilities:** ♠ ⊙ ⚘ ※ ⚓ ⚓ ★
Services: 🔌 ⊡ 🛢 ⌗ ⚡ ✗ ⏚ → ⊚ ⚠ ✚ ⚒ 🗲
💳 🧲 🗺 🛒

BRAMPTON   Map 21 NY56

► ► ► 68% **Irthing Vale Holiday Park
(NY522613)**
Old Church Ln CA8 2AA ☎ 016977 3600   GOLD
✉ glennwndrby@aol.com
🌐 www.ukparks.co.uk/irthingvale
*Dir: From A69 take A6071 to site, 0.5m outside town.
Turn opposite entrance to leisure centre by school. (NB
take care in narrow lane)*
🚐 🚙 **A**

Open Mar-Oct Booking advisable public hols & Jul-
Aug Last arrival 23.30hrs Last departure noon
*A grassy site on the outskirts of the market town on
the A6071. The friendly owners are gradually
improving the facilities. A 4.5-acre site with 20
touring pitches and 25 statics.*
Leisure: ♠
Facilities: ♠ ⊙ ※ ⚓ ⚓
Services: 🔌 ⊡ 🛢 🛒 → ∪ ▶ ✚ 🗲 🗺

CARLISLE   Map 18 NY35

► ► ► 74% **Dandy Dinmont Caravan & Camping
Park (NY399620)**
Blackford CA6 4EA ☎ 01228 674611
▤ 01228 674611
✉ Dandydinmont@btopenworld.com
🌐 www.caravan-camping-carlisle.itgo.com
*Dir: M6 junct 44, A7 north. Site 1.5m on right, after
Blackford sign*
🚐 £9-£9.25 🚙 £9-£9.25 **A** £7.75-£8.25

Open Mar-Nov Booking advisable bank hols Last
arrival 23.00hrs Last departure 15.00hrs
*A level sheltered site, screened on two sides by
hedgerows. The grass pitches are immaculately
kept, and there are some larger hardstandings for
motor homes. Keen owners maintain good
standards in all areas, and this rural park is only one*

contd.

Abbreviations: BH/bank hols-bank holidays   Etr-Easter   Whit-Whitsun   dep-departure   fr-from   hrs-hours   m-mile   mdnt-midnight
rdbt-roundabout   rs-restricted service   wk-week   wknd-weekend   ⊘-no dogs

mile from the M6 and Carlisle. A 4-acre site with 47 touring pitches, 20 hardstandings and 15 statics.

Facilities: ↟ ⊙ ☀ 짜

Services: ⊡ ⊟ ⓘ ∂ → ∪ ▶ ◎ ✈ ⚑

Notes: Dogs must be kept on leads at all times & exercised off site

---

▶ ▶ ▶ 85% **Green Acres Caravan Park** (NY416614)
High Knells, Houghton CA6 4JW ☎ 01228 675418
Ⓦ www.caravanpark-cumbria.com
Dir: Leave M6/A74(M) at junct 44, take A689 towards Brampton for 1m. Left at Scaleby sign and site 1m on left
★ ⚑ £7.50-£8.75 ⚑ £7.50-£8.75 ▲ £7.50-£8.75
Open Etr-Oct Booking advisable bank hols Last arrival 21.00hrs Last departure 14.00hrs
A small family touring park in rural surroundings with distant views of the fells. This pretty park is run by keen, friendly owners who maintain high standards throughout. A 3-acre site with 30 touring pitches, 15 hardstandings.

Leisure: ⚑ **Facilities:** ↟ ⊙ ☀ ⚑ **Services:** ⊡ ⊟ → ▶ ⚑

CARTMEL
Map 18 SD37

▶ ▶ ▶ 69% **Greaves Farm Caravan Park**
(SD391823)
Prospect House, Barber Green LA11 6HU
☎ 015395 36329 & 36587
Dir: From M6 junct 36 onto A590 signed Barrow. Approx 1m before Newby Bridge, turn left at x-roads signed Cartmel/Staveley. Site 2m on left just before church
★ ⚑ £11-£14 ⚑ £11-£14 ▲ £9-£14

Open Mar-Oct Booking advisable Last arrival 21.00hrs Last departure noon
A small family-owned park close to a working farm in a peaceful rural area. The well-tended grass and flower gardens distinguish this carefully nurtured park, and there is always a sparkle to the toilet facilities. A 3-acre site with 3 touring pitches and 20 statics.

Facilities: ↟ ⊙ ⚑ ☀ ⚑ ⊟ **Services:** ⊡ ⓘ → ∪ ▶ ⚑ ✈ ⚑ ⚑

CROOKLANDS
Map 18 SD58

▶ ▶ ▶ 78% **Waters Edge Caravan Park**
(SD533838)
LA7 7NN ☎ 015395 67708
Ⓔ dennis@watersedgecaravanpark.co.uk
Ⓦ www.watersedgecaravanpark.co.uk
Dir: From M6 follow signs for Kirkby Lonsdale A65, at 2nd rdbt follow signs for Crooklands/Endmoor. Site 1m on right at Crooklands garage, just beyond 40mph limit
⚑ ⚑ ▲

contd.

Open Mar-14 Nov Booking advisable bank hols Last arrival 22.00hrs Last departure noon
A peaceful, well-run park close to the M6, pleasantly bordered by streams and woodland. A Lakeland-style building houses a shop and bar, and the attractive toilet block is clean and modern. Ideal either as a stopover or for longer stays. A 3-acre site with 26 touring pitches and 20 statics.

Leisure: ⚐ ⊡ **Facilities:** ↟ ⊙ ⚑ ☀ ⚑ ⚑ ⚑ ⚑ 짜

Services: ⊡ ⚑ ⓘ ∂ ⊡ → ∪ ✈ 🍴 ▦

CUMWHITTON
Map 18 NY55

▶ ▶ ▶ 72% **Cairndale Caravan Park** (NY518523)
CA8 9BZ ☎ 01768 896280
Dir: Off A69 at Warwick Bridge on unclass road through Great Corby to Cumwhitton, left at village sign, site 1m
★ ⚑ £5.50-£6 ⚑ £5.50-£6
Open Mar-Oct Booking advisable school & public hols Last arrival 22.00hrs
Lovely grass site set in tranquil Eden Valley with good views to distant hills. The all-weather touring pitches have electricity, and are located close to the immaculate toilet facilities. A 2-acre site with 5 touring pitches, 5 hardstandings and 15 statics.

Facilities: ↟ ⊙ ☀

Services: ⊡ ⓘ ⊡ → ▶ ⚑ ⚑ ✈

DALSTON
Map 18 NY35

▶ ▶ ▶ 75% **Dalston Hall Caravan Park** (NY378519)
Dalston Hall Estate CA5 7JX ☎ 01228 710165
Ⓔ enquiries@dalstonhall.co.uk
Ⓦ www.dalstonhall.co.uk
Dir: 2.5m SW of Carlisle, just off B5299 & signed
⚑ £13-£16 ⚑ £13-£16 ▲ £7-£16
Open Mar-Oct Booking advisable Jul-Aug Last arrival 22.00hrs Last departure 13.00hrs
A neat, well-maintained site on level grass in the grounds of an estate located between Carlisle and Dalston. All facilities are to a very high standard, and amenities include a 9-hole golf course, a bar and clubhouse serving breakfast and bar meals, and salmon and trout fly fishing. A 3-acre site with 60 touring pitches, 26 hardstandings and 17 statics.

Leisure: ⚑ **Facilities:** ↟ ⊙ ☀ ⚑ ⚑ 짜 ⚑

Services: ⊡ ⊟ ⚑ ⓘ ∂ ⊡ ⊡ ✕ ▦ → ▶ 🍴 ✈
🍴 ▦ ▦ ⚑ ⚑

England

ESKDALE GREEN   Map 18 NY10

► ► ► 66% Fisherground Farm Campsite (NY152002)
CA19 1TF ☎ 01946 723349 🗐 01946 723349
🌐 camping@fishergroundcampsite.co.uk
🌐 www.fishergroundcampsite.co.uk
Dir: Leave A595 at Gosforth or Holmrook, follow signs on unclass road to Eskdale Green, on towards Boot. Site signed on left
★ 🚐 ▲ £10
Open Mar-Oct Last arrival 21.30hrs Last departure 11.00hrs
A mainly level grassy site on farmland amidst beautiful scenery, in Eskdale Valley below Hardknott Pass, between Eskdale and Boot. It has its own railway halt on the Eskdale-Ravenglass railway, 'The Ratty'. A 9-acre site with 215 touring pitches. Adventure playground, miniature railway, raft pond
Leisure: ⛰ Facilities: ╔⊙🔍※╚🏛
Services: 🔌🗑→ ►🤚🔧
Notes: No caravans, dogs must be on a lead

FLOOKBURGH   Map 18 SD37

77% Lakeland Leisure Park (SD372743)
Moor Ln LA11 7LT
☎ 01539 558556 🗐 01539 558559
🌐 www.havenholidays.com
Dir: On B5277 through Grange-over-Sands to Flookburgh. Left at village square, park 1m
★ 🚐 £11-£52 🚐 £11-£52 ▲ £8-£39
Open mid Mar-Oct Booking advisable at all times Last departure 10.00hrs
A complete leisure park with full range of activities and entertainments, making this flat, grassy site ideal for families. The touring area is quietly situated away from the main amenities, but the swimming pools, all-weather bowling green and evening entertainment are just a short stroll away. A 105-acre site with 145 touring pitches.
Leisure: 🏊 🎣🎱🔍⛰
Facilities: ╔⊙🔍╚🏛🍴🏺🔨
Services: 🔌🗑🍽🍴✗ 🚽→∪►◭
Notes: No cars by caravans or tents
Family park, no pets at Etr, May Day, Whitsun, and summer hols 💳 💳 💳 💳 💳

GRANGE-OVER-SANDS

See **Cartmel**

GREAT LANGDALE   Map 18 NY20

► ► ► 71% *Great Langdale National Trust Campsite (NY286059)*
LA22 9JU ☎ 015394 37668 🗐 015394 37668
🌐 langdale.camp@nationaltrust.org.uk
🌐 www.langdalecampsite.org.uk
Dir: Take A593 to Skelwith Bridge, then right onto B5343, approx 5m to New Dungeon Ghyll Hotel. Site entrance on left in 1m just before Old Dungeon Ghyll Hotel
▲ Open all year
Nestling in a green valley, sheltered by mature trees and surrounded by stunning fell views, this site is

an ideal base for campers, climbers and fell walkers. The large grass tent area has some gravel parking for cars, and there is a separate area for groups and one for families with a children's play area. Attractive wooden cabins house the toilets, a shop, and drying rooms. A 9-acre site.
Leisure: ⛰ Facilities: ╔⊙※╚🔧
Services: 🗑🍴🗃→ 🔧 Notes: No cars by tents
No noise after 11pm 💳 💳 💳 💳 🌀

GREYSTOKE   Map 18 NY43

► ► ► 72% *Hopkinsons Whitbarrow Hall Caravan Park (NY405289)*
Berrier CA11 0XB ☎ 01768 483456
Dir: From M6 junct 40 take A66 to Keswick, after 8m turn right, follow tourist signs to Hopkinsons
🚐 🚐 ▲
Open Mar-Oct Booking advisable bank hols & for electric hook up Last arrival 21.00hrs Last departure 13.00hrs
A rural park in a peaceful location surrounded by trees and shrubs, on the fringe of the Lake District National Park. This family-run park offers plenty of amenities including a small bar and clubhouse, a games room and a tennis court. There is a good mix of grass pitches and hardstandings, and very clean toilet facilities. An 8-acre site with 81 touring pitches and 167 statics.
Table tennis, pool table & video games.
Leisure: 🎱🎣⛰ Facilities: ╔⊙※╚🔧🏛🔨📶
Services: 🔌🗑🍽🍴🗃→∪►💳 💳 💳 🌀

HAVERTHWAITE   Map 18 SD38

► ► ► 72% **Bigland Hall Caravan Park (SD344833)**
LA12 8PJ ☎ 01539 531702 & 723339
🗐 01539 531702
Dir: From A590 in Haverthwaite turn left opposite steam railway, left at T-junct signed B5278, park on left after 1.5m
★ 🚐 £12-£15 🚐 £12-£15
Open Mar-16 Nov Booking advisable public hols Last arrival 22.30hrs Last departure 13.00hrs
A wooded site in lovely countryside 3m from the southern end of Lake Windermere and near the Haverthwaite Steam Railway. The various touring areas are dotted around this large park, and the three toilet blocks are strategically placed. A 30-acre site with 36 touring pitches and 29 statics.
Off-licence on site.
Facilities: ╔⊙╚🔧
Services: 🔌🗃🗑→∪🍴💳 💳 💳 🌀

KENDAL   Map 18 SD59

► ► ► 73% **Camping & Caravanning Club Site (SD526948)**
Millcrest, Shap Rd LA9 6NY ☎ 01539 741363
🌐 www.campingandcaravanningclub.co.uk
Dir: On A6, 1.5m N of Kendal. Site 100yds N of Skelsmergh sign
★ 🚐 £12.40-£16.70 🚐 £12.40-£16.70 ▲ £12.40-£16.70
Open Mar-Oct Booking advisable bank hols & peak periods Last arrival 21.00hrs Last departure noon
A sloping grass site, set in hilly wood and

contd.

contd.

---

meadowland, with some level all-weather pitches. Very clean, well kept facilities and attractive flower beds and tubs make a positive impression. The park is handy for nearby Kendal, with its shops and laundry (no laundry on site). Please see advertisement on page 11 for information on Club sites and membership. A 3.5-acre site with 50 touring pitches, 6 hardstandings.

Leisure: 🛝 Facilities: 🏪⊙🔦✳🔥❤️🛁🏇

Services: 🔌🛒🧺🗑️🔳🚮→🔾🍴🔺🔧🦽

🔲 🔲 🔲 🔲 🔲

Burns Farm Caravan Park

KESWICK   Map 18 NY22

▶ ▶ ▶ ▶ 92% *Castlerigg Hall*
Caravan & Camping Park (NY282227)
Castlerigg Hall CA12 4TE
☎ 017687 74499 📠 017687 74499
🅰 info@castlerigg.co.uk
🆆 www.castlerigg.co.uk
Dir: 1.5m SE of Keswick on A591, turn right at sign. Site 200mtrs on right past Heights Hotel.
🔌🔁🅰

Open mid Mar-15 Nov Last arrival 21.00hrs Last departure 11.30hrs
Spectacular views over Derwentwater to the mountains beyond are among the many attractions at this lovely Lakeland park. Old farm buildings have been tastefully converted into excellent toilets with private washing and family bathroom, reception and a well-equipped shop, and there is a kitchen/dining area for campers with a courtyard tearoom which also serves breakfast. An 8-acre site with 48 touring pitches, 48 hardstandings. Campers' kitchen, sitting room

Leisure: 🔦🗔

Facilities: ↩🏪⊙🔦✳🔥🛁🏇

Services: 🔌🛒🔳🅰🗑️🔳🚮→🍴🔺🔧🦽 🔲 🔲 🔲

▶ ▶ ▶ 80% *Burns Farm Caravan Park*
(NY307244)
St Johns in the Vale CA12 4RR
☎ 017687 79225 & 79112
🅰 info@burnsfarmcamping.co.uk
🆆 www.burns-farm.co.uk
Dir: Turn left off A66 signed Castlerigg Stone Circle/Youth Centre/Burns Farm. Site on right in 0.5m
🔌🔁🅰
Open Mar-4 Nov Last departure noon
Lovely views of Blencathra and Skiddaw can be enjoyed from this secluded park, set on a working

farm. *A warm welcome for families make this an attractive choice for exploring the beautiful and interesting countryside. Food can be found in the pub at Threlkeld village. A 2.5-acre site with 32 touring pitches.*

Facilities: 🏪⊙✳🔥❤️🛁

Services: 🔌🔳🅰🗑️🚮→🔾🍴◎🔺🔧🛎️🦽🔲

▶ ▶ ▶ 76% Camping & Caravanning
Club Site (NY258234)
Crow Park Rd CA12 5EP
☎ 01768 772392
🆆 www.campingandcaravanningclub.co.uk
Dir: From Penrith on A66 into Main Street (Keswick), right to pass 'Lakes' bus stn, past rugby club, turn right, site on right
★ 🔁 £16.10-£19.80 🔁 £16.10-£19.80 🅰 £16.10-£19.80
Open Feb-Nov Booking advisable bank hols & peak period Last arrival 21.00hrs Last departure noon
A well-situated lakeside site within walking distance of the town centre. Boat launching is available from the site onto Derwentwater, and this level grassy park also offers a number of all-weather pitches. Please see advertisement on page 11 for information on Club sites and membership. A 14-acre site with 250 touring pitches, 96 hardstandings.

Leisure: 🛝 Facilities: 🏪⊙🔦✳🔥❤️🛁🔲🏇

Services: 🔌🛒🔳🅰🗑️🔳🚮→🔺🔧

🔲 🔲 🔲 🔲 🔲

▶ ▶ ▶ 77% Camping & Caravanning
Club Site (NY257234)
Crow Park Rd CA12 5EN
☎ 01768 772579
🆆 www.campingandcaravanningclub.co.uk
Dir: Signed off B5289 in town centre
★ 🔁 £16.10-£19.80 🔁 £16.10-£19.80
Open Mar-Nov Booking advisable bank hols & peak period Last arrival 21.00hrs Last departure noon
A peaceful location close to Derwentwater for this well-managed and popular park which is divided into two areas for tourers. Keswick, with its shops and pubs, is just a 5 minute walk away. Please see the advertisement on page 11 for information on Club sites and membership. A 16-acre site with 44 touring pitches, 44 hardstandings.

Leisure: 🛝🛝 Facilities: 🏪⊙🔦✳🔥❤️🛁

Services: 🔌🛒🔳🅰🗑️🔳🚮→🔾🍴🔺🔧🦽

🔲 🔲 🔲 🔲 🔲

contd.

Leisure: 🏊 Indoor swimming pool 🏊 Outdoor swimming pool 🎾 Tennis court 🎱 Games room 🛝 Children's playground ∪ Stables
▶ 9/18 hole golf course ⚓ Boats for hire 🎬 Cinema 🎣 Fishing ◎ Mini golf 🌊 Watersports 🖵 Separate TV room

England

GILL HEAD CARAVAN AND CAMPING PARK
Troutbeck, Penrith, Cumbria CA11 0ST

With panoramic views of the surrounding fells we have a level, sheltered site in well cared for grounds run to a high standard. There are modern, spacious and well maintained shower, toilet and laundry facilities on site. Central for touring the Lake District.
Brochures on request.
www.gillheadfarm.co.uk
Tel/Fax: 017687 79652

▶ ▶ ▶ **80% Castlerigg Farm Camping & Caravan Site (NY283225)**
Castlerigg Farm CA12 4TE ☎ 017687 72479
🖷 017687 74718
✆ info@castleriggfarm.com
Ⓦ www.castleriggfarm.com
Dir: From Keswick on A591 towards Windermere, turn right at top of hill at camping sign. Farm 2nd site on left
★ 🚐 £10-£15 🚐 £10-£15 ⚑ £9.50-£10.60
Open Mar-Nov (rs Mar-Apr & Nov Shop not open all day) Last arrival 21.30hrs Last departure 11.00hrs
Nestling at the foot of Walla Crag, this tranquil fellside park enjoys lake views, and is popular with families and couples seeking a quiet base for fell walking. The modern facilities include a shop, laundry and spotless toilet facilities. Castlerigg Stone Circle and the attractions of Keswick are nearby. A 3-acre site with 48 touring pitches. Cycle storage
Facilities: ♠☉♋✳🌂♒🎋
Services: 🖭🗑🛢🖉🖪🔲⟶▶◉🛢↘🛁ᴊ **Notes:** No noise after 22.30, no fires on the ground

---

▶ ▶ ▶ **84% Gill Head Farm Caravan & Camping Park (NY380269)**
Troutbeck CA11 0ST ☎ 017687 79652
🖷 017687 79130
✆ enquiries@gillheadfarm.co.uk
Ⓦ www.gillheadfarm.co.uk
Dir: From M6 junct 40 take A66, then A5091 towards Troutbeck. Turn right after 100yds, then right again.
★ 🚐 £15-£18 🚐 £15-£18 ⚑ £10-£15

contd.

Open Apr-Oct Booking advisable bank hols Last arrival 22.30hrs Last departure noon
A family-run park on a working hill farm with lovely fell views. It has level touring pitches, and a new log cabin dining room that is popular with families. Tent pitches are gently sloping in a separate field. A 5.5-acre site with 42 touring pitches and 17 statics.
Leisure: ♫🏓 **Facilities:** ♠☉♋✳🌂♒🎋🏸🎋
Services: 🖭🗑🛢🖉⟶∪▶♒↘ᴊ **Notes:** No fires

KIRKBY LONSDALE   Map 18 SD67

▶ ▶ ▶ ▶ **77% New House Caravan Park (SD628774)**
LA6 2HR ☎ 015242 71590
✆ colinpreece9@aol.com
Dir: 1m SE of Kirkby Lonsdale on A65, turn right into site entrance 300yds past Whoop-Hall Inn
★ 🚐 £11 🚐 £11
Open Mar-Oct Booking advisable bank hols, peak season Last arrival 22.00hrs
A very pleasant base in which to relax or tour the surrounding area, developed around a former farm. The excellent toilet facilities are purpose built, and there are good roads and hardstandings, all in a lovely rural setting. A 3-acre site with 50 touring pitches, 50 hardstandings.
Facilities: ♠☉♋✳🌂♒🎋
Services: 🖭🗑🛢🖉🖪🔲⟶▶ᴊ🛁

▶ ▶ ▶ ▶ **83% Woodclose Caravan Park (SD618786)**
Casterton LA6 2SE ☎ 01524 271597
🖷 01524 272301
✆ info@woodclosepark.com
Ⓦ www.woodclosepark.com
Dir: On A65, 0.25m after Kirkby Lonsdale towards Skipton
🚐 £10-£20 🚐 £10-£20 ⚑ £11.50-£13.50

Open Mar-Oct (rs Nov-Dec) Booking advisable bank hols, Jul-Aug & Sep Last arrival 21.00hrs Last departure 13.00hrs
A peaceful park with excellent toilet facilities set in idyllic countryside in the beautiful Lune Valley. Ideal for those seeking quiet relaxation, and for visiting the Lakes and Dales, with the riverside walks at Devil's Bridge, and historic Kirkby Lonsdale both an easy walk from the park. Free view TV via a booster cable from reception is available. A 9-acre site with 29 touring pitches and 54 statics.
Leisure: ♫ **Facilities:** ♠☉♋✳🌂♒🎋🛒
Services: 🖭🗑🛢🖉⟶▶ᴊ

LAMPLUGH Map 18 NY02

▶ ▶ ▶ **77% Inglenook Caravan Park (NY084206)**
Fitz Bridge CA14 4SH ☎ 01946 861240
▤ 01946 861240
🄴 enquiry@inglenookcaravanpark.co.uk
🄦 www.inglenookcaravanpark.co.uk
Dir: On left of A5086 towards Egremont
★ ⊞ fr £14 ⊞ fr £12 ▲ £10-£15
Open all year (rs Oct-Etr shop closed) Last arrival
20.00hrs Last departure noon
*An ideal touring site, well-maintained and situated
in beautiful surroundings. The picturesque village
of Lamplugh is close to the western lakes of
Ennerdale, Buttermere and Loweswater, and a short
drive from sandy beaches. A 3.5-acre site with 12
touring pitches, 12 hardstandings and 40 statics.*
Leisure: ⚠ Facilities: 🝆⊙🝤✳⚅🝢🝙
Services: 🔲🝙🝔

LONGTOWN Map 21 NY36

▶ ▶ **72% Camelot Caravan Park (NY391666)**
CA6 5SZ ☎ 01228 791248 ▤ 01228 791248
*Dir: Leave M6 junct 44. Site 5m N on A7, 1m S of
Longtown*
★ ⊞ fr £8.50 ⊞ fr £8.50 ▲ fr £4
Open Mar-Oct Booking advisable Jul-Aug Last
arrival 22.00hrs Last departure noon
*Very pleasant level grassy site in a wooded setting
near the M6, with direct access from the A7.
This park is an ideal stopover site. A 1.5-acre site
with 20 touring pitches and 2 statics.*
Ice-cream, soft drinks, newspapers & milk to order
Facilities: 🝆⊙✳🝙 Services: 🔲🝙🝔→∪🝚🝓🝞

▶ ▶ **70% Oakbank Lakes (NY369700)**
CA6 5NA ☎ 01228 791108
▤ 01228 791108
🄴 oakbank@nlaq.globalnet.co.uk
*Dir: From Longtown take A7 towards
Langholm/Galashiels. Turn left after 1m signed Corries
Mill Chapelknowe, site in 200yds*
★ ⊞ £7-£9 ⊞ £7-£9 ▲ £6-£8
Open Mar-Nov Booking advisable Last arrival
20.00hrs Last departure 14.00hrs
*A wooded park in a peaceful setting with three
fishing lakes and a nature reserve, making a
relaxing haven for anglers and nature lovers. A
shop and self-service kitchen add to facilities here,
and the toilets are well kept and clean. A 60-acre
site with 22 touring pitches, 14 hardstandings.
Coarse fishing*
Facilities: 🝆⊙✳⚅🎋🝙 Services: 🔲→🝚🝔
Notes: No fires, no cars by tents 🔲 🔲 🔲 🝞

MEALSGATE Map 18 NY24

▶ ▶ ▶ **77% *Larches Caravan Park (NY205415)***
CA7 1LQ ☎ 016973 71379 & 71803 ▤ 016973 71782
Dir: On A595, Carlisle to Cockermouth road
⊞ ⊞ ▲
Open Mar-Oct (rs early & late season) Booking
advisable Etr Spring bank hol & Jul-Aug Last arrival
21.30hrs Last departure noon
This over 18s-only park is set in wooded rural
contd.

*surroundings on the fringe of the Lake District
National Park. Touring units are spread out over
two sections. The park offers well cared for
facilities, and a small indoor swimming pool. A
20-acre site with 73 touring pitches and 100 statics.*
Leisure: ⚛ Facilities: 🝆⊙🝤⚅🝢🝙
Services: 🔲🝔🝙🝚🝓🝙→▶🝚 Notes: Adults only

MILNTHORPE Map 18 SD48

▶ ▶ ▶ **75% Hall More Caravan Park (SD502771)**
Hale LA7 7BP ☎ 01524 718695 ▤ 01524 784815
🄴 enquiries@southlakeland-caravans.co.uk
🄦 www.southlakeland-caravans.co.uk
*Dir: M6 junct 35 onto A6 towards Milnthorpe for 4m.
Left at Lakeland Wildlife Oasis, follow brown signs*
★ ⊞ £10-£12 ⊞ £10-£12 ▲ £9-£10
Open Mar-Oct Booking advisable bank/school
holidays Last arrival 22.00hrs Last departure 10.00hrs
*A pleasant meadowland site adjacent to the main
road, with all hardstanding pitches. It is close to a
farm and stables offering pony trekking, and there
is trout fishing nearby. A 4-acre site with 38 touring
pitches, 7 hardstandings and 60 statics.*
Facilities: 🝆⊙🝤✳🝙🝙
Services: 🔲🝔🝙🝚→∪▶🝚🝓🝞 🔲🔲 🝞 🝞

NETHER WASDALE Map 18 NY10

▶ ▶ ▶ **77% Church Stile Farm
(NY126042)**
CA20 1ET ☎ 019467 26252
▤ 019467 26028
🄴 churchstile@campfarm.fsnet.co.uk
🄦 www.churchstile.com
*Dir: From Barrow on A595 towards Whitehaven, right
into Gosforth. Follow Wasdale signs for approx 4m. Right
at Nether Wasdale sign, left in village after pubs & church*
★ ⊞ £12-£14 ▲ £12-£14

Open Mar-Oct Booking advisable Last arrival
21.30hrs Last departure noon
*Idyllic fell views surround this sheltered, wooded
campsite in a quiet part of a working hill farm. The
friendly owners provide good facilities including a
boot-drying room in the laundry. Walkers,
backpackers and climbers are attracted by the
mountains and fells, and there are two inns and a
hotel serving meals within walking distance.
A 3-acre site with 50 touring pitches,
3 hardstandings and 40 statics.*
Woodland walks, football pitch
Leisure: ⚠ Facilities: 🝆⊙🝤✳⚅🝙🎋🝙
Services: 🔲🝔→🝚🝓🝞 🔲🔲 🝞 🝞

PATTERDALE   Map 18 NY31

► ► ► 78% Sykeside Camping Park
(NY403119)
Brotherswater CA11 0NZ ☎ 017684 82239
📠 017684 82558
🅔 info@sykeside.co.uk
🆆 www.sykeside.co.uk
Dir: Direct access off A592 Windermere to Ullswater road at the foot of Kirkstone Pass
★ 🏕 fr £15 🏕 fr £15 ⚑ £11.50-£13.25
Open all year Booking advisable bank hols & Jul-Aug Last arrival 22.30hrs Last departure 14.00hrs
A camper's delight, this family-run park is sited at the foot of Kirkstone Pass, under the 2000ft Hartsop Dodd in a spectacular area with breathtaking views. The park has mainly grass pitches with a few hardstandings, and for those campers without a tent there is bunkhouse accommodation. A small camper's kitchen and bar serves breakfast and bar meals. There is abundant wildlife. A 5-acre site with 86 touring pitches, 5 hardstandings.

Leisure: ⚠

Facilities: ♁⊙🍴✳☕🐕🛈

Services: 🔌🚾🖂⚡⌀🕀🅣✗→△↳🗡

🔵 🚋 🔲 🔳 🔲

PENRITH   Map 18 NY53
See also **Greystoke**

► ► ► ► 81% *Lowther Holiday Park*
(NY527265)
Eamont Bridge CA10 2JB
☎ 01768 863631 📠 01768 868126
🅔 sales@lowther-holidaypark.co.uk
🆆 www.lowther-holidaypark.co.uk
Dir: 3m S of Penrith on A6
🏕🏕⚑
Open mid Mar-mid Nov Booking advisable bank hols Last arrival 23.00hrs Last departure 22.00hrs
A secluded natural woodland site with lovely riverside walks and glorious surrounding countryside. The park is home to a rare colony of red squirrels, and trout fishing is available on the 2-mile stretch of the River Lowther which runs through it. A 50-acre site with 203 touring pitches, 43 hardstandings and 403 statics.

Leisure: ⚠

Facilities: ✇♁⊙🍴✳☕🐕🛈

Services: 🔌🚾🖂⚡⌀🕀🅣✗ 🛠→∪📍◉♨🗡

Notes: Families only, no cats, no rollerblades, no skateboards, no commerical vehicles

🔵 🚋 🔲 🔳 🔲

Services: 🅣 Toilet Fluid ✗ Café/ Restaurant 🍴 Fast Food/Takeaway 🍼 Baby Care 🔌 Electric Hook Up
🛠 Motorvan Service Point 🔲 Launderette ♨ Licensed Bar 🛢 Calor Gaz ⌀ Camping Gaz 🕀 Battery Charging

England

PENRUDDOCK   Map 18 NY42

▶ ▶ ▶ **71% Beckses Caravan Park (NY419278)**
CA11 0RX ☎ 01768 483224 ▤ 01768 483006
*Dir: M6 junct 40 onto A66 towards Keswick. Approx 6m
at caravan park sign turn right onto B5288. Site on right
in 0.25m*
★ ⊞ fr £8.50 ⊟ fr £8.50 Å fr £7.50

Open Etr-Oct Booking advisable public hols Last
arrival 20.00hrs Last departure 11.00hrs
*A small, pleasant site on sloping ground with level
pitches and views of distant fells, on the edge of the
National Park. This sheltered park is in a good
location for touring the North Lakes. A 4-acre site
with 23 touring pitches and 18 statics.*
Leisure: ⚠ **Facilities:** ↖⊙⚊❋↖↟
Services: ⊞▯⊘⊞▯→∪ ⚓

POOLEY BRIDGE   Map 18 NY42
See also **Greystoke**

▶ ▶ ▶ **72% Hillcroft Caravan & Camping Site
(NY478241)**
Roe Head Ln CA10 2LT ☎ 017684 86363
▤ 017684 86010
*Dir: From A592 into Pooley Bridge. Turn right at church,
straight across x-rds to Roe Head. Park on left*
★ ⊟ fr £20 ⊟ fr £20 Å fr £15
Open 7 Mar-14 Nov Booking advisable bank hols
Last departure noon
*A pleasant rural site close to the village and Ullswater,
with good fell views. There are spacious grassy
pitches for tents, and six hardstandings with electricity
for motor homes and caravans. A 10-acre site with 96
touring pitches, 6 hardstandings and 200 statics.*
Leisure: ⚠ **Facilities:** ↖⊙⚊❋⚏↖↟
Services: ⊞▯⊘→∪⚓⚒ ⚓
Notes: No groups, family camping only

▶ ▶ ▶ **76% Park Foot Caravan & Camping Park
(NY469235)**
Howtown Rd CA10 2NA ☎ 017684 86309
▤ 017684 86041
✉ holidays@parkfootullswater.co.uk
ⓦ www.parkfootullswater.co.uk
*Dir: M6 junct 40 onto A66 towards Keswick, then A592
to Ullswater. Turn left for Pooley Bridge, right at church,
right at x-roads signed Howtown*
⊟ £14-£27.50 ⊟ £10-£20 Å £10-£20
Open Mar-Oct (rs Mar-May, mid Sep-Oct Clubhouse
open wknds only) Booking advisable bank hols Last
arrival 22.00hrs Last departure noon

contd.

Park Foot Caravan & Camping Park
*A lively park with good outdoor sports facilities, and
boat launching directly onto Lake Ullswater. The
attractive mainly tenting park has many mature
trees and lovely views across the lake. The Country
Club bar and restaurant provides good meals,
as well as late-night discos, live music and
entertainment which may not appeal to those
seeking a quiet holiday. An 18-acre site with
323 touring pitches and 131 statics.*
Boat launch, pony trekking, pool table, table tennis
Leisure: ⚊⚫⚠⊟
Facilities: ↖⊙⚊❋⚏↖⚍↟↟
Services: ⊞▯⚏⊘⊞▯✗ ⚓→∪⚓⚒ ⚓
⬤ ⬛ ⬛ ⬛ ⬛

▶ ▶ ▶ **83% Waterfoot Caravan Park
(NY462246)**
CA11 0JF ☎ 017684 86302
▤ 017684 86728
✉ enquiries@waterfootpark.co.uk
ⓦ www.waterfootpark.co.uk
*Dir: From M6 junct 40 take A66 for 1m, then A592 for
4m, site on right before lake*
⊟ £14-£19.50 ⊟ £14-£19.50

GOLD

Open Mar-14 Nov Booking advisable telephone
bookings only Last arrival dusk Last departure
noon
*A quality touring park with neat pitches in a grassy
glade within the wooded grounds of an elegant
Georgian mansion. A lounge bar with a separate
family room enjoys lake views, and there is a path
to Ullswater. Aira Force waterfall, Dalemain House
and garden, and Pooley Bridge are all close by.
A 22-acre site with 37 touring pitches, 32
hardstandings and 146 statics.*
Leisure: ⚫⚠ **Facilities:** ↖⊙⚊❋⚏↖⚍↟↟
Services: ⊞⚏▯⚏⊟⊞▯→∪⚓⚒ ⚓

Leisure: ⚐ Indoor swimming pool   ⚐ Outdoor swimming pool   ⚏ Tennis court   ⚫ Games room   ⚠ Children's playground   ∪ Stables
▶ 9/18 hole golf course   ⚓ Boats for hire   🎬 Cinema   ⚓ Fishing   ◎ Mini golf   ⚄ Watersports   ▭ Separate TV room

England

► ► ► 79% **Waterside House Camp Site**
(NY462231)
Howtown Rd CA10 2NA ☎ 017684 86332
📠 017684 86332
🅴 enquire@watersidefarm-campsite.co.uk
🆆 www.watersidefarm-campsite.co.uk
Dir: From M6 junct 40 take A66 signed Keswick. After
1m left onto A592 signed Ullswater/Pooley Bridge. Turn
left by lake, over bridge. 1st right along Howtown Rd,
2nd site on right
🚐 Å

Open Mar-Sep Booking advisable bank holidays &
weekends Last departure noon
An established farm campsite in a very picturesque
location at the quiet end of Ullswater, with no bar or
club to spoil the peace. Children enjoy seeing the
lambs, ducks and calves, and there are sea cycles,
Canadian canoes and rowing boats for hire, with
direct lake access for sailing boats. The very good
                                                    contd.

toilet facilities are well maintained.
Boat, bike and canoe hire, table tennis
Leisure: 🏔 Facilities: 🏪⊙🍳✳🔌🛁🚻🖼
Services: 🗄🍴🍽🖥📺✗→∪♨⚡🔧

ST BEES   Map 18 NX91
NEW ► ► ► ► 78% **Seacote Park (NX962117)**
The Beach CA27 0ET ☎ 01946 822777
📠 01946 824442
🅴 reception@seacote.com
🆆 www.seacote.com
Dir: From St Bees main street follow signs to beach.
Take road past Seacote Hotel, through public car park to
site entrance
🚐 £15 🚙 £15 Å £7-£12
Open all year Booking advisable Last arrival
18.30hrs Last departure 11.00hrs
An ideal family holiday park with sweeping sea
views, beach access and cliff walks, set in the
charming village of St Bees. A smart new toilet
block with private cubicles is an obvious asset.
The facilities of an adjacent hotel are open to park
visitors, and include restaurant and bar meals,
games room and live entertainment. The park has a
play area and tea rooms, and there's a beach shop
nearby. A 20-acre site with 40 touring pitches, 40
hardstandings and 200 statics.
Leisure: ♣ Facilities: 🏪⊙🍳✳🛁🚻🖼🎠
Services: 🍳🛒🍽🍴🖥✗ ⬛→▶♨🔧
💳 ━━ 🔳 🔳 🅖

SANTON BRIDGE   Map 18 NY10

▶ ▶ **71% The Old Post Office Campsite (NY110016)**
CA19 1UY ☎ 01946 726286 📠 01946 726125
Dir: A595 to Holmbrook and Santon Bridge, 2.5m
🚐 fr £11 🚗 fr £11 🛆 fr £11
Open Mar-15 Nov Booking advisable bank & school hols Last departure noon
A family-run campsite in a delightful riverside setting next to an attractive stone bridge, with very pretty pitches. The simple, clean facilities include a new disabled toilet, laundry and reception. Permits for salmon, sea and brown trout fishing are available, and there is an adjacent pub serving excellent meals. A 2.25-acre site with 40 touring pitches, 5 hardstandings.

Leisure: ⚏
Facilities: 🏕☉🍴✻🛆🖃🐾
Services: 🕹🚾🖲🖃→∪🍴🔧

SILLOTH   Map 18 NY15

90% Stanwix Park Holiday Centre (NY108527)
Greenrow CA7 4HH ☎ 016973 32666
📠 016973 32555
📧 enquiries@stanwix.com
🌐 www.stanwix.com
Dir: 1m SW on B5300. From A596 (Wigton bypass), follow signs to Silloth on B5302. In Silloth follow signs to site, approx 1m on B5300.
★ 🚐 £16-£19.50 🚗 £16-£19.50 🛆 £16-£19.50

Open all year (rs Nov-Feb (ex New Year) no entertainment/shop closed) Booking advisable Etr, Spring bank hol, Jul-Aug & New Year Last arrival 22.00hrs Last departure 11.00hrs
A large well-run family park within easy reach of the Lake District. Attractively laid-out, with lots of amenities to ensure a lively holiday, including a 4-lane automatic 10-pin bowling alley. A 4-acre site with 121 touring pitches, 100 hardstandings and 212 statics.
Amusement arcade, gym, kitchen
Leisure: 🎱 ⚒ 🎣 ⚽ 🏊 ⚏ 🖳
Facilities: 🛁🏕☉🍴✻🛆🧴🐾
Services: 🕹🚾🖲🖃🍴⬀🗑✕ 🚿→❘◉🔧
💳 🚬 🔲 📶 🎬
See advertisement on opposite page

▶ ▶ ▶ ▶ **81% Hylton Caravan Park (NY113533)**
Eden St CA7 4AY ☎ 016973 31707 📠 016973 32555
📧 enquiries@stanwix.com
🌐 www.stanwix.com
Dir: On entering Silloth on B5302 follow signs Hylton Caravan Park, approx 0.5m on left, (end of Eden St)
★ 🚐 £14.40-£17.50 🚗 £14.40-£17.50 🛆 £14.40-£17.50

Open Mar-15 Nov Booking advisable school hols Last arrival 21.00hrs Last departure 11.00hrs
A smart, modern touring park with excellent toilet facilities including several bathrooms. This high quality park is a sister site to Stanwix Park, which is just a mile away and offers all the amenities of a holiday centre. An 18-acre site with 90 touring pitches and 213 statics.
Use of facilities at Stanwix Park Holiday Centre
Leisure: ⚏
Facilities: 🛁🏕☉🍴🛆🧴🖽
Services: 🕹🚾🖲🖃🗑⬀→❘◉🔧
Notes: Families only 💳 🚬 🔲 📶 🎬

▶ ▶ ▶ **66% *Tanglewood Caravan Park (NY131534)***
Causewayhead CA7 4PE ☎ 016973 31253
📧 tanglewoodcaravanpark@hotmail.com
🌐 www.tanglewoodcaravanpark.co.uk
Dir: Adjacent to B5302 (Wigton-Silloth), 4m from Abbeytown, on left
🚐 🚗 🛆
Open Mar-part Feb Booking advisable Etr, Whit & Jul-Aug Last arrival 23.00hrs Last departure 10.00hrs
A pleasant park sheltered by mature trees and shrubs, set in meadowland close to the town. There is a clubhouse and bar, and two small toilet blocks for tourers, both with underfloor heating. A 7-acre site with 31 touring pitches, 21 hardstandings and 58 statics.
Leisure: ⚑ ⚏ 🖳 Facilities: 🏕☉✻🖽🐾
Services: 🕹🖲🍴🖃→∪❘◉🔧

┌─────────────────────────────┐
│ THE PERCENTAGE RATING   │
│ FOR ALL PARKS RANGES FROM │
│   50% - 100%.   │
└─────────────────────────────┘

England

TEBAY   Map 18 NY60

▶ ▶ ▶ 72% **Tebay Caravan Site (NY609060)**
Orton CA10 3SB ☎ 015396 24511 ▤ 015396 24944
✉ caravans@westmorland.com
ⓦ www.tebaycaravanpark.co.uk
Dir: Leave M6 at Westmorland Services, 1m from junct
38. Site accessed through service area from either
N'bound or S'bound carriageways. Follow park signs.
★ ⊞ £10-£12.50 ⊞ £10-£12.50

Open Mar-Oct Booking advisable Jul-Aug & wknds
Last arrival anytime Last departure noon
An ideal stopover site adjacent to the Tebay service
station on the M6, and handy for touring the Lake
District. The park is screened by high grass banks,
bushes and trees, and is within walking distance of
a shop and restaurant. A 4-acre site with 70 touring
pitches, 70 hardstandings and 7 statics.
Facilities: ⋔ ⊙ �٩ ✳ ⅋ ⅃ ዬ ⌂ ⊞ ⋔
Services: ⊟ ▤ ▮ ⊤ ✕ ⅏ → ∪ ⅃
Notes: No cars by tents ⬤ ▰ ▦ ⓪ ▨ ⑨

ULVERSTON   Map 18 SD27

▶ ▶ ▶ ▶ 79% **Bardsea Leisure Park**
(SD292765)
Priory Rd LA12 9QE ☎ 01229 584712
▤ 01229 580413
✉ reception@bardsealeisure.co.uk
ⓦ www.bardsealeisure.co.uk
Dir: Off A5087
★ ⊞ £10-£25 ⊞ £10-£25 ⅄ £10-£12.50

Open all year Booking advisable bank hols & Jul-
Aug Last arrival 21.00hrs Last departure 18.00hrs
Attractively landscaped former quarry, making a
quiet and very sheltered site. Many of the
generously-sized pitches offer all-weather full
facilities, and a luxury toilet block provides plenty of
privacy. Set on the southern edge of the town,
convenient for both the coast and the Lake District.
contd.

A 5-acre site with 83 touring pitches, 83
hardstandings and 83 statics.
Leisure: ⋔ Facilities: ⋔ ⊙ ٩ ✳ ⅋ ⅃ ዬ ⌂ ⋔
Services: ⊟ ▤ ▮ ⅃ ⊞ ⊤ ⅏ → ∪ ▶ ⅏ ⅃ ⬤   ▰ ▦ ▨ ⑨

WASDALE HEAD   Map 18 NY10

▶ ▶ ▶ 71% *Wasdale Head National Trust*
Campsite (NY183076)
CA20 1EX ☎ 019467 26220
✉ wasdale.campsite@nationaltrust.org.uk
ⓦ www.nationaltrust.org.uk/campsites/lakedistrict
Dir: From A595(N) turn left at Gosforth; from A595(S)
turn right at Holmrook for Santon Bridge & follow signs
to Wasdale Head
⊞ ⅄
Open all year Last arrival 23.00hrs Last dep noon
Set in a remote and beautiful spot at Wasdale Head,
under the stunning Scafell peaks at the head of the
deepest lake in England. Clean, well-kept facilities
are set centrally amongst open grass pitches and
trees. The renowned Wasdale Head Inn is close by.
A 5-acre site .
Facilities: ⋔ ⊙ ٩ ✳ ⅋ ⅃ ዬ ⋔ Services: ▤ ▮ ⅆ → ⅋ ⅃
Notes: No cars by tents, groups by arrangement
⬤ ▰ ▦ ⓪ ▨ ⑨

WATERMILLOCK   Map 18 NY42

▶ ▶ ▶ 75% **Cove Caravan & Camping Park**
(NY431236)
Ullswater CA11 0LS ☎ 017684 86549
▤ 017684 86549
✉ info@cove-park.co.uk
ⓦ www.cove-park.co.uk
Dir: M6 junct 40 take A592 for Ullswater. Right at lake
junct, then right at Brackenrigg Hotel. Site 1.5m on right
★ ⊞ £13-£16 ⊞ £13-£16 ⅄ £11-£13

Open Mar-Oct Booking advisable bank & school
hols Last arrival 21.00hrs Last departure noon
A peaceful family site in an attractive and elevated
position with extensive fell views and glimpses of
Ullswater Lake. The ground is gently sloping grass,
but there are also hardstandings for motorhomes
and caravans. A 3-acre site with 50 touring pitches,
14 hardstandings and 39 statics.
Drinks machine.
Leisure: ⋔ Facilities: ⋔ ⊙ ٩ ✳ ⅋ ዬ ⌂ ⋔
Services: ⊟ ▤ ▮ ⅆ ⊞ ⊤ → ∪ ⅄ ⅃

See advertisement on opposite page

Services: ⊤ Toilet Fluid ✕ Café/ Restaurant ⅏ Fast Food/Takeaway ⅏ Baby Care ⅏ Electric Hook Up
⅏ Motorvan Service Point ⅏ Launderette ⅏ Licensed Bar ⅏ Calor Gaz ⅏ Camping Gaz ⅏ Battery Charging

▶ ▶ ▶ 79% **The Quiet Site** (NY431236)
Ullswater CA11 0LS
☎ 01768 486337 & 07768 727016
✉ info@thequietsite.co.uk
ⓦ www.thequietsite.co.uk
Dir: M6 junct 40, A592 towards Ullswater. Right at lake junct, then right at Brackenrigg Hotel. Site 1.5m on right
★ ⊞ £15-£25 ⊞ £15-£25 ⚠ £12-£25
Open Mar-Nov Booking advisable weekends, bank hols & Jul-Aug Last arrival 22.00hrs Last departure noon
A well-maintained site in a lovely, peaceful location, with very good facilities, including a family bathroom. A charming olde-worlde bar is another attraction. A 6-acre site with 60 touring pitches, 20 hardstandings and 23 statics.
Pets corner, pool/darts (for adults), caravan storage
Leisure: ⚫ ♨ ☐
Facilities: ⇥ ♠ ☉ ⚅ ✳ ⚗ ⚘ ⛌ ⛨
Services: ⚙ ⛎ ⊟ ⚎ ⌱ ⊞ ⊡ ⇥ → ∪ ⅄ ✈
Notes: Quiet from 10pm onwards

▶ ▶ ▶ 76% **Ullswater Caravan Camping Site & Marine Park** (NY438232)
High Longthwaite CA11 0LR
☎ 017684 86666 ▤ 017684 86095
✉ info@uccmp.co.uk
ⓦ www.uccmp.co.uk
Dir: M6 junct 40 take A592, W for Ullswater for 5m. Right alongside Ullswater for 2m, then right at phone box. Site 0.5m on right
★ ⊞ £14.50-£17.50 ⊞ £14.50-£17.50 ⚠ £12-£14.50

Open Mar-Nov bar open weekends only in low season Booking advisable public hols Last arrival 21.00hrs Last departure noon
A pleasant rural site with own nearby boat launching and marine storage facility making it ideal for sailors. The family-owned and run park enjoys fell and lake views, and there is a bar and café on site. Many of the pitches are fully serviced. A 12-acre site with 160 touring pitches, 58 hardstandings and 55 statics.
Boat launching & moorings.
Leisure: ⚫ ♨ ☐
Facilities: ♠ ☉ ⚅ ✳ ⚗ ⚘ ⛌ ⛨
Services: ⚙ ⊟ ⚎ ⌱ ⊞ ⊡ → ∪ ⚐ ⅄ ✈
Notes: No open fires ⬤ ▭ ▭ ▦ ◲

WINDERMERE   Map 18 SD49

PREMIER PARK

▶ ▶ ▶ ▶ ▶ 81% **Fallbarrow Park**
(SD401973)
Rayrigg Rd LA23 3DL
☎ 015394 44422 ▤ 015394 88736
✉ enquiries@southlakeland-caravans.co.uk
ⓦ www.southlakeland-caravans.co.uk/parks/1115/view
Dir: 0.5m N of Windermere on A591. At mini-rdbt take road to Bowness Bay & the Lake. Site 1.3m on right
★ ⊞ £17-£24 ⊞ £17-£24

GOLD

Open Mar-mid Nov Booking advisable bank hols & Jul-Aug Last arrival 22.00hrs Last departure 10.00hrs
A quality park with excellent facilities, a few minutes' walk from Bowness on the shore of Lake Windermere. There is direct access to
contd.

Leisure: ⚐ Indoor swimming pool   ⚐ Outdoor swimming pool   ⚽ Tennis court   ⚫ Games room   ♨ Children's playground   ∪ Stables   ▶ 9/18 hole golf course   ⅄ Boats for hire   ⚏ Cinema   ✈ Fishing   ◎ Mini golf   ⚐ Watersports   ☐ Separate TV room

the lake through the wooded park. A restaurant with a specialist chef is a popular feature. A 32-acre site with 38 touring pitches and 269 statics.
Boat launching

Leisure: ♦ ⚘ ♫ ❏ Facilities: ♺ ⊙ ♋ ✳ ⸆ ⚲ ♨ ⩎

Services: ⊡ ⅃ ⬚ ⊠ ♋ ⬚ ⊡ ⬚ ✗ ♣ ➡ → ∪ ♭ ◉ ◬ ⸆ ♨ ↗

Notes: ⌀ No tents ⬤ ▦ ▦ ▧ ◫

▶ ▶ ▶ ▶ ▶ 86% Limefitt Park (NY416032)
LA23 1PA ☎ 015394 32300
✉ enquiries@
    southlakeland-caravans.co.uk
ⓦ www.southlakeland-caravans.co.uk/
    parks/1117/view
Dir: From Windermere take A592 to Ullswater. Site 2.5m on right
★ ♞ £13-£20 ♞ £13-£20 ⚠ £11-£17

Open Mar-mid Nov Booking advisable bank hols & Jul-Aug Last arrival 22.00hrs Last departure 10.00hrs
An attractive family site with superb facilities in a lovely location in the Lake District National Park. Buildings are well-integrated into the landscape, and the River Troutbeck runs through the grounds. From its valley setting there are spectacular views of the surrounding hills, with direct access to the fells and plenty of walks. A 20-acre site with 72 touring pitches, 72 hardstandings and 91 statics.

Leisure: ♦ ⚘ ♫ ❏ Facilities: ♺ ⊙ ♋ ✳ ⸆ ⚲ ♨ ⩎

Services: ⊡ ⬚ ⊠ ♋ ⬚ ⊡ ✗ ♣ ➡ → ∪ ♭ ◉ ◬ ⸆ ♨ ↗

Notes: ⌀ ⬤ ▦ ▦ ▧ ◫

▶ ▶ ▶ ▶ 90% Camping & Caravanning Club Site (Ashes Lane) (SD478962)
Ashes Ln LA8 9JS ☎ 01539 821119
ⓦ www.campingandcaravanningclub.co.uk
Dir: Signed off A591, 0.75m from rdbt with B5284 towards Windermere
★ ♞ £16.20-£20.60 ♞ £16.20-£20.60 ⚠ £16.20-£20.60
Open Mar-Jan Booking advisable bank hols & peak periods Last arrival 21.00hrs Last departure noon
A top Club site in a beautifully landscaped setting bordered by bluebell woods. Many mature trees and shrubs add to the natural beauty, and there are rocky outcrops and lovely views to be enjoyed. First class toilet facilities, good security, a large

contd.

---

adventure playground, and a bar (The Whistling Pig) serving breakfasts, snacks and hot meals all add to the popularity of this very well-redeveloped site. Please see the advertisement on page 11 for information on Club sites and membership. A 24-acre site with 250 touring pitches, 88 hardstandings.

Leisure: ⚘ Facilities: ♺ ⊙ ♋ ✳ ⸆ ⚲ ♨ ⩎

Services: ⊡ ⅃ ⬚ ⊠ ♋ ⬚ ⊡ ⬚ ✗ → ∪ ♭ ◬ ↗ ⸆

⬤ ▦ ▦ ▧ ◫

▶ ▶ ▶ ▶ 77% Park Cliffe Camping & Caravan Estate (SD391912)
Birks Rd, Tower Wood LA23 3PG
☎ 01539 531344 ▤ 01539 531971
✉ info@parkcliffe.co.uk
ⓦ www.parkcliffe.co.uk
Dir: M6 junct 36 onto A590. Right at Newby Bridge onto A592. 4m right into site. (Due to difficult access from main road this is the only advised direction for approaching the site)
★ ♞ £20 ♞ £20 ⚠ £17-£20

Open Mar-15 Nov Booking advisable bank hols & Aug Last arrival 22.00hrs Last departure noon
A lovely hillside park set in 25 secluded acres of fell land. The camping area is sloping and uneven in places, but well drained and sheltered; some pitches have spectacular views of Lake Windermere and the Langdales. The park is very well equipped for families, and there is an attractive bar lounge. A 25-acre site with 250 touring pitches, 60 hardstandings and 50 statics.
Off-licence.

Leisure: ♦ ⚘ Facilities: ♣ ♺ ⊙ ♋ ✳ ⸆ ⚲ ♨ ⩎

Services: ⊡ ⅃ ⬚ ⊠ ♋ ⬚ ⊡ ✗ ♣ ➡ → ∪ ◉ ◬ ⸆ ♨ ↗

Notes: No noise 10.30pm -7.30am ⬤ ▦ ▦ ▧ ◫

▶ ▶ ▶ 88% Hill of Oaks & Blakeholme (SD386899)
Tower Wood LA12 8NR
☎ 015395 31578 ▤ 015395 30431
✉ enquiries@hillofoaks.co.uk
ⓦ www.hillofoaks.co.uk
Dir: M6 junct 36 onto A590 towards Barrow. At rdbt signed Bowness turn right onto A592. Site approx 3m on left
★ ♞ £12.50-£25 ♞ £12.50-£25
Open Mar-14 Nov Booking advisable bank holidays & school holidays
A secluded, heavily wooded park on the shores of Lake Windermere. Pretty lakeside picnic areas,

contd.

England

Hill of Oaks & Blakeholme

woodland walks and a good play area make this a delightful park for families, with excellent serviced pitches, a licensed shop and a heated toilet block. Watersports include sailing and canoeing, with private jetties for boat launching. A 31-acre site with 43 touring pitches and 215 statics.

Leisure: ⚓ **Facilities:** ♪ ⊙ ♀ ✻ ⚒ ℓ ⚑ ㅠ ✝
Services: ▣ ⛽ ☷ ⓘ 🛢 ⊤ ✇ → ∪ ▶ ▲ ♨ ⚲ ♫

DERBYSHIRE

ASHBOURNE   Map 10 SK14
See also Fenny Bentley & Osmaston

▶ ▶ ▶ 81% *Rivendale Touring Caravan & Leisure Park (SK162566)*
Buxton Rd, Alsop en le Dale DE6 1QU
☎ 01335 310311 & 01332 843000
🖶 01335 310311
🅔 rivendale@fsmail.net
🆆 www.rivendalecaravanpark.co.uk
Dir: Off A515 (Ashbourne-Buxton) opposite turn for Biggin
🚐 🚗 ⚲
Open Mar-Jan (rs low & mid season bar & cafe opening hours restricted) Booking advisable Jul & Aug Last arrival 21.00hrs Last departure 11.00hrs
A sheltered park centred around a long-closed quarry with all hardstandings. The site is well equipped with excellent facilities, and run by enthusiastic staff. It has a small country-style bar, and a restaurant serving food at busy holiday times. A 37-acre site with 105 touring pitches, 60 hardstandings and 20 statics.
Nature walk, dog walking field
Leisure: ♦ ⚓ ❑ **Facilities:** ♪ ⊙ ✻ ⚒ ℓ ⚑ ㅠ ✝
Services: ▣ ⛽ ♀ ⓘ ⚇ ⊤ ⊤ ✕ → ∪ 🍴 ☷ ⚲ ♫

▶ 85% Carsington Fields Caravan Park (SK251493)
Millfields Ln, Carsington Water DE6 3JS
☎ 01335 372872
🅔 judy@carsingtoncaravaning.co.uk
🆆 www.carsingtoncaravaning.co.uk
Dir: From Belper towards Ashbourne on A517 turn right approx 0.25m past Hulland Ward into Dog Lane. 0.75m right at x-roads signed Carsington. Site on right after approx 0.75m
🚐 £12-£14 🚗 £12-£14 ▲ £10-£14
Open end Mar-end Oct Booking advisable Last arrival 21.00hrs Last departure 18.00hrs
A very well presented and spacious park with open
contd.

views and a large fenced pond that attracts plenty of wildlife. The popular tourist attraction of Carsington Water is a short stroll away, with its variety of leisure facilities including fishing, sailing, windsurfing and children's play area. The park is also a good base for walkers. A 6-acre site with 10 touring pitches, 10 hardstandings.
Facilities: ♪ ✝
Services: ▣ → ∪ ♨ ⚲ ♫ ℓ ℡ **Notes:** No large groups

BAKEWELL   Map 16 SK26
See also **Youlgreave**

▶ ▶ ▶ 77% Greenhills Holiday Park (SK202693)
Crow Hill Ln DE45 1PX ☎ 01629 813052 & 813467
🖶 01629 815760
🅔 info@greenhillsleisure.com
🆆 www.greenhillsleisure.com
Dir: 1m NW of Bakewell on A6. Signed before Ashford in the Water, 50yds along unclass road on right
★ 🚐 £13.50-£16.50 🚗 £12.50-£15.50 ▲ £11-£13
Open May-Sep (rs Oct, Mar & Apr bar & shop closed) Booking advisable Etr-Sep Last arrival 22.00hrs Last departure noon
A well-established park set in lovely countryside within the Peak District National Park. Many pitches enjoy uninterrupted views, and there is easy accessibility to all facilities. A clubhouse, shop and children's playground are popular features. An 8-acre site with 172 touring pitches, 21 hardstandings and 63 statics.
Leisure: ⚓ **Facilities:** ♪ ⊙ ♀ ✻ ⚒ ℓ ℠ ⚑ ✝
Services: ▣ ⛽ ♀ ⓘ ⚇ ⊤ → ∪ 🍴 ◉ ♫
💳 ▦ ▦ ▦ ⚑

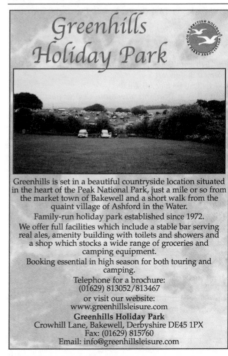

Greenhills
Holiday Park

Greenhills is set in a beautiful countryside location situated in the heart of the Peak National Park, just a mile or so from the market town of Bakewell and a short walk from the quaint village of Ashford in the Water.
Family-run holiday park established since 1972.
We offer full facilities which include a stable bar serving real ales, amenity building with toilets and showers and a shop which stocks a wide range of groceries and camping equipment.
Booking essential in high season for both touring and camping.
Telephone for a brochure:
(01629) 813052/813467
or visit our website:
www.greenhillsleisure.com
Greenhills Holiday Park
Crowhill Lane, Bakewell, Derbyshire DE45 1PX
Fax: (01629) 815760
Email: info@greenhillsleisure.com

Facilities: 🚿 Bath ♪ Shower ⊙ Electric Shaver ⚑ Hairdryer ✻ Ice Pack Facility ⚒ Disabled Facilities ℡ Public Telephone
ℒ Shop on Site or within 200yds ☷ Mobile Shop (calls at least 5 days a week) ㅠ BBQ Area ㅠ Picnic Area ✝ Dog Exercise Area

England

BUXTON   Map 16 SK07

▶ ▶ ▶ ▶ 77% **Lime Tree Park (SK070725)**
Dukes Dr SK17 9RP ☎ 01298 22988 🖪 01298 22988
🕲 limetreebuxton@dukes50.fsnet.co.uk
🌐 www.ukparks.co.uk/limetree
Dir: 1m S, between A515 & A6
★ 🚐 £15-£17 🚐 £15-£17 ▲ £12-£15

Open Mar-Oct Booking advisable bank hols & Jul-Aug Last arrival 21.00hrs Last departure noon
A most attractive and well-designed site, set on the side of a narrow valley in an elevated location. Its backdrop of magnificent old railway viaduct and views over Buxton and the surrounding hills make this a sought-after destination. A 10.5-acre site with 99 touring pitches, 8 hardstandings and 43 statics.
Leisure: ♦ ⚠ ☐ Facilities: ℕ ⊙ ☜ ✳ ♿ ℄ ⅀ ⌦
Services: ☺ ⓖ 🛢 ⊘ ☐ ⊤ → ∪ ▶ ⊙ ⬧
🚽 ⊞ 🔋 ✂ 🔌

NEW ▶ ▶ ▶ 74% **Clover Fields Touring Caravan Park (SK075704)**
1 Heath View, Harpur Hill SK17 9PU
☎ 01298 78731
🕲 cloverfields@tiscali.co.uk
Dir: A515 onto B5053, then immediately right. Park approx 0.5m on left
★ 🚐 £12.50 🚐 £12.50 ▲ £8
Open all year Booking advisable Last departure 18.00hrs
A newly developed, spacious park with very good facilities, just over a mile from the attractions of Buxton. All pitches are fully serviced including individual barbecues, and are set out on terraces, each with extensive views over the countryside. Children will enjoy the small animals which the enthusiastic owners rear in the surrounding meadows. A 12-acre site with 25 touring pitches, 25 hardstandings.
Facilities: ℕ ⊙ ✳ ♿ ℄ ⅀ ⌦ ⌦
Services: ☺ 🖊 🛢 ⊘ ☐ → ∪ ▶ 🛢
Notes: No cars by tents

▶ ▶ 78% **Cottage Farm Caravan Park (SK122720)**
Beech Croft, Blackwell in the Peak SK17 9TQ
☎ 01298 85330
🕲 mail@cottagefarmsite.co.uk
🌐 www.cottagefarmsite.co.uk
Dir: Off A6 midway between Buxton and Bakewell. Site is signed
★ 🚐 fr £10 🚐 fr £10 ▲ fr £8

contd.

Open mid Mar-Oct (rs Nov-Mar hook up and water tap only) Booking advisable Last arrival 21.30hrs
A small terraced site in an attractive farm setting with lovely views. Hardstandings are provided for caravans, and there is a separate field for tents. An ideal site for those touring or walking in the Peak District. A 3-acre site with 30 touring pitches, 25 hardstandings.
Facilities: ℕ ⊙ ✳ ℄ ⅀
Services: ☺ 🛢 ⊘ ☐

▶ ▶ 70% **Thornheyes Farm Campsite (SK084761)**
Thornheyes Farm, Longridge Ln, Peak Dale
SK17 8AD ☎ 01298 26421
Dir: 1.5m from Buxton on A6 turn E for Peak Dale. After 0.5m S at x-rds to site on right
★ 🚐 fr £12 🚐 fr £12 ▲ fr £12
Open Etr-Oct Booking advisable bank hols & high season Last arrival 21.30hrs Last departure evenings
A pleasant mainly-sloping farm site run by a friendly family team in the central Peak District. Toilet and other facilities are very simple but extremely clean. A 2-acre site with 10 touring pitches.
Facilities: ℕ ✳
Services: ☺ 🛢 ☐ → ∪ ▶ 🛢 ⅀
Notes: Site not suitable for children, no ball games, no bicycles, dogs on leads, unisex showers

CROWDEN   Map 16 SK09

▶ ▶ 70% **Camping & Caravanning Club Site (SK072992)**
SK13 1HZ ☎ 01457 866057
🌐 www.campingandcaravanningclub.co.uk
Dir: A628 (Manchester to Barnsley road). At Crowden follow sign for car park/youth hostel & camp site. Site approx 300yds from main road
★ ▲ £7.65-£12
Open Apr-Oct Booking advisable bank hols & peak periods Last arrival 21.00hrs Last departure noon
A beautifully located moorland site, overlooking the reservoirs and surrounded by hills. Tents only, with backpackers' drying room. Please see advertisement on page 11 for information on Club sites and membership. A 2.5-acre site with 45 touring pitches.
Facilities: ℕ ⊙ ☜ ✳ ℄ ⌦
Services: 🛢 🖊 ⊘ ☐ ⊤ → ∪ ▶ ⬧ ⅀ 🚽 ⊞ 🔋 ✂ 🔌

EDALE   Map 16 SK18

▶ ▶ 69% **Coopers Camp & Caravan Park (SK121859)**
Newfold Farm, Edale Village S33 7ZD
☎ 01433 670372
Dir: From A6187 at Hope take minor road for 4m to Edale. Right onto unclass road, site on left in 800yds opposite school
★ 🚐 fr £7.50 🚐 fr £7.50 ▲ fr £7.50
Open all year Booking advisable bank hols Last arrival 23.30hrs Last departure 15.00hrs

contd.

Coopers Camp & Caravan Park
Rising grassland behind a working farm, divided by a wall into two fields, culminating in the 2062ft Edale Moor. Facilities have been converted from original farm buildings, and include a café for backpackers, and a well-stocked shop. A 6-acre site with 135 touring pitches and 11 statics.
Facilities: ♠ ⊕ ⊛ ※ ↺ ▨
Services: ⊟ ▮ ⌀ ⊞ ✕ → ∪

FENNY BENTLEY   Map 16 SK14

▶ ▶ ▶ 69% Bank Top Farm (SK181498)
DE6 1LF ☎ 01335 350250
Dir: Leave Ashbourne on A515, take B5056, 200yds on right
★ ⊞ £10-£12.50 ⊟ £10-£12.50 ▲ £9.50
Open Mar/Etr-Sep Booking advisable peak periods Last arrival 20.00hrs Last departure 14.00hrs
A working farm with pitches laid out on gently-sloping grass and some level areas. There is a pub at the end of the driveway serving food. A 3-acre site with 36 touring pitches.
Facilities: ♠ ⊕ ⊛ ※ ▨
Services: ⊟ ⊞ → ∪ ▶ △ ⚲ ⊿

HAYFIELD   Map 16 SK08

▶ ▶ 75% Camping & Caravanning Club Site (SK048868)
Kinder Rd SK22 2LE ☎ 01663 745394
ⓦ www.campingandcaravanningclub.co.uk
Dir: Off A624, Glossop to Chapel-en-le-Frith (Hayfield by-pass). Well signed into village, follow wood-carved signs to site
★ ⊟ £12.40-£16.70 ▲ £12.40-£16.70
Open Mar-Oct Booking advisable bank hols & peak periods Last arrival 21.00hrs Last departure noon
On level ground along the River Sett valley, a peaceful location overlooked on three sides by mature woodland, with the hills of the North Derbyshire moors on the fourth side. The camping area is in two fields with central amenities. Please see the advertisement on page 11 for information on Club sites and membership. A 6-acre site with 90 touring pitches.
Facilities: ♠ ⊕ ⊛ ※ ↺ ⊞
Services: ▮ ⌀ ⊞ ⊡ → ∪ △ ⚲ ▨
⊜ ▭ ⑩ ▩ ▨ ◲

HOPE   Map 16 SK18

▶ 71% Pindale Farm Outdoor Centre (SK163825)
Pindale Rd S33 6RN ☎ 01433 620111
📠 01433 620729
📧 bookings@pindale.fsbusiness.co.uk
ⓦ www.pindale.fsbusiness.co.uk
Dir: From A625 in Hope turn into Pindale Lane between church and Woodroffe Arms. Pass cement works, over bridge, site in 400yds, well signed
★ ⊟ ▲ £8
Open Mar-Oct Booking advisable Last departure 11.00hrs
An ideal base for walking, climbing and various outdoor pursuits, offering basic facilities for campers and with a self-contained bunkhouse for up to 60 people. A new well appointed female amenity block is now open, with an upgrade to the male block planned for 2006 season. A 1-acre site with 10 touring pitches.
Facilities: ♠ ⊕ ※ ⊞ ⊓
Services: ⊟ → ∪ ▶ ⚲ ▨
Notes: No cars by caravans, dogs must be kept on leads

MATLOCK   Map 16 SK35

▶ ▶ ▶ ▶ 74% Lickpenny Caravan Site (SK339597)
Lickpenny Ln, Tansley DE4 5GF ☎ 01629 583040
📠 01629 583040
📧 lickpenny@btinternet.com
ⓦ www.lickpennycaravanpark.co.uk
Dir: From A615 between Alfreton & Matlock, approx 1m N of Tansley. Turn into Lickpenny Lane at x-rds
★ ⊟ £13.50-£17 ⊟ £13.50-£17
Open all year Booking advisable Last arrival 20.00hrs Last departure noon
A picturesque site in the grounds of an old plant nursery with areas broken up and screened by a variety of shrubs, and spectacular views. Pitches, several fully serviced, are spacious and well marked, and facilities are to a very good standard. A bistro/coffee shop is popular with visitors. A 16-acre site with 80 touring pitches, 80 hardstandings.
Child bath available
Leisure: ⋔ **Facilities:** ♠ ⊕ ⊛ ⅁ ↺ ⊓ ⋔
Services: ⊟ ⅄ ⊡ ▮ ↝ → ∪ ▶ ◉ △ ⚲ ▨
⊜ ▭ ⑩ ▩ ▨ ◲

NEWHAVEN   Map 16 SK16

▶ ▶ ▶ 77% Newhaven Holiday Camping & Caravan Park (SK167602)
SK17 0DT ☎ 01298 84300 📠 01332 726027
ⓦ www.newhavencaravanpark.co.uk
Dir: Halfway between Ashbourne & Buxton at junct with A515 & A5012
★ ⊟ £9-£10.25 ⊟ £9-£10.25 ▲ £9-£10.25
Open Mar-Oct Booking advisable public hols Last arrival 23.00hrs Last departure anytime
Pleasantly situated within the Peak District National Park, with mature trees screening the three touring areas. Very good toilet facilities cater for touring
contd.

Newhaven Holiday Camping & Caravan Park
vans and a large tent field, and there's a restaurant adjacent to the site. A 30-acre site with 125 touring pitches, 4 hardstandings and 73 statics.

Leisure: ◀ ⚠ Facilities: ♠☺☜❄☾☙☶🎕🐾
Services: 🖭🅑🛈⬷🛗🆃→♡△⚡♨🖲 🔳 🔳 🔳 🔳 🔳

OSMASTON   Map 10 SK14

▶ ▶ 70% *Gateway Caravan Park (SK194449)*
DE6 1NA ☎ 01335 344643 📠 01335 344643
📧 admin@gatewaycaravanpark.co.uk
🌐 www.gatewaycaravanpark.co.uk
Dir: 1m S of Ashbourne turn off A52 signed Osmaston, site 400yds on right
🚐🚐🛖
Open all year (rs Nov-Feb Bar closures) Booking advisable bank & school hols Last arrival 21.00hrs Last departure 17.00hrs
This park has been acquired by enthusiastic new owners and extensive upgrading began in early 2005, including a play-barn for children and a well-appointed bar/bistro. New carefully-planned landscaping has ensured an informal arrangement of pitches. There are numerous walks available from the park, with both the attractions of the Peak District and Alton Towers on the doorstep. A 13-acre site with 200 touring pitches, 20 hardstandings. Function room with entertainment, squash court
Leisure: ◀ 🖵 Facilities: ♠☺❄☾☙☶🎕🐾
Services: 🖭🅑🎵🛈🆃→♡▶△♨⚡ Notes: Family park, no large groups 🔳 🔳 🔳 🔳 🔳 🔳

ROSLISTON   Map 10 SK21

NEW ▶ ▶ 82% *Beehive Farm Woodland Lakes (SK249161)*
DE12 8HZ ☎ 01283 763981
Dir: Turn S off A444 at Castle Gresley onto Mount Road, follow Roliston signs. Park on left at T-junct at end of Linton road
🚐🛖 Open Mar-Nov
A small, informal caravan area secluded from an extensive woodland park in the heart of the forest. There is a newly constructed, fine quality amenity block. Young children will enjoy the on-site animal farm and playground, whilst anglers will appreciate fishing the three lakes within the park. The Honey Pot tearoom provides snacks and is open most days. A 2.5-acre site with 25 touring pitches.

ROWSLEY   Map 16 SK26

▶ ▶ ▶ 68% *Grouse & Claret (SK258660)*
Station Rd DE4 2EL ☎ 01629 733233
📠 01629 735194
🚐🚐🛖
Open all year Booking advisable wknds, bank hols & peak periods Last arrival 20.00hrs Last departure noon
A well-designed, purpose-built park at the rear of an eating house on the A6 between Bakewell and Chatsworth, and adjacent to the New Peak Shopping Village. The park comprises a level grassy area running down to the river, and all pitches have hardstandings and electric hook-ups. A 2.5-acre site with 29 touring pitches, 29 hardstandings.
Leisure: ⚠ Facilities: ♠☺☾🎕
Services: 🖭♀☓⬷→♡▶♨⚡
🔳 🔳 🔳 🔳 🔳

SHARDLOW   Map 11 SK43

▶ ▶ ▶ 68% Shardlow Marina Caravan Park (SK444303)
London Rd DE72 2GL ☎ 01332 792832
📠 01332 792832
Dir: M1 junct 24A, take A50 Derby. Exit junct 1 at rdbt signed Shardlow. Site 1m on right
★ 🚐 £9-£11.75 🚐 £9-£11.75 🛖 £9-£11.75
Open Mar-Jan Booking advisable all the time Last arrival 17.00hrs Last departure 14.00hrs
A large marina site with restaurant facilities, situated on the Trent/Merseyside Canal. Pitches are on grass surrounded by mature trees, and for the keen angler the site offers fishing within the marina. A new and attractive grass touring area overlooking the marina has been created. A 25-acre site with 70 touring pitches and 66 statics.
Facilities: ♠☺❄☾🎕🐾
Services: 🖭♀🛈⬷🛗🆃☓→♡▶♨🖲

YOULGREAVE   Map 16 SK26

▶ 70% Camping & Caravanning Club Site (SK206632)
c/o Hopping Farm DE45 1NA ☎ 01629 636555
🌐 www.campingandcaravanningclub.co.uk
Dir: A6/B5056, after 0.5m turn right to Youlgreave. Turn sharp left after church down Bradford Lane, opposite George Hotel. 0.5m to sign turn right
★ 🚐 £9.90-£11.40 🚐 £9.90-£11.40 🛖 £9.90-£11.40
Open Mar-Oct Booking advisable bank hols & peak periods Last arrival 21.00hrs Last departure noon
Ideal for touring and walking in the Peak District National Park, this gently sloping grass site is accessed through narrow streets and along unadopted hardcore. Own sanitary facilities essential. Please see the advertisement on page 11 for information on Club sites and membership. A 14-acre site with 100 touring pitches, 6 hardstandings.
Leisure: ⚠ Facilities: ❄☾🎕🐾
Services: 🖭🛈⬷🛗🆃→♡▶△♨⚡
🔳 🔳 🔳 🔳

DEVON

ASHBURTON
Map 03 SX77

► ► ► ► 75% **Parkers Farm Holidays**
(SX779713)
Higher Mead Farm TQ13 7LJ
☎ 01364 652598 📠 01364 654004
📧 parkersfarm@btconnect.com
🌐 www.parkersfarm.co.uk

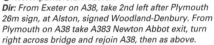

Dir: From Exeter on A38, take 2nd left after Plymouth 26m sign, at Alston, signed Woodland-Denbury. From Plymouth on A38 take A383 Newton Abbot exit, turn right across bridge and rejoin A38, then as above.
★ 🚐 £8-£14.50 🚐 £8-£14.50 ▲ £6-£14.50
Open Etr-end Oct Booking advisable Whitsun & school hols Last arrival 22.00hrs Last departure 10.00hrs

A well-developed site terraced into rising ground. Part of a working farm, this park offers beautifully maintained, quality facilities. Large family rooms with two shower cubicles, a large sink and a toilet are especially appreciated by families with small children. There are regular farm walks when all the family can meet and feed the various animals. An 8-acre site with 100 touring pitches and 25 statics.

Leisure: 🏊 ⚑

Facilities: 🅿 ⊙ ✳ ⚿ 🚻 🛒 🖨 🎋 🐕

Services: 🔌 🍽 🍴 ⌂ 🏧 🗑 ✕ 🚮 ➔ 🔧
🚌 🛒 📶 🖥

Set in 90 acres of spectacular parkland

Family touring site with cafe, bar, tennis courts
and heated outdoor pool
Extensive adventure playground
& pirate play lake
Instructor led activities in summer holidays

Self Catering

Play Lake

River Dart Adventures
at Holne Park, Ashburton, Devon
Follow the brown tourist signs from the A38

01364 652511

www.riverdart.co.uk

▶ ▶ ▶ ▶ **77% River Dart Adventures**
(SX734700)
Holne Park TQ13 7NP ☎ 01364 652511
🖷 01364 652020
🅴 enquiries@riverdart.co.uk
🆆 www.riverdart.co.uk
Dir: *From M5 take A38 towards Plymouth, turn off at*
Ashburton following brown signs to River Dart Country
Park. Site 1m on left
★ 🐾 £12-£19.50 🚐 £12-£19.50 🅰 £9.50-£17
Open Jul-Aug, wknds & school hols Apr-Sep (rs Etr
& Sep no evening facilities & no warden cover)
Booking advisable Spring bank hol & Jul-Aug Last
arrival 21.00hrs Last departure 11.00hrs
Set in 90 acres of magnificent parkland that was
once part of a Victorian estate, with many specimen
and exotic trees, and in spring a blaze of colour
from the many azaleas and rhododendrons. There
are numerous outdoor activities for all ages
including abseiling, caving and canoeing, plus high
quality, well-maintained facilities. The open
moorland of Dartmoor is only a few minutes away.
A 7-acre site with 170 touring pitches, 12
hardstandings.
Adventure playground, climbing, canoeing
Leisure: ⟑ ⚲ ◑ ⚲ ⊿ ⊡
Facilities: ➡ ⋔ ⊙ ⚲ ⚹ ⚹ ⚿ ⚿ 🛢 🛒 ⊓ ⋔
Services: 🖭 🚻 ⚤ ⚠ ◔ 🔋 ⊓ ✕ 🚿 🚐 → ∪ ▶ ✦

🖭 ▬▬▬ ▬▬▬ 🖼 🗓

See advertisement on previous page

AXMINSTER   Map 04 SY29

▶ ▶ ▶ ▶ **76% Andrewshayes Caravan Park**
(ST248088)
Dalwood EX13 7DY ☎ 01404 831225
🖷 01404 831893
🅴 enquiries@andrewshayes.co.uk
🆆 www.andrewshayes.co.uk
Dir: *On A35, 3m from Axminster. Turn N at Taunton*
Cross signed Stockland/Dalwood. Site 150mtrs on
right
🐾 £10-£20 🚐 £10-£17 🅰 £10-£17

Open Mar-Jan (rs Apr-21 May & Oct-Jan shop hrs
limited, pool closed Sep-mid May) Booking
advisable Spring bank hol & Jul-Aug Last arrival
22.00hrs Last departure noon
A lively park within easy reach of Lyme Regis,
Seaton, Branscombe and Sidmouth in an ideal
touring location. This popular park boasts an
attractive bistro beside the swimming pool, a bar,
laundry and shop. A 12-acre site with 150 touring
contd.

---

pitches, 105 hardstandings and 80 statics.
Licensed bistro May-Sep.
Leisure: ⟑ ⚲ ◑ ⊿ ⊡ **Facilities:** ⋔ ⊙ ⚲ ⚹ ⚿ ⚿ 🛢 ⋔
Services: 🖭 🚻 ⚤ ⚠ ◔ 🔋 ⊡ ✕ 🚿 → ✦
Notes: Dogs must be kept on leads
🖭 ▬▬▬ ▬▬▬ 🖼 🗓

BARNSTAPLE   Map 03 SS53

▶ ▶ ▶ **79% Tarka Holiday Park**
(SS533346)
Braunton Rd, Ashford EX31 4AU
☎ 01271 343691 🖷 01271 326355
🅴 info@tarkaholidaypark.co.uk
🆆 www.tarkaholidaypark.co.uk
Dir: *2m from Barnstaple on A361 towards Chivenor. (NB*
This is a fast dual-carriageway & care should be taken)
★ 🐾 £6-£14 🚐 £6-£14 🅰 £6-£14

Open 22 Jan-1 Jan Booking advisable all year Last
arrival 22.00hrs Last departure noon
A gently-sloping grass park divided into paddocks,
and close to the Tarka cycle trail. It offers a licensed
bar with occasional entertainment, pitch and putt, a
bouncy castle and children's playground. The site is
about 5m from sandy beaches. A 10-acre site with
35 touring pitches, 16 hardstandings and 82 statics.
Bouncy castle, eating area in clubhouse
Leisure: ⚲ ◑ **Facilities:** ⋔ ⊙ ⚹ ⚿ ⚿ 🛢 ⋔
Services: 🖭 🚻 ⚤ ⚠ ◔ ✕ 🚿 → ∪ ▶ ◎ ⚄ ⚤ ✦
🖭 ▬▬▬ ◎ ▬▬▬ 🖼 🗓

BICKINGTON (NEAR ASHBURTON) Map 03 SX87

▶ ▶ ▶ ▶ **65% *The Dartmoor Halfway Caravan***
Park (SX804719)
TQ12 6JW ☎ 01626 821270 🖷 01626 821820
🅴 BHUGG22430@aol.com
Dir: *Direct access from A383, 1m from A38 Exeter-*
Plymouth road
🐾 🚐

contd.

Open all year Booking advisable high season &
bank hols Last departure 10.00hrs
*A well-developed park tucked away on the edge of
Dartmoor, beside the River Lemon and adjacent to
the Halfway Inn. The neat and compact park has a
small toilet block with immaculate facilities, and
pitches separated by mature shrubs. An extensive
menu at the inn offers reasonably-priced food all
day and evening. A 2-acre site with 22 touring
pitches.*

Leisure: ⚙

Facilities: ⬡⊙✳&⛎☂🐾

Services: ⬡♀🖃✕→∪▶♨✍🗊🏧
⬤ ▬ ▦ ⓪ 🚫 🖳 🔟

▶ ▶ ▶ ▶ 80% **Lemonford Caravan Park**
(SX793723)
TQ12 6JR ☎ 01626 821242 & 821263
🖹 01626 821263
🅴 mark@lemonford.co.uk
🆆 www.lemonford.co.uk
*Dir: From Exeter A38 take A382, then 3rd exit on rdbt ,
follow Bickington signs*
★ ⊞ £7.50-£11.50 ⊞ £7.50-£11.50 🅐 £7.50-£11.50
Open mid Mar-Oct Booking advisable school hols
Last arrival 22.00hrs Last departure 11.00hrs
*Small, secluded and well-maintained park with a
good mixture of attractively laid out pitches. The
friendly owners pay a great deal of attention to
detail, and the toilets in particular are kept
spotlessly clean. This good touring base is only 1m
from Dartmoor and 10m from the seaside at
Torbay. A 7-acre site with 85 touring pitches,
55 hardstandings and 28 statics.*
Clothes drying area.

Leisure: ⚙

Facilities: ✈⬡⊙🍲✳&⛎🛍🙽☂🐾

Services: ⬡🖃🛢⚙🖃🅣→∪▶♨✍

BRATTON FLEMING   Map 03 SS63

▶ ▶ ▶ 72% **Greenacres Farm Touring Caravan**
Park (SS658414)
EX31 4SG ☎ 01598 763334
*Dir: M5 junct 27 onto A361 towards Barnstaple. At 2nd
rdbt near South Molton turn right onto A399 signed
Blackmoor Gate/Combe Martin. Approx 10m turn left at
Stowford Cross. Site signed on left. (Do not follow signs
to Bratton Fleming)*
★ ⊞ £4.75-£10 ⊞ £4.75-£10
Open Apr-Oct Booking advisable all times Last
arrival 23.00hrs Last departure 11.00hrs
*Located on the edge of Exmoor National Park, this
small park is sheltered behind mature hedges, and
well landscaped with a mix of grass and hard
pitches. There are extensive views, and very well
maintained facilities. A 4-acre site with 30 touring
pitches, 6 hardstandings.*

Leisure: ⚙

Facilities: ⬡⊙🍲✳&⛎☂🐾

Services: ⬡🛢🖃→∪✍🏧

BRAUNTON   Map 03 SS43

▶ ▶ ▶ 73% **Lobb Fields Caravan & Camping Park**
(SS475378)
Saunton Rd EX33 1EB ☎ 01271 812090
🖹 01271 812090
🅴 info@lobbfields.com
🆆 www.lobbfields.com
*Dir: At x-rds in Braunton take B3231 to Croyde. Site
signed on right leaving Braunton*
★ ⊞ £7.50-£21 ⊞ £7.50-£21 🅐 £6-£21

Open 24 Mar-29 Oct Booking advisable Jul-Aug,
Spring BH Last arrival 21.00hrs Last departure
10.30hrs
*A bright, tree-lined park with the gently-sloping
grass pitches divided into two open areas. Braunton
is an easy walk away, and the golden beaches of
Saunton Sands and Croyde are within easy reach.
A 14-acre site with 180 touring pitches,
7 hardstandings.*

contd.

Leisure: 🏊 Indoor swimming pool   🏊 Outdoor swimming pool   🎾 Tennis court   🎱 Games room   ⚙ Children's playground   ∪ Stables
▶ 9/18 hole golf course   ⛵ Boats for hire   🎬 Cinema   🎣 Fishing   ◎ Mini golf   🏄 Watersports   🖳 Separate TV room

England

Baby changing facilities.
Leisure: ⚙ Facilities: ⬢⊙ℚ⚒※⚘🚻
Services: ☎🗑⊘⊟→∪▷⚠🍴🚿
Notes: No under 18s unless accompanied by an adult 🅿 🚮 📶 🅟

BRIDESTOWE   Map 03 SX58

▶ ▶ ▶ 73% **Bridestowe Caravan Park**
(SX519893)
EX20 4ER ☎ 01837 861261
🅴 myoung@myoung.demon.co.uk
🅦 www.myoung.demon.co.uk/Index.html
Dir: Leave A30 at A386/Sourton Down junct, follow B3278 signed Bridestowe, turn left in 3m. In village centre, left down unclass road for 0.5m
★ 🚐 £10-£13 🚍 £10-£13 ▲ £8-£11
Open Mar-Dec Booking advisable summer Last arrival 22.30hrs Last departure noon
A small, well-established park in a rural setting close to Dartmoor National Park. This mainly static park has a small, peaceful touring space, and there are many activities to enjoy in the area including fishing and riding. A 1-acre site with 13 touring pitches, 3 hardstandings and 40 statics.
Leisure: ⚓⚙ Facilities: ⬢⊙※🚿
Services: ☎🗑🍴⊘⊟→∪♫

BRIDGERULE   Map 02 SS20

▶ ▶ ▶ 70% **Hedleywood Caravan & Camping Park**
(SS262013)
EX22 7ED ☎ 01288 381404 🖨 01288 382011
🅴 alan@hedleywood.co.uk
🅦 www.hedleywood.co.uk
Dir: From B3254 take Widemouth road (unclass) at the Devon/Cornwall border
🚐🚍▲
Open all year Bar/restaurant open at main holidays Booking advisable public hols & Jul-Aug
Set in a very rural location about 4 miles from Bude, this relaxed family-owned site has a peaceful, easy-going atmosphere. Pitches are in separate paddocks, some with extensive views, and this wooded park is quite sheltered in the lower areas. A 16.5-acre site with 120 touring pitches, 14 hardstandings and 16 statics.
Dog kennels, nature trail.
Leisure: ⚓⚙🖵 Facilities: ⬢⊙ℚ※⚘🚿🏪🖎🎣🚻
Services: ☎💈🗑🏧🍴⊘⊟🅣✕🚮→∪▷🍴♫

▶ ▶ 88% **Highfield House Camping & Caravanning**
(SS279035)
Holsworthy EX22 7EB ☎ 01288 381480
🅴 nikki@highfieldholidays.freeserve.co.uk
Dir: Exit A3072 at Red Post x-rds onto B3254 towards Launceston. Direct access just over Devon border on right.
🚐🚍▲
Open all year Booking advisable
Set in a quiet and peaceful rural location, this park has extensive views over the valley to the sea at Bude, 5 miles away. The friendly young owners, with small children of their own, offer a relaxing holiday for families, with the simple facilities

carefully looked after. A 4-acre site with 20 touring pitches and 2 statics.
Leisure: ⚙ Facilities: ⬢⊙※⚘🚻
Services: ☎🗑→▷◎♫🚿

BRIXHAM   Map 03 SX95

▶ ▶ ▶ 77% **Galmpton Touring Park**
(SX885558)
Greenway Rd TQ5 0EP
☎ 01803 842066
🅴 galmptontouringpark@hotmail.com
🅦 www.galmptontouringpark.co.uk
Dir: Signed from A3022 Torbay to Brixham road at Churston
★ 🚐 £8.40-£15 🚍 £8.40-£15 ▲ £8.40-£15

Open Etr-Sep Booking advisable Jul-Aug & bank hols Last arrival 22.00hrs Last departure 11.00hrs
An excellent location on high ground overlooking the River Dart, with outstanding views of the creek and anchorage. Pitches are set on level terraces, and facilities are bright and clean. A 10-acre site with 120 touring pitches.
Under 5's bathroom (charged)
Leisure: ⚙ Facilities: ⬢⊙ℚ※⚘🚻
Services: ☎🗑🍴⊘🅣🚮→▷◎♨🚻♫
Notes: Families and couples only, no dogs during peak season 🅿 🚮 📶 🅟

BRIXTON   Map 03 SX55

▶ ▶ 71% **Brixton Caravan & Camping Park**
(SX550520)
Venn Farm PL8 2AX ☎ 01752 880378
🖨 01752 880378
🅴 info@vennfarm.co.uk
🅦 www.vennfarm.co.uk
Dir: Leave A38 at Marsh Mills rdbt in Plymouth onto A379, signed Modbury and Kingsbridge. In approx 4m, turn right at mini-rdbt in centre of village, turn right into private road, site signed
🚐🚍▲
Open 15 Mar-14 Oct (rs 15 Mar-Jun & Sep-14 Oct no warden) Booking advisable Jul-Aug Last arrival 23.00hrs Last departure noon
A small park adjacent to a farm in the village, in a quiet rural area. The park is divided into two paddocks, and is just 100yds from the village services. A 2-acre site with 43 touring pitches.
Facilities: 🚿⬢⊙※🚿⊟
Services: ☎→∪▷♨🚻♫

contd.

BROADWOODWIDGER   Map 03 SX48

▶ ▶ **78% Roadford Lake (SX421900)**
Lower Goodacre PL16 0JL ☎ 01409 211507
🖩 01566 778503
✆ info@swlakestrust.org.uk
ⓦ www.swlakestrust.org.uk
Dir: Exit A30 between Okehampton & Launceston at
Roadford Lake signs, follow across dam wall to
watersports centre
★ 🚐 fr £10 ▲ fr £10

Open Apr-Oct (rs winter weekends only) Booking
advisable
*Located right at the edge of Devon's largest inland
water, this popular rural park is well screened by
mature trees and shrubs. It boasts an excellent
watersports school with hire and day launch
facilities, and is an ideal location for fly fishing for
brown trout. A 1.5-acre site with 30 touring pitches,
4 hardstandings.*
Fishing, sailing, watersports
Facilities: 🕯⊙✳&🏛
Services: 🔌→◭↘🥄🍴 🍽 🎬 🗑

BUCKFASTLEIGH   Map 03 SX76

▶ **84% Beara Farm Caravan & Camping Site
(SX751645)**
Colston Rd TQ11 0LW ☎ 01364 642234
Dir: From Exeter take Buckfastleigh exit at Dart Bridge,
follow South Devon Steam Railway/ Butterfly Farm
signs. 200mtrs 1st left to Old Totnes Rd, 0.5m right at
brick cottages signed Beara Farm.
★ 🚐 fr £7.50 🚐 fr £7.50 ▲ fr £7.50
Open all year Booking advisable peak periods
Jul-Aug
*A very good farm park with clean unisex facilities
and very keen and friendly owners. A well-trimmed
camping field offers peace and quiet. Close to the
River Dart and the Dart Valley steam railway line,
within easy reach of sea and moors. Approach is
narrow with passing places and needs care. A 3.75-
acre site with 30 touring pitches, 1 hardstanding.*
Facilities: 🕯⊙✳🏛🎋🐾 **Services:** 🎬→🥄🍴

▶ **84% Churchill Farm Campsite (SX743664)**
TQ11 0EZ ☎ 01364 642844
✆ a.pedrick@farmersweekly.net
Dir: A38 Dart Bridge exit for Buckfastleigh/Totnes
towards Buckfast Abbey. Pass Abbey entrance, proceed
up hill, and then left at x-roads to site opposite Holy
Trinity church
★ 🚐 £10-£11 🚐 £10-£11 ▲ £8-£11
contd.

Open Etr-Sep Booking advisable Jul & Aug Last
arrival 22.30hrs
*A working family farm in a relaxed and peaceful
setting, with keen, friendly owners. Set on the hills
above Buckfast Abbey, this attractive park is
maintained to a good standard. The spacious
pitches in the neatly trimmed paddock enjoy
extensive country views, and the clean, simple toilet
facilities have modern showers. A 3-acre site with
25 touring pitches.*
Facilities: 🕯⊙✳&
Services: 🔌🗐→🐾
Notes: Dogs must be kept on leads (working farm)

BUDLEIGH SALTERTON   Map 03 SY08
See also **Ladram Bay**

▶ ▶ **76% *Pooh Cottage Holiday Park (SY053831)***
Bear Ln EX9 7AQ ☎ 01395 442354
✆ info@poohcottage.co.uk
ⓦ www.poohcottage.co.uk
Dir: M5 junct 30 onto A376 towards Exmouth. Left onto
B3179 towards Woodbury & Budleigh Salterton. Left
into Knowle on B3178. Through village, at brow of
hill take sharp left into Bear Lane lane (very narrow).
Site 200yds
🚐 🚐 ▲

Open all year Booking advisable Jul-Aug & bank
hols Last arrival 23.00hrs Last departure 11.00hrs
*A rural park with widespread views of the sea and
surrounding peaceful countryside. Expect a friendly
welcome to this attractive site, with its lovely play
area, and easy access to plenty of local walks, as
well as the Buzzard Cycle Way. A 4-acre site with
42 touring pitches, 4 hardstandings and 3 statics.*
Leisure: ↘ ⚠ **Facilities:** 🕯✳&🐾🎋
Services: 🔌🗐→∪🍴⊙🥄🍴

CHAPMANS WELL   Map 03 SX39

▶ ▶ **78% Chapmanswell Caravan Park (SX354931)**
PL15 9SG ☎ 01409 211382 🖩 01409 211154
✆ george@chapmanswellcaravanpark.co.uk
ⓦ www.chapmanswellcaravanpark.co.uk
Dir: Off A388 midway between Launceston and
Holsworthy
★ 🚐 £9.50-£16.50 🚐 £9.50-£16.50 ▲ £7.50-£14.50
Open all year Booking advisable Jul & Aug
*Set on the borders of Devon and Cornwall in
peaceful countryside, this park is just waiting to be
discovered. It enjoys extensive views towards
Dartmoor from level pitches, and is within easy
driving distance of Launceston (7m) and the golden*
contd.

Facilities: 🚿 Bath 🕯 Shower ⊙ Electric Shaver 🧴 Hairdryer ✳ Ice Pack Facility & Disabled Facilities 📞 Public Telephone
🏪 Shop on Site or within 200yds 🚚 Mobile Shop (calls at least 5 days a week) 🏛 BBQ Area 🎋 Picnic Area 🐾 Dog Exercise Area

England

beaches at Bude (14m). A 10-acre site with
50 touring pitches, 35 hardstandings and 50 statics.
Leisure: ⚙ Facilities: ℝ⊙❄ℂ🐾ㅐ
Services: 🔌 ♨🚽🛢🔧🗑🄣✕→∪▶🔥⚡☇⚓

CHIVENOR   Map 03 SS53

▶ ▶ ▶ 72% Chivenor Caravan Park
(SS501351)
EX31 4BN ☎ 01271 812217
🖬 01271 812644
✉ chivenorcp@lineone.net
Ⓦ www.chivenorcaravanpark.co.uk
Dir: On rdbt at Chivenor Cross. Adjacent to RMB Chivenor
🚐 £8.50-£11 🚉 £8.50-£11 ▲ £7.50-£11

SILVER

Open mid Mar-mid Jan Booking advisable Jun-Aug
Last arrival 21.00hrs Last departure noon
*A nicely maintained grassy park with some hard
pitches, set in a good location for touring North Devon,
and handy for the bus stop in Barnstaple. The site is
about 5 miles from sandy beaches. A 3.5-acre site with
30 touring pitches, 5 hardstandings and 10 statics.
Off licence*
Leisure: ⚙ Facilities: ℝ⊙❄❄ℂ🐾
Services: 🔌🛢🔧🗑→∪▶♨⚡

CHUDLEIGH   Map 03 SX87

▶ ▶ ▶ 78% Holmans Wood Holiday Park
(SX881812)
Harcombe Cross TQ13 0DZ
☎ 01626 853785 🖬 01626 853792
✉ enquiries@holmanswood.co.uk
Ⓦ www.holmanswood.co.uk
*Dir: Follow M5 past Exeter onto A38 after racecourse at
top of Haldon Hill. Left at BP petrol station signed
Chudleigh, park entrance on left of slip road.*
★ 🚐 £10.50-£15.75 🚉 £10.50-£15.75 ▲ £10-£12
Open mid Mar-end Oct Booking advisable Last
arrival 22.00hrs Last departure 11.00hrs
*Delightful small park set back from the A38 in a
secluded wooded area, handy for touring Dartmoor
National Park, and the lanes and beaches of South
Devon. The facilities are bright and clean, and the
grounds are attractively landscaped. A 12-acre site with
85 touring pitches, 71 hardstandings and 25 statics.
Information room*
Leisure: ⚙ Facilities: ℝ⊙❄❄ℂ🐾
Services: 🔌🛢🔧⚡→∪♨
Notes: 🐕⊘

COLYTON   Map 04 SY29

NEW ▶ ▶ ▶ 87% Leacroft Touring Park
(SY217925)
Colyton Hill EX24 6HY
☎ 01297 552823

SILVER

*Dir: 1m from Stafford Cross on A3052 towards
Colyton*
★ 🚐 £13-£16 🚉 £13-£16 ▲ £13-£16
Open Etr-Oct Booking advisable Jul-Aug & Spring
bank hol Last arrival 21.00hrs Last departure
11.00hrs
*Located outside the little village of Colyton in the
east Devon countryside, the park has distant sea
views across Lyme Bay from its slightly elevated
position. A wooded area with walks is nearby, and
the traffic-free seaside resort of Seaton is about 2.5
miles away. The park is slightly sloping with all
pitches well spaced and level. A 10-acre site with
138 touring pitches, 10 hardstandings.
Off-licence.*
Leisure: ✎ ⚙
Facilities: ℝ⊙❄❄ℂ🐾🛢🄣ㅐ
Services: 🔌🛢🔧🗑🄣→∪▶♨⚡☇⚓

▶ ▶ 78% Ashdown Caravan Park (SY216922)
Colyton Hill EX24 6HY
☎ 01297 20292 & 22052
✉ ashdowncaravans@tiscali.co.uk
*Dir: From W take A3052 through Sidmouth towards
Seaton, left at Stafford Cross, site 0.5m on left. From
E turn off A35 onto A358 signed Seaton, right onto
A3052 signed Sidmouth. 4m at Stafford Cross turn right
for site*
★ 🚐 £11-£12 🚉 £9
Open Apr-Oct Booking advisable public hols Last
departure noon
*Sheltered by mature trees and shrubs in quiet,
unspoilt surroundings, this grassy park is divided
into two spacious areas around the perimeter. Most
pitches have electricity, and Seaton with its famous
tramway is only 3 miles away. A 9-acre site with
90 touring pitches and 3 statics.*
Facilities: ℝ❄ℂ🐾ㅐ
Services: 🔧🛢→▶⚡☇🗑
Notes: Dogs must be kept on leads

COMBE MARTIN   Map 03 SS54

▶ ▶ ▶ ▶ 83% Stowford Farm
Meadows (SS560427)
Berry Down EX34 0PW
☎ 01271 882476 🖬 01271 883053
✉ enquiries@stowford.co.uk
Ⓦ www.stowford.co.uk
*Dir: M5 junct 27 onto A361 to Barnstaple. Take A39 from
town centre towards Lynton, in 1m turn left onto B3230.
Right at garage at Lynton Cross onto A3123, site 1.5m
on right*
★ 🚐 £6.80-£18 🚉 £6.80-£18 ▲ £6.80-£21
Open all year (rs Winter Pool and bars closed)
Booking advisable bank hols & Jul-Aug Last arrival
20.00hrs Last departure 10.00hrs
Very gently sloping, grassy, sheltered and south-

GOLD

contd.

---

facing site approached down a wide, well-kept driveway. This large farm park is set in 500 acres, and offers many quality amenities, including a large swimming pool, horse riding and crazy golf. A 60-acre wooded nature trail is an added attraction, as is the mini zoo with its stock of friendly animals. A 100-acre site with 700 touring pitches, 30 hardstandings.
Horse rides, fun golf, mini zoo & cycle hire

Leisure: 🏊 🎱 /🛝\

Facilities: 🚽 🛞 ⊙ 🍴 ❋ 🛁 🔥 🛎

Services: 🔌 💷 🍴 🚰 🗑 🔲 ✕ 🛒 → ∪ ▶ ⓞ ♨ 🎣

🚙 💿 🌐 🗞

CROCKERNWELL   Map 03 SX79

► ► ► 71% Barley Meadow Caravan & Camping Park (SX757925)
EX6 6NR ☎ 01647 281629
✉ angela.waldron1@btopenworld.com
ⓦ www.barleymeadow.co.uk
Dir: M5 junct 31 take A30 to 3rd exit signed Woodleigh. Through Cheriton Bishop, park signed just beyond Crockernwell. From Cornwall take A30 to Merrymead rdbt, then 1st exit to Cheriton Bishop, park 3m on right
🏕 🚐 👤
Open 15 Mar-15 Nov Booking advisable bank hols & Jul-Aug Last arrival 22.00hrs Last departure 11.00hrs
A small, very well maintained park set on high ground in the Dartmoor National Park in a quiet

contd.

location. The grassy pitches are mostly level, and the park is well placed to explore Dartmoor. A 4-acre site with 40 touring pitches, 5 hardstandings.
Picnic tables.

Leisure: 🎱 /🛝\ 🔲

Facilities: 🛞 ⊙ 🍴 ❋ 🛁 🛎 🔥 🛎

Services: 🔌 💷 🍴 🗑 🔲 → ∪ ▶ 🎣

CROYDE   Map 03 SS43

► ► ► 75% Bay View Farm Caravan & Camping Park (SS443388)
EX33 1PN ☎ 01271 890501
ⓦ www.bayviewfarm.co.uk
Dir: M5 junct 27 onto A361, through Barnstaple to Braunton, turn left onto B3231. Site at entry to Croyde village
🏕 🚐 👤
Open Mar-Nov Booking advisable high season Last arrival 21.30hrs Last departure 11.00hrs
A very busy and popular park close to surfing beaches and rock pools, with a public footpath leading directly to the sea. Set in a stunning location with views out over the Atlantic to Lundy Island, it is just a short stroll from Croyde. Facilities are clean and well maintained, and there is a fish and chip shop on site. No dogs allowed. A 10-acre site with 70 touring pitches, 38 hardstandings.

Leisure: /🛝\ **Facilities:** 🛞 ⊙ 🍴 ❋ 🛁 🛎

Services: 🔌 💷 🍴 🗑 🛒 🚰 → ∪ ▶ 🎣

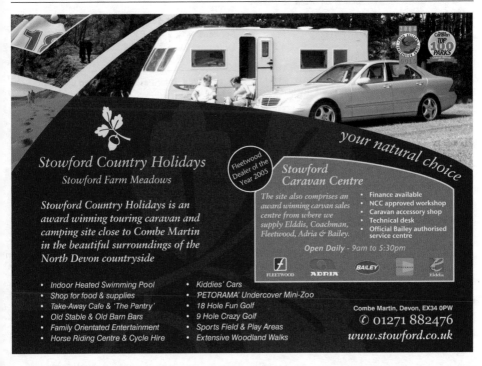

Leisure: 🏊 Indoor swimming pool 🏊 Outdoor swimming pool 🎾 Tennis court 🎱 Games room /🛝\ Children's playground ∪ Stables
▶ 9/18 hole golf course 🛶 Boats for hire 🎬 Cinema 🎣 Fishing ⊚ Mini golf 🌊 Watersports 🔲 Separate TV room

England

CROYDE BAY   Map 03 SS43

80% **Ruda Holiday Park (SS438397)**
EX33 1NY ☎ 01271 890671/ 890477 & 0870 420 2991
🖷 01271 890656
✆ enquiries@parkdeanholidays.co.uk
ⓦ www.parkdeanholidays.co.uk
Dir: M5 junct 27, follow A361 to Braunton. Left at main traffic lights and follow signs for Croyde
★ 🚐 £7-£27 🚎 £10-£31 ▲ £12-£35
Open mid Mar-Nov Booking advisable all times
Last arrival 21.00hrs Last departure 10.00hrs
A spacious, well-managed park with its own glorious blue flag sandy beach, a surfer's paradise. Set in well-landscaped grounds, and with a full leisure programme plus daytime and evening entertainment for all the family. Cascades tropical adventure pool and a nightclub are very popular features. A 220-acre site with 372 touring pitches and 280 statics. Live family entertainment, childen's club
Leisure: ॰ ৎ ◀ 🝢 ⏧ ▢
Facilities: ➡ ℹ ⊙ ☜ ※ ৬ ঙ ⬙ 🎋
Services: ▣ 🖺 ৪ ✓ ☈ ⊞ ✕ 🛒 → ∪ ▶ ৬ ✔
Notes: ⍓ 🍴 ▦ ▦ ▦ ▦

CULLOMPTON   Map 03 ST00
See **Kentisbeare**

DARTMOUTH   Map 03 SX85

▶ ▶ ▶ ▶ 78% **Little Cotton Caravan Park (SX858508)**
Little Cotton TQ6 0LB ☎ 01803 832558
🖷 01803 834887
✆ enquiries@littlecotton.co.uk
ⓦ www.littlecotton.co.uk
Dir: Exit A38 at Buckfastleigh, A384 to Totnes, A381 to Halwell, then A3122 Dartmouth Rd, park on right at entrance to town
🚐 🚎 ▲
Open 15 Mar-Oct Booking advisable Jul & Aug Last arrival 22.00hrs Last departure 11.00hrs
A very good grassy touring park set on high ground above Dartmouth, with quality facilities, and park and ride to the town from the gate. The toilet blocks are heated, and superbly maintained. The friendly owners are happy to offer advice on touring in this pretty area. A 7.5-acre site with 95 touring pitches, 20 hardstandings.
Facilities: ℹ ⊙ ☜ ※ ৬ ঙ ☈ ⬙ 🎋
Services: ▣ 🖺 ৪ ✓ ⊞ ⊤ → ▶ ◉ ৬ ✦ ✔
🍴 ▦ ▦ ▦ ▦

▶ ▶ ▶ ▶ 92% **Woodlands Leisure Park (SX813522)**
Blackawton TQ9 7DQ
☎ 01803 712598 🖷 01803 712680
✆ fun@woodlandspark.com
ⓦ www.woodlandspark.com
Dir: 4m from Dartmouth on A3122. From A38 take turn for Totnes & follow brown tourist signs
★ 🚐 £11-£17.50 🚎 £11-£17.50 ▲ £11-£17.50

Open Etr-6 Nov Booking advisable anytime Last departure 11.00hrs
An extensive woodland park with a terraced grass camping area, and quality facilities which are maintained to a very high standard. The park caters for all the family in a relaxed atmosphere under the supervision of the owner's family, and boasts the UK's biggest indoor venture zone, several water-coasters and rides, and a wildlife park. A 16-acre site with 350 touring pitches, 47 hardstandings. Watercoasters, toboggan run, gliders, falconry centre
Leisure: ৎ 🝢 ▢ Facilities: ➡ ℹ ⊙ ☜ ※ ৬ ঙ ⬙ 🎋
Services: ▣ 🖺 ৪ ✓ ⊞ ⊤ ✕ 🛒 → ∪ ✦ ✔
Notes: ⍓ 🍴 ▦ ▦ ▦ ▦

See advertisement on oppposite page

▶ ▶ ▶ 73% **Deer Park Caravan and Camping (SX864493)**
Dartmouth Rd, Stoke Fleming TQ6 0RF
☎ 01803 770253
✆ info@deerparkinn.co.uk
ⓦ www.deerparkinn.co.uk
Dir: Direct access from A379 from Dartmouth before Stoke Fleming
★ 🚐 £8.50-£16 🚎 £8.50-£16 ▲ £7.50-£16
Open mid Mar-mid Nov Booking advisable Jul-Aug, Bank hols Last arrival 21.00hrs Last departure 11.00hrs
Set on high ground with extensive sea views over Start Bay, this park is divided into three grassy paddocks. Good food is served next door at the Deer Park Inn, and there is a bus service to local beaches and Dartmouth. A 6-acre site with 160 touring pitches.
Leisure: ৎ ◀ 🝢 Facilities: ℹ ⊙ ※ ৬ ঙ ☈
Services: ▣ 🖺 ৪ ✓ ⊞ ⊤ ✕ 🛒 → ∪ ▶ ৬ ✦ ✔
Notes: Dogs must be kept on leads
🍴 ▦ ▦ ▦ ▦

Campsites in popular areas get very crowded at busy times – it is advisable to book well in advance.

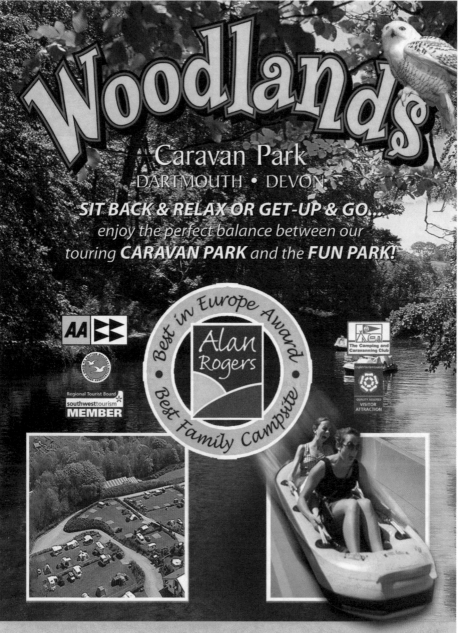

Woodlands

Caravan Park
DARTMOUTH • DEVON

SIT BACK & RELAX OR GET-UP & GO...
enjoy the perfect balance between our
touring **CARAVAN PARK** *and the* **FUN PARK!**

AA

The Camping and Caravanning Club

southwesttourism
MEMBER

Best in Europe Award
Alan Rogers
Best Family Campsite

QUALITY ASSURED
VISITOR
ATTRACTION

Woodlands Leisure Park, Blackawton, Totnes, South Devon TQ9 7DQ
Tel: 01803 712598 • Web: www.woodlandspark.com
Woodlands Leisure reserve the right to close the park or any attractions without prior notice.

Facilities: 🛁 Bath 🚿 Shower ☺ Electric Shaver 💇 Hairdryer ✳ Ice Pack Facility ♿ Disabled Facilities 📞 Public Telephone
🛒 Shop on Site or within 200yds 🚐 Mobile Shop (calls at least 5 days a week) 🍖 BBQ Area 🌲 Picnic Area 🐕 Dog Exercise Area

England

73% Golden Sands Holiday Park (SX968784)
Week Ln EX7 0LZ
☎ 01626 863099 🖷 01626 867149
🅴 info@goldensands.co.uk
🆆 www.goldensands.co.uk
Dir: M5 junct 30 onto A379 signed Dawlish. After 6m pass small harbour at Cockwood, signed on left in 2m
★ 🚐 £10-£20 🚕 £10-£20 ⛺ £10-£20
Open Etr-Oct Booking advisable May-Sep Last arrival 22.00hrs Last departure 10.00hrs
A holiday centre for all the family, offering a wide range of entertainment. The small touring area is surrounded by mature trees and hedges in a pleasant area, and visitors enjoy free use of the licensed club, and heated swimming pools. Organised children's activities are a popular feature. A 2.5-acre site with 54 touring pitches and 188 statics.
Leisure: 🏊 🎿 🎱 ⚅ Facilities: 🛁 ⊙ 🎱 & ♿ 🛒
Services: 🖵 🅱 🆀 💡 🕭 📅 🗙 🕍 → 🏐 ⊚ 🔧
Notes: 🐾 No pets 💳 ▭▭ ▭▭ 🔳 🔳 🅖
See advertisement on oppposite page

75% Lady's Mile Holiday Park (SX968784)
EX7 0LX ☎ 01626 863411
🖷 01626 888689
Dir: 1m N of Dawlish on A379
🚐 🚕 ⛺
Open 17 Mar-27 Oct Booking advisable bank hols & Jul-Aug Last arrival 20.00hrs Last departure 11.00hrs
A holiday site with all grass touring pitches, and plenty of activities for everyone. Two swimming pools with waterslides, a large adventure playground, 9-hole golf course, and a bar with entertainment in high season all add to the enjoyment of a stay here. Facilities are kept clean, and the surrounding beaches are easily accessed. A 16-acre site with 243 touring pitches and 43 statics.
Leisure: 🏊 🎿 🎱 ⚅ 🗔
Facilities: 🚻 🛁 ⊙ 🎱 ✳ & ♿ 🛒 🐾
Services: 🖵 🅱 🆀 💡 🖊 📅 🗙 🕍 → ∪ ▶ ⊚ 🔺 🔧 ♨ 🔧
💳 ▭▭ 🔳 🅖
See advertisement on oppposite page

73% Peppermint Park (SX978788)
Warren Rd EX7 0PQ
☎ 01626 863436 🖷 01626 866482
🅴 info@peppermintpark.co.uk
🆆 www.peppermintpark.co.uk
Dir: From A379 at Dawlish follow signs for Dawlish Warren. Site 1m on left
🚐 🚕 ⛺
Open Etr-Oct (rs early/late season shop, pool, club closed) Booking advisable Spring bank hol & Jul-Aug Last arrival 20.00hrs Last departure 11.00hrs
Well managed attractive park close to the coast, with excellent facilities including club and bar
contd.

Peppermint Park
which are well away from pitches. Nestling close to sandy beaches, the park offers individually marked pitches on level terraces in pleasant, sheltered grassland. The many amenities include a heated swimming pool and water chute, coarse fishing and launderette. A 26-acre site with 250 touring pitches. Licensed club, entertainment, coarse fishing lake
Leisure: 🎿 🎱 ⚅ Facilities: 🛁 ⊙ ✳ & ♿ 🛒 🐾
Services: 🖵 🅱 🆀 💡 ∅ 📅 🕭 → ▶ ♨ 🔧
💳 ▭▭ 🔳 🅖 See advertisement on page 106

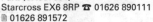

▶ ▶ ▶ ▶ **74% Cofton Country Holiday Park (SX967801)**
Starcross EX6 8RP ☎ 01626 890111
🖷 01626 891572
🅴 info@coftonholidays.co.uk
🆆 www.coftonholidays.co.uk
Dir: On A379 Exeter/Dawlish road 3m from Dawlish
★ 🚐 £12-£19.50 🚕 £12-£19.50 ⛺ £12-£19.50

Open Etr-Oct (rs Etr-Spring bank hol & mid Sep-Oct swimming pool closed) Booking advisable bank hols & Jul-Aug Last arrival 20.00hrs Last departure 11.00hrs
Set in a rural location surrounded by spacious open grassland, with plenty of well-kept flower beds throughout the park. Most pitches overlook either the swimming pool complex or the fishing lakes and woodlands. An on-site pub serves drinks, and meals or snacks, for all the family, and a mini-market caters for most shopping needs. A 16-acre site with 450 touring pitches, 20 hardstandings and 66 statics. Coarse fishing, pub with family room.
Leisure: 🎿 🎱 ⚅ Facilities: 🛁 ⊙ 🎱 ✳ & ♿ 🛒 🐾
Services: 🖵 🅱 🆀 💡 ∅ 📅 🕭 🗙 🕍 → ▶ ⊚ ♨ 🔧
💳 ▭▭ 🔳 🅖
See advertisement on page 107

Leisure: 🏊 Indoor swimming pool 🏊 Outdoor swimming pool 🎾 Tennis court 🎱 Games room 🛝 Children's playground ⛹ Stables ⛳ 9/18 hole golf course ⛵ Boats for hire 🎬 Cinema 🎣 Fishing ⛳ Mini golf 🌊 Watersports 📺 Separate TV room

▶ ▶ ▶ **74% Leadstone Camping (SX974782)**
Warren Rd EX7 0NG ☎ 01626 864411
🖹 01626 873833
🖃 info@leadstonecamping.co.uk
🌐 www.leadstonecamping.co.uk
Dir: From M5 junct 30 take A379 to Dawlish. Before
village turn left on brow of hill, signed Dawlish Warren.
Site 0.5m on right
★ ⚏ £13.90-£15.55 ⚏ £10.50-£11.80
⚑ £10.50-£11.80

Open 16 Jun-4 Sep Booking advisable 15 Jul-28
Aug Last arrival 22.00hrs Last departure noon
*A traditional, mainly level grassy camping park
approx 0.5m walk from sands and dunes at Dawlish
Warren, an Area of Outstanding Natural Beauty.
This mainly tented park has been run by the same
friendly family for many years, and is an ideal base
for touring south Devon. A regular bus service from
outside the gate takes in a wide area. An 8-acre site
with 137 touring pitches.*   *contd.*

Leisure: ⚑ Facilities: 🅙⊙🅠☀🅣🅢
Services: 🕿🖃🖩🖉🖵→∪🅟🛢🖉
Notes: No noise after 11pm 🖰 ⬛ ⬛ 🖰 🖰

NEW ▶ **72% Seaway Touring Park (SX969784)**
Warren Rd EX7 0LX ☎ 01626 866986
Dir: M5 junct 30 take A379 towards Dawlish. On brow of
hill before Dawlish turn left signed Dawlish Warren. Site
350yds on left
⚏ ⚑
Open Etr-Oct
*A developing park in an elevated position with
lovely views of the surrounding countryside and
glimpses of the sea. A downhill walk leads to the
beach at Dawlish Warren, a busy seaside holiday
village with lots to offer. An 18-acre site with 100
touring pitches.*

Facilities: 🅙

DREWSTEIGNTON   Map 03 SX79

▶ ▶ **77% Woodland Springs Adult Touring Park
(SX695912)**
Venton EX6 6PG ☎ 01647 231695
🖹 01647 231695
🖃 enquiries@woodlandsprings.co.uk
🌐 www.woodlandsprings.co.uk
Dir: Leave A30 at Merrymeet rdbt, turn left onto A382
towards Moretonhampstead. Site 1.5m on left
⚏ £8.50-£15.50 ⚏ £8.50-£15.50 ⚑ £5.50-£15.50
Open all year Booking advisable Last arrival
22.30hrs Last departure 11.00hrs   *contd.*

England

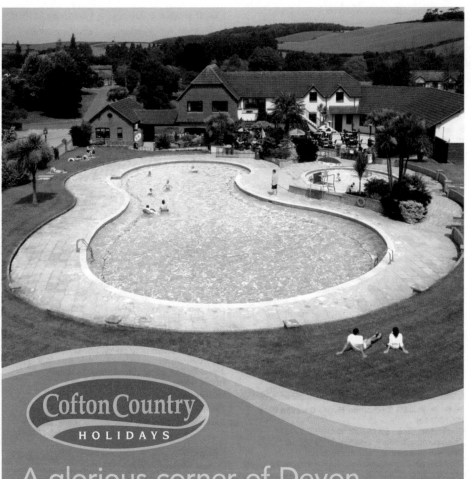

Cofton Country HOLIDAYS

A glorious corner of Devon

- Four star family-run holiday park in eighty acres of parkland, rolling meadows and mature woodland
- Fantastic facilities including outdoor swimming pools, Swan pub, take-away and mini-market
- Five well-stocked coarse fishing lakes

- Just minutes from Dawlish Warren's famous Blue Flag beach
- Described by David Bellamy as 'a green champion' for our positive contribution to the environment

0800 085 8649 www.coftonholidays.co.uk

touring caravans · camping · caravan holiday homes · cottages and apartments

Facilities: ⬛ Bath 🚿 Shower ☺ Electric Shaver 🔌 Hairdryer ✳ Ice Pack Facility ♿ Disabled Facilities 📞 Public Telephone
🛒 Shop on Site or within 200yds 🚐 Mobile Shop (calls at least 5 days a week) ⊞ BBQ Area 🅿 Picnic Area 🐕 Dog Exercise Area

England

An attractive park in a rural area within Dartmoor National Park. This site is surrounded by woodland and neighbouring farmland, and is very peaceful. Children are not admitted. A 4-acre site with 85 touring pitches, 20 hardstandings.

Facilities: ↖⊙✳🏭☐🐾
Services: 🔌🔋🖊⌀→∪▸✒🔧
Notes: Adults only, no fires, no noise 11pm-8am

EAST ALLINGTON   Map 03 SX74

▶ ▶ ▶ 73% **Mounts Farm Touring Park** (SX757488)
The Mounts TQ9 7QJ ☎ 01548 521591
✉ mounts.farm@lineone.net
Ⓦ www.mountsfarm.co.uk
Dir: From Totnes on A381 towards Dartmouth, beyond Kingsbridge (ignore signs for E Allington). Stay on A381 and Mounts Farm 0.5m on right.
★ 🚐 £12-£15 🚙 £12-£15 ⛺ £12-£15
Open 15 Mar-Oct Booking advisable bank hols & peak hol season Last arrival anytime Last departure flexible
A neat grassy park, no longer a working farm, divided into four paddocks by mature natural hedges. Three of the paddocks house the tourers and campers, and the fourth is the children's play area. There are adequate toilet facilities, and the laundry and well-stocked little shop are in converted farm buildings. A 7-acre site with 50 touring pitches.
Leisure: ⚠ **Facilities:** ↖⊙✳🐾
Services: 🔌🖊⌀🔋☐⊤→∪🔋↘⚕✒🔲
🔲 🚬 🅾️ 🔋 🔲 🔲 🔲

EAST ANSTEY   Map 03 SS82

▶ ▶ ▶ ▶ 81% **Zeacombe House Caravan Park** (SS860240)
Blackerton Cross EX16 9JU ☎ 01398 341279
✉ enquiries@zeacombeadultretreat.co.uk
Ⓦ www.zeacombeadultretreat.co.uk
Dir: M5 junct 27 onto A361 signed Barnstaple, turn right at next rdbt onto A396 signed Dulverton/Minehead. In 5m at Exeter Inn turn left onto B3227 towards South Molton, site in 7m on left
🚐 £14-£18 🚙 £14-£18 ⛺ £14-£18
Open 7 Mar-Oct Booking advisable BH's & Jul-Aug Last arrival 21.00hrs Last departure noon
Set on the southern fringes of Exmoor National Park, this 'garden' park is nicely landscaped in a tranquil location, and enjoys panoramic views towards Exmoor. This adult-only park offers a choice of grass or hardstanding pitches, and a unique restaurant-style delivery service allows you to eat an evening meal in the comfort of your own unit. A 5-acre site with 50 touring pitches, 12 hardstandings.
Off licence
Facilities: ↖⊙🔋✳⚙🔋🐾
Services: 🔌🚐🖊⌀☐⊤ ⚕→∪✒
Notes: Adults only 🔲 🚬 🔲 🔲 🔲

EAST WORLINGTON   Map 03 SS71

▶ ▶ ▶ ▶ 70% **Yeatheridge Farm Caravan Park** (SS768110)
EX17 4TN ☎ 01884 860330
✉ yeatheridge@talk21.com
Ⓦ www.yeatheridge.co.uk
Dir: M5 junct 27 onto A361, at 1st rdbt at Tiverton follow B3147 for 9m towards Witheridge. Fork left 1m past Nomansland onto B3042 & site on left in 3.5m. (Do not go to E Worlington.)
🚐 🚙 ⛺

Open Etr-Sep Booking advisable Etr, Spring bank hol & school hols Last arrival 22.00hrs Last departure 22.00hrs
Gently sloping grass site with mature trees, set in meadowland in rural Devon. There are good views of distant Dartmoor, and the site is of great appeal to families with its farm animals, horse riding, and two indoor swimming pools, one with flume. There are many attractive villages in this area. A 9-acre site with 85 touring pitches and 13 statics. Horse riding, fishing & pool table.
Leisure: 🎣 ⚓⚠☐
Facilities: ⚙↖⊙🔋✳⚙🔋🐾
Services: 🔌☐🔋🖊⌀☐⊤✕ ⚕→∪✒ 🔲 🚬 🔲

See advertisement under TIVERTON

EXETER
See **Kennford**

EXMOUTH   Map 03 SY08
See also **Woodbury Salterton**

 84% **Devon Cliffs Holiday Park** (SY036807)
Sandy Bay EX8 5BT
☎ 01395 226226 🖨 01395 223111
Ⓦ www.havenholidays.com
Dir: M5 junct 30/A376 towards Exmouth, follow brown signs to Sandy Bay
🚐 🚙 ⛺
Open mid Mar-Oct (rs mid Mar-May & Sep-Oct Some facilities may be reduced) Booking advisable School hols Last arrival 22.00hrs Last departure noon
A large and exciting holiday park on a hillside setting close to Exmouth, with spectacular views across Sandy Bay. The all-action park offers a superb entertainment programme for all ages throughout the day, with very modern sports and leisure facilities available for everyone.

contd.

A 163-acre site with 144 touring pitches and 2000 statics.
Leisure: ⚓ ⚓ ⚓ ⚓ ⚓ ⚓
Facilities: ⚓ ⚓
Services: ⚓ ⚓ ⚓ ⚓ ⚓ ⚓ ⚓ ⚓ ⚓ ⚓ ⚓ ⚓

▶ ▶ ▶ ▶ **83% Webbers Farm Caravan & Camping Park (SY018874)**
Castle Ln, Woodbury EX5 1EA
☎ 01395 232276 🖷 01395 233389
✉ reception@webberspark.co.uk
🌐 www.webberspark.co.uk
Dir: From M5 junct 30 take A376, then B3179 to Woodbury. Site 500yds E of village
⚓ £11-£18 ⚓ £11-£18 ▲ £11-£18
Open mid Mar-Oct Booking advisable peak season & BH's Last arrival 20.00hrs Last departure 11.00hrs
An unspoilt family park set in three areas, offering a quiet and relaxing touring location. A high quality toilet block provides ensuite family rooms and plenty of smart private facilities. The park has good views towards the Haldon Hills, and plenty to explore including 3,000 acres of Woodbury Common and nearby beaches. An 8-acre site with 115 touring pitches and 2 statics.
Pets corner, caravan storage facilities
Leisure: ⚓ **Facilities:** ⚓ ⚓ ⚓ ⚓ ⚓ ⚓ ⚓ ⚓ ⚓ ⚓ ⚓
Services: ⚓ ⚓ ⚓ ⚓ ⚓ ⚓ ⚓ ⚓ ⚓ ⚓
⚓ ⚓ ⚓ ⚓

▶ ▶ **76% St Johns Caravan & Camping Park (SY027834)**
St Johns Rd EX8 5EG ☎ 01395 263170
✉ st.johns.farm@amserve.net
Dir: M5 junct 30 follow A376/Exmouth signs. Left through Woodbury towards Budleigh Salterton on B3179 & B3180. Turn right 4m after Exmouth exit
★ ⚓ £9-£10 ⚓ £9-£10 ▲ £6-£10
Open mid Feb-Dec Booking advisable school summer hols Last arrival 22.00hrs Last departure noon
A quiet rural site with attractive country views, only 2 miles from Exmouth's sandy beaches, and half a mile from Woodbury Common. Owners are committed to upgrading the facilities over the next few years, and offer a warm welcome to visitors. A 6-acre site with 45 touring pitches, 5 hardstandings.
Farm shop
Leisure: ⚓ **Facilities:** ⚓ ⚓ ⚓ ⚓ ⚓ ⚓ ⚓ ⚓ ⚓
Services: ⚓ ⚓ ⚓ ⚓ ⚓ ⚓ ⚓ ⚓ ⚓ ⚓ ⚓
⚓ ⚓ ⚓ ⚓

HARTLAND — Map 02 SS22

▶ ▶ ▶ **71% Hartland Caravan & Camping Park (SS263243)**
South Ln EX39 6DG
☎ 01237 441242 & 441876 🖷 01237 441034
Dir: Leave A39 approx 0.25m past Clovelly road and take B3248 signed to Hartland. 3m after entering village park signed on left
⚓ ⚓ ▲
Open all year
A quiet family-run site on partly sloping ground, divided into four paddocks for privacy and shelter. It has good toilet facilities with baby-changing and family room, and a coarse fishing lake on site, plus a barbecue area. Village amenities just a short stroll away. A 6-acre site with 45 touring pitches and 2 statics.
Caravan storage all year
Leisure: ⚓ **Facilities:** ⚓ ⚓ ⚓
Services: ⚓ ⚓ ⚓ ⚓ ⚓ ⚓

HOLSWORTHY — Map 03 SS30

NEW ▶ **72% Noteworthy Caravan and Campsite (SS303052)**
Noteworthy, Bude Rd EX22 7JB ☎ 01409 253731
✉ jmsb.0603@virgin.net
Dir: on A3072 between Holsworthy & Bude. 3m from Holsworthy on right
★ ⚓ fr £8 ⚓ fr £8 ▲ fr £8

Open all year Booking advisable
A newly established campsite owned by a friendly young couple with their own small children. There are good views from the quiet rural location, and simple toilet facilities. A 5-acre site with 5 touring pitches.
Leisure: ⚓ **Facilities:** ⚓ ⚓ ⚓ ⚓
Services: ⚓ ⚓ ⚓ ⚓ ⚓ ⚓ **Notes:** No open fires

ILFRACOMBE — Map 03 SS54
See also **West Down**

NEW ▶ ▶ ▶ ▶ **80% Hele Valley Holiday Park (SS533472)**
Hele Bay EX34 9RD ☎ 01271 862460
🖷 01271 867926
✉ holidays@helevalley.co.uk
🌐 www.helevalley.co.uk
Dir: M5 junct 27 onto A36. Through Barnstaple & Braunton to Ilfracombe. Then A399 towards Combe Martin. Follow brown Hele Valley signs. 400mtrs sharp right, then to T-junct. Site on right
★ ⚓ ▲ £10-£17

contd.

Open Mar-Dec Booking advisable Last arrival
18.00hrs Last departure 11.00hrs
*A deceptively spacious park set in a picturesque
valley with glorious tree-lined hilly views from most
pitches. High quality new toilet facilities are
provided, and the park is close to a lovely beach,
with the harbour and other attractions of Ilfracombe
just a mile away. A 17-acre site with 12 touring
pitches and 80 statics.*

Leisure: ⚊

Facilities: ⬤⊙🔍✳⬤⬤🛒🚿🛎

Services: ⬤🛒⬤⬤⬤⬤↗⬤▶⬤⬤⬤⬤⬤
⬤ ⬤ ⬤ ⬤

Watermouth Cove Holiday Park

swimming. The site is two miles from both Combe
Martin and Ilfracombe. A 6-acre site with 90 touring
pitches, 10 hardstandings.
Coastal headland fishing.

Leisure: ⚊ ⬤ ⚊ ⬤

Facilities: ⬤⊙🔍✳⬤⬤🛒🚿🛎

Services: ⬤⬤⬤⬤⬤⬤⬤✗⬤↗⬤▶⬤⬤⬤⬤⬤
⬤ ⬤ ⬤ ⬤

► ► ► 71% Watermouth Cove Holiday Park
(SS558477)
Berrynarbor EX34 9SJ ☎ 01271 862504
🅴 info@watermouthcoveholidays.co.uk
🅦 www.watermouthcoveholidays.co.uk
*Dir: From M5 junct 27, take A361 to 2nd rdbt at South
Molton, then A399 through Coombe Martin. Turn left at
seafront & site 2m on right*
★ 🚐 £8-£24.70 🚙 £8-£24.70 ▲ £8-£24.70
Open Etr-Oct (rs Etr-Whit & Sep-Nov pool,
takeaway, club & shop limited) Booking advisable
Whit & Jul-Aug Last arrival anytime Last dep 11.00hrs
*A popular site in very attractive surroundings, set
amidst trees and bushes in meadowland with
access to sea, beach and main road. This beautiful
cove has a private sandy beach, and offers
launching for boats and other water craft, as well as*

contd.

KENNFORD   Map 03 SX98

► ► ► ► 73% Kennford International Caravan
Park (SX912857)
EX6 7YN ☎ 01392 833046 📠 01392 833046
🅴 ian@kennfordint.fsbusiness.co.uk
🅦 www.kennfordint.co.uk
*Dir: At end of M5, take A38, site signed at Kennford slip
road*
★ 🚐 £10-£12.70 🚙 £10-£12.70 ▲ £10-£12.70

Open all year Booking advisable Last arrival
21.00hrs Last departure 11.00hrs
*Screened by trees and shrubs from the A38, this
park offers many pitches divided by hedging for
privacy. A high quality toilet block complements the
park's facilities. A good, centrally-located base for
touring the coast and countryside of Devon, and
Exeter is easily accessible via a nearby bus stop. A
15-acre site with 127 touring pitches and 15 statics.*

Leisure: ⬤ ⚊

Facilities: ⬤⬤⊙🔍✳⬤⬤🛒🚿🛎

Services: ⬤⬤⬤⬤⬤✗→⬤▶⬤⬤⬤
⬤ ⬤ ⬤ ⬤

KENTISBEARE | Map 03 ST00

▶ ▶ ▶ ▶ **76% Forest Glade Holiday Park (ST100075)**
Cullompton EX15 2DT
☎ 01404 841381
🖷 01404 841593
✆ enquiries@forest-glade.co.uk
ⓦ www.forest-glade.co.uk

Dir: Tent traffic from A373, signed at Keepers Cottage Inn, 2.5m E of M5 junct 28. Touring caravans via Honiton/Dunkeswell road: phone for access details
🚐 £11.50-£15 🚐 £11.50-£15 ▲ £9.30-£12.75
Open 2 wks before Etr-end Oct (rs low season limited shop hours) Booking advisable school hols Last arrival 21.00hrs
A quiet, attractive park in a forest clearing with well-kept gardens and beech hedge screening. One of the main attractions is the immediate proximity of the forest, which offers magnificent hillside walks with surprising views over the valleys. Please telephone for route details. A 15-acre site with 80 touring pitches, 40 hardstandings and 57 statics.
Adventure play area & paddling/ball pools.

Leisure: ⚑ ⚙ 🏊 ⋀

Facilities: 🏧 ⊙ ⚑ ✳ ㏿ ₠ ⅃ 冎 ⵂ

Services: ☎ ⵜ 🖳 ⅈ ⌀ 🖵 ⏢ ⏢ → ∪ ⅃

Notes: Couples & families only

KENTISBURY | Map 03 SS64

▶ ▶ ▶ **83% Kentisbury Grange Country Park (SS628428)**
EX31 4NL ☎ 01271 883454
🖷 01271 882040
✆ info@kentisburygrange.co.uk
ⓦ www.kentisburygrange.co.uk
Dir: turn off A399 onto A39 towards Barnstaple, site 1m on right
★ 🚐 £10-£15 🚐 £10-£15 ▲ £9-£14
Open Etr-Oct Booking advisable mid Jul-mid Sep Last arrival 18.00hrs Last departure 11.00hrs
A country park set in seven acres of mature grounds on the fringe of Exmoor National Park, with extensive open countryside views. It offers a quiet base for nature lovers, and is located midway between Lynton/Lynmouth and Ilfracombe, close to Combe Martin. A 7-acre site with 20 touring pitches, 20 hardstandings.
TV hook ups

Facilities: 🏧 ⊙ ⚑ ㏿ ₠ ⅃ 冎

Services: ☎ ⵜ 🖳 ⅈ 🖵 → ∪ ⅃

Notes: Dogs on lead all times, no skateboarding, cycling or noisy ball games

LYDFORD | Map 03 SX58

▶ ▶ ▶ **70% Camping & Caravanning Club Site (SX512853)**
EX20 4BE ☎ 01822 820275
ⓦ www.campingandcaravanningclub.co.uk
Dir: From A30 take A386 signed to Tavistock & Lydford. Past Fox & Hounds on left, turn right at sign for Lydford. Right at war memorial, keep right to site in 200yds
★ 🚐 £13.60-£17.80 🚐 £13.60-£17.80 ▲ £13.60-£17.80
Open Mar-Oct Booking advisable bank hols & peak periods Last arrival 21.00hrs Last departure noon
Site on mainly level ground looking towards the western slopes of Dartmoor at the edge of the village, near the spectacular gorge. This popular park is close to the Devon coast to coast cycle route, between Tavistock and Okehampton. Please see advertisement on page 11 for information on Club sites and membership. A 7.75-acre site with 70 touring pitches.

Facilities: 🏧 ⊙ ⚑ ✳ ₠ 冎 ⵂ

Services: ☎ 🖳 ⅈ ⌀ 🖵 ⏢ → ∪ ⵗ ⅃ ₠

CHANNEL VIEW CARAVAN & CAMPING PARK

BARBROOK, LYNTON, NORTH DEVON EX35 6LD

Tel: (01598) 753349 Fax: (01598) 752777

www.channel-view.co.uk

Email: relax@channel-view.co.uk

A warm welcome awaits you at this quiet family run site, which is situated on the edge of Exmoor National Park, overlooking Lynton and Lynmouth and the Bristol Channel. With some of the most spectacular views in the area. First class camping and touring facilities. Electric hook-ups, fully serviced pitches, site shop, site café, public telephone, launderette. Dogs welcome.

LYNTON   **Map 03 SS74**
See also **Oare (Somerset)**

▶ ▶ ▶ ▶ 69% **Channel View Caravan and Camping Park** (SS724482)
Manor Farm EX35 6LD ☎ 01598 753349
▤ 01598 752777

➌ relax@channel-view.co.uk
ⓦ www.channel-view.co.uk
Dir: A39 E for 0.5m on left past Barbrook
★ ⊞ £8.50-£14 ⊞ £8-£13 ▲ £8-£13
Open 15 Mar-15 Nov Booking advisable Jul-Aug Last arrival 22.00hrs Last departure noon
On the top of the cliffs overlooking the Bristol Channel, a well-maintained park on the edge of Exmoor, and close to both Lynton and Lynmouth. Pitches can be selected from a hidden hedged area, or with panoramic views over the coast. A 6-acre site with 76 touring pitches, 15 hardstandings and 36 statics.
Parent & baby room
Leisure: ⚠ **Facilities:** ➜ ♟ ☉ ☜ ✻ ⎙ ⛽ ☃
Services: ☎ ⛟ ⛽ ⛾ ⌀ ☰ ⊞ ✕ → ∪ ☺ ☖ ☙ ✈
Notes: Groups by prior arrangement only
⬛ ⬛ ⬛ ⬛ ⬛

▶ ▶ ▶ 72% **Camping & Caravanning Club Site** (SS700484)
Caffyns Cross EX35 6JS ☎ 01598 752379
ⓦ www.campingandcaravanningclub.co.uk
Dir: M5 junct 27 onto A361 to Barnstable. Turn right to Blackmoor Gate signed Lynmouth & Lynton. Approx 5m to Caffyns Cross, immediately right to site in 1m
★ ⊞ £12.40-£16.70 ⊞ £12.40-£16.70 ▲ £12.40-£16.70
Open Mar-Oct Booking advisable bank hols & peak periods Last arrival 21.00hrs Last departure noon
Set on high ground with excellent views over the Bristol Channel, and close to the twin resorts of Lynton & Lynmouth. This area is known as Little Switzerland because of its wooded hills, and the park is ideal for walking, and cycling on the nearby National Cycle Network. Please see the advertisement on page 11 for information on Club sites and membership. A 5.5-acre site with 105 touring pitches, 10 hardstandings.
Leisure: ⚠ **Facilities:** ➜ ☉ ♟ ✻ ⛽ ☃ ☃
Services: ☎ ⛟ ⛽ ⛾ ⌀ ⊞ ⊞ → ∪ ☖ ● ⬛ ⬛ ⬛ ⬛

▶ ▶ ▶ 76% **Sunny Lyn Holiday Park** (SS719486)
Lynbridge EX35 6NS
☎ 01598 753384 ▤ 01598 753273
➌ info@caravandevon.co.uk
ⓦ www.caravandevon.co.uk
Dir: M5 junct 27 onto A361 to South Molton. Right onto A399 to Blackmoor Gate, right onto A39, left onto B3234 towards Lynmouth. Site 1m on right
★ ⊞ £12.50-£13 ⊞ £12.50-£13 ▲ £10.50-£11

Open Mar-Oct (rs Mar-Dec Log cabins open)
Booking advisable Etr, spring bank hol & mid Jul-Aug Last arrival 20.00hrs Last departure 11.00hrs
Set in a sheltered riverside location in a wooded combe within a mile of the sea, in Exmoor National Park. This family-run park offers good facilities including an excellent café. A 4.5-acre site with 37 touring pitches, 4 hardstandings and 31 statics.
Table tennis & trout fishing
Facilities: ➜ ☉ ♟ ✻ ⛽ ☃ ☃
Services: ☎ ⛽ ⛾ ⌀ ⊞ ✕ ⛟ → ∪ ☺ ☖ ☙ ✈
⬛ ⬛ ⬛ ⬛ ⬛

Practise setting up your tent at home before you take it on holiday, and check that all guy ropes, pegs and poles are present and intact.

Remember that prices and opening times are liable to change within the currency of this guide. It is always best to telephone in advance.

Services: ⊤ Toilet Fluid ✕ Café/ Restaurant ⛽ Fast Food/Takeaway ➜ Baby Care ☺ Electric Hook Up
⛟ Motorvan Service Point ⊟ Launderette ☖ Licensed Bar ⛽ Calor Gaz ⌀ Camping Gaz ⊞ Battery Charging

MODBURY   Map 03 SX65

▶ ▶ ▶ 79% **Camping & Caravanning Club Site**
(SX705530)
PL21 0SG ☎ 01548 821297
Ⓦ www.campingandcaravanningclub.co.uk
*Dir: Leave A38 at Wrangton Cross onto A3121, continue
to x-rds. Cross over onto B3196, left after California
Cross sign before petrol station, site on right*
★ ⊕ £12.40-£16.70 ⊕ £12.40-£16.70 ▲ £12.40-£16.70
Open Apr-Oct Booking advisable bank hols & peak
periods Last arrival 21.00hrs Last departure noon
*A gently sloping site with some terracing, set in a
rural location midway between Ivybridge and
Kingsbridge. This well ordered site is protected by
high hedging, and is an ideal base for exploring the
lovely South Devon countryside. Please see
advertisement on page 11 for information on
Club sites and membership. A 3.75-acre site with
80 touring pitches, 11 hardstandings.*

Leisure: � Facilities: ❘ⓧ⦿⦿❉✻ⓒⓒ⛁
Services: ⊞⛽⛟⓪◫⌸⊞⊡→U⚡⚡⛾⛾ ▒▒ ▒▒ ⑨

▶ ▶ ▶ 89% **Moor View Touring Park**
(SX705533)
California Cross PL21 0SG
☎ 01548 821485 ▤ 01548 821485
Ⓔ info@moorviewtouringpark.co.uk
Ⓦ www.moorviewtouringpark.co.uk
*Dir: Leave A38 at Wrangaton Cross, turn left at top of
slip road onto B3121. Over x-rds for 4m past petrol
station. Park 0.5m*
★ ⊕ £8.85-£17.85 ⊕ £8.85-£17.85 ▲ £8.85-£9.85
Open all year Booking advisable Last arrival
18.00hrs Last departure 11.00hrs
*A compact terraced park in picturesque South
Hams, with wide views of Dartmoor. Many pitches
are divided by low mature hedging, and most are
hardstandings with electricity, water and grey
waste. The excellent facilities include a bright,
modern toilet block, and a games room/TV lounge.
The park is for adults only. A 5.5-acre site with
68 touring pitches, 65 hardstandings.*

Leisure: ⚘⛛ Facilities: ❘ⓧ⦿⦿❉ⓒⓒⒹⓜ⛾
Services: ⊞⛽⛟◫⌸⊞⊡▥→U▸⚡⛾ ▒▒ ▒▒ ⑨

▶ ▶ ▶ 72% **Pennymoor Camping & Caravan Park**
(SX685516)
PL21 0SB ☎ 01548 830542 & 830020 ▤ 01548 830542
Ⓔ enquiries@pennymoor-camping.co.uk
Ⓦ www.pennymoor-camping.co.uk
*Dir: Leave A38 at Wrangaton Cross. Turn left & straight
over x-roads. Then 4m, pass petrol station & 2nd left.
Site 1.5m on right*
★ ⊕ £6-£12 ⊕ £5-£9 ▲ £6-£12
Open 15 Mar-15 Nov (rs 15 Mar-mid May 1 toilet &
shower block only open) Booking advisable Jul-Aug
Last arrival 20.00hrs Last departure noon
*A well-established rural park on gently sloping
grass with good views over distant Dartmoor and
the countryside in between. The park is very
carefully tended, and has a relaxing atmosphere. A
new toilet block is planned for 2006. A 12.5-acre site
with 145 touring pitches and 76 statics.*

Leisure: ⚫ Facilities: ❘ⓧ⦿⦿❉✻ⓒⓒ⛾
Services: ⊞⛽◫⌸⊞⊡→U⚡

MOLLAND   Map 03 SS82

▶ ▶ ▶ 74% **Yeo Valley Holiday Park**
(SS788265)
EX36 3NW ☎ 01769 550297
▤ 01769 550101
Ⓔ info@yeovalleyholidays.com
Ⓦ www.yeovalleyholidays.com
*Dir: From A361 onto B3227 towards Bampton. Follow
brown signs for Blackcock Inn. Site opposite*
★ ⊕ £9-£13.50 ⊕ £9-£13.50 ▲ £9-£13.50
Open all year (rs Sep-Mar swimming pool closed)
Booking advisable Jul-Aug Last arrival 22.30hrs Last
departure 10.00hrs
*Set in a beautiful secluded valley on the edge of
Exmoor National Park, this family-run park has easy
access to both the moors and the North Devon
coastline. The park is adjacent to the Blackcock Inn
(under the same ownership), and has a very good
heated indoor pool. A 7-acre site with 65 touring
pitches, 16 hardstandings.*
Fishing lake & bike hire

Leisure: ⚞ ⚫ ⚫⛛ Facilities: ❘ⓧ⦿⦿❉✻ⓒⓒⓜ⛾
Services: ⊞⛽⛟⚷⛟◫X→U⚡⛾ ▒▒ ▒▒ ⑨

England

MORTEHOE   Map 03 SS44
See also **West Down & Woolacombe**

72% Twitchen Parc (SS465447)
Station Rd EX34 7ES
☎ 01271 870343 ▤ 01271 870089
🅔 goodtimes@woolacombe.com
Ⓦ www.woolacombe.com
*Dir: From Mullacott Cross rdbt take B3343
(Woolacombe road) to Turnpike Cross junct.
Take right fork, site 1.5m on left*
★ ⊞ £14-£47.50 ⊞ £14-£47.50 ▲ £9-£30
Open Mar-Oct Booking advisable Etr/Whit &
Jul-Aug Last arrival mdnt Last departure
10.00hrs
*A very attractive park with good leisure facilities.
Visitors can use the amenities at all three of
Woolacombe Bay holiday parks, and a bus
service connects them all with the beach. The
touring areas features pitches offering either sea
views or a country and woodland outlook.
A 45-acre site with 334 touring pitches,
110 hardstandings and 278 statics.*
Table tennis, sauna, bus to beach, kids' club
Leisure: ⚑ ⚓ ♦ 🎱 ▢
Facilities: 🏪 ⊙ ℚ ✳ 🚿 ☕ 🧺 ⛱ 🔥 🐾
Services: 🔌 🗑 🍴 ⛽ 🏧 ⊞ ▣ ✕ 🛒 → ∪ ▶ ◎ △ ♨ ☎ 🗑 ⚓
💳 ▭▭ ▭▭ ▭▭ 🗲

▶ ▶ ▶ **72% Easewell Farm Holiday Parc & Golf
Club (SS465455)**
EX34 7EH ☎ 01271 870343 ▤ 01271 870089
🅔 goodtimes@woolacombe.com
Ⓦ www.woolacombe.com
*Dir: From Mullacott Cross take B3343 to Mortehoe. Turn
right at fork, site 2m on right*
★ ⊞ £14-£47.50 ⊞ £14-£47.50 ▲ £9-£30
Open Etr-Oct (rs Etr no shop) Booking advisable Jul-
Aug, Etr, Whitsun Last arrival 22.00hrs Last
departure 10.00hrs
*A peaceful clifftop park with full facility pitches for
caravans and motorhomes, and superb views. The
park offers a range of activities including indoor
bowling and a golf course, and all the facilities of
the three other nearby holiday centres within this
group are open to everyone. A 17-acre site with
302 touring pitches, 50 hardstandings.*
9-hole golf on site, indoor bowls, snooker
Leisure: ⚑ ♦ ⚠ Facilities: 🏪 ⊙ ℚ ✳ 🚿 ☕ 🧺 ⛱ 🔥
Services: 🔌 🗑 🍴 ⛽ 🏧 ⊞ ▣ ✕ 🛒 → ∪ ▶ ◎ △ ♨ ☎
💳 ▭▭ ▭▭ ▭▭ 🗲

See advertisement under WOOLACOMBE

▶ ▶ ▶ **82% North Morte Farm Caravan &
Camping Park (SS462455)**
North Morte Rd EX34 7EG ☎ 01271 870381
▤ 01271 870115
🅔 info@northmortefarm.co.uk
Ⓦ www.northmortefarm.co.uk
*Dir: Turn off B3343 into Mortehoe, then right at post
office. Park 500yds on left*
★ ⊞ £11-£18.50 ⊞ £10-£18.50 ▲ £10-£14
Open Etr-Sep (rs Oct Caravan owners only) Booking

North Morte Farm Caravan & Camping Park
advisable school hols Last arrival 22.30hrs Last
departure noon
*Set in spectacular coastal countryside close to
National Trust land and 500yds from Rockham
Beach. This attractive park is very well run and
maintained by friendly family owners, and the
quaint village of Mortehoe with its cafés, shops and
pubs is just a 5 minute walk away. A 22-acre site
with 180 touring pitches, 14 hardstandings and
73 statics.*
Leisure: ⚠ Facilities: 🏪 ⊙ ℚ ✳ ☕ 🧺 ⛱ 🔥
Services: 🔌 🗑 🍴 🏧 ⊞ → ∪ ▶ ☎
Notes: No large groups, dogs must be on lead at all
times 💳 ▭▭ ▭▭ 🗲

▶ ▶ ▶ **84% *Warcombe Farm Caravan
& Camping Park (SS478445)***
Station Rd EX34 7EJ
☎ 01271 870690 & 07774 428770
▤ 01271 871070
🅔 info@warcombefarm.co.uk
Ⓦ www.warcombefarm.co.uk
*Dir: N towards Mortehoe from Mullacot Cross rdbt at
A361 junct with B3343. Site 2m on right*
⊞ ⊞ ▲
Open 15 Mar-Oct Booking advisable Jul & Aug Last
arrival 10.00hrs Last departure noon
*Extensive views over the Bristol Channel can be
enjoyed from the open areas of this attractive park,
while other pitches are sheltered in paddocks with
maturing trees. The superb sandy beach with Blue
Flag award at Woolacombe Bay is only 1.5m away,
and there is a fishing lake with direct access from
some pitches. A 19-acre site with 100 touring
pitches, 5 hardstandings.*
Private fishing.
Leisure: ⚠
Facilities: ➔ 🏪 ⊙ ℚ ✳ ☕ 🧺 ⛱ 🔥
Services: 🔌 ⛽ 🗑 🍴 🏧 ⊞ ▣ ✕ 🛒 → ∪ ▶ ◎ ♨ ☎
Notes: No groups unless booked in advance
💳 ▬ ▭▭ ▭▭ 🗲

Remember to check your tent or
caravan thoroughly before leaving home
to ensure everything is in good order.

---

contd.

NEWTON ABBOT
See also **Bickington**

Map 03 SX87

PREMIER PARK

▶ ▶ ▶ ▶ ▶ 86% **Dornafield**
(SX838683)
Dornafield Farm, Two Mile Oak
TQ12 6DD ☎ 01803 812732
🖷 01803 812032
✆ enquiries@dornafield.com
ⓦ www.dornafield.com
Dir: Take A381 (Newton Abbot-Totnes) for 2m. At Two Mile Oak Inn turn right, then left at x-roads in 0.5m to site on right
★ ♣ £11.50-£18 ♣ £11.50-£18 ▲ £18

Open Mar-Oct Booking advisable bank hols & Jul-Aug Last arrival 22.00hrs Last departure 11.00hrs
An excellent park in a secluded wooded valley setting, with well laid out pitches and a peaceful atmosphere. A lovely 15th-century farmhouse sits at the entrance, and reception and the shop are housed in converted barns around a courtyard. The park is divided into three separate areas, served by two modern, heated toilet blocks, and the friendly family owners are always available. A 30-acre site with 135 touring pitches, 82 hardstandings.
Caravan storage (all year)

Leisure: ⚲ ⚑ ⚏ **Facilities:** ⌂ ⊙ ☖ ✳ ⚓ ℃ ⚑ ⚏ ♅
Services: ⚑ ⚏ ⚐ ⚓ ◑ ⊞ ⊤ ⚑ → ∪ ▶ ♨ ✦
⚫ ⚌ ⚑ ⚏

PREMIER PARK

▶ ▶ ▶ ▶ ▶ 95% **Ross Park**
(SX845671)
Park Hill Farm, Ipplepen TQ12 5TT
☎ 01803 812983 🖷 01803 812983
✆ enquiries@rossparkcaravanpark.co.uk
ⓦ www.rossparkcaravanpark.co.uk
Dir: Off A381, 3m from Newton Abbot towards Totnes, signed opposite Jet garage towards 'Woodland'
★ ♣ £11.50-£17.95 ♣ £11.50-£17.95
▲ £10.50-£16.95
Open end Feb-1 Jan (rs Nov-Feb & 1st 3wks of Mar Restaurant/bar closed (ex Xmas/New Year)) Booking advisable Jul, Aug & BH's Last arrival 21.00hrs Last departure 10.00hrs
A top-class park in every way, with large secluded pitches, high quality toilet facilities and

contd.

Ross Park

lovely floral displays throughout the 26 acres. The beautiful tropical conservatory also offers a breathtaking show of colour. This very rural park enjoys superb views of Dartmoor, and good quality meals to suit all tastes and pockets are served in the restaurant. A 26-acre site with 110 touring pitches, 82 hardstandings.
Snooker, table tennis, badminton, croquet.

Leisure: ⚲ ⚑ ⚏
Facilities: ⌂ ⊙ ☖ ✳ ⚓ ℃ ⚑ ⚏ ♅
Services: ⚑ ⚏ ⚐ ⚓ ◑ ⊞ ⊤ ✗ ⚑ → ∪ ▶ ♨ ✦

▶ ▶ ▶ 78% *Twelve Oaks Farm Caravan Park*
(SX852737)
Teigngrace TQ12 6QT ☎ 01626 352769
🖷 01626 352769
✆ info@twelveoaksfarm.co.uk
ⓦ www.twelveoaksfarm.co.uk
Dir: A38 from Exeter left signed Teigngrace (only), 0.25m before Drumbridges rdbt. 1.5m, through village, site on left. From Plymouth pass Drumbridges rdbt, take slip road for Chudleigh Knighton. Right over bridge, rejoin A38 towards Plymouth. Left for Teigngrace (only), then as above
♣ ♣ ▲

Open all year Booking advisable Last arrival 21.00hrs Last departure 11.00hrs
An attractive small park on a working farm close to Dartmoor National Park, and bordered by the River Teign. The tidy pitches are located amongst trees and shrubs, and the modern facilities are very well maintained. Children will enjoy all the farm animals, and nearby is the Templar Way walking route. A 2-acre site with 35 touring pitches, 17 hardstandings.

Leisure: ⚲ **Facilities:** ⌂ ⊙ ☖ ✳ ⚓ ℃ ⚑
Services: ⚑ ◑ → ∪ ▶ ♨ ✦ ⚐ ⚫ ⚌ ⚑

PAIGNTON	Map 03 SX86

82% Beverley Parks Caravan & Camping Park
(SX886582)
Goodrington Rd TQ4 7JE
☎ 01803 661979 📠 01803 845427
ⓔ info@beverley-holidays.co.uk
ⓦ www.beverley-holidays.co.uk
Dir: On A380/A3022, 2m S of Paignton turn left into Goodrington Rd
🚐 £13.50-£30.80 🚐 £13.50-£30.80
⛺ £8.50-£24.50
Open Feb-Nov Booking advisable Jun-Sep Last arrival 22.00hrs Last departure 10.00hrs
A high quality family-run park with extensive views of the bay, and plenty of on-site amenities. The park boasts indoor and outdoor heated swimming pools, and the toilet facilities are very modern and clean. The park complex is attractively laid out. A 12-acre site with 187 touring pitches, 36 hardstandings and 190 statics.
Table tennis, pool, spa bath, crazy golf, sauna.
Leisure: ⚓ 🎣 ⚘ 🎱 ♨
Facilities: ➡ ♠ ⊙ ⚑ ✳ ♿ 🍴 ⛽ 🎪
Services: 🔌 🅾 💧 🚽 🗑 👶 ➡ ∪ 🍴 ⊙ ♨ 🛒 ♨ ⚓
Notes: ❌ 🐕 ⬛ ⬛ ⬛ 🏴 🇬

▶ ▶ ▶ ▶ **78% Widend Touring Park**
(SX852619)
Berry Pomeroy Rd, Marldon TQ3 1RT
☎ 01803 550116 📠 01803 550116
Dir: Signed from Torbay ring road
🚐 🚐 ⛺

Open Apr-end Sep (rs Apr-mid May & mid Sep swimming pool & club house closed) Booking advisable Jul-Aug & Whit Last arrival 21.00hrs Last departure 10.00hrs
A terraced grass park paddocked and screened on high ground overlooking Torbay with views of Dartmoor. This attractive park is well laid out, divided up by mature trees and bushes but with plenty of open grassy areas. Facilities are of a high standard and offer a heated outdoor swimming pool with sunbathing area, a small lounge bar and a well-stocked shop. A 22-acre site with 207 touring pitches, 6 hardstandings.
Leisure: ⚓ 🎣 ♨
Facilities: ♠ ⊙ ✳ ♿ 🍴 🐾 🎪
Services: 🔌 🅾 💧 🗑 🚽 🗑 👶 ➡ ∪ 🍴 ⊙ ♨ 🛒 ♨ 🍴
Notes: No dogs mid Jul-Aug ⬛ ⬛ ⬛ 🏴 🇬

NEW ▶ ▶ ▶ **69% Barton Pines (SX847611)**
Blagdon Rd TQ3 3YG ☎ 01803 553350
Dir: From A380 (Torbay ring road) at 2nd rdbt follow Marldon signs. At next rdbt 2nd left into Five Lanes (Singmore Hotel on corner) towards Pomeroy & Totnes. Follow brown site signs (approx 1m)
🚐 Open all year
Set in the grounds of a beautiful country manor

contd.

Barton Pines

house amidst pine trees, this quiet park has a relaxed atmosphere, and modern toilet facilities. The very rural location is within easy reach of the beach and coast of Torbay. A 4-acre site with 33 touring pitches.

Facilities: ⚕ → ▥

► ► ► **85% Byslades International Touring & Camping Park (SX853603)**
Totnes Rd TQ4 7PY ☎ 01803 555072
🖷 01803 555669
🅰 info@byslades.co.uk
🌐 www.byslades.co.uk
Dir: on A385, halfway between Paignton & Totnes
★ ⚏ £6-£11.50 ⚏ £6-£11.50 ⚊ £6-£13
Open Whit-Aug BH (rs May & Sep bar & swimming pool closed) Booking advisable Jul-Aug Last arrival 18.00hrs Last departure 10.00hrs
A well-kept terraced park in beautiful countryside,
contd.

only 2m from Paignton. It offers a good mix of amenities, and a licensed club with high season entertainment, plus a children's playground, and large heated outdoor swimming pool with special area for toddlers. A 23-acre site with 190 touring pitches, 40 hardstandings.
Crazy golf.

Leisure: ⚘ ⚘ ⚘ ⚙   **Facilities:** ⚕ ⊙ ⚒ ✳ ⚕ ⚕ ⚒ ⚔ ⚔
Services: ⚏ ⚏ ⚏ ⚏ ⚏ ⚏ ⚏ ✕ ⚏ → ⚑ ⚏ ⚏ ⚏ ⚏
Notes: No commercial vehicles, no dogs mid Jul-Aug ⚏ ⚏ ⚏ ⚏ ⚏

NEW ► ► ► 80% Whitehill Country Park (SX857588)
Stoke Rd TQ4 7PF ☎ 01803 782338 🖷 01803 782722
🅰 info@whitehill-park.co.uk
🌐 www.whitehill-park.co.uk
★ ⚏ £11.50-£22 ⚏ £11.50-£22 ⚊ £9.50-£16
Open 13 Apr-Sep Booking advisable Jul-Aug Last arrival 21.00hrs Last departure 10.00hrs
A family-owned and run park set in rolling countryside, with many scenic beaches just a short drive away. This extensive country park covers 40 acres with woodland walks, and plenty of flora and fauna. It offers ideal facilities for an excellent holiday. A 40-acre site with 260 touring pitches and 60 statics.

Leisure: ⚘ ⚘ ⚙ ⚏   **Facilities:** ⚒ ✳ ⚕ ⚕
Services: ⚏ ⚏ ⚏ ⚏ ⚏ ✕ ⚏ → ⚌ ⚑ ⊙ ⚏ ⚏ ⚏ ⚏ ⚏
Notes: ⚏ ⚏ ⚏ ⚏ ⚏ ⚏

Leisure: ⚘ Indoor swimming pool ⚘ Outdoor swimming pool ⚘ Tennis court ⚘ Games room ⚙ Children's playground ⚌ Stables
► 9/18 hole golf course ⚏ Boats for hire ⚏ Cinema ⚏ Fishing ⊙ Mini golf ⚏ Watersports ⚏ Separate TV room

England

RIVERSIDE
CARAVAN PARK
Longbridge Road, Marsh Mills, Plymouth
Telephone: Plymouth (01752) 344122

"The award-winning touring park that'll stop you touring!"

"Riverside" the conveniently situated, secluded, countryside park has all the amenities, scenery, and relaxed atmosphere that will make you want to stay for the rest of your holiday. Surrounded by woodlands, and bordered by the River Plym, this pleasant site has the luxury of permanent facilities without losing the country charm.

Within a short distance you can also reach the freedom of Dartmoor, the shops and history of Plymouth, and the fun of many beaches and coves. The numerous sports, activities and attractions of the whole area mean "Riverside" can be the centre of a complete holiday experience. Ring or write for details.

★ Bar, Restaurant and Takeaway ★ Heated swimming pool ★ Games room ★ TV room and play areas ★ Shop and Telephone ★ Coffee bar ★ Off licence ★ Level pitches ★ Electricity ★ Tarmac roads ★ Street lights ★ Toilet and shower blocks ★ Laundry and dishwashing facilities ★ Special over 50's rates.

PLYMOUTH	Map 03 SX45

► ► ► ► 78% *Riverside Caravan Park*
(SX515575)
Leigham Manor Dr PL6 8LL ☎ 01752 344122
🖷 01752 344122
🌐 info@riversidecaravanpark.com
🆆 www.riversidecaravanpark.com
Dir: A38 follow signs at Marsh Mills rdbt, take 3rd exit, then left. 400yds turn right (keep River Plym on right) to park
🚐🚙▲

Open all year (rs Oct-Etr Bar, Restaurant & Take-away closed) Booking advisable Jun-Aug Last arrival 22.00hrs Last departure 10.00hrs
A well-groomed site on the outskirts of Plymouth on the banks of the River Plym, in a quiet location surrounded by woodland. The toilet facilities are to a very good standard, and include private cubicles. This park is an ideal stopover for the ferries to

contd.

France, and makes an excellent base for touring Dartmoor and the coast. An 11-acre site with 293 touring pitches.
Leisure: ⚡🎱⛰️🏊 Facilities: 🚻☉🍴✳️♿🐕🏹
Services: 🚰🔌🅿️🛢️🚿🚽🛒✕ 💧→ᑌ🅿️☺🔥🔥⚡🐾🍴
🍺 🍽️ 🎫 🔊

PRINCETOWN	Map 03 SX57

NEW ► ► 76% **The Plume of Feathers Inn** (SX592734)
Plymouth PL20 6QQ ☎ 01822 890240
Dir: Site accessed directly from B3212 rdbt (beside Plume of Feathers Inn) in centre of Princetown
🚐 fr £9 ▲ fr £9

Open all year
Set amidst the rugged beauty of Dartmoor not far from the notorious prison, this campsite boasts new toilet facilities and all the amenities of the inn. The Plume of Feathers is Princetown's oldest building, and serves all day food in an atmospheric setting. The campsite is mainly for tents. A 3-acre site with 85 touring pitches.
Facilities: 🚻 Notes: No caravans

SALCOMBE	Map 03 SX73

► ► ► 71% *Bolberry House Farm Caravan & Camping Park (SX687395)*
Bolberry TQ7 3DY ☎ 01548 561251
🌐 bolberry.house@virgin.net
🆆 www.bolberryparks.co.uk
Dir: At Malborough on A381 turn right signed Hope Cove/Bolberry. Take left fork after village signed Soar/Bolberry. 0.6m right again. Site signed in 0.5m
🚐🚙▲

Open Etr-Oct Booking advisable Jun-Sep Last arrival 20.00hrs Last departure 11.00hrs
A level, well maintained family run park in peaceful setting on coastal farm with sea views, fine cliff

contd.

walks and nearby beaches. Discount in low season for senior citizens. A 6-acre site with 70 touring pitches and 10 statics.
Children's play area & play barn.

Leisure: ⚲ **Facilities:** ⬡☉🕊✳🔥⛟🛒🐕
Services: 🔌🔋💧🛢🏪🗓→∪❙◉♨🚻♨🔧

► ► ► **71% Higher Rew Caravan & Camping Park** (SX714383)
Higher Rew, Malborough TQ7 3BW ☎ 01548 842681
📠 01548 843681
✉ enquiries@higherrew.co.uk
ⓦ www.higherrew.co.uk
Dir: Follow A381 to Marlborough. Turn right at Townsend Cross & follow signs to Soar for 1m. Left at Rew Cross
🚐 £8-£14 🚐 £8-£14 ▲ £7-£12
Open Etr-Oct Booking advisable Spring bank hol & mid Jul-Aug Last arrival 22.00hrs Last departure noon
A long-established park in a remote location in sight of the sea. The spacious, open touring field has some tiered pitches in the sloping grass, and there are lovely countryside or sea views from every pitch. Friendly family owners are continually improving the facilities. A 5-acre site with 85 touring pitches.
Play barn

Leisure: ⚲ ♣ **Facilities:** ⬡☉🕊✳🔥⛟🛒🐕
Services: 🔌🔋💧🛢🏪🗓→∪♨🔧 **Notes:** No groups of young people in peak season.

► ► ► **76% *Karrageen Caravan & Camping Park*** (SX686395)
Bolberry, Malborough TQ7 3EN ☎ 01548 561230
📠 01548 560192
✉ phil@karrageen.co.uk
ⓦ www.karrageen.co.uk
Dir: At Malborough on A381, turn sharp right through village, after 0.6m right again, after 0.9m site on right.
🚐🚐▲

Open 15 Mar-Sep Booking advisable bank & school hols Last arrival 21.00hrs Last departure 11.30hrs
A small friendly, family-run park with terraced grass pitches giving extensive sea and country views. There is a varied takeaway menu available every evening, and a well-stocked shop. This park is just 1m from the beach and pretty hamlet of Hope Cove. A 7.5-acre site with 70 touring pitches and 25 statics.
Baby room, licensed shop, 2 play areas, family shower

Facilities: ⬡☉🕊✳⛟🛒🚿
Services: 🔌🔋💧🛢🏪🗓 ♨→♨🔧

► ► **68% Alston Farm Camping & Caravan Site** (SX716406)
Malborough, Kingsbridge TQ7 3BJ ☎ 01548 561260 & 0780 803 0921 📠 01548 561260
✉ alston.campsite@ukgateway.net
ⓦ www.welcome.to/alstonfarm
Dir: 1.5m W of town off A381 towards Malborough
★ 🚐 £8-£10.50 🚐 £7-£10.50 ▲ £7-£8.50
Open 15 Mar-Oct Booking advisable Aug
An established farm site in a rural location adjacent to the Kingsbridge/Salcombe estuary. The site is well sheltered and screened, and approached down a long well-surfaced narrow farm lane with passing places. The toilet facilities are basic. A 16-acre site with 90 touring pitches and 58 statics.

Leisure: ⚲ **Facilities:** ⬡☉🕊✳⛟🛒🐎🐕
Services: 🔌💧🛢🏪🗓→∪❙♨🔧🚻🔧◉

SAMPFORD PEVERELL   **Map 03 ST01**

► ► ► ► **85% Minnows Touring Park** (SS042148)
Holbrook Ln EX16 7EN
☎ 01884 821770 📠 01884 829199
ⓦ www.ukparks.co.uk/minnows
Dir: From M5 junct 27 take A361 signed Tiverton and Barnstaple, after 600yds take 1st slip rd, then turn right over bridge, site ahead
★ 🚐 £10.60-£18.60 🚐 £10.60-£18.60 ▲ £8.60-£16.60
Open 6 Mar-13 Nov Booking advisable bank hols & Jun-Sep Last arrival 20.00hrs Last departure 11.30hrs
A small, well-sheltered park, peacefully located amidst fields and mature trees. The toilet facilities are of a high quality in keeping with the rest of the park, and there is a good laundry. The park has direct gated access to the canal towpath. A 5.5-acre site with 45 touring pitches, 34 hardstandings and 1 static.
Tourist Info Centre

Leisure: ⚲ **Facilities:** ⬡☉🕊✳⛟&🎣🐕
Services: 🔌♨🔋💧🛢🏪🗓→♨🔧⛟
Notes: No cycling, no groundsheets on the grass

SEATON
See **Colyton**

SHALDON   **Map 03 SX97**

NEW **71% Coast View Holiday Park** (SX935716)
Torquay Rd TQ14 0BG
☎ 01626 872392
Dir: from M5 junct 31 take A38 then A380 towards Torquay. Then A381 towards Teignmouth. Right in 4m at lights, over Shaldon Bridge. 0.75m, up hill, site on right
🚐▲
Open mid Mar-mid Jan
This park has stunning coast and sea views from both its level terraced pitches and slightly sloping grass pitches. The family-run park has a full entertainment programme every night for all the family, plus outdoor and indoor activities for

---

Facilities: 🛁 Bath 🕊 Shower ☉ Electric Shaver 🕊 Hairdryer ✳ Ice Pack Facility & Disabled Facilities 🔧 Public Telephone
🛒 Shop on Site or within 200yds 🗓 Mobile Shop (calls at least 5 days a week) 🍖 BBQ Area 🏕 Picnic Area 🐕 Dog Exercise Area

Coast View Holiday Park

children, and will appeal to lively families.
A 3-acre site with 186 touring pitches.

Facilities: 🛈

Caravan & Camping Park,
Salcombe Regis, Sidmouth,
Devon EX10 0PD
Tel:/Fax: 01297 680313
Web: www.ukparks.co.uk/kingsdowntail
E-mail: info@kingsdowntail.co.uk

A quiet, tree sheltered park personally operated by the
proprietors Ian & Sue McKenzie-Edwards

- Ideal centre to explore East Devon
- Easy Access
- Free hot showers
- Games room & childrens play area
- Secure caravan storage available

Coloured brochure on request

Devon's Coast & Countryside ...

simply different

SIDMOUTH   Map 03 SY18

▶ ▶ ▶ ▶ **81% Oakdown Touring &
Holiday Home Park (SY167902)**
Weston EX10 0PH ☎ 01297 680387
🗎 01297 680541
🅔 enquiries@oakdown.co.uk
🅦 www.oakdown.co.uk
Dir: Off A3052, 2.5m E of junct with A375
★ 🚐 £9.30-£22.20 🚗 £9.30-£22.20 ▲ £9.30-£17
Open Apr-Oct Booking advisable Spring bank hol &
Jul-Aug Last arrival 22.00hrs Last departure
10.30hrs
*Friendly, well-maintained park with good
landscaping and plenty of maturing trees. Pitches*

contd.

---

*are grouped in paddocks surrounded by shrubs,
and the park is well screened from the A3502. The
park's conservation areas with their natural flora
and fauna offer attractive walks, and there is a hide
by the Victorian reed bed for both casual and
dedicated bird watchers. A 13-acre site with 100
touring pitches, 90 hardstandings and 62 statics.
Free use of microwave.*

Leisure: 🅰 ⌧

Facilities: ➡ 🛈 ⊙ 🟡 ✳ ⅋ ⅃ 🛖 🏚 🖈

Services: 🔌 🖳 🖥 🛢 ⌀ 🗔 🅣 ✗ ➡ ➜ ∪ ▶ ◎ ⅏ ❄ 💩 🌙 🔋

Notes: Dogs must be kept on leads & exercised off
park, no bikes, no skateboards, no kite flying
🚌 🔳 🔳 🔳 🔳

▶ ▶ ▶ **72% Kings Down Tail Caravan & Camping
Park (SY173907)**
Salcombe Regis EX10 0PD ☎ 01297 680313
🗎 01297 680313
🅔 info@kings-down-tail.co.uk
🅦 www.kings-down-tail.co.uk
Dir: Off A3052 3m E of junct with A375
★ 🚐 £11.80-£13.80 🚗 £11.80-£13.80
▲ £9.20-£11.20
Open 15 Mar-15 Nov Booking advisable Whit, bank
hols & mid Jul-Sep Last arrival 22.00hrs Last
departure noon
*A well-kept site on level ground in a tree-sheltered
spot on the side of the Sid Valley. This neat family-
run park makes a good base for exploring the East
Devon coast. A 5-acre site with 100 touring pitches,
41 hardstandings.*

Leisure: 🎣 🅰

Facilities: 🛈 ⊙ 🟡 ✳ ⅋ ⅃ 🏚 🖈

Services: 🔌 🛢 ⌀ 🗔 ➜ ∪ ▶ ❄ 💩 🌙 🖥
🚌 🔳 🔳 🔳 🔳

▶ ▶ ▶ **79% Salcombe Regis Caravan & Camping
Park (SY153892)**
Salcombe Regis EX10 0JH ☎ 01395 514303
🗎 01395 514314
🅔 info@salcombe-regis.co.uk
🅦 www.salcombe-regis.co.uk
*Dir: Off A3052 1m E of junct with A375. From other
direction take left past Donkey Sanctuary*
★ 🚐 £7.95-£13.50 🚗 £7.95-£13.50
▲ £7.95-£13.50
Open Etr-Oct Booking advisable bank hols & Jul-
Aug Last arrival 20.15hrs Last departure 10.30hrs
*Set in quiet countryside with glorious views, this
spacious park has well-maintained facilities, and a
good mix of grass and hardstanding pitches. A
footpath runs from the park to the coastal path and
the beach. A 16-acre site with 100 touring pitches,
40 hardstandings and 10 statics.*
Off licence and putting.

Leisure: 🅰

Facilities: ➡ 🛈 ⊙ 🟡 ✳ ⅋ ⅃ 🏚 🖈

Services: 🔌 🖥 🛢 ⌀ 🗔 🅣 ➜ ∪ ▶ ◎ ⅏ ❄ 💩 🌙
🚌 🔳 🔳 🔳 🔳

SLAPTON — Map 03 SX84

▶ ▶ ▶ **75% Camping & Caravanning Club Site**
(SX825450)
Middle Grounds TQ7 2QW ☎ 01548 580538
Ⓦ www.campingandcaravanningclub.co.uk
*Dir: On A379 from Kingsbridge. Site entrance 0.25m
from A379, beyond brow of hill approaching Slapton*
★ ⚐ £13.60-£19.80 ▲ £13.60-£19.80
Open Mar-Oct Booking advisable bank hols & peak
periods Last arrival 21.00hrs Last departure noon
*A very attractive location and well-run site
overlooking Start Bay, with extensive views from
some pitches, and glimpses of the sea from others.
The shingle beach of Slapton Sands, and the Blue
Flag beach at Blackpool Sands are among
attractions, along with a nearby freshwater lake and
nature reserve. Please see the advertisement on
page 11 for information on Club sites and
membership. A 5.5-acre site with 115 touring
pitches, 10 hardstandings.*
Leisure: ⚏ Facilities: ⬤⊙⬤✳⬤⬤⬤⬤
Services: ⬤⬤⬤⬤⬤⬤⬤→⬤▶⬤⬤⬤ Notes:
Members' touring caravans only ⬤ ⬤ ⬤ ⬤

SOURTON CROSS — Map 03 SX59

▶ ▶ ▶ **70% Bundu Camping & Caravan Park**
(SX546916)
EX20 4HT ☎ 01837 861611 ▤ 01837 861611
Ⓔ frances@bundusargent.wanadoo.co.uk
Ⓦ www.bundu.co.uk
*Dir: W on A30, past Okehampton. Take A386 to
Tavistock. Take 1st left & left again*
★ ⚐ £8.50-£10.50 ⚐ £8.50-£10.50 ▲ £6-£8.50
Open all year Booking advisable Jul & Aug Last
arrival 23.30hrs Last departure 14.00hrs
*Welcoming, friendly owners set the tone for this
well-maintained site, ideally positioned on the
border of the Dartmoor National Park. Along with
fine views and level grassy pitches, the Granite Way
cycle track from Lydford to Okehampton along the
old railway line passes the edge of the park. A 4.5-
acre site with 38 touring pitches, 8 hardstandings.*
Facilities: ⬤⊙⬤✳⬤⬤⬤
Services: ⬤⬤⬤⬤⬤→⬤▶⬤⬤

STARCROSS
See **Dawlish**

STOKE GABRIEL — Map 03 SX85

NEW ▶ ▶ ▶ **72% Broadleigh Farm Park**
(SX851587)
Coombe House Ln, Aish TQ9 6PU
☎ 01803 782309 & 782110
*Dir: from Exeter on A38 then A380 towards Tor Bay. Right
onto A385 for Totnes. After 0.5m at Parkers Arms left for
Stoke Gabriel. Right after Whitehill Country Park to site*
⚐ ⚐
*Set in a very rural location on a working farm which
borders Paignton and Stoke Gabriel. The large
sloping field with a new timber-clad toilet block in
the centre is sheltered and peaceful, surrounded by
rolling countryside but handy for the beaches.
A 3-acre site with 35 touring pitches.*
Facilities: ⬤

▶ ▶ ▶ 81% Higher Well Farm Holiday Park
(SX857577)
Waddeton Rd TQ9 6RN ☎ 01803 782289
Ⓔ higherwell@talk21.com
Ⓦ www.ukparks.co.uk/higherwell
*Dir: From Exeter A380 to Torbay turn right onto
A385 for Totnes, after 0.5m turn left for Stoke Gabriel
following signs*
⚐ £7.50-£12.50 ⚐ £7.50-£12.50 ▲ £7.50-£12.50
Open 7 Apr-30 Oct Booking advisable bank hols &
mid Jul-Aug Last arrival 22.00hrs Last departure
10.00hrs
*Set on a quiet farm yet only 4 miles from
Paignton, this rural holiday park is on the outskirts
of the picturesque village of Stoke Gabriel. A toilet
block with some en suite facilities is a
considerable amenity, and tourers are housed
in an open field with some very good views.
A 10-acre site with 80 touring pitches,
3 hardstandings and 20 statics.*
Facilities: ⬤⊙⬤✳⬤⬤⬤⬤⬤
Services: ⬤⬤⬤⬤⬤⬤→▶⬤
Notes: No commercial vehicles ⬤ ⬤ ⬤

STOKENHAM — Map 03 SX84

▶ ▶ ▶ **75% *Old Cotmore Farm***
(SX804417)
TQ7 2LR ☎ 01548 580240 & 581252
▤ 01548 580875
Ⓔ graham.bowsher@btinternet.com
Ⓦ www.oldcotmorefarm.co.uk
*Dir: Leave Kingsbridge on A379 Dartmouth rd, passing
through Frogmore & Chillington to mini rdbt at
Stokenham. Right towards Beesands, site 1m on right*
⚐ ⚐ ▲

BRONZE

Open mid Mar-Oct Booking advisable Jul & Aug
Last arrival 20.00hrs Last departure 11.00hrs
*A quiet park with some gentle slopes and mainly
flat pitches set in an Area of Outstanding Natural
Beauty. The family-run park enjoys fine views of the
picturesque countryside of the South Hams.
Facilities are modern and well maintained, and
pebble and sandy beaches with cliff walks through
woods and fields are within walking distance. A 3-
acre site with 30 touring pitches, 11 hardstandings.*
Leisure: ⬤ ⚏
Facilities: ⬤⊙⬤✳⬤⬤⬤⬤⬤⬤
Services: ⬤⬤⬤⬤⬤⬤→⬤⬤⬤
Notes: Dogs must be kept on leads
⬤ ⬤ ⬤ ⬤ ⬤

Leisure: 🏊 Indoor swimming pool 🏊 Outdoor swimming pool ⚋ Tennis court ● Games room ⚏ Children's playground ⋃ Stables
▶ 9/18 hole golf course ⚓ Boats for hire ⚏ Cinema 🎣 Fishing ◎ Mini golf ⬤ Watersports ⬛ Separate TV room

TOURING CARAVANS, TENTS AND MOTORHOMES
PLUS SELF CATERING COTTAGES

Small friendly family run park. Ideal for touring
Dartmoor, Devon & Cornwall
Level, spacious grass & all weather pitches
available all with lovely views of Dartmoor.
Deluxe toilet block with free showers & hot water,
Bath, Shop, Take Away, Off Licence,
Campers Lounge, TV & Games Room, Launderette.
Dogs Welcome Free.
Multi-serviced & Seasonal Pitches. Caravan Storage.
Plus 4 stone built self catering cottages

Higher Longford Caravan & Camping Park
Tel: 01822 613360
Email: Stay@higherlongford.co.uk
Website: www.higherlongford.co.uk
Moorshop, Tavistock, Devon, PL19 9LQ

TAVISTOCK   **Map 03 SX47**

▶ ▶ ▶ ▶ 86% **Higher Longford Caravan**
& Camping Park (SX520747)
Moorshop PL19 9LQ
☎ 01822 613360 & 07717 507434
🖷 01822 618722
📧 stay@higherlongford.co.uk
🌐 www.higherlongford.co.uk
*Dir: From A30 to Tavistock take B3357 towards
Princetown. 2m on right before hill onto moors*
★ ♫ £11-£15 ♫ £11-£15 🅰 £11-£15

GOLD

Open all year Booking advisable Etr, Jun-Aug Last
arrival 22.30hrs Last departure noon
*A very pleasant park in Dartmoor National Park,
with panoramic views of the moors. The mainly
grassy pitches are sheltered, and some are
secluded for extra peace and quiet. Higher Longford
is surrounded by moorland parks, lanes and pretty
rivers, yet Tavistock is only 2.5m away. The park is*
                                            contd.

---

open all year round, and is well served with a shop.
A 7-acre site with 82 touring pitches,
20 hardstandings.
Pool table, campers' lounge, off licence
Leisure: ✎ 🎱 🖵 **Facilities:** ➡ 🏕 ☺ 🍴 ⚡ ❄ 🚿 ♿ 🛒 🔧 🏪 ♨ ✂
Services: 🚐 🖴 🛢 🚰 🖻 🗑 ➜ ∪ ▶ 🐕 ✂
Notes: Dogs must be kept on leads
🐕 ▬ 💳 ▬ ▬ 🔲

▶ ▶ ▶ ▶ 78% **Woodovis Park**
(SX431745)
Gulworthy PL19 8NY
☎ 01822 832968 🖷 01822 832948
📧 info@woodovis.com
🌐 www.woodovis.com
*Dir: From Tavistock take A390 signed to Callington &
Gunnislake. At top of hill turn right at x-roads signed
Lamerton & 'Chipshop'. Park 1m on left*
★ ♫ £17-£19 ♫ £17-£19 🅰 £15-£17
Open Apr-Oct Booking advisable Jun-Aug Last
arrival 22.00hrs Last departure noon
*A well-kept park in a remote woodland setting on
the edge of the Tamar Valley. This peacefully-
located park is set at the end of a half-mile private
tree-lined road, and has lots of on-site facilities.
The toilets are excellent, and there is an indoor
swimming pool, all in a friendly, purposeful
atmosphere. A 14.5-acre site with 50 touring
pitches, 18 hardstandings and 35 statics.
Mini-golf, sauna, jacuzzi.*
Leisure: ♥ ✎ 🎱 **Facilities:** ➡ 🏕 ☺ 🍴 ❄ 🚿 ♿ 🛒 🏪 ♨ ✂
Services: 🚐 🖴 🛢 🚰 🗑 ➜ ∪ ▶ ◎ ✂ **Notes:** Dogs must
be kept on leads 🐕 ▬ 💳 ▬ 🔲

The Best of British

▶ ▶ ▶ 77% **Harford Bridge Holiday**
Park (SX504767)
Peter Tavy PL19 9LS ☎ 01822 810349
🖷 01822 810028
📧 enquiry@harfordbridge.co.uk
🌐 www.harfordbridge.co.uk
*Dir: 2m N of Tavistock, off A386 Okehampton Rd, take
Peter Tavy turn, entrance 200yds on right.*
★ ♫ £7.50-£12.75 ♫ £7.50-£12.75 🅰 £7.50-£12.75

GOLD

Open all year (rs Nov-Mar Statics only & 5
hardstanding pitches) Booking advisable Aug, Etr,
BH's Last arrival 21.00hrs Last departure noon
*This beautiful spacious park is set beside the River
Tavy in the Dartmoor National Park. Pitches are
located beside the river and around the copses, and
the park is very well equipped for the holidaymaker.
An adventure playground and games room*
                                            contd.

---

entertain children, and there is fly-fishing and a free tennis court. A 16-acre site with 120 touring pitches, 5 hardstandings and 80 statics.
Fly fishing.

Leisure: ৭ ৭ ⚲ ☐
Facilities: ⋔ ⊙ ৭ ☀ ৬ ᄂ ⊞ 爲 ♣
Services: ⊒ ⎍ ⑤ ▯ ⌀ ⊞ → ∪ ⏵ ◎ ♨ ৶ ⅏
◉ ▦ ⇶ ⬡

► ► ► 80% **Langstone Manor Camping & Caravan Park (SX524738)**
Moortown PL19 9JZ ☎ 01822 613371
🖷 01822 613371
✉ jane@langstone-manor.co.uk
🌐 www.langstone-manor.co.uk
Dir: Take B3357 from Tavistock to Princetown, after approx 1.5m turn right at x-rds, follow signs
★ 🚐 £8-£10 🚐 £8-£10 ▲ £8-£10

Open 15 Mar-15 Nov Booking advisable bank hols & Jul-Aug Last arrival 22.00hrs Last departure 11.00hrs
A secluded site set in the well-maintained grounds of a manor house in Dartmoor National Park. Many attractive mature trees provide a screen within the park, and there is a popular lounge bar with an excellent menu of reasonably priced evening meals. Plenty of activities and places of interest can be found within the surrounding moorland. A 5.5-acre site with 40 touring pitches, 5 hardstandings and 25 statics.

Leisure: ♣ ⚲
Facilities: ⋔ ⊙ ৭ ☀ ᄂ 爲 爲
Services: ⊒ 🖸 ৭ ▯ ⌀ ⊞ ☐ ✕ → ∪ ⏵ ◎ ♨ ৶ ⅏
◉ ▦ ⇶ ⬡

---

contd.

TEDBURN ST MARY   Map 03 SX89

NEW ► ► ► 72% **Springfield Holiday Park (SX788935)**
Tedburn Rd EX6 6EW ☎ 01647 24242
🖷 01647 24131
✉ springfielddevon@aol.com
🌐 www.springfieldholidaypark.co.uk
Dir: Exit A30 at Woodleigh junct. Follow signs to site
★ 🚐 £10-£12 🚐 £10-£12
Open 15 Mar-15 Nov (rs 15 Nov-15 Jan Static home owners only) Booking advisable Jul-Aug Last arrival 18.00hrs Last departure noon
Set in a quiet rural location with countryside views, this park is being upgraded to a smart standard by new owners. It has the advantage of being located

contd.

---

close to Dartmoor National Park, with village pubs and stores just 2 miles away. A 9-acre site with 48 touring pitches, 38 hardstandings and 49 statics.
Family bathroom

Leisure: ⳇ ♣ ⚲ **Facilities:** ⋔ ⊙ ৭ 爲 ♣
Services: ⊒ ▯ ⌀ → ⏵ ৶ ⅏
Notes: Dogs must be kept on leads

TIVERTON
See **East Worlington**

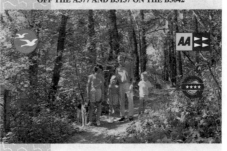

TORQUAY   Map 03 SX96
See also **Newton Abbot**

► ► ► ► 80% **Widdicombe Farm Tourist Park (SX880650)**
Marldon TQ3 1ST ☎ 01803 558325
🖷 01803 559526
✉ g.glynn@farmersweekly.net
🌐 www.widdicombefarm.co.uk
Dir: On A380 midway between Torquay & Paignton
★ 🚐 £7-£17.50 🚐 £7-£17.50 ▲ £7-£17.50
Open mid Mar-mid Oct Booking advisable Whit & Jul-Aug Last arrival 21.30hrs Last departure 11.00hrs
A friendly family-owned and run park on a working farm, with good quality facilities and extensive views. The level pitches are terraced to take advantage of the views towards the coast and Dartmoor. A quiet but happy atmosphere pervades this park, encouraged by a large children's play

contd.

---

area. Other amenities include a well-stocked shop, a restaurant, and a lounge bar. An 8-acre site with 200 touring pitches, 180 hardstandings and 3 statics. Family bathrooms, BBQ patio

Leisure: ◕ /Λ

Facilities: ➡ ৌ ⊙ ❑ ※ & ৬ ৯ ৯ ৯ ৯

Services: ◲ ৬ ৺ ৺ ৹ ৹ ⊞ ⏳ ✕ ◕ ➡ → ∪ ᐅ ◎ ☺ ৴

Notes: Families & couples only

▣ ▤ ▥ ▦ ▧

▶ ▶ **70% Manor Farm Campsite (SX903678)**
Daccombe TQ12 4ST ☎ 01803 328294
▤ 01803 328294
Dir: From A380 Newton Abbot to Torquay road, up hill to Kingskerswell Rd, follow camp site signs
☙ ▲

Open Etr-1 Oct Booking advisable peak times
A spacious grassy campsite enjoying unbelievable panoramic views of Devon's countryside and Dartmoor. This peaceful park is on a working farm, with flat pitches on a lovely sloping field. Facilities are simple but adequate and clean. A 3-acre site with 75 touring pitches.

Facilities: ৌ ⊙ ※ ৬ ৯

Services: ৹ ৴ → ᐅ ◎ ◕ ☺ ৴ ▣

Notes: Families and couples only

▶ ▶ ▶ **74% Camping & Caravanning Club Site (SS606242)**
Over Weir EX37 9DU ☎ 01769 560009
ⓦ www.campingandcaravanningclub.co.uk
Dir: On A377 from Barnstaple turn right at Umberleigh sign.
★ ☙ £13.60-£17.80 ☙ £13.60-£17.80 ▲ £13.60-£17.80
Open Apr-Oct Booking advisable bank hols & peak periods Last arrival 21.00hrs Last departure noon
There are fine country views from this compact site set on high ground. The site has the advantage of a games room with table tennis and skittle alley, and two quality tennis courts, with an adjacent wooded area for walks, and a nearby fishing pond. Please see advertisement on page 11 for information on Club sites and membership. A 3-acre site with 60 touring pitches, 12 hardstandings.

Leisure: ৎ ◕ /Λ **Facilities:** ৌ ⊙ ❑ ※ & ৬ ৯ ৯

Services: ◲ ৬ ▣ ৹ ৹ ⊞ ⏳ → ∪ ৴ ৬

▣ ▤ ▥ ▦ ▧

▶ ▶ ▶ ▶ **80% Hidden Valley Park (SS499408)**
EX34 8NU ☎ 01271 813837
▤ 01271 814041
ⓔ relax@hiddenvalleypark.com
ⓦ www.hiddenvalleypark.com
Dir: Direct access off A361, 8m from Barnstaple & 2m from Mullacott Cross
☙ £7-£22.50 ☙ £7-£22.50 ▲ £7-£17.50

GOLD

Open all year (rs 15 Nov-15 Mar All weather pitches only) Booking advisable peak season Last arrival 21.30hrs Last departure 10.00hrs
A delightful, well-appointed family site set in a wooded valley, with superb facilities and a café. The park is set in a very rural, natural position not far from the beautiful coastline around Ilfracombe. A 25-acre site with 135 touring pitches, 74 hardstandings.
Gardens, woodland walks & lake

Leisure: ◕ /Λ

Facilities: ➡ ৌ ⊙ ❑ ※ & ৬ ৯ ৯ ৯

Services: ◲ ▣ ৹ ৺ ৹ ⊞ ⏳ ✕ ◕ → ∪ ᐅ ◊ ☺ ৴

▣ ▤ ▥ ▦ ▧

See advertisement under ILFRACOMBE

NEW ▶ ▶ **71% West Middlewick Farm Caravan & Camping Site (SS826136)**
Nomansland EX16 8NP
☎ 01884 861235 ▤ 01884 861235
ⓔ stay@westmiddlewick.co.uk
ⓦ www.westmiddlewick.co.uk
Dir: From M5 junct 27, A361 to Tiverton. Take B3137, follow Witheridge signs. Site 1m past Nomansland on right (8m from Tiverton)
☙ £6-£9 ☙ £6-£9 ▲ £6-£8
Open all year Booking advisable Jul-Aug Last arrival 22.00hrs Last departure noon
A working dairy farm on a ridge west of the hamlet of Nomansland, with extensive rural views. The newly upgraded park offers campers a quiet and relaxing break, and the country's official best village shop is nearby. A 3.5-acre site with 25 touring pitches, 8 hardstandings.

Facilities: ৌ ⊙ ※ & ৯ ৯ **Services:** ◲ ⊞ → ∪ ৴ ৬

Notes: Dogs must be kept on leads, children must be supervised

WOODBURY SALTERTON Map 03 SY08

► ► ► 85% **Browns Farm Caravan Park (SY016885)**
Browns Farm EX5 1PS ☎ 01395 232895
Dir: From M5 junct 30 take A3052 for 3.7m. Right at White Horse Inn follow sign to Woodbury, at village road junct turn right, site on left
★ ⊞ £7-£9.50 ⊞ £7-£10.50 Å £6-£9.50
Open all year Booking advisable all times
A small farm park adjoining a 14th-century thatched farmhouse, and located in a quiet village. Pitches back onto hedgerows, and friendly owners keep the facilities spotlessly clean. The tourist information and games room with table tennis, chess etc is housed in a purpose-built building. The park is just a mile from the historic heathland of Woodbury Common with its superb views. A 2.5-acre site with 20 touring pitches, 12 hardstandings.
Hard standings for winter period, caravan storage
Leisure: ✎
Facilities: ⚑⊙☜✼⚐✆
Services: ⊞⛽⊟→∪▶⬎⚐
Notes: No ground sheets in awnings, no music

WOOLACOMBE Map 03 SS44
See also **Mortehoe & West Down**

76% **Golden Coast Holiday Village (SS482436)**
Station Rd EX34 7HW
☎ 01271 870343 ⧉ 01271 870089
✉ goodtimes@woolacombe.com
ⓦ www.woolacombe.com
Dir: Follow road to Woolacombe Bay from Mullacott & site is 1.5m on left
★ ⊞ £12.50-£45 ⊞ £12.50-£45 Å £9-£30
Open Feb-Dec (rs mid Sep-May Outdoor pools closed) Booking advisable bank hols & mid Jul-end Aug Last arrival 24.00hrs Last departure 10.00hrs
A holiday village offering excellent leisure facilities as well as the amenities of the other Woolacombe Bay holiday parks. There is a neat touring area with a new unisex toilet block, maintained to a high standard. Bowling alleys, a number of bars and plenty of activities add to the holiday experience. A 10-acre site with 93 touring pitches, 53 hardstandings and 519 statics.
Sauna, solarium, jacuzzi, tennis, golf, fishing, snooker
Leisure: ☃ ☂ ❈ ✎ ⚑ ☐
Facilities: ⚑⊙☜✼✆⚐⚑
Services: ⊞⛽⛽⬭⊟⊟✕⬆⬌→∪▶◎⚐⚑⬎⚐
Notes: ⬥ ⊞ ⬛⬛ ⬛ ⬛ ⬛

77% **Woolacombe Bay Holiday Village (SS465442)**
Sandy Ln EX34 7AH ☎ 01271 870343
⧉ 01271 870089
✉ goodtimes@woolacombe.com
ⓦ www.woolacombe.com
Dir: From Mullacott Cross rdbt take B3343 (Woolacombe rd) to Turnpike Cross junct. Right towards Mortehoe, site approx 1m on left
★ Å £9-£30
Open Mar-Oct (rs Mar-mid May, mid Sep-Oct No camping) Booking advisable Whit & summer holidays Last arrival midnight Last departure 10.00hrs
A well-developed touring section in a holiday complex with a full entertainment and leisure programme. This tents-only park offers excellent facilities including a steam room and sauna. For a small charge a bus takes holidaymakers to the other Woolacombe Bay holiday centres where they can take part in any of the activities offered, and there is also a bus to the beach. An 8.5-acre site with 237 statics.
Entertainment, children's club, health suite, bowls
Leisure: ☃ ☂ ❈ ✎ ⚑ ☐
Facilities: ⚑⊙☜✼✆⚐⚑⬛⚑
Services: ⊞⛽⛽⬭⊟⊟✕⬆→∪▶◎⚐⬎⚐⬛
⊞ ⬛⬛ ⬛ ⬛
See advertisement on page 126

73% **Woolacombe Sands Holiday Park (SS471434)**
Beach Rd EX34 7AF ☎ 01271 870569
⧉ 01271 870606
✉ lifesabeach@woolacombe-sands.co.uk
ⓦ www.woolacombe-sands.co.uk
Dir: From M5 junct 27 take A361 to Barnstaple. Follow signs to Ilfracombe, until Mullacott Cross. Turn left onto B3343 to Woolacombe. Site on left
⊞ ⊞ Å
Open Apr-Oct Booking advisable 24-31 May & 19 Jul-30 Aug Last arrival 22.00hrs Last departure 10.00hrs
Set in rolling countryside with grassy terraced pitches, most with spectacular views overlooking the sea at Woolacombe. The lovely blue flag beach can be accessed directly by footpath in 10-15 minutes, and there is a full entertainment programme for all the family in high season. A 20-acre site with 200 touring pitches and 80 statics.
Leisure: ☃ ☂ ❈ ⚑ Facilities: ⚑⊙☜✼✆⚐⬛⚑
Services: ⊞⛽⛽⬭⊟⊟✕⬆→∪▶◎⬎
⊞ ⬛⬛ ⬛ ⬛
See advertisement on page 127

THE PERCENTAGE RATING
FOR ALL PARKS RANGES FROM
50% - 100%.

The number of touring pitches listed for each site includes tents, caravans and motorvans.

Leisure: ☃ Indoor swimming pool ☂ Outdoor swimming pool ❈ Tennis court ✎ Games room ⚑ Children's playground ∪ Stables ▶ 9/18 hole golf course ⬆ Boats for hire ☰ Cinema ⬎ Fishing ◎ Mini golf ⬥ Watersports ☐ Separate TV room

England

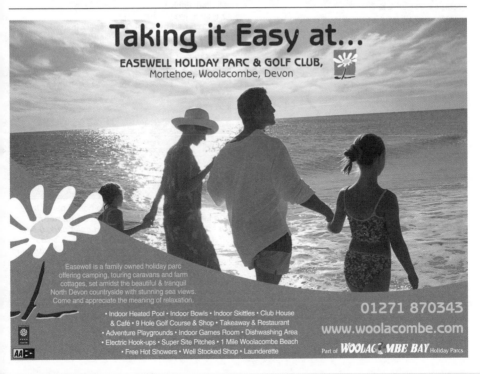
Facilities: ♨ Bath 🚿 Shower ⊙ Electric Shaver ✂ Hairdryer ✳ Ice Pack Facility ♿ Disabled Facilities ☏ Public Telephone 🛒 Shop on Site or within 200yds 📠 Mobile Shop (calls at least 5 days a week) ⊞ BBQ Area 🪑 Picnic Area 🐕 Dog Exercise Area

England

▶ ▶ ▶ **77%** *Europa Park (SS475435)*
Beach Rd EX34 7AN ☎ 01271 871425
🖷 01271 871425
✉ europaparkwoolacombe@yahoo.co.uk
*Dir: M5 junct 27, A361 through Barnstaple to Mullacott
Cross. Left onto B3343 signed Woolacombe. Site on
right at Spa shop/garage*
🚐 🚙 Å

Open all year Booking advisable bank hols & high
season Last arrival 23.00hrs
*Set high above Woolacombe with probably the best
views across the bay from all pitches, this park
offers superb holiday facilities. All pitches are set on
mainly level terraces, and visitors can enjoy the
indoor pool and sauna, games room,
restaurant/café/bar and clubhouse. A 16-acre site
with 180 touring pitches, 20 hardstandings and
22 statics.*
Leisure: ❄ ✎ ⚁ ▢
Facilities: ⋒ ⊙ ☼ ⚲ ☎ 🜨
Services: ⊡ ⱳ ⬚ ⵛ ⅋ ⌀ ⊞ Ⓣ ✗ 🔌 → ∪ ▶ ◎ ⚠ ⚲ ✎
▭ ▭ ▭ ▧ 🔋

DORSET

BERE REGIS   Map 04 SY89

▶ ▶ ▶ **77%** *Rowlands Wait
Touring Park (SY842933)*
Rye Hill BH20 7LP
☎ 01929 472727 🖷 01929 472727
✉ aa@rowlandswait.co.uk
ⓦ www.rowlandswait.co.uk
*Dir: On approach to Bere Regis follow signs to
Bovington Tank Museum. At top of Rye Hill, 0.75m from
village turn right. 200yds to site*
🚐 🚙 Å

Rowlands Wait Touring Park
Open mid Mar-Oct (winter by arrangement)
Booking advisable bank hols & Jul-Aug Last arrival
21.30hrs Last departure noon
*This park lies in a really attractive setting
overlooking Bere and the Dorset countryside, set
amongst undulating areas of trees and shrubs.
Within a few miles of the Tank Museum, and the
mock tank battles are an attraction of the area.
An 8-acre site with 71 touring pitches.*
Leisure: ❡ ✎
Facilities: ⇥ ⋒ ⊙ ⚲ ☼ ☎ 🜨 ⊞ 🞡 ᚛
Services: ⊡ ⵛ ⬚ ⌀ ⊞ Ⓣ → ∪ ▶ ◎ ✎
▭ ▭ ▭ ▧ 🔋

BLANDFORD FORUM   Map 04 ST80

▶ ▶ ▶ ▶ **75%** The Inside Park (ST869046)
Down House Estate DT11 9AD ☎ 01258 453719
🖷 01258 459921
✉ inspark@aol.com
ⓦ http://members.aol.com/inspark/inspark
*Dir: From town cross River Stour and follow signs for
Winterborne Stickland. Site in 1.5m*
★ 🚐 £12.45-£16.05 🚙 £12.45-£16.05 Å £12.45-£16.05

Open Etr-Oct Booking advisable bank hols & Jul-
Aug Last arrival 22.00hrs Last departure noon
*An attractive, well-sheltered and quiet park, 0.5m
off a country lane in a wooded valley. Spacious
pitches are divided by mature trees and shrubs, and
amenities are housed in an 18th-century coach
house and stables. There are some lovely woodland
walks within the park. A 12-acre site with 125
touring pitches.*
Farm trips (main season), kennels for hire.
Leisure: ❡ ✎ Facilities: ⋒ ⊙ ⚲ ☼ ⚲ & ⬚ ☎ ᚛
Services: ⊡ ⬚ ⬚ ⌀ ⊞ Ⓣ ⇥ → ∪ ▶ ✎
▭ ▭ ▭ ▧ 🔋

contd.

Services: Ⓣ Toilet Fluid ✗ Café/ Restaurant 🍟 Fast Food/Takeaway ⇥ Baby Care ❡ Electric Hook Up
ⱳ Motorvan Service Point ⬚ Launderette ⵛ Licensed Bar ⬚ Calor Gaz ⌀ Camping Gaz ⊞ Battery Charging

BRIDPORT Map 04 SY49

**80% Freshwater Beach
Holiday Park** (SY493892)
Burton Bradstock DT6 4PT
☎ 01308 897317 🖹 01308 897336
📧 enquiries@freshwaterbeach.co.uk
🌐 www.freshwaterbeach.co.uk
Dir: Take B3157 from Bridport towards Burton
Bradstock. Site 1.5m on right from Crown rdbt
★ 🚐 £8-£30 🚐 £8-£30 ▲ £8-£30

Open 15 Mar-10 Nov Booking advisable Jul-Aug
Last arrival 23.30hrs Last departure 10.00hrs
*A family holiday centre sheltered by a sandbank
and enjoying its own private beach. The park
offers a wide variety of leisure and
entertainment programmes for all the family.
It is well placed at one end of the
Weymouth/Bridport coast with spectacular*

contd.

*views of Chesil Beach. There are three
immaculate toilet blocks. A 40-acre site with
500 touring pitches and 250 statics.*
Entertainment, amusement arcade, horse riding
Leisure: 🏊 🎣 ⛰ **Facilities:** 🏪 ☉ 🍴 ☀ ♿ 🚿 🛒 🐾
Services: 🔌 🚽 🍴 🧊 📶 🗑 🛒 ⇨ ∪ 🅿 ⊚ ⚡ 🎣 🎵
🔵 💳 🔲 🔳

**73% West Bay Holiday
Park** (SY461906)
West Bay DT6 4HB
☎ 01308 422424/459491 &
0870 420 2991 🖹 01308 421371
📧 enquiries@parkdeanholidays.co.uk
🌐 www.parkdeanholidays.co.uk
Dir: From A35 Dorchester road, W towards Bridport,
take 1st exit at 1st rdbt, 2nd exit at 2nd rdbt into
West Bay, park on right
★ 🚐 £7-£25 🚐 £10-£28.50 ▲ £7-£25
Open 23 Mar-2 Nov (rs 6 Apr-25 May & 14-19
Sep Entertainment restricted) Booking advisable
Last arrival 21.00hrs Last departure 10.00hrs
*Overlooking the pretty little harbour at West
Bay, and close to the shingle beach, this park
offers a full entertainment programme for all
ages. There are children's clubs and sports
activities for all the family, and plenty of evening
fun with talent shows and cabaret etc. The
grassy touring area is terraced to enjoy the
seaward views. A large adventure playground is
very popular. A 6-acre site with 131 touring
pitches and 307 statics.*

contd.

Leisure: 🏊 Indoor swimming pool 🏊 Outdoor swimming pool 🎾 Tennis court 🎱 Games room ⛰ Children's playground ∪ Stables
🏌 9/18 hole golf course 🚣 Boats for hire 🎬 Cinema 🎣 Fishing ⊚ Mini golf 🌊 Watersports 📺 Separate TV room

Live family entertainment & children's clubs
Leisure: ✈ ✦ ⚲ **Facilities:** ♖⊙☜☀🅱⛾💺🅻🎏
Services: 🔌🗑🍴♨🧺⊞✕ ⬛↝→∪▶⊚♨🗲
🍺 🚃 📶 🔧

Dir: *1m W of Bridport on A35, turn south for Eype.
Park signed*
★ 🚐 £11.25-£20 � £11.25-£20 ▲ £8.25-£14.50
Open mid Mar-early Nov Booking advisable
public hols & Jul-Aug Last arrival 22.00hrs Last
departure 11.00hrs
*A well-screened site with magnificent clifftop
views over the Channel and Dorset coast,
adjacent to National Trust land and overlooking
Lyme Bay. Pitches are mostly sheltered by
hedging and well spaced on hardstandings.
There is a mixture of statics and tourers, but the
tourers enjoy the best clifftop positions. A 9-acre
site with 195 touring pitches, 45 hardstandings
and 160 statics.*
Gym, steam room, sauna, pitch & putt
Leisure: ✈ ✦ ⚲ **Facilities:** ♖⊙☜☀🅱⛾💺🅻🎏
Services: 🔌♨🗑🍴♨🧺⊞⊤✕ ⬛→▶🗲
🍺 🚃 📶

CERNE ABBAS   **Map 04 ST60**

▶ ▶ ▶ 78% **Lyons Gate Caravan and Camping
Park** (ST660062)
Lyons Gate DT2 7AZ ☎ 01300 345260
❷ info@lyons-gate.co.uk
ⓦ www.lyons-gate.co.uk
Dir: *Signed with direct access off A352, 3m N of Cerne
Abbas*
🚐🚐▲

Open all year Booking advisable peak times Last
arrival 20.00hrs Last departure 11.30hrs
*A peaceful park with pitches set out around the four
attractive coarse fishing lakes. It is surrounded by
mature woodland, with many footpaths and
bridleways. Other easily accessible attractions
include the Cerne Giant carved into the hills, the old
market town of Dorchester, and the superb sandy
beach at Weymouth. A 10-acre site with 90 touring
pitches, 4 hardstandings.*
4 fishing lakes on site
Facilities: ♖⊙☜☀🅱🎏🎏🎏
Services: 🔌♨🍴→∪▶🗲
Notes: No ball games, bikes, scooters or
skateboards allowed

───────────────

▶ ▶ 70% **Giant's Head Caravan & Camping Park**
(ST675029)
Giants Head Farm, Old Sherborne Rd DT2 7TR
☎ 01300 341242
❷ holidays@giantshead.co.uk
ⓦ www.giantshead.co.uk
Dir: *From Dorchester into town avoiding by-pass, at Top
O'Town rdbt take Sherborne road, 500yds right fork at
Esso (Loder's garage) site signed*
★ 🚐 £7-£12 🚐 £7-£12 ▲ £7-£12
Open Etr-Oct (rs Etr shop & bar closed) Booking
advisable Aug Last arrival anytime Last departure
13.00hrs
*A pleasant though rather basic park set in Dorset
downland near Cerne Giant (a figure cut into the
chalk) with stunning views. A good stopover site,
ideal for tenters and backpackers on the Ridgeway
route. A 4-acre site with 50 touring pitches.*
Two holiday chalets.
Facilities: ♖⊙☜☀🎏🎏
Services: 🔌🗑🍴♨⊞→▶🗲🅻

┌─────────────────────────────────┐
│   **For full details of the AA pennant**   │
│   **ratings scheme see pages 7-8**   │
└─────────────────────────────────┘

───

CHARMOUTH   Map 04 SY39

► ► ► ► 80% **Camping & Caravanning
Club Site (SY330965)**
Monkton Wylde Farm DT6 6DB
☎ 01297 32965
GOLD
🌐 www.campingandcaravanningclub.co.uk
*Dir: From Dorchester on A35 turn right onto B3165
signed Hawkchurch, site on left in 0.25m*
★ 🚐 £16.10-£19.80 🚐 £16.10-£19.80 ▲ £16.10-£19.80
Open Mar-Oct Booking advisable bank hols & peak
periods Last arrival 21.00hrs Last departure noon
*Located in a rural setting almost on the
Devon/Dorset border, this attractively terraced park
with high quality toilet facilities is ideally placed for
visiting the resorts of Charmouth, Lyme Regis and
the Jurassic Coast. Friendly managers keep the
whole park in tiptop condition. Please see the
advertisement on page 11 for information on Club
sites and membership. A 12-acre site with
80 touring pitches, 34 hardstandings.*
Leisure: ⚲
Facilities: 🏕☉🕤✳☉🕻🛏
Services: 🚐🚘🛢🔌🖭🔽→∪🏪▲🗑🛒
🈁 🈁 🈁 🈁

► ► ► ► 78% **Monkton Wyld Farm
Caravan Park (SY336964)**
DT6 6DB ☎ 01297 34525 &
631131 (May-Sep) 🖷 01297 33594
GOLD
🌐 holidays@monktonwyld.co.uk
🌐 www.monktonwyld.co.uk
*Dir: From Charmouth on A35 towards Axminster, after
approx 3m (ignore 1st sign to Monkton Wyld - road very
steep) take next right signed Marshwood. Site 500mtrs
on left*
★ 🚐 £8.50-£16.40 🚐 £8.50-£16.40 ▲ £8.50-£16.40

Open Etr-Oct Booking advisable school hols Last
arrival 22.00hrs Last departure 11.00hrs
*An attractive family park in a secluded location yet
central for Charmouth, Lyme and the coast. It has
been tastefully designed in a maturing landscape,
with perimeter trees providing a screen, and every
pitch backed by hedges or shrubs. A 6-acre site with
60 touring pitches, 45 hardstandings.*
Family shower room.
Leisure: ⚲
Facilities: 🏕☉🕤✳☉🕻🛏🏠
Services: 🚐🛢🔌🖭→∪🏪▲🗑🛒
🈁 🈁 🈁 🈁

► ► ► ► 85% **Wood Farm
Caravan & Camping Park (SY356940)**
Axminster Rd DT6 6BT
☎ 01297 560697 🖷 01297 561243
SILVER
🌐 holidays@woodfarm.co.uk
🌐 www.woodfarm.co.uk
*Dir: Park entered directly off A35 rdbt on Axminster side
of Charmouth.*
★ 🚐 £12-£19 🚐 £12-£19 ▲ £10-£19
Open Etr-Oct Booking advisable school hols Last
arrival 19.00hrs Last departure noon
*A pleasant, well-established and mature park
overlooking Charmouth, the sea and the Dorset hills
and valleys. It stands on a high spot, and the four
camping fields are terraced, each with its own
impressive toilet block. Convenient for Lyme Regis,
Axminster, and this famous fossil coastline.
A 13-acre site with 216 touring pitches,
175 hardstandings and 81 statics.*
Coarse fishing lake.
Leisure: 🎣 🔍 ⚲ ⚲ 🖵
Facilities: 🛁🏕☉🕤✳☉🕻🛏🐾
Services: 🚐🛢🔌🖭 →∪🏪☉▲🗑🛒
Notes: No skateboards, scooters or roller skates
🈁 🈁 🈁 🈁

► ► ► 75% **Manor Farm Holiday Centre
(SY368937)**
DT6 6QL ☎ 01297 560226
🌐 enquiries@manorfarmholidaycentre.co.uk
🌐 www.manorfarmholidaycentre.co.uk
Dir: W on A35 to Charmouth, site 0.75m on right
★ 🚐 £9-£15 🚐 £9-£15 ▲ £9-£15

Open all year (rs End Oct-mid Mar statics only)
Booking advisable high season Last arrival 20.00hrs
Last departure 10.00hrs
*Set just a short walk from the safe sand and shingle
beach at Charmouth, this popular family park offers
a good range of facilities. Children enjoy the activity
area and outdoor swimming pool (so do their
parents!), and the park is well placed for touring
this beautiful area. A 15-acre site with 250 touring
pitches, 80 hardstandings and 29 statics.*
Leisure: 🎣 ⚲ ⚲
Facilities: 🏕☉🕤✳☉🕻🛏🐾
Services: 🚐🛢🔌🍴✖ →∪🏪☉▲🗑🛒
🈁 🈁 🈁 🈁

England

▶ ▶ ▶ 91% **Newlands Caravan & Camping Park (SY374935)**
DT6 6RB ☎ 01297 560259
🖹 01297 560787
ⓔ enq@newlandsholidays.co.uk
ⓦ www.newlandsholidays.co.uk
Dir: 4m W of Bridport on A35
★ 🚐 £11-£30 🚐 £11-£30 Å £10-£24
Open all year (rs Nov-Mar restaurant, bar & shop closed) Booking advisable school hols Last arrival 22.30hrs Last departure 10.00hrs
A very smart site with excellent touring facilities, including five 'millennium' pitches complete with water, electricity, chemical disposal point, washing machine and tumble dryer. The park offers a full cabaret and entertainment programme for all ages, and boasts an indoor swimming pool with spa and an outdoor pool with water slide. Set on gently sloping ground in hilly countryside near the sea. A 23-acre site with 240 touring pitches, 52 hardstandings and 86 statics.
Leisure: ♥ ♥ ◕ ⚏ ▢
Facilities: ⋔ ⊙ �ℚ ✻ ♿ ⚐ ♨ ★
Services: ▦ ▣ ♀ 🗑 🖉 Ⓣ ✕ ⬆ → ∪ ▶ ◎ ◭ ✦ ⚏ ✈
▦ ▭ ▦ ▩ ⑨

SILVER

▶ ▶ ▶ ▶ 83% **Golden Cap Caravan Park (SY422919)**
Seatown DT6 6JX
☎ 01297 489341 & 01308 422139
🖹 01297 489788
ⓔ holidays@wdlh.co.uk
ⓦ www.wdlh.co.uk
Dir: On A35, in Chideock turn S for Seatown
★ 🚐 £10.75-£23 🚐 £10.75-£23 Å £10.75-£16.50
Open mid Mar-early Nov Booking advisable public hols & Jul-Aug Last arrival 22.00hrs Last departure 11.00hrs
A grassy site, overlooking sea and beach and surrounded by National Trust parkland. This uniquely placed park slopes down to the sea, although pitches are generally level. A slight dip hides the beach view from the back of the park, but this area benefits from having trees, scrub and meadows, unlike the barer areas closer to the sea. Ideal base for touring Dorset and Devon. An 11-acre site with 108 touring pitches, 29 hardstandings and 234 statics.
Fishing lake
Leisure: ⚏ **Facilities:** ⋔ ⊙ ℚ ✻ ♿ ⚐ ♨ 🗑 ★
Services: 🗑 ▣ 🖉 ⊟ Ⓣ → ▶ ✦ ✈ ▦ ▭ ⑨

The Best of British
TOURING AND HOLIDAY PARKS
GOLD

Services: Ⓣ Toilet Fluid   ✕ Café/ Restaurant   🍴 Fast Food/Takeaway   🍼 Baby Care   🔌 Electric Hook Up
🚐 Motorvan Service Point   🗑 Launderette   ♀ Licensed Bar   🛢 Calor Gaz   🔥 Camping Gaz   🔋 Battery Charging

CHRISTCHURCH   Map 05 SZ19

► ► ► ► 83% **Grove Farm Meadow Holiday Caravan Park** (SZ136946)

Stour Way BH23 2PQ ☎ 01202 483597
🗎 01202 483878
🖃 enquiries@meadowbank-holidays.co.uk
🌐 www.meadowbank-holidays.co.uk
Dir: Take Christchurch/Airport exit off A338, turn left for Christchurch and follow signs
★ 🚐 £7-£25 🚐 £7-£25
Open Mar-Oct Booking advisable at all times Last arrival 21.00hrs Last departure noon
A very smart park on the banks of the River Stour, with a colourful display of hanging baskets and flower-filled tubs around the superb reception area. Toilet facilities are modern and spotless, and there is excellent play equipment for children. Visitors can choose between pitch sizes, including some luxury fully-serviced ones. A 2-acre site with 41 touring pitches, 22 hardstandings and 180 statics. Fishing on site, 21 fully serviced pitches

Leisure: 🎣 🅰
Facilities: ➡🏕⊙🍳🔥♿👜🖷
Services: 🖳🔋🅱🚿🛒→🅄🛒📮⚠🚬🐕🛠
Notes: 🐾 💳 🔳 🔳 🔳 🔳

See advertisement on opposite page

CORFE CASTLE   Map 04 SY98

► ► ► 79% **Woodland Caravan & Camping Park** (SY953818)
The Glebe, Bucknowle Farm, Bucknowle BH20 5PQ
☎ 01929 480280 🗎 01929 480280
🖃 hazelparker@btconnect.com
Dir: From Wareham A351 towards Swanage. In 4m turn right at foot of Corfe Castle signed Church Knowle. 0.75m right into site
🚐 £12-£14 🚐 £12-£14 ⛺ £12-£14

Open Mar-Oct Last departure 11.00hrs
A quiet family park set in a clearing within a wooded area, with touring pitches spread around the perimeter in secluded areas. The central grass area is kept free as a play space, and there are many walks from the park. A toilet and amenities block provides very good facilities. A 5-acre site with 65 touring pitches.
Baby changing area

Leisure: 🅰 **Facilities:** 🏕⊙🍳✳♿🔥🔋🖷
Services: 🖳🅱♿🚿🛒→🅄📮🛠
Notes: Quiet after 22.30

DORCHESTER
See **Cerne Abbas**

EVERSHOT   Map 04 ST50

► ► ► 74% **Clay Pigeon Caravan Park** (ST610077)
Wardon Hill DT2 9PW ☎ 01935 83492
Dir: Turn off A37 onto unclassified road signed Batcombe, site on right 150yds
🚐🚐⛺

Open all year Booking advisable Last arrival 21.00hrs
A level, close-mown park with mature trees in a rural area. The refurbished toilet block is well equipped, and adjacent to the site is a go-kart track and clay pigeon shooting range. A 3-acre site with 60 touring pitches, 12 hardstandings and 6 statics.

Leisure: 🅰 **Facilities:** 🏕⊙🍳♿🔥🖷🐕🏕
Services: 🖳🚿🅱🅱♿🛒✖ ♿
Notes: Dogs must be kept on leads

See advertisement on page 134

FERNDOWN   Map 05 SU00

NEW ► ► ► 68% **St Leonards Farm Caravan & Camping Park** (SU093014)
Ringwood Rd, West Moors BH22 0AQ
☎ 01202 872637 🗎 01202 855683
🖃 james@love5.fsnet.co.uk
🌐 www.stleonardsfarm.biz
Dir: from Ringwood follow Poole & Dorchester signs on A31. 5m to site entrance opposite Texaco garage.
★ 🚐 £8-£15 🚐 £8-£15 ⛺ £8-£15
Open Apr-Sep Last departure 14.00hrs
The private road off A31 leads to this well-screened park divided into paddocks, spacious pitches. This is one of the nearest parks to Bournemouth with its many holiday amenities. A 12-acre site with 151 touring pitches.

Leisure: 🅰
Facilities: 🏕✳♿🔥🖷🐕
Services: 🖳🔋🅱♿→🅄🛠
Notes: Dogs on leads

> Don't forget matches, a torch and spare batteries, and the means to make a drink. Packet soups are sustaining until the shops open.

Leisure: 🏊 Indoor swimming pool 🏊 Outdoor swimming pool 🎾 Tennis court 🎱 Games room 🅰 Children's playground ♿ Stables
▶ 9/18 hole golf course 🚣 Boats for hire 🎬 Cinema 🎣 Fishing ◎ Mini golf ⛵ Watersports 📺 Separate TV room

HOLTON HEATH   Map 04 SY99

76% *Sandford Holiday Park*
(SY939916)
BH16 6JZ ☎ 0870 0667793 &
01202 622513 📠 01202 625678
GOLD
🅔 bookings@weststarholidays.co.uk
Ⓦ www.weststarholidays.co.uk
*Dir: From Poole take A35 towards Dorchester, at
lights turn onto A351 towards Wareham. Right
at Holton Heath. Park 100yds on left on Organford
Road*
🚐🚍🅐
Open Mar-Nov Booking advisable Jul-Aug &
bank hols Last arrival 22.00hrs Last departure
10.00hrs
*With touring pitches set individually in 20 acres
surrounded by woodland, this park offers a full
range of leisure activities and entertainment for
the whole family. The touring area is neat and
well maintained, and there are children's clubs
in the daytime and nightly entertainment.
A 64-acre site with 500 touring pitches and
284 statics.*
Fun factory, bowling, entertainment, crazy golf.
Leisure: ⚽ 🎾 🏊 🎱 🎮 🖵
Facilities: ⚓ 🐾 ⊙ ✻ 👶 🔌 💺 🛒 🖪 🐕
Services: 🚰 🔋 ⚡ 🍴 ✗ 👕 → ∪ 🅿 ⊚ 🔥 👕 🥄

💳   💳   💳   💳   💳

See advertisement under POOLE

HORTON   Map 05 SU00

▶ ▶ ▶ 75% Meadow View Caravan Park
(SU045070)
Wigbeth BH21 7JH ☎ 01258 840040
📠 01258 840040
🅔 mail@meadowviewcaravanpark.co.uk
Ⓦ www.meadowviewcaravanpark.co.uk
*Dir: Follow unclass road from Horton to site, 0.5m from
Druscilla pub*
★ 🚐 £8-£12.50 🚍 £8-£12.50 🅐 £8-£12.50
Open all year Booking advisable Jul-Aug Last
arrival 21.00hrs Last departure 11.00hrs
*A small family-owned park, part of a specialised
commercial turf farm, and set in a very rural area
with its own lake and nature reserve. This very good
park is always neatly trimmed and clean. A 1.5-acre
site with 15 touring pitches, 7 hardstandings.*
Coarse fishing
Facilities: 🐾 ⊙ 🔌 ✻ 🛒 🖪 🐕
Services: 🚰 🔋 🖪 → ∪ 🅿 🥄
Notes: Dogs must be kept on leads

LYME REGIS   Map 04 SY39
See also **Charmouth**

▶ ▶ ▶ 77% *Hook Farm Caravan & Camping Park*
(SY323930)
Gore Ln, Uplyme DT7 3UU ☎ 01297 442801
📠 01297 442801
🅔 information@hookfarm-uplyme.co.uk
Ⓦ www.hookfarm-uplyme.co.uk
Dir: From A35 towards Lyme Regis & Uplyme take

contd.

Abbreviations: BH/bank hols-bank holidays   Etr-Easter   Whit-Whitsun   dep-departure   fr-from   hrs-hours   m-mile   mdnt-midnight
rdbt-roundabout   rs-restricted service   wk-week   wknd-weekend   🐕̸-no dogs

B3165 at Hunters Lodge pub. 2m turn right into Gore
Lane, site 400yds on right
🏕 ⚊

Open all year (rs Nov-Feb shop not open/booking
required) Booking advisable Etr, May BH, Jul & Aug
Last arrival 22.00hrs Last departure 11.00hrs
*Set in a peaceful and very rural location with views
of Lym Valley and just a mile from the seaside at
Lyme Regis. The modern toilet facilities are part of
an upgrading programme, and there are good on-
site amenities. Most pitches are level due to
excellent terracing. A 5.5-acre site with 100 touring
pitches and 17 statics.*

Leisure: ⚊ Facilities: ⬤⬤⬤⬤⬤⬤⬤⬤
Services: ⬤⬤⬤⬤⬤→⬤⬤⬤⬤⬤⬤⬤⬤

▶ ▶ ▶ **75% Shrubbery Touring Park (SY300914)**
Rousdon DT7 3XW ☎ 01297 442227
🖷 01297 442227
ⓦ www.ukparks.co.uk/shrubbery
Dir: 3m W of Lyme Regis on A3052 coast road
★ 🏕 £8.25-£12.25 🏕 £7.75-£11.50 ⚊ £7.75-£11.50

Open Mar-Oct Booking advisable BH's & Jul-Aug
Last arrival 23.00hrs Last departure 11.00hrs
*Mature trees enclose this peaceful park which has
distant views of the lovely surrounding countryside.
The modern facilities are well kept, and there is
plenty of space for children to play in the grounds.
Located on the Devon/Dorset borders, just 3 miles
from Lyme Regis. A 10-acre site with 120 touring
pitches.*
Crazy golf

Leisure: ⚊ Facilities: ⬤⬤⬤⬤⬤⬤
Services: ⬤⬤⬤⬤⬤→⬤⬤⬤⬤⬤⬤
💳 💳 💳 💳 💳

LYTCHETT MINSTER   Map 04 SY99

▶ ▶ ▶ **71% South Lytchett Manor Caravan Park
(SY954926)**
The Lodge, Dorchester Rd BH16 6JB
☎ 01202 622577 🖷 01202 622620
🅔 slmcp@talk21.com
ⓦ www.eluk.co.uk/camping/dorset/slytchett
Dir: On B3067, off A35, 1m E of Lytchett Minster
★ 🏕 £11-£17 🏕 £11-£17 ⚊ £11-£17
Open Mar-Oct Booking advisable bank hols & mid
Jul-Aug Last arrival 22.00hrs Last departure
11.00hrs
*A pleasant family-owned park set along the tree-
lined driveway of the old manor house, with pitches
enjoying open views of pastureland. Facilities are*
contd.

*basic but clean and well cared for, and the park is
only 3m from Poole. A 15-acre site with 150 touring
pitches, 7 hardstandings.*
Pool table & table tennis

Leisure: ⚊ ⬤ Facilities: ⬤⬤⬤⬤⬤⬤⬤⬤
Services: ⬤⬤⬤⬤⬤⬤⬤→⬤⬤⬤⬤⬤
Notes: Dogs must be kept on leads
💳 💳 💳 💳 💳

MORETON   Map 04 SY88

▶ ▶ ▶ **79% Camping & Caravanning Club Site
(SY782892)**
Station Rd DT2 8BB ☎ 01305 853801
ⓦ www.campingandcaravanningclub.co.uk
*Dir: From Poole on A35, past Bere Regis, left onto B3390
signed Alfpuddle. After approx 2m site on left before
Moreton Station and next to public house*
★ 🏕 £13.60-£19.80 🏕 £13.60-£19.80
⚊ £13.60-£19.80
Open Mar-Nov Booking advisable bank hols & peak
periods Last arrival 21.00hrs Last departure noon
*Modern purpose-built site on level ground with
good amenities. This tidy, well-maintained park
offers electric hook-ups to most pitches, and there
is a first class play area for children. Please see the
advertisement on page 11 for information on Club
sites and membership. A 7-acre site with
118 touring pitches, 10 hardstandings.*

Leisure: ⚊ Facilities: ⬤⬤⬤⬤⬤⬤⬤⬤
Services: ⬤⬤⬤⬤⬤⬤⬤→⬤⬤⬤ 💳 💳 💳 💳

England

ORGANFORD   Map 04 SY99

▶ ▶ ▶ ▶ **83% Pear Tree Touring Park** (SY938915)
Organford Rd, Holton Heath BH16 6LA
☎ 01202 622434
✉ info@visitpeartree.co.uk
🌐 www.visitpeartree.co.uk
Dir: *From Poole take A35 towards Dorchester, onto A351 towards Wareham, at 1st lights turn right, park 300yds on left*
★ 🚐 £10.50-£18 🚐 £10.50-£18 ▲ £10-£18

Open Etr & Apr-Oct Booking advisable Etr, Spring bank hol & end Jul-Aug Last arrival 22.00hrs Last departure 11.00hrs
A quiet, sheltered country park, with refurbished toilet facilities offering quality and comfort. The touring area is divided into terraces with mature hedges for screening, with a separate level tenting area on the edge of woodland. The friendly atmosphere at this attractive park, and the many colourful flower beds help to ensure a relaxing holiday. A bridle path leads into Wareham Forest. A 7.5-acre site with 125 touring pitches, 10 hardstandings.
Leisure: ⚙ **Facilities:** ⌐⊙🍴✳🕭↻🛒🎋🎠
Services: 🍴🖥🛢🅿🗑🚽↻↻🅿🔺🔌🧹
🈸 🖾 🖾 🏴 🔲

▶ ▶ ▶ **75% Organford Manor** (SY943926)
BH16 6ES ☎ 01202 622202 & 623278
🖷 01202 623278
✉ organford@lds.co.uk
🌐 www.organfordmanor.co.uk
Dir: *On A35 1st on left after Lytchett rdbt at junct with A351. Site entrance on right*
🚐 🚐 ▲

Open 15 Mar-Oct Booking advisable peak periods Last arrival 22.00hrs Last departure noon
A quiet, secluded site in the grounds of the manor house with level grassy areas amongst trees and shrubs. Set midway between Poole and Wareham
                             contd.

---

in an attractive rural location, it boasts smart toilet facilities and an efficient laundry. An 8-acre site with 70 touring pitches, 1 hardstanding and 45 statics.
Facilities: ⌐⊙🍴✳↻🛒
Services: 🍴🖥🛢🗑🅱🚽↻↻🅿🔌

OSMINGTON MILLS   Map 04 SY78

▶ ▶ ▶ **75% Osmington Mills Holidays** (SY736820)
DT3 6HB ☎ 01305 832311 🖷 01305 835251
✉ holidays@osmingtonmills.fsnet.co.uk
🌐 www.osmington-mills-holidays.co.uk
Dir: *Take A353 towards Weymouth. At Osmington Mills sign (opposite garage) turn left to site*
★ ▲ £10-£18
Open May-Oct (rs mid Mar-May & Oct-mid Nov pool closed, shop closed to Etr) Booking advisable Last departure 10.00hrs
A large, slightly sloping field with hedging and natural screening providing bays, in a peaceful setting close to the Dorset coastline and footpaths. The upgraded facilities are of a very good quality. The park offers seasonal entertainment in a ranch-style bar, and an outdoor swimming pool with paddling pools. A 14-acre site with 225 touring pitches and 83 statics.
Riding stables & coarse fishing
Leisure: 🎣 **Facilities:** ⌐⊙🍴✳↻🛒
Services: 🍴🖥🍽🛢🗑🅱🚽✖🧹↻🅿🔌
Notes: 🐕 No stag or hen parties 🈸 🖾 🖾 🏴 🔲

OWERMOIGNE   Map 04 SY78

▶ ▶ ▶ **80% Sandyholme Caravan Park** (SY768863)
Moreton Rd DT2 8HZ ☎ 01305 852677
🖷 01305 854677
✉ smeatons@sandyholme.co.uk
🌐 www.sandyholme.co.uk
Dir: *From A352 (Wareham to Dorchester road) turn right to Owermoigne for 1m. Site on left.*
★ 🚐 £11-£16 🚐 £8.50-£16 ▲ £8.50-£16

GOLD

Open Apr-Oct Booking advisable peak periods Last arrival 21.30hrs Last departure 10.30hrs
A quiet family-run site in a tree-lined rural setting within easy reach of the coast at Lulworth Cove, and handy for several seaside resorts. The facilities are very good, including a superb toilet block, and decent food is available in the lounge/bar. A 6-acre site with 50 touring pitches and 55 statics.
Table tennis
Leisure: 🎣 ⚙ **Facilities:** ⌐⊙🍴✳↻🛒🎋
Services: 🍴🖥🍽🛢🗑🅱🚽✖↻↻🅿🔌 **Notes:** Dogs must be kept on leads 🈸 🖾 🖾 🏴 🔲

POOLE
Map 04 SZ09
See also **Lytchett Minster, Organford & Wimborne Minster**

76% Rockley Park (SY982909)
Hamworthy BH15 4LZ
☎ 01202 679393
📠 01202 683159
ⓦ www.havenholidays.com
Dir: Take A31 off M27 to Poole centre, then follow signs to park

Open mid Mar-Oct (rs mid Mar-May & Sep-Oct Some facilities may be reduced) Booking advisable school hols Last departure 10.00hrs
A complete holiday experience including a wide range of day and night entertainment, and plenty of sports and leisure activities. Water sports are comprehensively covered, and there is also mooring and launching from the park. The touring area has been upgraded to provide good quality facilities. A 90-acre site with 101 touring pitches, 68 hardstandings and 1077 statics.
Sailing school

Leisure: 🏊 🏊 🎱 🛝 **Facilities:** ⊙ ✳ ⅋ ⅃ 🏪 🏛

Services: 🗑 🍴 ✕ 🕍 → ◎ ⅃ ⅃ 🎣

Notes: Dogs not allowed on touring pitches

▶ ▶ ▶ **77% *Beacon Hill Touring Park (SY977945)***
Blandford Rd North BH16 6AB
☎ 01202 631631
📠 01202 625749
ⓔ bookings@beaconhilltouringpark.co.uk
ⓦ www.beaconhilltouringpark.co.uk
Dir: On A350, 0.25m N of junct with A35, 4m N of Poole

🚐 🚐 ⅃

Open Etr-Sep (rs low & mid season some services closed/restricted opening) Booking advisable Etr, Whit & Jul-Aug Last arrival 23.00hrs Last departure 11.00hrs
Set in attractive, wooded area with conservation very much in mind. Two large ponds are within the grounds and the terraced pitches, informally sited so that visitors can choose their favourite spot, offer some fine views. A 30-acre site with 170 touring pitches, 10 hardstandings.
Fishing & view point.

Leisure: 🏊 🎱 🛝 🖥

Facilities: 🏪 ⊙ ⅃ ✳ ⅃ ⅃ 🏪 🐕

Services: 🗑 🍴 🅿 🛒 🕍 ✕ 🕍 → ∪ 🅿 ⅃ 🎣 🍴 🎣

Notes: Groups of young people accepted at management's discretion

Leisure: 🏊 Indoor swimming pool 🏊 Outdoor swimming pool 🎾 Tennis court 🎱 Games room 🛝 Children's playground ∪ Stables ▶ 9/18 hole golf course 🛥 Boats for hire 🎬 Cinema 🎣 Fishing ◎ Mini golf 🌊 Watersports 🖥 Separate TV room

PORTESHAM   Map 04 SY68

NEW ► ► ► ► 78% **Portesham Dairy Farm Campsite (SY602854)**
DT3 4HG ☎ 01305 871297
Dir: from Dorchester on A35 towards Bridport. After 5m left at Winterbourne Abbas, follow Portesham signs. Through village, left at Kings Arms pub, site in 350yds on right
🚐 🚐 Å
Open mid Mar-Oct
Located at the edge of the picturesque village of Portesham, this family run park is part of a small working dairy farm in a quiet rural location. This level park has a local pub near the site entrance where meals are served, and with a garden for children. An 8-acre site with 78 touring pitches.
Facilities: 🌐

PUNCKNOWLE   Map 04 SY58

NEW ► ► 72% **Home Farm Caravan and Campsite (SY535887)**
Home Farm, Rectory Ln DT2 9BW ☎ 01308 897258
Dir: from Dorchester on A35 towards Bridport, turn left at start of dual carriageway to Litton Cheney. Through village, 2nd left to Puncknowle. Left at T-junct, left at phone box. Site 150mtrs on right
★ 🚐 £8-£12 🚐 £8-£12 Å £6-£10
Open Apr or Etr-Oct Booking advisable May Day BH & Jul-Aug Last arrival 21.00hrs Last departure noon
A quiet site hidden away on the edge of this little hamlet. It offers sweeping views of the Dorset countryside from most pitches, and is just 5 miles from Abbotsbury, and 1.5m from the South West Coastal Footpath. A 6.5-acre site with 47 touring pitches.
Facilities: 🌐 ⊙ 🔧 ✳ 🕻 🗛 **Services:** 🖭 🎱 🔌 🍴 🔲
Notes: Dogs must be kept on leads, no cats

ST LEONARDS   Map 05 SU10

 76% *Oakdene Forest Park (SU095023)*
BH24 2RZ ☎ 01590 648331
🖨 01590 645610
🌐 holidays@shorefield.co.uk
🌐 www.shorefield.co.uk
Dir: 3m W of Ringwood off A31, turn left after foot bridge over A31
🚐 Å
Open Feb-2 Jan Booking advisable all times Last arrival 22.00hrs Last departure 10.00hrs
Set in 55 acres of parkland beside the beautiful Avon Forest, this full-entertainment park offers 'fun and games' for the whole family, and there are both indoor and outdoor pools, and a riding stable on site. A special children's programme is offered during high season. A 55-acre site with 81 touring pitches and 350 statics.
Woodland walks & crazy golf
Leisure: 🏊 🏊 🎣 🎮 **Facilities:** 🌐 ⊙ 🔧 ✳ 🕻 🛎 🗛 🐾
Services: 🖭 🎱 🍴 🔌 🔲 🎫 ✕ 🚽 → ∪ 🛒 🍴 🎵
🔳 🔳 🔳 🔳 🎴

See advertisement on page 153

► ► ► ► 77% **Back of Beyond Touring Park (SU103034)**
234 Ringwood Rd BH24 2SB ☎ 01202 876968
🖨 01202 876968
🌐 melandsuepike@aol.com
🌐 www.backofbeyondtouringpark.co.uk
Dir: W along A31, in St Leonards turn right at Boundary Lane rdbt. Follow signs for 0.5m down lane.
★ 🚐 £11-£15.50 🚐 £11-£15.50 Å £11-£15.50
Open Mar-Oct Booking advisable summer Last arrival 21.00hrs Last departure noon
Set well off the beaten track in natural woodland surroundings, with its own river and lake yet close to many attractions. This tranquil park has been completely redeveloped by keen, friendly owners, and the quality facilities are for adults only. A 28-acre site with 80 touring pitches.
Lake & river fishing, 9-hole pitch & putt course
Facilities: 🌐 ⊙ 🔧 ✳ 🕻 🛎 🗛 🗛 🐾
Services: 🖭 🎱 🔌 🍴 🔲 🎫 ✕ 🚽 → ∪ 🛒 🎵
Notes: Adults only, no commercial vehicles
🔳 🔳 🔳 🔳 🎴

► ► ► 78% *Forest Edge Touring Park (SU104024)*
229 Ringwood Rd BH24 2SD ☎ 01590 648331
🖨 01590 645610
🌐 holidays@shorefield.co.uk
🌐 www.shorefield.co.uk
Dir: 3m W of Ringwood off A31, turn left at rdbt into Boundary Lane
🚐 🚐 Å
Open Feb-Dec (rs mid Jul-Aug pool only open school & summer holidays) Booking advisable at all times Last arrival 21.00hrs Last departure 10.00hrs
A tree-lined park set in grassland with plenty of excellent amenities for all the family, including an outdoor heated swimming pool and toddlers' pool, an adventure playground, and two launderettes. Visitors are invited to use the superb leisure club plus all amenities and entertainment at the sister site of Oakdene Forest Park less than a mile away. Some pitches may experience traffic noise from the nearby A31. A 9-acre site with 202 touring pitches.
Leisure: 🏊 🎣 🎮 **Facilities:** 🌐 ⊙ 🔧 ✳ 🕻 🛎
Services: 🖭 🎱 🍴 🔌 🔲 🎫 → ∪ 🛒 🎵 **Notes:** 1 dog & car per pitch 🔳 🔳 🔳 🎴

See advertisement on page 153

► ► ► 77% **Shamba Holiday Park (SU105029)**
230 Ringwood Rd BH24 2SB ☎ 01202 873302
🖨 01202 873392
🌐 enquiries@shambaholidays.co.uk
🌐 www.shambaholidays.co.uk
Dir: Off A31, from Poole turn left into Eastmoors Lane, 100yds past 2nd rdbt from Texaco garage. Park 0.25m on right, just past the Hungry Poacher inn
★ 🚐 £15-£20 🚐 £15-£20 Å £15-£20
Open Mar-Oct (rs Low season some facilities only open at weekends) Booking advisable bank hols & Jul-Aug Last arrival 22.00hrs Last departure 11.00hrs

contd.

Abbreviations: BH/bank hols-bank holidays   Etr-Easter   Whit-Whitsun   dep-departure   fr-from   hrs-hours   m-mile   mdnt-midnight   rdbt-roundabout   rs-restricted service   wk-week   wknd-weekend   ✂-no dogs

A relaxed touring park in pleasant countryside between the New Forest and Bournemouth. The park is very well equipped for holidaymakers, with swimming pool, good playground, and bar, shop and takeaway. A 7-acre site with 150 touring pitches.
Phone card top-up facility

Leisure: ﹩ ♦ ⋔

Facilities: ⇢ ⋔ ⊙ ℞ ✳ ⅋ ⅄ ⅏ ⋔

Services: ⊞ ⊟ ❢ ⅃ ⌀ ⊞ ⊤ ⅏ → ∪ ▶ ⌁

Notes: No large groups ⊛ ▭ ▦ ▧ ⊡

SHAFTESBURY   Map 04 ST82

▶ ▶ **76% Blackmore Vale Caravan & Camping Park** (ST835233)
Sherborne Causeway SP7 9PX
☎ 01747 851523 & 852573 ▤ 01747 851671
ⓦ www.caravancampingsites.co.uk/
    dorset/blackmorevale.htm
Dir: *From Shaftesbury's Ivy Cross rdbt take A30 signed Sherborne. Site 2m on right*
★ ⊞ £8.50-£10 ⊞ £8-£9 ▲ £7-£8
Open all year Booking advisable bank hols Last arrival 21.00hrs
A comfortable touring park with spacious pitches and well-maintained facilities. Set behind a caravan sales showground and dealership, and about 2m from Shaftesbury. A 3-acre site with 26 touring pitches, 6 hardstandings and 12 statics.
Caravan sales & accessories

Facilities: ⋔ ⊙ ✳ ⅋ ⅄ ⅏ ⋔

Services: ⊞ ❢ ⌀ ⊞ ⊤ → ∪ ▶ ⌁ ⊡
⊛ ▭ ▦ ▧ ⊡

SIXPENNY HANDLEY   Map 04 ST91

▶ ▶ ▶ **75% Church Farm Caravan & Camping Park** (ST994173)
The Bungalow, Church Farm High St SP5 5ND
☎ 01725 552563 ▤ 01725 552563
ⓔ churchfarmcandcpark@yahoo.co.uk
ⓦ www.churchfarmcandcpark.co.uk
Dir: *A354, between Salisbury and Blandford, turn off towards Sixpenny Handley, and site at top of village, by church and war memorial.*
★ ⊞ £9-£11 ⊞ £9-£11 ▲ £9-£11
Open all year Booking advisable BHs May & Aug Last arrival 21.00hrs Last departure anytime
A spacious, open park located within the Cranborne Chase in an Area of Outstanding Natural Beauty. There are good quality toilet facilities, and the pretty village of Sixpenny Handley with all its amenities is 200yds away. A 5-acre site with 20 touring pitches, 2 hardstandings and 2 statics.
Recycling facilities & caravan storage

Leisure: ⋔

Facilities: ⋔ ⊙ ✳ ⅋ ⅄ ⅏ ⋔

Services: ⊞ ⅄ ⌀ ❢ ⌀ ⊤ ✗ → ▶

Notes: Dogs must be kept on leads, quiet after 11pm

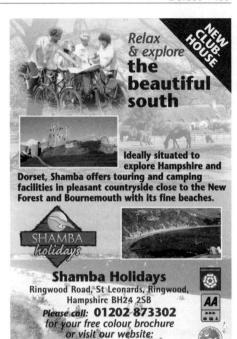

SWANAGE   Map 05 SZ07

NEW ▶ ▶ ▶ **75% Swanage Coastal Park** (SZ024797)
Priestway BH19 2RS ☎ 01590 648331
▤ 01590 645610
ⓔ holidays@shorefield.co.uk
ⓦ www.shorefield.co.uk
Dir: *A351 from Wareham. 1m past 'Welcome to Swanage' sign, right into High St. 1st right into Bell St. Up hill, 1st left into Priests Rd, 1st right into Priestway to site*
★ ⊞ £10-£19.50 ⊞ £10-£19.50 ▲ £8-£15
Open 24 Mar-Oct Booking advisable At all times Last arrival 22.00hrs Last departure 10.00hrs
Newly acquired by Shorefield Holidays, this 15-acre site is set in stunning countryside with views over Swanage Bay and the Purbeck Hills. The shops and beaches at Swanage are less than a mile away, and the adjacent holiday park offers day membership to its health and fitness club, including bar, indoor swimming pool, gym, sauna, solarium, shop and restaurant. A 15-acre site with 10 touring pitches, 10 hardstandings and 52 statics.

Leisure: ⋔

Facilities: ⅃ ⅄ → △ ⅋ ⅏ ⌁ ⊡

Notes: Dogs must be kept on leads
⊛ ▭ ▦ ▧ ⊡

See advertisement on page 153

Facilities: ⇢ Bath ⋔ Shower ⊙ Electric Shaver ℞ Hairdryer ✳ Ice Pack Facility � Disabled Facilities ⅃ Public Telephone ⅄ Shop on Site or within 200yds ⊡ Mobile Shop (calls at least 5 days a week) ⅏ BBQ Area ⋔ Picnic Area ⋔ Dog Exercise Area

England

► ► ► 78% **Ulwell Cottage Caravan Park** (SZ019809)
Ulwell Cottage, Ulwell BH19 3DG
☎ 01929 422823 📠 01929 421500

SILVER

E enq@ulwellcottagepark.co.uk
W www.ulwellcottagepark.co.uk
Dir: From Swanage N for 2m on unclass road towards Studland
★ 🚐 £12.50-£30 🚐 £10-£30 ▲ £10-£30
Open Mar-7 Jan (rs Mar-Spring bank hol & mid Sep-early Jan takeaway closed, shop open variable hours) Booking advisable bank hols & Jul-Aug Last arrival 22.00hrs Last departure 11.00hrs
Nestling under the Purbeck Hills surrounded by scenic walks and only 2 miles from the beach. This family-run park caters well for families and couples, offering high quality facilities including an indoor heated swimming pool and village inn. A 13-acre site with 77 touring pitches, 19 hardstandings and 140 statics.
Leisure: 🏊 🅰 Facilities: 🕅 ⊙ ✳ ⚬ 🖫 🎢
Services: 🚐 🔋 🍴 🛒 🎯 🚿 🍳 🗙 → ∪ ▶ ⊙ 🛆 ↘ ✈
💳 🚬 🔔 🔕

NEW ► 72% **Acton Field Camping Site** (SY991785)
Acton Field, Langton Matravers BH19 3HS
☎ 01929 424184 & 439424
Dir: from Wareham take A351 towards Swanage. Turn right onto B3069. Turn right for site before entering Langton Matravers
🚐 £8-£12 🚐 £8-£12 ▲ £5-£10
Open mid Jul-early Sep

contd.

An informal campsite bordered by farmland on the outskirts of Langton Maltravers. There are superb views of the Purbeck Hills and towards the Isle of Wight, and a footpath leads to the coastal path. The site was once a stone quarry, and rock pegs are required. A 7-acre site with 50 touring pitches.
Facilities: 🕅

THREE LEGGED CROSS — Map 05 SU00

► ► ► 74% **Woolsbridge Manor Farm Caravan Park** (SZ103050)
BH21 6RA ☎ 01202 826369

SILVER

📠 01202 820603
E woolsbridge@btconnect.com
W www.woolsbridgemanorfarmcaravanpark.co.uk
Dir: 2m off A31, 3m W of Ringwood. From Three Legged Cross continue S to Woolsbridge. Site 1.75m on left
★ 🚐 £11.50-£16.50 🚐 £11.50-£16.50 ▲ £11.50-£16.50

Open Etr-Oct Booking advisable bank hols & Aug Last arrival 20.00hrs Last departure 10.30hrs
A small farm site with spacious pitches on a level field. This quiet site is an excellent central base for touring the New Forest, Salisbury and the South coast, and is close to Moors Valley Country Park for outdoor family activities. A 6.75-acre site with 60 touring pitches.
Leisure: 🅰 Facilities: 🕅 ⊙ ⚲ ✳ ⚬ 🖢 🖫 🎢 🎠
Services: 🚐 🔋 🍴 🛒 🎯 → ∪ ▶ ✈ 🔕
💳 🚬 🔔 🔕 🔕
See advertisement under WIMBORNE MINSTER

VERWOOD — Map 05 SU00

► ► ► 75% **Camping & Caravanning Club Site** (SU069098)
Sutton Hill, Woodlands BH21 8NQ ☎ 01202 822763
W www.campingandcaravanningclub.co.uk
Dir: Turn left on A354 13m from Salisbury onto B3081, site is 1.5m W of Verwood
★ 🚐 £13.60-£17.80 🚐 £13.60-£17.80 ▲ £13.60-£17.80
Open Mar-Oct Booking advisable bank hols & peak periods Last arrival 21.00hrs Last departure noon
Set on rising ground between the woodland of the New Forest and the rolling downs of Cranborne Chase and Salisbury Plains. This comfortable site is well kept by very keen wardens. Please see the advertisement on page 11 for information on Club sites and membership. A 12.75-acre site with 150 touring pitches, 17 hardstandings.
Leisure: 🎱 🅰 Facilities: 🕅 ⊙ ⚲ ✳ ⚬ 🖢 🎢 🎠
Services: 🚐 🔋 🍴 🛒 🎯 → ▶ 🎯 💳 🚬 🔔 🔕 🔕

WAREHAM — Map 04 SY98

► ► ► ► 85% **Wareham Forest Tourist Park** (SY894912)
North Trigon BH20 7NZ
☎ 01929 551393 ▤ 01929 558321
✉ holiday@wareham-forest.co.uk
ⓦ www.wareham-forest.co.uk
★ ➡ £12-£18 ➡ £12-£18 ▲ £9.50-£18

SILVER

Open all year (rs off-peak season limited services)
Booking advisable Spring bank hol & Jul-Aug Last
arrival 21.00hrs Last departure 10.30hrs
*A friendly woodland park ideally located within the
tranquil Wareham Forest, with its many walks and
proximity to Poole, Dorchester and the Purbeck
coast. It offers excellent facilities in two luxury
blocks, with combined washbasin/WCs for total
privacy, and a high standard of cleanliness. A
heated outdoor swimming pool, off licence, snack
bar, shop and games room add to the pleasure of a
stay here. A 42-acre site with 200 touring pitches, 62
hardstandings.*

Leisure: ⌇ ◕ ⋒
Facilities: ⋔ ⊙ �ℚ ✻ ⅋ ℄ ⅋ ⊞ ⊓ ⅋
Services: ⊡ ⅃ ⊟ ▯ ∅ ⊞ ⊤ → ∪ ⅂ ⅋ ⅋ ⅃
Notes: Couples & families only, no group bookings

⬤ ▭ ▭ 🎦

► ► ► 81% *Birchwood Tourist Park* (SY896905)
Bere Rd, North Trigon BH20 7PA ☎ 01929 554763
▤ 01929 556635
ⓦ www.birchwoodtouristpark.co.uk
Dir: From Poole (A351) or Dorchester (A352) on N side
of railway line at Wareham, follow road signed Bere
Regis (unclassified). 2nd tourist park after 2.25m
➡ ➡ ▲
Open Mar-Oct (rs Nov-Feb Some restrictions)
Booking advisable bank hols & Jul-Aug Last arrival
21.00hrs Last departure 11.30hrs
*Set in 50 acres of parkland located within Wareham
Forest, this site offers direct access into ideal areas
for walking, mountain biking, and horse and pony
riding. The modern facilities are centrally located
and well-organised. A 25-acre site with 175 touring
pitches, 8 hardstandings.*
Games field, bike hire, pitch & putt, paddling pool

Leisure: ◕ ⋒
Facilities: ⋔ ⊙ ⅂ ✻ ℄ ⅋ ⅋ ⅋
Services: ⊡ ⅃ ▯ ∅ ⊞ ⊤ ⅋ → ∪ ⅂ ⅋ ⅋ ⅃
Notes: No generators, no groups at Bank Hols

⬤ ▭ ▭

► ► ► 73% **East Creech Camping & Caravan Park**
(SY928827)
East Creech Farm, East Creech BH20 5AP
☎ 01929 480519 & 481312
✉ east.creech@virgin.net
ⓦ www.eastcreechfarm.co.uk
Dir: From Wareham on A351 S towards Swanage.
On bypass at 3rd rdbt take Furzebrook/Blue Pool Rd
exit, approx 2m site on right
★ ➡ £7.50-£13 ➡ £7.50-£13 ▲ £7.50-£13
Open Apr-Oct Booking advisable bank holidays &
peak season
*A grassy park set in a peaceful location beneath the
Purbeck Hills, with extensive views towards Poole
and Brownsea Island. The park boasts a woodland
play area, bright, clean toilet facilities, and a farm
shop selling milk, eggs and bread. There are also
three coarse fishing lakes teeming with fish.
A 2.5-acre site with 80 touring pitches.*

Leisure: ⋒
Facilities: ⋔ ⊙ ✻ ℄
Services: ⊡ ⊞ → ⅋ ⅃ ▯ ⅋

Practise setting up your tent at home
before you take it on holiday, and check
that all guy ropes, pegs and poles are
present and intact.

England

▶ ▶ ▶ **77% Lookout Holiday Park (SY927858)**
Stoborough BH20 5AZ ☎ 01929 552546
📠 01929 556662
✉ enquiries@caravan-sites.co.uk
🌐 www.caravan-sites.co.uk
Dir: Take A351 through Wareham, after crossing River Frome & through Stoborough, site signed on left
🚐 🚐 Å

Open all year Booking advisable bank hols & Jul-Aug Last arrival 22.00hrs Last departure noon
Divided into two paddocks and set well back from the Swanage road, this touring park is separated from the static part of the operation. A superb children's playground and plenty of other attractions make this an ideal centre for families. A 5-acre site with 150 touring pitches, 94 hardstandings and 90 statics.
Leisure: 🐟 ⛰ **Facilities:** 🍴 ⊙ 🍳 ✳ ⏦ ℃ 🚿
Services: 🚿 🔋 🛢 ⊘ 🖽 🖫 ♨ → ∪ ▶ ⅄ 🐶 ⟍
Notes: ⌀ 🍶 💳 📶 🔲

▶ ▶ ▶ **70% Ridge Farm Camping & Caravan Park (SY939868)**
Barnhill Rd, Ridge BH20 5BG ☎ 01929 556444
✉ info@ridgefarm.co.uk
🌐 www.ridgefarm.co.uk
Dir: From Wareham take B3075 towards Corfe Castle, cross river to Stoborough, then left to Ridge and follow site signs for 1.5m
★ 🚐 £9-£11 🚐 £9-£11 Å £9-£11
Open Etr-Sep Booking advisable Jul & Aug Last arrival 21.00hrs Last departure noon
A quiet rural park, adjacent to a working farm and surrounded by trees and bushes. This away-from-it-all park is ideally located for touring this part of Dorset, and especially for bird watchers, or those who enjoy walking and cycling. A 3.5-acre site with 60 touring pitches, 2 hardstandings.
Facilities: 🍴 ⊙ 🍳 ✳ ℃ 🚿
Services: 🚿 🔋 🛢 ⊘ 🖽 🖫 → ∪ ▶ ⅄ 🐶 ⟍
Notes: No dogs Jul-Aug

▶ ▶ ▶ **75% Woodlands Camping Park (SY867861)**
Bindon Ln, East Stoke BH20 6AS ☎ 01929 462327
📠 01929 462327
✉ stay@woodlandscampingpark.co.uk
🌐 www.woodlandscampingpark.co.uk
Dir: From Wool - at rail crossing turn off A352 onto B3071, at right bend turn left into Bindon Lane. Park 1.5m on right. From Wareham – A352 onto B3070 at junct for East Stoke, right into Bindon/Holme Lane. Park 1.5m on left
Å fr £14
Open Apr-Sep Booking advisable May-Aug & bank hols Last arrival 21.30hrs Last departure noon
A rural tents-only park set in an Area of Outstanding Natural Beauty surrounded by woodland. The park is divided into three areas by trees, and is appreciated by people looking for peace and quiet. Facilities are well kept, and security is good. Conversational French, German and Spanish are spoken. A 2.75-acre site with 50 touring pitches. Fridge-freezer
Facilities: 🍴 ⊙ 🍳 ✳ ⅊ 🚿 → ∪ 🖩
Notes: ⌀ No camp fires, no loud radios, no groups apart from award schemes

WARMWELL   Map 04 SY78

▶ ▶ ▶ **77% Warmwell Country Touring Park (SY764878)**
DT2 8JD ☎ 01305 852313 📠 01305 851824
✉ stay@warmwell-country-touring-park.co.uk
🌐 www.warmwell-country-touring-park.co.uk
Dir: On B3390 which joins A35 and A352
★ 🚐 £11.95-£15.95 🚐 £11.95-£15.95 Å £9.40-£13.40
Open Mar-Dec Booking advisable Etr-Sep & Xmas Last arrival 21.00hrs Last departure 11.00hrs
A lovely setting in an old quarry, with small open areas or sheltered pitches amongst evergreen trees. The site is visited by plenty of wildlife including deer, badgers and foxes, and is in an Area of Outstanding Natural Beauty around the Purbeck Peninsula. A 15-acre site with 170 touring pitches and 20 statics.
Facilities: 🍴 ⊙ 🍳 ✳ ⅊ ℃ 🚿
Services: 🚿 🔋 ♉ 🛢 🖽 ✗ → ∪ ▶ ⊚ ◬ ⅄ ⟍
Notes: Adults only 🍶 💳 📶 🔲

WEYMOUTH — Map 04 SY67

 78% Littlesea (SY654783)
Lynch Ln DT4 9DT
☎ 01305 774414
📠 01305 760038
 SILVER
ⓦ www.havenholidays.com
Dir: A35 onto A354 signed Weymouth. Right at 1st rdbt, 3rd exit at 2nd rdbt towards Chickerell. Left into Lynch Lane after lights. Park at far end of road
🏕🚐⛺

Open mid Mar-Oct (rs mid Mar-May & Sep-Oct Facilities may be reduced) Booking advisable School hols Last arrival 22.00hrs Last departure noon
Just 3 miles from Weymouth with its lovely beaches and many attractions, Littlesea has a cheerful family atmosphere and fantastic facilities. Indoor and outdoor entertainment and activities are on offer for all the family, and the toilet facilities on the touring park are of a good quality. A 75-acre site with 220 touring pitches and 720 statics.

Leisure: 🏊 ⚲ ⚽ 🎯 ♨ ☐ Facilities: 🛍
Services: 🔌♀✕ 🔥🍴 🍺 🏧 Ⓓ 📶 🛒 🎵

 70% Seaview Holiday Park (SY707830)
Preston DT3 6DZ ☎ 01305 833037
📠 01305 833169
ⓦ www.havenholidays.com
Dir: A354 to Weymouth, signs for Preston/Wareham onto A353. Park 3m on right just after Weymouth Bay Holiday Park
🏕🚐⛺

Open mid Mar-Oct (rs mid Mar-May & Sep-Oct Facilities may be reduced) Booking advisable School hols Last arrival 22.00hrs Last departure noon

contd.

A fun-packed holiday centre for all the family, with plenty of activities and entertainment during the day and evening. Terraced pitches are provided for caravans, and there is a separate field for tents. The park is close to Weymouth and other coastal attractions. A 20-acre site with 96 touring pitches and 259 statics.

Leisure: 🏊 ⚲ ⚽ 🎯 ♨ ☐ Facilities: 🛍
Services: 🔌♀🛒✕ 🔥🍴 🍺 🏧 Ⓓ 📶 🛒 🎵

 82% Waterside Holiday Park (SY702822)
Bowleaze Cove DT3 6PP
☎ 01305 833103 📠 01305 832830
🌐 info@watersideholidays.co.uk
ⓦ www.watersideholidays.co.uk
Dir: From Weymouth take A353 E for 2m, then right fork to park in 0.5m
★ 🚐 £18-£32 🚐 £18-£32
Open Apr-Oct Booking advisable peak holidays Last arrival 21.30hrs Last departure 10.00hrs
A top quality leisure park with a full range of activities and entertainment. The touring area of this large complex is ideal for families of all ages, offering individual grass pitches divided by hedging. The beach is a short distance away, and a frequent bus service connects this holiday centre with Weymouth. The private owners maintain very high standards in all areas. A 35-acre site with 70 touring pitches and 540 statics.

Leisure: 🏊 ⚲ ⚽ ♨
Facilities: 🏪⊙♀☀⛽♿🛍🏧🚿
Services: 🔌♀🛒✕ 🔥→∪🍴⊙△🔥♨🎵
Notes: No tents, no commercial vehicles & no pets
🍴 🏧 📶 🎵

▶▶▶▶ **80% East Fleet Farm Touring Park (SY640797)**
Chickerell DT3 4DW ☎ 01305 785768
🌐 enquiries@eastfleet.co.uk
ⓦ www.eastfleet.co.uk
GOLD
Dir: On B3157 (Weymouth-Bridport road), 3m from Weymouth
★ 🚐 £5.50-£14 🚐 £5.50-£14 ⛺ £5.50-£14
Open 16 Mar-Oct Booking advisable peak season Last arrival 22.00hrs Last departure 10.30hrs

contd.

Set on a working organic farm overlooking Fleet Lagoon and Chesil Beach, with a wide range of amenities and quality toilet facilities. The friendly owners are welcoming and helpful, and their family bar serving meals and take-away food is open from Easter, with glorious views from the patio area. A 21-acre site with 270 touring pitches, 26 hardstandings.

Leisure: ♦ ⚠ Facilities: ↦ ⋒ ☉ ☜ ✳ ᴔ ↻ ☳ ⅏ ⊞ ♬ ★
Services: ⌷ ∀⅃ ⬚ ☲ ⚑ ⊘ ⊞ ⊤ ✕ ♨ → ∪ ┃ ☺ ◬ ♨ ⅃
◉ ☲☲☲ ☒ ☯

▶ ▶ ▶ 71% **Bagwell Farm Touring Park (SY627816)**
Knights in the Bottom, Chickerell DT3 4EA
☎ 01305 782575 🗎 01305 780554
🅔 aa@bagwellfarm.co.uk
🆆 www.bagwellfarm.co.uk
Dir: 4m W of Weymouth on B3157 (Weymouth-Bridport), past Chickerell, turn left into park 500yds after Victoria Inn.
★ 🚐 £8-£22 🚐 £8-£22 ▲ £8-£17

Open all year (rs Winter bar closed) Booking advisable bank/school hols Last arrival 21.00hrs Last departure 11.00hrs
An idyllically-placed terraced site on a hillside and a valley overlooking Chesil Beach. The park is well equipped with mini-supermarket, children's play area and pets corner, and a bar and grill serving food in high season. A 14-acre site with 320 touring pitches, 10 hardstandings.
Wet suit shower, camper's shelter.

Leisure: ⚠ Facilities: ↦ ⋒ ☉ ☜ ✳ ᴔ ↻ ☳ ⅏ ⊞ ★
Services: ⌷ ∀⅃ ⬚ ☲ ⚑ ⊘ ⊞ ⊤ ✕ ♨ → ∪
Notes: Families only, dogs must be kept on a lead
◉ ☲☲☲ ☒ ☯

▶ ▶ ▶ 69% *Pebble Bank Caravan Park (SY659775)*
Camp Rd, Wyke Regis DT4 9HF ☎ 01305 774844
🅔 info@pebblebank.co.uk
🆆 www.pebblebank.co.uk
Dir: From Weymouth take Portland road. At last rdbt turn right, then 1st left to Army Tent Camp. Site opposite
🚐 🚐 ▲

Open Etr-mid Oct bar open high season & wknds only Booking advisable peak times Last arrival 21.00hrs Last departure 11.00hrs
Overlooking Lyme Bay and Chesil Beach, this gently sloping grass site is only 1.5m from Weymouth town centre. The tenting field shares the same
contd.

wonderful views, and there is a friendly little bar. A 4-acre site with 40 touring pitches and 80 statics.

Leisure: ⚠ Facilities: ⋒ ☉ ☜ ✳ ↻
Services: ⌷ ⬚ ☲ ⚑ ⊘ ⊞ → ∪ ┃ ☺ ◬ ♨ ⅏ ⅃ ☳
◉ ☲☲☲ ☒ ☯

▶ ▶ 72% **Sea Barn Farm (SY625807)**
Fleet DT3 4ED ☎ 01305 782218 🗎 01305 775396
🅔 fleetcamp@lineone.net
🆆 www.seabarnfarm.co.uk
Dir: From Weymouth take B3157 towards Bridport for 3m. Turn left at mini-rdbt towards Fleet. Site 1m on left
★ £10-£12 ▲ £10-£12

Open Etr-Oct (rs pool open May-15 Sep) Booking advisable Spring & Aug bank hols & school hols Last arrival 22.30hrs Last departure noon
A quiet site bordering the Fleet nature reserve, and close to the Dorset coastal path. Optional use of the clubhouse and swimming pool at West Fleet Holiday Farm is available. Pitches are sheltered by hedging, and there is plenty of space for games. A 12-acre site with 250 touring pitches and 1 static. Café & fast food available from next door site

Leisure: ↘ ⚠ Facilities: ⋒ ☉ ✳ ↻ ☳ ⅏ ★
Services: ⌷ ⬚ ☲ ⚑ ⊘ ⊞ ⊤
Notes: Non family groups by arrangement, dogs must be kept on lead at all times

▶ ▶ 72% **West Fleet Holiday Farm (SY625811)**
Fleet DT3 4EF ☎ 01305 782218 🗎 01305 775396
🅔 fleetcamp@lineone.net
🆆 www.westfleetholidays.co.uk
Dir: From Weymouth take B3157 towards Bridport for 3m. Turn left at mini-rdbt to Fleet, 1m on right
★ £10-£14 ▲ £10-£14

Open Etr-Oct (rs pool closed 20 Sep-Apr) Booking advisable BH's & school hols Last arrival 22.30hrs Last departure noon
A spacious farm site with both level and sloping pitches divided into paddocks, and screened with hedging. Good views of the Dorset countryside, and a relaxing site for a family holiday with its heated outdoor pool and club house. A 12-acre site with 250 touring pitches.

Leisure: ↘ ♦ ⚠ ⊡ Facilities: ⋒ ☉ ✳ ↻ ☳ ⅏ ⊞ ★
Services: ⌷ ⬚ ☲ ⚑ ⊘ ⊞ ⊤ ✕ ♨
Notes: Non family groups by arrangement, dogs must be kept on leads at all times & are restricted to certain camping areas

▶ 69% *Higher South Buckland Farm (SY652818)*
Nottington DT3 4BQ ☎ 01305 813188
Dir: Leave A354 (Dorchester/Weymouth) at Broadway onto unclass road to Nottington. At T-junct in village, turn left signed Chickerell. Site on right in 0.75m
🚐 ▲

Open Apr-Oct Booking advisable Last departure noon
A quiet and friendly working farm site, set in lovely countryside but just 2 miles from Weymouth Beach. The toilet facilities are housed within the farmhouse buildings a short walk from this secluded site,
contd.

making it more ideal for those with their own
facilities. A 0.5-acre site with 14 touring pitches.

Facilities: ⚹ ☀ ⌂

Services: 🖭 ⬌ → ∪ ► ◎ ♨ ⌟ ♨ ♩ ⊡ ⚓

WIMBORNE MINSTER   Map 05 SZ09

▶ ▶ ▶ ▶ ▶ 76% **Merley Court
Touring Park (SZ008984)**
Merley BH21 3AA
☎ 01202 881488 📠 01202 881484
🅴 holidays@merley-court.co.uk
🆆 www.merley-court.co.uk
*Dir: Merley Court is clearly signed on A31
Wimborne by-pass & Poole junct rdbt*
★ 🚐 £11-£16 🚙 £11-£16 ▲ £11-£16
Open Mar-7 Jan (rs low season pool closed &
bar, shop open limited hrs) Booking advisable
bank hols & Jun-Sep Last arrival 21.00hrs Last
departure 11.00hrs
*A superb site in a quiet rural position on the
edge of Wimborne, with woodland on two sides
and good access roads. The park is well
landscaped, and offers generous individual
pitches in sheltered grassland. There are plenty
of amenities for all the family, including heated
outdoor pool, tennis court and adventure
playground. A 20-acre site with 160 touring
pitches, 50 hardstandings.*
Badminton, mini football, table tennis, crazy golf

Leisure: ⚿ ⚼ ⚫ ∕◻ ⊡

Facilities: ➔ ⚿ ☉ ☀ ⚹ ⚹ ⚓ ⚓ ⊞ ⍲ ⚹

Services: 🖭 ♈ 🖥 ⚹ 🍴 ⊘ ⊞ ⟭ ✕ ⚫ → ∪ ► ◎ ♨ ⚰ ♩

Notes: Couples and families only,
No dogs 17 Jul-3 Sep 💳 💳 💳 📷 🅖

▶ ▶ ▶ ▶ ▶ 86% **Wilksworth Farm
Caravan Park (SU004018)**
Cranborne Rd BH21 4HW
☎ 01202 885467 📠 01202 885467
🅴 rayandwendy@wilksworthfarmcaravanpark.co.uk
🆆 www.wilksworthfarmcaravanpark.co.uk
Dir: 1m N of Wimborne on B3078
★ 🚐 £10-£20 🚙 £10-£20 ▲ £10-£20
Open Apr-Oct (rs Apr & Oct no shop or coffee
shop) Booking advisable Spring bank hol &
Jul-Aug Last arrival 20.00hrs Last departure
11.00hrs
*A popular and attractive park set in the grounds
of a listed house, tranquilly placed in the heart
of rural Dorset. The spacious site has much to
offer visitors, including a heated swimming
pool, take-away and café, and games room. The
ultra-modern toilet facilities contain en suite
rooms. An 11-acre site with 85 touring pitches,
20 hardstandings and 77 statics.*
Paddling pool, volley ball, mini football pitch.

Leisure: ⚿ ⚼ ⚫ ∕◻

Facilities: ⚿ ☉ ⚑ ☀ ⚹ ⚓ ⚓ ⊞ ⍲ ⚹

Services: 🖭 🖥 🍴 ⊘ ⊞ ⟭ ✕ ⚫ → ∪ ◎ ⚰ ♩
💳 💳 💳 📷 🅖

**WILKSWORTH FARM
CARAVAN PARK**
Cranborne Road,
Wimborne BH21 4HW
Telephone: (01202) 885467 ▶▶▶▶▶
www.wilksworthfarmcaravanpark.co.uk

AA Best Campsite for South of England 1994
Runner up for Park of the Year 2003 (Calor Gas Awards)
Practical Caravan Regional Winner for Dorset 2004 and 2005
A family run park for families. A high standard
awaits you at our peaceful secluded park, close
to Kingston Lacy, Poole and Bournemouth. An
attractively laid out touring and camping park,
with heated outdoor swimming pool and tennis
court. No statics to hire.
Completely re-furbished toilet block with
family bathroom and disabled shower room.
Coffee shop and takeaway.

▶ ▶ ▶ 74% **Charris Camping & Caravan Park
(SY992988)**
Candy's Ln, Corfe Mullen BH21 3EF
☎ 01202 885970 📠 01202 881281
🅴 enquiries@charris.co.uk
🆆 www.charris.co.uk
*Dir: Turn L off Wimborne bypass (A31) W end. 300yds
after Caravan Sales, follow brown sign.*
★ 🚐 £9-£10 🚙 £9-£10 ▲ £8-£10

Open Mar-Jan Booking advisable at all times Last
arrival 21.00hrs Last departure 11.00hrs
*A sheltered park of grassland lined with trees, on
the edge of the Stour Valley. The owners are
friendly and welcoming, and they maintain the park
facilities to a good standard. Barbecues are a
popular occasional event. A 3.5-acre site with
45 touring pitches, 12 hardstandings.*

Facilities: ⚿ ☉ ⚑ ☀ ⚹ ⚓

Services: 🖭 🍴 ⊘ ⊞ → ∪ ► ♩ 🖥

Notes: Earliest arrival time 11.00hrs

England

WOOLSBRIDGE MANOR FARM CARAVAN PARK

THREE LEGGED CROSS WIMBORNE, DORSET BH21 6RA

Tel: (01202) 826369

Situated approx. 3½ miles from the New Forest Market town of Ringwood – easy access to the South Coast. 7 acres of level, semi sheltered, well drained spacious pitches. Quiet country location on a working farm – ideal and safe for families. Childrens play area on site. Fishing, Moors Valley Country Park, Golf Course, Pub/Restaurant all close by. AA 3 pennant grading

▶ ▶ ▶ 77% **Springfield Touring Park (SY987989)**
Candys Ln, Corfe Mullen BH21 3EF ☎ 01202 881719
Dir: Turn left off Wimborne by-pass (A31) western end, after Caravan Sales follow brown sign.
★ ♨ £10-£14 ♨ £10-£14 ▲ £7-£14
Open Apr-Oct Booking advisable bank hols & Jul-Aug Last arrival 22.00hrs Last departure 11.00hrs
A small touring park with extensive views over the Stour Valley, with a quiet and friendly atmosphere. The park is maintained immaculately, and has a well-stocked shop. A 3.5-acre site with 45 touring pitches, 18 hardstandings.
Leisure: ⚏ Facilities: ⬚⊙⚑✳⬚⬚
Services: ⬚⬚⬚⬚⬚→∪▶⬚⬚⬚⬚

WOOL	Map 04 SY88

▶ ▶ ▶ ▶ 77% **Whitemead Caravan Park (SY841869)**
East Burton Rd BH20 6HG
☎ 01929 462241 ▤ 01929 462241
✉ whitemeadcp@aol.com
⬚ www.whitemeadcaravanpark.co.uk
Dir: Signed from A352 at level crossing on Wareham side of Wool
★ ♨ £7.50-£14.50 ♨ £7.50-£14.50 ▲ £7.50-£12.50
Open mid Mar-Oct Booking advisable public hols & mid Jul-Aug Last arrival 22.00hrs Last dep noon
A well laid-out site in the valley of the River Frome, close to the village and surrounded by woodland. A shop and games room enhance the facilities here, and the newly refurbished toilets are heated,

Whitemead Caravan Park
providing an excellent amenity. A 5-acre site with 95 touring pitches.
Leisure: ◣ ⚏ Facilities: ⬚⊙⚑✳⬚⬚⬚⬚
Services: ⬚⬚⬚⬚⬚⬚⬚ ⬚→∪▶⬚

CO DURHAM

BARNARD CASTLE	Map 19 NZ01

▶ ▶ ▶ ▶ 77% **Camping & Caravanning Club Site (NZ025168)**
Dockenflatts Ln, Lartington DL12 9DG
☎ 01833 630228
⬚ www.campingandcaravanningclub.co.uk
Dir: Take B6277 to Middleton-in-Teesdale. After 1m turn left signed Raygill Riding Stables. Site 500mtrs on left
★ ♨ £13.60-£17.80 ♨ £13.60-£17.80
▲ £13.60-£17.80
Open Mar-Oct Booking advisable bank hols & peak periods Last arrival 21.00hrs Last departure noon
A peaceful site surrounded by mature woodland and meadowland, with first class facilities. This immaculately maintained park is set in the heart of the countryside. Pitches are well laid out and generous, on mainly level grass with some hardstandings. Please see the advertisement on page 11 for information on Club sites and membership. A 10-acre site with 90 touring pitches, 19 hardstandings.
Leisure: ⚏ Facilities: ⬚⊙⚑✳⬚⬚⬚
Services: ⬚⬚⬚⬚⬚⬚⬚→∪▶⬚⬚
⬚ ⬚⬚⬚ ⬚⬚ ⬚

▶ ▶ ▶ 75% **Pecknell Farm Caravan Park (NZ028178)**
Lartington DL12 9DF ☎ 01833 638357
Dir: 1.5m from Barnard Castle. From A66 take B6277. Site on right 1.5m from junction with A67
★ ♨ £7.50-£10 ♨ fr £7.50
Open Apr-Oct Booking advisable Jul, Aug & bank hols Last arrival 21.00hrs Last departure flexible
A small well laid out site on a working farm in beautiful rural meadowland, with spacious marked pitches on level ground. A 1.5-acre site with 15 touring pitches, 5 hardstandings.
Facilities: ⬚⊙⚑⬚
Services: ⬚⬚⬚→∪▶⊙⬚⬚
Notes: Showers are unisex

contd.

England

BEAMISH
Map 19 NZ25

► ► ► 72% **Bobby Shafto Caravan Park (NZ232545)**
Cranberry Plantation DH9 0RY ☎ 0191 370 1776
🖹 0191 370 1783
Dir: From A1693 signed Beamish to sign for Beamish Museum. Take approach road and turn right immediately before museum, left at pub to site 1m on right
★ ⚏ £12.50-£18.50 ⚏ £12.50-£18.50 Å £12.50-£15.50
Open Mar-Oct Booking advisable school hols Last arrival 23.00hrs Last departure 11.00hrs
A tranquil rural park surrounded by trees, with very clean and well-organised facilities. The suntrap touring area has plenty of attractive hanging baskets, and there is a clubhouse with bar, TV and pool. New hardstandings and fully serviced pitches enhance the amenities. A 9-acre site with 83 touring pitches, 30 hardstandings and 54 statics.
Leisure: ♦ ⚄ ⛁ Facilities: 🝙⊙🝙⚹🝙🝙🝙
Services: 🝙🝙🝙🝙🝙🝙→🝙▶🝙🝙🝙🝙🝙
🝙🝙 🝙🝙 🝙🝙 🝙🝙 🝙🝙 🝙

CASTLESIDE
Map 19 NZ04

► ► ► 64% *Allensford Caravan & Camping Park (NZ083505)*
DH8 9BA ☎ 01207 505572
Ⓦ www.snootyfoxresorts.co.uk
Dir: 2m SW of Consett, N on A68 for 1m, then right at Allensford Bridge
⚏ ⚏ Å
Open Mar-Oct Booking advisable wknds & peak periods Last arrival 22.00hrs Last departure noon
Level parkland with mature trees, in hilly moor and woodland country near the urban area adjacent to River Derwent and A68. Durham is readily accessible, and there are plenty of attractions in the area including Hadrian's Wall, Beamish Open Air Museum, and Hamsterley Forest. A 2-acre site with 40 touring pitches and 50 statics.
Tourist information centre.
Leisure: ⚄ Facilities: 🝙⊙🝙⚹🝙🝙🝙🝙
Services: 🝙🝙🝙🝙→▶🝙🝙🝙
Notes: Dogs must be kept on leads, no motorcycles
🝙🝙 🝙🝙 🝙🝙 🝙🝙 🝙🝙 🝙

CONSETT
Map 19 NZ15

► ► 78% **Byreside Caravan Site (NZ122560)**
Hamsterley NE17 7RT ☎ 01207 560280
🖹 01207 560280
Dir: From A694 on to B6310 and follow signs
★ ⚏ £7.50-£9 ⚏ £7.50-£9 Å £6-£10
Open all year Booking advisable bank hols & Jul-Aug Last arrival 22.00hrs Last departure noon
A small, secluded family-run site on a working farm, with well-maintained facilities. It is immediately beside the coast to coast cycle track so makes an ideal location for walkers and cyclists. Handy for Newcastle and Durham; the Roman Wall and Northumberland National Park are within an hour's drive. A 1.5-acre site with 31 touring pitches, 29 hardstandings.
Caravan storage
contd.

Facilities: 🝙⊙⚹🝙🝙🝙🝙
Services: 🝙🝙🝙🝙→ ▶🝙🝙🝙 Notes: No ball games on site, dogs on leads

DURHAM
Map 19 NZ24

► ► ► 79% **Strawberry Hill Farm (NZ337399)**
Old Cassop DH6 4QA ☎ 0191 372 3457 & 372 2512
🖹 0191 372 2512
🅴 howarddunkerley
  @strawberryhillfarm.freeserve.co.uk
Dir: Approx 3m from A1(M) junct 61. Site can only be accessed from eastbound carriageway of A181
★ ⚏ £12.50-£14.50 ⚏ £12.50-£14.50 Å £11.50-£12.50

Open Mar-Dec Booking advisable Jun-Aug & bank hols Last arrival 21.00hrs Last departure 18.00hrs
An attractive park, planted with many young trees and shrubs and well screened from the road. The terraced pitches have superb panoramic views across lovely wooded countryside. Good toilet and laundry facilities, and a useful base for visiting Durham Castle and Cathedral, Beamish Museum and the coast. A 6.5-acre site with 45 touring pitches, 10 hardstandings and 1 static.
Facilities: 🝙⊙🝙⚹🝙🝙🝙🝙🝙
Services: 🝙🝙🝙🝙🝙🝙→▶🝙 🝙🝙 🝙🝙 🝙🝙 🝙

ESSEX

BRENTWOOD
Map 06 TQ59

► ► ► 72% **Camping & Caravanning Club Site (TQ577976)**
Warren Ln, Doddington, Kelvedon Hatch CM15 0JG
☎ 01277 372773
Ⓦ www.campingandcaravanningclub.co.uk
Dir: M25 junct 28. Brentwood 2m left on A128 signed Ongar. After 3m turn right. Site signed
★ ⚏ £12.40-£16.70 ⚏ £12.40-£16.70 Å £12.40-£16.70
Open Mar-Oct Booking advisable bank hols & peak periods Last arrival 21.00hrs Last departure noon
A very pretty rural site with many separate areas amongst the trees, and a secluded field for campers. This peaceful site has older-style toilet facilities which are kept very clean, and smart laundry equipment. Please see the advertisement on page 11 for information on Club sites and membership. A 12-acre site with 90 touring pitches, 23 hardstandings.
Leisure: ⚄ Facilities: 🝙⊙🝙⚹🝙🝙🝙🝙
Services: 🝙🝙🝙🝙🝙🝙→🝙▶🝙🝙🝙
🝙🝙 🝙🝙 🝙🝙 🝙🝙 🝙

Facilities: 🝙 Bath 🝙 Shower ⊙ Electric Shaver ⚹ Hairdryer ✳ Ice Pack Facility 🝙 Disabled Facilities 🝙 Public Telephone
🝙 Shop on Site or within 200yds 🝙 Mobile Shop (calls at least 5 days a week) 🝙 BBQ Area 🝙 Picnic Area 🝙 Dog Exercise Area

England

COLCHESTER   Map 13 TL92

▶ ▶ ▶ ▶ **79% Colchester Camping Caravan Park** (TL971252)
Cymbeline Way, Lexden CO3 4AG
☎ 01206 545551 ▤ 01206 710443
🅔 enquiries@colchestercamping.co.uk
🆆 www.colchestercamping.co.uk
Dir: Follow tourist signs from A12, then A133 Colchester Central slip road
🚐 🚐 🅰
Open all year Booking advisable school and bank holidays Last arrival 20.30hrs Last departure noon
A well-designed campsite on level grassland, on the west side of Colchester near the town centre. Close to main routes to London (A12) and east coast. There is good provision for hardstandings, and the owner's attention to detail is reflected in the neatly trimmed grass and well-cut hedges. Toilet facilities are housed in three buildings, two of which are modern and well equipped. A 12-acre site with 168 touring pitches, 44 hardstandings. Badminton court
Leisure: ⚅
Facilities: ♠☉🎾⚒♿🖩🐕🪒
Services: 🔌🅔🛢🔥▥→∪▶♨🐾✒
Notes: No commercial vehicles
💳 🚬 🏦 📶 🄶

MERSEA ISLAND   Map 07 TM01

69% Waldegraves Holiday Park (TM033133)
CO5 8SE ☎ 01206 382898
▤ 01206 385359
🅔 holidays@waldegraves.co.uk
🆆 www.waldegraves.co.uk
Dir: B1025 to Mersea Island across the Strood. Left to East Mersea, 2nd turn on right, follow tourist signs to park
★ 🚐 £16-£22 🚐 £16-£22 🅰 £16-£22
Open Mar-Nov Booking advisable all times Last arrival 22.00hrs Last departure noon
A spacious and pleasant site, located between farmland and its own private beach on the Blackwater Estuary. Facilities include two freshwater fishing lakes, heated swimming pool, club, amusements, café and golf, and there is generally good provision for families. A 25-acre site with 60 touring pitches and 250 statics. Boating and fishing on site.
Leisure: ⛵🎣⚅🎮
Facilities: ♠☉🎾⚒♿🖩🐕🖩🪒🐕
Services: 🔌🕎🅔🛢🔥▥🍽✗🍴→▶◉♨✒
Notes: No large groups
💳 🚬 🄳 🏦 📶 🄶

If you are dissatisfied with any aspect of a campsite, discuss the problem at the time with a member of staff.

ROYDON   Map 06 TL41

▶ ▶ ▶ **69% Roydon Mill Leisure Park** (TL403104)
CM19 5EJ ☎ 01279 792777 ▤ 01279 792695
🅔 info@roydonpark.com
🆆 www.roydonpark.com
Dir: From A414 between Harlow & A10. Follow tourist signs to park. Situated at N end of High Street by railway station
★ 🚐 £11.50-£13 🚐 £11.50-£13 🅰 £11.50-£13
Open all year Booking advisable bank & school hols Last arrival 22.00hrs Last departure 22.00hrs
A busy complex with caravan sales and water sports. The attractive camping field is behind an old mill in a hedged meadow, and the caravan pitches have hardstandings. An 11-acre site with 120 touring pitches, 6 hardstandings and 149 statics. Large lake
Facilities: ♠☉🎾♿🖩🐕🖩🪒
Services: 🔌🕎🅔🛢🔥🗑▥✗🍴→∪▶♨🐾✒
Notes: 🚫 No unaccompanied children
💳 🚬 🏦 📶 🄶

GLOUCESTERSHIRE

BERKELEY   Map 04 ST69

▶ ▶ ▶ *72% Hogsdown Farm Caravan & Camping Park (ST710974)*
Hogsdown Farm, Lower Wick GL11 6DD
☎ 01453 810224
Dir: M5 junct 14 (Falfield), take A38 towards Gloucester, turn right for site
🚐
Open all year
A pleasant site with good toilet facilities, located between Bristol and Gloucester. It is well positioned for visiting Berkeley Castle and the Cotswold Edge country, and makes an excellent overnight stop when travelling to or from the West Country. A 5-acre site with 45 touring pitches.
Leisure: ⚅ **Facilities:** ♠🖩🐕
Services: 🛢→▶✒

CHELTENHAM   Map 10 SO92

▶ ▶ ▶ *77% Briarfields (SO899215)*
Gloucester Rd GL51 0SX ☎ 01242 235324
▤ 01242 262216
Dir: From Cheltenham take A40 to Golden Valley rdbt, then 3rd turning left onto B4063 and follow signs
🚐 🚐 🅰
Open all year Booking advisable Last arrival 22.00hrs Last departure noon
A well-designed level park with motel facilities adjacent. The park is well-positioned between Cheltenham and Gloucester, with easy access to the Cotswolds. A 6-acre site with 72 touring pitches, 72 hardstandings.
Facilities: ♠☉🎾♿🖩🐕🖩
Services: 🔌🕎🅔🛢🗑→∪▶◉♨🐾✒
Notes: No cars by tents 💳 🚬 🏦 📶 🄶

England

CIRENCESTER   Map 05 SP00

▶ ▶ ▶ **77% Mayfield Touring Park** (SP020055)
Cheltenham Rd GL7 7BH ☎ 01285 831301
✉ mayfield-park@cirencester.fsbusiness.co.uk
Ⓦ www.mayfieldpark.co.uk
Dir: From Cirencester bypass take Burford rd/A429 junct exit towards Cirencester, then via A417 to A435, direct access onto site on left in 0.5m
★ ⊞ £9-£13 ⊞ £9-£13.50 ▲ £7-£11
Open all year Booking advisable bank hols & Fairford Air Display Last arrival 22.00hrs Last departure 18.00hrs
A gently sloping park on the edge of the Cotswolds, with level pitches and a warm welcome. Popular with couples and families, it offers a good licensed shop selling a wide selection of home cooked takeaway food. Although some traffic noise can be heard at times, this lovely park makes an ideal base. A 12-acre site with 72 touring pitches, 19 hardstandings.
Off licence
Facilities: 🅝 ⊙ ⚲ ☀ 🝖 🐕
Services: 🔌 🚽 🛁 🔥 🖵 → ▶ ♨ ♪
Notes: Dogs only allowed if pre-booked
💳 ▦ ▦ ▦ ▦ ▦

COLEFORD   Map 04 SO51

▶ ▶ **79% Woodlands View Camping & Caravan Park** (SO582085)
Sling GL16 8JA ☎ 01594 835127 & 01989 750468
✉ woodlandsview@tiscali.co.uk
Dir: From Coleford take B4228 towards Chepstow. Appox 0.5m pass Puzzle Wood on right. 0.5m site signed on left
★ ⊞ £10-£13.50 ⊞ £10-£13.50 ▲ £10-£13.50
Open Mar-Oct Booking advisable Bank hols & Jul-Aug Last arrival 22.00hrs Last departure noon
A small peaceful park in the Forest of Dean, next to the charming village of Clearwell. The friendly owners provide a warm welcome, and maintain the park to a good standard. The four fully-serviced pitches are ideal for large motorhomes. A 1.5-acre site with 26 touring pitches.
Facilities: 🅝 ⊙ ☀ 🝖 🐕
Services: 🔌 🛁 🔥 → ▶ ♨ ♪
💳 ▦ ▦ ▦ ▦ ▦

GLOUCESTER   Map 10 SO81

▶ ▶ ▶ **73% Red Lion Camping & Caravan Park** (SO849258)
Wainlode Hill, Norton GL2 9LW ☎ 01452 730251
🖷 01452 730251
Ⓦ www.redlioninn-caravancampingpark.co.uk
Dir: Turn off A38 at Norton and follow road to river
⊞ ⊞ ▲
Open all year Booking advisable Spring bank hol Last arrival 22.00hrs Last departure 11.00hrs
An attractive meadowland park, adjacent to a traditional pub, with the River Severn just across a country lane. This is an ideal touring and fishing base. A 13-acre site with 60 touring pitches, 10 hardstandings and 20 statics.
Freshwater fishing & private lake
contd.

Red Lion Camping & Caravan Park

Leisure: 🅐 **Facilities:** 🅝⊙⚲☀🝖🛡🝖🐕
Services: 🔌🚽🛁🛒🔥🖵✕🛏→∪▶♪
💳 ▦ ▦ ▦ ▦

SLIMBRIDGE   Map 04 SO70

▶ ▶ ▶ **75% Tudor Caravan & Camping** (SO728040)
Shepherds Patch GL2 7BP
☎ 01453 890483 & 07702 989940
✉ aa@tudorcaravanpark.co.uk
Ⓦ www.tudorcaravanpark.com
Dir: From M5 junct 13 follow signs for WWT Wetlands Wildlife Centre-Slimbridge. Site at rear of Tudor Arms pub
★ ⊞ £9-£10 ⊞ £9-£10 ▲ £6-£10

Open all year Booking advisable bank & school hols Last arrival 21.00hrs Last departure noon
An orchard-style park sheltered by mature trees and shrubs, set in an attractive meadow beside a canal. This tidy site offers both level grass and gravel pitches complete with electric hook-ups, and there is a separate area for adults only. Slimbridge Wetlands Centre is close by, and there is much scope locally for bird-watching. An 8-acre site with 75 touring pitches, 48 hardstandings.
Facilities: 🅝⊙⚲☀🝖🛡🝖🐕
Services: 🔌🛁🛒🔥🖵✕→∪♪

WINCHCOMBE   Map 10 SP02

▶ ▶ ▶ **79% Camping & Caravanning Club Site** (SP007324)
Brooklands Farm, Alderton GL20 8NX
☎ 01242 620259
Ⓦ www.campingandcaravanningclub.co.uk
Dir: Leave M5 junct 9 onto A46, keep straight on at rdbt and onto B4077 signed Stow-on-the-Wold. Site 3m on right
★ ⊞ £16.10-£17.80 ⊞ £16.10-£17.80 ▲ £16.10-£17.80
Open Mar-Jan Booking advisable BH's & peak
contd.

Leisure: 🐟 Indoor swimming pool 🐟 Outdoor swimming pool 🎾 Tennis court 🎱 Games room 🅐 Children's playground ∪ Stables
▶ 9/18 hole golf course ⚓ Boats for hire 🎬 Cinema ♪ Fishing ◎ Mini golf 🌊 Watersports 🖵 Separate TV room

England

periods Last arrival 21.00hrs Last departure noon
*A pleasant rural park with pitches spaced around
two attractive lakes offering good fishing, and the
benefit of a long season. This flower-filled park is in
an area of historic buildings and picturesque
villages between Cheltenham and Tewkesbury.
Please see advertisement on page 11 for
information on Club sites and membership. A
20-acre site with 80 touring pitches, 43 hardstandings.
Fishing, pool table, table tennis*
Leisure: ♦ ⚑ Facilities: ⌐ ⊙ 🅟 ✳ & ⌐ 🏠 ♀
Services: 🖭 🗑 🖹 🅰 🗓 → ∪ 🛆 🥄 🐾 ● 🎗 🖩 🎦 🚊

GREATER MANCHESTER

LITTLEBOROUGH   Map 16 SD91

▶ ▶ ▶ 69% **Hollingworth Lake Caravan Park**
(SD943146)
Round House Farm, Rakewood Rd, Rakewood OL15
0AT ☎ 01706 378661 & 373919
*Dir: From Littleborough or Milnrow (M62 junct 21),
follow 'Hollingworth Lake Country Park' signs to
Fishermans Inn. Take 'No Through Road' to Rakewood,
then 2nd on right.*
★ 🚐 £10-£14 🚐 £10-£14 ▲ £10-£14

Open all year Booking advisable Apr-Sep Last
arrival 20.00hrs Last departure 14.00hrs
*A popular park adjacent to Hollingworth Lake, at the
foot of the Pennines, within easy reach of many
local attractions. Backpackers walking the Pennine
Way are welcome at this family-run park, and there
are also large rally fields. A 5-acre site with 50
touring pitches, 25 hardstandings and 53 statics.
Pony Trekking.*
Facilities: ⌐ ⊙ ✳ & ∟ 🐾 🏠
Services: 🖭 ♨ 🗑 🖹 🅰 🗓 → ∪ ▶ 🛆 ❅ 🥄 Notes: Dogs
must be kept on leads, family groups only

ROCHDALE   Map 16 SD81

▶ ▶ ▶ 74% **Gelder Wood Country Park**
(SD852127)
Ashworth Rd OL11 5UP ☎ 01706 364858 &
620300 🖹 01706 364858
❸ gelderwood@aol.com
Ⓦ www.ukparks.co.uk/gelderwood
*Dir: Signed midway off B6222 Bury/ Rochdale Road.
Turn into Ashworth Rd, continue past the mill and uphill
for 800yds, site on right*
★ 🚐 £13 🚐 £13 ▲ £11

contd.

Open Mar-Oct Booking advisable Etr Last departure
11.00hrs
*A very rural site in a peaceful private country park
with excellent facilities. All pitches have extensive
views of the moor, and this is a popular base for
walkers and birdwatchers. The park is for adults
only, and children are not allowed to visit.
A 10-acre site with 34 touring pitches.*
Facilities: ⌐ ⊙ & ♀
Services: 🖭 🗑 🅰 🗓 → ∪ 🥄 🗓 🐾
Notes: Adults only

HAMPSHIRE

BRANSGORE   Map 05 SZ19

▶ ▶ ▶ 77% *Harrow Wood Farm Caravan Park*
(SZ194978)
Harrow Wood Farm, Poplar Ln BH23 8JE
☎ 01425 672487 🖹 01425 672487
❸ harrowwood@caravan-sites.co.uk
Ⓦ www.caravan-sites.co.uk
*Dir: Leave village from S and take last turning on left.
Site at top of lane*
🚐 🚐

Open Mar-6 Jan Booking advisable bank & school
hols Last arrival 22.00hrs Last departure noon
*A well laid out site in a pleasant rural position
adjoining onto woodland and fields. Free on-site
coarse fishing is available at this peaceful park.
A 6-acre site with 60 touring pitches.*
Facilities: ⌐ ⊙ 🗻 ✳ ∟
Services: 🖭 🗑 🖹 🅰 🗓 → 🥄 🐾
Notes: ✀ ● 🖩 🎦 🚊
See advertisement on opposite page

CRAWLEY   Map 05 SU43

▶ ▶ 76% **Folly Farm Touring Caravan Park**
(SU415337)
Crawley SO21 2PH ☎ 01962 776486
*Dir: Midway between Winchester and Stockbridge on
B3049. Site 0.75m past Rack & Manger Pub*
★ 🚐 £10-£12 🚐 £10-£12 ▲ £10-£12
Open all year Booking advisable all year Last arrival
22.00hrs
*A small farm site set in rural mid-Hampshire
between Stockbridge and Winchester, ideal for
visiting the ancient capital of Wessex, the New
Forest, and the south coast, a short drive away. The
clean facilities are located in farm outbuildings, and
there is a small campers' kitchen. A 2.5-acre site
with 30 touring pitches.*
Leisure: ⚑ Facilities: ⌐ ⊙ 🗻 ✳ & 🏠 🗒 ♀
Services: 🖭 🗑 → ∪ 🥄 🗓 🐾
Notes: No children on farm area & dogs must be on
a lead

THE PERCENTAGE RATING
FOR ALL PARKS RANGES FROM
50% - 100%.

Abbreviations: BH/bank hols-bank holidays Etr-Easter Whit-Whitsun dep-departure fr-from hrs-hours m-mile mdnt-midnight
rdbt-roundabout rs-restricted service wk-week wknd-weekend ✀-no dogs

FORDINGBRIDGE — Map 05 SU11

88% Sandy Balls Holiday Centre (SU167148)
Sandy Balls Estate Ltd, Godshill SP6 2JY
☎ 01425 653042 📠 01425 653067
✉ post@sandy-balls.co.uk
🌐 www.sandy-balls.co.uk
Dir: Leave M27 at junct 1 & take B3078/B3079, W 8m to Godshill. Park 0.25m after cattle grid
★ 🚐 £12.75-£19.50 🚐 £12.75-£19.50
▲ £12.75-£19.50
Open all year (rs Nov-Feb pitches reduced, no activities) Booking advisable bank & school hols & wknds Last arrival 21.00hrs Last departure 11.00hrs
A large, mostly wooded New Forest holiday complex with good provision of touring facilities on terraced, well laid-out fields. Pitches are fully serviced with shingle bases, and groups can be sited beside the river and away from the main site. Excellent sport, leisure and entertainment facilities for the whole family. A 120-acre site with 230 touring pitches, 230 hardstandings and 267 statics.
Jacuzzi, sauna, sunbeds, gym, horse riding, cycle hire
Leisure: 🏊 🎣 🎮 🎠
Facilities: 🚿 ...
Services: ...
Notes: Groups by arrangement

FRITHAM
See **Landford (Wiltshire)**

HAMBLE — Map 05 SU40

▶ ▶ ▶ **69% Riverside Holidays (SU481081)**
Satchell Ln SO31 4HR ☎ 023 8045 3220
📠 023 8045 3611
✉ enquiries@riversideholidays.co.uk
🌐 www.riversideholidays.co.uk
Dir: M27 junct 8, follow signs to Hamble B3397. Turn left into Satchell Lane, 1m down lane on left
🚐 £15-£20 🚐 £15-£20 ▲ £11-£17
Open all year (rs Nov-Feb No camping or touring) Booking advisable bank hols, peak season & boat show wk Last arrival 22.00hrs Last departure 11.00hrs
A small, peaceful park next to the marina, and close to the pretty village of Hamble. The park is neatly kept, though the toilet facilities are dated. A pub and restaurant are very close by. A 6-acre site with 75 touring pitches and 38 statics.
Bike hire, baby changing facilities
Facilities: ...
Services: ...

See advertisement on page 152

Facilities: 🛁 Bath ⚲ Shower ⊙ Electric Shaver ⚑ Hairdryer ✳ Ice Pack Facility ♿ Disabled Facilities ✆ Public Telephone 🛒 Shop on Site or within 200yds 📱 Mobile Shop (calls at least 5 days a week) 🍖 BBQ Area 🍴 Picnic Area 🐕 Dog Exercise Area

---

LINWOOD   Map 05 SU10

▶ ▶ ▶ **72% Red Shoot Camping Park** (SU187094)
BH24 3QT ☎ 01425 473789 📠 01425 471558
✉ enquiries@redshoot-campingpark.com
🌐 www.redshoot-campingpark.com
Dir: A31 onto A338 towards Fordingbridge & Salisbury. Right at brown signs for caravan park towards Linwood on unclassified roads, park signed
★ ⊕ £10.16-£15.20 ⊕ £10.16-£15.20 ▲ £10.16-£15.20
Open Mar-Oct Booking advisable Last arrival 20.30hrs Last departure 13.00hrs
Sitting behind the Red Shoot Inn in one of the most attractive parts of the New Forest, this park is in an ideal spot for nature lovers, walkers and tourers. It is personally supervised by friendly owners, and offers many amenities including a children's play area. A 3.5-acre site with 130 touring pitches.
Mountain bike hire
Leisure: ⚴ **Facilities:** ⬏⊙⬱⚹⬤⬢⬡⬢
Services: ⬡⬢⬣⬤⬥⬦⬧✗→⬨⬩⬪ ⬫⬬⬭ ⬮

MILFORD ON SEA   Map 05 SZ29

▶ ▶ ▶ **81%** *Lytton Lawn Touring Park* (SZ293937)
Lymore Ln SO41 0TX ☎ 01590 648331
📠 01590 645610
✉ holidays@shorefield.co.uk
🌐 www.shorefield.co.uk
Dir: From Lymington A337 to Christchurch for 2.5m to Everton. Left onto B3058 to Milford-on-Sea. After 0.25m left onto Lymore Lane
⊕ ⊕ ▲

contd.

Open Feb-2 Jan (rs Xmas/New year no grass pitches available) Booking advisable at all times Last arrival 22.00hrs Last departure 10.00hrs
A pleasant well-run park with good facilities, located near the coast. The park is peaceful and quiet, but the facilities of a sister park 2.5 miles away are available to campers, including swimming pool, tennis courts, bistro and bar/carvery, and large club with family entertainment. Fully-serviced pitches provide good screening, and standard pitches are on gently-sloping grass. A 5-acre site with 136 touring pitches, 48 hardstandings. Free use of Shorefield Leisure Club
Leisure: ⚴ ⚴ **Facilities:** ⬏⊙⬱⚹⬤⬢⬡⬢⬣
Services: ⬡⬢⬣⬤⬥⬦→⬨⬩⬪⬫
Notes: Family park only ⬤ ⬛⬛ ⬛⬛ ⬛⬛ ⬮

See advertisement on opposite page

OWER   Map 05 SU31

▶ ▶ ▶ **79% Green Pastures Farm** (SU321158)
SO51 6AJ ☎ 023 80814444
✉ enquiries@greenpasturesfarm.com
🌐 www.greenpasturesfarm.com
Dir: M27 junct 2. Follow Salisbury signs for 0.5m. Then follow brown tourist signs for Green Pastures. Also signed from A36 & A3090 at Ower
⊕ £14 ⊕ £14 ▲ £14
Open 15 Mar-Oct Booking advisable bank hols & peak periods Last departure noon
A pleasant site on a working farm, with good screening of trees and shrubs around the perimeter. The touring area is divided by a border of shrubs and at times colourful foxgloves. This peaceful location is close to the M27 and New Forest. A 5-acre site with 45 touring pitches, 2 hardstandings.
Day kennels
Facilities: ⬏⊙⚹⬤⬢⬡⬢⬣
Services: ⬡⬢⬣⬤⬥⬦→⬪⬫

RINGWOOD   Map 05 SU10
See St Leonards (Dorset)

ROMSEY   Map 05 SU32

▶ ▶ ▶ ▶ **85% Hill Farm Caravan Park** (SU287238)
Branches Ln, Sherfield English SO51 6FH
☎ 01794 340402 📠 01794 342358
✉ gjb@hillfarmpark.com
🌐 www.hillfarmpark.com
Dir: Signed off A27 Salisbury to Romsey road in Sherfield English, 4m NW of Romsey and M27 junct 2
★ ⊕ £16-£25 ⊕ £16-£25 ▲ £12-£22

contd.

England

Leisure: 🏊 Indoor swimming pool 🏊 Outdoor swimming pool 🎾 Tennis court 🎱 Games room 🛝 Children's playground ♆ Stables
▶ 9/18 hole golf course ⚓ Boats for hire 🎬 Cinema 🎣 Fishing ⛳ Mini golf 🌊 Watersports 📺 Separate TV room

England

Open Mar-Oct Booking advisable bank & school hols Last arrival 20.00hrs Last departure noon
A small, well-sheltered park peacefully located amidst mature trees and meadows. The two toilet blocks offer smart unisex showers as well as a fully en suite family/disabled room and plenty of privacy in the wash rooms. The owners are continuing to develop this attractive park, and with its proximity to Salisbury and the New Forest, it makes an appealing holiday location. A 10.5-acre site with 70 touring pitches, 16 hardstandings and 6 statics.
9-hole pitch and putt, goal posts, badminton
Leisure: /A
Facilities: 🏕 ⊙ ⬚ ✳ ⬚ ⬚ ⬚ ⬚
Services: ⬚ ⬚ ⬚ ⬚ ⬚ ⬚ ⬚ ✕ ⬚ → ∪ ⬚ ⬚
Notes: Minimal noise after 11pm, one unit per pitch.

WARSASH   Map 05 SU40

▶ ▶ ▶ **79% Dibles Park (SU505060)**
Dibles Rd SO31 9SA ☎ 01489 575232
Dir: M27 junct 8 onto A27 to Fareham. At 1st rdbt 3rd exit, at next rdbt 2nd exit. Straight to bottom of road, turn left at Warsash Motors. Right in 1m, then 2nd right
★ ⬚ fr £10 ⬚ fr £10 ▲ fr £8
Open all year Booking advisable bank hols & Jul-Aug Last arrival 20.30hrs Last departure 13.00hrs
A small grassy touring area with hardstandings, adjacent to a private residential park. This site continues to improve, and there is always a warm welcome for visitors. Within easy reach of the River Hamble and the Solent. A 0.75-acre site with 14 touring pitches and 46 statics.
Facilities: 🏕 ⊙ ⬚ ✳ ⬚ ⬚
Services: ⬚ ⬚ ⬚ ⬚ → ∪ ⬚ ⬚ ⬚

HEREFORDSHIRE

HEREFORD   Map 10 SO53

NEW ▶ **66% Ridge Hill Caravan and Campsite (SO509355)**
☎ 01432 351293
ⓔ ridgehill@fsmail.net
ⓦ www.ridgehillcaravanandcampsite.co.uk
Dir: from Hereford on A49 take B4399 towards Holme Lacy. Turn left after Post Office to Dinedor. Through Dinedor & Dinedor Cross to T-junct. Turn right then left (Ridgeway Hill). Site 2nd left
⬚ £9 ⬚ £8 ▲ £7
Open Mar-Oct Booking advisable Last departure noon
A simple, basic site set high on Ridge Hill 3 miles south of Hereford. This peaceful site offers outstanding views over the surrounding countryside. It does not have toilets or showers, and therefore own facilities are essential. A 1.5-acre site with 5 touring pitches.
Services: → ⬚ ⬚ ⬚ ⬚
Notes: Dogs must be kept on leads

LITTLE TARRINGTON   Map 10 SO64

▶ ▶ ▶ **81% The Millpond (SO625410)**
HR1 4JA ☎ 01432 890243 📠 01432 890243
ⓔ enquiries@millpond.co.uk
ⓦ www.millpond.co.uk
GOLD
Dir: 300yds off A438 on Ledbury side of Tarrington, entrance on right, 50yds before railway bridge
⬚ £12.50-£15 ⬚ £12.50-£15 ▲ £10-£15
Open Mar-Oct Booking advisable peak periods Last arrival 20.30hrs Last departure 11.00hrs
A spacious grassy park set beside a fishing lake in a peaceful location. Well-planted trees and shrubs help to divide and screen the park, and the modern toilet block provides good facilities. A 4.5-acre site with 55 touring pitches, 20 hardstandings.
3 acre coarse fishing lake.
Facilities: 🏕 ⊙ ⬚ ✳ ⬚ ⬚ ⬚   **Services:** ⬚ ⬚ → ⬚
Notes: Dogs must be kept on lead at all times

MORTIMER'S CROSS   Map 09 SO46

▶ ▶ **83% The Beeches Touring Caravan Site (SO408623)**
HR6 9NY ☎ 01568 709286
ⓔ reg76@btinternet.com
ⓦ www.beechescampsite.co.uk
Dir: A4110 onto B4362 at Mortimers Cross, site 0.75m on left
★ ⬚ £8-£10 ⬚ £7-£9 ▲ £5-£7
Open Mar-Oct Booking advisable Last arrival dusk Last departure noon
A very small developing site with excellent facilities, located in an Area of Outstanding Natural Beauty near the village of Shobdon. The gently sloping site is south facing with level pitches, and provides pleasant views of the countryside. A 1.5-acre site with 5 touring pitches, 2 hardstandings.
Facilities: 🏕 ⊙ ✳ ⬚
Services: ⬚ ⬚ ⬚ → ∪ ⬚ ⬚

PETERCHURCH   Map 09 SO33

▶ ▶ ▶ ▶ **83% Poston Mill Caravan & Camping Park (SO355373)**
HR2 0SF ☎ 01981 550225
📠 01981 550885
ⓔ enquiries@poston-mill.co.uk
ⓦ www.bestparks.co.uk
GOLD
Dir: 11m SW of Hereford on B4348
★ ⬚ £12-£16 ⬚ £12-£16 ▲ £8-£16
Open all year (rs Nov-Mar limited toilet facilities)
Booking advisable bank & summer hols Last departure noon
Delightfully set in the Golden Valley and surrounded by hills, with beautiful views. This quality park has excellent facilities including sporting amenities which are to one side of the site. There is also an adjoining restaurant, The Mill, and a pleasant walk alongside the River Dore. A 33-acre site with 93 touring pitches, 63 hardstandings and 95 statics.
Leisure: ⬚ ⬚ /A ⬚   **Facilities:** 🏕 ⊙ ⬚ ✳ ⬚ ⬚ ⬚ ⬚ ⬚ ⬚
Services: ⬚ ⬚ ⬚ ⬚ ⬚ ⬚ ⬚ ⬚ ✕ ⬚ ⬚ → ⬚ ⬚ ⬚
⬚ ⬚ ⬚ ⬚ ⬚

STANFORD BISHOP   Map 10 SO65

▶ ▶ ▶ 79% **Boyce Caravan Park (SO692528)**
WR6 5UB ☎ 01886 884248
e enquiries@boyceholidaypark.co.uk
w www.boyceholidaypark.co.uk
*Dir: From B4220 Malvern road take sharp turn opposite
Herefordshire House pub, then right after 0.25m. Signed
Linley Green, then first drive on right.*
★ ⊞ £10-£11.50 ⊞ £10-£11.50 ▲ fr £10

Open Feb-Dec (rs Feb-Mar & Oct-Dec) Booking
advisable bank hols & Jun-Aug Last arrival 18.00hrs
Last departure noon
*A friendly and peaceful park with access allowed
onto the 100 acres of farmland. Coarse fishing is
also available in the grounds, and there are
extensive views over the Malvern and Suckley
Hills. A 10-acre site with 25 touring pitches and
100 statics.*
Coarse fishing available
Leisure: ⋒
Facilities: ℕ⊖🏖⚡※&🔔🎋🐕
Services: 🔌🎣🛢🚰⊞→🍴🔥🛒
Notes: Certain dog breeds not accepted

SYMONDS YAT (WEST)   Map 10 SO51

▶ ▶ 91% **Doward Park Camp Site (SO539167)**
Great Doward HR9 6BP ☎ 01600 890438
e enquiries@doward-park.co.uk
w www.doward-park.co.uk
*Dir: 2m from A40 between Ross-on-Wye & Monmouth.
Take Symonds Yat (West) turn, then Crockers Ash,
follow signs to site*
★ ⊞ £10.50-£14 ⊞ £10.50-£14 ▲ £10.50-£14
Open Mar-Oct Booking advisable wknds, BH's &
Jul-Aug Last arrival 20.00hrs Last departure
11.30hrs
*A very attractive site set in woodland on the hillside
above the River Wye, and ideal for campers. New
owners are planning to refurbish the toilet block
and add laundry equipment, but existing facilities
are kept to a good standard. A 1.5-acre site with
33 touring pitches, 2 hardstandings.*
Leisure: ⋒
Facilities: ℕ⊖🏖※&🛒
Services: 🔌🛢⊞→🍴🔥🛒🔥
Notes: No fires, quiet after 10pm, dogs on leads
🐕 📶 📷 🅟

▶ ▶ 67% **Symonds Yat Caravan & Camping Park
(SO554174)**
HR9 6BY ☎ 01600 890883 & 891069
e enquiries@campingandcaravan.com
w www.campingandcaravan.com
*Dir: On A40 between Ross-on-Wye & Monmouth, take
Symonds Yat (West) exit. Follow signs*
★ ⊞ £9-£11 ⊞ £9-£11 ▲ £9-£21
Open Mar-Oct Booking advisable BHs & weekends
Last departure noon
*A popular little park next to the River Wye, with its
own canoe hire and launching ramp. An
amusement/leisure park next door can be very
noisy, but this park is well suited for young tenters
who enjoy canoeing. A 1.25-acre site with 35
touring pitches, 10 hardstandings.*
Fishing from site, fishing permits sold, canoe hire
Facilities: ℕ⊖※🔔
Services: 🔌🎣⊞→🍴🔥🛒🛢🛒🔥 Notes: No
cycling or ball games on site 🐕 📶 📷 🅟

HERTFORDSHIRE

HERTFORD   Map 06 TL31

▶ ▶ ▶ ▶ 77% **Camping & Caravanning
Club Site (TL334113)**
Mangrove Rd SG13 8QF
☎ 01992 586696
w www.campingandcaravanningclub.co.uk
*Dir: From A10 follow A414 Hertford signs to next rdbt
(Foxholes) straight over. After 200yds turn left signed
Balls Park & Hertford University. Left at T-junct into
Mangrove Rd. Site on left*
★ ⊞ £16.10-£17.80 ⊞ £16.10-£17.80 ▲ £16.10-£17.80
Open all year Booking advisable BH's & peak
periods Last arrival 21.00hrs Last departure noon
*A spacious, well-landscaped club site in a rural
setting one mile south of Hertford, with immaculate
modern toilet facilities. There are several hedged
areas with good provision of hardstandings, and a
cosy camping section in an old orchard. All kinds of
wildlife flourish around the lake. Please see
advertisement on page 11 for information on Club
sites and membership. A 32-acre site with
250 touring pitches, 54 hardstandings.*
Leisure: ⋒ Facilities: ℕ⊖🏖⚡&🔔🎋🐕
Services: 🔌🛗🛢🛢🛢⊞⏲→🍴🍴🛒🛢🛒
🐕 📶 📷 🅟

HODDESDON   Map 06 TL30

▶ ▶ ▶ 77% **Lee Valley Caravan Park (TL383082)**
Dobbs Weir, Essex Rd EN11 0AS ☎ 01992 462090
📠 01992 462090
e caravanpark@leevalleypark.org.uk
w www.leevalleypark.org.uk
*Dir: Leave A10 at Hoddesdon junct, 2nd rdbt turn left
signed Dobbs Weir. On right in 1m*
⊞⊞▲
Open Mar-Nov Booking advisable public hols
*A neat, well-kept site in a peaceful field surrounded
by hedges and tall trees. The tenting field is on the*

contd.

England

banks of the River Lee, and there are good local walks as well as a useful playing field. Everything is beautifully managed and maintained. An 8-acre site with 100 touring pitches and 100 statics.
Fishing, library

Leisure: ⚙ **Facilities:** ⬛️☉◑⚡✳⬛🔥🕭
Services: 🔌🚐🔋🔧🚽🎨⬛️→🥄♨🍴 **Notes:** No double axle caravans 💳 🚊🔷 📠 🚫 🈯

See advertisement on page 170

WALTHAM CROSS Map 06 TL30

▶ ▶ **70% Camping & Caravanning Club Site (TL344005)**
Theobalds Park, Bulls Cross Ride EN7 5HS
☎ 01992 620604
ⓦ www.campingandcaravanningclub.co.uk
Dir: M25 junct 25. A10 towards London keep in right lane. Right at 1st lights. Right at T-junct, right behind dog kennels. Site towards top of lane on right
★ 🚐 £11.30-£14.80 🚐 £11.30-£14.80 ▲ £11.30-£14.80
Open Mar-Oct Booking advisable bank hols & peak periods Last arrival 21.00hrs Last departure noon
A lovely open site surrounded by mature trees, and set in parkland at Theobalds Hall. The portacabin toilet facilities are freshly painted and extremely clean, and there are two separate glades for tents. Please see the advertisement on page 11 for information on Club sites and membership.
A 14-acre site with 90 touring pitches.
Leisure: ♦ ⚙ **Facilities:** ⬛️☉✳🕯⬛🔥🕭
Services: 🔌🔋🔧🚽⬛️→🥄♨🍴🚫💳 🚊🔷 📠 🈯

KENT

ASHFORD Map 07 TR04

▶ ▶ ▶ ▶ **83% Broad Hembury Holiday Park (TR009387)**
Steeds Ln, Kingsnorth TN26 1NQ
☎ 01233 620859 📠 01233 620918
ⓔ holidays@broadhembury.co.uk
ⓦ www.broadhembury.co.uk
Dir: From M20 junct 10 take A2070 for 3m. Left at 2nd rdbt signed Kingsnorth, then left at 2nd x-roads in village
★ 🚐 £10-£17 🚐 £10-£15 ▲ £10-£15
Open all year Booking advisable Jul-Aug & bank hols Last arrival 23.00hrs Last departure noon
Well-run and maintained small family park surrounded by open pasture and neatly landscaped, with pitches sheltered by mature hedges. Some super pitches have proved a popular addition, and there is a well-equipped campers' kitchen.
A 10-acre site with 60 touring pitches, 14 hardstandings and 25 statics.
Football, volleyball & kitchen appliances
Leisure: ♦ ⚙ 🖵
Facilities: ⬛️☉⚡✳⬛🕯🔥🕭
Services: 🔌🚐🔋🔧🚽⬛️🈯→🔄♨🍴♨🍴🛒
💳 🚊🔷 🈯

Services: 🅣 Toilet Fluid ✖ Café/ Restaurant 🍴 Fast Food/Takeaway 🍼 Baby Care 🔌 Electric Hook Up 🚐 Motorvan Service Point 🅖 Launderette 🍷 Licensed Bar 🛢 Calor Gaz 🔥 Camping Gaz 🔋 Battery Charging

BIDDENDEN   Map 07 TQ83

▶ ▶ ▶ 66% **Woodlands Park (TQ867372)**
Tenterden Rd TN27 8BT
☎ 01580 291216 🖷 01580 291216
📧 woodlandsp@aol.com
🌐 www.campingsite.co.uk
Dir: From A28 onto A262. Site 1.5m on right
🚐 🚐 ▲

Open Mar-Oct (rs Mar-Apr weather permitting)
Booking advisable bank hols & Jul-Aug
A site of level grassland bordered by hedges and
trees, with two ponds and a smart and well-
maintained modern toilet block. Ideal centre for
Kent, Sussex and Channel ports. A 9-acre site with
200 touring pitches and 205 statics.
Camping accessory sales & small site shop.
Facilities: 🖍⊙🕾✻🕭🗣🖫🏂⊞
Services: 🖵🖩🛢🖎🗓⊞⊺→∪▶◎🅙

BIRCHINGTON   Map 07 TR36

▶ ▶ ▶ 77% **Quex Caravan Park**
(TR321685)
Park Rd CT7 0BL
☎ 01843 841273
📧 info@keatfarm.co.uk
🌐 www.keatfarm.co.uk
Dir: From Birchington (A28) turn SE into Park Road to
site in 1m
★ 🚐 £11-£13.50 🚐 £11-£13.50
Open Mar-Nov Booking advisable BH's Last arrival
anytime Last departure noon
A small parkland site in a quiet and secluded
woodland glade, with a very clean toilet block
housed in a log cabin. This picturesque site is just
one mile from the village of Birchington, while
Ramsgate, Margate and Broadstairs are all within
easy reach. An 11-acre site with 48 touring pitches
and 145 statics.
Leisure: 🖾
Facilities: 🖍⊙🕾✻🗣🖫🏂
Services: 🖵🖩🛢🖎🗓⊞→∪▶🗲🖇🅙 🞐 🞑 🞒

▶ ▶ ▶ 77% **Two Chimneys Caravan Park**
(TR320684)
Shottendane Rd CT7 0HD
☎ 01843 841068 & 843157 🖷 01843 848099
📧 info@twochimneys.co.uk
🌐 www.twochimneys.co.uk
Dir: From A28 to Birchington Sq, turn right into Park
Lane (B2048). Left at Manston Rd (B2050) then 1st left
★ 🚐 £12-£20 🚐 £12-£20 ▲ £12-£20

Open Mar-Oct (rs Mar-May & Sep-Oct shop, bar,
pool & takeaway restricted) Booking advisable bank
& school hols Last arrival 23.00hrs Last departure
noon
An impressive entrance leads into this well-
managed site, which boasts two swimming pools
and a fully-licensed clubhouse. Other attractions
include a tennis court and children's play area, and
the immaculately clean toilet facilities fully meet
the needs of this busy family park. A 30-acre site
with 200 touring pitches, 5 hardstandings and
100 statics.
Amusement arcade.
Leisure: 🕾 🖳 🖾
Facilities: 🖍⊙🕾✻🗣🖫
Services: 🖵🖩🞀🖎🗓⊞⊺ 🖲→∪▶◎🖇🖇🗲🅙
🞐 🞑 🞒 🞓 🞔

England

CANTERBURY   Map 07 TR15

▶ ▶ ▶ 85% **Camping & Caravanning Club Site (TR172577)**
Bekesbourne Ln CT3 4AB
☎ 01227 463216

GOLD

Ⓦ www.campingandcaravanningclub.co.uk
Dir: From Canterbury follow A257 signs (Sandwich), turn right opposite golf course
★ ⚏ £13.60-£17.80 ⚏ £13.60-£17.80 ▲ £13.60-£17.80
Open all year Booking advisable bank hols & peak periods Last arrival 21.00hrs Last departure noon
An attractive tree-screened site in pleasant rural surroundings yet within walking distance of the city centre. The park is well landscaped, and offers very smart toilet facilities in one block, with another older but well-kept building housing further facilities. Please see the advertisement on page 11 for information on Club sites and membership. A 20-acre site with 200 touring pitches, 11 hardstandings.
Leisure: ⚠ Facilities: 🚿⊙🔧⚒✳⚘🚻🛒🐕
Services: 🔌🔃🚽🍴🧺🚰🚻↝∪▶▲🚮🔩
💳 ▭ ▭ 🔗 🔵

▶ ▶ 78% **Ashfield Farm (TR138508)**
Waddenhall, Petham CT4 5PX ☎ 01227 700624
Ⓔ mpatterson@ashfieldfarm.freeserve.co.uk
Dir: 7m S of Canterbury on B2068
⚏⚏▲

Open Apr-Oct Booking advisable Jul & Aug Last arrival anytime Last departure noon
Small rural site with simple facilities and well-drained pitches, set in beautiful countryside and enjoying lovely open views. Located south of Canterbury, and with very security-conscious owners. A 4.5-acre site with 30 touring pitches and 1 static.
Mini golf, short term kennelling.
Facilities: 🚿⊙✳⚘🚻🐕
Services: 🔌🚽🍴🚰🚻↝∪▶🔩

DOVER   Map 07 TR34

▶ ▶ ▶ ▶ 74% **Hawthorn Farm Caravan Park (TR342464)**
Station Rd, Martin Mill CT15 5LA
☎ 01304 852658 & 852914
🖷 01304 853417
Ⓔ info@keatfarm.co.uk
Ⓦ www.keatfarm.co.uk/touringparks/hawthorn.htm
Dir: Signed from A258
★ ⚏ £11-£13.50 ⚏ £11-£13.50 ▲ £11-£13.50

Best of British
GOLD

contd.

Hawthorn Farm Caravan Park
Open Mar-Nov (rs winter water off if weather cold) Booking advisable bank hols & Jul-Aug Last arrival anytime Last departure noon
This pleasant rural park set in 28 acres of beautifully-landscaped gardens is screened by young trees and hedgerows, in grounds which include woods and a rose garden. The decent facilities include a shop and laundry. A 28-acre site with 147 touring pitches, 5 hardstandings and 176 statics.
Facilities: 🚿⊙🔧✳⚘🐕
Services: 🔌🚽🍴🚰✕🧺↝∪▶◎▲🚮🐕🔩
💳 ▭ ▭ 🔗 🔵

See advertisement under BIRCHINGTON

FAVERSHAM   Map 07 TR06

▶ ▶ ▶ 68% *Painters Farm Caravan & Camping Site (TQ990591)*
Painters Forstal ME13 0EG
☎ 01795 532995
Dir: Leave A2 at Faversham, signs to Painters Forstal & Eastling. 1.5m down 'No through road' at Forstal
⚏⚏▲
Open Mar-Oct Booking advisable bank hols Last arrival 23.59hrs
A delightful farm site in an extremely attractive and peaceful former cherry and plum orchard, with mature trees and hedging. The spotless toilets are housed in converted farm buildings, along with a laundry, dishwashing area, and function room. The village playground is nearby. A 3-acre site with 50 touring pitches.
Facilities: 🚿⊙✳⚘🐕
Services: 🔌🚽🍴🚰🚻↝∪▶🚮🔩

FOLKESTONE   Map 07 TR23

▶ ▶ ▶ 83% **Camping & Caravanning Club Site (TR246376)**
The Warren CT19 6PT
☎ 01303 255093
Ⓦ www.campingandcaravanningclub.co.uk
Dir: From A2 or A20 join A260 and turn left at island into Folkstone. Continue straight over x-rds into Wear Bay Road and 2nd left turn past Martello Tower, site 0.5m on right
★ ⚏ £13.60-£19.80 ▲ £13.60-£19.80
Open Mar-Oct Booking advisable bank hols & peak periods Last arrival 21.00hrs Last departure noon
This site commands marvellous views across the Strait of Dover, and is well located for the Channel

contd.

ports. It nestles on the side of the cliff, and is tiered in some areas. The toilet facilities are modern and tasteful, with cubicled wash basins in both blocks. Please see the advertisement on page 11 for information on Club sites and membership. A 4-acre site with 80 touring pitches, 9 hardstandings.

Facilities: ♠⊙☜※♿⚓

Services: ♥🚐🗑♨⚡☎→∪►♿🗲🕭

🔲 ▨ ▨ ▨ 🔊

▶ ▶ ▶ **77% Little Satmar Holiday Park (TR260390)**

Winehouse Ln, Capel Le Ferne CT18 7JF
☎ 01303 251188 📠 01303 251188
📧 info@keatfarm.co.uk
🌐 www.keatfarm.co.uk/touringparks/
   littlesatmar.htm

Dir: Signed off B2011
★ 🚐 £11-£13.50 🚐 £11-£13.50 ▲ £11-£13.50
Open Mar-Nov Booking advisable bank hols & Jul-Aug Last arrival 23.00hrs Last departure 14.00hrs
A quiet, well-screened site well away from the road and statics, with clean and tidy facilities. A useful base for visiting Dover and Folkestone, and just a short walk from cliff paths with their views of the Channel, and sandy beaches below. A 5-acre site with 60 touring pitches and 80 statics.

Leisure: 🅰 **Facilities:** ♠⊙☜※♿⚓

Services: ♥🗑♨⚡☎→∪►♿🗲🔲 ▨ ▨ 🔊
See advertisement under BIRCHINGTON

▶ ▶ **74% Little Switzerland Camping & Caravan Site (TR248380)**

Wear Bay Rd CT19 6PS ☎ 01303 252168
📧 btony328@aol.com
🌐 www.caravancampingsites.co.uk/
   kent/littleswitzerland.htm

Dir: Signed from A20 E of Folkestone. Approaching from A259 or B2011 on E outskirts of Folkestone, follow signs for Wear Bay/Martello Tower, then tourist sign to site, follow signs to country park.
★ 🚐 £8-£16 🚐 £8-£16 ▲ £5-£10
Open Mar-Oct Booking advisable from Mar Last arrival mdnt Last departure noon
Set on a narrow plateau below the 'white cliffs', this unusual site enjoys fine views across Wear Bay and the Strait of Dover. A licensed café with an alfresco area is popular; the basic toilet facilities are unsuitable for the disabled. A 3-acre site with 32 touring pitches and 13 statics.

Facilities: ♠⊙※♿⚓

Services: ♥🚐🗑♨♿♨⚡☒✕♿→∪►⊙♿✚🗲🕭

▶ ▶ ▶ **71% Priory Hill (TR038704)**

Wing Rd ME12 4QT
☎ 01795 510267 📠 01795 511503
📧 philip@prioryhill.co.uk
🌐 www.prioryhill.co.uk

Dir: Take A249 signed to Sheerness then B2231 to Leysdown, follow brown tourist signs.
★ 🚐 £11-£20 🚐 £11-£20 ▲ £11-£20
Open Mar-Oct (rs low season shorter opening times
contd.

---

of pool & club) Booking advisable bank hols, wknds & Jul-Aug Last arrival 20.00hrs Last departure noon. *A small well-maintained touring area on an established family-run holiday park close to the sea, with views of the North Kent coast. Amenities include a clubhouse and a swimming pool. A 1.5-acre site with 50 touring pitches.*

Leisure: 🔗 ♦▢ **Facilities:** ♠⊙☜※♿⚓🕭🐕

Services: ♥🗑♨⚓♨✕ ♨→🗲

🔲 ▨ ▨ ▨ 🔊

▶ ▶ ▶ **81% Pine Lodge Touring Park (TQ815549)**

Ashford Rd, Bearsted, Hollingbourne ME17 1XH
☎ 01622 730018 📠 01622 734498
📧 booking@pinelodgetouringpark.co.uk
🌐 www.pinelodgetouringpark.co.uk

Dir: M20 junct 8, keep to right. Right at next rdbt. 0.5m on A20 towards Maidstone East on left
★ 🚐 £13-£15.25 🚐 £14-£18.25 ▲ £10-£12
Open all year Booking advisable bank hols/weekends Last arrival 22.00hrs Last departure noon
A well-run park suitable for all touring units from large motorhomes to small tents. The modern facilities are maintained to a high standard by the owners, and the site is handy for the M20 and visiting Leeds Castle. A 7-acre site with 100 touring pitches.
Waste disposal points.

Leisure: 🅰

Facilities: ♠⊙☜※♿⚓🕭

Services: ♥🚐🗑♨♨⚡☎→∪►♨🗲

Notes: ✂ No commercial vehicles

🔲 ▨ ▨ ▨ 🔊

▶ ▶ ▶ **79% Manston Caravan & Camping Park (TR348662)**

Manston Court Rd CT12 5AU ☎ 01843 823442
📧 enquiries@manston-park.co.uk
🌐 www.manston-park.co.uk

Dir: From B2050, N of Manston Airport, take minor road (Manston Court Rd) to site in 0.24m on right
🚐 🚐 ▲
Open Apr/Etr-Oct (rs Apr shop open weekends only (off-peak)) Booking advisable bank hols & Jul-Aug Last arrival 23.55hrs Last departure 11.00hrs
A neatly-kept grassy park broken up by mature trees, handy for Manston Airport and the seaside resorts on the Isle of Thanet. The older-style toilet facilities are well maintained, and there is an excellent children's play area. A 5-acre site with 100 touring pitches and 46 statics.

Leisure: 🅰

Facilities: ♠⊙※♿🕭⚓🐕

Services: ♥♨⚓♨⚡☎→∪►⊙♿✚🗲🕭

🔲 ▨ ▨ 🔊

Homing Park

Church Lane, Seasalter, Whitstable,
Kent CT5 4BU tel 01227 771777

Fully serviced pitches including TV & drainage.
Six miles from Historic City of Canterbury.
Seasalter beach about fifteen minutes walk.
Tennis court, gym, & children's playground.
5 star Loo of the Year award winners.

www.coastandcountryleisure.com

SANDWICH   Map 07 TR35

► ► ► ► 81% Sandwich Leisure
Park (TR326581)

Woodnesborough Rd CT13 0AA
☎ 01304 612681 ▤ 01304 615252
🄴 info@sandwichleisurepark.co.uk
🆆 www.sandwichleisurepark.co.uk
*Dir: From Sandwich town centre, then follow brown
tourist signs*
★ 🚐 £9.80-£14.75 🚐 £9.80-£14.75 ▲ £6.50-£14.75
Open Mar-Oct Booking advisable Etr, Spring bank
hol & Jul-Aug Last arrival 20.00hrs Last departure
11.00hrs
*A large site with impressive toilet facilities,
including a suite of family rooms, and 18 fully-
serviced pitches. Visitors can choose between
pitches with hook-ups or those in a separate field
with a more natural ambience. The park backs onto
open farmland on the edge of Sandwich, and is well
planted with mature and newer trees. A 15-acre site
with 187 touring pitches, 34 hardstandings and
103 statics.*
Leisure: 🅐
Facilities: 🌣 ⊙ ⌇ ✳ ☷ ⛿ 🎇
Services: 🔌 🛒 🏴 🅰 ⌀ → ▶ ◎ ⏏ ⚓ ✈ 🐾 ⌇
Notes: No groups of under 17yrs without adult
present, no commercial vehicles 💳 🚉 🔵

SEVENOAKS   Map 06 TQ55

► ► ► 70% Camping & Caravanning Club Site
(TQ577564)
Styants Bottom, Seal TN15 0ET ☎ 01732 762728
🆆 www.campingandcaravanningclub.co.uk
*Dir: Take A25 from Sevenoaks towards Borough Green.
Left just after Crown Point Inn, on right, down narrow
lane to Styants Bottom. Site on left*
★ 🚐 £12.40-£16.70 🚐 £12.40-£16.70 ▲ £12.40-£16.70
Open Mar-Oct Booking advisable bank hols & peak
periods Last arrival 21.00hrs Last departure
noon
*A remarkably tranquil site in the centre of National
Trust woodland, with buildings blending well into
the surroundings. Expect the usual high standard of
customer care found at all Club sites. Please see the
advertisement on page 11 for information on Club
sites and membership. A 6-acre site with 60 touring
pitches.*
Leisure: 🅐 **Facilities:** 🌣 ⊙ ⌇ ✳ ☷ ⛿ 🎇
Services: 🔌 🛒 🏴 🅰 ⏏ 🅣 → ∪ ▶ 🅰 ✈ ⌇
💳 🚉 🔵

ST NICHOLAS AT WADE   Map 07 TR26

► 72% St Nicholas Camping Site (TR254672)
Court Rd CT7 0NH ☎ 01843 847245
*Dir: Signed off A299 and A28, at W end of village near
church*
★ 🚐 £12-£14.50 🚐 £11-£12.50 ▲ £9.50-£14

Open Etr-Oct Booking advisable Jul-Aug Last arrival
22.00hrs Last departure 14.00hrs
*A gently-sloping field with mature hedging, on the
edge of the village close to the shop. This rustic site
offers simple facilities, and is conveniently located
close to primary routes. A 3-acre site with 75
touring pitches.*
Leisure: 🅐 **Facilities:** 🌣 ⊙ ✳ 🎇
Services: 🔌 🅰 ⌀ 🅣 → ∪ ✈ 🛒 ⌇

WHITSTABLE   Map 07 TR16

► ► ► ► 77% Homing Park (TR095645)
Church Ln, Seasalter CT5 4BU
☎ 01227 771777 ▤ 01227 273512
🄴 info@homingpark.co.uk
🆆 www.coastandcountryleisure.com
*Dir: Turn off A299 for Whitstable and Canterbury, left at
brown camping/caravan sign into Church Lane. Park
entrance has 2 large flag poles*
★ 🚐 £9.80-£15.75 🚐 £9.80-£15.75 ▲ £6.50-£15.75

contd.

Homing Park
Open Mar-Oct Booking advisable Etr, bank hols & Aug Last arrival 20.00hrs Last departure 11.00hrs
A small touring park with a new toilet block, close to Seasalter Beach and Whitstable, which is famous for its oysters. All pitches are generously sized and fully serviced, and most are separated by hedging and shrubs. A clubhouse and swimming pool are available on the adjacent residential park at a small cost. A 12.75-acre site with 43 touring pitches and 195 statics. Fitness centre

Leisure: ₹ ९ ∧ Facilities: ⋔⊙⊀⋇ ᏪᏆ
Services: ⊟⊟ⴹ♀ᔑ⌀✕ ♨→ ♭Å ☎♩ ᏏᏏ
Notes: No commercial vehicles/pre-booking for large units, no unaccompanied groups of under 18's
⊜ ⊞ ⊉   See advertisement on opposite page

▶ ▶ ▶ 75% **Seaview Holiday Village (TR145675)**
St John's Rd CT5 2RY
☎ 01227 792246 ▤ 01227 792247
✉ mail@seaviewpark.fsnet.co.uk
Dir: From A299 take A2990 then B2205 to Swalecliffe, site between Herne Bay & Whitstable
★ ⊞ fr £12.50 ⊞ fr £12.50 ⚑ fr £12.50
Open Mar-Oct (rs Feb & Nov limited facilities) Booking advisable all times Last arrival 21.30hrs Last departure noon
A pleasant open site on the edge of Whitstable, set well away from the static area, with a smart, modern toilet block and both super and hardstanding pitches. A 12-acre site with 171 touring pitches, 32 hardstandings and 452 statics. Amusements in games room & adventure trail
Leisure: ♣ ∧ ☐ Facilities: ⋔⊙⊀⋇ ᏪᏆᏏ⋥₹
Services: ⊟⛬Ꮕ♀ᔑ⌀Ⅱ✕ ♨♩→∪♭◉△⅍ᏏᎫ
⊜ ⊞ ⊞ ⊠ ⊉
                   See advertisement under ASHFORD

WROTHAM HEATH   Map 06 TQ65

▶ ▶ ▶ 77% **Gate House Wood Touring Park (TQ635585)**
Ford Ln TN15 7SD ☎ 01732 843062
✉ gatehousewood@btinternet.com
ⓦ www.gatehousewoodtouringpark.co.uk
Dir: From M26 junct 2A take A20 S towards Maidstone, through traffic lights at Wrotham Heath. Take 1st left turn signed Trottiscliffe turn left at next junct into Ford Lane, Gate House Wood 100yds on left.
★ ⊞ £11-£14.50 ⊞ £11-£14.50 ⚑ £6.50-£14.50
Open Mar-Nov Booking advisable bank holidays Last arrival 22.00hrs Last departure noon
A well-sheltered and mature site in a former quarry
                                          contd.

surrounded by tall deciduous trees and gorse banks. The well-designed facilities include reception, shop and smart toilets, and there is good entrance security. A 3.5-acre site with 55 touring pitches.
Leisure: ∧ Facilities: ⋔⊙⊀⋇ᏪᏆ⋥
Services: ⊟ᴧⴹᔑ⌀Ⅱ→∪♭
Notes: No commercial vehicles, no pets

LANCASHIRE

See also sites under **Greater Manchester & Merseyside**

BLACKPOOL   Map 18 SD33
See also **Lytham St Annes & Thornton**

73% **Marton Mere Holiday Village (SD347349)**
Mythop Rd FY4 4XN
☎ 01253 767544
▤ 01253 791544
ⓦ www.havenholidays.com
Dir: From M55 junct 4 onto A583 towards Blackpool. Turn right at Clifton Arms traffic lights, onto Mythop Rd. Park 150yds on left.
★ ⊞ £11-£60 ⊞ £11-£60
Open mid Mar-Oct Booking advisable School holidays Last departure 10.00hrs
A very attractive holiday centre in an unusual setting on the edge of the mere, with plenty of birdlife to be spotted. The on-site entertainment is directed at all ages, and includes a superb show bar. There's a regular bus service into Blackpool for those who want to explore further afield. The separate touring area is well equipped with hardstandings and electric pitches, and there are good quality facilities. A 30-acre site with 205 touring pitches.
Leisure: ₹ ९ ♣ ∧ Facilities: ⋔⊙⊀Ꮪᴧ ₹
Services: ⊟⛬Ꮕᔑ⌀✕ ♨→∪♭◉△⅍Ꮫ
Notes: No more than 2 dogs per group
⊜ ⊞ ⊞ ⊠ ⊉

BOLTON-LE-SANDS   Map 18 SD46

▶ ▶ ▶ 83% *Sandside Caravan & Camping Park (SD472681)*
The Shore LA5 8JS
☎ 01524 822311 ▤ 01524 822311
ⓦ www.sandside.co.uk
Dir: From M6 junct 35 follow A6 through Carnforth, turn right after far Pavillion in Bolton-le-Sands, and over level crossing to site
⊞ ⊞ ⚑
Open Mar-Oct Booking advisable bank hols & Jul-Aug Last arrival 22.00hrs Last departure 13.00hrs
A well-kept park located in a pleasant spot overlooking Morecambe Bay, with distant views of the Lake District. The site is next to a busy main West Coast railway line with a level crossing. A new shop and reception are an asset to this welcoming park. A 9-acre site with 70 touring pitches, 42 hardstandings and 33 statics.
Facilities: ⋔⊙⊀⋇Ꮟ₹⋥ᏆᏏ
Services: ⊟ⴹᔑ→∪♭◉△⅍ᏏᎫ

England

► ► 76% *Detron Gate Farm (SD478683)*
LA5 9TN ☎ 01524 732842 & 733617 (night)
Dir: W of A6, 1m N of Bolton-le-Sands
🚐🚐⚠
Open Mar-Oct (rs Mar-May shop hours restricted)
Booking advisable bank hols Last arrival 22.00hrs
Last departure 18.00hrs
*A rural grassy site with lovely views out over
Morecambe Bay to the Lakeland hills, on slightly
sloping ground close to a small farm. An attractive
barn houses the shop, paperback library and table
tennis. A 10-acre site with 100 touring pitches and
42 statics.*
Leisure: ❀⚠▭
Facilities: ₦⊙❊✆🛁
Services: 🖵🗑🛢🛒☎📺🗑→∪▶✖🐾♪

► ► 72% *Red Bank Farm (SD472681)*
LA5 8JR ☎ 01524 823196 📠 01524 824981
✉ archer-mark@lycos.co.uk
🌐 www.redbankfarm.co.uk
Dir: Take A5105 (Morecambe road), after 200mtrs right
on Shore Lane. At rail bridge, turn right to Red Bank
🚐⚠
Open Mar-Oct Booking advisable
*A gently sloping grassy field with mature hedges,
close to the sea shore and a RSPB reserve. This
farm site has superb views across Morecambe Bay
to the distant Lake District hills, and is popular with
tenters. The basic toilet facilities are clean and
bright. A 3-acre site with 60 touring pitches,
40 hardstandings.*
Pets corner
Facilities: ₦⊙❊❊
Services: 🖵🛒→▶◎⚠☀♪🗑🛒
Notes: Dogs on lead

CAPERNWRAY   Map 18 SD57

► ► ► 92% **Old Hall Caravan Park**
(SD533716)
LA6 1AD ☎ 01524 733276
📠 01524 734488
✉ info@oldhall.uk.com
🌐 www.oldhall.uk.com
Dir: M6 junct 35 follow signs to Over Kellet, left onto
B6254, left at village green signed Capernwray. Site
1.5m on right
★ 🚐 £16-£18 🚐 £16-£18
Open Mar-Oct (rs Nov-10 Jan only for seasonal
tourers & static vans) Booking advisable wknds,
bank hols & Jul-Aug
*A lovely secluded park set in a clearing amongst
trees at the end of a half-mile long drive. This
peaceful park is home to a wide variety of wildlife,
and there are marked walks in the woods. Facilities
are well maintained by friendly owners. A 3-acre
site with 38 touring pitches, 38 hardstandings and
220 statics.*
Leisure: ⚠
Facilities: ₦⊙🍴⚙✆🖵🐾
Services: 🖵🗑🛒⚙📺→∪◎✖♪🛒
💳 ▭▭ 🏧 🗑

SILVER

CLITHEROE   Map 18 SD74

► ► ► ► 79% **Camping & Caravanning Club Site**
(SD727413)
Edisford Rd BB7 3LA ☎ 01200 425294
🌐 www.campingandcaravanningclub.co.uk
Dir: From W follow A671 to Clitheroe. Look for sign for
left turn to Longridge/Sports Centre. Turn into
Greenacre Rd approx 25mtrs after pelican crossing.
To T-junct. (Sports Centre on right). Site 50mtrs on left
★ 🚐 £13.60-£17.80 🚐 £13.60-£17.80 ⚠ £13.60-£17.80
Open Mar-Oct Booking advisable bank hols & peak
periods Last arrival 21.00hrs Last departure noon
*Set on the banks of the River Ribble, this park is
attractively landscaped with mature trees and
shrubs. An ideal spot for walking and fishing, and
the site is also adjacent to a park with a café, pitch
and putt, leisure centre, swimming pool and
miniature steam railway. The Ribble Country Way is
nearby. Please see the advertisement on page 11
for information on Club sites and membership.*
*A 6-acre site with 80 touring pitches, 30
hardstandings.*
Facilities: ₦⊙🍴❊🖵✆🖾
Services: 🖵🚽🛢⚙📺→▶◎♪🛒
💳 ▭▭ 🏧 🗑

COCKERHAM   Map 18 SD45

► ► ► ► 80% *Mosswood Caravan
Park (SD456497)*
Crimbles Ln LA2 0ES
☎ 01524 791041 📠 01524 792444
✉ info@mosswood.co.uk
🌐 www.mosswood.co.uk
Dir: Approx 4m from A6/M6 junct 33, 1m W of
Cockerham on A588
🚐🚐⚠

GOLD

Open Mar-Oct Booking advisable bank hols & Jul-
Sep Last arrival 20.00hrs Last departure 16.00hrs
*A tree-lined grassy park with sheltered, level pitches,
located on peaceful Cockerham Moss. The modern
toilet block is attractively clad in stained wood, and
the facilities include cubicled washing facilities and a
launderette. A 25-acre site with 25 touring pitches,
25 hardstandings and 143 statics.*
Woodland walks
Leisure: ⚠ Facilities: ₦⊙🍴❊🖵✆🖾🎣🐾
Services: 🖵🛢⚙📺→∪▶♪💳 ▭▭ 🏧 🗑

CROSTON   Map 15 SD41

► ► ► 82% *Royal Umpire Caravan Park
(SD504190)*
Southport Rd PR26 9JB
☎ 01772 600257 📠 01772 600662
🌐 www.royalumpire.co.uk
Dir: From Chorley take A581, 3.5m & on approach to
Croston, park on right
🚐🚐⚠
Open all year (rs 7 Nov-22 Dec hardstandings only)
Booking advisable bank hols & peak season Last
arrival 22.00hrs Last departure noon
*A pleasant level site set in open countryside, with
an attractive sunken garden and seating area.
Plenty of leisure opportunities include a large*

contd.

Abbreviations: BH/bank hols-bank holidays   Etr-Easter   Whit-Whitsun   dep-departure   fr-from   hrs-hours   m-mile   mdnt-midnight
rdbt-roundabout   rs-restricted service   wk-week   wknd-weekend   🐾-no dogs

games room, an interesting children's playground, and a large playing field. The toilets, laundry and dishwashing area are of a very good quality. A 60-acre site with 200 touring pitches, 130 hardstandings.
Assault course, five-a-side football pitch.

Leisure: ♦ ⚠

Facilities: ℝ ☉ ☜ ✳ ዼ ᘯ ☎ ᛒ ☨ 🛏

Services: ▦ ⓢ ▯ ᵃ ⊞ ⊤ ♣ → ∪ ▮ ✗ ♪

Notes: No large groups of young people

▦ ▤ ▨ ▩ ◪

GARSTANG   Map 18 SD44

▶ ▶ ▶ ▶ **80% Claylands Caravan Park (SD496485)**
Cabus PR3 1AJ ☎ 01524 791242
🖹 01524 792406
✉ alan@claylands.com
🌐 www.claylands.com
Dir: From M6 junct 33 S to Garstang, approx 6m pass Little Chef, signed off A6 into private road on Lancaster side of Garstang
★ ⊞ £16-£18 ⚐ £16-£18 ▲ £14-£18
Open Mar-4 Jan (rs Jan & Feb Holiday park only)
Booking advisable bank hols & Jul-Aug Last arrival 23.00hrs Last departure 14.00hrs
A well-maintained site with lovely river and woodland walks and good views over the River Wyre towards the village of Scorton. This friendly park is set in delightful countryside. Guests can enjoy fishing, and the atmosphere is very relaxed. The quality facilities and amenities are of a high standard, and everything is immaculately maintained. A 14-acre site with 30 touring pitches, 30 hardstandings and 68 statics.

Leisure: ⚠

Facilities: ℝ ☉ ✳ ዼ ☎ ᛒ ᘯ ☨ 🛏

Services: ▦ ⓢ ☸ ▯ ᵃ ⊞ ⊤ ✗ ᵗ ♣ → ∪ ▮ ✗ ♪

▦ ▤ ▨ ◪

▶ ▶ ▶ **74% Bridge House Marina & Caravan Park (SD483457)**
Nateby Crossing Ln, Nateby PR3 0JJ
☎ 01995 603207 🖹 01995 601612
✉ edwin@bridgehousemarina.co.uk
🌐 www.bridgehousemarina.co.uk
Dir: Off A6 at pub and sign for Knott End, immediately right into Nateby Crossing Lane, over canal bridge to site on left
★ ⊞ £12.50-£16 ⚐ £12.50-£16
Open Mar-4 Jan Booking advisable bank hols Last arrival 22.00hrs Last departure 13.00hrs
A well-maintained site in attractive countryside by the Lancaster Canal, with good views towards the Trough of Bowland. The boatyard atmosphere is interesting, and there is a super children's playground. A 4-acre site with 50 touring pitches, 45 hardstandings and 20 statics.

Leisure: ⚠ **Facilities:** ℝ ☉ ✳ ዼ ☎ ᛒ ☨ 🛏

Services: ▦ ⓢ ▯ ᵃ ⊞ ⊤ → ▮ ✗ ♪

▦ ▤ ▨ ◪

GISBURN   Map 18 SD84

▶ ▶ ▶ **85% Rimington Caravan Park (SD825469)**
Hardacre Ln, Rimington BB7 4EE ☎ 01200 445355
🖹 01200 445355
✉ rimingtoncaravanpark@btinternet.com
Dir: Off A682 1m S of Gisburn, site on right in 1m
★ ⚐ fr £16 ⊞ fr £16 ▲ fr £12
Open Apr-Oct (rs Mar hardstanding available only)
Booking advisable bank hols & Jul-3 Sep Last arrival 18.00hrs Last departure noon
A very well-cared for park set in an attractive rural valley close to the Pendle Hills. The high quality facilities are kept spotless, and the family owners pay a great deal of attention to customer needs. An 11-acre site with 4 touring pitches, 4 hardstandings and 150 statics.

Facilities: ℝ ☉ ✳ ዼ ☎ ᛒ

Services: ▦ ⓢ ☸ ▯ ᵃ ⊞ ⊤ → ∪ ♪

Notes: No cars by caravans or tents

HEYSHAM   Map 18 SD46

72% Ocean Edge Leisure Park (SD407591)
Moneyclose Ln LA3 2XA
☎ 01524 855657 🖹 01524 855884
✉ enquiries@southlakeland-caravans.co.uk
🌐 www.southlakeland-caravans.co.uk
Dir: From M6 junct 34 follow A683 to Heysham. In Heysham site signed before ferry port
★ ⚐ £14-£16 ⊞ £15-£18 ▲ £10-£12
Open mid Feb-Jan Booking advisable bank/school hols Last arrival 22.00hrs Last departure 10.00hrs
An open touring area of a large holiday complex adjacent to the sea, and with good sea views. Facilities include a large bar and café, and nightly entertainment including bingo, quizzes, cabaret and singsongs. A 10-acre site with 94 touring pitches and 600 statics.

Leisure: ☇ ♦ ⚠ **Facilities:** ℝ ☉ ዼ ☎ ᛒ 🛏

Services: ▦ ⓢ ☸ ▯ ᵃ ✗ ♣ → ∪ ▮ △ ⚇ ♪

▦ ▤ ▨ ◪

LANCASTER   Map 18 SD46

▶ ▶ **86% New Parkside Farm Caravan Park (SD507633)**
Denny Beck, Caton Rd LA2 9HH
☎ 01524 770723 & 770337
🌐 www.ukparks.co.uk/newparkside
Dir: From M6 junct 34 onto A683 E towards Kirkby Lonsdale. Park 0.75m on right
⚐ ⊞ ▲
Open Mar-Oct Booking advisable bank hols & Jul-Aug Last arrival 22.00hrs Last departure 16.00hrs
Peaceful, friendly grassy park on a working farm with extensive views of Lune Valley and Ingleborough. A 3-acre site with 40 touring pitches and 10 statics.

Facilities: ℝ ☉ ☜ ✳ ዼ ᘯ 🛏

Services: ▦ ▯ ᵃ → ▮ ⚇ ♪ ◙ ᛒ

Notes: Dogs must be kept on leads

England

LONGRIDGE   Map 18 SD63

▶ ▶ ▶ 72% **Beacon Fell View Caravan Park (SD618382)**
110 Higher Rd PR3 2TF ☎ 01772 785434 & 783233
🖷 01772 784204
✆ enquiries@hagansleisure.co.uk
ⓦ www.hagansleisure.co.uk
Dir: Leave A6 at Broughton on B5269 into Longridge & follow B6243 out of town centre. Take left fork signed Jeffrey Hill. Site 0.75m on right
★ ⚏ £5-£23.50 ⚏ £5-£23.50 ⚑ £5-£23.50
Open 3 Mar-Nov (rs 3 Mar-10 Apr & 25-30 Nov limited entertainment Booking advisable Last departure 10.00hrs
An elevated park with views over Beacon Fell. This tiered park with level pitches provides an extensive free evening entertainment programme in the clubhouse. There is a superb heated pool with fitness room, small arcade, small adult-only bar, and large modern reception with tourist information. A 32-acre site with 43 touring pitches. Internet café, gym.
Leisure: ⚜ ⚛ ⚙ **Facilities:** ⚐⊙⚑⚙⚘⚉🔭
Services: ⚑⚏⚒⚎⚘⚅⊞⚓→▶⊙⚒⚇⚏⚏⚏⚏

LYTHAM ST ANNES   Map 18 SD32

▶ ▶ ▶ 72% *Eastham Hall Caravan Site (SD379291)*
Saltcotes Rd FY8 4LS
☎ 01253 737907
SILVER
Dir: Leave M55 junct 3. Straight over 3 rdbts onto B5259. Through Wrea Green & Moss Side, park 1m after level crossing
⚏ ⚏

Open Mar-Oct Booking advisable bank hols & Jul Last arrival 21.00hrs Last departure 16.00hrs
Secluded park with trees and hedgerows in a rural setting. Helpful owners ensure that facilities are maintained to a high standard. A 15-acre site with 200 touring pitches, 30 hardstandings and 200 statics.
Leisure: ⚜ **Facilities:** ⚐⊙⚑⚛⚉🔭
Services: ⚑⚏⚘⚅⊙⚓→⊙▶⚘⚒
Notes: No tents, no groundsheets in awnings
⚏ ⚏ ⚏ ⚏

For full details of the AA pennant
ratings scheme see pages 7-8

MIDDLETON (NEAR MORECAMBE) Map 18 SD45

▶ ▶ ▶ 65% **Melbreak Caravan Park (SD415584)**
Carr Ln LA3 3LH ☎ 01524 852430
Dir: M6 junct 34 onto A683. After 6m turn left at rdbt, pass Middleton & turn right into village. Site in 0.5m
★ ⚏ £9 ⚏ £9 ⚑ £8.50
Open Mar-Oct Booking advisable Jul-Aug Last arrival 22.00hrs Last departure noon
A small rural park run by friendly owners, in open country south of Morecambe. It offers simple but clean facilities and ample hardstands. Good access to historic Sunderland Point, Heysham Port for Isle of Man ferries, and the seaside attractions of Morecambe. A 2-acre site with 10 touring pitches and 32 statics.
Facilities: ⚐⊙⚑⚛⚉
Services: ⚑⚎⚒⊞⚘⚅⊞ ⚓→▶⚒

MORECAMBE   Map 18 SD46

▶ ▶ ▶ 66% **Riverside Caravan Park (SD448615)**
Lancaster Rd, Snatchems LA3 3ER
☎ 01524 844193
✆ info@riverside-morecambe.co.uk
ⓦ www.riverside-morecambe.co.uk
Dir: On unclass road off B5273 near Heaton
★ ⚏ £12-£14 ⚏ £12-£14

Open Mar-Oct Booking advisable public hols & high season Last arrival 20.00hrs Last departure noon
A grassy site with views over the River Lune and Morecambe Bay. The sanitary facilities in a modern toilet block are clean and fresh. Road access is subject to tidal river flooding, and it is advisable to check tide times before crossing. A 2-acre site with 50 touring pitches and 52 statics.
Leisure: ⚜ **Facilities:** ⚐⊙⚑⚛⚉⚙🔭
Services: ⚑⚎⚘⚅→⊙▶⚐⚏⚇⚒⚏⚏ ⚏

▶ ▶ ▶ 76% **Venture Caravan Park (SD436633)**
Langridge Way, Westgate LA4 4TQ
☎ 01524 412986 🖷 01524 422029
✆ mark@venturecaravanpark.co.uk
ⓦ www.venturecaravanpark.co.uk
Dir: From M6 junct 34 follow Morecambe signs. At rdbt take road towards Westgate & follow park signs. 1st right after fire station
★ ⚏ £9.65-£11.65 ⚏ £9.65-£11.65 ⚑ £9.65-£11.65
Open all year (rs 6 Jan-22 Feb touring vans only, one toilet block open) Booking advisable bank hols & peak periods Last arrival 22.00hrs Last departure noon

contd.

A large park with good modern facilities, including a small indoor heated pool, a licensed clubhouse and a family room with children's entertainment. The site has many statics, and is close to the town centre. A 17.5-acre site with 56 touring pitches, 40 hardstandings and 304 statics.
Amusement arcade & off licence.

Leisure: ⌇ ✦ ⊿ ☐

Facilities: ⇥ ⋔ ⊙ ⍦ ✳ ⚲ ⚃ ⚑

Services: ⚘ ⚇ ⚏ ⚑ ⊞ ⊤ ⚒ → ⌇ ⚓ ✦

⚇ ⚏ ⚌ ⚑ ⚑ ⚑

ORMSKIRK — Map 15 SD40

▶ ▶ ▶ ▶ 78% *Abbey Farm Caravan Park* (SD434098)
Dark Ln L40 5TX ☎ 01695 572686
🖷 01695 572686
📧 abbeyfarm@yahoo.com
🌐 www.abbeyfarmcaravanpark.co.uk
Dir: M6 junct 27 onto A5209 to Burscough. 4m left onto B5240. Immediate right into Hobcross Ln. Park 1.5m on right
🚐 🚐 ⚑

Open all year Booking advisable public hols & Jul-Aug Last arrival 22.00hrs Last departure 13.00hrs
Delightful hanging baskets and flower beds brighten this garden-like rural park which is sheltered by hedging and mature trees. Modern, very clean facilities include a family bathroom, and there are special pitches for the disabled near the toilets. A superb recreation field caters for children of all ages, and there is an indoor games room, large library, fishing lake and dog walk. Tents have their own area with BBQ and picnic tables. A 6-acre site with 56 touring pitches and 44 statics.
Off-licence, farm walk

Leisure: ✦ ⊿

Facilities: ⇥ ⋔ ⊙ ⍦ ✳ ⚲ ⚃ ⚑ ⚑ ⚑ ⚑

Services: ⚘ ⚏ ⚑ ⊞ ⊤ → ∪ ⌇ ✦

⚇ ⚏ ⚌ ⚑ ⚑

▶ ▶ ▶ 73% *Shaw Hall Caravan Park* (SD397119)
Smithy Ln, Scarisbrick L40 8HJ
☎ 01704 840298 🖷 01704 840539
📧 shawhall@btconnect.com
🌐 www.shawhall.co.uk
Dir: 200yds S of canal bridge at Scarisbrick, 0.25m off A570 at Smithy Lane
★ 🚐 £18-£23 🚐 £18-£23

Open Mar-7 Jan Booking advisable bank hols & peak periods Last arrival 20.30hrs
A large, pleasant park with 20 super pitches and good toilets. The clubhouse and bar offer cabaret and discos which are popular with families. The park also boasts canal walks from its direct access to the Leeds-Liverpool Canal, a football field, and putting and bowling greens. A 26-acre site with 45 touring pitches and 300 statics.
Fishing

Leisure: ⊿ ☐

Facilities: ⋔ ⊙ ⍦ ✳ ⚲ ⚃ ⚑ ⚑ ⚑

Services: ⚘ ⚏ ⚑ ⊞ ⚒ → ∪ ⌇ ✦

⚇ ⚌ ⚑ ⚑

SILVERDALE — Map 18 SD47

▶ ▶ ▶ ▶ ▶ 92% *Holgate's Caravan Park* (SD455762)
Middlebarrow Plain, Cove Rd LA5 0SH
☎ 01524 701508 🖷 01524 701580
📧 caravan@holgates.co.uk
🌐 www.holgates.co.uk
Dir: M6 junct 35. 5m NW of Carnforth. From Carnforth centre take unclass Silverdale road & follow tourist signs after Warton
★ 🚐 £27.75-£29.50 🚐 £27.75-£29.50
⚑ £25-£26.75

Open 22 Dec-5 Nov Booking advisable school hols, public hols & wknds Last arrival 22.00hrs Last departure noon
A superb family holiday park set in wooded countryside next to the sea. This park demonstrates high quality in all areas, and offers a wide range of leisure amenities. Its relaxing position overlooking Morecambe Bay combined with excellent touring facilities mark this park out as special. A 10-acre site with 70 touring pitches, 70 hardstandings and 339 statics.
Sauna, spa bath, steam room, mini-golf, gym

Leisure: ⌇ ✦ ⊿

Facilities: ⋔ ⊙ ⍦ ✳ ⚲ ⚃ ⚑ ⚑

Services: ⚘ ⚏ ⚑ ⚒ ⊞ ✕ ⚒ → ∪ ⌇ ✦

Notes: No unaccompanied children

⚇ ⚌ ⚑ ⚑ ⚑

contd.

Leisure: ⌇ Indoor swimming pool ⌇ Outdoor swimming pool ⚲ Tennis court ✦ Games room ⊿ Children's playground ∪ Stables
⌇ 9/18 hole golf course ⚓ Boats for hire ⚏ Cinema ✦ Fishing ⊚ Mini golf ⚃ Watersports ☐ Separate TV room

England

THORNTON   Map 18 SD34

▶ ▶ ▶ ▶ 79% **Kneps Farm Holiday Park**
(SD353429)
River Rd, Stanah FY5 5LR
☎ 01253 823632 ▤ 01253 863967
✉ enquiries@knepsfarm.co.uk
🌐 www.knepsfarm.co.uk
*Dir: Leave A585 at rdbt onto B5412 to Little Thornton.
Right at mini-rdbt after school onto Stanah Rd, over 2nd
mini-rdbt, leading to River Rd*
★ 🚏 £12-£16 🚐 £12-£16 ▲ £12-£16
Open Mar-mid Nov Booking advisable at all times
Last arrival 20.00hrs Last departure noon
*A quality park adjacent to the River Wyre and the
Wyre Estuary Country Park, handily placed for the
attractions of Blackpool and the Fylde coast. This
family-run park offers an excellent toilet block with
immaculate facilities, and a mixture of hard and
grass pitches. The park is quietly located, but
there is some noise from a nearby plastics plant.
A 10-acre site with 60 touring pitches,
40 hardstandings and 68 statics.*
Leisure: ⚲ **Facilities:** ◪♠⊖♥※⑤♨♒
Services: ⚡❀▯⌀⌂▥↻♨→▶◐♨♫ ⚐ ⬛ ⌷ ▣

LEICESTERSHIRE

CASTLE DONINGTON   Map 11 SK42

▶ ▶ ▶ 70% **Donington Park Farmhouse Hotel**
(SK414254)
Melbourne Rd, Isley Walton DE74 2RN
☎ 01332 862409 ▤ 01332 862364
✉ info@parkfarmhouse.co.uk
🌐 www.parkfarmhouse.co.uk
*Dir: M1 junct 24, pass airport to Isley Walton, right
towards Melbourne. Park 0.5m on right*
★ 🚏 £15-£20 🚐 £14-£19 ▲ £9-£16
Open Jan-23 Dec (rs winter months hardstanding
only) Booking advisable summer season Last arrival
21.00hrs Last departure noon
*An extremely pleasant secluded touring site at the
rear of a hotel beside Donington Park motor racing
circuit. Booking is essential on race days, but this is
a quiet rural site at other times. A 7-acre site with
60 touring pitches, 10 hardstandings.*
Bread & milk sold, hotel on site for bar/dining
Leisure: ⚲ **Facilities:** ♠⊖※⑤♨♒
Services: ⚡❀♀▮※→↻▶♨♫▥
⬛ ⬛ ⌷ ⬤ ⬛ ▣ ▣

ULLESTHORPE   Map 11 SP58

▶ 72% **Ullesthorpe Garden Centre** (SP515872)
Lutterworth Rd LE17 5DR
☎ 01455 202144 ▤ 01455 202585
✉ enquiries@ullesthorpegardencentre.co.uk
🌐 www.ullesthorpegardencentre.co.uk
*Dir: From M1 junct 20 take A4303 through Lutterworth,
then B577 for 2m. Site just SE of Ullesthorpe*
★ 🚏 £5-£7 🚐 £5-£7
Open Mar-Oct Booking advisable at all times Last
arrival 18.00hrs Last departure sunset

*A pleasant site next to the garden centre, ideal for
the self-contained caravanner, with nature walk and
fishing on site. A 7-acre site with 150 touring
pitches.*
Facilities: ※♒ **Services:** ⚡※♨→↻▶♫▥
Notes: Tents only allowed with a caravan
⬛ ⌷ ⬛ ▣

LINCOLNSHIRE

ANCASTER   Map 11 SK94

▶ ▶ ▶ 76% **Woodland Waters** (SK979435)
Willoughby Rd NG32 3RT
☎ 01400 230888 ▤ 01400 230888
✉ info@woodlandwaters.co.uk
🌐 www.woodlandwaters.co.uk
Dir: On A153 W of x-roads with B6403
★ 🚏 £9-£15.50 🚐 £9-£15.50 ▲ £7-£11
Open all year Booking advisable BH's Last arrival
21.00hrs Last departure noon
*Peacefully set around impressive fishing lakes, with
a few log cabins in a separate area, a pleasant open
park. The access road is through mature woodland,
and there is a very good heated toilet block, and a
pub/club house with restaurant. A 5-acre site with
62 touring pitches.*
5 fishing lakes
Leisure: ♠⚲ **Facilities:** ♠⊖♥⑤♨♒♒♒
Services: ⚡❀♀▯※♨→↻▶♫
Notes: Dogs must be kept on leads at all times

BOSTON   Map 12 TF34

▶ ▶ ▶ ▶ 77% **Orchard Park** (TF274432)
Frampton Ln, Hubbert's Bridge
PE20 3QU ☎ 01205 290328 ▤ 01205 290247
🌐 www.orchardpark.co.uk
*Dir: On B1192, between A52 (Boston-Grantham) &
A1121 (Boston-Sleaford)*
★ 🚏 £12-£14 🚐 £12-£14 ▲ £6-£14
Open Mar-Nov (rs Dec-Jan statics only, no café)
Booking advisable bank hols Last arrival 22.30hrs
Last departure 11.00hrs
*Ideally located for exploring the unique fenlands,
this rapidly-improving park has two lakes - one for
fishing and the other set aside for conservation.
A very attractive restaurant and bar are popular
with visitors. A 36-acre site with 87 touring pitches,
3 hardstandings and 128 statics.*
Angling lake
Leisure: ♨♠ **Facilities:** ◪♠⊖♥※⑤♨♒♒♒
Services: ⚡❀♀▯⌀⌂※→↻▶◐♫
Notes: Adults only

▶ ▶ ▶ ▶ 80% **Pilgrims Way** (TF358434)
Church Green Rd, Fishtoft PE21 0QY
☎ 01205 366646 ▤ 01205 366646
✉ info@pilgrims-way.co.uk
🌐 www.pilgrims-way.co.uk
*Dir: From Boston N on A16 (T), right onto A52, right
again at Ball House pub to Fishtoft 1m on left*
★ 🚏 fr £12 🚐 fr £12 ▲ fr £12

contd.

contd.

England

Open Etr & Apr-Sep Booking advisable bank hols
Last arrival 20.00hrs Last departure noon
*A very attractive site in the gardens of the Grange,
with individually screened pitches and purpose-
built toilet facilities. This park is ideal for those
seeking peace and tranquillity, and is ideally-placed
for touring around the Boston area, and visiting the
Pilgrim Fathers Memorial. A 1-acre site with 22
touring pitches.*

Facilities: �📶 ⊖ 🥤 ✳ 🍴 ᴸ 🛒 🏪

Services: 🖭 🍴 🔌 🎵 ⊞ → ∪ ▶ 🛆 ⅃ ᴝ 🍴

Notes: Adults only

CLEETHORPES   Map 17 TA30

**77% Thorpe Park Holiday
Centre (TA321035)**
DN35 0PW ☎ 01472 813395
📠 01472 812146
ⓦ www.havenholidays.com
*Dir: Take unclass road off A180 at Cleethorpes,
signed Humberstone and Holiday Park*
★ 🚐 £12-£64 🚐 £12-£64 ▲ £9-£46
Open mid Mar-Oct (rs mid Mar-May & Sep-Oct
Some facilities may be reduced) Booking
advisable bank & school hols Last departure
10.00hrs
*A large static site with touring facilities,
including fully-serviced pitches, adjacent to the
beach. This holiday centre offers excellent
recreational and leisure activities, including an
indoor pool with bar, bowling greens, crazy golf,
tennis courts, and a games area. Parts of the site
overlook the sea. A 300-acre site with
113 touring pitches, 64 hardstandings.*
Pitch and putt, roller ring, fishing lakes

Leisure: 🥤 🔍 🎾 🅰

Facilities: 📶 ⊖ 🥤 🛆 ᴸ 🛒 🏪 🍴

Services: 🖭 🍴 🥤 ✕ ♨ → ∪ ▶ ⊙ 🛆 ᴝ 🍴

Notes: Maximum of 2 dogs per group
🖭 💳 🖩 🖼 📶

FLEET HARGATE   Map 12 TF32

▶ ▶ ▶ **83% Delph Bank Touring
Caravan & Camping Park (TF388248)**
Old Main Rd PE12 8LL ☎ 01406 422910
🅔 enquiries@delphbank.co.uk
ⓦ www.delphbank.co.uk
*Dir: Turn off A17, King's Lynn to Sleaford road, into
Fleet Hargate and follow signs*
🚐 🚐 ▲
Open Mar-Nov Booking advisable 1-10 May & BH's
Last arrival 22.30hrs Last departure noon
*A quiet, well-screened park, neatly laid out in two
fields with trimmed grass and colourful flower
beds. The older-style toilet facilities are
immaculately maintained. This adult-only park
which is being improved constantly, is set well
away from the village and the A17, and there is no
traffic noise. A 3-acre site with 45 touring pitches,
13 hardstandings.*

Facilities: 📶 ⊖ 🥤 ✳ ᴸ 🛒 🏪

Services: 🖭 🍴 🔌 🎵 ⊞ ⊞ → 🍴 **Notes:** Adults only

LOUTH   Map 17 TF38

▶ ▶ **72% *Manby Caravan Park (TF392876)***
Manby Leisure Ltd, Middlegate, Manby LN11 8SY
☎ 01507 328232 📠 01507 327867
Dir: Approx 3m E of Louth off B1200
🚐 🚐 ▲
Open Apr-Oct Booking advisable all bank hols Last
arrival 20.00hrs Last departure noon
*A simple touring park behind a health and leisure
club, with level, well-drained pitches. A 5-acre site
with 80 touring pitches and 7 statics.*
Temporary membership to Health Club

Leisure: 🥤 🅰 **Facilities:** 📶 ⊖ 🥤 ✳ 🛆 🛒 🏪 🍴

Services: 🖭 → ∪ ▶ ᴝ 🍴 🖩

MABLETHORPE   Map 17 TF58

**73% Golden Sands Holiday
Park (TF501861)**
Quebec Rd LN12 1QJ
☎ 01507 477871 📠 01507 472066
ⓦ www.havenholidays.com
*Dir: From centre of Mablethorpe turn left on
seafront road towards north end. Park is on this
road on left.*
★ 🚐 £9-£43 🚐 £9-£43 ▲ £6-£29
Open mid Mar-Oct Booking advisable school
hols Last departure 10.00hrs
*A large, well-equipped seaside holiday park with
separate touring facilities on two sites, including
fully modernised toilets. The first floor
entertainment rooms are only accessible via
stairs (no lifts). A 7-acre site with 195 touring
pitches.*
Mini bowling alley, snooker/pool, indoor fun
palace.

Leisure: 🥤 🔍 🎾 🅰 **Facilities:** 📶 ⊖ ✳ 🛆 ᴸ 🛒

Services: 🖭 🍴 🥤 🔌 🎵 ✕ ♨ → ▶ ⊙ 🛆 ᴝ 🍴

Notes: Maximum of 2 dogs per group
🖭 💳 🖩 🖼 📶

▶ ▶ ▶ **75% Camping & Caravanning Club Site
(TF499839)**
Highfield, 120 Church Ln LN12 2NU
☎ 01507 472374
ⓦ www.campingandcaravanningclub.co.uk
*Dir: On outskirts of Mablethorpe, on A1104, just after
the 'Welcome to Mablethorpe' sign turn right into
Church Ln. 800yds to end of lane. Site on right*
★ 🚐 £12.40-£16.70 🚐 £12.40-£16.70 ▲ £12.40-£16.70
Open Mar-Oct Booking advisable bank hol & peak
periods Last arrival 21.00hrs Last departure noon
*Located next to flat agricultural land 1m from the
sea, and well away from the road. The camping
area is in two hedged fields with rural views, and
the modern toilet facilities and laundry are centrally
sited. Please see advertisement on page 11 for
information on Club sites and membership.
A 6-acre site with 105 touring pitches.*

Leisure: 🅰 **Facilities:** 📶 ⊖ 🥤 ✳ 🛆 ᴸ 🛒

Services: 🖭 🍴 🔌 🎵 ⊞ ⊞ → ∪ ▶ 🛆 🍴 🛒
🖭 💳 🖩 🖼 📶

England

▶ ▶ ▶ 77% **Kirkstead Holiday Park** (TF509835)
North Rd, Trusthorpe LN12 2QD
☎ 01507 441483 ▯ 08700 336723
✉ mark@kirkstead.co.uk
🌐 www.kirkstead.co.uk
Dir: From Mablethorpe town centre take A52 S towards Sutton-on-Sea. 1m turn sharp right at 2 phone boxes into North Rd. Site signed in 300yds
★ ⛺ £14-£20 ⛺ £14-£20 ⛺ £10-£16
Open Mar-Nov Booking advisable bank hols & Jul-Aug Last arrival mdnt Last departure 15.00hrs
Controlled entry is a welcome security feature of this pleasant family-run site. The touring area and good quality toilets are centrally located, and the grounds are particularly well maintained. A 10-acre site with 80 touring pitches and 75 statics.
Snooker, volleyball, football pitch, basketball

Leisure: ♦ ⋀ ☐
Facilities: ♠ ⊙ ☜ ☀ ⅋ ⅃ ☎ ⊞ 禾 ⼤
Services: ☐ ☺ ☙ ⅃ ⼀ ☒ ✕ ⼦ → ∪ ⼁ ◎ ☺ ♪
🕲 🔳 🅾 🔳 🔳 🕈

▶ ▶ ▶ 73% **Racecourse Caravan Park**
(TF123883)
Legsby Rd LN8 3EA
☎ 01673 842307 & 843434 ▯ 01673 844532
✉ marketrasen@rht.net
🌐 www.marketrasenraces.co.uk
Dir: E of Market Rasen on A631, turn right 300yds after lights into Legsby Rd, site racecourse entrance is 0.75m on left
★ ⛺ £9.35-£13.60 ⛺ £9.35-£13.60 ⛺ £12.60-£14.60

Open 29 Mar-7 Oct (rs race days shared toilet & shower) Booking advisable bank hols & race days
Last arrival 20.00hrs Last departure 14.00hrs
Set in a grass paddock adjacent to but separate from the racecourse, and screened by a hedge. The site has a golf course with a discount for campers, and there is a large children's playground. A 3-acre site with 55 touring pitches.
Reduced rate for racing & golf

Leisure: ♦ ⋀
Facilities: ♠ ⊙ ☀ ⅃ ⼤ ☎ ⼤
Services: ☐ ☙ ⅃ ⼀ ☒ ⊞ → ∪ ⼁ ☒
Notes: Family park 🕲 🔳 🔳 🔳 🕈

▶ ▶ ▶ 70% **White Cat Caravan & Camping Park**
(TF415498)
Shaw Ln PE22 9LQ ☎ 01205 870121 ▯ 01205 871749
✉ kevin@klannen.freeserve.co.uk
🌐 www.whitecatpark.com
Dir: Just off A52, 7m NE of Boston, opposite B1184
★ ⛺ £9-£11 ⛺ £9-£11 ⛺ £9-£11
Open Apr-Oct Booking advisable bank hols Last arrival 22.00hrs Last departure noon
A pleasant, well-maintained small touring park set down a rural lane just off the A52, surrounded by the typical quiet character of the Fenlands. It makes a peaceful base for exploring Boston and the Lincolnshire coast. A 2.5-acre site with 30 touring pitches, 4 hardstandings and 10 statics.

Leisure: ⋀　Facilities: ♠ ⊙ ☀ ⅃ ⼤ ☎
Services: ☐ ⼀ ⼀ ⊞ ⊞ → ∪ ♪

▶ ▶ ▶ 80% *Heron's Mead Fishing Lake & Touring Park* (TF508673)
Marsh Ln PE24 5JA ☎ 01754 811340
✉ heronsmead@freeuk.com
🌐 www.ukparks.co.uk/herons
Dir: From A158 Lincoln to Skegness road turn left at rdbt, through Orby for 0.5m
⛺ ⛺ ⛺
Open Etr-Oct Booking advisable bank & school hols Last arrival 21.00hrs Last departure noon
A pleasant fishing and touring park with coarse fishing and an 8-acre woodland walk. Quiet couples and elderly visitors are particularly welcome. A 4-acre site with 30 touring pitches.
Fishing on site, 2 disabled pegs

Facilities: ♠ ⊙ ☜ ☀ ⅃ ⼤
Services: ☐ ⼦ → ∪ ⼁ ◎ ⼀ ♪ ⊞ ⼀
Notes: No ball games

▶ ▶ ▶ 80% **Saltfleetby Fisheries** (TF425892)
Main Rd LN11 7SS ☎ 01507 338272
✉ saltfleetbyfish@aol.com
🌐 www.saltfleetbyfisheries.co.uk
Dir: On B1200, 6m E of junct with A16; 3m W of A103
★ ⛺ fr £8 ⛺ fr £8 ⛺ fr £8

Open Mar-Nov Booking advisable bank hols Last arrival 18.00hrs Last departure noon
A pretty little site beside a well-stocked fishing lake behind the owner's house. An excellent toilet block
contd.

offers quality facilities, and there are electric hook ups and spacious hardstandings. A 12-acre site with 18 touring pitches, 12 hardstandings and 1 static.
2 acre coarse fishing pond & 2 fishing lakes
Facilities: ⁿ※&⅃⊼⼐
Services: ⊡⑤🔌📶📺↻↩⼐💈⼐
Notes: Adults only park

SUTTON ST EDMUND   Map 12 TF31

► ► ► **64% Orchard View Caravan & Camping Park (TF365108)**
Broadgate PE12 0LT ☎ 01945 700482
✉ orchardview@hotmail.co.uk
Dir: A47 Peterborough to Wisbech at Guyhirn. Turn towards Wisbech St Mary & Murrow. Through Murrow, over double bridge, then 2nd right. Site 0.5m on right
★ ⊞ £6-£8 ⊞ £6-£8 Å £5-£8
Open 31 Mar-Oct Booking advisable Bank hols & Spalding Flower Festival
A neat meadowland site with good planting for shelter and screening, located in remote and unspoilt fenland. The park has its own clubhouse. A 6-acre site with 35 touring pitches, 3 hardstandings and 2 statics.
Rally field
Leisure: ⚆⼐ **Facilities:** ⁿ⊙🔍※&⅃⊡⼐⼐
Services: ⊡⑤🔌📶↻↩⼐⼐

SUTTON ST JAMES   Map 12 TF31

► ► ► **80% Foremans Bridge Caravan Park (TF409197)**
Sutton Rd PE12 0HU ☎ 01945 440346
✉ foremans.bridge@btinternet.com
🌐 www.foremans-bridge.co.uk
Dir: 2m from A17 on B1390
★ ⊞ £8.50-£11.50 ⊞ £8.50-£11.50 Å £5-£10.50
Open Mar-Nov Booking advisable bank hols Last arrival 21.00hrs Last departure 10.00hrs
A lovely, well-maintained little site set beside the South Holland Main Drain which flows past, and offers good fishing. The enthusiastic hands-on owners keep the facilities in immaculate condition, and their quiet park is mainly used by adults. A 2.5-acre site with 40 touring pitches, 20 hardstandings and 7 statics.
Cycle hire centre, fishing on site.
Facilities: ⁿ⊙🔍※&⅃⊡⼐⼐⼐
Services: ⊡🚐⑤📶🔌📺⼐→↻↩⼐
Notes: No cycling or ball games in park

WADDINGHAM   Map 17 SK99

► **69% Brandy Wharf Leisure Park (TF014968)**
Brandy Wharf DN21 4RT
☎ 01673 818010 📠 01673 818010
✉ brandywharflp@freenetname.co.uk
🌐 www.brandywharfleisurepark.co.uk
Dir: From A15 onto B1205 through Waddingham. Site 3m from Waddingham
★ ⊞ fr £10 ⊞ fr £10 Å fr £9
Open Etr-Oct (rs Nov-Etr caravans only) Booking advisable Etr-Sep
A simple, quiet site in a very rural area on the banks of the River Anholme, where fishing is available.
contd.

Brandy Wharf Leisure Park
The basic unisex facilities are clean, and there are level grassy pitches, all with electricity, and a playing/picnic area. A 5-acre site with 30 touring pitches.
Fishing & boat mooring, pets corner
Leisure: ⚆ **Facilities:** ⁿ🔍※&⊡⼐⼐
Services: ⊡⑤📶📺⼐→⼐

WOODHALL SPA   Map 17 TF16

PREMIER PARK

► ► ► ► ► **86% Bainland Country Park (TF215640)**
Horncastle Rd LN10 6UX
☎ 01526 352903 & 353572
📠 01526 353730
✉ bookings@bainland.co.uk
🌐 www.bainland.co.uk
Dir: 1.5m from town, on B1191
★ ⊞ £12-£34 ⊞ £12-£34 Å £10-£24

The Best of British TOURING AND HOLIDAY PARKS

Open all year Booking advisable all year Last arrival 21.30hrs Last departure 11.30hrs
More a country club than a purely touring park, this is one of the best equipped parks in the country with an impressive array of leisure facilities, combined with high standards of maintenance. The touring pitches are all screened by shrubs and trees, and many are fully serviced. Children are well catered for, and there is an indoor swimming pool. A 12-acre site with 170 touring pitches, 51 hardstandings and 10 statics.
Jacuzzi, solarium, sauna, par 3, bowling green
Leisure: 🏊 🎾 ⚇ ⚆ ⼐
Facilities: ↩ⁿ⊙🔍※&↻⅃⊡⼐⼐⼐
Services: ⊡🚐⑤📶🔌📺⼐✕⼐⼐→↻↩◎△💈⼐⼐
Notes: Children must be accompanied by an adult 💳 💳 💳 💳

See advertisement on page 170

Leisure: 🏊 Indoor swimming pool 🏊 Outdoor swimming pool 🎾 Tennis court ⚆ Games room ⚇ Children's playground ↻ Stables
⼐ 9/18 hole golf course ⼐ Boats for hire 💈 Cinema ⼐ Fishing ◎ Mini golf △ Watersports ⼐ Separate TV room

▶ ▶ ▶ 77% **Camping & Caravanning Club Site (TF225633)**
Wellsyke Ln, Kirkby-on-Bain LN10 6YU
☎ 01526 352911
ⓦ www.campingandcaravanningclub.co.uk
Dir: From Sleaford or Horncastle take A153 to Haltham. At garage turn onto side road. Over bridge, left towards Kirkby-on-Bain. 1st turn right, signed
★ ♞ £13.60-£17.80 ♞ £13.60-£17.80
▲ £13.60-£17.80
Open Mar-Oct Booking advisable bank hols & peak periods Last arrival 21.00hrs Last departure noon
A pleasant site in silver birch wood and moorland, with pitches laid out around a central lake (no fishing). Facilities include a family room, and a unisex room with en suite facilities. Please see the advertisement on page 11 for information on Club sites and membership. A 6-acre site with 90 touring pitches.
Facilities: ⚛⊙🔍⚒&⚓🐕🏕
Services: 🍴🛒🖉🔌🗓🚾🗑→🏪🛒
⊜ 🔲🔲 🔲 🔲

LONDON

E4 CHINGFORD   Map 06 TQ39

▶ ▶ ▶ 81% **Lee Valley Campsite (TQ381970)**
Sewardstone Rd E4 7RA
☎ 020 8529 5689 🖨 020 8559 4070
🅔 scs@leevalleypark.org.uk
ⓦ www.leevalleypark.com
Dir: From M25 junct 26 to A112 and signed
★ ♞ fr £12.30 ♞ fr £12.30 ▲ fr £12.30
Open Apr-Oct Booking advisable bank hols & Jul-Aug Last arrival 21.00hrs Last departure noon
Overlooking King George's Reservoir and close to Epping Forest, this parks has excellent modern facilities and a very peaceful atmosphere. A bus calls at the site hourly to take passengers to the nearest tube station, and Enfield is easily accessible. This impressive park is maintained to a high standard. A 12-acre site with 200 touring pitches, 20 hardstandings.
Leisure: ⚘
Facilities: ⚛⊙🔍⚒&⚓🐕🏕
Services: 🍴🛒🖉🔌🗓🚾→∪🏪⊙🍴⚲
Notes: Under 18's must be accompanied by an adult ⊜ 🔲 🔲 🔲 🔲

N9 EDMONTON   Map 06 TQ39

▶ ▶ ▶ 84% **Lee Valley Camping & Caravan Park (TQ360945)**
Meridian Way N9 0AS
☎ 020 8803 6900 🖨 020 8884 4975
🅔 leisurecentre@leevalleypark.org.uk
ⓦ www.leevalleypark.com
Dir: From M25 junct 25, A10 S, 1st left on A1055, approx 5m to Leisure Centre. From A406 (North Circular), N on A1010, left after 0.25m, right (Pickets Lock Ln)
★ ♞ £12.10 ♞ £12.10 ▲ £12.10

contd.

Booking advisable Jul-Aug Last arrival 22.00hrs Last departure noon
A pleasant, open site within easy reach of London yet peacefully located close to two large reservoirs. The very good toilet facilities are beautifully kept by dedicated wardens, and the site has the advantage of being adjacent to a restaurant and bar, and a multi-screen cinema. A 4.5-acre site with 160 touring pitches, 32 hardstandings.
Kitchen, cinema, 18-hole golf course

Leisure: ⚲ ⋀

Facilities: ⟡ ⊙ ⚲ ✳ ᴑ Ꮝ 🛒 🖼 🐾

Services: ⊟ ⛽ 🛢 🔌 🔲 ✕ 🍴 🐕 → ᐟ △ ⚡ ⚌ ✒

Notes: No commercial vehicles, max length of units 26 feet 🚍 ⊞ ⊞ ⊠ ⑤

See advertisement on opposite page

MERSEYSIDE

SOUTHPORT | **Map 15 SD31**

▶ ▶ ▶ **77%** *Brooklyn Park and Country Club (SD392196)*
Gravel Ln PR9 8BU ☎ 01704 228534
Dir: Signed from A565, E of Southport.
🚐 🚐
Open Mar-7 Jan
A developing park with two areas for tourers, one with gravel hardstands. The country club provides meals, music and entertainment, with separate areas for families and couples. A 15-acre site with 95 touring pitches and 181 statics.

Leisure: ⋀

Facilities: ⟡ ⊙ ⚲ ᴑ Ꮝ 🐾

Services: ⛽ ✕

▶ ▶ ▶ **76% Hurlston Hall Country Caravan Park** (SD398107)
Southport Rd L40 8HB
☎ 01704 841064 🖷 01704 841700
Dir: On A570, 3m from Ormskirk towards Southport
★ 🚐 £10-£15 🚐 £10-£15
Open Etr-Oct Booking advisable bank hols Last arrival 21.00hrs Last departure 17.00hrs
A peaceful tree-lined touring park next to a static site in attractive countryside about 10 minutes' drive from Southport. The park is maturing well, with growing trees and a coarse fishing lake. No dogs permitted. A 5-acre site with 60 touring pitches and 68 statics.
Coarse fishing, golf facilities

Leisure: ⋀

Facilities: ⟡ ⚲ ᴑ Ꮝ

Services: ⊟ ⛽ 🛢 🔌 ✕ → ᐟ ✒ 🛒

Notes: ⊘ No tents

▶ ▶ ▶ **79% Riverside Holiday Park** (SD405192) PR9 8DF
☎ 01704 228886 🖷 01704 505886
ⓦ www.riversideleisurecentre.com
Dir: M6 junct 27, A5209 towards Parbold/Burscough, right onto A59. Left onto A565 at lights in Tarleton. Continue to dual carriageway. At rdbt straight across, park 1m on left
★ 🚐 £10-£16 🚐 £10-£16 ⚊ £7-£24
Open Mar-6 Jan Booking advisable bank & school hols Last arrival 17.00hrs Last departure 11.00hrs
A large, spacious park with a lively family entertainment complex for cabaret, dancing and theme nights. Children have their own club and entertainer plus food and games. An 80-acre site with 260 touring pitches and 355 statics.

Leisure: ⋀

Facilities: ⟡ ᴑ Ꮝ 🛒 🖼 🐾

Services: ⊟ ⛽ 🛢 🔌 🔲 🍴 → ∪ ᐟ △ ✒ 🍴 🚍 ⊞ ⑤

▶ ▶ ▶ **83% Willowbank Holiday Home & Touring Park** (SD305110)
Coastal Rd, Ainsdale PR8 3ST
☎ 01704 571566 🖷 01704 571566
ⓔ info@willowbankcp.co.uk
ⓦ www.willowbankcp.co.uk
Dir: From A565 between Formby and Ainsdale turn at the Woodvale lights onto coastal road, site 150mtrs on left
★ 🚐 £10.50-£13.50 🚐 £10.50-£13.50 ⚊ fr £10

Open Mar-10 Jan Booking advisable bank hols & special events Last arrival 21.00hrs Last departure 16.00hrs
Set in a wooded clearing on a nature reserve next to the beautiful sand dunes, this attractive park is just off the coastal road to Southport. The immaculate toilet facilities are well equipped. A 6-acre site with 54 touring pitches, 30 hardstandings and 228 statics.
Baby changing facility

Leisure: ⋀

Facilities: ⟡ ⊙ ⚲ ᴑ Ꮝ 🍴 🐾

Services: ⊟ 🛢 🔌 🔲 → ∪ ᐟ ⊙ △ ✒ 🛒
🚍 ⊞ ⊞ ⊠ ⑤

Facilities: 🛁 Bath 🚿 Shower ⊙ Electric Shaver ⚲ Hairdryer ✳ Ice Pack Facility Ꮝ Disabled Facilities ᴑ Public Telephone
🛒 Shop on Site or within 200yds 🚍 Mobile Shop (calls at least 5 days a week) 🖼 BBQ Area 🗲 Picnic Area 🐾 Dog Exercise Area

England

NORFOLK

BARNEY　　　　　　　　　Map 13 TF93

▶ ▶ ▶ ▶ 92% **The Old Brick Kilns**
(TG007328)
Little Barney Ln NR21 0NL
☎ 01328 878305 🖷 01328 878948
✉ enquiries@old-brick-kilns.co.uk
⊕ www.old-brick-kilns.co.uk
Dir: Follow brown tourist signs from A148 (Fakenham-Cromer) to Barney, then left into Little Barney Lane - site at end of lane
🚐 🚃 ⛺

Open Mar-6 Jan (rs low season bar food/takeaway selected nights only) Booking advisable bank hols & Jul-Aug Last arrival 22.00hrs Last departure noon
A secluded and peaceful park approached via a quiet leafy country lane. The park is on two levels with its own boating and fishing pool and many mature trees. Excellent, well-planned toilet facilities can be found in two blocks, and there is a short dog walk. A 12.75-acre site with 65 touring pitches, 65 hardstandings.
Outdoor draughts, chess, family games area.
Leisure: ◀ ⋀ ▯ **Facilities:** ⌐◉⛱⋇க୧⛐鬲冎㈇
Services: ⊟⋓⛽⧟⌀㊙ⓣ✕→✈
💳 💳 ⑩ 🔲 📷 🔟

BELTON　　　　　　　　　Map 13 TG40

65% **Wild Duck Holiday Park**
(TG475028)
Howards Common NR31 9NE
☎ 01493 780268 🖷 01493 782308
⊕ www.havenholidays.com
Dir: From A47 towards Gt Yarmouth take A143 towards Beccles. Turn right at Burgh Castle, right at T-junct, left at next T-junct, park is 200mtrs on right.
🚐 🚃 ⛺
Open mid Mar-Oct (rs mid Mar-May & Sep-Oct Some facilities may be reduced) Booking advisable school hols Last arrival 23.00hrs Last departure noon
This a large holiday complex with plenty to do for all ages both indoors and out. This level grassy site is set in a forest with small cleared areas for tourers and well laid out facilities. Clubs for children and teenagers, sporting activities and evening shows all add to the fun

contd.

of a stay here. A 97-acre site with 125 touring pitches and 365 statics.
Sauna & jacuzzi
Leisure: ⋟ ⋠⋞◀ ⋀ **Facilities:** ⌐◉⛱⋇க୧⛐⚓
Services: ⊟⋓⛽⧟⌀✕ ▥→∪▶⋌⚒✈
💳 💳 💳 📷 🔟

▶ ▶ ▶ ▶ 83% **Rose Farm Touring & Camping Park (TG488033)**
Stepshort, nr Great Yarmouth, NR31 9JS
☎ 01493 780896 🖷 01493 780896
⊕ www.rosefarmtouringpark.co.uk
Dir: Follow signs to Belton off A143, right at lane called Stepshort, site 1st on right
★ 🚐 £10-£14 🚃 £10-£14 ⛺ £10-£14

Open all year Booking advisable Jul-Aug
A former railway line is the setting for this very peaceful site which enjoys rural views and is beautifully presented throughout. The ever-improving toilet facilities are spotlessly clean and inviting to use, and the park is brightened with many flower and herb beds. Customer care is truly exceptional. A 6-acre site with 80 touring pitches.
Leisure: ◀ ⋀ ▯ **Facilities:** ⌐◉⛱⋇க⚓
Services: ⊟⛽⧟⌀▥→∪▶⋌✈⚒

CLIPPESBY　　　　　　　Map 13 TG41

▶ ▶ ▶ ▶ 80% **Clippesby Hall**
(TG423147)
Clippesby Hall NR29 3BL
☎ 01493 367800 🖷 01493 367809
✉ holidays@clippesby.com
⊕ www.clippesby.com
Dir: From A47 follow tourist signs for The Broads. At Acle rdbt take A1064, after 2m left onto B1152, 0.5m turn left opposite village sign, 400yds on right
🚐 £13-£19.50 🚃 £13-£19.50 ⛺ £13-£19.50

contd.

Open Spring BH-30 Oct (rs Etr-23 May No swimming/tennis. Pub/cafe BH wknds) Booking advisable school hols Last arrival 17.30hrs Last departure 11.00hrs
A lovely country house estate with secluded pitches hidden among the trees or in sheltered sunny glades. The toilet facilities have been upgraded to a very good standard, providing a wide choice of cubicle. Amenities include a café, clubhouse and family crazy-golf. A 30-acre site with 100 touring pitches.
Bicycle hire & mini golf

Leisure: ⌖ ⌖ ⌖ ⌖ Facilities: ⌖⌖⌖⌖⌖⌖⌖⌖⌖

Services: ⌖⌖⌖⌖⌖⌖⌖⌖⌖→⌖⌖⌖⌖⌖

Notes: Dogs must be kept on leads

⌖⌖ ⌖⌖ ⌖⌖ ⌖⌖ ⌖

CROMER   Map 13 TG24

▶ ▶ ▶ ▶ 76% *Seacroft Camping Park*
(TG206424)
Runton Rd NR27 9NH
☎ 01263 511722 ▤ 01263 511512
Ⓦ www.ukparks.co.uk/seacroft
BRONZE
Dir: 1m W of Cromer on A149 coast road
⌖⌖⌖
Open Mar-Oct Booking advisable school hols, 22-31 May & 4 Sep Last arrival 23.00hrs Last departure 11.00hrs
A very good touring site, well laid out and landscaped. Touring pitches are well screened for privacy, and there is a separate large playing field with children's play equipment. Toilets and showers in the sanitary buildings are tiled and spotless. There is a heated swimming pool and bar/restaurant. A 5-acre site with 120 touring pitches.
Baby change.

Leisure: ⌖ ⌖ ⌖ ⌖ Facilities: ⌖⌖⌖⌖⌖⌖⌖⌖⌖⌖
Services: ⌖⌖⌖⌖⌖⌖⌖⌖⌖⌖→⌖⌖⌖⌖⌖⌖

⌖⌖ ⌖⌖ ⌖⌖ ⌖⌖ ⌖

▶ ▶ ▶ 73% *Forest Park Caravan Site*
(TG233405)
Northrepps Rd NR27 0JR
☎ 01263 513290 ▤ 01263 511992
Ⓔ forestpark@netcom.co.uk
Ⓦ www.forest-park.co.uk
GOLD
Dir: A140 from Norwich, left at T-junct signed Cromer, right signed Northrepps, right then immediate left, left at T-junct, park on right
★ ⌖ £9-£17 ⌖ £9-£17 ⌖ £9-£17

contd.

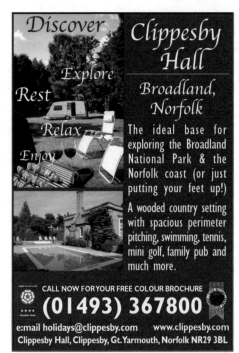
Open mid Mar- mid Jan Booking advisable Etr, Spring bank hol & Jul-Aug Last arrival 22.00hrs Last departure 14.00hrs
Surrounded by forest, this gently sloping park offers a wide choice of pitches. Visitors have the use of a heated indoor swimming pool, and a large clubhouse with entertainment. An 85-acre site with 344 touring pitches and 372 statics.
BMX track, hair salon

Leisure: ⌖ ⌖ ⌖ Facilities: ⌖⌖⌖⌖⌖⌖⌖⌖⌖
Services: ⌖⌖⌖⌖⌖⌖⌖⌖⌖→⌖⌖⌖⌖⌖⌖⌖⌖

⌖⌖ ⌖⌖ ⌖⌖ ⌖⌖ ⌖

▶ ▶ ▶ 66% *Manor Farm Caravan & Campsite*
(TG198416)
East Runton NR27 9PR ☎ 01263 512858
Ⓔ manor-farm@ukf.net
Ⓦ www.manorfarmcaravansite.co.uk
Dir: 1m W of Cromer, turn off A148 or A149 at Manor Farm sign
★ ⌖ £9-£10.50 ⌖ £9-£10.50 ⌖ £9-£10.50
Open Etr-Sep Booking advisable bank hols & all season for EHU points Last arrival 20.30hrs Last departure noon
A well-established family-run site on a working farm enjoying panoramic sea views. There are good modern facilities on the caravan-only area, and there is a decent toilet block on the tenting field. A 17-acre site with 250 touring pitches.
2 dog-free fields

Leisure: ⌖ Facilities: ⌖⌖⌖⌖⌖⌖⌖
Services: ⌖⌖⌖⌖⌖→⌖⌖⌖⌖⌖⌖⌖⌖⌖

Leisure: ⌖ Indoor swimming pool   ⌖ Outdoor swimming pool   ⌖ Tennis court   ⌖ Games room   ⌖ Children's playground   ⌖ Stables
▶ 9/18 hole golf course   ⌖ Boats for hire   ⌖ Cinema   ⌖ Fishing   ◎ Mini golf   ⌖ Watersports   ⌖ Separate TV room

DISS
See **Scole**

DOWNHAM MARKET Map 12 TF60

► ► ► 79% *Lakeside Caravan Park & Fisheries (TF608013)*
Sluice Rd, Denver PE38 0DZ
☎ 01366 387074 & 07770 663237
Dir: Off A10 towards King's Lynn
🚐 🚐 ⅄
Open all year
A peaceful, rapidly improving park set around three pretty fishing lakes. Several grassy touring areas are sheltered by mature hedging and trees. There is a function room, shop and laundry. A 10-acre site with 100 touring pitches and 1 static.
Four fishing lakes
Facilities: 🖰 ⅄ 🏪 Services: 🗑

FAKENHAM Map 13 TF92

► ► ► 77% **Caravan Club M.V.C. Site (TF926288)**
Fakenham Racecourse NR21 7NY ☎ 01328 862388
📄 01328 855908
✉ caravan@fakenhamracecourse.co.uk
🌐 www.fakenhamracecourse.co.uk
Dir: 0.75m SW of Fakenham off A1065 Swaffham road
★ 🚐 £8.30-£20.20 🚐 £8.30-£20.20 ⅄ fr £6
Open all year (rs race days all caravans moved to centre of course) Booking advisable Jun-Sep Last arrival 21.00hrs Last departure 14.00hrs
A very well laid out site set around the racecourse, with a grandstand offering smart modern toilet
contd.

facilities. Tourers move to the centre of the course on race days, and enjoy free racing, and there's a wide range of sporting activities in the club house. An 11.5-acre site with 120 touring pitches, 25 hardstandings. TV aerial hook-ups, hostel accommodation available
Facilities: 🖰 ⊙ 🗑 ✻ ⅄ 🛒 🏪 🎣
Services: 🔌 🗑 🍴 🚿 🛒 🖍 🗑 × 🚽 → ∪ ▶ ♨ ┘
💳 💳 💳 💳 💳

► ► 70% **Crossways Caravan & Camping Park (TF961321)**
Crossways, Holt Rd, Little Snoring NR21 0AX
☎ 01328 878335
✉ hollands@mannasolutions.com
🌐 www.crosswayscaravan.co.uk
Dir: From Fakenham take A148 towards Cromer. After 3m pass turn off for Little Snoring. Site on A148 on left behind Post Office
★ 🚐 £4-£9 🚐 £4-£9 ⅄ £4-£9
Open all year Booking advisable in high season, bank & school holidays Last departure noon
Set on the edge of the peaceful hamlet of Little Snoring, this level site enjoys views across the fields towards the North Norfolk coast some 7 miles away. Visitors can use the health suite for a small charge, and there is a shop on site, and a good village pub.
A 2-acre site with 26 touring pitches, 10 hardstandings.
Health suite, sauna, sunbed, hot spa bath
Facilities: 🖰 ⊙ ✻ ⅄ 🛒 🏪 🎣
Services: 🔌 🗑 🖍 🗑 → ∪ ▶ ☺ ♨ ┘ 🗑 Notes: Dogs must be kept on leads 💳 💳 💳 💳 💳

GREAT YARMOUTH   Map 13 TG50

 74% Vauxhall Holiday Park (TG520083)
4 Acle New Rd NR30 1TB
☎ 01493 857231 ▤ 01493 331122
✉ vauxhall.holidays@virgin.net
🌐 www.vauxhall-holiday-park.co.uk
Dir: On A47 approaching Great Yarmouth
🚐🚐🅰

Open Etr, mid May-Sep & Oct half term Booking
advisable mid Jul-Aug Last arrival 21.00hrs Last
departure 10.00hrs

*A very large holiday complex with plenty of
entertainment and access to beach, river,
estuary, lake and main A47. The touring pitches
are laid out in four separate areas, each with its
own amenity block, and all arranged around the
main entertainment. A 40-acre site with
220 touring pitches and 421 statics.*
Children's pool, sauna, solarium, fitness centre.

Leisure: ⚓ ⚲ ⚫ 🎱 ☐

Facilities: ⋔ ⊙ ※ ⧖ ⚫ 🛒

Services: 🗄 🗄 🗄 ⊿ 🗄 🗄 ✕ 🗄 🚐 → ∪ ▶ ⊚ ⊿ ⋋ ⚐ ⤴

Notes: ※ 💳 ▭ ▭ ▭ 🗄

See advertisement on opposite page

HUNSTANTON   Map 12 TF64

 78% Searles Leisure Resort (TF671400)
South Beach Rd PE36 5BB
☎ 01485 534211 ▤ 01485 533815
🌐 www.searles.co.uk
*Dir: A149 from King's Lynn to Hunstanton. At rdbt
follow signs for South Beach. Straight on at 2nd
rdbt. Site on left*
★ 🚐 £11-£33 🚐 £11-£33 🅰 £10-£32

Open Feb (half term)-New Year (rs Feb-May &
Oct-Dec outdoor pool closed) Booking advisable
bank hols & Jul-Aug Last arrival 20.45hrs Last
departure 11.00hrs

*A large seaside holiday complex with well-
managed facilities, adjacent to sea and beach.
The tourers have their own areas, including two
excellent toilet blocks, and pitches are
individually lined with small maturing shrubs for
privacy. The bars and entertainment, restaurant,
bistro and takeaway, heated indoor and outdoor
pools, golf, fishing and bowling green make this
park popular throughout the year. A 50-acre site*
                                            contd.

---

with 332 touring pitches, 100 hardstandings and
460 statics.
Entertainment programme, hire shop, golf
course

Leisure: ⚓ ⚲ ⚫ 🎱 🅰

Facilities: ⋔ ⊙ ⊙ 🎱 ⧖ ⚫ 🛒 📮 🅰 🐕

Services: 🗄 🗄 🗄 ⊿ 🗄 🗄 ✕ 🚐 → ∪ ▶ ⊚ ⊿ ⋋ ⚐ ⤴

💳 ▭ ▭ ▭ 🗄

See advertisement on page 176

KING'S LYNN

See Saddle Bow & Stanhoe

MUNDESLEY   Map 13 TG33

▶ ▶ **70% Links Caravan Site (TG305365)**
Links Rd NR11 8AE ☎ 01263 720665
*Dir: From B1159 at Mundesley into Church Rd, then
right into Links Rd. From B1145 to village centre, &
left up hill to Links Rd*
🚐🚐🅰

Open Etr-1st wk Oct Booking advisable bank hols &
peak season Last arrival 22.00hrs Last departure
noon

*A pleasant site on a south-facing slope with level
pitches, with distant rural views. The site is popular
with those who enjoy peace and simplicity, and
there is a golf course adjacent. A 2-acre site with
55 touring pitches.*
Golf driving range

Leisure: 🅰

Facilities: ⋔ ⊙ ※

Services: 🗄 → ∪ ▶ ⊚ ⤴ 🗄 🛒

NORTH WALSHAM   Map 13 TG23

▶ ▶ ▶ ▶ **90% Two Mills Touring
Park (TG291286)**
Yarmouth Rd NR28 9NA
☎ 01692 405829 ▤ 01692 405829
✉ enquiries@twomills.co.uk
🌐 www.twomills.co.uk
*Dir: 1m S of North Walsham on Old Yarmouth rd past
police station & hospital on left*
★ 🚐 £12.50-£17.50 🚐 £12.50-£17.50
🅰 £12.50-£16.50

Open Mar-3 Jan Booking advisable Jul & Aug Last
arrival 20.30hrs Last departure noon

*Set in superb countryside in a peaceful spot which
is also convenient for touring. Some fully-serviced
pitches offer panoramic views over the site, and the
layout of pitches and facilities is excellent. The very
friendly and helpful owners keep the park in
immaculate condition. This park does not accept
children. A 5-acre site with 50 touring pitches,
50 hardstandings.*
Tourist information room & library

Leisure: ☐

Facilities: ⋔ ⊙ ※ ⧖ ⚫ 🛒 🅰 🐕

Services: 🗄 🗄 ⊿ 🗄 🗄 → ⤴

Notes: Adults only, 2 dogs max per pitch
💳 ▭ ▭ ▭ 🗄

Facilities: ⋔ Bath ⋔ Shower ⊙ Electric Shaver ⊿ Hairdryer ※ Ice Pack Facility ⧖ Disabled Facilities ⚫ Public Telephone
🛒 Shop on Site or within 200yds 💳 Mobile Shop (calls at least 5 days a week) 📮 BBQ Area 🅰 Picnic Area 🐕 Dog Exercise Area

England

NORWICH　Map 13 TG20

► ► ► 72% **Camping & Caravanning Club Site** (TG237063)

Martineau Ln NR1 2HX ☎ 01603 620060

Ⓦ www.campingandcaravanningclub.co.uk

Dir: From A47 onto A146 towards city centre. Left at lights to next lights, under low bridge to Cock pub, turn left. Site 150yds on right

★ ⊕ £13.60-£17.80 ⊕ £13.60-£17.80 Å £13.60-£17.80

Open Mar-Oct Booking advisable bank hols & peak periods Last arrival 21.00hrs Last departure noon

A very pretty small site on the outskirts of the city, close to the River Yare. The park is built on two levels, with the lower meadow enjoying good rural views, and there is plenty of screening from nearby houses. The older-style toilet block is kept immaculately clean. Please see the advertisement on page 11 for information on Club sites and membership. A 2.5-acre site with 50 touring pitches.

Facilities: ♠⊙ℚ☀ℂ🏧♀

Services: ♀🛈⌀🖃🅣→∪♨♪🔋🎴 ▭▭ ▨ 🎱

SADDLE BOW　Map 12 TF61

► ► ► 78% **Bank Farm Caravan Park** (TF593157)

Fallow Pipe Rd PE34 3AS

☎ 01553 617305 🖨 01553 617305

Dir: Leave A47 at signs for Saddle Bow. In village cross river bridge. After 1m turn right into Fallow Pipe Rd. Farm at end of road

★ ⊕ £8 ⊕ £8 Å £5-£8

Open Mar-Sep Booking advisable bank hols Last

contd.

arrival 23.00hrs Last departure 11.00hrs

A very pleasant, quiet park on a working farm on the banks of the River Ouse. Pitches are well laid out among mature trees, and facilities are housed in converted farm buildings, including a games room, and a utility room where soft drinks, milk and eggs are on sale via an honesty box. A 1.5-acre site with 15 touring pitches.

Snooker table

Leisure: ♠ **Facilities:** ♠⊙ℚ☀ℂ🏧♀

Services: ♀🖃🛈🖃🅣→♪ **Notes:** Adults only, no ball games, dogs must be on leads

ST JOHN'S FEN END　Map 12 TF51

► ► ► ► 73% **Virginia Lake Caravan Park** (TF538113)

Smeeth Rd PE14 8JF

☎ 01945 430332 & 430585 🖨 01945 430676

Ⓦ www.virginialake.co.uk

Dir: From A47 E of Wisbech follow tourist board signs to Terrington St John. Park on left

⊕ ⊕ Å

Open all year Booking advisable Last arrival 23.30hrs Last departure noon

A well-established park beside a 2-acre fishing lake with good facilities for both anglers and tourers. The toilet facilities are very good, and security is carefully observed throughout the park. A clubhouse serves a selection of meals. A 5-acre site with 100 touring pitches, 20 hardstandings.

Fishing

Leisure: ⋀ **Facilities:** ♠⊙ℚ☀♿ℂ🏧☲♀

Services: ♀🛒♀🛈⌀🖃🅣✕👢→∪▸◎🎱♪🔋

Services: 🅣 Toilet Fluid　✕ Café/ Restaurant　👢 Fast Food/Takeaway　🍼 Baby Care　♀ Electric Hook Up
🚐 Motorvan Service Point　◎ Launderette　♀ Licensed Bar　🛢 Calor Gaz　⌀ Camping Gaz　🖃 Battery Charging

SANDRINGHAM — Map 12 TF62

▶ ▶ ▶ ▶ 85% Camping & Caravanning Club Site (TF683274)
The Sandringham Estate,
Double Lodges PE35 6EA ☎ 01485 542555
Ⓦ www.campingandcaravanningclub.co.uk
Dir: From A148 onto B1440 signed West Newton. Follow signs to site. Or take A149 turn left & follow site signs
★ ♧ £16.10-£19.80 ♧ £16.10-£19.80
Å £16.10-£19.80
Open Feb-Nov Booking advisable bank hols & peak periods Last arrival 21.00hrs Last departure noon
A prestige park, very well landscaped and laid out in mature woodland, with toilets and other buildings blending in with the scenery. There are plenty of walks from the site, and this is a good touring base for the rest of Norfolk. Please see the advertisement on page 11 for information on Club sites and membership. A 28-acre site with 275 touring pitches, 2 hardstandings.
Leisure: ⚠
Facilities: ⚄⊙⚄※⚄⚄⚄⚄
Services: ⚄⚄⚄⚄⚄⚄⚄→∪▶
⚄ ⚄ ⚄ ⚄ ⚄

SCOLE — Map 13 TM17

▶ ▶ 70% Willows Camping & Caravan Park (TM146789)
Diss Rd IP21 4DH ☎ 01379 740271
▤ 01379 740271
Dir: At Scole rdbt on A140 turn onto A1066, site 150yds on left
★ ♧ £10-£12 ♧ £10-£12 Å £9-£11

Open Etr-Oct Booking advisable Spring bank hol & school hols Last arrival 23.00hrs Last departure noon
A quiet garden site on the banks of the River Waveney, bordered by willow trees. The park is well placed on the Norfolk/Suffolk border, and ideal for touring both counties. A 4-acre site with 32 touring pitches, 8 hardstandings.
Leisure: ⚠
Facilities: ⚄⊙※⚄
Services: ⚄⚄⚄⚄⚄→▶⚄⚄⚄

> Not all campsites accept pets.
> It is advisable to check at the time
> of booking.

SCRATBY — Map 13 TG51

▶ ▶ ▶ 74% Scratby Hall Caravan Park (TG501155)
NR29 3PH ☎ 01493 730283
Dir: N of Great Yarmouth exit A149 onto B1159, site signed
♧ £5.50-£13 ♧ £5.50-£13 Å £5.50-£13

Open Spring bank hol-mid Sep (rs Etr-Spring bank hol & mid Sep-Oct reduced hours & shop closed)
Booking advisable Spring bank hol wk & Jul-Aug
Last arrival 22.00hrs Last departure noon
A neatly-maintained site with a popular children's play area, well-equipped shop and outdoor swimming pool with sun terrace. The toilets are kept spotlessly clean, and the beach and the Norfolk Broads are close by. A 5-acre site with 108 touring pitches.
Food preparation room.
Leisure: ⚄ ⚠ Facilities: ⚄⊙⚄※⚄⚄⚄
Services: ⚄⚄⚄⚄⚄⚄→∪▶⚄⚄
Notes: No commercial vehicles

STANHOE — Map 13 TF83

▶ ▶ ▶ 78% The Rickels Caravan & Camping Park (TF794355)
Bircham Rd PE31 8PU ☎ 01485 518671
Dir: A148 from King's Lynn to Hillington, B1153 to Great Bircham. B1155 to x-rds, straight over, site on left
★ ♧ £10.50-£12 ♧ £10.50-£12 Å £10.50-£12

Open Mar-Oct Booking advisable bank hols Last arrival 21.00hrs Last departure 11.00hrs
Set in three acres of grassland, with sweeping country views and a pleasant, relaxing atmosphere. The meticulously maintained grounds and facilities are part of the attraction, and the slightly sloping land has some level areas and sheltering for tents. Children using the play equipment can be safely watched from all pitches. A 3-acre site with 30 touring pitches.
Field available to hire for rallies
Leisure: ⚠ ⚄ Facilities: ⚄⊙※⚄
Services: ⚄⚄⚄⚄→⚄⚄
Notes: Dogs must be on leads, no ground sheets

England

SWAFFHAM — Map 13 TF80

▶ ▶ ▶ 81% **Breckland Meadows Touring Park (TF809094)**
Lynn Rd PE37 7PT ☎ 01760 721246
🅴 info@brecklandmeadows.co.uk
🆆 www.brecklandmeadows.co.uk
Dir: 1m W of Swaffham on old A47
🚐 🚐 🛆
Open all year Booking advisable bank hols Last arrival 21.00hrs Last departure noon
An immaculate, well-landscaped little park on the edge of Swaffham. The impressive toilet block is well equipped, and there are hardstandings, full electricity and a laundry equipment. Plenty of planting is resulting in attractive screening. A 3-acre site with 45 touring pitches, 9 hardstandings. Tourist info centre
Facilities: ⋔ ⊙ ✳ ⅙ 🗐 🎋 🏕
Services: ⛽ 🗐 🛉 ⧄ 🖭 → ∪ ▶ 🏕 🍴 🔧
Notes: Adult only park

SYDERSTONE — Map 13 TF83

▶ ▶ ▶ 78% **The Garden Caravan Site (TF812337)**
Barmer Hall Farm PE31 8SR ☎ 01485 578220 & 578178 📠 01485 578178
🅴 nigel@mason96fsnet.co.uk
🆆 www.gardencaravansite.co.uk
Dir: Signed off B1454 at Barmer between A148 and Docking, 1m W of Syderstone
★ 🚐 £11-£13 🚐 £11-£13 🛆 £11-£13
Open Mar-Nov Booking advisable at all times Last departure noon
In the tranquil setting of a former walled garden beside a large farmhouse, with mature trees and shrubs, a secluded site surrounded by woodland. The site is run mainly on trust, with a daily notice indicating which pitches are available, and an honesty box for basic foods. An ideal site for the discerning camper, and well placed for touring north Norfolk. A 3.5-acre site with 30 touring pitches.
Facilities: ⋔ ⊙ ℡ ✳ ⅙ 🗐 🎋 🏕
Services: ⛽ 🛉 🗐 → ∪ ▶ 🔧

TRIMINGHAM — Map 13 TG23

▶ ▶ ▶ 70% **Woodlands Leisure Park (TG274388)**
NR11 8AL ☎ 01263 579208 📠 01263 576477
🅴 info@woodland-park.co.uk
🆆 www.woodland-park.co.uk
Dir: 4m SE on B1159 coast road
🚐 £15-£18 🚐 £15-£18

contd.

Open Mar-Dec Booking advisable public hols & Jul-Aug Last arrival 23.00hrs Last departure noon
A secluded woodland site in an open enclosure, close to the sea but well sheltered from the winds by tall trees. Facilities include two bars, a restaurant, an indoor swimming pool, bowling green and sauna, and entertainment is provided in the clubhouse. A 55-acre site with 55 touring pitches and 230 statics.
Leisure: ⚑ ℠ ⚓ ♨
Facilities: ⋔ ⊙ ℡ ✳ ⅙ ⅃ 🛒 🎋
Services: ⛽ ℠ 🗐 🖭 ✕ 🍴 → ∪ ▶ 🏕 🔧 🖲
🍴 🚬 🏧 📶 🗐

WEST RUNTON — Map 13 TG14

▶ ▶ ▶ ▶ 85% **Camping & Caravanning Club Site (TG189419)**
Holgate Ln NR27 9NW ☎ 01263 837544
🆆 www.campingandcaravanningclub.co.uk
Dir: From King's Lynn on A148 towards West Runton. Left at Roman Camp Inn. Site track on right at crest of hill, 0.5m to site opposite National Trust sign
★ 🚐 £16.10-£19.80 🚐 £16.10-£19.80 🛆 £16.10-£19.80
Open Mar-Oct Booking advisable bank hols & peak periods Last arrival 21.00hrs Last departure noon
A lovely, well-kept site with some gently sloping pitches on pleasantly undulating ground. This peaceful park is surrounded on three sides by woodland, with the fourth side open to fields and the coast beyond. The very well equipped family rooms and refurbished toilet blocks are excellent. Please see the advertisement on page 11 for information on Club sites and membership. A 15-acre site with 200 touring pitches.
Facilities: ⋔ ⊙ ℡ ✳ ⅙ 🛒 🎋
Services: ⛽ 🛉 🗐 🛉 ⧄ 🖭 🖭 → ∪ ▶ 🛆 🔧 🖲
🍴 🚬 🏧 📶 🗐

WORTWELL — Map 13 TM28

▶ ▶ ▶ ▶ 81% **Little Lakeland Caravan Park (TM279849)**
IP20 0EL ☎ 01986 788646 📠 01986 788646
🅴 information@littlelakeland.co.uk
🆆 www.littlelakeland.co.uk
Dir: From W leave A143 at sign for Wortwell. In village turn right 300yds past garage. From E on A143, left onto B1062, then right. After 800yds turn left
🚐 £9.80-£14.20 🚐 £9.80-£14.20 🛆 £9.80-£14.20
Open 15 Mar-Oct (rs Mar-Etr restricted laundry facilities) Booking advisable bank hols & peak periods Last arrival 22.00hrs Last departure noon
A well-kept and pretty site built round a fishing lake, and accessed by a lake-lined drive. The individual pitches are sited in hedged enclosures for complete privacy, and the purpose-built toilet facilities are excellent. A 4.5-acre site with 38 touring pitches, 6 hardstandings and 20 statics.
Library & fishing on site.
Leisure: ♨ Facilities: ⋔ ⊙ ℡ ✳ ⅙ 🔧
Services: ⛽ 🛉 ⧄ 🖭 🖭 → ▶ 🔧 🍴

England

NORTHUMBERLAND

BAMBURGH   Map 21 NU13

► ► ► ► 72% **Waren Caravan Park (NU155343)**

Waren Mill NE70 7EE
☎ 01668 214366 📠 01668 214224
✉ waren@meadowhead.co.uk
🌐 www.meadowhead.co.uk
Dir: 2m E of town. From A1 onto B1342 signed Bamburgh. Take unclass road past Waren Mill, signed Budle
★ ➤ £9.50-£18 ➤ £9.50-£18 ▲ £9.50-£15
Open Apr-Oct (rs Nov-Feb Bar, shop and restaurant closed) Booking advisable Spring bank hol & Jul-Aug Last arrival 20.00hrs Last departure noon
Attractive seaside site with footpath access to the beach, surrounded by a slightly sloping grassy embankment giving shelter to caravans. The park offers excellent facilities including several family bathrooms. A 4-acre site with 180 touring pitches, 11 hardstandings and 300 statics. 100 acres of private heathland.
Leisure: ₹ ♦ ⚠
Facilities: ➤ ⚑ ⊙ ⌦ ✳ ⚴ ⚦ ⚑ ⚓ ⚒ ⚓ ↑
Services: ⚡ ⚐ ⚑ ⚒ ⚙ ⚒ ⚐ ⚓ ✗ ⚓ → ∪ ▶ ⊚ ♪
⚌ ⚌ ⚌ ⚌ ⚌

► ► ► 67% **Glororum Caravan Park (NU166334)**

Glororum Farm NE69 7AW ☎ 01668 214457
📠 01688 214622
✉ info@glororum-caravanpark.co.uk
🌐 www.glororum-caravanpark.co.uk
Dir: Leave A1 at junct with B1341 (Purdy's Lodge). In 3.5m left onto unclass rd. Site 300yds on left
★ ➤ £14-£16 ➤ £14-£16 ▲ £14-£16
Open Apr-Oct Booking advisable school & bank hols Last arrival 22.00hrs Last departure 11.00hrs
A pleasantly situated site where tourers have their own well-established facilities. The open countryside setting affords good views of Bamburgh Castle and surrounding farmland. A 6-acre site with 100 touring pitches and 150 statics.
Leisure: ⚲ ⚠
Facilities: ⚑ ⊙ ⌦ ✳ ⚴ ⚒ ⚓ ↑
Services: ⚡ ⚐ ⚒ ⚙ ⚒ → ∪ ▶ ⊚ ⚴ ✦ ♪

BEADNELL   Map 21 NU22

► ► 70% **Camping & Caravanning Club Site (NU231297)**

NE67 5BX ☎ 01665 720586
🌐 www.campingandcaravanningclub.co.uk
Dir: A1 onto B1430 signed Seahouses. At Beadnell ignore signs for Beadnell village. Site on left after village, just after left bend
★ ➤ £12.40-£16.70 ▲ £12.40-£16.70
Open Apr-Oct Booking advisable bank hols & peak period Last arrival 21.00hrs Last departure noon
A level grassy site in a coastal area just across the road from the sea and sandy beach. Popular with
contd.

divers, anglers, surfboarders and canoeists, and ideal for visiting many tourist attractions. Motorvans and tents only. Please see page 11 for information on Club sites and membership. A 6-acre site with 150 touring pitches.
Facilities: ⚑ ⊙ ⌦ ✳ ⚴ ⚓
Services: ⚡ ⚐ ⚒ ⚙ ⚒ ⚐ → ∪ ▶ ⚴ ♪ ⚴
⚌ ⚌ ⚌ ⚌ ⚌

BELLINGHAM   Map 21 NY88

► ► ► ► 77% **Brown Rigg Caravan & Camping Park (NY835826)**

NE48 2JY ☎ 01434 220175
✉ enquiries@northumberlandcaravanparks.com
🌐 www.northumberlandcaravanparks.com
Dir: from A69 take A68 N. Take B6318 to Chollerford and B6320 to Bellingham. Pass Forestry Commission land, site 0.5m S of Bellingham
★ ➤ £12-£15 ➤ £12-£15 ▲ £12-£15

Open 31 Mar-Oct Booking advisable at all times Last arrival 20.00hrs Last departure noon
Set in a pleasant rural location, this quiet park is surrounded by trees on one side and extensive views on the other. The camping area is flat and grassy, with marked pitches for caravans. The first class sanitary facilities have spacious showers and toilets. The park is handy for the various attractions of Northumberland. A 5-acre site with 70 touring pitches, 15 hardstandings.
Leisure: ♦ ⚠ Facilities: ⚑ ⊙ ⌦ ✳ ⚴ ⚒ ⚓ ↑
Services: ⚡ ⚐ ⚒ ⚙ ⚒ → ∪ ▶ ♪
Notes: Dogs on leads, no groups, quiet policy 23.00-07.30 ⚌ ⚌ ⚌ ⚌ ⚌

BERWICK-UPON-TWEED   Map 21 NT95

 74% **Haggerston Castle (NU041435)**

Beal TD15 2PA
☎ 01289 381333 📠 01289 381433
🌐 www.havenholidays.com
Dir: On A1, 7m S of Berwick-upon-Tweed and signed
★ ➤ £12-£64 ➤ £12-£64
Open mid Mar-Oct (rs mid Mar-May & Sep-Oct Some facilities may be reduced) Booking advisable school hols Last departure 10.00hrs
A large holiday centre with a very well equipped touring park, offering comprehensive holiday activities. The entertainment complex contains amusements for the whole family, and there are
contd.

Facilities: ➤ Bath ⚑ Shower ⊙ Electric Shaver ⌦ Hairdryer ✳ Ice Pack Facility ⚴ Disabled Facilities ⚦ Public Telephone
⚒ Shop on Site or within 200yds ⚐ Mobile Shop (calls at least 5 days a week) ⚓ BBQ Area ⚒ Picnic Area ↑ Dog Exercise Area

England

Haggerston Castle

several bars, an adventure playground, boating on the lake, a children's club, a 9-hole golf course, tennis courts, and various eating outlets. A 7-acre site with 157 touring pitches, 157 hardstandings and 1200 statics.

Leisure: 🏊 ⚴ 🎯 🎱 🚲 ⚲

Facilities: 🖄 ⊙ 🄌 🖑 🛁 🕹 🖤 🐶 🎠 🎋 🕈

Services: 🔌 🛒 🖥 🍴 🛗 Ⓣ ✕ 🖑 ⇥ ⟶ 🖱 ▶ 🔥 ✦

Notes: No cars by tents

💳 💳 💳 ▨ 🟡

▶ ▶ ▶ ▶ ▶ 80% Ord House
Country Park (NT982515)
East Ord TD15 2NS
☎ 01289 305288 📠 01289 330832
🅴 enquiries@ordhouse.co.uk
🆆 www.ordhouse.co.uk
Dir: On A1, Berwick bypass, turn off at 2nd rdbt at East Ord, follow 'Caravan' signs
★ 🚐 £11.50-£17.90 🚙 £11.50-£17.90
🅰 £6.50-£17.90
Open all year Booking advisable bank hols & Jul-Aug Last arrival 23.00hrs Last departure noon
A very well run park set in the pleasant grounds of an 18th-century country house. Touring pitches are marked and well spaced, some of them fully-serviced. The very modern toilet facilities include family bath and shower suites, and first class disabled rooms. There is a six-hole golf course and an outdoor leisure shop with a good range of camping and caravanning spares, as well as clothing and equipment. A 42-acre site with 79 touring pitches, 46 hardstandings and 255 statics.
Crazy golf, table tennis

Leisure: ⚲

Facilities: ⇥ 🖄 ⊙ 🄌 🖑 🛁 🐶 🎠 🖤 🕈

Services: 🔌 🛗 🖥 🍴 🛒 🖱 Ⓣ ✕ ⇥ ⟶ ▶ ◎ ✦ 🥤 🔧

💳 💳 💳 ▨ 🟡

Never set up or dismantle a tent
in high winds. Double-peg the main guy
ropes by driving pegs in at different
angles.

▶ ▶ 72% Old Mill Caravan Site (NU055401)
West Kyloe Farm, Beal TD15 2PG
☎ 01289 381279 📠 01289 381279
🅴 treasasmalley@westkyloe.demon.co.uk
🆆 www.westkyloe.co.uk
Dir: Take B6353 off A1, 9m S of Berwick-upon-Tweed. Road signed to Lowick. Farm 1m up road
★ 🚐 £8-£14 🚙 £7-£9 🅰 fr £8
Open Etr-Oct Booking advisable at all times Last arrival 19.00hrs Last departure 11.00hrs
Small, secluded site accessed through a farm complex, and overlooking a mill pond complete with resident ducks. Some pitches are in a walled garden, and the amenity block is simple but well kept. Delightful walks can be enjoyed on the 600-acre farm. A 2.5-acre site with 12 touring pitches.
Facilities: 🖄 ⊙ 🄌 🕈   Services: 🔌 🛗 ⟶ 🖱
Notes: Dogs must be kept on lead when on site

CRASTER	Map 21 NU21

▶ ▶ ▶ 77% Camping & Caravanning Club Site (NU236214)
Dunstan Hill, Dunstan NE66 3TQ ☎ 01665 576310
🆆 www.campingandcaravanningclub.co.uk
Dir: From A1, just N of Alnwick, take B1340 signed Seahouses. Continue to T-junct at Criston Bank, turn right. Next right signed Embleton. Right at x-rds then 1st left signed Craster
★ 🚐 £13.60-£17.80 🚙 £13.60-£17.80 🅰 £13.60-£17.8
Open Mar-Oct Booking advisable BH's & peak periods Last arrival 21.00hrs Last departure noon
An immaculately maintained site with pleasant landscaping, close to the beach and Craster harbour. The historic town of Alnwick is nearby, as is the ruined Dunstanburgh Castle. Please see the advertisement on page 11 for information on Club sites and membership. A 14-acre site with 150 touring pitches, 20 hardstandings.
Leisure: ⚲   Facilities: 🖄 ⊙ 🄌 🕹 🛁 🄌 🖤 🐶 🎠 🕈
Services: 🔌 🛗 🖥 🍴 🖱 Ⓣ ⟶ ▶ 🔥 🔧 🥤
💳 💳 💳 ▨ 🟡

HALTWHISTLE	Map 21 NY76

▶ ▶ ▶ 72% Camping & Caravanning Club Site (NY685621)
Burnfoot Park Village NE49 0JP ☎ 01434 320106
🆆 www.campingandcaravanningclub.co.uk
Dir: From A69 Haltwhistle bypass (NB do not go into town) take Alston Rd S signed A689, then right signed Kellan
★ 🚐 £11.30-£14.80 🚙 £11.30-£14.80 🅰 £11.30-£14.8
Open Mar-Oct Booking advisable bank hols & peak periods Last arrival 21.00hrs Last departure noon
An attractive site on the banks of the River South Tyne amidst mature trees, on the Bellister Castle estate. This peaceful, relaxing site is a good cross country transit stop in excellent walking country. Please see the advertisement on page 11 for information on Club sites and membership. A 3.5-acre site with 50 touring pitches, 15 hardstandings.
Facilities: 🖄 ⊙ 🄌 🕹 🛁 🖤 🐶 🕈
Services: 🔌 🛗 🖥 🍴 🖱 Ⓣ ⟶ 🖱 ▶ 🔥 🔧 🥤
💳 💳 💳 ▨ 🟡

Services: Ⓣ Toilet Fluid   ✕ Café/ Restaurant   🛗 Fast Food/Takeaway   🖑 Baby Care   🔌 Electric Hook Up
🛗 Motorvan Service Point   🖥 Launderette   🛒 Licensed Bar   🖱 Calor Gas   🥤 Camping Gaz   🔋 Battery Charging

HEXHAM   Map 21 NY96

▶ ▶ ▶ 77% **Causey Hill Caravan Park**
(NY925625)
Causey Hill NE46 2JN
☎ 01434 602834 📠 01434 609086
🖎 causeyhillcp@aol.com
🌐 www.causeyhill.co.uk
Dir: Take B6306 from Hexham, 1st right to Whitley
Chapel. Right for Hexham Racecourse, right again for
site
★ 🚐 £12-£16 🚐 £12-£16 ▲ £11-£15
Open Mar-Oct Booking advisable public hols &
May-Sep Last departure noon
A well-maintained site on very sloping ground, with
plenty of terracing to create level pitches. The site is
attractively screened by trees, and a new reception
area/shop/disabled facility provides a quality
amenity. A 6-acre site with 35 touring pitches,
20 hardstandings and 105 statics.
Leisure: ⚏ Facilities: 🅿⊙🍴✻&🛒🐴🐾
Services: 🔌🛢🛢🚿🚽→∪🅿🍴✚🔧🧺♨

▶ ▶ ▶ 66% **Hexham Racecourse Caravan Site**
(NY919623)
Hexham Racecourse NE46 3NN
☎ 01434 606847 & 606881 📠 01434 605814
🖎 hexrace@aol.com
Dir: From Hexham take B6305 signed Allendale/Alston.
Left in 3m signed to racecourse. Site 1.5m on right
★ 🚐 fr £12 🚐 fr £12 ▲ fr £9
Open May-Sep Booking advisable wknds & bank
hols for electric hook-up Last arrival 20.00hrs Last
departure noon
A part-level and part-sloping grassy site on
racecourse overlooking Hexhamshire Moors.
The facilities are functional and well-maintained.
A 4-acre site with 40 touring pitches.
Leisure: ♠ ⚏ Facilities: 🅿⊙🍴✻🛒🐾
Services: 🔌🛢🛢🚿🚽→∪🅿⊙✚🔧🧺♨

ROTHBURY   Map 21 NU00

▶ ▶ ▶ 76% **Coquetdale Caravan Park (NU055007)**
Whitton NE65 7RU ☎ 01669 620549 📠 01669 620559
🖎 enquiries@coquetdalecaravanpark.co.uk
🌐 www.coquetdalecaravanpark.co.uk
Dir: 0.5m SW of Rothbury towards Newtown
★ 🚐 £12-£15 🚐 £12-£15
Open Etr-Oct Booking advisable At all times Last
arrival 21.00hrs Last departure 14.00hrs
A very pleasant mainly static site in a lovely
location beside the River Coquet, with good open
views of moorland and the Simonside Hills. Tourers
are on the site's upper area with their own purpose-
built toilet facilities. An ideal place for relaxing and
touring. A 13-acre site with 30 touring pitches and
160 statics.
Adventure playground for older children/adults
Leisure: ⚏ Facilities: 🅿⊙✻🛒🐴🐾
Services: 🔌🛢🚿→🅿🔧🛒
Notes: Families & couples only

NOTTINGHAMSHIRE

CHURCH LANEHAM   Map 17 SK87

NEW ▶ ▶ ▶ 78% **Trentfield Farm (SK815774)**
DN22 0NJ ☎ 01777 228651
Dir: from A1 take A57 towards Lincoln for 6m. 2nd left
turn for Laneham, 1.5m through Laneham & Church
Laneham (pass Ferry boat pub on left). Site 300yds on
right.
🚐▲
Open Etr-Oct
A delightfully rural, level grass park tucked away on
the banks of the River Trent. The park has its own
river frontage with free coarse fishing available to
park residents. The cosy village pub which serves
food is a 5-minute walk from the park. A new
quality amenity block will be completed for the 2006
season. An on-site dog sitting service is available.
A 12-acre site with 25 touring pitches.

NEWARK
See **Southwell & Wellow**

RADCLIFFE ON TRENT   Map 11 SK63

▶ ▶ ▶ 71% **Thornton's Holt Camping Park**
(SK638377)
Stragglethorpe Rd, Stragglethorpe NG12 2JZ
☎ 0115 933 2125 & 933 4204 📠 0115 933 3318
🖎 camping@thorntons-holt.co.uk
🌐 www.thorntons-holt.co.uk
Dir: Take A52, 3m E of Nottingham. Turn S at lights
towards Cropwell Bishop. Park 0.5m on left. Or A46 SE
of Nottingham. N at lights. Park 2.5m on right
★ 🚐 £9-£13 🚐 £9-£13 ▲ £9-£13
Open all year (rs 2 Nov-24 Mar No pool, shop or
games room) Booking advisable bank hols & wknds
mid May-Oct Last arrival 21.00hrs Last departure
13.00hrs
A well-run family site in former meadowland, with
pitches located among young trees and bushes for
a rural atmosphere and outlook. The toilets are
housed in converted farm buildings, and an indoor
swimming pool is a popular attraction. A 13-acre
site with 155 touring pitches, 35 hardstandings.
Pub & Restaurant within 150mtrs
Leisure: 🏊 ♠⚏🖵
Facilities: 🅿⊙🍴✻&🛒🐴🐾
Services: 🔌🚾🛢🛢🚿🚽→∪🅿♨✚🔧🧺♨
Notes: 10.30pm noise curfew
💳 💳 💳 💳 💳   See advertisement on page 182

Remember that prices and opening times
are liable to change within the currency
of this guide. It is always best
to telephone in advance.

Leisure: 🏊 Indoor swimming pool 🏊 Outdoor swimming pool ✻ Tennis court ♠ Games room ⚏ Children's playground ∪ Stables
🅿 9/18 hole golf course 🚣 Boats for hire 🎬 Cinema 🎣 Fishing ◎ Mini golf 🌊 Watersports 🖵 Separate TV room

England

Thorntons Holt

Camping Park ▶▶▶

**Stragglethorpe, Radcliffe-on-Trent,
Nottingham NG12 2JZ**
Tel: 0115 9332125 Fax: 0115 9333318
www.thorntons-holt.co.uk

'The Play Area'
Situated off the A52, Nottingham to Grantham Road
**Where the peace of the countryside meets the
culture and entertainment of Nottingham**
13 acres of sheltered, landscaped, level grassland and
orchards for approximately 100 caravans or tents.
Open 1st April to 1st November with full facilities
2nd November to 31st March with limited facilites

★ 87 pitches with electric hook-ups ★
★ Pub and restaurants 100m away ★
★ Good toilet/shower/laundry ★
★ Indoor heated swimming pool ★
★ Shop and information centre ★
★ Play area and games room ★
★ Rallies catered for ★

SOUTHWELL   Map 17 SK65

NEW ▶ ▶ ▶ 73% **New Hall Farm Touring Park**
(SK660550)
New Hall Farm, New Hall Ln NG22 8BS
☎ 01623 883041 ▤ 01623 883041
ⓔ new.hall@care4free.net
ⓦ www.newhallfarm.co.uk
*Dir: New Hall Lane is off the Farnsfield - Southwell road,
at the top of Edingley Hill.*
★ 🚐 £10-£12 🚐 £10-£12

Open Mar-Oct Booking advisable Last arrival
21.00hrs Last departure 13.00hrs
*A newly developed park on a working stock farm
with the elevated pitching area enjoying
outstanding panoramic views. It is within a short
drive of medieval Newark and Sherwood Forest. A
log cabin viewing gantry offers a place to relax and
take in the spectacular views. A 2.5-acre site with
25 touring pitches, 5 hardstandings.*

contd.

Facilities: ⬡⊙✳🏛️🎪🐕
Services: 🔌🎱→∪▶🍴⬛🔋
Notes: Adults only, no pets ex dogs (must be on
leads)

TEVERSAL   Map 16 SK46

▶ ▶ ▶ ▶ 92% **Shardaroba Caravan**
Park (SK472615)
Silverhill Ln NG17 3JJ
☎ 01623 551838 & 0771 259 0158
▤ 0870 70 58 416
ⓔ stay@shardaroba.co.uk
ⓦ www.shardaroba.co.uk
*Dir: M1 junct 28 onto A38 towards Mansfield. 1st traffic
lights left onto B6027. Top of hill, over x-rds. After
200yds at next x-rds left at Peacock Hotel & Workpeople
Inn. After 1.4m at T-junct right onto B6014 signed
Stanton Hill at Carnarvon Arms turn left onto Silverhill
Ln, site 300yds on left*
★ 🚐 £12-£16 🚐 £12-£16 ▲ £10-£14
Open all year Booking advisable peak season Last
arrival 22.30hrs Last departure noon
*A top notch park with excellent purpose-built
facilities, set in a rural former mining area. Each
pitch is spacious, and there are views of and access
to the surrounding countryside and nearby
Silverhill Community Woods. The attention to detail
and all-round quality are truly exceptional. A 6-acre
site with 100 touring pitches, 95 hardstandings.
Tourist info & book lending room*
Leisure: ⛰️
Facilities: ⬡⊙🍴✳⬛🛒🏛️🎪🐕
Services: 🔌🚽⬛🍴🔥🎱🚰→∪▶🍴♨️🍴
⬛ ▦ ▦ ▦ 🔋

TUXFORD   Map 17 SK77

▶ ▶ ▶ 79% **Orchard Park Touring Caravan &**
Camping Park (SK754708)
Marnham Rd NG22 0PY ☎ 01777 870228
▤ 01777 870320
ⓔ info@orchardcaravanpark.co.uk
ⓦ www.orchardcaravanpark.co.uk
*Dir: A1 at Tuxford exit onto A6075 towards Lincoln.
0.5m, right into Marnham Rd. Site 0.75m on right*
🚐 £15 🚐 £15 ▲ £15
Open mid Mar-Oct (rs Nov-Dec Winter use
restricted to hard standings) Booking advisable
bank hols & Jul-Aug Last arrival mdnt Last
departure 18.00hrs
*A rural site set in an old fruit orchard with spacious
pitches arranged in small groups separated by
shrubs. Many of them are served with water and
electricity. A network of grass pathways and picnic
clearings have been created in a woodland area,
and there's a superb adventure playground. A 7-
acre site with 60 touring pitches, 30 hardstandings.
Family shower room.*
Leisure: ⛰️ **Facilities:** ⬡⊙🍴✳⬛🛒🏛️🐕
Services: 🔌🍴🔥🎱🚰→∪🍴 ⬛ ▦ ▦ ▦ 🔋

WELLOW   Map 17 SK66

▶ ▶ 76% *The Shannon Caravan & Camping Park* (SK665666)

Wellow Rd NG22 9AP ☎ 01623 869002 & 07979 018565 ▤ 01623 869002

Dir: From Ollerton follow A616 towards Newark, park 1.5m left just after Ollerton House Hotel.

⊞ ⊞ ⚠

Open all year Booking advisable bank hols Last arrival anytime Last departure flexible

A well-equipped site with a modern toilet block and good facilities throughout. There is a separate tenting area, and the park is 0.5m from Ollerton on the edge of the village of Wellow, which is famous for its maypole celebrations and local hostelries. A 4-acre site with 37 touring pitches, 37 hardstandings. Caravan storage

Leisure: � **Facilities:** ⚏⊙⚹⚒戸✝

Services: ⚑⛟→∪⚑⚙▣⚆

Notes: Open to all age groups

WORKSOP   Map 16 SK57

NEW ▶ ▶ ▶ 77% **Riverside Caravan Park** (SK582790)

Central Av S80 1ER ☎ 01909 474118

Dir: From Newcastle Ave in Worksop town centre turn left onto Stubbing Lane, then right onto Central Ave, site is left at pet shop.

★ ⊞ £11-£12 ⊞ £11-£12 ⚠ £11-£12

Open all year Booking advisable Wknds and Bank hols Last arrival 20.00hrs Last departure 14.00hrs

A very well maintained park within the attractive market town of Worksop and next door to the cricket/bowls club where Riverside customers are made welcome. This is an ideal park for those wishing to be within walking distance of all amenities yet within a 10 minute car journey of the extensive Clumber Park and numerous good garden centres. The towpath of the adjacent Chesterfield Canal provides excellent walking opportunities. A 4-acre site with 60 touring pitches, 52 hardstandings.

Facilities: ⚏⊙⚹⚒⚙✝

Services: ⚑⛟▣⌀▣→⚑⚙⚙▣

Notes: Dogs must be kept on leads

OXFORDSHIRE

BANBURY   Map 11 SP44

▶ ▶ ▶ ▶ 79% **Barnstones Caravan & Camping Site** (SP455454)

Great Bourton OX17 1QU ☎ 01295 750289

Dir: Take A423 from Banbury signed Southam. In 3m turn right signed Gt Bourton/Cropredy, site 100yds on right, (3m N of M40 junct 11)

★ ⊞ £8.50-£10.50 ⊞ £8.50-£10.50 ⚠ £5.50-£8

Open all year Booking advisable public hols

Popular, neatly laid-out site with plenty of hardstandings, some fully serviced pitches, and a smart up-to-date toilet block. Well run by personable owner. A 3-acre site with 49 touring pitches, 44 hardstandings.

Leisure: ⚤ **Facilities:** ⚏⊙⚹⚒⛒戸✝

Services: ⚑▣⚙⌀▣⚱→∪⚑⊙⚙⚘⚙▣

▶ ▶ ▶ ▶ 77% **Bo Peep Farm Caravan Park** (SP481348)

Bo Peep Farm, Aynho Rd, Adderbury OX17 3NP

☎ 01295 810605 ▤ 01295 810605

🄴 warden@bo-peep.co.uk

🆆 www.bo-peep.co.uk

Dir: 1m E of Adderbury & A4260, on B4100 Aynho Road

★ ⊞ £11.50-£17 ⊞ £11.50-£17 ⚠ £11-£12.50

Open Mar-Oct Booking advisable bank hols, British Grand Prix Last arrival 20.00hrs Last departure noon

A delightful park with good views and a spacious feel. Four well laid camping areas including two with hard standings and a separate tent field are all planted with maturing shrubs and trees. The two facility blocks are in attractive Cotswold stone. Unusually there is a bay in which you can clean your caravan or motorhome. A 13-acre site with 114 touring pitches.

Facilities: ⚏⊙⚑⚹⚒⛒⚙戸✝

Services: ⚑⛟▣⌀▣⚱→⚑⚙

Facilities: ⚍ Bath ⚏ Shower ⊙ Electric Shaver ⚑ Hairdryer ⚹ Ice Pack Facility ⚒ Disabled Facilities ⚙ Public Telephone ⚱ Shop on Site or within 200yds ▣ Mobile Shop (calls at least 5 days a week) 戸 BBQ Area 戸 Picnic Area ✝ Dog Exercise Area

England

▶ ▶ ▶ 78% **Anita's Touring Caravan Park**
(SP443477)
The Yews, Mollington OX17 1AZ ☎ 01295 750731 &
07966 171959 ▤ 01295 750731
ⓔ anitagail@btopenworld.com
*Dir: From M40 junct 11 onto A422 signed Banbury. Take
A423 signed Southam, site 3.5m on left. (Do not go into
village, site on main road just past village entrance)*
★ 🚐 £9-£10 🚙 £9-£10 ▲ £6-£7

Open all year Booking advisable bank hols Last
arrival 20.00hrs
*A neat, well-run small farm site with brick-built
toilet facilities. On the edge of the village, adjacent
to A423, the farm is a centre for rearing pedigree
Suffolk sheep and Welsh mountain ponies.
There is a large area for ball games. A 2-acre site
with 36 touring pitches, 24 hardstandings.*
Field play area.

Facilities: ⋒ ⊙ ❡ ✳ ⅓ ♒
Services: 🔌 ⅏ → ∪ ◎ ⤴ ⅃

BLETCHINGDON   **Map 11 SP51**

▶ ▶ ▶ 84% *Diamond Farm Caravan & Camping
Park (SP513170)*
Islip Rd OX5 3DR ☎ 01869 350909 ▤ 01869 350059
ⓔ warden@diamondpark.co.uk
ⓦ www.diamondpark.co.uk
*Dir: From M40 junct 9 onto A34 S for 3m, then B4027 to
Bletchingdon. Site 1m on left*
🚐 🚙 ▲
Open Mar-Nov Booking advisable bank hols & Jul-
Sep Last arrival 22.00hrs Last departure noon
*A well-run, quiet rural site in good level
surroundings, and ideal for touring the Cotswolds.
Situated 7m N of Oxford in the heart of the Thames
Valley. This popular park has excellent facilities, and
offers a heated outdoor swimming pool and a
games room for children. A 3-acre site with
37 touring pitches, 13 hardstandings.*

Leisure: ⌇ ☚ ⅏ **Facilities:** ➡ ⋒ ⊙ ❡ ✳ ⌈ ⅓
Services: 🔌 ⅟ ⅄ ⅍ ⅃ ⅀ ⅏ → ⅌ ⤴

<u>NEW</u> ▶ ▶ ▶ 69% **Greenhill Leisure Park
(SP488178)**
Greenhill Farm, Station Rd OX5 3BQ
☎ 01869 351600 ▤ 01869 350918
ⓔ info@greenhill-leisure-park.co.uk
ⓦ www.greenhill-leisure-park.co.uk
*Dir: M40 junct 9, A34 south for 3m. Take B4027 to
Bletchingdon. Site 0.5m after village on left*
🚐 £8-£10 🚙 £8-£10 ▲ £8-£10

contd.

Greenhill Leisure Park

Open all year (rs Oct-Mar Shop closed) Booking
advisable Bank hols & Jul-Aug Last arrival 22.00hrs
Last departure noon
*A newly developed all year round park set in open
countryside near the village of Bletchingdon. Fishing
is available in the nearby river, and the park has its
own farm shop. It makes an ideal base for touring
the Cotswolds, and Oxford. Please note the park
officially opens from Easter 2006 although limited
facilities may be available before this. A 7-acre site
with 36 touring pitches, 25 hardstandings.*
Fishing, pets corner

Leisure: ⅏ **Facilities:** ⋒ ⊙ ❡ ✳ ⅓ ⅔ ♒ ➡
Services: 🔌 🔋 ⅟ ⅄ ⅍ ⅃ → ⅌ ⤴
🍴 ▦ ▤▤ ▦ 🔋 ⅏

CHARLBURY   **Map 11 SP31**

▶ ▶ ▶ ▶ 78% *Cotswold View Touring Park
(SP365210)*
EnstoneRd OX7 3JH
☎ 01608 810314 ▤ 01608 811891
ⓔ bookings@gfwiddows.f9.co.uk
ⓦ www.cotswoldview.co.uk
Dir: Signed from A44 on to B4022
🚐 🚙 ▲

Open Etr or Apr-Oct Booking advisable bank hols
Last arrival 21.00hrs Last departure noon
*A good Cotswold site, well screened and with
attractive views across the countryside. The toilet
facilities include fully-equipped family rooms and
bathrooms, and there are spacious, sheltered
pitches, some with hardstandings. Breakfast and
take-away food available from the shop. A 10-acre
site with 125 touring pitches.*
Off-licence, cycle hire, skittle alley.

Leisure: ☚ ☚ ⅏ **Facilities:** ➡ ⋒ ⊙ ❡ ✳ ⅓ ⅔ ♒ ➡
Services: 🔌 🔋 ⅟ ⅍ ⅃ ⅀ ➡ → ⤴ 🍴 ▦▦ ▦▦ ▦ ⅏

England

CHIPPING NORTON
Map 10 SP32

▶ ▶ ▶ 76% Camping & Caravanning Club Site
(SP315244)
Chipping Norton Rd, Chadlington OX7 3PE
☎ 01608 641993
Ⓦ www.campingandcaravanningclub.co.uk
Dir: Take A44 to Chipping Norton, on to A361 Burford road. Turn left at x-rds and site in 150yds
★ ⌑ £13.60-£17.80 ⌑ £13.60-£17.80
Å £13.60-£17.80
Open Mar-Oct Booking advisable bank hols & peak periods Last arrival 21.00hrs Last departure noon
A hilltop site surrounded by trees but close to a busy main road. The toilets are very clean and visitors are given the usual warm Club welcome. Please see the advertisement on page 11 for information on Club sites and membership. A 4-acre site with 105 touring pitches.

Leisure: 𝄢

Facilities: ℕ⊖🔍❄️&🛁⛴

Services: 🔌🔋🔍🍴🗑️⊞Ⓣ→▶️🔺🐾
📧 💳 🔲 🏴 🔵

HENLEY-ON-THAMES
Map 05 SU78

▶ ▶ ▶ 70% *Swiss Farm International Camping* (SU759837)
Marlow Rd RG9 2HY ☎ 01491 573419
ⓔ enquiries@swissfarmcamping.co.uk
Ⓦ www.swissfarmcamping.co.uk
Dir: On A4155, N of Henley, next left after rugby club, towards Marlow.
⌑ ⌑ Å

Open Mar-Oct Booking advisable all year Last arrival 21.00hrs Last departure noon
A conveniently-located site within a few minutes walk of Henley. Visitors are invited to fish in the park's well-stocked lake, which is set in a secluded wooded area. A 6-acre site with 165 touring pitches, 12 hardstandings and 6 statics.
Fishing lake.

Leisure: 🎣 ♠ 𝄢

Facilities: 🚰ℕ⊖🔍❄️&🛁⛴🐴

Services: 🔌🔋🍴🔍🗑️Ⓣ→∪▶️🔱🎪🐾
Notes: No groups 📧 💳 🔲 🏴 🔵

For full details of the AA pennant ratings scheme see pages 7-8

OXFORD
Map 05 SP50

▶ ▶ ▶ 70% Camping & Caravanning Club Site
(SP518041)
426 Abingdon Rd OX1 4XG ☎ 01865 244088
Ⓦ www.campingandcaravanningclub.co.uk
Dir: From M40 leave A34 at A423 for Oxford. Turn left immediately after junct into Abingdon Road, site on left behind Touchwood Sports
★ ⌑ £13.60-£17.80 ⌑ £13.60-£17.80
Å £13.60-£17.80
Open all year Booking advisable bank hols & peak period Last arrival 21.00hrs Last departure noon
A very busy town site with handy park-and-ride into Oxford. All pitches are on grass, and most offer electric hook-ups. Please see advertisement on page 11 for information on Club sites and membership. A 5-acre site with 85 touring pitches.

Facilities: ℕ⊖❄️&⛴

Services: 🔌🔋🔍🍴⊞Ⓣ→∪🔺🐾
📧 💳 🔲 🏴 🔵

STANDLAKE
Map 05 SP30

PREMIER PARK

▶ ▶ ▶ ▶ ▶ 92% Lincoln Farm Park
(SP395028)
High St OX29 7RH ☎ 01865 300239
🖥 01865 300127
ⓔ info@lincolnfarm.touristnet.uk.com
Ⓦ www.lincolnfarmpark.co.uk
Dir: In village off A415 between Abingdon & Witney, 5m SE of Witney
★ ⌑ £13-£19 ⌑ £13-£19 Å £11-£17

Open Feb-Nov Booking advisable bank hols, Jul-Aug & most wknds Last arrival 21.00hrs Last departure noon
An attractively landscaped park in a quiet village setting, with superb facilities and a high standard of maintenance. Family rooms, fully-serviced pitches, two indoor swimming pools and a fully-equipped gym are part of the comprehensive amenities. A 9-acre site with 90 touring pitches, 42 hardstandings and 19 statics.
Indoor leisure centre, putting green, outdoor chess

Leisure: 🎣 𝄢

Facilities: 🚰ℕ⊖🔍❄️&🛁🐾🎡🐴

Services: 🔌♨️🔋🍴🔍⊞Ⓣ→∪▶️🔺🎪🐾
📧 💳 🔲 🏴 🔵

Leisure: 🎣 Indoor swimming pool 🎣 Outdoor swimming pool ♀ Tennis court ♠ Games room 𝄢 Children's playground ∪ Stables
▶ 9/18 hole golf course 🔱 Boats for hire 🎪 Cinema 🐾 Fishing ◎ Mini golf 🔺 Watersports 🔲 Separate TV room

England

WESTON-ON-THE-GREEN   Map 11 SP51

▶ ▶ 71% Godwin's Caravan Park (SP534185)
Manor Farm OX25 3QL
☎ 01869 351647 🖥 01869 351647
🌐 neil@westononthegreen.freeserve.co.uk
Dir: From A34 take B430 & site on right just before village
★ 🚐 £10.50-£12.50 🚐 £10.50-£12.50 ▲ £7-£10
Open Mar-Oct Booking advisable bank hols Last arrival 20.00hrs Last departure noon
A developing caravan park on a working dairy farm which makes its own ice cream and sells it in a café bar. The open farmland setting is ideal for nature lovers, walkers and cyclists. A 2-acre site with 60 touring pitches.
Ice cream parlour, farm shop, pet supplies shop
Facilities: ⬡ ⊙ ✳ & 🐾 🚿
Services: ⊡ ✗ ♨ → ∪ ▶ 🗑

RUTLAND

GREETHAM   Map 11 SK91

▶ ▶ ▶ 77% Rutland Caravan & Camping (SK925148)
LE15 7NX ☎ 01572 813520 🖥 01572 812616
🌐 info@rutlandcaravanandcamping.co.uk
🌐 www.rutlandcaravanandcamping.co.uk
Dir: From A1 onto B668 towards Greetham. Before Greetham turn right at x-rds, then 2nd left to site
★ 🚐 £10.50-£13.50 🚐 £10.50-£13.50
▲ £8.50-£11.50

Open all year Booking advisable BH's
A pretty caravan park built to a high specification, and surrounded by well-planted banks which will provide good screening. The spacious grassy site is close to the Viking Way and other footpath networks, and well sited for visiting Rutland Water and the many picturesque villages in the area. A 3-acre site with 30 touring pitches, 8 hardstandings.
Leisure: ⚠
Facilities: ⬡ ⊙ 🔲 ✳ & 🐾 ⟊
Services: ⊡ ⛟ 🛢 ⌁ ⊞ ♨ → ∪ ▶ ⊙ △ ⅄ ⌇ 🐾

THE PERCENTAGE RATING
FOR ALL PARKS RANGES FROM
50% - 100%.

SHROPSHIRE

BRIDGNORTH   Map 10 SO79

▶ ▶ ▶ ▶ 90% Stanmore Hall Touring Park (SO742923)
Stourbridge Rd WV15 6DT ☎ 01746 761761
🖥 01746 768069
🌐 stanmore@morris-leisure.co.uk
Dir: 2m E of Bridgnorth on A458
★ 🚐 £14.85-£35 🚐 £14.85-£35 ▲ £14.85-£35

Open all year Booking advisable school & bank hols & Jul-Aug Last arrival 20.00hrs Last departure noon
An excellent park in peaceful surroundings offering outstanding facilities. The pitches, many fully serviced, are arranged around the lake in Stanmore Hall, home of the Midland Motor Museum. Handy for touring Ironbridge and the Severn Valley Railway, while Bridgnorth itself is an attractive old market town. A 12.5-acre site with 131 touring pitches, 44 hardstandings.
Leisure: ⚠
Facilities: ⬡ ⊙ 🔲 ✳ & (🐾 ⟊ 🐾
Services: ⊡ ⛟ 🗑 🛢 ⌁ ⊞ ⊤ ♨ → ∪ ▶ ⅄ ⚒ ⌇
Notes: max of 2 dogs
💳 💳 💳 💳 🗑

BROOME   Map 09 SO48

▶ ▶ 71% Engine & Tender Inn (SO399812)
SY7 0NT ☎ 01588 660275
Dir: W from Craven Arms on B4368, fork left to B4367, site in village, 2m on right
★ 🚐 £7-£10 🚐 £7-£10 ▲ £6
Open all year Booking advisable bank hols Last arrival 21.00hrs Last departure 14.00hrs
A rural site in a pleasant setting adjacent to the country pub, and accessible through the pub car park. The site has clean but fairly basic facilities. A 1-acre site with 20 touring pitches and 2 statics.
Leisure: ⚘
Facilities: ⬡ ⊙ ✳ 🚿
Services: ⊡ ⛾ ⊞ ✗ ♨ → ∪ ▶ ⌇ 🗑 🐾
💳 💳 🗑

ELLESMERE
See Lyneal

HAUGHTON Map 10 SJ51

▶ **85% Camping & Caravanning Club Site (SJ546164)**
Ebury Hill, Ring Bank TF6 6BU
☎ 01743 709334
Ⓦ www.campingandcaravanningclub.co.uk
Dir: 2.5m through Shrewsbury on A53. Turn left signed Haughton & Upton Magna. Continue 1.5m site on right
★ ⊞ £9.90-£11.40 ⊞ £9.90-£11.40 Å £9.90-£11.40
Open Mar-Oct Booking advisable bank hols & peak periods Last arrival 21.00hrs Last departure noon
A wooded hill fort with a central lake overlooking the Shropshire countryside. The site is well screened by mature trees, and there is good fishing in a disused quarry. Though there are no toilet or shower facilities, this lovely park is very popular with discerning visitors. Please see the advertisement on page 11 for information on Club sites and membership. An 18-acre site with 100 touring pitches, 21 hardstandings.
Leisure: ⚠ **Facilities:** ✳ ℂ ⛺ ✝
Services: ⊞ ⛊ ⓘ ⊘ ⊞ ⊤ → ∪ ⟁ ⟆ ⛏
⬛ ▦ ⊠ ⬛

HUGHLEY Map 10 SO59

▶ ▶ ▶ **74% Mill Farm Holiday Park (SO564979)**
SY5 6NT ☎ 01746 785208
Ⓔ mail@millfarmcaravanpark.co.uk
Ⓦ www.millfarmcaravanpark.co.uk
Dir: On unclass road off B4371 through village of Hughley, 3m SW of Much Wenlock, 11m SW of Church Stretton
★ ⊞ fr £12 ⊞ fr £12 Å fr £12
Open Mar-Jan Booking advisable peak periods Last arrival 20.00hrs Last departure noon
A well-established farm site set in meadowland adjacent to river, with mature trees and bushes providing screening, situated below Wenlock Edge. A 20-acre site with 20 touring pitches and 90 statics. Fishing & horse riding.
Facilities: ℝ ⊙ ⅋ ✳ ℂ ⛺ ☰ ✝
Services: ⊞ ⛊ ⓘ ⊘ ⊞ → ∪ ⟆

LYNEAL (NEAR ELLESMERE) Map 15 SJ43

▶ ▶ ▶ ▶ **76% Fernwood Caravan Park (SJ445346)**
SY12 0QF ☎ 01948 710221
🖷 01948 710324
Ⓔ fernwood@caravanpark37.fsnet.co.uk
Ⓦ www.ranch.co.uk
Dir: From A495 in Welshampton take B5063, over canal bridge, turn right as signed
★ ⊞ £14.50-£18.75 ⊞ £14.50-£18.75
Open Mar-Nov Booking advisable bank hols Last arrival 21.00hrs Last departure 17.00hrs
A peaceful park set in wooded countryside, with a screened, tree-lined touring area and fishing lake. The approach is past flower beds, and the static area which is tastefully arranged around an attractive children's playing area. There is a small child-free touring area for those wanting complete
contd.

relaxation, and the park has 20 acres of woodland walks. A 26-acre site with 60 touring pitches, 2 hardstandings and 165 statics.
Lake for coarse fishing on site.
Leisure: ⚠ **Facilities:** ℝ ⊙ ⅋ ✳ ⅃ ℂ ⛺ ✝
Services: ⊞ ⛊ ⓘ ⊞ ⊤ → ⅄ ⟆ ⬛ ▦ ⊠ ⬛ ⬛

MINSTERLEY Map 15 SJ30

▶ ▶ **90% The Old School Caravan Park (SO322977)**
Shelve SY5 0JQ ☎ 01588 650410 🖷 01588 650410
Dir: 6.5m SW of Minsterley on A488
★ ⊞ fr £11 ⊞ fr £11 Å fr £11

Open Mar-Jan Booking advisable bank hols Last arrival 21.00hrs Last departure 10.30hrs
A very well designed park in a beautiful setting, with impressive facilities housed in an attractive brick and stone building. Self-contained cubicles with shower, wash basin and toilet are an added bonus of this small park, and the grounds are immaculate. A 1.5-acre site with 22 touring pitches, 3 hardstandings.
TV aerial connection.
Facilities: ℝ ⊙ ✳ ℂ ⛺ ✝
Services: ⊞ ⊞ → ∪ ⟆ ⛏

SHREWSBURY Map 15 SJ41

PREMIER PARK

▶ ▶ ▶ ▶ ▶ **80% Beaconsfield Farm Caravan Park (SJ522189)**
Battlefield SY4 4AA
☎ 01939 210370 & 210399
🖷 01939 210349
Ⓔ mail@beaconsfield-farm.co.uk
Ⓦ www.beaconsfield-farm.co.uk
Dir: At Hadnall, 1.5m NE of Shrewsbury, follow sign for Astley off A49.
★ ⊞ £14-£18 ⊞ £16-£18 Å fr £14

contd.

Open all year Booking advisable bank hols Last arrival 19.00hrs Last departure noon
A purpose-built family-run park on farmland in open countryside. This pleasant park offers quality in every area, including superior toilets, heated indoor swimming pool, and attractive landscaping. Fly and coarse fishing are available from the park's own fishing lake, and broadband internet links are available for laptops. The Bothy restaurant is relaxed and welcoming, and offers a freshly prepared menu using local produce. Only adults are accepted. A 16-acre site with 50 touring pitches, 40 hardstandings and 35 statics.
Fly fishing, coarse fishing, bowling green & wi-fi

Leisure: ᛩ

Facilities: ⇥ ⋔ ⊙ ☖ ✳ �୬ ↻ ☐ 㝵 ⊢

Services: ▦ 🚽 ☐ 🛈 ✕ → ⧙ ⊙ ☕ ◢ 🔋

Notes: Adults only (over 21yrs)

AA Campsite of the Year for England, and Overall Winner of the AA Best Campsite of the Year 2006

▶ ▶ ▶ ▶ 90% **Oxon Hall Touring Park (SJ455138)**
Welshpool Rd SY3 5FB
☎ 01743 340868 📠 01743 340869
🖂 oxon@morris-leisure.co.uk
Ⓦ www.morris-leisure.co.uk
Dir: Leave A5 ring road at junct with A458. Park shares entrance with 'Oxon Park & Ride'
★ 🏕 £14.60-£19.60 🚐 £14.60-£19.60 ▲

Open all year Booking advisable high season Last arrival 21.00hrs
A delightful park with quality facilities, and a choice of grass and fully-serviced pitches. An adults-only section is very popular with those wanting a peaceful holiday, and there is an inviting patio area next to reception and the shop, overlooking a small lake. This site is ideally located for visiting Shrewsbury and the surrounding countryside, and there is always a warm welcome here. A 15-acre site with 124 touring pitches, 72 hardstandings and 42 statics.

Leisure: ⚠

Facilities: ⋔ ⊙ ☖ ୬ ↻ 㝵 ⊢

Services: ▦ 🚽 ☐ 🛈 ◢ ☐ ⇥ → ⧙ ⊢ ☕ ◢
📠 ▭ ▭ 📶 🖩

▶ ▶ ▶ 89% **Severn Gorge Park (SJ705051)**
Bridgnorth Rd, Tweedale TF7 4JB ☎ 01952 684789
🖂 info@severngorgepark.co.uk
Ⓦ www.severngorgepark.co.uk
Dir: Signed off A442, 1m S of Telford
★ 🏕 £14.55-£16.25 🚐 £14.55-£16.25
▲ £10.15-£12.15

Open all year Booking advisable bank hols & wknds summer months Last arrival 23.00hrs Last departure noon
A very pleasant wooded site in the heart of Telford, well-screened and maintained. The sanitary facilities are fresh and immaculate, and landscaping of the grounds is carefully managed. An upgrade makes it a really delightful park to stay on, and it is also well positioned for visiting nearby Ironbridge. A 6-acre site with 40 touring pitches, 40 hardstandings.

Leisure: ⚠ **Facilities:** ⋔ ⊙ ☖ ✳ ୬ ↻ 㝵 ⊞ ⊢ ⊢

Services: ▦ 🚽 ☐ 🛈 ◢ ⊞ ⊤ → ∪ ⊢ ⊙ ◢ ☕ ◢
📠 ▭ ▭ 📶 🖩

▶ ▶ ▶ 74% **Lower Lacon Caravan Park (SJ534304)**
SY4 5RP ☎ 01939 232376 📠 01939 233606
🖂 info@llcp.co.uk
Ⓦ www.lowerlacon.co.uk
Dir: Take A49 to B5065. Site 3m on the right

🏕 £15-£19 🚐 £15-£19 ▲ £15-£19
Open all year (rs Nov-Mar club wknds only, toilets closed if frost) Booking advisable public hols & Jul-Aug Last arrival 20.00hrs Last departure 16.00hrs
A large, spacious park with lively club facilities and an entertainments barn, set safely away from the main road. The park is particularly suitable for families, with an outdoor swimming pool and

contd.

---

livestock. A 48-acre site with 270 touring pitches, 30 hardstandings and 50 statics.
Crazy golf

Leisure: ↝ ♦ ⚑ ▭ **Facilities:** ➡ ▶ ⊙ ⅊ ※ ⟁ ⟍ ⟐ ☰
Services: ⊟ ⿴ ⊠ ♀ ⓘ ◿ ⊞ ▭ ✕ ⛟ → ▶ ⟍

⊜ ⤏ ☰ ⟍ ⣿

WENTNOR   Map 15 SO39

▶ ▶ ▶ 72% **The Green Caravan Park**
(SO380932)
SY9 5EF ☎ 01588 650605
⊖ info@greencaravanpark.co.uk
ⓦ www.greencaravanpark.co.uk

GOLD

Dir: 1m NE of Bishop's Castle on A489. Turn right at brown tourist sign
⊞ fr £9.50 ⊞ fr £9.50 ⚑ fr £9.50
Open Etr-Oct Booking advisable bank hols & wknds
Last arrival 21.00hrs Last departure 14.00hrs
A pleasant site in a peaceful setting convenient for visiting Ludlow or Shrewsbury. The grassy pitches are mainly level. A 15-acre site with 140 touring pitches, 4 hardstandings and 20 statics.

Leisure: ⚑ **Facilities:** ▶ ⊙ ⅊ ※ ⟍ ⟐
Services: ⊟ ⿴ ♀ ⓘ ◿ ⊞ ▭ ✕ → ∪ ⟍
Notes: Dogs must be kept on leads at all times

⊜ ⤏ ☰ ⟍ ⣿

SOMERSET

BATH   Map 04 ST76

▶ ▶ ▶ ▶ 83% **Newton Mill Caravan
and Camping Park (ST715649)**
Newton Rd BA2 9JF ☎ 01225 333909
⊖ newtonmill@hotmail.com
ⓦ www.campinginbath.co.uk

GOLD

Dir: From Bath W on A4 to A39 rdbt, immediate left, site 1m on left
★ ⊞ £14.50-£18.50 ⊞ £14.50-£18.50 ⚑ £11-£16

Open all year Booking advisable public hols & Jul-Aug Last arrival 21.00hrs Last departure noon
An attractive, high quality park set in a sheltered valley and surrounded by woodland, with a stream running through. It offers excellent toilet facilities with private cubicles and rooms, and there is an appealing restaurant and bar offering a wide choice of menus throughout the year. The city is easily accessible by bus or via the Bristol to Bath cycle path. A 42-acre site with 195 touring pitches, 85 hardstandings.   *contd.*

Fishing & satellite TV hook ups.

Leisure: ♦ ⚑ **Facilities:** ➡ ▶ ⊙ ⅊ ※ ⟁ ⟍ ⟐ ☰
Services: ⊟ ⿴ ⊠ ♀ ⓘ ◿ ⊞ ▭ ✕ ⛟ → ∪ ▶ ⟍ ⟐ ⟍ ⟐

⊜ ⤏ ☰ ⟍ ⣿

▶ ▶ ▶ 76% **Bath Marina & Caravan Park
(ST719655)**
Brassmill Ln BA1 3JT ☎ 01225 424301 & 428778
🖷 01225 424301
Dir: From Bath centre towards suburb of Newbridge. Site signed off A4, 1.5m W towards Bristol/Wells
⊞ ⊞
Open all year Booking advisable bank hols & Jun-Sep Last departure noon
A pleasant site on the edge of Bath in park-like grounds among maturing trees and shrubs. A footpath to the nearby 'Park and Ride' gives good access to the city, and there is also a riverside walk into the centre. A 4-acre site with 88 touring pitches.

Leisure: ⚑ **Facilities:** ▶ ⊙ ⅊ ※ ⟁ ⟍ ⟐ ⟐
Services: ⊟ ⿴ ⓘ ◿ ⊞ ▭ → ∪ ▶ ⊙ ⟍ ⟐ ⟍ ⟐

⊜ ⤏ ☰ ⟍ ⣿

BREAN   Map 04 ST25

HOLIDAY CENTRE

78% **Warren Farm Holiday Centre
(ST297564)**
Brean Sands TA8 2RP
☎ 01278 751227
⊖ enquiries@warren-farm.co.uk
ⓦ www.warren-farm.co.uk
Dir: M5 junct 22 onto B3140 through Burnham-on-Sea to Berrow and Brean. Park 1.5m past Brean Leisure Park
★ ⊞ £6-£12.50 ⊞ £6-£12.50 ⚑ £6-£12.50
Open Apr-Oct Booking advisable BH's & school hols Last arrival 20.00hrs Last departure noon
A large family-run holiday park close to the beach, divided into several fields each with its own designated facilities. Pitches are spacious and level, and enjoy panoramic views of the Mendip Hills and Brean Down. A bar and restaurant are part of the complex, which provide entertainment for all the family, and there is also separate entertainment for children. A 100-acre site with 575 touring pitches and 800 statics.
Fishing lake & ponds, indoor play area

Leisure: ♦ ⚑ ▭
Facilities: ➡ ▶ ⊙ ⅊ ※ ⟁ ⟍ ⟐ ☰ ⟐
Services: ⊟ ⿴ ⊠ ♀ ⓘ ◿ ⊞ ▭ ✕ ⛟ → ∪ ▶ ⟍
Notes: No commerical vehicles ⊜ ⤏ ☰ ⟍ ⣿
See advertisement on page 190

▶ ▶ ▶ ▶ 77% **Northam Farm Caravan & Touring
Park (ST299556)**
TA8 2SE ☎ 01278 751244 🖷 01278 751150
⊖ enquiries@northamfarm.co.uk
ⓦ www.northamfarm.co.uk
Dir: From M5 junct 22 to Burnham-on-Sea. In Brean, Northam Farm on right 0.5m past Brean leisure park
★ ⊞ £5.50-£17.50 ⊞ £5.50-£17.50 ⚑ £5.50-£17.50
Open Apr-Oct (rs Mar & Oct shop/cafe/ takeaway   *contd.*

Leisure: ⚞ Indoor swimming pool ⚟ Outdoor swimming pool ⚬ Tennis court ♦ Games room ⚑ Children's playground ∪ Stables
▶ 9/18 hole golf course ⚓ Boats for hire ⚏ Cinema ⟍ Fishing ⊙ Mini golf ⚑ Watersports ▭ Separate TV room

England

open limited hours) Booking advisable bank & school hols Last arrival 21.00hrs Last departure 10.30hrs
An attractive site a short walk from the sea with game, coarse and sea fishing close by. The quality park also has lots of children's play areas, and is near a long sandy beach. It also runs the Seagull Inn about 600yds away, which includes a restaurant and entertainment. A 30-acre site with 350 touring pitches, 137 hardstandings and 112 statics. Fishing lake

Leisure: 🅰 **Facilities:** ➕ 🛞 ⊙ ⚲ ✳ & ⚲ ⌨ 🎗 ★
Services: 🔲 🔲 🛇 ∅ 🔲 🔲 ✕ 🧹 → ∪ ▶ ⊚ ♪
Notes: Families & couples only, no motorcycles
💳 💳 💳 🔲 🔲

See advertisement on opposite page

BRIDGETOWN   Map 03 SS93

▶ ▶ ▶ 81% **Exe Valley Caravan Site (SS923333)**
Mill House TA22 9JR ☎ 01643 851432
✉ paul@paulmatt.fsnet.co.uk
🌐 www.exevalleycamping.co.uk
Dir: Take A396 (Tiverton to Minehead road). Turn W in centre of Bridgetown, site 40yds on right
🚐 £7.50-£12.50 🚛 £7.50-£12.50 🅰 £7.50-£12.50
Open 17 Mar-16 Oct Booking advisable anytime Last arrival 22.00hrs
Set in the Exmoor National Park, this 'adults only' park occupies an enchanting, peaceful spot in a wooded valley alongside the River Exe. There is free fly fishing, and an abundance of wildlife, with excellent walks directly from the park. The inn opposite serves

contd.

lunchtime and evening meals. A 4-acre site with 50 touring pitches, 10 hardstandings.
Operating 17th-century mill*
Facilities: 🛞 ⊙ ⚲ ✳ & ⚲ ⌨ 🏛 🎗
Services: 🔲 🔲 🛇 ∅ 🔲 🔲 → ∪ 🛆 ⚲ ♪
Notes: adults only site

BRIDGWATER   Map 04 ST23

▶ ▶ ▶ ▶ 71% *Mill Farm Caravan & Camping Park (ST219410)*
Fiddington TA5 1JQ ☎ 01278 732286
Dir: From Bridgwater take A39 W, turn left at Cannington rdbt for 2m, then right just beyond Apple Inn towards Fiddington and follow camping signs
🔲 🚐 🅰
Open all year Booking advisable peak periods Last arrival 23.00hrs Last departure 10.00hrs
An established, mature site with plenty to interest all the family, and helpful owners. A waterfall, stream and safe boating pool are popular features, and there are heated indoor and outdoor swimming pools, the latter with a 50 metre waterslide, a games room, and pony and horse riding school. The park is divided into three caravan areas and a large space for tents, each with its own facilities and play equipment. A 6-acre site with 125 touring pitches. Canoeing, pool table, trampolines, entertainment
Leisure: ⚲ ⚲ ⚲ 🅰 🔲
Facilities: ➕ 🛞 ⊙ ⚲ ✳ & ⚲ ⌨ 🎗 ★
Services: 🔲 🔲 🛇 ∅ 🔲 🔲 🧹 → ▶ ⊚ ♪
💳 💳 💳 🔲 🔲

See advertisement on page 192

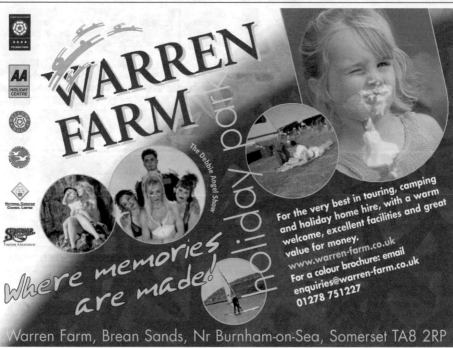

Abbreviations: BH/bank hols-bank holidays   Etr-Easter   Whit-Whitsun   dep-departure   fr-from   hrs-hours   m-mile   mdnt-midnight
rdbt-roundabout   rs-restricted service   wk-week   wknd-weekend   🐕-no dogs

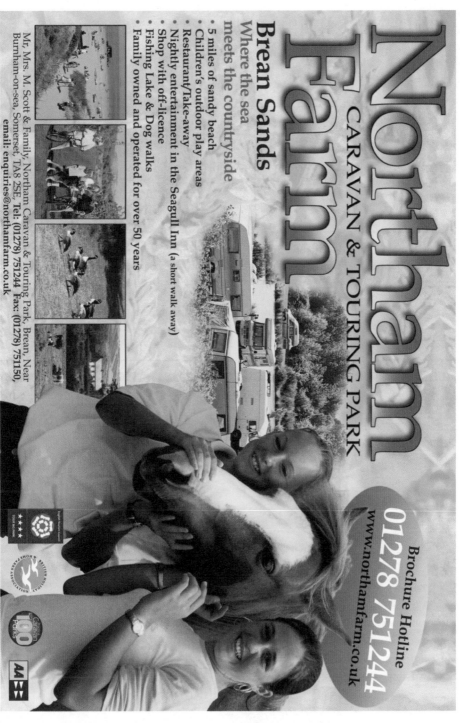

Northam Farm
CARAVAN & TOURING PARK

Brean Sands

Where the sea meets the countryside

- 5 miles of sandy beach
- Children's outdoor play areas
- Restaurant/Take-away
- Nightly entertainment in the Seagull Inn (a short walk away)
- Shop with off-licence
- Fishing Lake & Dog walks
- Family owned and operated for over 50 years

Mr, Mrs, M. Scott & Family, Northam Caravan & Touring Park, Brean, Near Burnham-on-sea, Somerset, TA8 2SE, **Tel:** (01278) 751244 **Fax** (01278) 751150, **email:** enquiries@northamfarm.co.uk

Brochure Hotline
01278 751244
www.northamfarm.co.uk

England

Services: T Toilet Fluid ✗ Café/ Restaurant 🏠 Fast Food/Takeaway 🍼 Baby Care 🔌 Electric Hook Up
🚐 Motorvan Service Point 🧺 Launderette 🍺 Licensed Bar 🔵 Calor Gaz 🔷 Camping Gaz 🔋 Battery Charging

► ► ► 67% **Somerset View Caravan Park**
(ST286314)
Taunton Rd, North Petherton TA6 6NW
☎ 01278 661294
✉ someview@somerset-view.co.uk
🌐 www.somerset-view.co.uk
Dir: S of N Petherton on A38, and entrance next to
rugby club at entrance to layby.
★ ⊞ £10-£12 ⊞ £10-£12
Open Feb-Dec Booking advisable
A popular site with people travelling to and from
Devon and Cornwall, handy for the M5. It is set in
open countryside south of Bridgwater, and Taunton
and the North Somerset coast are within easy
driving distance. A 3-acre site with 50 touring
pitches.
Facilities: ℞ ⊙ ⅄ ℄
Services: ♨ ⓤ 🛢 → ▶ ⚒ ♪ 🎬

BRUTON   **Map 04 ST63**

► ► 72% **Batcombe Vale Caravan & Camping Park**
(ST681379)
Batcombe Vale BA4 6BW ☎ 01749 830246
✉ donaldsage@compuserve.com
🌐 www.batcombevale.co.uk
Dir: Follow signs from Evercreech or Bruton
★ ⊞ £13 ⊞ Å
Open May-Sep Booking advisable bank hols, wknds
& Jul-Aug Last arrival 22.00hrs Last departure
noon
A very attractive site approached down a steep hill
into a secluded valley, with three lakes which offer
coarse fishing. This lovely remote location has
superb views and a peaceful environment, with
rustic facilities. A 4-acre site with 30 touring pitches.
Coarse fishing, free boats for use.
Leisure: 🅰 **Facilities:** ℞ ⊙ ⚡ ℄ 🎋 🐾
Services: ♨ 🛢 ⌀ 🗄 → ∪ ⚒ ♪ 🎬
Notes: No motorcycle groups

BURNHAM-ON-SEA   **Map 04 ST34**

77% **Burnham-on-Sea**
Holiday Village (ST305485)
Marine Dr TA8 1LA
☎ 01278 783391 🖨 01278 793776
🌐 www.havenholidays.com
Dir: On A38 to Highbridge, cross rail bridge, turn
right to Burnham-on-Sea. 1m turn left into Marine
Parade, follow signs to site on left
⊞ ⊞ Å

contd.

Open mid Mar-Oct (rs mid Mar-May & Sep-Oct
Facilities may be reduced) Booking advisable
Jul-Aug Last departure 10.00hrs
A large family-orientated holiday village
complex with a separate touring park containing
43 super pitches. There is a wide range of
activities including excellent indoor and outdoor
pools, plus bars, restaurants and entertainment
for all the family. The coarse fishing lake is very
popular, and the seafront at Burnham is only
0.5m away. A 76-acre site with 75 touring pitches.
Leisure: 🏊 🏊 ⚆ 🎱 🅰 🖵 **Facilities:** ⚙
Services: ♨ ♀ 🛢 ✗ 🚿
Notes: 🚫 🍴 💳 💳 💳 📀 🎬 📺 🎵
See advertisement on opposite page

BURTLE   **Map 04 ST34**

► 72% **Orchard Camping (ST397434)**
Ye Olde Burtle Inn, Catcott Rd TA7 8NG
☎ 01278 722269 & 722123 🖨 01278 722269
✉ chris@theburtleinn.co.uk
🌐 www.theburtleinn.co.uk
Dir: From M5 junct 23 onto A39, approx 4m turn left
onto unclass road to Burtle, site by pub in village centre
★ Å £8.90-£9.80
Open all year Booking advisable bank hols & peak
season Last arrival anytime
A simple campsite set in an orchard at the rear of a
lovely 17th-century family inn in the heart of the
Somerset Levels. The restaurant offers a wide range
of meals, and breakfast can be pre-ordered by
campers. A shower and disabled toilet have been
added and these facilities are available to campers
outside pub opening hours. A 0.75-acre site with
30 touring pitches.
Bicycle & tent hire
Leisure: 🎱 🅰 **Facilities:** ℞ ⊙ ⚡ ✳ ⅄ ℄ 🎋 🎋 🐾
Services: ♀ 🗄 ✗ 🚿 → ∪ ♪ 🎬
🍴 💳 💳 📀 🎬 📺 🎵

CHARD   **Map 04 ST30**

► ► ► 80% **Alpine Grove Touring Park**
(ST342071)
Forton TA20 4HD ☎ 01460 63479
🖨 01460 63479
✉ stay@alpinegrovetouringpark.com
🌐 www.alpinegrovetouringpark.com
Dir: Turn off A30 between Chard & Crewkerne towards
Cricket St Thomas, follow signs. Park 2m on right
★ ⊞ £8.50-£11 ⊞ £8.50-£11 Å £8.50-£11
Open 1 wk before Etr-Sep Booking advisable bank
hols & Jul-Aug Last arrival 21.00hrs Last departure
11.00hrs
An attractive, quiet wooded park with both
hardstandings and grass pitches, close to Cricket St
Thomas wildlife park, in a rural location. The park's
nature trails are popular. An 8.5-acre site with
40 touring pitches, 15 hardstandings.
Dog-sitting service
Leisure: 🥎 🅰 **Facilities:** ℞ ⊙ ⚡ ✳ ℄ ⅄ 🎋 🎋 🐾
Services: ♨ ⓤ 🛢 ⌀ 🗄 🗓 → ∪ ▶ ♪
Notes: Dogs must be kept on leads
See advertisement under LYME REGIS

QUANTOCK ORCHARD CARAVAN PARK

in the beautiful Quantock Hills –
The small, clean and friendly park for
Touring Caravans, Motor Homes & Camping
Situated at the foot of the Quantock Hills, our small
family-run park is close to Exmoor and the coast in a
designated area of outstanding natural beauty. This
beautiful area offers diverse landscapes and interesting
landscapes to explore on foot, bicycle, or by car.
To complement our beautiful outdoor heated swimming
pool we have now opened the millennium fitness and
leisure suite. This exciting new facility will be open all
year and includes – sauna, steam room, jacuzzi – full range
of superior exercise equipment – rest area conservatory
with coffee-tea machine. This development will provide a
superior all weather extension to complement our existing
award winning facilities.

For more information ring for our colour brochure on
01984 618618 – or visit our website:
www.flaxpool.freeserve.co.uk
Mr & Mrs Barrett
QUANTOCK ORCHARD CARAVAN PARK,
Flaxpool, Crowcombe, Taunton,
Somerset TA4 4AW
Tel: (01984) 618618

OPEN ALL YEAR

AA
Deluxe Park

CHEDDAR	Map 04 ST45

PREMIER PARK

▶ ▶ ▶ ▶ ▶ 69% **Broadway House**
Holiday Caravan & Camping Park
(ST448547) Axbridge Rd BS27 3DB
☎ 01934 742610 🖳 01934 744950
🅔 info@broadwayhouse.uk.com
*Dir: From M5 junct 22 follow signs to Cheddar
Gorge & Caves (8m). The Park is midway between
Cheddar & Axbridge on A371*
★ 🚐 £11-£20 🚐 £9-£16.50 Å £9.50-£18.50
Open Mar-mid Nov (rs Mar-end May & Oct-Nov
No bar or pool open, limited shop hours)
Booking advisable bank hols & end Jul-Aug Last
arrival 23.00hrs Last departure noon
*A well-equipped family park on the slopes of the
Mendips with an exceptional range of activities for
all ages. This is a busy and lively park in the main
holiday periods, but can be quiet and peaceful off-
peak. Broadway has its own activity centre based
on the site, providing archery, shooting, climbing,
caving, ballooning and much more. The slightly
terraced pitches face south, and are backed by the
Mendips. A 30-acre site with 200 touring pitches,
35 hardstandings and 37 statics.*
Sunbed, table tennis, crazy golf
Leisure: 🏵 ⚜ 🎣 🎱 💻
Facilities: ➡ 🚿 ⊙ 🎱 ✳ & 🔧 🛒 📮 🎠 ✂
Services: 🔌 💨 🗄 🎱 🍴 🛢 🎱 🔟 ✕ 🛒 → ∪ ▶ ⊙ 🍴
Notes: Children to be supervised at all times.
💳 💳 💳 💳 💳 💳 🅖

▶ ▶ ▶ 81% **Cheddar Bridge**
Touring Park (ST459529)
Draycott Rd BS27 3RJ
☎ 01934 743048 🖳 01934 743048
🅔 enquiries@cheddarbridge.co.uk
🕸 www.cheddarbridge.co.uk
*Dir: From M5 junct 22 (Burnham-on-Sea) take A38
towards Cheddar & Bristol, for approx 5m. Right onto
A371 at Cross, follow Cheddar signs. Through Cheddar
village towards Wells, site on right just before Caravan
Club site*
★ 🚐 £13-£15 🚐 £13-£15 Å £12-£14

SILVER

Open Mar-Oct Booking advisable Last arrival
22.00hrs Last departure 11.00hrs
*A peaceful adults-only park on the edge of the
village of Cheddar, with the River Yeo passing
attractively through its grounds. It is handy for
exploring the Cheddar Gorge and Wookey Hole,
Wells and Bath. The toilet facilities are very good.
A 4-acre site with 45 touring pitches,
10 hardstandings and 3 statics.*
Table tennis
Facilities: ➡ 🚿 ⊙ 🎱 ✳ & 🔧 🛒 📮 🎠
Services: 🔌 💨 🛢 🎱 → ∪ ▶ 🛢 🍴 🔟
Notes: Adults only

CROWCOMBE	Map 03 ST13

▶ ▶ ▶ ▶ 83% *Quantock Orchard Caravan Park*
(ST138357)
TA4 4AW ☎ 01984 618618 🖳 01984 618618
🅔 qocp@flaxpool.freeserve.co.uk
🕸 www.flaxpool.freeserve.co.uk
Dir: Site set back from A358
🚐 🚐 Å

Open all year Booking advisable bank hols & Jul-
Aug Last arrival 22.00hrs Last departure noon
*An attractive, quiet site with wonderful views,
sitting at the western foot of the Quantocks midway
between Taunton and Minehead. The park is laid*
contd.

out in an old orchard with plenty of colourful flower beds, and the quality facilities are very well maintained. A fitness complex next to the swimming pool offers jacuzzi, sauna and exercise machines. Ideal for visiting Exmoor National Park, and the nearby West Somerset Steam Railway. A 3.5-acre site with 75 touring pitches.
Gym & leisure suite, off-licence on site

Leisure: ⸯ ⚄ 🅿 Facilities: ➡ ⬧⊙⋇⅍ 🛒 🎱
Services: 🔌🗑️⬧⬧🖥️T→∪▶🧺 🍲 ▭ ▦ 🚮 🔁

See advertisement on opposite page

DULVERTON   Map 03 SS92
See also East Anstey, Devon

▶ ▶ ▶ 70% *Wimbleball Lake (SS960300)*
TA22 9NU ☎ 01398 371257
ⓦ www.swlakestrust.org.uk
Dir: From A396 (Tiverton-Minehead road) take B3222 signed Dulverton Services, follow signs to Wimbleball Lake. Ignore 1st entry (fishing) take 2nd entry for watersports & camping. Care needed on narrow roads
🚐 ▲

Open Apr-1 Nov Booking advisable high season Last departure 14.00hrs
A grassy site overlooking Wimbleball Lake, set high up on Exmoor National Park. The camping area is in its own paddock with toilet facilities, and surrounded by farmland in a quiet setting. The lake is nationally renowned for its trout fishing, and boats can be hired with advance notice. A 1.25-acre site with 30 touring pitches, 4 hardstandings.
Watersports centre

Leisure: ⚄ Facilities: ⬧⊙⅍🛒
Services: 🔌✕→∪⌬⤵⚒🛒
Notes: Dogs must be kept on leads
▭ ▦ 🚮 🔁

EMBOROUGH   Map 04 ST65

▶ ▶ ▶ 81% Old Down Touring Park (ST628513)
Old Down House BA3 4SA
☎ 01761 232355 ▤ 01761 232355
ⓔ olddown@talk21.com
ⓦ www.olddowntouringpark.co.uk
Dir: On A37 from Farrington Gurney through Ston Easton. After 2m left onto B3139 to Radstock. Site opposite Old Down Inn on right
★ 🚐 £9.50-£13 🚐 £9.50-£13 ▲ £9.50-£10.50
Open Mar-Nov Booking advisable bank hols & Jul-Aug Last arrival 20.00hrs Last departure noon
A small family-run site set in open parkland,

contd.

---

surrounded by well-established trees. The toilet facilities are excellent, and well maintained along with every other aspect of the park. Children are welcome. A 4-acre site with 30 touring pitches, 15 hardstandings.

Facilities: ⬧⊙⅍⋇🛒🛒🎱
Services: 🔌⬧🗑️🖥️T→∪▶🧺
Notes: Dogs must be kept on leads at all times
▭ ▦ 🚮 🔁

EXFORD   Map 03 SS83

▶ ▶ 75% Westermill Farm
(SS825398)
TA24 7NJ
☎ 01643 831238 ▤ 01643 831216
ⓔ aa@westermill.com
ⓦ www.westermill.com
Dir: Leave Exford on Porlock road. After 0.25m fork left, continue along valley until 'Westermill' sign on tree. Take left fork
★ 🚐 fr £10 ▲ fr £10

Open all year (rs Nov-May larger toilet block & shop closed) Booking advisable Spring bank hol & Jul-Aug
An idyllic site for peace and quiet, in a sheltered valley in the heart of Exmoor, which has won awards for conservation. Four waymarked walks over 500 acre working farm. Approach not suitable for caravans. A 6-acre site with 60 touring pitches. Shallow river for fishing/bathing, marked walks

Facilities: ⬧⊙⅍⋇🛒🎱🐾
Services: 🗑️⬧🖋️→⤵

FROME   Map 04 ST74

▶ ▶ ▶ 75% Seven Acres Caravan & Camping Site
(ST777444)
Seven Acres, West Woodlands BA11 5EQ
☎ 01373 464222
Dir: On B3092 approx 0.75m from rdbt with A361, Frome bypass
★ 🚐 fr £8 🚐 fr £8 ▲ fr £7
Open Mar-Oct Booking advisable
A level meadowland site beside the shallow River Frome, with a bridge across to an adjacent field, and plenty of scope for families (though no laundry, but launderette 0.5m away). Set on the edge of the Longleat Estate with its stately home, wildlife safari park, and many other attractions. A 3-acre site with 22 touring pitches, 22 hardstandings.

Leisure: ⚄ Facilities: ⬧⊙⅍⋇⅍🎱🐾
Services: 🔌→∪▶🍴⤵🛒
Notes: Dogs must be kept on leads

Facilities: ➡ Bath ⬧ Shower ⊙ Electric Shaver ⅍ Hairdryer ⋇ Ice Pack Facility ⅍ Disabled Facilities ⎁ Public Telephone
🛒 Shop on Site or within 200yds ▭ Mobile Shop (calls at least 5 days a week) 🎱 BBQ Area 🎋 Picnic Area 🐾 Dog Exercise Area

England

GLASTONBURY   Map 04 ST53

PREMIER PARK

▶ ▶ ▶ ▶ ▶ 88% **Old Oaks**
Touring Park (ST521394)
Wick Farm, Wick BA6 8JS
☎ 01458 831437 🖹 01458 833238
Best of British / *GOLD*
🅔 info@theoldoaks.co.uk
🆆 www.theoldoaks.co.uk
Dir: From Glastonbury on A361 towards Shepton Mallet in 1.75m turn left at sign Wick, site in 1m
🚐 £11-£14 🚐 £11-£14 🛆 £11-£14
Open mid Mar-Oct (rs Oct shop hours)
Booking advisable bank hols & main season Last arrival 20.00hrs Last departure noon
An idyllic park on a working farm with panoramic views towards the Mendip Hills. Old Oaks offers sophisticated services whilst retaining a farming atmosphere, and there are some 'super' pitches as well as en suite toilet facilities. Glastonbury's two famous 1,000-year-old oak trees, Gog and Magog, are on site. This is an adult-only park. A 10-acre site with 80 touring pitches, 18 hardstandings.
Fishing, bicycle hire & off-licence on site.
Facilities: 📶 🏧 ☉ 🥤 ✳ 🔥 🍴 🖴 🏕 🔭
Services: 🔌 🎝 🖴 🛢 🖉 🔳 🖂 → 🔧
Notes: Adults only. Group or block bookings at owners' discretion 💳 💳 💳 💳 💳 🌀

▶ ▶ ▶ ▶ 72% **Isle of Avalon Touring Caravan Park** (ST494397)
Godney Rd BA6 9AF ☎ 01458 833618
🖹 01458 833618
Dir: M5 junct 23, A39 to outskirts of Glastonbury, 2nd exit signed Wells at B&Q rdbt, straight over next rdbt, 1st exit at 3rd rdbt (B3151), 200yds right
★ 🚐 £8-£9 🚐 £8-£9 🛆 £8-£12
Open all year Booking advisable mid Jul-mid Aug Last arrival 21.00hrs Last departure 11.00hrs
A popular site on the south side of this historic town and within easy walking distance of the town centre. This level park offers a quiet environment in which to stay and explore the many local attractions including the Tor, Wells, Wookey Hole and Clark's Village. An 8-acre site with 120 touring pitches, 70 hardstandings.
Cycle hire.
Leisure: ⚑ **Facilities:** 🏧 ☉ 🥤 ✳ 🔥 🍴 🖴 🏕 🔭
Services: 🔌 🖴 🛢 🖉 🔳 🔲 ⬆ → 🔆 🎝
💳 💳 💳 💳 💳 🌀

▶ ▶ 92% **Greenacres Camping** (ST553416)
Barrow Ln, North Wootton BA4 4HL
☎ 01749 890497
Dir: A361 to Glastonbury. Turn at Steanbow Farm, from A39 turn at Browns Garden Centre. Follow campsite signs
★ 🚐 £10 🛆 £10
Open Apr-Oct Booking advisable school hols, Glastonbury Festival Last arrival 21.00hrs Last departure noon
An immaculately maintained site peacefully set

within sight of Glastonbury Tor. Mainly family orientated with many thoughtful extra facilities provided. A 4.5-acre site with 30 touring pitches.
Free use of fridges & freezers
Leisure: ⚑ **Facilities:** 🏧 ☉ 🥤 ✳
Services: 🔌 🛢 🖉 🔳 → 🔆 🔲 🏕 🎝 🖴 🔋
Notes: 🚫 No caravans

LANGPORT   Map 04 ST42

NEW ▶ ▶ ▶ 77% **Bowdens Crest Caravan & Camping Park** (ST414288)
Bowdens TA10 0DD
☎ 01458 250553 🖹 01458 253360
🅔 bowcrest@btconnect.com
🆆 www.bowdenscrest.co.uk
Dir: Off A372 Langport to Bridgwater road, signed.
★ 🚐 £8-£16 🚐 £8-£16 🛆 £5-£16

Open all year Booking advisable bank hols & Aug Last arrival 22.00hrs Last departure noon
A tranquil family-run park with spectacular panoramic views over the Somerset levels and the distant Blackdown Hills. The tasteful new restaurant with adjoining patio is a pleasant place to relax, and this quiet park will appeal to both couples and families. A 16.5-acre site with 30 touring pitches, 2 hardstandings and 13 statics.
Special diets catered for
Leisure: 🔵 ⚑ 🖵 **Facilities:** 🏧 ☉ ✳ 🔥 🍴 🖴 🖴 🏕 🔭
Services: 🔌 🛢 🥤 🖉 🔳 ✕ → 🔆 🎝 💳 💳 💳 💳 🌀

▶ ▶ ▶ 67% **Thorney Lakes Caravan Park** (ST430237)
Thorney Lakes, Muchelney TA10 0DW
☎ 01458 250811   *GOLD*
🆆 www.thorneylakes.co.uk
Dir: From A303 at Podimore rdbt take A372 to Langport. At Huish Episcopi Church turn left for Muchelney, then in 100yds left again (signed Muchelney & Crewkerne). Site 300yds after John Leach Pottery
★ 🚐 £10-£12 🚐 £10-£12 🛆 £10-£12
Open Apr-Oct Booking advisable
A small, basic but very attractive park set in a cider apple orchard, with coarse fishing in the three well-stocked on-site lakes. The famous John Leach pottery shop is nearby. A 6-acre site with 36 touring pitches.
Coarse fishing on site.
Facilities: 🏧 ☉ ✳
Services: 🔌 → 🍴 🎝 🔋

contd.

MARTOCK — Map 04 ST41

▶ ▶ ▶ ▶ 77% **Southfork Caravan Park (ST448188)**
Parrett Works TA12 6AE ☎ 01935 825661
🖨 01935 825122
🅔 southforkcaravans@btconnect.com
🆆 www.southforkcaravans.co.uk
Dir: 8m NW of Yeovil, 2m off A303. From E take exit after Cartgate rdbt. From W 1st exit off rdbt signed South Petherton, follow camping signs.
🅰

Open all year Booking advisable bank hols & Jul-Aug Last arrival 23.00hrs Last departure noon
A neat grass park in a quiet rural area, offering spotless facilities to those who enjoy the countryside. Located on the outskirts of a pretty village, with good amenities. A 2-acre site with 25 touring pitches and 3 statics.
Caravan service/repair centre & accessories shop.
Leisure: 🄰
Facilities: 🅝 ⊙ ℞ ✳ 🅛 🐾 🛒
Services: 🔧 🗑 🅘 🖉 🔲 🅣 → ▶ 🥄
💳 ▬ ▭ ▦ 🔀 🎿

MINEHEAD — Map 03 SS94

▶ ▶ ▶ 77% **Camping & Caravanning Club Site (SS958471)**
Hill Rd, North Hill TA24 5LB ☎ 01643 704138
🆆 www.campingandcaravanningclub.co.uk
Dir: From A39 towards town centre. In main street turn opposite W H Smith to Blenheim Rd. Left in 50yds (by pub) into Martlet Rd, continue up hill and site on right
★ 🚐 £7.65-£12 🅰 £7.65-£12
Open Apr-Oct Booking advisable bank hols & peak periods Last arrival 21.00hrs Last departure noon
A secluded site on a hilltop with glorious views of the Bristol Channel and the Quantocks. Good clean facilities plus a laundry and information room make this a popular choice for those seeking an isolated holiday. Please see advertisement on page 11 for information on Club sites and membership. A 3.75-acre site with 60 touring pitches, 12 hardstandings.
Facilities: 🅝 ⊙ ℞ ✳ 🅛 🏛
Services: 🔧 🛒 🗑 🅘 🖉 🔲 🅣 → U ▶ 🥄 🥄 🐾
💳 ▭ ▦ 🔀 🎿

▶ ▶ ▶ 67% Minehead & Exmoor Caravan & Camping Site (SS950457)
Porlock Rd TA24 8SW ☎ 01643 703074
Dir: 1m W of Minehead centre, close to A39
★ 🚐 fr £10 🚐 fr £10 🅰 fr £10
Open all year (rs Nov-Feb reduced no. of pitches)
Booking advisable bank hols & Jul-Aug Last arrival 22.00hrs Last departure noon
A small terraced park on the edge of Exmoor, spread over five paddocks and screened by the mature trees that surround it. The level pitches provide a comfortable space for each unit on this family-run park. There is a laundrette in nearby Minehead. A 2.5-acre site with 50 touring pitches, 4 hardstandings.
Leisure: 🄰
Facilities: 🅝 ⊙ ℞ ✳ 🅛 🅛 🛒
Services: 🔧 🗑 🅘 🖉 🔲 → U ▶ 🥄 🥄 🐾 🥄 🗑 🐾

MUCHELNEY — Map 04 ST42

NEW ▶ ▶ ▶ 69% **Muchelney Caravan & Camping Site (ST429249)**
Abbey Farm TA10 0DQ ☎ 01458 250112 & 07881 524426 🖨 01458 250112
Dir: from A303 at Podimore rdbt take A372 towards Langport. At church in Huish Episcopi follow Muchelney Abbey sign. In Muchelney left at village cross. Site in 50mtrs
🚐 £7-£7.50 🚐 £7-£7.50 🅰 £7-£7.50
Open all year Booking advisable bank & school hols
This small developing site is situated opposite Muchelney Abbey, an English Heritage property. This quiet and peaceful site will appeal to all lovers of the countryside, and is well positioned for visiting the Somerset Levels. A 3-acre site with 40 touring pitches, 5 hardstandings.
Fishing
Facilities: 🅝 ⊙ ✳ 🅛 🏛 🛒
Services: 🔧 🛒 🔲 🅣 → 🥄 🐾
Notes: Dogs must be kept on leads

OARE — Map 03 SS74

NEW ▶ ▶ ▶ 68% **Doone Valley Holidays (SS795468)**
EX35 6NU ☎ 01598 741234 🖨 01598 741154
🅔 doonevalleyholidays@hotmail.com
🆆 www.doonevalleyholidays.co.uk
Dir: Exit A39 between Lynton & Porlock at Doone Valley/Oare//Oareford sign. To T-junct, turn right. Site signed in 0.75m on left (NB do not pass site due to narrow bridge & no-turning area)
🚐 £10-£15 🚐 £10-£15 🅰 £10-£15
Open all year Booking advisable
Set in the heart of Exmoor's Doone Valley, this quiet, sheltered park is arranged over four riverside fields, with new toilet facilities. It offers a good café and a little shop, with a large garden for outdoor eating. A 110-acre site with 70 touring pitches.
Off-licence
Facilities: 🅝 ⊙ ℞ ✳ 🅛 🅛 🏛 🍴
Services: 🗑 🅘 🖉 🔲 ✕ → U 🥄
💳 ▬ ▭ ▦ ⓓ 🔀 🎿

PORLOCK   Map 03 SS84

▶ ▶ ▶ 87% *Burrowhayes Farm Caravan & Camping Site (SS897460)*
West Luccombe TA24 8HT ☎ 01643 862463
e info@burrowhayes.co.uk
w www.burrowhayes.co.uk
Dir: A39 from Minehead towards Porlock for 5m. Left at Red Post to Horner & West Lucombe, site 0.25m on right, immediately before humpback bridge
🚐🚗⋏

Open 15 Mar-Oct shop closed until Sat before Etr
Booking advisable Etr, Spring bank hol & Jul-Aug
Last arrival 22.00hrs Last departure noon
A delightful site on the edge of Exmoor, sloping gently down to Horner Water in glorious surroundings. The farm buildings have been converted into riding stables which offers escorted rides on the moors, and the excellent new toilet facilities are housed in timber-clad buildings. An ideal site for exploring the surrounding area, with many walks directly into the countryside. An 8-acre site with 120 touring pitches, 3 hardstandings and 20 statics.
Pony-trekking available, riding stables
Facilities: ♠⊙♥☀♿⚙☕⋔
Services: 🔌🔋🍴🔧🚿→∪▶☺♦⋆⬝
🔲🔲🔲🔲🔲🔲🔲

▶ ▶ ▶ 85% *Porlock Caravan Park (SS882469)*
TA24 8ND ☎ 01643 862269
📠 01643 862239
e info@porlockcaravanpark.co.uk
w www.porlockcaravanpark.co.uk
Dir: Through village fork right signed Porlock Weir, site on right
🚐🚗⋏
Open 15 Mar-Oct Booking advisable Etr, Whitsun & Jul-Aug Last arrival 22.30hrs Last departure noon
A sheltered touring park offering a quiet resting place in the centre of lovely countryside on the edge of the village, with Exmoor right on the doorstep. The toilets facilities are superb, with private washing facilities and an en suite family room. A kitchen area with microwave and freezer is a popular feature. This very well kept parks provides quality facilities throughout. A 3-acre site with 40 touring pitches, 10 hardstandings and 56 statics.
Facilities: ♠⊙♥☀⚙☕⋔
Services: 🔌🔋🍴🔧🚿→∪⋆☺⬝

REDHILL   Map 04 ST46

▶ ▶ ▶ 75% *Brook Lodge Farm Camping & Caravan Park (ST486620)*
Cowslip Green BS40 5RB
☎ 01934 862311 📠 01934 862311
e brooklodgefarm@aol.com
w www.brooklodgefarm.com
Dir: M5 junct 18/22 follow signs for Bristol Airport. Park 3m on left of A38 at bottom of hill after Darlington Arms
🚐🚗⋏

Open Mar-Oct Booking advisable 22 May-4 Sep Last arrival 22.30hrs Last departure noon
A naturally sheltered country touring park nestling in a valley of the Mendip Hills, surrounded by trees and a historic walled garden. Country walks can be enjoyed from the park, and there is trout fishing nearby. A 3.5-acre site with 29 touring pitches, 3 hardstandings.
Bicycle hire & walking maps provided
Leisure: ⚖
Facilities: ♠⊙♥☀♿⚙☕⋔
Services: 🔌🍴🔧🚿→∪▶⬝
Notes: Small dogs only & must be on lead
🔲🔲🔲🔲🔲

RODNEY STOKE   Map 04 ST44

▶ ▶ ▶ ▶ 72% *Bucklegrove Caravan & Camping Park (ST487502)*
Wells Rd BS27 3UZ ☎ 01749 870261
📠 01749 870101
e info@bucklegrove.co.uk
w www.bucklegrove.co.uk
Dir: On A371 midway between Cheddar & Wells
★ 🚐 £5-£18 🚗 £5-£18 ⋏ £5-£18
Open 5 Mar-2 Jan (rs Nov-Dec & Mar-Etr Pool closed) Booking advisable bank hols & peak periods Last arrival 21.00hrs Last departure noon
A well-sheltered site on the southern slopes of the Mendip Hills providing superb views of Somerset. This popular park offers good facilities and amenities including an indoor swimming pool and a bar/restaurant. An ideal touring base, and a pleasant suntrap. A 7.5-acre site with 120 touring pitches, 24 hardstandings and 35 statics.
Separate tourist information room.
Leisure: ⚓ ♠ ⚖
Facilities: ⬌♠⊙♥☀♿⚙☕⏛
Services: 🔌🔋🍽🔧🚿☕✗🛒→∪▶☺♨⬝
Notes: 🚫 🔲🔲🔲🔲🔲

SPARKFORD   Map 04 ST62

► ► ► 79% **Long Hazel Park (ST602262)**
High St BA22 7JH
☎ 01963 440002 📄 01963 440002
📧 longhazelpark@hotmail.com
🌐 www.sparkford.f9.co.uk/lhi.htm
Dir: *Turn off A303 at Hazlegrove rdbt follow signs for Sparkford. Park 400yds on left*
★ 🚐 £14 🚎 £14 🏕 £14
Open 16 Feb-16 Jan Booking advisable Jul-Sep and Bank hols Last arrival 22.00hrs Last dep 11.30hrs
A very neat, smart site next to the Sparkford Inn in the village high street. This attractive park is run by a friendly owner to a good standard. There are luxury lodges on site. A 3.5-acre site with 75 touring pitches, 40 hardstandings and 3 statics. Badminton

Leisure: ⚆ **Facilities:** 🅁 ⊙ 🕈 ✳ & 🖳 🚿 🎍
Services: 🕿 ⅏ 🗔 📶 🗒 → ∪ ▶ ⊙ ✦
Notes: Dogs on leads & exercised off site

TAUNTON   Map 04 ST22

► ► ► 73% **Ashe Farm Camping & Caravan Site (ST279229)**
Thornfalcon TA3 5NW
☎ 01823 442567 📄 01823 443372
📧 camping@ashe-farm.fsnet.co.uk
Dir: *From M5 junct 25 take A358 E for 2.5m. Turn right at Nags Head pub. Site 0.25m on right*
★ 🚐 fr £10 🚎 fr £10 🏕 fr £8.50

Open Apr-Oct Booking advisable Jul-Aug Last arrival 22.00hrs
A well-screened site surrounded by mature trees and shrubs, with two large touring fields. A facilities block includes smart toilets and a separate laundry room, while the old portaloos remain very clean and well-maintained. Not far from the bustling market town of Taunton, and handy for both coasts. A 7-acre site with 30 touring pitches, 8 hardstandings. Baby changing facilities

Leisure: ⚄ ⚆ **Facilities:** 🅁 ⊙ 🕈 ✳ & 🎋
Services: 🕿 🗔 🗑 ⅋ 🗒 🚾 → ∪ ▶ 🚼 ✦ 🖳

NEW ► ► ► 87% **Cornish Farm Touring Park (ST235217)**
Shoreditch TA3 7BS ☎ 01823 327746
📄 01823 354946
📧 warden@cornishfarm.com
🌐 www.cornishfarm.com
Dir: *M5 junct 25 towards Taunton. At lights left onto*
contd.

B3170. 3rd left in Ilminster Road (follow Corfe signs). Right at rdbt, left at next. Right at T-junct, left into Killams Drive, 2nd left into Killams Ave. Follow road over motorway bridge. Site on left, take 2nd entrance
★ 🚐 £10 🚎 £10 🏕 £10
Open all year Booking advisable race days & bank hols Last departure noon
This new park provides really top quality facilities throughout. Although only 2 miles from Taunton, the park is set in open countryside and is a very convenient base for visiting the many attractions of the area such as Clarke's Village, Glastonbury and Cheddar Gorge. A 3.5-acre site with 50 touring pitches, 25 hardstandings.

Facilities: 🅁 ⊙ 🕈 &
Services: 🕿 ⅏ 🗔 🗒 → ∪ ▶ 18 ⊚ 🚼 🖳
Notes: 💳 💳 💳 🚫 🚭

► ► ► 77% **Holly Bush Park (ST220162)**
Culmhead TA3 7EA ☎ 01823 421515
📧 info@hollybushpark.com
🌐 www.hollybushpark.com
Dir: *M5 junct 25 towards Taunton. Left at 1st lights signed Corfe/Taunton Racecourse. 3.5m past Corfe on B3170 right at top of hill on unclass road towards Wellington. Right at next junct, site 150yds*
🚐 £10-£14 🚎 £10-£14 🏕 £10-£12

Open all year Booking advisable bank hols & high season Last arrival 21.00hrs Last departure 11.00hrs
An immaculate little park set in an orchard in attractive countryside, with easy access to Wellington and Taunton. The friendly owners are welcoming and keen to help, and keep the facilities in good order. A 2-acre site with 40 touring pitches, 5 hardstandings.

Facilities: 🅁 ⊙ ✳ 🕽 🖳 🚿 🎋
Services: 🕿 🗔 🗑 ⅋ 🗒 → ∪ ▶ ✦ 💳 💳 💳 🚫 🚭

WATCHET   Map 03 ST04

► ► ► 80% **Home Farm Holiday Centre (ST106432)**
St Audries Bay TA4 4DP ☎ 01984 632487
📄 01984 634687
📧 dib@homefarmholidaycentre.co.uk
🌐 www.homefarmholidaycentre.co.uk
Dir: *Follow A39 towards Minehead, fork right onto B3191 at West Quantoxhead after St Audries garage, then right after 0.25m*
★ 🚐 £10-£15 🚎 £10-£15 🏕 £10-£15
Open all year Booking advisable all year Last arrival dusk Last departure noon
In a hidden valley beneath the Quantock Hills, this
contd.

England

park overlooks its own private beach. The atmosphere is friendly and quiet, and there are lovely sea views from the level pitches. Flower beds, woodland walks, and a koi carp pond all enhance this very attractive site, along with a lovely indoor swimming pool and a beer garden. A 45-acre site with 40 touring pitches, 35 hardstandings and 230 statics.

Leisure: ⌘ 🅰 **Facilities:** ⋒⊙🔍✳️⚿♿🏖️🐾
Services: 🖧🛢️🅿️🏴✉️📧🔳→ ◢ **Notes:** No cars by caravans or tents ☎ 💳 📮 🔲

WELLINGTON   Map 03 ST12

▶ ▶ ▶ 71% **Gamlins Farm Caravan Park (ST083195)**
Gamlins Farm House, Greenham TA21 0LZ
☎ 01823 672859 & 07986 832516 📠 01823 672859
Dir: From M5 junct 26 take A38 towards Tiverton. 4m turn right for Greenham, site 1m on right
★ 🅿️ £8-£10 🚐 £8-£10 ▲ £5.50-£7.50
Open Etr-Sep Booking advisable bank hols Last arrival 20.00hrs
A well-planned site in a secluded position with panoramic views. The friendly owners keep the toilet facilities to a good standard of cleanliness. A 3-acre site with 25 touring pitches, 3 hardstandings. Free coarse fishing on site

Leisure: ⚓ **Facilities:** ⋒⊙🔍✳️🎏🐾
Services: 🖧🔳→ ∪ 🏴✉️◢🛢️
Notes: Dogs must be kept on leads, no loud noise after 22.00

Tel: 01934 627595

- Heated Swimming Pool • Licenced Bar
- Shop • Children's Play Area
- Games Room
- Superb New Toilet/Shower Block
- Quiet Family Run Site
- Just 200 yards from Sand Bay Beach
- All Pitches with Electric

SEASONAL PITCHES AVAILABLE

WELLS   Map 04 ST54

▶ ▶ 81% **Homestead Park (ST532474)**
Wookey Hole BA5 1BW ☎ 01749 673022
📠 01749 673022
🅔 enquiries@homesteadpark.co.uk
🅦 www.homesteadpark.co.uk
Dir: 0.5m NW off A371 Wells to Cheddar road (weight limit on bridge into touring area now 1 tonne)
★ 🅿️ £12 🚐 £12 ▲ £12
Open Etr-Oct Booking advisable bank hols Last arrival 20.00hrs Last departure noon
Attractive small site by a stream, with mature trees. Set in hilly woods and meadowland with access to the river and Wookey Hole. This park is for adults only. A 2-acre site with 30 touring pitches and 28 statics.

Facilities: ⋒⊙🔍✳️⚿🛢️
Services: 🖧🛢️◢🔳→∪🏴✉️◢🔲
Notes: Adults only

WESTON-SUPER-MARE   Map 04 ST36

▶ ▶ ▶ 76% **Country View Caravan Park (ST335647)**
Sand Rd, Sand Bay BS22 9UJ
☎ 01934 627595
Dir: From M5 junct 21 take A370 towards Weston-Super-Mare. Immediately take left lane & follow signs for Kewstoke/Sand Bay. Straight over 3 rdbts onto Norton Ln. At Sand Bay right into Sand Rd
🚐 🚐 ▲

Open Mar-Jan Booking advisable bank hols, wknds & peak periods Last arrival 20.00hrs Last departure noon
A pleasant open site in a rural area a few hundred yards from Sandy Bay and beach. The park is also well placed for energetic walks along the coast at either end of the beach. Facilities are of a good standard.
An 8-acre site with 120 touring pitches, 90 hardstandings and 65 statics.

Leisure: ⏃ ⚓ 🅰
Facilities: ⋒⊙🔍✳️⚿♿🛢️🏖️
Services: 🖧🛢️🅿️🛢️◢🔳→∪🏴⊙🔺💧�🧺✉️◢
See advertisement on this page

Not all campsites accept pets.
It is advisable to check at the time of booking.

► ► ► 68% *Purn International Holiday Park (ST332568)*
Bridgwater Rd, Bleadon BS24 0AN
☎ 01934 812342 ▤ 01934 811104
✉ purninternational@snootyfoxresorts.co.uk
ⓦ www.snootyfoxresorts.co.uk
BRONZE
Dir: From Weston-Super-Mare take A370 towards Burnham-on-Sea, site on right by Anchor Inn, about 1m from hospital rdbt
⚑ 🚐 ⚺

Open Mar-Oct (rs Nov-Jan Club & shop restricted opening) Booking advisable Jul-Aug, Etr & bank hols Last arrival mdnt Last departure 10.30hrs
A tree-lined park in a handy position for touring the Somerset coast. The town centre and beaches are only 2 miles away, and the park is well geared towards the family. An 11-acre site with 96 touring pitches and 120 statics.
River with fishing.

Leisure: ⚓ ◆ ⚿
Facilities: ⋔ ⊙ ⚖ ✳ ⚸ ⚐ 🖳 ⚑ 🜖 ⋔
Services: ⚐ ⚙ ⚑ ⚓ ⌷ ⚡ → ∪ ▶ ◎ ⚖ ⚘ ⚞ ⚘
⬤ ▬ ▬ ▨ ▤

► ► ► 77% **West End Farm Caravan & Camping Park (ST354600)**
Locking BS24 8RH
☎ 01934 822529 ▤ 01934 822529
Dir: From M5 junct 21 onto A370. Follow International Helicopter Museum signs. Right at rdbt, follow signs to site
★ 🚐 £12.50-£14.50 🚐 £12.50-£14.50 ⚺ £10-£12.50
Open all year Booking advisable peak periods Last arrival 18.00hrs Last departure noon
A delightful park bordered by hedges, with good landscaping and well-kept facilities. It is handily located next to a helicopter museum, and offers good access to Weston-Super-Mare and the Mendips. A 10-acre site with 75 touring pitches and 20 statics.

Leisure: ◆ ⚿ Facilities: ⋔ ⊙ ⚖ ✳ ⚸ ⚑ ⋔
Services: ⚐ ⚙ ⚑ ⚓ → ∪ ▶ ◎ ⚖ ⚘ ⚞ ⚘

► ► ► 66% **Weston Gateway Caravan Site (ST370621)**
West Wick BS24 7TF ☎ 01934 510344
Dir: From M5 junct 21, take A370 towards Weston-Super-Mare, then immediately take left lane, then 1st left signed Banwell & Westwick, site on right
⚑ 🚐 ⚺

Open Apr-Oct (rs Apr-mid Jun weekends only) Booking advisable Jul-Aug Last arrival 23.00hrs Last departure noon
A pleasant site set amongst trees and shrubs, with quite simple toilet facilities. Site security is very tight, and there is some entertainment, as well as several seasonal pitches. A 15-acre site with 175 touring pitches.

Leisure: ◆ ⚿ Facilities: ⋔ ⊙ ⚖ ✳ ⚸ ⚑ ⋔
Services: ⚐ ⚙ ⚑ ⚓ ⌷ → ∪ ▶ ⚞ ⚘ ⚘
Notes: Families only, no commercial vehicles, no vehicle access after 23.00

► ► ► 77% **Halse Farm Caravan & Camping Park (SS894344)**
TA24 7JL ☎ 01643 851259
▤ 01643 851592
GOLD
ⓔ enquiries@halsefarm.co.uk
ⓦ www.halsefarm.co.uk
Dir: Signed from A396 at Bridgetown. In Winsford turn left and bear left past pub. 1m up hill, entrance on left immediately after cattle grid
🚐 £9-£11 🚐 £9-£11 ⚺ £9-£11

Open 22 Mar-Oct Booking advisable bank hols & mid Jul-Aug Last arrival 22.00hrs Last departure noon
A peaceful little site on Exmoor overlooking a wooded valley with glorious views. This moorland site is quite remote, but it provides good modern toilet facilities which are kept immaculately clean. A 3-acre site with 44 touring pitches, 11 hardstandings.

Leisure: ⚿
Facilities: ⋔ ⊙ ⚖ ✳ ⚸ ⚑ ⋔
Services: ⚐ ⚙ ⚑ ⚓ ⚡ → ∪ ⚘ ⚞
⬤ ▬ ▬ ▨ ▤

► ► ► ► 86% **Waterrow Touring Park (ST053251)**
TA4 2AZ ☎ 01984 623464
▤ 01984 624280
GOLD
ⓦ www.waterrowpark.co.uk
Dir: From M5 junct 25 take A358 (signed Minehead) around Taunton, then B3227 through Wiveliscombe. Site after 3m at Waterrow, 0.25m past Rock Inn
🚐 £11-£16 🚐 £11-£16 ⚺ £11-£16
Open all year Booking advisable bank hols, Jul-Aug Last arrival 20.30hrs Last departure 11.30hrs
A pretty park for adults only with individual pitches and plenty of hardstandings. The River Tone runs along a valley beneath the park, accessed by steps to a nature area created by the owners, where fly fishing is permitted. Painting and photographic workshops are available, and the local pub is a short walk away. A 6-acre site with 45 touring pitches, 27 hardstandings and 1 static.
Fly fishing on River Tone, watercolour painting

Facilities: ⋔ ⊙ ⚖ ✳ ⚸ ⚑ 🜖 ⋔
Services: ⚐ ⚙ ⚑ ⌷ → ⚘ ⚞
Notes: Adults only ⬤ ▬ ▨ ▤

STAFFORDSHIRE

CANNOCK　　　　　　　　　　Map 10 SJ91

▶ ▶ ▶ 79% Camping & Caravanning Club Site
(SK039145)
Old Youth Hostel, Wandon WS15 1QW
☎ 01889 582166
ⓦ www.campingandcaravanningclub.co.uk
Dir: on A460 to Hednesford, right at Rawnsley/
Hazelslade sign, 1st left, site is 0.5m past golf club
★ ⊞ £13.60-£17.80 ⊞ £13.60-£17.80 ▲ £13.60-£17.80
Open Mar-Oct Booking advisable bank hols & Jul-
Aug Last arrival 21.00hrs Last departure noon
Very popular and attractive site in an excellent
location in the heart of the Chase, with gently sloping
ground and timber-built facilities. Walks from the site
into this Area of Outstanding Natural Beauty are a
pleasant feature of this park, just 2.5 miles from
Rugeley. Please see the advertisement on page 11
for information on Club sites and membership.
A 5-acre site with 60 touring pitches,
6 hardstandings.
Facilities: ⎯⊙⎯※⎯⎯⎯
Services: ⎯⎯⎯⎯⎯⎯⎯→∪▶⎯⎯⎯
⎯ ⎯ ⎯ ⎯ ⎯

CHEADLE　　　　　　　　　　Map 10 SK04

▶ ▶ ▶ 79% Quarry Walk Park (SK045405)
Coppice Ln, Croxden Common, Freehay ST10 1RQ
☎ 01538 723412 ⎙ 01538 723495
ⓔ quarry@quarrywalkpark.co.uk
ⓦ www.quarrywalkpark.co.uk
Dir: From A522 (Uttoxeter-Cheadle road) turn at Crown
Inn at Mabberley signed Freehay. In 1m at rdbt by Queen
pub turn to Great Gate. Site signed on right in 1.25m
★ ⊞ £14-£14.50 ⊞ £14-£14.50 ▲£10-£10.50
Open all year Booking advisable bank hols Last
arrival 21.00hrs Last departure noon
A pleasant park in an old quarry with well-screened
pitches, all with water and electricity. Mature trees
and shrubs enhance the peaceful ambience.
Facilities include a small shop and information area,
and family toilets. For children, there is a well
equipped play area while Alton Towers is nearby.
A 14-acre site with 40 touring pitches,
40 hardstandings.
Leisure: ⎯ Facilities: ⎯⊙※⎯⎯⎯⎯
Services: ⎯⎯⎯⎯→⎯

LEEK　　　　　　　　　　　Map 16 SJ95

▶ ▶ ▶ 82% Camping & Caravanning Club Site
(SK008599)
Blackshaw Grange, Blackshaw Moor ST13 8TL
☎ 01538 300285
ⓦ www.campingandcaravanningclub.co.uk
Dir: 2m from Leek on A53 Leek to Buxton road. Site
200yds past sign for 'Blackshaw Moor' on left
★ ⊞ £13.60-£17.80 ⊞ £13.60-£17.80 ▲ £13.60-£17.80
Open all year Booking advisable BH's & peak
periods Last arrival 21.00hrs Last departure noon
A beautifully located club site with well-screened

pitches. The very good facilities are kept in pristine
condition, and children will enjoy the enclosed play
area. Please see the advertisement on page 11 for
information on Club sites and membership. A 6-acre
site with 70 touring pitches, 40 hardstandings.
Leisure: ⎯ Facilities: ⎯⊙⎯※⎯⎯⎯⎯
Services: ⎯⎯⎯⎯⎯⎯⎯→∪▶⎯⎯
⎯ ⎯ ⎯ ⎯ ⎯

OAKAMOOR　　　　　　　　Map 10 SK04

▶ ▶ ▶ 81% The Star Caravan & Camping Park
(SK066456)
Star Rd, Cotton ST10 3DW ☎ 01538 702219
⎙ 01538 703704
ⓦ www.starcaravanpark.co.uk
Dir: 1.25m N of Oakamoor on B5417
★ ⊞ £12-£14 ⊞ £14-£16 ▲ £12-£14

Open Mar-Nov Booking advisable especially for
EHU Last arrival 22.00hrs Last departure noon
This is a well maintained and efficiently managed
grassland park with an open outlook over the
countryside. It is ideally placed for a variety of
outdoor leisure activities including fishing, country
walking and cycling and conveniently located for
Alton Towers. Ye Olde Starr Inn, a traditional
country pub serving good bar meals, is a two
minute walk away. A 25-acre site with
120 touring pitches, 20 hardstandings and 63 statics.
Leisure: ⎯ Facilities: ⎯⊙※⎯⎯⎯⎯
Services: ⎯⎯⎯⎯⎯→ ▶⎯⎯
Notes: Quiet after 23.00, no ground fires/disposable
barbecues, no large groups

SUFFOLK

BECCLES　　　　　　　　　Map 13 TM48

▶ ▶ 78% Beulah Hall Caravan Park (TM478892)
Dairy Ln, Mutford NR34 7QJ ☎ 01502 476609
⎙ 01502 476453
ⓔ carol.stuckey@fsmail.net
Dir: 0.5m from A146, midway between Beccles &
Lowestoft. At Barnby turn off A146 into 'New Road',
turn right at T-junct, park 2nd on right (300yds)
★ ⊞ £8-£10 ⊞ £8-£10 ▲ £8-£10
Open Apr-Oct Booking advisable Jul-Aug Last
arrival 22.00hrs Last departure noon
Small secluded site in well kept grounds with
mature trees and hedging. The neat pitches and

contd.

contd.

pleasant tent area are beneath large trees opposite the swimming pool, and there are clean and well maintained portaloo toilets. A peaceful spot for those wishing to visit the Broads and the Suffolk coast. A 2.5-acre site with 30 touring pitches.

Facilities: ⊓ ⊙ ✻ ⊮

Services: ♨ ⬚ ⬚ ⬚ → ⯈ ⬚ ⬚ ⬚ ⬚

BUNGAY   Map 13 TM38

► ► ► 68% **Outney Meadow Caravan Park** (TM333905)

Outney Meadow NR35 1HG ☎ 01986 892338

🖅 01986 896627

🅔 c.r.hancy@ukgateway.net

🅦 www.outneymeadow.co.uk

Dir: *At Bungay park signed from rdbt junction of A143 & A144*

★ ♨ £11-£15 ♨ £11-£15 ⅄ £11-£15

Open Mar-Oct Booking advisable public hols Last arrival 21.00hrs Last departure 17.00hrs

Three pleasant grassy areas beside the River Waveney, with screened pitches. The toilets are dated but quite functional. The views from the site across the wide flood plain could be straight out of a Constable painting. Canoeing and boating, coarse fishing and cycling are all available here. A 6-acre site with 45 touring pitches, 5 hardstandings and 30 statics.

Fishing, boat, canoe and bike hire.

Facilities: ⊓ ⊙ ⬚ ✻ ⬚ ⬚ ⊮

Services: ♨ ⬚ ⬚ ⬚ ⬚ ⬚ → ⬚ ⯈ ⬚ ⬚ ⬚

Notes: Dogs must be kept on leads

BURY ST EDMUNDS   Map 13 TL86

► ► ► ► 85% **The Dell Touring & Caravan Park** (TL928640)

Beyton Rd, Thurston IP31 3RB ☎ 01359 270121

🖅 01359 270121

🅔 thedellcaravanpark@btinternet.com

Dir: *Signed off A14 at Beyton/Thurston, 4m E of Bury St Edmunds. Also signed off A143 at Barton/Thurston*

★ ♨ £12 ♨ £12 ⅄ £10-£20

Open all year Booking advisable bank hols

A small site with enthusiastic owners which has been developed to a high specification. Set in a quiet spot with lots of mature trees, the quality purpose-built toilet facilities include family rooms, dishwashing and laundry. An ideal base for exploring this picturesque area. More

contd.

The Dell Touring & Caravan Park

improvements are planned. A 6-acre site with 100 touring pitches, 12 hardstandings.

Facilities: ⇥ ⊓ ⊙ ⬚ ✻ ⬚ ⬚ ⊮

Services: ♨ ⬚ ⬚ ⬚ ⬚ ⬚ → ⯈ ⬚

BUTLEY   Map 13 TM35

► ► ► 69% **Forest Camping** (TM355485)

Rendlesham Forest IP12 3NF ☎ 01394 450707

🅔 admin@forestcamping.co.uk

🅦 www.forestcamping.co.uk

Dir: *From junct of A12 with A1152, follow tourist signs to Rendlesham Forest Centre on B1084*

★ ♨ £12.50-£13 ♨ £12.50-£13 ⅄ £12.50-£13

Open Apr-Oct Booking advisable at all times Last arrival 22.00hrs Last departure noon

Set off the beaten track deep in Rendlesham Forest, this peaceful park is in an open grassy area surrounded by pine trees. The facilities are quite good. A 7-acre site with 90 touring pitches.

Leisure: ⋒

Facilities: ⊓ ⊙ ⬚ ✻ ⬚ ⬚ ⬚

Services: ♨ ⬚ ⬚ ⬚ ⬚ ⬚ → ⬚ ⯈

Notes: No fires, dogs must be kept on leads

⬚ ⬚ ⬚ ⬚ ⬚

DUNWICH   Map 13 TM47

► ► 70% **Haw Wood Farm Caravan Park** (TM421717)

Hinton IP17 3QT ☎ 01986 784248

Dir: *Turn right off A12, 1.5m N of Darsham level crossing at Little Chef. Park 0.5m on right*

♨ ♨ ⅄

Open Apr-Oct Booking advisable bank hols, Jul & Aug Last arrival 21.00hrs Last departure noon

An unpretentious family-orientated park set in two large fields surrounded by low hedges. The toilets are clean and functional, and there is plenty of space for children to play. An 8-acre site with 65 touring pitches and 25 statics.

Leisure: ⋒

Facilities: ⊓ ⊙ ✻ ⊮

Services: ♨ → ⬚ ⯈ ⬚ ⬚

> Remember to check your tent or caravan thoroughly before leaving home to ensure everything is in good order.

Facilities: ⇥ Bath ⊓ Shower ⊙ Electric Shaver ⬚ Hairdryer ✻ Ice Pack Facility ⬚ Disabled Facilities ⬚ Public Telephone ⬚ Shop on Site or within 200yds ⬚ Mobile Shop (calls at least 5 days a week) ⬚ BBQ Area ⬚ Picnic Area ⊮ Dog Exercise Area

FELIXSTOWE   Map 13 TM33

▶ ▶ ▶ 71% **Peewit Caravan Park** (TM290338)
Walton Av IP11 2HB ☎ 01394 284511
📠 01473 659824
✉ peewitpark@aol.com
ⓦ www.peewitcaravanpark.co.uk
Dir: Signed from A14 in Felixstowe, 100mtrs past dock gate, first on left
★ ⛟ £9-£16.70 ⛟ £9-£16.70 ▲ £9-£16.70
Open Apr or Etr-Oct Booking advisable school & bank hols Last arrival 21.00hrs Last departure 11.00hrs
A grass touring area fringed by trees, with well-maintained grounds and a colourful floral display. This handy urban site is not overlooked by houses, and the toilet facilities are clean and well cared for. A function room contains a TV and library. The beach is a few minutes away by car. A 3-acre site with 45 touring pitches and 200 statics.
Boules area, bowling green, adventure trail
Leisure: ⚠ **Facilities:** ⬤⊙⚑✳⬤⚒ ⛆ 🛉
Services: ⚙▣🅸⊞→▶⊚⚠⚌⚌♩⚒

IPSWICH   Map 13 TM14

▶ ▶ ▶ ▶ 86% **Priory Park** (TM198409)
IP10 0JT ☎ 01473 727393 & 726373 📠 01473 278372
✉ jwl@priory-park.com
ⓦ www.priory-park.com
Dir: Leave A14 at Ipswich southern by-pass towards town centre. 300mtrs left towards Priory Park. Follow single track road into park
contd.

⛟ £16-£24 ⛟ £16-£24 ▲ £16-£24
Open Apr-Oct (rs Apr-Jun & Sep-Oct limited number of pitches, club/pool closed) Booking advisable at all times Last arrival 18.00hrs Last departure 14.00hrs
A well-screened and very peaceful south-facing park set close to the banks of the tidal River Orwell, and with panoramic views out over the water. The park is attractively landscaped, and offers superb toilet facilities with smartly-tiled, fully-serviced cubicles. A 100-acre site with 75 touring pitches, 59 hardstandings and 260 statics.
9-hole golf, small boat launching, table tennis
Leisure: ⚄ ⚅ ⚠
Facilities: ➔⬤⊙⚑✳⚒ ⬤⛆ 🛉
Services: ⚙▣🅿🅸∅✕→▶⚠⚌♩⚒
Notes: No commercial vehicles, pup tents or group bookings

▶ ▶ ▶ 77% *Low House Touring Caravan Centre* (TM227425)
Bucklesham Rd, Foxhall IP10 0AU
☎ 01473 659437 & 07710 378029 📠 01473 659880
✉ low.house@btopenworld.com
Dir: From A14 south ring road take slip road to A1156 signed East Ipswich. Right in 1m, right again in 0.5m. Site on left
⛟ ⛟ ▲
Open all year Booking advisable Last arrival anytime Last departure 14.00hrs
An appealing, secluded site with immaculate
contd.

Services: ⊤ Toilet Fluid   ✕ Café/ Restaurant   🍟 Fast Food/Takeaway   🍼 Baby Care   ⚡ Electric Hook Up
🚐 Motorvan Service Point   ▣ Launderette   🍺 Licensed Bar   🛢 Calor Gas   ∅ Camping Gaz   ⊞ Battery Charging

facilities and a very caring owner. A beautifully kept garden contains ornamental trees and plants, and there are unusual breeds of rabbits, bantams and guinea fowl. Tents accepted only if room available. A 3.5-acre site with 30 touring pitches.

Leisure: ⚐ **Facilities:** ⬠⊙⊕❄⛴⌂

Services: ⬚🅿️🔌🅱️→∪🅿️◉🗑️🛢️🐾

Notes: Dogs must be kept on leads

KESSINGLAND	Map 13 TM58

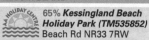 65% *Kessingland Beach Holiday Park (TM535852)*

Beach Rd NR33 7RW
☎ 01502 740636 🖷 01502 740907
Ⓦ www.park-resorts.com
⚐🏕️Å

Open Etr-2 Nov Booking advisable Last arrival mdnt Last departure 10.00hrs
A large holiday centre with direct access onto the beach, and a variety of leisure facilities. The touring area is tucked away from the statics, and served by a clean and functional toilet block. A fish and chip shop and Boat House Restaurant are popular features. A 69-acre site with 90 touring pitches.

Leisure: ⬡ ⬡ ⚬ ⚫ ⚐ **Facilities:** ⬠⊙❄⛴⌂⚿

Services: ⬚🅿️🅱️⚬🔌✕ ⛽→⚬🧺🛢️🐾
🌐 💳 💳 💳 🅿️

▶ ▶ ▶ ▶ 77% **Camping & Caravanning Club Site** (TM520860)
Suffolk Wildlife Park, Whites Ln NR33 7SL
☎ 01502 742040
Ⓦ www.campingandcaravanningclub.co.uk
Dir: On A12 from Lowestoft at Kessingland rdbt, follow Wildlife Park signs, turn right through park entrance
★ 🚐 £13.60-£19.80 🚐 £13.60-£19.80 Å £13.60-£19.80
Open Mar-Oct Booking advisable bank hols & peak period Last arrival 21.00hrs Last departure noon
A well screened open site next to Suffolk Wildlife Park, where concessions are available for visitors. An extensive renovation has created superb facilities, including three family rooms, a disabled unit, and smart reception. A well-equipped laundry and covered dishwashing sinks add to the quality amenities. Please see the advertisement on page 11 for information on Club sites and membership. A 5-acre site with 90 touring pitches.

Leisure: ⚐ **Facilities:** ⬠⊙⊕❄⛴⌂🐎⚿

Services: ⬚🅿️🅱️⚬🅱️Ⓣ→∪🛢️🌐 💳💳💳 🅿️🅿️

▶ ▶ ▶ 81% **Heathland Beach Caravan Park** (TM533877)
London Rd NR33 7PJ ☎ 01502 740337
🖷 01502 742355
Ⓔ heathlandbeach@btinternet.com
Ⓦ www.heathlandbeach.co.uk
Dir: 1m N of Kessingland off A12 onto B1437
★ 🚐 £17-£21 🚐 £17-£21 Å £7-£21
Open Apr-Oct Booking advisable peak periods Last arrival 21.00hrs Last departure 11.00hrs
A well-run and maintained park offering superb toilet facilities. The park is set in meadowland, with

contd.

---

level grass pitches, and mature trees and bushes. There is direct access to the sea and beach, and good provisions for families on site with a heated swimming pool and three play areas. A 5-acre site with 63 touring pitches and 200 statics. Freshwater/sea fishing.

Leisure: ⬡ ⚬ ⚐ **Facilities:** ⬠⊙❄⛴⌂🛢️⌂🐎

Services: ⬚🅿️🅱️🔌⚬→∪🅿️🧺🛢️🐾 **Notes:** 1 dog only per unit 🌐 💳💳💳 🅿️🅿️

LEISTON	Map 13 TM46

▶ ▶ ▶ 77% **Cakes & Ale** (TM432637)
Abbey Ln, Theberton IP16 4TE
☎ 01728 831655 & 01473 736650 🖷 01728 831998
Ⓔ cake.ale@virgin.net
Dir: From Saxmundham E on B1119. 3m follow minor road over level crossing, turn right, after 0.5m straight on at x-roads, entrance 0.5m on left
★ 🚐 £14-£20 🚐 £14-£20 Å £14-£20

contd.

Leisure: 🏊 Indoor swimming pool 🏊 Outdoor swimming pool 🎾 Tennis court 🎱 Games room ⛼ Children's playground ∪ Stables
▶ 9/18 hole golf course 🚣 Boats for hire 🎬 Cinema 🎣 Fishing ◎ Mini golf ⚓ Watersports 📺 Separate TV room

England

Open Apr-Oct (rs low season club, shop & reception limited hours) Booking advisable public & school hols Last arrival 20.00hrs Last departure 13.00hrs
A large, well spread out site with many trees and bushes on a former Second World War airfield. The spacious touring area includes plenty of hardstandings and super pitches, and there is a good bar and a well-maintained toilet block. A 5-acre site with 50 touring pitches, 50 hardstandings and 200 statics.
Tennis, 5-acre recreation ground, driving range & net
Leisure: ？ ⋀ Facilities: ➡ ⋔ ☉ ⍾ ✷ ☾ ⛤ 🐾
Services: ▣ ⬒ ℧ ⅃ ℰ ∅ → ∪ ♨ ✦ Notes: No group bookings, no noise between 21.00-08.00
⬛ ⬛ ⬛ ⬛ ⬛

LOWESTOFT
See **Kessingland**

POLSTEAD　　　　　　　　　　　Map 13 TL93

▶ ▶ ▶ ▶ **83% Polstead Touring Park (TL986480)**
Holt Rd CO6 5BZ ☎ 01787 211969 📄 01787 211969
Ⓦ www.polsteadtouring.co.uk
Dir: 150yds off A1071 between Boxford & Hadleigh, opposite Brewers Arms Inn, 1m N of Polstead
★ 🚐 £11-£13 🚙 £11-£13 ⛺ £8-£11

Open all year Booking advisable Jul & Aug Last arrival 22.30hrs Last departure noon
A gradually maturing and immaculately maintained site in the heart of unspoilt Suffolk countryside close to Lavenham and Sudbury, and near the distinctive high water tower. A well-equipped purpose-built toilet block provides very spacious showers, and the sheltered pitches are attractively laid out. The site is for adults only. A 2.5-acre site with 30 touring pitches, 24 hardstandings.
Rally field
Facilities: ⋔ ☉ ⍾ ✷ ⅋ ☾ ⛤ 🐾
Services: ▣ ⬒ ∅ ⊞ ⊤ → ∪ ▶ ⅃ ▤
Notes: Adults only

SAXMUNDHAM　　　　　　　　Map 13 TM36

▶ ▶ ▶ **73% Whitearch Touring Caravan Park (TM379610)**
Main Rd, Benhall IP17 1NA
☎ 01728 604646 & 603773
Dir: At junct of A12 & B1121
★ 🚐 fr £12 🚙 fr £12 ⛺ fr £10
Open Apr-Oct Booking advisable bank hols Last arrival 20.45hrs
contd.

A small, maturing park set around an attractive coarse-fishing lake, with decent toilet facilities and secluded pitches tucked away among trees and shrubs. The park is popular with anglers. There is some traffic noise from the adjacent A12.
A 14.5-acre site with 50 touring pitches.
Fishing lake, tennis courts
Leisure: ？ ⋀ Facilities: ⋔ ☉ ⍾ ✷ ⅋ ☾ ⛤ ⛫ 🐾
Services: ▣ ▤ ⬒ ∅ → ⅃ Notes: No cars by caravans

▶ ▶ **68% *Carlton Park Caravan Park (TM383632)***
Carlton Park IP17 1AT ☎ 01728 604413
Dir: Turn off A12 at sign for Carlton Park Ind Est, park is adjacent
🚐 🚙 ⛺
Open Etr or Apr-Oct Booking advisable
Set in the grounds of a sports club on the edge of Saxmundham, and sharing the club's toilet facilities. The gently-sloping touring field is well trimmed and tidy. A 6.5-acre site with 75 touring pitches.
Leisure: ？ ⋀ Facilities: ⋔ ☉
Services: ▣ → ⅋

▶ ▶ **78% Marsh Farm Caravan Site (TM385608)**
Sternfield IP17 1HW ☎ 01728 602168
Dir: From A12 take A1094 Aldeburgh road, at Snape x-roads turn left signed Sternfield, follow signs to farm
🚐 🚙 ⛺
Open all year Booking advisable Jun-Aug Last arrival 21.00hrs Last departure 17.00hrs
A very pretty site overlooking reed-fringed lakes which offer excellent coarse fishing. The facilities are very well maintained, and the park is a truly peaceful haven. A 30-acre site with 45 touring pitches.
Fishing lakes
Facilities: ⋔ ✷ ⅋ ⛤ ⛫ 🐾
Services: ▣ ⊞ → ∪ ▶ ♨ ⅃
Notes: Dogs must be kept on leads

SHOTTISHAM　　　　　　　　　Map 13 TM34

▶ **66% *St Margaret's House (TM323447)***
Hollesley Rd IP12 3HD ☎ 01394 411247
🅐 ken.norton@virgin.net
Dir: Turn off B1083 at village. Site in 150yds on left past Sorrel House pub
🚐 🚙 ⛺
Open Apr or Etr-Oct Booking advisable bank hols & Jul-Aug Last arrival 22.00hrs Last departure noon
A pleasant little family-run site in an attractive village setting beside the church. This lovely peaceful site is in an ideal position for touring the Suffolk coast. A 3-acre site with 30 touring pitches.
Milk & newspapers to order.
Facilities: ⋔ ☉ ✷
Services: ▣ ⬒ ∅ ⊞ ⊤ → ∪ ▶ ♨ ⅃ ▤ ⅋

SUDBURY　　　　　　　　　　　Map 13 TL84

▶ ▶ ▶ **76% Willowmere Caravan Park (TL886388)**
Bures Rd, Little Cornard CO10 0NN ☎ 01787 375559
Dir: 1.5m S of Sudbury on B1508 Bures road
★ 🚐 £10-£12 🚙 £10-£12 ⛺ £8-£12
Open Etr-Sep Booking advisable bank hols Last arrival any Last departure noon
contd.

A pleasant little site in a quiet location tucked away beyond a tiny residential static area, offering spotless facilities. A 3-acre site with 40 touring pitches and 9 statics.
Fishing

Facilities: ⎛⊙⚹⚹⚹

Services: ⎕⎕→∪⏵⊙⚹⚹⚹

WOODBRIDGE	Map 13 TM24

PREMIER PARK

▶ ▶ ▶ ▶ ▶ 92% **Moon & Sixpence**
(TM263454)
Newbourn Rd, Waldringfield IP12 4PP
☎ 01473 736650 📠 01473 736270
📧 moonsix@dircon.co.uk
🌐 www.moonsix.dircon.co.uk
Dir: Follow caravan & Moon & Sixpence signs from A12 Ipswich (East bypass). Turn left at x-roads 1.5m from A12
🚐 £16-£24 🚐 £16-£24 ⛺ £16-£24
Open Apr-Oct (rs low season club, shop, reception open limited hours) Booking advisable school & bank hols Last arrival 20.00hrs Last departure noon
A well-planned site, with tourers occupying a sheltered valley position around an attractive boating lake with a sandy beach. Toilet facilities are housed in a smart Norwegian cabin, and there is a laundry and dishwashing area. Leisure facilities include two tennis courts, a bowling green, fishing, boating and a games room.
contd.

There is an adult-only area, and a strict no groups and no noise after 9pm policy. A 5-acre site with 65 touring pitches and 225 statics. Lake, cycle trail, 10-acre sports area, 9-hole golf

Leisure: ⚹ ⚹ ⚹ **Facilities:** ⚹⎛⊙⚹⚹⚹⚹⚹⚹⚹

Services: ⎕⎕⎕⎕⎕⎕⚹⚹✕→⏵⎕⚹⚹

Notes: No group bookings or commercial vehicles. Quiet 21.00-08.00 💳 💳

▶ ▶ 83% **Moat Barn Touring Caravan Park**
(TM269530)
Dallinghoo Rd, Bredfield IP13 6BD
☎ 01473 737520
🌐 www.moat-barn.co.uk
Dir: Turn off A12 at Bredfield, take 1st right at village pump. Through village, 1m site on left
★ 🚐 fr £12 🚐 fr £12 ⛺ fr £12
Open Mar-15 Jan Booking advisable bank hols Last arrival 22.00hrs Last departure noon
An attractive small park set in idyllic Suffolk countryside, ideally located for touring the heritage coastline and Sutton Hoo. The modern toilet block is well equipped and maintained. Bed and breakfast and cycle hire are available, but there are no facilities for children. A 2-acre site with 25 touring pitches.

Facilities: ⎛⊙⚹⚹

Services: ⎕⎕→∪⏵⚹⎕

Notes: No ball games, breathable groundsheets only, dogs on leads

---

Facilities: ⎘ Bath ⎛ Shower ⊙ Electric Shaver ⎘ Hairdryer ⚹ Ice Pack Facility ⎍ Disabled Facilities ⎍ Public Telephone ⎍ Shop on Site or within 200yds ⎍ Mobile Shop (calls at least 5 days a week) ⎍ BBQ Area ⎍ Picnic Area ⎍ Dog Exercise Area

England

SURREY

CHERTSEY   Map 06 TQ06

▶ ▶ ▶ 87% Camping & Caravanning Club Site
(TQ052667)
Bridge Rd KT16 8JX ☎ 01932 562405
Ⓦ www.campingandcaravanningclub.co.uk
*Dir: M25 junct 11, follow A317 to Chertsey. At rdbt take
1st exit to lights. Straight over at next lights. Turn right
400yds turn left into site*
★ ⚑ £16.20-£20.60 ⚑ £16.20-£20.60
🛆 £16.20-£20.60
Open all year Booking advisable bank hols & peak
period Last arrival 21.00hrs Last departure noon
*A pretty Thames-side site set amongst trees and
shrubs in well-tended grounds, ideally placed for
the M3/M25 and for visiting London. Some
attractive riverside pitches are very popular, and
fishing and boating is allowed from the site on the
river. The toilet facilities are very good. Please see
the advertisement on page 11 for information on
Club sites and membership. A 12-acre site with
200 touring pitches, 65 hardstandings.*

Leisure: ⚓ ⚕

Facilities: ♠ ⊙ ⚑ ✳ ♿ 🚻 🛒 🐶

Services: 🔌 💌 🗑 🛢 🖉 🚽 🕾 → ∪ ▶ 🔧 🎿 🛠
🔳 🔳 🔳 🔳 🔳

EAST HORSLEY   Map 06 TQ05

▶ ▶ ▶ ▶ 74% Camping & Caravanning Club Site
(TQ083552)
Ockham Rd North KT24 6PE ☎ 01483 283273
Ⓦ www.campingandcaravanningclub.co.uk
*Dir: M25 junct 10, proceed S & take 1st major turn
signed Ockham, Southend & Ripley, then left & site
2.5m on right. From S take A3 past Guildford & turn off
towards Ripley on B2215*
★ ⚑ £13.60-£19.80 ⚑ £13.60-£19.80
🛆 £13.60-£19.80
Open Mar-Oct Booking advisable bank hols & peak
period Last arrival 21.00hrs Last departure noon
*A beautiful lakeside site with plenty of trees and
shrubs and separate camping fields, providing a
tranquil base within easy reach of London. Toilet
facilities are well maintained and clean. Please see
the advertisement on page 11 for information on
Club sites and membership. A 9.5-acre site with
130 touring pitches, 41 hardstandings.*

Leisure: ⚓ ⚕

Facilities: ♠ ⊙ ⚑ ✳ ♿ 🛒 🐶

Services: 🔌 💌 🗑 🛢 🖉 🚽 🕾 → ∪ ▶ 🛆 🎿 🛠
🔳 🔳 🔳 🔳 🔳

All of the campsites in this directory
are inspected annually by a team of
experienced inspectors

SUSSEX, EAST

BATTLE   Map 07 TQ71

▶ ▶ ▶ 74% Brakes Coppice Park (TQ765134)
Forewood Ln TN33 9AB ☎ 01424 830322
Ⓔ brakesco@btinternet.com
Ⓦ www.brakescoppicepark.co.uk
*Dir: From Battle on A2100 towards Hastings. After 2m
turn right for Crowhurst. Site 1m on left*
★ ⚑ £12-£13.75 ⚑ £12-£13.75 🛆 £12-£13.75

Open Mar-Oct Booking advisable public hols & Jul-
Aug Last arrival 21.30hrs Last departure noon
*Secluded farm site in meadow surrounded by
woodland with small stream and fishing lake, and a
raised garden in the centre. Pitches are neatly laid
out on a terrace, and tents are pitched on grass
edged by woodland. A 3-acre site with 30 touring
pitches, 10 hardstandings.*
Fishing

Leisure: ⚕

Facilities: ♠ ⊙ ⚑ ✳ 🛒 🐶 ♿

Services: 🔌 🗑 🛢 🖉 🚽 🕾 → ∪ ▶ 🎿 🔳 🔳 🔳

CROWBOROUGH   Map 06 TQ53

▶ ▶ ▶ 81% Camping & Caravanning Club Site
(TQ520315)
Goldsmith Recreation Ground TN6 2TN
☎ 01892 664827
Ⓦ www.campingandcaravanningclub.co.uk
*Dir: Turn off A26 into entrance to 'Goldsmiths Ground',
signed Leisure Centre. At top of road right onto site lane*
★ ⚑ £13.60-£17.80 ⚑ £13.60-£17.80
🛆 £13.60-£17.80
Open Mar-Dec Booking advisable bank hols & peak
period Last arrival 21.00hrs Last departure noon
*A spacious terraced site with stunning views across
the Weald to the North Downs in Kent. This good
quality site has clean, modern toilets, a kitchen and
eating area for campers, a recreation room, and
good provision of hard standings. An excellent
leisure centre is adjacent to the park. Please see the
advertisement on page 11 for information on Club
sites and membership. A 13-acre site with 90
touring pitches, 26 hardstandings.*

Leisure: ⚓ Facilities: ♠ ⊙ ⚑ ✳ ♿ 🛒 🐶

Services: 🔌 💌 🗑 🛢 🖉 🚽 🕾 → ∪ ▶ 🎿 🛠
🔳 🔳 🔳 🔳 🔳

Services: 🚽 Toilet Fluid ✖ Café/ Restaurant 🍟 Fast Food/Takeaway 🍼 Baby Care 🔌 Electric Hook Up
💌 Motorvan Service Point 🗑 Launderette 🍺 Licensed Bar 🛢 Calor Gaz 🖉 Camping Gaz 🔋 Battery Charging

FURNER'S GREEN
Map 06 TQ42

▶ ▶ 76% **Heaven Farm** (TQ403264)
TN22 3RG ☎ 01825 790226 📠 01825 790881
🌐 www.heavenfarm.co.uk
Dir: On A275 between Lewes and East Grinstead, 1m N of Sheffield Park Gardens
★ 🚐 fr £11 🚐 fr £11 ▲ fr £11
Open Apr-Oct (rs Nov-Mar caravans only allowed on concrete area) Booking advisable Last arrival 21.00hrs Last departure noon
Delightful small rural site on a popular farm complex incorporating a farm museum, craft shop, tea room and nature trail. Good clean facilities in well-converted outbuildings. A 1.5-acre site with 25 touring pitches.
Fishing, nature trail

Facilities: �📶⊙❋🕭🚾👪🗛🛏

Services: 🔌✕→∪▶🌙

Notes: Prefer no children between 6-18yrs

HASTINGS & ST LEONARDS
Map 07 TQ80

▶ ▶ 74% **Shearbarn Holiday Park** (TQ842112)
Barley Ln TN35 5DX
☎ 01424 423583 📠 01424 718740
🅑 shearbarn@haulfryn.co.uk
🌐 www.shearbarn.co.uk
Dir: From A259 to Rye-Folkstone, right at Stables Theatre into Harold Rd, right into Gurth Rd, left at end into Barley Lane. Site signed
🚐🚐▲
Open Apr-Oct Booking advisable bank hols Last arrival 21.00hrs Last departure noon
A large touring area set away from the statics and clubhouse on a hill high above Hastings with good views. Pitches are spacious, and good planting provides shade and shelter. Children will enjoy the many playgrounds and sandpits, as well as the amusement arcade and other entertainments. A 16-acre site with 400 touring pitches.

Leisure: 🔴 ⚆ **Facilities:** 📶⊙❋🕭🚾👪🗛🛏

Services: 🔌🍴🛇⌀🕛✕♨→⊙△👪🌙🍴🎦▦🏧🎣

SILVER

HEATHFIELD
Map 06 TQ52

▶ ▶ 72% **Greenviews Caravan Park** (TQ605223)
Burwash Rd, Broad Oak TN21 8RT
☎ 01435 863531 📠 01435 863531
Dir: Through Heathfield on A265 for 1m. Site on left after Broad Oak sign
🚐🚐▲
Open Apr-Oct (rs Mar-Apr & Oct-Dec bookings only, subject to weather) Booking advisable Jul-Aug Last arrival 22.00hrs Last departure 10.30hrs
A small touring area adjoining a residential park, with a smart clubhouse. The facility block includes a room for disabled visitors. The owners always offer a friendly welcome, and they take pride in the lovely flower beds which adorn the park. A 3-acre site with 10 touring pitches and 51 statics.

Facilities: 📶⊙❋🕭

Services: 🔌🍴🍴🛇⌀ **Notes:** 🐾

HORAM
Map 06 TQ51

▶ ▶ ▶ 76% **Horam Manor Touring Park** (TQ579170)
TN21 0YD ☎ 01435 813662
🅑 camp@horam-manor.co.uk
🌐 www.horam-manor.co.uk
Dir: On A267, 3m S of Heathfield and 10m N of Eastbourne
★ 🚐 £13.50 🚐 £13.50 ▲ £13.50
Open Mar-Oct Booking advisable peak periods Last arrival 22.00hrs Last departure 18.00hrs
A well landscaped park in a peaceful location on former estate land, set in gently-sloping grassland surrounded by woods and fishing lakes. There is free entry to nearby nature trails and a farm museum for site visitors. A 7-acre site with 90 touring pitches.
Parent and toddler room

Leisure: 🔴 ⚆ **Facilities:** 📶⊙❋🕭🚾👪🗛🛏

Services: 🔌🛇⌀🕛→∪▶🌙

PEVENSEY
Map 06 TQ60

▶ ▶ ▶ 77% **Camping & Caravanning Club Site** (TQ682055)
Norman's Bay BN24 6PR ☎ 01323 761190
🌐 www.campingandcaravanningclub.co.uk
Dir: From rdbt junct of A27/A259 follow A259 signed Eastbourne. In Pevensey Bay village take 1st left signed Beachlands only. 1.25m site on left
★ 🚐 £13.60-£19.80 🚐 £13.60-£19.80 ▲ £13.60-£19.80
Open Mar-Oct Booking advisable bank hols & peak period Last arrival 21.00hrs Last departure noon
A well kept site with immaculate toilet block, right beside the sea. This popular family park enjoys good rural views towards Rye and Pevensey. Please see the advertisement on page 11 for information on Club sites and membership. A 13-acre site with 200 touring pitches, 5 hardstandings.

Leisure: 🔴 ⚆ **Facilities:** 📶⊙🔧❋🕭🚾👪🗛🛏

Services: 🔌🛒🍴🛇⌀🕛🕛→⊙△🚾
🍴🏧▦▧🎣🔲

PEVENSEY BAY
Map 06 TQ60

▶ ▶ ▶ 76% **Bay View Park** (TQ648028)
Old Martello Rd BN24 6DX
☎ 01323 768688 📠 01323 769637
🅑 holidays@bay-view.co.uk
🌐 www.bay-view.co.uk
Dir: Signed from A259 W of Pevensey Bay. On sea side of A259 along private road towards beach
★ 🚐 £12-£15 🚐 £12-£15 ▲ £11-£12
Open Etr-Oct Booking advisable bank & school hols Last arrival 22.00hrs Last departure noon
A pleasant well-run site just yards from the beach, in an area east of the town centre known as 'The Crumbles'. The level grassy site is very well maintained. A 6-acre site with 79 touring pitches, 9 hardstandings.

Leisure: ⚆ **Facilities:** 📶⊙🔧❋🕭🚾

Services: 🔌🛇⌀🕛→▶⊙△👪🌙

Notes: Couples & families only, no commercial vehicles 🍴▦🏧🎣🔲

GOLD

Leisure: 🏊 Indoor swimming pool 🏊 Outdoor swimming pool ⚆ Tennis court 🔴 Games room ⚆ Children's playground ∪ Stables
▶ 9/18 hole golf course 🚣 Boats for hire 🎦 Cinema 🎣 Fishing ⊙ Mini golf △ Watersports 🔲 Separate TV room

England

SUSSEX, WEST

NEW ► ► ► 84% **Sumners Ponds Fishery & Campsite (TQ125268)**
Chapel Rd RH13 0PR ☎ 01403 732539
Dir: From A272 at Coolham x-rds, N towards Barnes Green. In 1.5m take 1st left at small x-rds. 1m, over level crossing. Site on left just after right bend
🚐 Å
Open all year
A newly created touring area on a working farm on the edge of the quiet village of Barnes Green, with purpose built facilities of a high standard. There are three well-stocked fishing lakes set in attractive surroundings, and a woodland walk with direct access to miles of footpaths. Horsham and Brighton are within easy reach. A 4-acre site with 57 touring pitches.
Facilities: 🛈

► ► 71% **Limeburners Arms Camp Site (TQ072255)**
Lordings Rd, Newbridge RH14 9JA ☎ 01403 782311
🖃 limeburners.campingltd@virgin.net
Dir: From A29 turn W onto A272 for 1m, then left onto B2133. Site 300yds on left
🚐 🚐 Å

Open Apr-Oct Booking advisable bank hols & Jul-Aug Last arrival 22.00hrs Last departure 14.00hrs
A secluded site in rural West Sussex, at the rear of the Limeburners Arms public house, and surrounded by fields. It makes a pleasant base for touring the South Downs and the Arun Valley. The toilets are basic but very clean. A 2.75-acre site with 40 touring pitches.
Leisure: ⋔ **Facilities:** 🛈 ⊕ ✻ ⌕
Services: 🚰 ⇄ 🖉 🖟 🖄 ✕ → ∪ ► 🛒
💳 📷 📷 📷 📷

► ► ► 76% **Ellscott Park (SU829995)**
Sidlesham Ln, Birdham PO20 7QL
☎ 01243 512003 🖨 01243 512003
🖃 camping@ellscottpark.co.uk
🖰 www.ellscottpark.co.uk
Dir: Take A286 Chichester/Wittering road for approx 4m, left at Butterfly Farm sign, site 500yds right
★ 🚐 £10-£14 🚐 £10-£14 Å £8-£11

contd.

Open Mar-Oct Booking advisable bank hols & Aug
A well-kept park set in meadowland behind the owners' nursery and van storage area. The park attracts a peace-loving clientele, and is handy for the beach and other local attractions. Home-grown produce and eggs are for sale. A 2.5-acre site with 50 touring pitches.
Leisure: ⋔ **Facilities:** 🛈 ⊕ ✻ ⌕ 🛒 🐾
Services: 🚰 🖟 🖉 🖄 → ∪ ► ⌕ ✤ 🖉 🛒

► ► ► ► 83% **Honeybridge Park (TQ152183)**
Honeybridge Ln RH13 8NX
☎ 01403 710923 🖨 01403 710923
🖃 enquiries@honeybridgepark.co.uk
🖰 www.honeybridgepark.co.uk
Dir: 10m S of Horsham on A24. Turn left 1m past Dial Post sign at Old Barn Nurseries, park 300yds on right
★ 🚐 £15-£20 🚐 £15-£20 Å £13-£18

GOLD

Open all year Booking advisable bank hols & high season Last arrival 22.00hrs Last departure 20.00hrs
An attractive and very popular park on gently-sloping ground surrounded by hedgerows and mature trees. A comprehensive amenities building houses upmarket toilet facilities including luxury family and disabled rooms, as well as a laundry, shop, takeaway and off-licence. There are plenty of hardstandings and electric hook-ups, and an excellent children's play area includes an aerial runway and other adventure equipment. A 15-acre site with 200 touring pitches, 75 hardstandings and 50 statics.
Holiday lodges
Leisure: ⦁ ⋔ **Facilities:** ➔ 🛈 ⊕ 🖳 ✻ ⌕ ⌕ 🛒 🐾
Services: 🚰 🖳 🖟 🖉 🖄 🖄 ➔ ∪ ► 🛒 🖉
Notes: No groups of under 18s 💳 📷 📷 🇬

FORD
Map 06 SU90

▶ ▶ 73% **Ship & Anchor Marina** (TQ002040)
Station Rd BN18 0BJ
☎ 01243 551262 🗎 01243 555256
✉ ysm36@dial.pipex.com
Dir: From A27 at Arundel take road S signed Ford. Site is 2m on left after level crossing
★ ⚑ £11.50-£14.50 ⚑ £11.50-£14.50 ▲ £11.50-£14.50
Open Mar-Oct Last arrival 21.00hrs Last departure noon
A neat and tidy site in a pleasant position beside the Ship & Anchor pub and the tidal River Arun. There are good walks from the site both to Arundel and to the coast. A 12-acre site with 160 touring pitches. River fishing from site

Leisure: ⚑ Facilities: ➡ ⚑ ☉ ☜ ✳ ⅋ ⅃ ⅃ ⅃
Services: ⚑ ⅀ ⅃ ⅃ ⅃ ⅃ ✗ → ∪ ⅃ ◉ ⅃ ⅃ ⅃ ⅃
⅃ ⅃ ⅃ ⅃

GRAFFHAM
Map 06 SU91

▶ ▶ ▶ 77% **Camping & Caravanning Club Site** (SU941187)
Great Bury GU28 0QJ ☎ 01798 867476
🌐 www.campingandcaravanningclub.co.uk
Dir: From Petworth on A285 pass Badgers pub on left & BP garage on right. Next right signed Selham Graffham. Follow sign to site
★ ⚑ £13.60-£17.80 ⚑ £13.60-£17.80 ▲ £13.60-£17.80
Open Mar-Oct Booking advisable bank hols & peak period Last arrival 21.00hrs Last departure noon
A superb woodland site with some pitches occupying their own private, naturally-screened areas. A peaceful retreat, or base for touring the South Downs, Chichester and the south coast. Please see the advertisement on page 11 for information on Club sites and membership. A 20-acre site with 90 touring pitches.

Facilities: ⅃ ☉ ⅃ ✳ ⅃ ⅃ ⅃
Services: ⚑ ⅃ ⅃ ⅃ ⅃ ⅃ → ∪ ⅃ ⅃ ⅃ ⅃ ⅃ ⅃ ⅃ ⅃ ⅃

HORSHAM
See **Barns Green & Dial Post**

LITTLEHAMPTON
Map 06 TQ00

▶ ▶ ▶ 80% **White Rose Touring Park** (TQ029039)
Mill Ln, Wick BN17 7PH ☎ 01903 716176
🗎 01903 732671
✉ snowdondavid@hotmail.com
🌐 www.whiterosetouringpark.co.uk
Dir: From A27 take A284 turn left into Mill Lane, after approx 1.5m just after Six Bells Pub.
★ ⚑ £12-£18 ⚑ £12-£14 ▲ £12-£14
Open 15 Mar-14 Dec Booking advisable bank hols & Jul-Aug Last arrival 22.00hrs Last departure noon
Farmland surrounds this carefully maintained site located on well-drained ground close to Arundel and Littlehampton. The family-run site offers a choice of super pitches and mini pitches for tents, and there is good hedging and landscaping. A 7-acre site with 127 touring pitches and 13 statics.

Leisure: ⚑ Facilities: ⅃ ☉ ⅃ ✳ ⅃ ⅃ ⅃ ⅃
Services: ⚑ ⅃ ⅃ ⅃ ⅃ ⅃ ⅃ → ∪ ⅃ ⅃ ◉ ⅃ ⅃ ⅃ ⅃
⅃ ⅃ ⅃ ⅃ ⅃

SELSEY
Map 05 SZ89

78% **Warner Farm Touring Park** (SZ845939)
Warner Ln, Selsey PO20 9EL
☎ 01243 608440 & 604499 🗎 01243 604095
✉ touring@bunnleisure.co.uk
🌐 www.bunnleisure.co.uk
Dir: Turn right onto School Lane & follow signs
★ ⚑ £16.50-£28.50 ⚑ £16.50-£28.50
▲ £14.50-£26.50

Open Mar-Oct Booking advisable 4 wks prior to arrival Last arrival 20.00hrs Last departure 10.00hrs
A well-screened touring site adjoining the three static parks under the same ownership. A courtesy bus runs around the complex to entertainment areas and supermarkets. The park backs onto open grassland, and the leisure facilities with bar, amusements and bowling
contd.

England

alley, and swimming pool/sauna complex are also accessible to tourers. A 10-acre site with 250 touring pitches, 60 hardstandings and 1500 statics.

Leisure: ◈ ◈ ◈ ◈ ◈ ⌂
Facilities: ◈ ⊙ ◈ ◈ ◈ ◈ ◈ ◈ ◈ ◈
Services: ◈ ◈ ◈ ◈ ◈ ⊙ ◈ ✕ ◈ → ∪ ◈ ◈ ◈ ◈ ◈
◈ ◈ ◈ ◈ ◈ ◈

See advertisement on page 211

SLINDON   **Map 06 SU90**

▶ 80% **Camping & Caravanning Club Site (SU958084)**
Slindon Park BN18 0RG ☎ 01243 814387
Ⓦ www.campingandcaravanningclub.co.uk
Dir: From A27 Fontwell to Chichester turn right at sign for Brittons Lane & 2nd right to Slindon. Site on this road
★ ◈ £9.90-£11.40 ◈ £9.90-£11.40
▲ £9.90-£11.40
Open Mar-Oct Booking advisable bank hols & peak period Last arrival 21.00hrs Last departure noon
A beautiful former orchard, completely screened by National Trust trees, and very quiet. It is ideal for the self-contained camper, and own sanitary facilities are essential. The entrance gate is narrow and on a bend, and touring units are advised to take a wide sweep on approach from private gravel roadway. Please see the advertisement on page 11 for information on Club sites and membership. A 2-acre site with 40 touring pitches.

Facilities: ✳ ◈ ◈ ◈
Services: ◈ ◈ ◈ ◈ ◈ ◈ → ∪ ◈ ◈
◈ ◈ ◈ ◈ ◈

SOUTHBOURNE   **Map 05 SU70**

▶ ▶ ▶ 79% **Camping & Caravanning Club Site (SU774056)**
Main Rd PO10 8JH ☎ 01243 373202
Ⓦ www.campingandcaravanningclub.co.uk
Dir: From Chichester take A259 to Southampton, site on right past Inlands Rd
★ ◈ £16.10-£19.80 ◈ £16.10-£19.80
▲ £16.10-£19.80
Open Feb-Nov Booking advisable bank hols & peak periods Last arrival 21.00hrs Last departure noon
Situated in open meadow and orchard, a very pleasant, popular site with well looked after, clean facilities. Well placed for Chichester, South Downs and the ferry ports. Please see the advertisement on page 11 for information on Club sites and membership. A 3-acre site with 58 touring pitches, 42 hardstandings.

Facilities: ◈ ⊙ ◈ ✳ ◈ ◈ ◈
Services: ◈ ◈ ◈ ◈ ◈ ◈ → ◈
◈ ◈ ◈ ◈ ◈

┌─────────────────────────────────────┐
│ The number of touring pitches listed for │
│ each site includes tents, caravans and │
│   motorvans.   │
└─────────────────────────────────────┘

WEST WITTERING   **Map 05 SZ79**

▶ ▶ ▶ 79% **Wicks Farm Holiday Park (SZ796995)**
Redlands Ln PO20 8QD
☎ 01243 513116 🗎 01243 511296
🅔 wicks.farm@virgin.net
Ⓦ www.wicksfarm.co.uk
Dir: From Chichester take A286/B2179 to West Wittering. Follow for 6m and 2nd right after Lamb Inn
◈ ▲
Open 14 Mar-Oct Booking advisable peak periods Last arrival 21.00hrs Last departure noon
A pleasant rural site, well screened by trees and with good clean toilet facilities. The park has a spacious recreation field, and good local walks, with the beach just 2m away. A 14-acre site with 40 touring pitches.

Leisure: ◈ ◈ **Facilities:** ◈ ⊙ ◈ ✳ ◈ ◈ ◈
Services: ◈ ◈ ◈ ◈ ◈ ◈ → ◈ ◈ ◈ ◈
Notes: No touring caravans ◈ ◈ ◈ ◈ ◈

TYNE & WEAR

SOUTH SHIELDS   **Map 21 NZ36**

▶ ▶ ▶ 66% *Lizard Lane Caravan & Camping Site (NZ399648)*
Lizard Ln NE34 7AB ☎ 0191 454 4982 & 455 7411 🗎 0191 427 0469
Dir: 2m S of town centre on A183 (Sunderland road)
◈ ◈ ▲
Open Mar-Oct Booking advisable for complete wks Jul-5 Sep Last arrival anytime Last departure 11.00hrs
A well-kept site on sloping ground near the beach, not far from the city of Sunderland with its many attractions. A 2-acre site with 45 touring pitches and 70 statics.
9-hole putting green

Leisure: ◈ **Facilities:** ◈ ⊙ ◈ ✳ ◈ ◈ ◈ ◈
Services: ◈ ◈ ◈ ◈ → ∪ ◈ ◈ ◈ ◈ ◈ ◈ ◈

▶ ▶ ▶ 71% *Sandhaven Caravan & Camping Park (NZ376672)*
Bents Park Rd NE33 2NL
☎ 0191 454 5594 & 455 7411 🗎 0191 455 7411
Dir: On A183, 0.5m from town centre with entrance on Bents Park Rd
◈ ◈ ▲
Open Mar-Oct Booking advisable for complete wks Jul-5 Sep Last arrival anytime Last departure 11.00hrs
A delightful park setting with flowerbeds and trees, close to a beach and boating lake which make this an ideal holiday base. Tents have their own hedged area amongst cherry trees, and the good portakabin facilities are clean and well located. Plenty of attractions locally include the Catherine Cookson festival, the Souter lighthouse, and an Anglo-Saxon farm. A 3.5-acre site with 75 touring pitches and 50 statics.

Facilities: ◈ ⊙ ◈ ✳ ◈ ◈ ◈ ◈
Services: ◈ ◈ ◈ → ∪ ◈ ◈ ◈ ◈ ◈

WARWICKSHIRE

ASTON CANTLOW   Map 10 SP16

► ► ► **77% Island Meadow Caravan
Park** (SP137596)
The Mill House B95 6JP
☎ 01789 488273 📠 01789 488273
🅔 holiday@islandmeadowcaravanpark.co.uk
🆆 www.islandmeadowcaravanpark.co.uk
*Dir: From A46 or A3400 for Aston Cantlow. Park 0.25m
W off Mill Lane*
★ 🚐 fr £15 🚐 fr £15 ▲ fr £12
Open Mar-Oct Booking advisable peak periods Last
arrival 21.00hrs Last departure noon
*A small well-kept site bordered by the River Alne on
one side and its mill stream on the other. Mature
willows line the banks, and this is a very pleasant
place to relax and unwind. A 7-acre site with
24 touring pitches, 14 hardstandings and 56 statics.
Free fishing for guests.*
Facilities: ♠ ⊙ ⊕ ✳ & ⚟ ⛾ 🖛
Services: 🚐 🛢 ⌀ ⊞ 🗔 → ▶ ◎ ♪

KINGSBURY   Map 10 SP29

► ► ► ► **85% Camping & Caravanning Club Site**
(SP202968)
Kingsbury Water Park, Bodymoor,
Heath Ln B76 0DY ☎ 01827 874101
🆆 www.campingandcaravanningclub.co.uk
*Dir: From M42 junct 9 take B4097 Kingsbury road. Left
at rdbt, past main entrance to water park, over
motorway, take next right. Follow lane for 0.5m to site*
★ 🚐 £16.10-£17.80 🚐 £16.10-£17.80
▲ £16.10-£17.80
Open all year Booking advisable bank hols & peak
period Last arrival 21.00hrs Last departure noon
*A completely refurbished site with new facilities
block, roadways and landscaping bringing it up to
an extremely high standard. Along with private
washing facilities in the quality toilets, there is good
security on this attractive former gravel pit, with its
complex of lakes, canals, woods and marshland,
with good access roads. Please see the
advertisement on page 11 for information on Club
sites and membership. An 18-acre site with
150 touring pitches, 60 hardstandings.*
Facilities: ♠ ⊙ ⊕ ✳ & ⚟ 🚽
Services: 🚐 ⛟ 🛢 ⌀ ⊞ 🗔 → ∪ ▶ ◢ ♪ ⚟
🟦 🔲 🔲 🔲 🟩

advertisement on page 11

► **66% *Tame View Caravan Site* (SP209979)**
Cliff B78 2DR ☎ 01827 873853
*Dir: 400yds off A51 (Tamworth-Kingsbury road), 1m N
of Kingsbury opp pub. Signed 'No through road'*
🚐 🚐 ▲
Open all year Booking advisable 1 month in
advance Last arrival 23.00hrs Last departure
23.00hrs
*A secluded spot overlooking the Tame Valley and
river, sheltered by high hedges. Sanitary facilities
are minimal, but the site is popular with many
return visitors. A 5-acre site with 55 touring pitches.
Fishing.*
Facilities: ✳ ⚟ ⛾ 🖛
Services: ⊞ → ∪ ▶ ◎ ◢ ⚟ ♪ 🖥

RUGBY   Map 11 SP57

► ► **70% Lodge Farm Campsite** (SP476748)
Bilton Ln, Long Lawford CV23 9DU
☎ 01788 560193 📠 01788 550603
🅔 alec@lodgefarm.com
🆆 www.lodgefarm.com
*Dir: From Rugby take A428 (Lawford Road) 1.5m
towards Coventry. At Sheaf & Sickle pub left into Bilton
Lane, site 500yds*
★ 🚐 £10 🚐 £10 ▲ £8
Open Etr-Nov Booking advisable bank hols Last
arrival 22.00hrs
*A small, simple farm site set behind the friendly
owner's home and self-catering cottages, with
converted stables housing the toilet facilities. Rugby
is only a short drive away, and the site is tucked
well away from the main road. A 2.5-acre site with
35 touring pitches, 3 hardstandings and 10 statics.*
Facilities: ♠ ⊙ ✳ & ⚟ 🖛
Services: 🚐 🛢 ⊞ → ∪ ▶ ◎ ◢ ⚟ ♪ 🖥 ⚟
🟦 🔲 🔲 🔲 🟩

WOLVEY   Map 11 SP48

► ► ► **72% Wolvey Villa Farm Caravan &
Camping Site** (SP428869)
LE10 3HF ☎ 01455 220493 & 220630
🆆 www.wolveycaravanpark.itgo.com
*Dir: From M6 junct 2 take B4065 follow Wolvey signs.
Or M69 junct 1 & follow Wolvey signs*
★ 🚐 £10-£11 🚐 £10-£11 ▲ £8-£9
Booking advisable Spring bank hol-mid Aug Last
arrival 22.00hrs Last departure noon
*A level grass site surrounded by trees and shrubs,
on the borders of Warwickshire and Leicestershire.
This quiet country site has its own popular fishing
lake, and is convenient for visiting the major cities
of Coventry and Leicester. A 7-acre site with
110 touring pitches, 24 hardstandings.
Fishing, putting green & off licence.*
Leisure: ◣ ⊡ **Facilities:** ♠ ⊙ ✳ & ⚟ ⛾ 🖛
Services: 🚐 🖥 🛢 ⌀ ⊞ 🗔 → ∪ ▶ ♪
Notes: No twin axles

Campsites in popular areas get very
crowded at busy times – it is advisable
to book well in advance.

Leisure: ⚑ Indoor swimming pool ⚑ Outdoor swimming pool ⚌ Tennis court ◣ Games room ⛰ Children's playground ∪ Stables
▶ 9/18 hole golf course ⚓ Boats for hire 🎬 Cinema ♪ Fishing ◎ Mini golf ◢ Watersports ⊡ Separate TV room

England

WIGHT, ISLE OF

BEMBRIDGE
See **Whitecliff Bay**

COWES   Map 05 SZ49

 77% **Thorness Bay Holiday Park**
(SZ448928)
Thorness PO31 8NJ
GOLD
☎ 01983 523109 📠 01983 822213
✉ holidaysales.thornessbay@park-resorts.com
🌐 www.park-resorts.com
Dir: On A3054 towards Yarmouth, 1st right after BMW garage, signed Thorness Bay
★ 🚐 £5-£25 🚐 £5-£25 ▲ £3-£22
Open 2 Mar-5 Jan Booking advisable Jul-Aug
Last arrival anytime Last departure 10.00hrs
*Splendid views of the Solent can be enjoyed
from this rural park located just outside Cowes.
A footpath leads directly to the coast, while on
site there is an all-weather sports court,
entertainment clubs for children, and cabaret,
shows and a bar for all the family. This park has
been upgraded to a high standard, and now
offers 23 serviced pitches with TV boosters.
A 148-acre site with 80 touring pitches,
20 hardstandings and 560 statics.*
Leisure: ₹ ⚙ **Facilities:** 🜂 ⊙ ℄ ⅊ ⊼
Services: ⊕ ⎈ ▤ ℥ ⌀ ✕ ⇟ → ∪ ⚓ ⌇
⊞ ⊠ ⊟ ⊠ ⊡

FRESHWATER   Map 05 SZ38

▶ ▶ ▶ 81% **Heathfield Farm**
Camping (SZ335879)
Heathfield Rd PO40 9SH
GOLD
☎ 01983 756756 📠 01983 756756
✉ web@heathfieldcamping.co.uk
🌐 www.heathfieldcamping.co.uk
*Dir: 2m W from Yarmouth ferry port on A3054, left to
Heathfield Rd, entrance 200yds on right.*
🚐 £9.50-£14 🚐 £9.50-£14 ▲ £8-£12.50

Open May-Sep Booking advisable bank hols & Jul-
Aug Last arrival 22.00hrs Last departure 22.00hrs
*A good quality park with friendly owners and lovely
views across the Solent to Hurst Castle. The toilet
facilities which include a family room are
immaculate, and this park is constantly improving
to meet the needs of campers and caravanners.
A 10-acre site with 60 touring pitches.*

contd.

Abbreviations: BH/bank hols-bank holidays Etr-Easter Whit-Whitsun dep-departure fr-from hrs-hours m-mile mdnt-midnight
rdbt-roundabout rs-restricted service wk-week wknd-weekend 🚫-no dogs

Separate playing field for ball games etc.

Facilities: 🅿️⊙🔌✳️🚿👶🍴⛺🐕

Services: 🔋🚮🚽🧺→∪🍴⊙🔧🧺🔌🔋

Notes: Family camping only

NEWBRIDGE   Map 05 SZ48

PREMIER PARK

▶ ▶ ▶ ▶ ▶ 86% **Orchards**
Holiday Caravan Park (SZ411881)
PO41 0TS ☎ 01983 531331
& 531350 🖹 01983 531666
🅔 info@orchards-holiday-park.co.uk
🅦 www.orchards-holiday-park.co.uk
Dir: 4m E of Yarmouth and 6m W of Newport on B3401.
★ 🚐 £11.40-£15.90 🚐 £11.40-£15.90
🅰 £11.40-£15.90
Open 11 Feb-2 Jan (rs Nov-Jan & Feb-mid Mar
shop/takeaway closed, pool closed Sep-May)
Booking advisable Etr, Spring BH, Jun-Aug, Oct half
term Last arrival 23.00hrs Last departure 11.00hrs
*A really excellent, well-managed park set in a
peaceful village location amid downs and
meadowland, with glorious downland views.
Pitches are terraced, and offer a good provision
of hardstandings, including super pitches. The
toilet facilities are immaculate, and the park has
indoor and outdoor swimming pools. There is
excellent provision for families, and disabled
access to all facilities on site, plus disabled
toilets. An 8-acre site with 171 touring pitches,
74 hardstandings and 65 statics.*
Coarse fishing, petanque
Leisure: 🎣 🎿 🏊 🎮 🎱
Facilities: 🚿🅿️🔌⊙🚿✳️👶🍴🐕
Services: 🔋🛢🚮🧺🖲🅃✖️🚮→∪🔧
🅔 💳 💳 📶 🅂

NEWCHURCH   Map 05 SZ58

PREMIER PARK

▶ ▶ ▶ ▶ ▶ 88% **Southland**
Camping Park (SZ557847)
PO36 0LZ
☎ 01983 865385 🖹 01983 867663
🅔 info@southland.co.uk
🅦 www.southland.co.uk
*Dir: A3056 towards Sandown. 2nd left after Fighting
Cocks pub towards Newchurch. Site 1m on left*
🚐 £10.20-£15.20 🚐 £10.20-£15.20
🅰 £10.20-£15.20

contd.

Open Etr-Sep Booking advisable Jun-Aug Last
arrival 21.30hrs Last departure 11.00hrs
*Beautifully maintained site, peacefully located
and impressively laid out on the outskirts of the
village in the Arreton Valley. Spotless sanitary
facilities including spacious family rooms
enhance the park. Pitches are well screened
by lovely trees and shrubs. A 9-acre site with
120 touring pitches.*

Leisure: 🎮
Facilities: 🚿🅿️🔌⊙🚿✳️👶🍴🐕⛺🍴🐕
Services: 🔋🛢🚮🧺🖲🅃🚮→∪🍴⊙🔧🧺🔧
🅔 💳 💳 📶 🅂

PONDWELL   Map 05 SZ69

▶ ▶ ▶ 74% *Pondwell Camp Site* (SZ622911)
PO34 5AQ ☎ 01983 612330 🖹 01983 613511
*Dir: From Ryde take A3055 then left on B3350 to
Seaview. Site next to Wishing Well pub*
🚐🚐🅰
Open May-26 Sep Booking advisable Aug Last
arrival 23.00hrs Last departure 11.00hrs
*A secluded site in quiet rural surroundings close to
the sea, on slightly sloping ground with some level
areas. The village is within easy walking distance.
A 9-acre site with 250 touring pitches.*

Leisure: 🎣 🎮 🎱
Facilities: 🚿🅿️🔌⊙🚿👶🍴⛺🍴
Services: 🔋🛢🚮🖲→🍴⊙🔧🚽🔧
Notes: 🚫 🅔 💳 🅂

England

ROOKLEY   Map 05 SZ58

NEW ► ► ► 80% **Rookley Country Park**
(SZ512838)
Island View Holidays, Main Rd PO38 3LU
☎ 01983 721606 ▤ 01983 721607
❸ info@islandviewhols.co.uk
Ⓦ www.islandviewhols.co.uk
*Dir: from Newport take A3020 towards Godshill.
Through Rookley, site on left*
★ ♣ £9-£13 ♣ £9-£13 ▲ £8-£10
Open all year (ex 25 Dec) Booking advisable all year
Last arrival 23.00hrs Last departure 10.00hrs
*A newly created park within an established holiday
park. The touring pitches are on hard stands next to
grass, and the tent area is in a peaceful meadow
with mature trees. All amenities except fishing are
included in the price. A 22-acre site with 78 touring
pitches, 19 hardstandings and 108 statics.*
Fishing lake
Leisure: ⧉ ❅ ⦿ ⏜ Facilities: ⛕ ⊙ ⚑ ✲ ⎣ ⅏ ⧖ ⚲
Services: ⚡ ⛽ ⅏ ⊞ ⊡ ✖ ⅏ → ∪ ⑨ ⚲
Notes: ⦿ ▭ ▦ ▨ ⑨

RYDE   Map 05 SZ59

NEW **Roebeck Camping and Caravan Park**
(SZ581903)
Gatehouse Rd, Upton Cross PO33 4BP
☎ 01983 611475 & 07930 992080
*Dir: turn right from Fishbourne ferry terminal (west of
Ryde). At lights turn left onto A3054 towards Ryde. In
outskirts straight on at 'All Through Traffic' sign. At end
of Pellhurst Rd right in Upton Rd. Site 50yds*
♣ ▲ Open Apr-Nov
*At the time of going to press, the pennant
classification for this site was not confirmed.
A 3-acre site with 37 touring pitches.*

Facilities: ⛕

ST HELENS   Map 05 SZ68

74% **Nodes Point Holiday Park**
(SZ636897)
Nodes Rd PO33 1YA GOLD
☎ 01983 872401 ▤ 01983 874696
❸ gm.nodespoint@park-resorts.com
Ⓦ www.park-resorts.com
*Dir: From Ryde take B3330 signed Seaview/
Puckpool. At junct for Puckpool bear right. 1m past
Road Side Inn in Nettlestone, on left*
★ ♣ £8-£28 ♣ £8-£28 ▲ £5-£22
Open Apr-Oct (rs Mar park open, no facilities)
Booking advisable May-Aug Last arrival 21.00hrs
Last departure 10.00hrs
*A well-equipped holiday centre on an elevated
position with direct access to the beach. The
touring area is mostly sloping with some
terraces, and toilet facilities are dated but clean.
Activities are organised for youngsters, and
there is entertainment for the whole family.
Buses pass the main entrance road. A 16-acre
site with 147 touring pitches, 4 hardstandings
and 162 statics.*
Leisure: ❅ ⏜ Facilities: ⛕ ⊙ ⚑ ✲ ⎣ ⅏ ⧖ ⚲
Services: ⚡ ⛽ ⅏ ⧫ ✖ ⅏ → ∪ ⑨ ⊙ ⚲ ⚲ ✦
Notes: Family park ⦿ ▭ ▦ ▨ ⑨
See advertisement on page 214

SANDOWN   Map 05 SZ58

PREMIER PARK

► ► ► ► ► 80% **Camping & Caravanning
Club Site** (SZ590855)
Lower Adgestone Rd PO36 0HL ☎ 01983 403432
Ⓦ www.campingandcaravanningclub.co.uk
*Dir: Turn off A3055 (Sandown/Shanklin road) at
Manor House pub, in Lake. Past school & golf
course on left, turn right at T-junct, park 200yds on
right*
★ ♣ £16.20-£20.60 ♣ £16.20-£20.60
▲ £16.20-£20.60
Open Apr-Oct Booking advisable bank hols &
peak period Last arrival 21.00hrs Last departure
noon
*A popular, well-managed park in a quiet, rural
location not far from Sandown. The level pitches
are imaginatively laid out, and surrounded by
beautiful flower beds and trees set close to a
small river. This planting offers good screening
as well as enhancing the appearance of the park.
Spotless sanitary facilities include two family
rooms, and there is excellent provision for
families in general. Please see advertisement on
page 11 for information on Club sites and
membership. A 22-acre site with 270 touring
pitches.*
Leisure: ❅ ⏜ Facilities: ⛕ ⊙ ⚑ ✲ ⎣ ⅏ ⧖ ⚲
Services: ⚡ ⛽ ⅏ ⧫ ⊞ ⊡ → ∪ ⑨ ⚲ ⚲
⦿ ▭ ▦ ▨ ⑨

► ► ► ► 77% **Old Barn Touring Park**
(SZ573833)
Cheverton Farm, Newport Rd,
Apse Heath PO36 9PJ ☎ 01983 866414
▤ 01983 865988 GOLD
❸ oldbarn@weltinet.com
Ⓦ www.oldbarntouring.co.uk
Dir: On A3056 from Newport, site on left after Apse Heath
★ ♣ £10-£13.50 ♣ £10-£13.50 ▲ £10-£13.50

Open May-Sep Booking advisable bank hols & peak
periods Last arrival 21.00hrs Last departure noon
*A terraced site with good quality facilities,
bordering on open farmland. The spacious pitches
are secluded and fully serviced, and there is a
decent modern toilet block. A 5-acre site with
60 touring pitches, 9 hardstandings.*
Leisure: ⦿ ⏛ Facilities: ⛕ ⊙ ⚑ ✲ ⎣ ⅏ ⧖ ⚲
Services: ⚡ ⛽ ⅏ ⊞ ⊡ ✦ → ∪ ⑨ ⊙ ⚲ ⚲ ✦ ⚲
⦿ ▭ ▦ ▨ ⑨

► ► ► 77% **Cheverton Copse Holiday Park (SZ570833)**
Scotchells Brook Ln PO36 0JP
☎ 01983 403161 📠 01983 408942
🖃 holidays@cheverton-copse.co.uk
🌐 www.cheverton-copse.co.uk
Dir: 400yds from A3056 towards Newport, 1m from Lake
🚐 £9-£18 🚑 £9-£18 ▲ £9-£15
Open Apr-Sep (rs Apr-Whit Clubhouse closed)
Booking advisable 20 Jul-1 Sep Last arrival 21.00hrs
Last departure noon
A small park on the edge of open farmland close to the resort attractions of Sandown and Shanklin. The smart toilets offer excellent sanitary facilities, and many of the pitches are set on cut-away terraces in the slightly-sloping land. A 1-acre site with 14 touring pitches and 57 statics.

Leisure: ♣ ⚠ **Facilities:** ↖ ☉ ⚹ ☀ ↙ 🚿
Services: 🖵🖥♀→ ∪ ⓘ ☺ △ ↘ ↗ 🖳
Notes: ⊗ No cars by caravans 🚐 ═══ 🚘 🅈

► 78% **Queen Bower Dairy Caravan Park (SZ567846)**
Alverstone Rd, Queen Bower PO36 0NZ
☎ 01983 403840 & 407392 📠 01983 409671
🖃 qbdcaravanpark@aol.com
🌐 www.queenbowerdairy.co.uk
Dir: 3m N of Sandown off A3056 turn right towards Alverstone, site 1m on left
★ 🚐 £4-£6.50 🚑 £4-£6.50 ▲ £4-£6.50
Open May-Oct Booking advisable Jul-Aug
A small site with basic amenities that will appeal to campers keen to escape the crowds and the busy larger sites. The enthusiastic owners keeps the facilities clean. A 2.5-acre site with 20 touring pitches.

Facilities: ☀ **Services:** 🖵🖥→ ⓘ △ ↘ ↗ 🖥🖳
Notes: Dogs must be kept on leads & exercised off site

SHANKLIN	Map 05 SZ58

80% **Lower Hyde Holiday Park (SZ575819)**
Landguard Rd PO37 7LL
☎ 01983 866131 📠 01983 862532
🖃 holidaysales.lowerhyde@park-resorts.com
🌐 www.park-resorts.com
Dir: From Fishbourne ferry terminal follow A3055 to Shanklin. Park signed just past lake
🚐 ▲
Open 17 Apr-1 Nov Booking advisable all year
Last arrival anytime Last departure 10.00hrs
A popular holiday park on the outskirts of Shanklin, close to the sandy beaches. There is an outdoor swimming pool and plenty of organised activities for youngsters of all ages. In the evening there is a choice of family entertainment. The touring facilities are located in a quiet area away from the main complex, with good views over the downs. A 65-acre site with 115 touring pitches, 25 hardstandings and 318 statics.

Leisure: 🏊 ⚛ ⚾ ⚠ **Facilities:** ↖ ☀ ☀ ↙ 🖳
Services: 🖵🖥♀ⓘ ⌀🖥✕ 🖳→∪ⓘ☺↘↗
Notes: No cars by caravans 🚐 ═══ 🚘 🅈
See advertisement on page 214

► ► ► 80% **Landguard Camping Park (SZ577825)**
Landguard Manor Rd PO37 7PH
☎ 01983 867028 📠 01983 865988
🖃 landguard@weltinet.com
🌐 www.landguard-camping.co.uk
Dir: Take A3056 to Sandown turn right after passing Safeways at Lake into Whitecross Lane. Follow signs
★ 🚐 £10.50-£15 🚑 £10.50-£15 ▲ £10.50-£15

Open Etr-Sep Booking advisable school hols Last arrival 20.00hrs Last departure noon
Surrounded by trees in a rural setting, this peaceful and secluded touring park is within walking distance of Shanklin. Facilities are clean and tidy, and the park benefits from a very good outdoor pool. A 7-acre site with 150 touring pitches, 6 hardstandings.

Leisure: ⚛ ⚠ **Facilities:** ↖ ☉ ⚹ ☀ ↙ 🖳
Services: 🖵 ∀ 🖥♀ ⌀🖥🖵 🚿🖳→ ⓘ ☺ △ ↘ ↗
Notes: ⊗ Families only
🚐 ═══ 🚘 🅈

► ► ► 78% **Ninham Country Holidays (SZ573825)**
Ninham PO37 7PL
☎ 01983 864243 & 866040 📠 01983 868881
🖃 info@ninham.fsnet.co.uk
🌐 www.ninham-holiday.co.uk
Dir: Signed off A3056 (Newport to Sandown road)
★ 🚐 £8-£16 🚑 £8-£16 ▲ £8-£16
Open May-Sep (rs 1-27 May & 10-30 Sep Outdoor pool & launderette closed) Booking advisable Jun-Sep
Enjoying a lofty rural position with fine country views, this delightful, spacious park occupies two separate well-maintained areas in a country park setting near the sea and beach. A 14-acre site with 200 touring pitches and 6 statics.
Coarse fishing.

Leisure: ⚛ ⚠
Facilities: ↖ ☉ ⚹ ☀ ↙ 🖳 🚿 ╥ 🐾
Services: 🖵🖥 ⌀🖥🖵✕ 🖳→∪ⓘ☺△↘ ☸ ↗
🚐 ═══ 🚘 🅈

Remember that prices and opening times are liable to change within the currency of this guide. It is always best to telephone in advance.

England

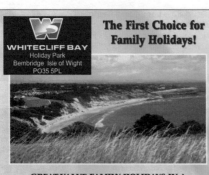
TOTLAND BAY   Map 05 SZ38

▶ ▶ 75% **Stoats Farm Camping** (SZ324865)
PO39 0HE ☎ 01983 755258 & 753416
📄 01983 755258
📧 david@stoats-farm.co.uk
🌐 www.stoats-farm.co.uk
Dir: On Alum Bay road, 1.5m from Freshwater & 0.75m from Totland
★ ⊞ £9.50-£11 ⊞ £9.50-£11 ▲ £8.50-£9.50

Open Mar-Oct Booking advisable Aug
A friendly, personally run site in a quiet country setting close to Alum Bay, Tennyson Down and The Needles. It has good laundry and shower facilities, and the shop, though small, is well stocked. Popular with families, walkers and cyclists. A 10-acre site with 100 touring pitches.
Facilities: ⋔ ⊙ ✳ ⅙ ℂ ℠ 🜍 ⋔
Services: ⦾ ⅏ ◫ ⊞ → ∪ ▷ ◎ ⟁ �ⱽ ⟍

WHITECLIFF BAY   Map 05 SZ68

 78% **Whitecliff Bay
Holiday Park** (SZ637862)
Hillway Rd, Bembridge PO35 5PL
☎ 01983 872671 📄 01983 872941
📧 holiday@whitecliff-bay.com
🌐 www.whitecliff-bay.com
Dir: 1m S of Bembridge, signed off B3395 in village
★ ⊞ £8.40-£14.70 ⊞ £8.40-£14.70
▲ £8.40-£14.70

Open Mar-Oct Booking advisable Jul-Aug Last arrival 21.00hrs Last departure 10.30hrs
A large seaside complex on two sites, with tourers and tents on one, and tourers and statics on the other. There is an indoor and outdoor swimming pool, a leisure centre, and plenty of traditional on-site entertainment, plus easy access to a lovely sandy beach. A 49-acre site with 400 touring pitches, 50 hardstandings and 227 statics.
Leisure centre with fun pool, spa bath & sauna
Leisure: ॰ ॰ ◉ ⋔
Facilities: ⊬ ⋔ ⊙ ◰ ✳ ⅙ ℂ ℠ ⋔
Services: ⦾ ⅏ ◫ ◻ ⓘ ⌀ ⊞ 🅃 ✕ 🜍 → ∪ ▷ ◎ ⟁ ⟍
Notes: Adults and families only, no dogs during high season 💳 💳 💳 ⑤

WOOTTON BRIDGE   Map 05 SZ59

▶ ▶ ▶ 76% **Kite Hill Farm Caravan Park**
(SZ549906)
Firestone Copse Rd PO33 4LE
☎ 01983 882543 & 883261 📄 01983 883883
📧 barry@kitehillfarm.freeserve.co.uk
🌐 www.campingparkisleofwight.com
Dir: Signed off A3054 at Wootton Bridge, between Ryde and Newport
★ ⊞ £10-£11 ⊞ £10-£11 ▲ £8-£9
Open all year Booking advisable Jun-Aug
The park, on a gently sloping field, is tucked away behind the owners' farm, just a short walk from the village and attractive river estuary. Facilities are well maintained and the atmosphere pleasantly relaxing. A 12.5-acre site with 50 touring pitches, 10 hardstandings.
Leisure: ⋔
Facilities: ⋔ ⊙ ✳ ⅙ ⋔
Services: ⦾ ⓘ ⌀ ⊞ → ∪ ▷ ➿ ⟍ ◫ ℠

WROXALL   Map 05 SZ57

▶ ▶ ▶ 77% Appuldurcombe Gardens Caravan & Camping Park (SZ546804)
Appuldurcombe Rd PO38 3EP ☎ 01983 852597
🖹 01983 856225
📧 info@appuldurcombegardens.co.uk
🌐 www.appuldurcombegardens.co.uk
Dir: From Newport take A3020 towards Shanklin. Through Rookley & Godshill. Right at Whiteley Bank rdbt towards Wroxall, then follow brown signs
🚐🚙🛖

Open Mar-Oct (rs Mar-Spring bank hol & Aug bank hol-Oct) Booking advisable Jul-Aug Last arrival 22.00hrs Last departure noon
An attractive secluded site close to the ruins of Appuldurcombe House, with a stream running through it. The facilities include a good swimming pool, shop, bar/café and entertainment room, and plenty of tree planting will result in excellent screening. A 12-acre site with 100 touring pitches and 40 statics.
Crazy golf, pitch & putt.
Leisure: ⚲ ◕ ⌂   **Facilities:** ⬕ ⊙ ⚲ ✱ ⚷ ⚬ ⬒ ⬚
Services: ⬚ ⬜ ⬛ ⊗ ⚚ ⬜ ⊞ ⊤ ✕ ⬛ → ∪ ⬧ ⊙ ⬧ ⬛ ⚲ ⬦
Notes: No cars by caravans, family groups during high season 🔵 💳 💳 💳 🔳 🔳

YARMOUTH
See **Newbridge**

WILTSHIRE

CALNE   Map 04 ST97

▶ ▶ ▶ 77% Blackland Lakes Holiday & Leisure Centre (ST973687)
Stockley Ln SN11 0NQ
☎ 01249 813672 🖹 01249 811346
📧 info@blacklandlakes.co.uk
🌐 www.blacklandlakes.co.uk
Dir: From Calne take A4 E for 1.5m, right at camp sign. Site 1m on left
🚐🚙🛖

Open all year (rs Nov-mid Mar bookings only (pre paid)) Booking advisable all year Last arrival 23.00hrs Last departure noon
A rural site surrounded by the North and West Downs. The park is divided into several paddocks separated by hedges, trees and fences, and there are two well-stocked carp fisheries for the angling enthusiast. Some excellent walks close by, and the interesting market town of Devizes is a few miles away. A 15-acre site with 180 touring pitches, 25 hardstandings.
Wildfowl sanctuary, fishing facilities, bike trail
Leisure: ⌂   **Facilities:** ⬕ ⊙ ⚲ ✱ ⚷ ⚬ ⬛ ⬚ ⬒ ⬅
Services: ⬚ ⬜ ⬛ ⊗ ⚚ ⊞ ⊤ → ∪ ⬧ ⚲ 🔵 💳 💳 🔳 🔳

DEVIZES   Map 04 SU06

▶ ▶ ▶ ▶ 81% Camping & Caravanning Club Site (ST950621)
Scout Ln, Seend, Melksham SN12 6RN
☎ 01380 828839
🌐 www.campingandcaravanningclub.co.uk
Dir: From Devizes on A361 turn right onto A365, over canal, next left down lane beside 3 Magpies pub. Site on right
★ 🚐 £16.10-£17.80 🚙 £16.10-£17.80
🛖 £16.10-£17.80

Open all year Booking advisable BH's & peak period Last arrival 21.00hrs Last departure noon
An excellent club site with well-designed, quality facilities and a high level of staff commitment. This popular park is set beside the Kennet and Avon Canal, with a gate to the towpath for walking and cycling, and with fishing available in the canal. Well situated for exploring Salisbury Plain and the Marlborough Downs. Please see the advertisement on page 11 for information on Club sites and membership. A 13.5-acre site with 90 touring pitches, 50 hardstandings.
Leisure: ⌂
Facilities: ⬕ ⊙ ⚲ ✱ ⚷ ⚬ ⬛ ⬅
Services: ⬚ ⚚ ⬜ ⬛ ⊞ ⊤ → ∪ ⬧ ⊙ ⚲ ⬛
🔵 💳 💳 🔳 🔳

LACOCK   Map 04 ST96

▶ ▶ ▶ 84% Piccadilly Caravan Park Ltd (ST913683)
Folly Ln West SN15 2LP
☎ 01249 730260 🖹 01249 730260
📧 piccadillylacock@aol.com
Dir: 4m S of Chippenham. On A350 from towards Lacock for 3m. Left at Gastard sign. Site 200yds on left
🚐🚙🛖

Open Apr-Oct Booking advisable school & bank hols Last arrival 22.00hrs Last departure noon
A peaceful, pleasant site, well established and beautifully laid out, close to the village of Lacock. Facilities and grounds are immaculately kept, and there is very good screening. A 2.5-acre site with 41 touring pitches, 12 hardstandings.
Leisure: ⌂
Facilities: ⬕ ⊙ ⚲ ✱ ⚬ ⬅
Services: ⬚ ⬛ ⚚ ⬜ ⊞ → ∪ ⬧ ⬛ ⚲ ⬛

England

LANDFORD — Map 05 SU21

▶ ▶ ▶ 67% **Greenhill Farm Camping & Caravan Park (SU266183)**
Greenhill Farm, New Rd SP5 2AZ
☎ 01794 324117 & 023 8081 1506 📠 023 8081 3209
✉ greenhillcamping@aol.co.uk
🌐 www.newforest-uk.com/greenhill.htm
Dir: M27 junct 2, A36 towards Salisbury, approx 3m after Hants/Wilts border, (Shoe Inn pub on right, BP garage on left) take next left into New Rd, signed Nomansland, 2nd site on left
★ 🚐 fr £12 🚐 fr £12 🛆 fr £10

Open all year Booking advisable bank hols, Jul-Aug Last arrival 21.30hrs Last departure 13.00hrs
A tranquil, well-landscaped park hidden away in unspoilt countryside on the edge of the New Forest. Pitches overlooking the fishing lake include hardstandings. Facilities are housed in portable type buildings. This park is for adults only. A 13-acre site with 80 touring pitches, 30 hardstandings.
Fishing, disposable BBQs
Facilities: ↑ ⊙ ❄ ⬤ ↑
Services: 🔌 ⛽ 🧴 🔋 🚽 → ∪ ► ⊚ 🜄 ↓ ✈ 🛒
Notes: Adults only, dogs must be on leads
🍴 🚬 🔦 🔦

MARSTON MEYSEY — Map 05 SU19

▶ ▶ 71% **Second Chance Touring Park (SU140960)**
SN6 6SZ ☎ 01285 810675 & 810939
Dir: Take A419 from Cirencester towards Swindon, at junct with Cotswold Water Park turn left to Latton. Through Latton and turn left at next mini rdbt, towards Fairford. Follow signs to site
★ 🚐 £8 🚐 £8 🛆 £6-£10
Open Mar-Nov (rs Dec-Feb short stay) Booking advisable peak periods & bank hols Last arrival 21.00hrs Last departure 13.30hrs
An attractive, quiet site located near the source of the Thames, and well positioned for those wishing to visit the nearby Cotswold Water Park. The facilities are a bit dated but clean. A 1.75-acre site with 22 touring pitches, 10 hardstandings and 4 statics.
Fishing, access for canoes
Facilities: ↑ ⊙ ❄ 🎏
Services: 🔌 🧴 → ► ⊚ 🜄 ✈ 🛒
Notes: ✂ No loud music or parties

ORCHESTON — Map 05 SU04

▶ ▶ ▶ 74% **Stonehenge Touring Park (SU061456)**
SP3 4SH ☎ 01980 620304
✉ stay@stonehengetouringpark.com
🌐 www.stonehengetouringpark.com
Dir: Off A360
★ 🚐 £6.50-£11.50 🚐 £6.50-£11.50 🛆 £6.50-£11.50
Open all year Booking advisable bank hols & Jul-Aug Last arrival 21.00hrs Last departure 11.00hrs
A quiet site adjacent to the small village of Orcheston near the centre of Salisbury Plain and 4m from Stonehenge. A 2-acre site with 30 touring pitches, 12 hardstandings.
Leisure: 🅰 **Facilities:** ↑ ⊙ 🔧 ❄ ⬤ 🔋 🛆 🎏
Services: 🔌 ⛽ 🧴 🚽 🔋 ⬤ 🚬 🔦 🔦

SALISBURY — Map 05 SU12

▶ ▶ ▶ ▶ 77% **Coombe Touring Park (SU099282)**
Race Plain, Netherhampton SP2 8PN
☎ 01722 328451 📠 01722 328451
Dir: Turn off A36 onto A3094, then 2m SW, adjacent to Salisbury racecourse
★ 🚐 £8-£12 🚐 £8-£12 🛆 £8-£12

Open all year (rs Oct-Apr Shop closed) Booking advisable bank hols (by letter only) Last arrival 21.00hrs Last departure noon
A very neat and attractive site adjacent to the racecourse with views over the downs, and outstanding flower beds. The park is well landscaped with shrubs and maturing trees, and the very colourful beds are stocked from the owner's greenhouse. A comfortable park with a superb luxury toilet block. A 3-acre site with 50 touring pitches.
Children's bathroom
Facilities: ↑ ⊙ 🔧 ❄ ⬤
Services: 🔌 ⛽ 🧴 🚽 🔋 → ∪ ► 🛒

▶ ▶ ▶ 72% ***Alderbury Caravan & Camping Park (SU197259)***
Southampton Rd, Whaddon SP5 3HB
☎ 01722 710125
✉ alderbury@aol.com
Dir: Just off A36, 3m from Salisbury, opposite The Three Crowns
🚐 🚐 🛆
Open all year Booking advisable anytime Last arrival 21.00hrs Last departure 12.30hrs
A pleasant, attractive park set in the village of

contd.

Services: 🅃 Toilet Fluid ✗ Café/ Restaurant 🍟 Fast Food/Takeaway 🍼 Baby Care 🔌 Electric Hook Up
🚐 Motorvan Service Point ⬚ Launderette ♀ Licensed Bar ▮ Calor Gaz ⬮ Camping Gaz 🔋 Battery Charging

Alderbury Caravan & Camping Park
Whaddon not far from Salisbury. The small site is
well maintained by friendly owners, and is well
positioned near the main A36 for overnight stops
for ferry ports of Southampton. A 1.5-acre site with
39 touring pitches, 12 hardstandings and 1 static.
Microwave

Leisure: ⚠ Facilities: 🌂⊙☀☻👤🛒🏛
Services: 📞🛅🛢🗑→∪▶🍴💈🎱♨🔥

▶ ▶ ▶ 85% Camping & Caravanning Club Site
(SU140320)
Hudsons Field, Castle Rd SP1 3RR
☎ 01722 320713
ⓦ www.campingandcaravanningclub.co.uk
Dir: 1.5m from Salisbury on A345. (Large open field
next to Old Sarum)
★ 🚐 £13.60-£17.80 🚏 £13.60-£17.80
🛖 £13.60-£17.80
Open Mar-Oct Booking advisable bank hols & peak
period Last arrival 21.00hrs Last departure noon
Well placed within walking distance of Salisbury,
this tidy site has friendly and helpful wardens, and
immaculate toilet facilities with cubicled wash
basins. Please see the advertisement on page 11
for information on Club sites and membership.
A 4.5-acre site with 150 touring pitches,
16 hardstandings.
Facilities: 🌂⊙☜☀♨☻🏛
Services: 📞🛅🛢🛅🛢🗑🖥→▶♨🔥♨
💳 🚪 🏦 📶 🔵

TROWBRIDGE   Map 04 ST85

▶ 73% Stowford Manor Farm (ST810577)
Stowford, Wingfield BA14 9LH ☎ 01225 752253
ⓔ stowford1@supanet.com
ⓦ www.stowfordmanorfarm.co.uk
Dir: From Trowbridge take A366 W towards Radstock.
Site on left in 3m
★ 🚐 £7-£8.50 🚏 £7-£8.50 🛖 £5-£7
Open Etr-Oct Booking advisable school & Bank Hols
A very simple farm site set on the banks of the River
Frome behind the farm courtyard. The owners are
friendly and relaxed, and the park enjoys a similarly
comfortable ambience. A 1.5-acre site with
15 touring pitches.
Riverside site, fishing, boating, swimming
Facilities: 🌂⊙☀🐾
Services: 📞🖥✖→∪▶♨⚓🔥🛢🛒

WESTBURY   Map 04 ST85

▶ ▶ ▶ 77% Brokerswood Country
Park (ST836523)
Brokerswood BA13 4EH
☎ 01373 822238 🖨 01373 858474
ⓔ woodland.park@virgin.net
ⓦ www.brokerswood.co.uk
Dir: From M4 south on A350. Right at Yarnbrook to
Rising Sun pub at North Bradley, then left at rdbt. Left
on bend approaching Southwick, follow lane for 2.5m,
site on right.
★ 🚐 £8-£20 🚏 £8-£20 🛖 £8-£20
Open all year Booking advisable peak season &
bank hols Last arrival 21.30hrs Last departure
11.00hrs
A pleasant site on the edge of an 80-acre woodland
park with nature trails and fishing lakes. An
adventure playground offers plenty of fun for all
ages, and there is a miniature railway of one-third
of a mile, an indoor play centre, and a licensed café.
A 5-acre site with 69 touring pitches,
21 hardstandings.
Country park with play grounds & fishing lake
Leisure: ⚠
Facilities: 🌂⊙☜☀☻🛒🏛☴🐾
Services: 📞🛅🛢🖥✖🚮→♨
Notes: Families only, no cycling, no disposable
BBQ's 💳 🚪 🔵

WORCESTERSHIRE

CLENT HILLS
See Romsley

HANLEY SWAN   Map 10 SO84

▶ ▶ ▶ 78% Camping & Caravanning Club Site
(SO812440)
Blackmore Camp Site No 2 WR8 0EE
☎ 01684 310280
ⓦ www.campingandcaravanningclub.co.uk
Dir: A38 to Upton on Severn. Turn N over river bridge.
2nd left, then 1st left signed Hanley Swan. Site 1m on
right
★ 🚐 £16.10-£17.80 🚏 £16.10-£17.80
🛖 £16.10-£17.80
Open all year Booking advisable bank hols & peak
period Last arrival 21.00hrs Last departure noon
Blackmore is a well-established, level wooded park,
ideally located for exploring the Malvern Hills and
Worcester. The excellent toilet facilities are
spotlessly maintained. Please see the advertisement
on page 11 for information on Club sites and
membership. A 17-acre site with 200 touring
pitches, 66 hardstandings.
Leisure: ♣ ⚠
Facilities: 🌂⊙☜☀☻🏛🐾
Services: 📞🚽🛅🛢🛅🛢🖥🗑→∪♨🔥♨
💳 🚪 🏦 📶 🔵

England

HONEYBOURNE   Map 10 SP14

▶ ▶ ▶ ▶ 80% **Ranch Caravan Park (SP113444)**
Station Rd WR11 7PR
☎ 01386 830744 📠 01386 833503
📧 enquiries@ranch.co.uk
🌐 www.ranch.co.uk

GOLD

Dir: Through village x-rds towards Bidford, entrance 400mtrs on left
★ 🚐 £14.50-£18.75 🚐 £14.50-£18.75
Open Mar-Nov (rs Mar-May & Sep-Nov swimming pool closed, shorter club hours) Booking advisable school hols Last arrival 20.00hrs Last departure noon
An attractive and well-run park set amidst farmland in the Vale of Evesham and landscaped with trees and bushes. Tourers have their own excellent facilities in two locations, and the use of an outdoor heated swimming pool in peak season. There is also a licensed club serving meals. Tents not accepted. A 12-acre site with 120 touring pitches, 30 hardstandings and 195 statics.
Leisure: ⚡ ♦ 🄰 ▢
Facilities: 🅝 ⊙ 🔧 ✳ ➰ 🐾 ♜
Services: 🔌 ♨ 🗑 ♑ ₤ ⌀ 🄷 🄣 ✕ 🛒 → ∪ ⚓
Notes: No unaccompanied minors, no tents
💳 🎫 🔳 💷

CARAVAN PARK HOLIDAY CENTRE

● Established family-run park
● Located in the vale of Evesham
● Tourers welcome
● Electric hook-ups available
● multi-service hook-ups
● Licensed club serving meals
● Heated outdoor swimming pool
● Shop
● Laundry

**HONEYBOURNE
EVESHAM
WORCS
WR11 7PR**

AA ◀✚▶

Tel: Evesham (01386) 830744
www.ranch.co.uk

MALVERN   Map 10 SO74

▶ ▶ ▶ 72% **Riverside Caravan Park (SO833463)**
Little Clevelode WR13 6PE ☎ 01684 310475
📠 01684 310475
Dir: From A449 signed onto B4424
★ 🚐 fr £13 🚐 fr £13 ▲ fr £13

Open Mar-Dec (rs Mar, Nov-Dec Closed for tourers)
Booking advisable bank hols & end May-end Aug
Last arrival 20.00hrs Last departure noon
An open grassy field close to the Malvern Hills, with fishing in the River Severn which runs past the lower part of the park. The toilet facilities are good, and there is a bar/restaurant/shop. A 25-acre site with 70 touring pitches and 130 statics.
Fishing on river.
Leisure: ⚡ ♦ 🄰 ▢ **Facilities:** 🅝 ⊙ ✳ 🐾 ♜
Services: 🔌 🗑 ♑ ₤ ⌀ 🄣 → ∪ ▶ ⚓ ⚓
Notes: 🚫🐕 No bicycles & skateboards, barrier gate closes at night

---

ROMSLEY   Map 10 SO98

▶ ▶ ▶ 79% **Camping & Caravanning Club Site (SO955795)**
Fieldhouse Ln B62 0NH ☎ 01562 710015
🌐 www.campingandcaravanningclub.co.uk
Dir: From M5 junct 3 take A456. Left on B4551 to Romsley. Turn right past Sun Hotel, take 5th left, then next left. Site 330yds on left
★ 🚐 £13.60-£17.80 🚐 £13.60-£17.80 ▲ £13.60-£17.80
Open Mar-Oct Booking advisable bank hols & peak period Last arrival 21.00hrs Last departure noon
A very pretty, well tended park surrounded by wooded hills. The site offers excellent facilities, including hardstandings to provide flat pitches for motorhomes. Lovely views of the Clent Hills can be enjoyed from this park, and there are plenty of local scenic walks. Please see the advertisement on page 11 for information on Club sites and membership. A 7.5-acre site with 95 touring pitches, 18 hardstandings.
Leisure: 🄰 **Facilities:** 🅝 ⊙ 🔧 ✳ ⚓ 🛁
Services: 🔌 🗑 ⌀ 🄷 🄣 → ∪ ▶ ⚓ 🚆 💳 🎫 🔳 💷

Remember that prices and opening times are liable to change within the currency of this guide. It is always best to telephone in advance.

Abbreviations: BH/bank hols-bank holidays Etr-Easter Whit-Whitsun dep-departure fr-from hrs-hours m-mile mdnt-midnight rdbt-roundabout rs-restricted service wk-week wknd-weekend 🚫🐕-no dogs

WOLVERLEY   Map 10 SO87

▶ ▶ ▶ 73% **Camping & Caravanning Club Site**
(SO833792)
Brown Westhead Park DY10 3PX ☎ 01562 850909
ⓦ www.campingandcaravanningclub.co.uk
Dir: From Kidderminster A449 to Wolverhampton, turn
left at lights onto B4189 signed Wolverley. Follow
brown camping signs, turn right. Site on left
★ ⚍ £13.60-£17.80 ⚐ £13.60-£17.80
▲ £13.60-£17.80
Open Mar-Oct Booking advisable bank hols & peak
period Last arrival 21.00hrs Last departure noon
A very pleasant grassy site on the edge of the
village, with the canal lock and towpath close to the
entrance, and a pub overlooking the water. The site
has good access to and from nearby motorways.
Please see the advertisement on page 11 for
information on Club sites and membership.
A 12-acre site with 115 touring pitches.

Leisure: ♣ ⚙ Facilities: ⋔ ⊙ ⚏ ✶ ⅋ ⅃ ⚏ ⋔
Services: ⚏ ⅃ ⊟ ⅃ ⊟ ⊟ → ∪ ▶ ⚊ ⚖ ⚒
⚏ ⚏ ⚏ ⚏ ⚏

YORKSHIRE, EAST RIDING OF

BRANDESBURTON   Map 17 TA14

▶ ▶ ▶ 75% **Dacre Lakeside Park (TA118468)**
YO25 8RT
☎ 01964 543704 & 542372 ⓕ 01964 543851
ⓔ dacresurf@aol.com
ⓦ www.dacrepark.co.uk
Dir: Off A165 bypass, midway between Beverley and
Hornsea
★ ⚍ £8.50-£10.50 ⚐ £8.50-£10.50 ▲ £8.50-£10.50

Open Mar-Oct Booking advisable bank hols Last
arrival 21.00hrs Last departure noon
A large lake popular with watersports enthusiasts is
the focal point of this grassy site. The clubhouse
offers plenty of indoor activities, and a fish and chip
shop and Chinese takeaway can be found in the
village. The lake is used for windsurfing, sailing and
canoeing. An 8-acre site with 120 touring pitches.
Windsurfing, fishing, canoeing, sailing & bowling
Leisure: ⚌ ♣ Facilities: ⋔ ⊙ ⚏ ✶ ⅋ ⅃ ⚏ ⋔
Services: ⚏ ⅃ ⅃ ⊟ ⅃ ⊟ → ∪ ▶ ⚊ ⚖ ⅃
⚏ ⚏ ⚏ ⚏ ⚏

Dacre LAKESIDE PARK
Luxury Lakeside Living

Brandesburton, Driffield, East Yorks
Tel: (01964) 543704 (Site Office)
(01964) 542372 (Admin)
Fax: (01964) 543851
www.dacrepark.co.uk

Excellent landscaped park with 25 timber lodges
to buy or holiday let set around an 8 acre lake
for windsurfing, sailing, canoeing and fishing.
Ideally situated for East coast resorts and historic
towns of York and Beverley. Tennis on site with
golf, bowling and jet skiing nearby.
Attractive village with pubs, Chinese restaurant
and shops within walking distance.

BRIDLINGTON   Map 17 TA16
See also **Rudston**

▶ ▶ ▶ 80% **Fir Tree Caravan Park (TA195702)**
Jewison Ln, Sewerby YO16 6YG
☎ 01262 676442 ⓕ 01262 676442
ⓔ info@flowerofmay.com
ⓦ www.flowerofmay.com
Dir: 1.5m from centre of Bridlington. Turn left off B1255
at Marton Corner & site is 600yds on left
★ ⚍ £13-£17.50 ⚐ £13-£17.50
Open Apr-Oct (rs Etr & late season) Booking
advisable Jul-Aug & bank hols Last arrival 21.00hrs
Last departure noon
Fir Park has a well laid out touring area with its own
facilities within a large, mainly static park. It has an
excellent swimming pool complex, and the adjacent
bar-cum-conservatory serves meals. There is also a
family bar, games room and outdoor children's play
area. A 22-acre site with 45 touring pitches,
45 hardstandings and 400 statics.

Leisure: ⚏ ♣ ⚙ Facilities: ⋔ ⊙ ✶ ⅋ ⚏ ⚏ ⋔
Services: ⚏ ⅃ ⚏ ⅃ ⊟ ✗ → ∪ ⅃ ⊙ ⚊ ⚖ ⚒ ⅃
Notes: Dogs by arrangement only
                    See advertisement under SCARBOROUGH

▶ ▶ 88% **Poplars Touring Park (TA194701)**
45 Jewison Ln, Sewerby YO15 1DX ☎ 01262 677251
ⓦ www.the-poplars.co.uk
Dir: B1255 towards Flamborough, take 2nd bend off
Z-bend, 1st left after Marton Hall, site 0.33m on left
★ ⚍ £10.50-£13.50 ⚐ £10.50-£13.50 ▲ £8.30-£15.70
                                              contd.

England

EAST YORKSHIRE'S QUALITY SITE
Quiet, sheltered within kitchen garden walls. Centrally heated toilet block. Toilet and bathroom for disabled persons. Dogs welcome. Own Coarse Fishery.
Thorpe Hall Caravan and Camping Site, Rudston, Driffield, East Yorkshire YO25 4JE
Tel: 01262 420393 Fax: 01262 420588
Manager Mrs Jayne Chatterton
Residence: 01262 420574
Web: www.thorpehall.co.uk

Open Mar-Oct Booking advisable bank hols & school summer hols Last arrival 21.00hrs Last departure noon
A small, peaceful park with immaculate facilities including a well-appointed toilet block. The friendly owners also run a B & B next door, and there is a good pub close by. A 1.25-acre site with 30 touring pitches, 10 hardstandings.
Facilities: ⁣
Services: ⁣
Notes: No large groups

FANGFOSS   Map 17 SE75
► ► ► 72% *Fangfoss Park* (SE747527)
YO41 5QB ☎ 01759 380491 ▤ 01759 388497
✆ info@fangfosspark.fsbusiness.co.uk
Dir: Turn off A1079 at Wilberfoss, follow sign in centre of Wilberfoss, 1.5m towards Fangfoss
Open Mar-1 Jan Booking advisable High season Last arrival 22.00hrs Last departure noon
A popular site in a pleasant rural area. The track and sidings of the old railway station are grassed over and provide excellent hardstanding with a level landscaped field adjacent. A 5-acre site with 75 touring pitches.
Off licence
Leisure: ⁣
Facilities: ⁣
Services: ⁣

KINGSTON UPON HULL   Map 17 TA02
See **Sproatley**

LITTLE WEIGHTON   Map 17 SE93
NEW ► ► ► ► 83% Croft Park (SE982333)
55 Rowley Rd HU20 3XJ
☎ 01482 840600 ▤ 01482 840600
ⓦ www.croftpark.net
Dir: On outskirts of village near water tower
🚐 £19 🚐 £19

Open mid Mar-2 Jan Booking advisable Last arrival 21.00hrs Last departure noon
A newly developed, tranquil and up-market park exclusively for adults on the edge of the village of Little Weighton. The spacious gravel pitches are thoughtfully laid out in what was the owner's garden, and are fully serviced including TV connection. The park has a tasteful on-site coffee shop and a very comfortable TV lounge/reading room. A 2-acre site with 10 touring pitches.
Leisure: ⁣ **Facilities:** ⁣
Services: ⁣
Notes: Adults only, dogs must be kept on leads

RUDSTON   Map 17 TA06
► ► ► 77% Thorpe Hall Caravan & Camping Site (TA108677)
Thorpe Hall YO25 4JE
☎ 01262 420393 & 420574 ▤ 01262 420588
✆ caravansite@thorpehall.co.uk
ⓦ www.thorpehall.co.uk
Dir: 5m from Bridlington on B1253
★ 🚐 £10-£19.50 🚐 £10-£19.50 ▲ £6.50-£15

Open Mar-Oct reception & shop limited opening hours Booking advisable bank hols & peak periods Last arrival 22.00hrs Last departure noon
A delightful, peaceful small park within the walled

contd.

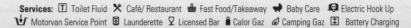

England

gardens of Thorpe Hall yet within a few miles of the bustling seaside resort of Bridlington. There are numerous walks available locally, and a number of stately homes are within easy reach. The manager is welcoming. A 4.5-acre site with 90 touring pitches.

Fishing, golf practice holes

Leisure: ♦ � △ ⊡

Facilities: ⌂ ⊙ ⦿ ✳ & ⌧ ⦰ ⊼ ✝

Services: ⊡ ⊡ ✎ ⊡ ⊡ → ⋃ ⌖ ⦿ ⊡ ⊠

SKIPSEA — Map 17 TA15

84% Low Skirlington Leisure Park (TA188528)
YO25 8SY ☎ 01262 468213 & 468466 🖷 01262 468105
📧 info@skirlington.com
🌐 www.skirlington.com

Dir: From M62 towards Beverley then Hornsea. Between Skipsea & Hornsea on B1242

⊞ ⊞ Å

Open Mar-Oct Booking advisable Mar-Oct
A large well-run seaside park set close to the beach in partly-sloping meadowland with young trees and shrubs. The site has five toilet blocks, a supermarket and an amusement arcade, with occasional entertainment in the clubhouse. The wide range of family amenities include an indoor heated swimming pool complex with sauna, jacuzzi and sunbeds. A 10-pin bowling alley and indoor play area for children are new additions. A 24-acre site with 285 touring pitches, 9 hardstandings and 450 statics.
Sauna, sunbed, jacuzzi, putting green, pony trekking

Leisure: 🏊 ♦ ⸫ ⊡

Facilities: ⇒ ⌂ ⊙ ⦿ ✳ & ⌧ ⦰ ⊼ ✝

Services: ⊡ ⊡ ⊡ ✎ ⊡ ✕ ⬚ → ⋃ ⌖ ⦿ ⊿ ⋋ ⌖
⊡ ⊠ ⊟ ⊡

► ► 76% Mill Farm Country Park (TA168554)
Mill Ln YO25 8SS ☎ 01262 468211
Dir: From A165 (Hull/Bridlington) take B1249 at Beeford to Skipsea. At x-rds right then 1st left into Cross St, leads onto Mill Lane. Booking office at Mill Farm on right

★ ⊞ £8.25-£11.90 ⊞ £8.25-£11.90
Å £8.25-£11.90

Open 10 Mar-1 Oct Booking advisable all times
A meadow site on an arable farm, well run by competent, friendly owners. The toilet facilities are maintained to a high standard, and there is a large area for ball games, plus good walks around the farm. A 3-acre site with 56 touring pitches, 7 hardstandings.
Children's playfield, farm walk

Facilities: ⌂ ⊙ & ✝

Services: ⊡ → ⌖ ⊿ ⌖ ⊡ ⊞

SPROATLEY — Map 17 TA13

► ► ► 80% Burton Constable Holiday Park (TA186357)
Old Lodges HU11 4LN
☎ 01964 562508 🖷 01964 563420
📧 info@burtonconstable.co.uk
🌐 www.burtonconstable.co.uk

Dir: Off A165 onto B1238 to Sproatley. Follow signs to park
★ ⊞ £12-£14 ⊞ £12-£14 Å £11-£12

Open Mar-Oct (rs Nov-Jan Static caravans and cabins only) Booking advisable bank hols & wknds Last arrival 22.00hrs Last departure 16.00hrs
A very attractive parkland site overlooking the fishing lakes, in the grounds of Burton Constable Hall. The toilet facilities are kept spotlessly clean, and the Lakeside Club provides a focus for relaxing in the evening. Children will enjoy the extensive adventure playground. A 50-acre site with 200 touring pitches, 14 hardstandings and 233 statics.
Two 10-acre fishing lakes

Leisure: ⸫

Facilities: ⌂ ⊙ ⦿ & ⌧ ⦰ ⊼ ✝

Services: ⊡ ⩗ ⊡ ⊡ ✎ ⊡ ⊡ → ⋃ ▶ ⌖

Notes: Dogs must be kept on leads
⊡ ⊟ ⊠ ⊡

All of the campsites in this directory are inspected annually by a team of experienced inspectors

If you are dissatisfied with any aspect of a campsite, discuss the problem at the time with a member of staff.

England

YORKSHIRE, NORTH

ACASTER MALBIS   Map 16 SE54

▶ ▶ 76% **Moor End Farm (SE589457)**
YO23 2UQ ☎ 01904 706727 & 07860 405872
🄴 moorendfarm@acaster99.fsnet.co.uk
🔴 www.ukparks.co.uk/moorend
*Dir: Follow signs to Acaster Malbis from A64/A1237
junct at Copmanthorpe*
★ ⊕ £11-£14 ⊕ £10-£13 ▲ £10-£15

Open Etr or Apr-Oct Booking advisable bank hols &
end Jul-Aug Last arrival 22.00hrs Last departure
14.00hrs
*A very pleasant, quiet farm site with clean,
modernised toilet facilities. The friendly owners
keep the grass well trimmed, and have now added a
disabled/family room. A riverboat pickup to York is
150yds from the site entrance, and the village inn
and restaurant are a short stroll away. A good place
to hire a boat or simply watch the boats go by. A 1-
acre site with 10 touring pitches and 7 statics.*
Use of fridge/freezer & microwave
Leisure: ⚠ **Facilities:** ⬤⊙◖❋⚒⛟⛱
Services: ⊕⊡→▶⅗⚇⌿⊚

ALLERSTON   Map 19 SE88

▶ ▶ ▶ 79% **Vale of Pickering Caravan
Park (SE879808)**
Carr House Farm YO18 7PQ
☎ 01723 859280 ⓘ 01723 850060
🄴 tony@valeofpickering.co.uk
🔴 www.valeofpickering.co.uk   SILVER
*Dir: On B1415, 1.75m off A170 (Pickering-Scarborough
road)*
⊕⊕▲
Open Mar-8 Jan (rs Mar) Booking advisable BH's
Last arrival 21.00hrs Last departure noon
*An attractively maintained park with high quality
facilities, and surrounded by mature hedges with
lots of colourful landscaping. Set in open
countryside within the North Yorkshire Moors
National Park. A 13-acre site with 120 touring
pitches, 80 hardstandings.*
Microwave
Leisure: ⚠
Facilities: ➔⬤⊙◖❋⚒⛟⛱
Services: ⊕⊡⬤⌀⊞⊡➔⊍▶⊚⌿
⊕⊟⊞⊡

ALNE   Map 19 SE46

▶ ▶ ▶ ▶ 76% **Alders Caravan Park (SE497654)**
Home Farm YO61 1RY
☎ 01347 838722 ⓘ 01347 838722
🄴 enquiries@homefarmalne.co.uk
🔴 www.alderscaravanpark.co.uk
*Dir: From A19 turn off at signs to Alne, in 1.5m turn left
at T-junct, 0.5m Alders on left in village centre in Monk
Green left off Main St.*
★ ⊕ £10-£11.50 ⊕ £10-£11.50 ▲ fr £9

Open Mar-Oct Booking advisable bank hols Last
arrival 21.00hrs Last departure 14.00hrs
*A tastefully developed park on a working farm with
pitches laid out in horseshoe-shaped areas, and
individually screened by trees and shrubs. This well
designed park offers excellent toilet facilities
including bathroom and fully-serviced washing and
toilet cubicles which offer total privacy. A woodland
and a water meadow are pleasant places to walk
and enjoy the local fauna and flora. This park has
no laundry. A 6-acre site with 40 touring pitches,
3 hardstandings.*
Summer house & herb garden
Facilities: ➔⬤⊙◖❋⚒⛟⛱
Services: ⊕⬤⊡→▶⌿⊚

ARNCLIFFE   Map 18 SD97

▶ ▶ ▶ 81% **Hawkswick Cote Caravan Park
(SD947703)**
BD23 5PX ☎ 01756 770226 ⓘ 01756 770327
🄴 hawkswick@lakelandleisureestates.co.uk
*Dir: From B6160 1m N of Kilnsey, take unclass road
signed Arncliffe. Site 1.5m on left*
★ ⊕ £15-£20 ⊕ £15-£20 ▲ fr £15
Open Mar-14 Nov Booking advisable bank hols &
Jul-Aug Last arrival 22.00hrs Last departure noon
*A spacious site in the Dales, with mature
landscaping and views of the surrounding fells.
Various camping areas are divided by traditional
dry stone walling, which complement the stone
park buildings, some of which have been converted
from farm buildings. There are pleasant views in all
directions. A 3-acre site with 50 touring pitches,
19 hardstandings and 90 statics.*
Licensed shop
Leisure: ⚠
Facilities: ⬤⊙◖❋⚒⛟⛱⛱
Services: ⊕⊡⬤⌀⊡→⊍⌿
Notes: Dogs must be kept on leads

England

AYSGARTH   Map 19 SE08

▶ ▶ ▶ 82% *Westholme Caravan & Camping Park*
(SE016882)
DL8 3SP ☎ 01969 663268
Dir: 1m E of Aysgarth off A684
🏠🏠⚠

Open Mar-Oct Booking advisable Bank hols & Jul-
Aug Last arrival 22.00hrs Last departure noon
A beckside site with level grassy pitches in various
paddocks set into the hillside. There is a well-
equipped children's playground, a well-stocked
shop, and a licensed bar and family room. The
famous Aysgarth Falls are nearby. A 22-acre site
with 70 touring pitches and 44 statics.
Fishing free on site.

Leisure: 🎮 🖵
Facilities: 🏠☉🍴☀✇🔌🐾
Services: 🚫📧🍴🛒🔌🔵🔄→ 🗯

BEDALE   Map 19 SE28

NEW ▶ ▶ ▶ 73% **Lindale Holiday Park**
(SE215883)
Newton Le Willows DL8 1TA
☎ 01677 450842 🖨 01677 450869
🖂 info@lindalepark.co.uk
🌐 www.lindalepark.co.uk
Dir: Exit A1 at Leeming Bar onto A684 to Leyburn.
Turn off at x-rds W of Patrick Brompton, signed
Newton le Willows. After 2.5m take minor rd for
Thornton Stewart after sharp left bend park 200mtrs
on right
⚠ £12

Open 31 Mar-Oct (rs Mar-5 Jan Statics only)
Booking advisable Aug Last arrival 22.00hrs Last
departure noon
A newly developed, secluded park in a valley,
surrounded by trees and shrubs. The tenting area is
situated on an elevated position overlooking the
larger upmarket mobile home area, and the toilet
facilities are very good. The park is a good base for
the country walker, and those who wish to explore
the surrounding area by car. A 5-acre site with
15 touring pitches and 36 statics.

Facilities: ➡🏠🍴☀♿🎠🐾
Services: 🍴→🔵🔘◐🔄🗯🐾
Notes: No music to be played in the open, dogs
allowed by prior arrangement
💳 💳 💳 🔘 💳 🔵

BISHOP MONKTON   Map 19 SE36

NEW ▶ ▶ ▶ 69% **Church Farm Caravan Park**
(SE328660)
Knaresborough Rd HG3 3QQ
☎ 01765 677668 🖨 01765 677668
🖂 mervyn@churchfarmcaravans.wanadoo.co.uk
Dir: Park is opposite church.
★ 🚐 £7.50-£10.50 🚐 £7.50-£10.50 ⚠ £6.50-£12
Open Mar-Oct Booking advisable Bank hols Last
arrival 22.30hrs Last departure 15.30hrs
A very pleasant rural site on a working farm, on the
edge of the attractive village of Bishop Monkton
with its well-stocked shop and pubs. Whilst very
                                           contd.

much a place to relax, there are many attractions
close by including Fountains Abbey, Newby Hall,
Ripon and Harrogate. A 4-acre site with 45 touring
pitches and 3 statics.

Facilities: 🏠☉☀♿🔌
Services: 🚫📧🍴🛒→🔵🔘🔄🗯🔵
Notes: No ball games, pets must be kept on leads

BOLTON ABBEY   Map 19 SE05

▶ ▶ ▶ 81% **Howgill Lodge**
(SD065593)
Barden BD23 6DJ
☎ 01756 720655
🖂 info@howgill-lodge.co.uk
🌐 www.howgill-lodge.co.uk
Dir: From Bolton Abbey take B6160 signed Burnsall. 3m
and at Barden Tower turn right signed Appletreewick.
1.5m at phone box turn into lane on right to Howgill
★ 🚐 fr £13 🚐 fr £13 ⚠ fr £12
Open mid Mar-Oct (rs Nov-mid Mar Static caravans
only for hire) Booking advisable Last arrival
21.00hrs
A beautifully-maintained and secluded site offering
panoramic views of Wharfedale. The spacious
hardstanding pitches are mainly terraced, and there
is a separate tenting area with numerous picnic
tables. There are three toilet facilities spread
throughout the site, and a well-stocked shop.
A 4-acre site with 40 touring pitches,
20 hardstandings.

Facilities: 🏠☉🍴☀✇🔌🐾
Services: 🚫📧🍴🔄🔵🔄→ 🗯
💳 💳 💳 🔵 🔵

BOROUGHBRIDGE   Map 19 SE36

▶ ▶ ▶ ▶ 77% **Camping & Caravanning Club Site**
(SE384662)
Bar Ln, Roecliffe YO51 9LS ☎ 01423 322683
🌐 www.campingandcaravanningclub.co.uk
Dir: From A1(M) junct 48 follow signs for Bar Lane Ind
Est & Roecliffe. Site 0.25m from rdbt
★ 🚐 £16.10-£17.80 🚐 £16.10-£17.80
⚠ £16.10-£17.80
Open all year Booking advisable bank hols & peak
period Last arrival 21.00hrs Last departure noon
A quiet riverside site with direct access onto the
River Ure, with fishing and boating available. Close
enough to the A1(M) but far enough away to hear
little traffic noise, this site is a perfect stopover for
longer journeys. The popular tourist centres of
Ripon, Knaresborough, Harrogate and York are
within easy reach, while the friendly little town of
Boroughbridge offers plenty of facilities just a short
walk away. Please see the advertisement on page
11 for information on Club sites and membership.
A 5-acre site with 85 touring pitches,
13 hardstandings.
Fishing.

Leisure: 🎣 🎮
Facilities: 🏠☉🍴☀♿🔌🐾
Services: 🚫📧📧🍴🔄🔵🔄→◐🔄🐾
💳 💳 💳 🔵 🔵

England

CAWOOD   Map 16 SE53

▶ ▶ ▶ ▶ 74% **Cawood Park (SE563385)**
Ryther Rd YO8 3TT ☎ 01757 268450
✉ cawoodpark@aol.com
ⓦ www.cawoodpark.com
*Dir: from A1 take B1222, turn at Cawood lights signed
Tadcaster onto B1223 for 1m, park on left*
★ ⚍ £13-£21 ⚏ £13-£21 ▲ £13-£21

Booking advisable bank hols & Jul-Aug Last arrival
21.00hrs Last departure 11.00hrs
*An attractive park in a rural area with its own
fishing lake, overlooked by the camping area. The
site is bordered by hedges and mature trees, and is
well away from the road, with modern amenities.
The lakeside club house provides regular
entertainment, and coarse fishing is available.
A 12-acre site with 60 touring pitches,
3 hardstandings and 10 statics.*
Leisure: ◣ ◻
Facilities: ↑⊙ℚ❄ & ㄥ 🐾 ⬛ 🎋
Services: 🔌 🖥 ♀ ⚓ ⏲ → ∪ ▶ ▲ ⌁
💳 🚘 💳 ⑩ 💳 🚗 🔃

CONSTABLE BURTON   Map 19 SE19

▶ ▶ ▶ 80% **Constable Burton Hall Caravan Park
(SE158907)**
DL8 5LJ ☎ 01677 450428
Dir: Off A684 (screened behind old deer park wall)
★ ⚍ £11-£14 ⚏ £11-£14 ▲
Open Apr-Oct Booking advisable public hols Last
arrival 20.00hrs Last departure noon
*A pretty site in the former deer park of the adjoining
Constable Burton Hall, screened from the road by
the deer park walls and surrounded by mature trees
in a quiet rural location. The laundry is housed in a
converted 18th-century deer barn, and there is a
pub and restaurant opposite. A 10-acre site with
120 touring pitches.*
Facilities: ↑⊙ℚ❄ & ㄥ 🎋
Services: 🔌 ⚓ ⌁ ⏲ ✗ → ▶ ♨ 🛒
Notes: Dogs on leads, no commercial vehicles, no
games

Practise setting up your tent at home
before you take it on holiday, and check
that all guy ropes, pegs and poles are
present and intact.

EASINGWOLD   Map 19 SE56

▶ ▶ 64% *Folly Garth (SE543687)*
Green Ln YO61 3ES ☎ 01347 821150
*Dir: From Easingwold take Stillington road for 1.5m, site
on right*
⚍ ⚏ ▲
Open Feb-Dec
*A small country site tucked away at the end of a
lane, just 1.5 miles from the Georgian market town
of Easingwold. Facilities include a kitchen and a
lounge with table and chairs, opening onto a
decking area. The toilets are to a good standard.
A 3-acre site with 20 touring pitches.*
Facilities: ↑
Services: 🔌

FILEY   Map 17 TA18

 72% **Blue Dolphin Holiday
Park (TA095829)** Gristhorpe Bay YO14 9PU
☎ 01723 515155 🖷 01723 512059
ⓦ www.havenholidays.com
Dir: Park is off A165 2m N of Filey.
★ ⚍ £9-£46 ⚏ £9-£46 ▲ £6-£29
Open mid Mar-Oct (rs mid Mar-May &
Sep-Oct Some facilities may be reduced)
Booking advisable School hols Last departure
10.00hrs
*There are great clifftop views to be enjoyed from
this fun-filled holiday centre with an extensive
and separate touring area. The emphasis is on
non-stop entertainment, with organised sports
and clubs, all-weather leisure facilities, heated
swimming pools and plenty of well-planned
amusements. Pitches are mainly on level or
gently-sloping grass plus some fully-serviced
hardstandings, and the beach is just 2 miles
away. There is also an interesting nature trail.
An 85-acre site with 385 touring pitches,
10 hardstandings.*
Multi-sports court
Leisure: ➹ ⊰ ◣ ⚙
Facilities: ⊙ℚ❄ & ㄥ 🐾 🎋
Services: 🔌 ⚙ 🖥 ♀ ⚓ ⌀ ✗ ⬆ → ▶ ◎ ▲ ⌁ ⌁
Notes: Maximum of 2 dogs per group
💳 💳 💳 🚗 🔃

 88% **Flower of May Holiday
Park (TA085835)** Lebberston Cliff YO11 3NU
☎ 01723 584311 🖷 01723 581361
✉ info@flowerofmay.com
ⓦ www.flowerofmay.com
Dir: Signed off A165 on Scarborough side of Filey
★ ⚍ £13-£17.50 ⚏ £13-£17.50 ▲ £10-£17.50
Open Etr-Oct (rs early & late season) Booking
advisable Spring BH wk, Jul-Aug & BH's Last
arrival 21.00hrs Last departure noon
*A well-run, high quality family holiday park with
top class facilities. This large landscaped park
offers a full range of recreational activities, with
plenty to occupy everyone. Grass or hard
pitches are available, all on level ground, and*
contd.

Services: Ⓣ Toilet Fluid ✗ Café/ Restaurant 🍴 Fast Food/Takeaway ➡ Baby Care 🔌 Electric Hook Up
🚐 Motorvan Service Point 🖥 Launderette ♀ Licensed Bar 🛢 Calor Gaz ⌀ Camping Gaz ⬆ Battery Charging

Flower of May Holiday Park
arranged in avenues screened by shrubs.
A 13-acre site with 270 touring pitches,
100 hardstandings and 193 statics.
Squash, bowling, 9-hole golf & basketball court

Leisure: 🏊 � ⚑ ☐

Facilities: ⚐ ☉ ⚐ ✳ ⚑ ⚑ ⚑ ☂ ⚑

Services: ⚑ ⚑ ⚑ ⚑ ⚑ ⚑ ⚑ ✕ ⚑ → ∪ ⚑ ☉ ⚑ ⚑ ⚑ ⚑ ⚑

Notes: Dogs by arrangement only
See advertisement under SCARBOROUGH

 77% Primrose Valley
Holiday Park (TA123778)
YO14 9RF ☎ 01723 513771
& 0870 405 0126 🖷 01723 513777
Ⓦ www.havenholidays.com
Dir: Signed off A165 (Scarborough-Bridlington
road), 3m S of Filey
★ ⚑ £13-£64 ⚑ £13-£64
Open mid Mar-Oct Booking advisable At all
times Last departure 10.00hrs
A large all-action holiday centre with a wide
range of sports and leisure activities to suit
everyone from morning until late in the evening.
A completely new touring area, with its own
entrance and toilet facility, was completed in
2005. All touring pitches are fully-serviced hard-
standings with grassed awning strips.
A 160-acre site with 49 touring pitches and
1800 statics.

Leisure: 🏊 ⚑ ⚑ ⚑ ⚑

Facilities: ⚐ ☉ ⚑ ⚑ ⚑ ⚑

Services: ⚑ ⚑ ⚑ ⚑ ⚑ ✕ ⚑ → ⚑ ☉ ⚑ ⚑ ⚑

Notes: Maximum of 2 dogs
per group ⚑ ⚑ ⚑ ⚑ ⚑

 66% Reighton Sands
Holiday Park (TA142769)
Reighton Gap YO14 9SH
☎ 01723 890476 🖷 01723 891043
Ⓦ www.havenholidays.com
Dir: On A165 5m S of Filey at Righton Gap, signed
⚑ ⚑ ⚑
Open mid Mar-Oct (rs mid Mar-May & Sep-Oct
Some facilities may be reduced) Booking
advisable School hols Last arrival 22.00hrs Last
departure noon
A large, lively holiday centre with a wide range
of entertainment and all-weather leisure
facilities, located just 10 minutes' walk from a
contd.

Reighton Sands Holiday Park
long sandy beach. Each of the three touring
areas has its own facilities block, and the site is
particularly geared towards families with young
children. A 229-acre site with 160 touring
pitches, 160 hardstandings and 800 statics.
Indoor play area

Leisure: 🏊 ⚑ ⚑

Facilities: ☉ ✳ ⚑ ⚑ ⚑

Services: ⚑ ⚑ ⚑ ✕ ⚑
⚑ ⚑ ⚑ ⚑ ⚑ ⚑ ⚑

▶ ▶ ▶ ▶ **83% Lebberston Touring Park**
(TA077824)
Filey Rd YO11 3PE ☎ 01723 585723
Ⓔ info@lebberstontouring.co.uk
Ⓦ www.lebberstontouring.co.uk
Dir: Off A165 (Filey to Scarborough road). Site signed
★ ⚑ £12-£18 ⚑ £12-£18

Open Mar-Oct Booking advisable bank hols &
school holidays Last arrival 21.00hrs Last departure
noon
A peaceful family park in a gently-sloping rural
area, where the quality facilities are maintained to a
high standard of cleanliness. The keen owners are
friendly and helpful, and create a relaxing
atmosphere. A natural area offers views of the
surrounding countryside through the shrubbery.
A 7.5-acre site with 125 touring pitches,
25 hardstandings.

Facilities: ⚑ ⚐ ☉ ⚑ ✳ ⚑ ⚑ ⚑ ⚑

Services: ⚑ ⚑ ⚑ ⚑ → ∪ ⚑ ☉ ⚑ ⚑ ⚑ ⚑

Notes: No tents, dogs on lead
⚑ ⚑ ⚑ ⚑ ⚑

For full details of the AA pennant
ratings scheme see pages 7-8

Leisure: 🏊 Indoor swimming pool ⚑ Outdoor swimming pool ⚑ Tennis court ⚑ Games room ⚑ Children's playground ∪ Stables
▶ 9/18 hole golf course ⚑ Boats for hire ⚑ Cinema ⚑ Fishing ☉ Mini golf ⚑ Watersports ☐ Separate TV room

England

▶ ▶ ▶ 75% **Centenary Way Camping & Caravan Park** (TA115798)
Muston Grange YO14 0HU
☎ 01723 516415 & 512313
Dir: Just off A1039 near junct with A165 on Bridlington side of Filey
★ ⊕ £8-£12 ⊕ £8-£12 Å £3.50-£12

Open Mar-Oct Booking advisable bank hols & Jul-Aug Last arrival 21.00hrs Last departure noon
A well set-out family-owned park, with footpath access to nearby beach. Close to the seaside resort of Filey, and caravan pitches enjoy views over open countryside. A 3-acre site with 75 touring pitches, 25 hardstandings.

Leisure: ⚊
Facilities: ⬤⊙✻⬤⬤⬤
Services: ⬤⬤⬤⬤→⬤⬤⬤⬤

▶ ▶ ▶ 74% **Crows Nest Caravan Park** (TA094826)
Gristhorpe YO14 9PS
☎ 01723 582206 ▤ 01723 582206
ⓦ www.crowsnestcaravanpark.com
Dir: 5m S of Scarborough, and 2m N of Filey. On seaward side of A165, signed off rdbt, near petrol station.
★ ⊕ fr £14 ⊕ fr £12 Å fr £12
Open Mar-Oct Booking advisable Last departure noon
A beautifully situated park on the coast between Scarborough and Filey, with excellent panoramic views. This large and mainly static park offers lively entertainment, and two bars. The touring caravan area is near the entertainment complex, whilst the tenting pitches are at the top of the site. A 20-acre site with 49 touring pitches, 49 hardstandings and 217 statics.

Leisure: ⬤⬤⚊
Facilities: ⬤⊙✻⬤⬤⬤
Services: ⬤⬤⬤⬤⬤⬤⬤→⬤⬤⬤⬤⬤
⬤⬤⬤⬤⬤⬤⬤

Don't forget matches, a torch and spare batteries, and the means to make a drink. Packet soups are sustaining until the shops open.

▶ ▶ ▶ 74% **Filey Brigg Touring Caravan & Country Park** (TA115812)
North Cliff YO14 9ET ☎ 01723 513852
Dir: 0.5m from Filey town centre on coast road from Scarborough, A165
⬤⬤Å

Open Etr-30 Oct Booking advisable bank hols & Jul-Aug Last arrival 18.00hrs Last departure noon
A municipal park overlooking Filey Brigg with splendid views along the coast, and set in a country park. The beach is just a short walk away, as is the resort of Filey. Heating has now been installed in the main toilet block, and 50 all-weather pitches are available. A 9-acre site with 158 touring pitches, 55 hardstandings.

Leisure: ⚊ Facilities: ⬤⊙✻⬤⬤⬤⬤⬤⬤
Services: ⬤⬤⬤✕⬤→⬤⬤⬤⬤⬤
⬤⬤⬤⬤⬤

GRASSINGTON
See **Threshfield**

HARROGATE　　　　　　　　　　　Map 19 SE35
PREMIER PARK

▶ ▶ ▶ ▶ ▶ 72% **Ripley Caravan Park** (SE289610)
Knaresborough Rd, Ripley HG3 3AU
☎ 01423 770050 ▤ 01423 770050
Dir: 3m N of Harrogate on A61. Right at rdbt onto B6165 signed Knaresborough. Park 300yds left
★ ⊕ £10.50-£13.50 ⊕ £10.50-£13.50
Å £10.50-£13.50
Open Etr-Oct Booking advisable bank hols Last arrival 21.00hrs Last departure noon
A well-run rural site in attractive meadowland which has been landscaped with mature tree plantings. The resident owners lovingly maintain their facilities, and there is a heated swimming pool and sauna, a games room, and a covered play room for small children. An 18-acre site with 100 touring pitches, 35 hardstandings and 50 statics.
Nursery playroom, sauna, football, TV in games room

Leisure: ⬤⬤⚊ Facilities: ⬤⊙⬤✻⬤⬤⬤⬤
Services: ⬤⬤⬤⬤⬤⬤→⬤⬤⬤⬤⬤⬤
Notes: Family camping only, dogs on leads, BBQs must be off the ground ⬤⬤⬤⬤⬤

PREMIER PARK

▶ ▶ ▶ ▶ ▶ 80% **Rudding Holiday Park** (SE333531)
Follifoot HG3 1JH ☎ 01423 870439
🖷 01423 870859
🅴 holiday-park@ruddingpark.com
🆆 www.ruddingpark.com
Dir: From A1 take A59 to A658, then S signed Bradford. 4.5m then right, follow signs
★ ⚏ £14.50-£28 ⚏ Å £8-£21

Open Mar-Jan (rs Nov-Jan) Booking advisable bank hols & wknds Last arrival 22.30hrs Last departure 14.00hrs
A spacious park set in the stunning 200-acres of mature parkland and walled gardens of Rudding Park. The setting has been tastefully enhanced with terraced pitches and dry-stone walls. A separate area houses super pitches where all services are supplied including a picnic table and TV connection. The toilet blocks are first class. There is an 18-hole golf course, and a heated outdoor swimming pool, plus the Deer House bar and restaurant, and a children's play area. A 55-acre site with 141 touring pitches, 60 hardstandings and 95 statics.
18-hole golf course, driving range
Leisure: ⚈ ⚉ ⚊
Facilities: ⚌ ⚍ ⚎ ⚏ ⚐ ⚑ ⚒ ⚓ ⚔ ⚕ ⚖ ⚗
Services: ⚘ ⚙ ⚚ ⚛ ⚜ ⚝ ⚞ ⚟ ⚠ ⚡ ⚢ ⚣ ⚤ ⚥
Notes: Under 18's must be accompanied by adult ⚦ ⚧ ⚨ ⚩ ⚪ ⚫

▶ ▶ ▶ ▶ 77% **High Moor Farm Park** (SE242560)
Skipton Rd HG3 2LT ☎ 01423 563637 & 564955
🖷 01423 529449
Dir: On A59 Harrogate-Skipton road
⚏ £13-£17.50 ⚏ £13-£17.50

contd.

Open Etr or Apr-Oct Booking advisable public hols Last arrival 23.30hrs Last departure 15.00hrs
An excellent site with first class facilities, set beside a small wood and surrounded by thorn hedges. The numerous touring pitches are located in meadowland fields, each area with its own toilet block. A large heated indoor swimming pool and a games room are very popular, and there is a golf course, a full-sized crown bowling green, and a bar serving meals and snacks. A 15-acre site with 320 touring pitches, 51 hardstandings and 158 statics.
Coarse fishing, 9-hole golf course, bowling green
Leisure: ⚈ ⚉ ⚊ **Facilities:** ⚌ ⚍ ⚎ ⚏ ⚐ ⚑ ⚒ ⚓ ⚔ ⚕ ⚖ ⚗
Services: ⚘ ⚙ ⚚ ⚛ ⚜ ⚝ ⚞ ⚟ ⚠ ⚡ ⚢ ⚣
Notes: ⚦ ⚧ ⚨ ⚩

▶ ▶ ▶ 63% **Shaws Trailer Park** (SE325557)
Knaresborough Rd HG2 7NE ☎ 01423 884432
🖷 01423 883622
🆆 www.shawstrailerpark.co.uk
Dir: On A59 1m from town centre. 0.5m SW of Starbeck railway crossing, by Johnsons dry cleaners
★ ⚏ fr £12.50 ⚏ fr £12.50 Å fr £12
Open all year Booking advisable public hols Last arrival 20.00hrs Last departure noon
A long-established site just a mile from the centre of Harrogate. The all-weather pitches are arranged around a carefully kept grass area, and the toilets are basic but functional and clean. The entrance is on the bus route to Harrogate. An 11-acre site with 60 touring pitches, 24 hardstandings and 146 statics.
Facilities: ⚌ ⚍ ⚎ ⚖ **Services:** ⚘ ⚙ ⚚ ⚟ ⚠ ⚣ ⚤ ⚥
Notes: Adults only

England

FOXHOLME ▶▶▶
CARAVAN PARK
Campsite of the Year North Region Winner 1986
60 Touring Vans, Motor Caravans & Tents

AA ▶◀

English
Tourist Council
✓✓✓✓✓

ADULTS
ONLY

Ryedale, North Yorkshire, (4 miles from Helmsley and the North York Moors National Park). A quiet site suitable for exploring North Yorkshire.
60 pitches set in individual clearings in the woodland. Luxury toilet blocks, AA graded Excellent for environment, wc's, hot water, showers, wash basins in cubicles and shaver points.
Reception, late arrival park, shop and mains hook-up points. Some pitches for tents.
Caravan Club approved. Camping Club listed.
For brochure, please send stamp to:

FOXHOLME CARAVAN PARK
**(AA), Harome, Helmsley, North Yorkshire
YO62 5JG
Tel. (01439) 771241 Fax: (01439) 771744**

NEW ▶ ▶ 78% **Bilton Park (SE317577)**
Village Farm, Bilton Ln HG1 4DH
☎ 01423 863121
Dir: Turn E off A59 at Skipton Inn into Bilton Lane.
Site approx 1m
🚐🚐
Open Apr-Oct
An established family-owned park in open countryside yet only 2 miles from the shops and tearooms of Harrogate. The spacious grass pitches are complemented by a well appointed new toilet block with private facilities. This is an excellent walking area with the Nidd Gorge right on the doorstep. A 4-acre site with 50 touring pitches.
Facilities: ↑ 🛒

HAWES	Map 18 SD88

▶ ▶ 86% **Bainbridge Ings Caravan & Camping Site (SD879895)**
DL8 3NU ☎ 01969 667354
🅱 janet@bainbridge-ings.co.uk
🆆 www.bainbridge-ings.co.uk
Dir: Approaching Hawes from Bainbridge on A684, turn left at sign marked Gayle, 300yds on left
🚐 £10 🚐 £9.50 ⛺ £9.50
Open Apr-Oct Booking advisable school hols Last arrival 22.00hrs Last departure noon
A quiet, well-organised site in open countryside close to Hawes in the heart of Upper Wensleydale, popular with ramblers. Pitches are sited around the perimeter of several fields, each bounded by

contd.

traditional stone walls. A 5-acre site with 70 touring pitches, 4 hardstandings and 15 statics.
Facilities: ↑ ☉ 🍴 ✳
Services: 🚐 🔋 🛢 🛒 ⊞ → 🍴 🛒

HELMSLEY	Map 19 SE68

▶ ▶ ▶ ▶ 78% **Golden Square Touring Caravan Park (SE604797)**
Oswaldkirk YO62 5YQ
☎ 01439 788269 📠 01439 788236
🅱 barbara
@goldensquarecaravanpark.freeserve.co.uk
🆆 www.goldensquarecaravanpark.com
Dir: 1m from Ampleforth towards Helmsley on caravan route. Turn off B1257 to Ampleforth, 0.5m on right
★ 🚐 £9.50-£13.50 🚐 £9.50-£13.50 ⛺ £9.50-£13.50

GOLD

Open Mar-Oct Booking advisable bank hols Last arrival 21.00hrs Last departure noon
An excellent, popular family site with manicured grounds and first class toilets. This friendly park is set in a quiet rural situation with lovely views over the North Yorks Moors. The park is terraced on three levels surrounded by trees, and caters particularly for families. Country walks and mountain bike trails start here. Caravans are banned from the A170 at Sutton Bank between Thirsk and Helmsley.
A 12-acre site with 129 touring pitches and 1 static. Microwave
Leisure: ♦ ⚙ **Facilities:** ↝ ↑ ☉ 🍴 ✳ ⓰ 🛒 🛒 🎏 ⟙
Services: 🚐 ↯ 🛢 🛒 ⊞ ⊞ ↝ → 🍴 ▶ ◉ 🍴

▶ ▶ ▶ 75% **Foxholme Caravan Park (SE658828)**
Harome YO62 5JG ☎ 01439 770416 & 771241
📠 01439 771744
Dir: A170 from Helmsley towards Scarborough, right signed Harome, left at church, through village follow signs
★ 🚐 £12.50-£14 🚐 £12.50-£14 ⛺ £12.50-£14
Open Etr-Oct Booking advisable bank & school hols Last arrival 23.00hrs Last departure noon
A quiet adults only park set in secluded wooded countryside, with well-shaded pitches in individual clearings divided by mature trees. The facilities are well maintained, and the site is ideal as a touring base or a place to relax. Caravans are prohibited on the A170 at Sutton Bank between Thirsk and Helmsley. A 6-acre site with 60 touring pitches.
Facilities: ↑ ☉ 🍴 ✳ ⓰ 🛒 🛒 🎏
Services: 🚐 ↯ 🛢 🛒 ⊞ ⊞ → 🍴 ▶ 🍴
Notes: Adults only

► ► ► 66% **Wrens of Ryedale Touring Park**
(SE656840)
Gale Ln, Nawton YO62 7SD ☎ 01439 771260
🖃 dave@wrensofryedale.fsnet.co.uk
ⓦ www.wrensofryedale.fsnet.co.uk
Dir: On A170 3m E of Helmsley, turn right in villages of
Nawton/Beadlam into Gale Lane. Park 400mtrs on right
🚐🚐⚕
Open Apr-Oct Booking advisable bank & school
hols Last arrival 22.00hrs Last departure flexible
A small family-owned park divided into three areas
by mature trees and shrubs. The sheltered grass
pitches are ideal for those seeking a quiet and
relaxing holiday. Caravans are prohibited on the
A170 at Sutton Bank between Thirsk and Helmsley.
A 2.5-acre site with 45 touring pitches.
Bike hire.

Leisure: ⚙ Facilities: 🌣⊙🥤⚹🛠🛁🎣
Services: 🔌🖳👜⊘🖂→∪▶🍴

| HIGH BENTHAM | Map 18 SD66 |

► ► ► ► 79% **Riverside Caravan**
Park (SD665688)
LA2 7LW ☎ 015242 61272 &
62163 🖨 015242 62163
🖃 info@riversidecaravanpark.co.uk
ⓦ www.riversidecaravanpark.co.uk
Dir: Off B6480, signed from town centre
🚐🚐⚕
Open Mar-Nov Booking advisable bank hols Last
arrival 20.00hrs Last departure noon
A well-managed riverside park with level grass
pitches set in avenues separated by trees. This
attractive park has a well-equipped amenities block
including excellent facilities for family tenters. The
games room and adventure playground are popular
with families, and the market town of High Bentham
is close by. A 12-acre site with 61 touring pitches,
12 hardstandings and 205 statics.
Free permits for private fishing

Leisure: ⚙ ⚙
Facilities: 🌣⊙🥤⚹🛠🛁🎣
Services: 🔌🖳🖳👜⊘🖂⊡→▶🍴🌮🚬🚬🔋🔌📶 🔲

► 78% **Lowther Hill Caravan Park (SD696695)**
LA2 7AN ☎ 01524 261657
Dir: From A65 at Clapham onto B6480 signed Bentham.
3m to site on right
★ 🚐 £10-£12.50 🚐 £10-£12.50 ⚕ £3-£4

Open Mar-Nov Booking advisable Last arrival
20.00hrs Last departure 14.00.hrs
contd.

A simple site with stunning panoramic views from
every pitch. Peace reigns on this little park, though
the tourist villages of Ingleton, Clapham and Settle
are not far away. All pitches have electricity, and
there is a heated toilet/washroom. A 1-acre site with
9 touring pitches and 1 static.

Services: 🔌→▶🖂🖳🔋

| HUNMANBY | Map 17 TA07 |

► ► ► 79% **Orchard Farm Holiday Village**
(TA105779)
Stonegate YO14 0PU
☎ 01723 891582
🖨 01723 891582
🖃 s.dugdale@virgin.net
ⓦ www.orchardfarmholidayvillage.co.uk
Dir: From Scarborough take A165 towards Bridlington.
Turn right signed Hunmanby, park on right just after
railway bridge
★ 🚐 £10-£16 🚐 £10-£16 ⚕ £10-£16
Open Mar-Oct (rs Nov-Mar not all facilities open)
Booking advisable bank hols & peak season Last
arrival 23.00hrs Last departure 11.00hrs
Pitches are arranged around a large coarse fishing
lake at this grassy park. The young owners are keen
and friendly, and offer a wide range of amenities
including an indoor heated swimming pool and a
licensed bar. A 14-acre site with 91 touring pitches,
34 hardstandings and 46 statics.
Fishing

Leisure: 🏊 ⚙ ⚙ 🔲
Facilities: 🌣⊙🥤⚹🛁🛠🎣🐾🍴
Services: 🔌🖳🚰👜🖂⊡ 🍺→▶🌮♨🔋🍴

| HUTTON-LE-HOLE | Map 19 SE79 |

► ► ► 82% **Hutton-le-Hole Caravan Park**
(SE705895)
Westfield Lodge YO62 6UG
☎ 01751 417261 🖨 01751 417876
🖃 rwstrickland@farmersweekly.net
ⓦ www.westfieldlodge.co.uk
Dir: from A170 onto Hutton-le-Hole road, N for approx
2m, over cattle grid, 500yds left into Park Drive, signed
into site
★ 🚐 £10-£11.50 🚐 £10-£11.50 ⚕ £8-£10
Open Etr-Oct Booking advisable bank hols Last
arrival 22.00hrs Last departure noon
A small high quality park within a working farm in
the North York Moors National Park. Pitches are
on a well-maintained lawn with surrounding
hedges and trees. The purpose-built toilet block
achieves a very high standard with its en suite
family rooms. The village with its shop and pubs
is a 10 minute walk away. Caravans are prohibited
from using the A170 at Sutton Bank between
Thirsk and Helmsley. A 2.5-acre site with
22 touring pitches.
Farm walks

Facilities: 🌣⊙🥤⚹🛁🛠🎣🍴
Services: 🔌👜🖂⊡→∪▶♨🔋

England

KNARESBOROUGH　　　Map 19 SE35

▶ ▶ ▶ 73% **Kingfisher Caravan Park** (SE343603)
Low Moor Ln, Farnham HG5 9JB
☎ 01423 869411 ▤ 01423 869411
Dir: From Knaresborough take A6055. After 1m turn left towards Farnham & left again in village signed Scotton. Site 1m on left
★ ⊞ £10-£14 ⊞ £10-£12 ▲ £10-£12
Open Mar-Oct Booking advisable bank hols & 15 Jul-1 Sep Last arrival 23.00hrs Last departure 16.00hrs
A large grassy site with open spaces set in a wooded area in rural countryside. Whilst Harrogate, Fountains Abbey and York are within easy reach, anglers will want to take advantage of on-site coarse and fly fishing lakes. A 4-acre site with 35 touring pitches and 30 statics.

Leisure: ⚏

Facilities: ⋔⊙⊑⋇⅋⌁⊡⊞⊓⋔

Services: ⊡⊡⊟⌑⊡→∪⋇⇲⊿

LONG PRESTON　　　Map 18 SD85

▶ ▶ ▶ ▶ 77% **Gallaber Park** (SD840570)
BD23 4QF ☎ 01729 851397 ▤ 01729 851398
☻ info@gallaberpark.co.uk
ⓦ www.gallaberpark.com
Dir: On A682 between Long Preston & Gisburn
★ ⊞ £12-£18 ⊞ £12-£18 ▲ £12
Open mid Mar-Oct Booking advisable Bank hols
Set in the picturesque Ribble Valley, this park enjoys lovely views across the Dales. A stone barn houses excellent toilets and a family bathroom, and there are various types of pitches including some fully serviced ones. The emphasis is on quiet relaxation, and the spacious grounds and plentiful young shrubs and trees support this impression. 63 touring pitches, 27 hardstandings and 21 statics.
Family bathroom

Facilities: ⋔⊙⅋⋔

Services: ⊡⩜⊟⊡→⅃⊜⊞⊞⊠⊠

MARKINGTON　　　Map 19 SE26

▶ ▶ ▶ 76% **Yorkshire Hussar Inn Holiday Caravan Park** (SE288650)
High St HG3 3NR ☎ 01765 677327
☻ yorkshirehussar@yahoo.co.uk
Dir: Between Harrogate & Ripon (A61) turn W at Wormald Green, 1m into Markington
★ ⊞ £14-£15 ⊞ £14-£15 ▲ £8-£15
Open Etr-Oct Booking advisable bank hols Last arrival 22.00hrs Last departure noon
A terraced site behind the village inn with well-kept grass. This pleasant site offers spacious pitches with some hardstandings and electricity. A 5-acre site with 20 touring pitches, 2 hardstandings and 73 statics.
Paddling pool

Leisure: ⚏

Facilities: ⋔⊙⊑⋇⅋⊑

Services: ⊡⊟⊑⊟⊞→∪▶

Notes: Dogs must be kept on leads

MASHAM　　　Map 19 SE28

▶ ▶ ▶ 71% *Black Swan Holiday Park* (SE192808)
Fearby HG4 4NF
☎ 01765 689477 ▤ 01765 689477
☻ info@blackswanholiday.co.uk
ⓦ www.blackswanholiday.co.uk
Dir: Turn left off A6108 0.25m NW of Masham onto Fearby Road, site 2m on left at rear Black Swan Hotel
⊞⊞▲
Open Mar-Oct Booking advisable at all times Last arrival 22.00hrs Last departure noon
A sloping site at the rear of the Black Swan Inn, with central toilet facilities, and good open views over a wooded hillside. The Black Swan is a country pub serving restaurant/bar meals, with regular weekend entertainment. A 4-acre site with 50 touring pitches, 2 hardstandings and 3 statics.

Leisure: ⚏⊡

Facilities: ⋔⊙⋇⅋⊑⊓⋔

Services: ⊡⊡⊑⊟⌑⊡⊡⋇⇲→∪▶⊿⅊
⊞⊞⊞⊙⊞⊠⊡

NEW ▶ ▶ ▶ 75% **Old Station Caravan Park** (SE232812)

Old Station Yard, Low Burton HG4 4DF
☎ 01765 689569
Dir: Exit A1 onto B6267 signed Masham & Thirsk. In 8m left onto A6108. In 100yds left into site
⊞▲
Open Mar-Nov
An interesting and developing site on a former station. The enthusiastic and caring family owners have maintained the railway theme in creating a park with high quality facilities. The small town of Masham with its Theakston and Black Sheep breweries are within easy walking distance of the park. A new reception and café, together with a number of fully serviced pitches are due to be completed for the 2006 season. A 3-acre site with 50 touring pitches.

Facilities: ⋔

NABURN　　　Map 16 SE54

▶ ▶ ▶ 75% *Naburn Lock Caravan Park* (SE596446)
YO19 4RU ☎ 01904 728697 ▤ 01904 728697
☻ wilks@naburnlock.co.uk
ⓦ www.naburnlock.co.uk
Dir: From A64 take on A19 N, turn left signed Naburn, site on right 0.5m past village
⊞⊞▲

contd.

Open Mar-6 Nov Booking advisable anytime Last arrival 22.00hrs
A family park whose enthusiastic owners are steadily improving its quality. The mainly grass pitches are arranged in small groups separated by mature hedges. The park is close to the River Ouse, and the river towpath provides excellent walking and cycling opportunities. The riverbus to nearby York leaves from a jetty beside the park. A 7-acre site with 100 touring pitches.
River fishing
Facilities: �ⓒ🔍⚡✳⚓ㅿ🎍⛺
Services: 🚇♨️🛢🍴🔌🍽🚹→∪⚓
🍷🏧🍺◎🏧🍴🐕🅿️

NORTHALLERTON   Map 19 SE39

NEW ▶ ▶ ▶ ▶ 76% **Otterington Park (SE378882)**
Station Park, South Otterington DL7 9JB
☎ 01609 780656 & 780263
Dir: Turn W off A168 midway between Northallerton & Thirsk, signed South Otterington. Site on right just before South Otterington
🚐

Open Mar-Oct
A newly developed high quality park on a working farm with open outlooks across the Vale of York. The attractions of Northallerton and Thirsk are a few minutes drive away. On site, peace and tranquillity reigns, with a first class nature walk and on-site fishing being popular. Young children will enjoy the play area. Toilet facilities are very good. A warm Yorkshire welcome is ensured from the enthusiastic owners. A 5-acre site with 40 touring pitches.
Facilities: ⚓

NORTH STAINLEY   Map 19 SE27

▶ ▶ ▶ 77% **Sleningford Water Mill Caravan Camping Park (SE280783)**
HG4 3HQ ☎ 01765 635201
🌐 www.ukparks.co.uk/sleningford
Dir: Adjacent to A6108. 4m N of Ripon & 1m N of North Stainley
🚐🚐🅰️
Open Etr & Apr-Oct Booking advisable bank & school hols Last arrival 22.00hrs Last departure 12.30hrs
The old watermill and the River Ure make an attractive setting for this touring park which is laid out in two areas. Pitches are placed in meadowland and close to mature woodland, and the park is
contd.

---

carefully maintained. The park is popular with canoeists. A 14-acre site with 80 touring pitches. Off-licence, canoe access, fly fishing.
Leisure: 🔍 🏔
Facilities: 🛐ⓒ✳⚓🍴🎍ㅿ🎍
Services: 🚇♨️🛢🍴🔌🍽→ ▶ ㅿ⚓
Notes: Youth groups by prior arrangement only

OSMOTHERLEY   Map 19 SE49

▶ ▶ ▶ 77% **Cote Ghyll Caravan & Camping Park (SE459979)**
DL6 3AH ☎ 01609 883425 📠 01609 883425
ⓔ hills@coteghyll.com
🌐 www.coteghyll.com
Dir: Exit A19 at A684 (Northallerton junct). Follow signs to Osmotherley. Left in village centre. Site entrance 0.5m on right
★ 🚐 £10.50-£12.50 🚐 £10.50-£12.50 🅰️ £10.50-£12.50
Open Mar-Oct Booking advisable bank hols Last arrival 23.00hrs Last departure noon
Quiet, peaceful site in a pleasant valley on the edge of moors, close to the village. The park is divided into terraces bordered by woodland, and the amenities are being progressively upgraded. There are pubs and shops nearby. A 7-acre site with 77 touring pitches, 3 hardstandings and 18 statics.
Tourist info, packed lunch service
Leisure: 🏔
Facilities: ⛯🛐ⓒ✳⚓🍴🎍🐕🎍
Services: 🚇♨️🛢🍴🔌🍽⚓→∪⚓
Notes: Family park, dogs must be kept on lead at all times

PICKERING   Map 19 SE78

▶ ▶ ▶ 80% **Upper Carr Touring Park (SE804816)**
Upper Carr Ln, Malton Rd YO18 7JP
☎ 01751 473115 📠 01751 473115
ⓔ harker@uppercarr.demon.co.uk
🌐 www.uppercarr.demon.co.uk
Dir: Off A169 (Malton-Pickering road), approx 1.5m from Pickering. Signed opposite Black Bull pub
★ 🚐 £10.50-£15 🚐 £10.50-£15 🅰️ £10.50-£15

Open Mar-Oct Booking advisable Last arrival 21.00hrs Last departure noon
Attractive and well-maintained rural touring park set amongst mature trees and hedges, with an animal corner and adjacent 9-hole golf course. A nature trail leads to the quaint village of
contd.

Upper Carr Touring Park

Upper Carr is a quiet Country Park near Pickering. Everyone is made welcome whether Towing a Caravan, Pitching a Tent or Driving a Motor Home.

UPPER CARR offers:
* Timber Holiday Chalet for hire
* Amenity block, laundry & disabled facilities to a good standard
* Quiet secluded Country Park
* Level pitches with 10amp Hook-ups
* Attractive children's Play area
* Pets Corner
* Nature walk and cycle trail
* Many nearby attractions

NEARBY ATTRACTIONS:
Family Country Pub serving Meals (2 minutes walk away) • Small 9-hole Golf Course and Tennis Courts (opposite) • Fishing • Swimming • Walking • Riding • Duncombe Park • North Yorkshire Moors Steam Railway • Flamingoland Theme Park • Eden Camp Military Museum • Eden Farm

TIMBER HOLIDAY CHALET FOR HIRE
(accommodates four people)

Upper Carr Lane,
Malton Road, Pickering
North Yorkshire YO18 7JP
Telephone/Fax: 01751-473115
E-mail: harker@uppercarr.demon.co.uk
www.uppercarr.demon.co.uk

Thornton-le-Dale, which has streams running through the centre. There is a family pub serving food directly opposite the park. A 6.25-acre site with 80 touring pitches.
Off-licence, rare hens & owls

Leisure: 🅰 Facilities: 🌂⊙🎱❋⅙❤🎿🐾
Services: 🖥🗑📦🔌🚰📷 →▶🎪🍴💻 ▦ 🔋 🎯

▶ ▶ ▶ 77% **Wayside Caravan Park (SE764859)**
Wrelton YO18 8PG ☎ 01751 472608 🖨 01751 472608
🅔 waysideparks@freenet.co.uk
🆆 www.waysideparks.co.uk
Dir: 2.5m W of Pickering off A170, follow signs at Wrelton
★ 🚐 £10.50-£13 🚐 £10-£12.50 ▲ £10

Open Etr-early Oct Booking advisable Etr, Spring bank hol & Jul-Aug Last arrival 23.00hrs Last departure noon
Located in the village of Wrelton, this well-

maintained park is divided into small paddocks by mature hedging. The village pub and restaurant are within a few minutes walk of the park. Caravans are prohibited from using the A170 at Sutton Bank between Thirsk and Helmsley. A 10-acre site with 75 touring pitches and 88 statics.

Leisure: 🅰 Facilities: 🌂⊙🎱❋⅙❤🎿🐾
Services: 🖥🚐🗑📦🔌🚰📷 →▶🎪🍴💻
🛢 ▦ 🔋 🎯

RICHMOND   Map 19 NZ10

▶ ▶ ▶ ▶ 72% **Brompton-on-Swale Caravan & Camping Park (NZ199002)**
Brompton-on-Swale DL10 7EZ
☎ 01748 824629 🖨 01748 826383
🅔 brompton.caravanpark@btinternet.com
🆆 www.bromptoncaravanpark.co.uk
Dir: Take B6271 off A1 signed Richmond, site 1m on left
★ 🚐 £14-£17 🚐 £14-£17 ▲ £5-£17

GOLD

Open all year (rs Oct-Jan Closed to tourers) Last arrival 20.00hrs Last departure noon
A peaceful riverside park on former meadowland with mature trees and other natural features. Fishing is available on the River Swale which flows through the park, and there is a good children's playground. A 14.5-acre site with 177 touring pitches and 22 statics.
Fishing on site

Leisure: 🅰 Facilities: 🌂⊙🎱❋⅙❤🎿🐾
Services: 🖥🗑📦🔌🚰📷 →▶▲🍴
🛢 ▦ 🔋 🎯

▶ ▶ ▶ 76% *Swale View Caravan Park (NZ134013)*
Reeth Rd DL10 4SF
☎ 01748 823106 🖨 01748 823106
🅔 swaleview@teesdaleonline.co.uk
Dir: 3m W of Richmond on A6108 (Reeth to Leyburn road)
🚐 🚐 ▲

Open Mar-Jan Booking advisable bank & summer hols Last arrival 21.00hrs Last departure noon
Shaded by trees and overlooking the River Swale is this attractive, mainly grassy site. The facilities have been extensively upgraded by enthusiastic owners, and this park is a short distance from Richmond, and well situated for exploring Swaledale and Wensleydale. A 13-acre site with 60 touring pitches and 139 statics.

Leisure: ❤🅰🗂 Facilities: 🌂⊙🎱❋⅙❤🎿🛢🧺🔋🐾
Services: 🖥🚐🗑📦🔌🚰📷🚽→▶🍴💻 ▦ 🎯

contd.

Services: 🔲 Toilet Fluid ❌ Café/ Restaurant 🍟 Fast Food/Takeaway 🍼 Baby Care 🔌 Electric Hook Up
🚐 Motorvan Service Point 🗑 Launderette 🍺 Licensed Bar 🛢 Calor Gaz 🔥 Camping Gaz 🔋 Battery Charging

RIPON Map 19 SE37
See also **North Stainley & Winksley**

▶ ▶ ▶ 80% **Riverside Meadows Country Caravan Park (SE317726)**
Ure Bank Top HG4 1JD
☎ 01765 602964 ▤ 01765 604045
✉ info@flowerofmay.com
🌐 www.flowerofmay.com
Dir: On A61 at N end of bridge from Ripon, W along river, do not cross river. Site 400yds, signed
★ ⊞ £13-£17.50 ⊞ £13-£17.50 ▲ £13-£17.50
Open Etr-Oct (rs Mar-Apr bar open wknds only)
Booking advisable bank hols & high season Last arrival 21.00hrs Last departure noon
This pleasant, well-maintained site stands on high ground overlooking the River Ure, 1m from the town centre. The site has an excellent club with family room and quiet lounge. There is no access to the river from the site. A 28-acre site with 131 touring pitches and 269 statics.
Leisure: ♦ ⚠ ▢ Facilities: 🏧⊙✳🔥🍴📞🎣🐾
Services: 🔌🔵🅿🚿▢▢→∪▶♨☂♨🌙
Notes: Dogs by arrangement only
See advertisement under SCARBOROUGH

ROBIN HOOD'S BAY Map 19 NZ90
See also **Whitby**

▶ ▶ ▶ 77% **Grouse Hill Caravan Park (NZ928002)**
Flask Bungalow Farm, Fylingdales YO22 4QH
☎ 01947 880543 & 880560 ▤ 01947 880543
Dir: Off A171 (Whitby-Scarborough road), entered via loop road at Flask Inn
★ ⊞ £12-£14 ⊞ £12-£14 ▲ £12-£14

Open Spring bank hol-Sep (rs Etr-May shop & reception restricted) Booking advisable public hols Last arrival 22.00hrs Last departure noon
A spacious site on a south-facing slope, with many terraced pitches overlooking the North Yorkshire Moors National Park. The owners are constantly improving the park, and it is an ideal base for walking and touring. A 14-acre site with 175 touring pitches.
Leisure: ♦ ⚠ Facilities: 🏧⊙✳🔥📞🎣🐾
Services: 🔌🔵🅿🚿▢▢→∪▶
Notes: No motorcycles

Remember to check your tent or caravan thoroughly before leaving home to ensure everything is in good order.

Middlewood Farm Holiday Park
Robin Hood's Bay, Whitby, N. Yorkshire YO22 4UF
Tel: 01947 880414   www.middlewoodfarm.com
E-mail: info@middlewoodfarm.com

Small, peaceful family park. Walkers, artists and wildlife paradise. Magnificent panoramic views of the sea, moors and "Heartbeat Country".
· SUPERIOR LUXURY HOLIDAY HOMES for HIRE
· TOURERS/TENTS/MOTOR HOMES welcome
· Electric Hook-ups
· SUPERB heated facilities
· FREE HOT SHOWERS/Dishwashing
· Children's Adventure Play Area
· Village PUB – 5 minutes walk
· BEACH – 10 minutes walk
· OPEN: 1st March to 4th January
We're waiting to make you Welcome!

▶ ▶ ▶ 80% *Middlewood Farm Holiday Park (NZ945045)*
Middlewood Ln, Fylingthorpe YO22 4UF
☎ 01947 880414 ▤ 01947 880871
✉ info@middlewoodfarm.com
🌐 www.middlewoodfarm.com
Dir: From A171 towards Robin Hood's Bay & into Fylingthorpe. Park signed from A171
⊞ ⊞ ▲

Open Mar-4 Jan Booking advisable bank & school hols Last arrival 22.00hrs Last departure noon
A peaceful, friendly family park enjoying panoramic views in a picturesque fishing village. The toilet facilities are very good, and the park is well maintained. The pub is 5 minutes walk away, and the beach is 10. A 7-acre site with 100 touring pitches, 9 hardstandings and 30 statics.
Leisure: ⚠ Facilities: 🏧⊙🔥✳📞🐾
Services: 🔌🔵🅿🚿▢🚰→∪▶♨🌙🛒 Notes: Dogs on lead at all times, dangerous breeds not accepted, no radios/noise after 22.00 💳 💳 💳 🔌 🅶

ROSEDALE ABBEY   Map 19 SE79

▶ ▶ ▶ 71% **Rosedale Caravan & Camping Park**
(SE725958)

YO18 8SA ☎ 01751 417272
🅔 info@flowerofmay.com
🅦 www.flowerofmay.com

Dir: From Pickering take A170 towards Sinnington for
2.25m. At Wrelton turn right onto unclass road signed
Cropton & Rosedale, 7m. Park on left in village
★ 🚐 £13-£17.50 🚐 £13-£17.50 ▲ £10-£17.50
Open Mar-Oct Booking advisable BH's & high
season Last arrival 21.00hrs Last departure noon
*Set in a sheltered valley in the centre of the North
Yorkshire Moors National Park, and divided into
separate areas for tents, tourers and statics. A very
popular park, with well-tended grounds, and close
to the pretty village of Rosedale Abbey. Toilets are
basic but functional. A 10-acre site with 100 touring
pitches and 37 statics.*

Leisure: ◖ ⅍   Facilities: ↖ ⊙ ✳ ᠔ ᠘ ᠌ ⊞ ⴼ ☂
Services: 🔌 🖭 🛢 ⬚ ⊞ ⬚ → ∪ ▶ ┛
Notes: Dogs by arrangement only
See advertisement on opposite page

SCARBOROUGH   Map 17 TA08
See also **Filey**

▶ ▶ ▶ ▶ 77% **Camping & Caravanning Club Site**
(TA025911)

Field Ln, Burniston Rd YO13 0DA ☎ 01723 366441
🅦 www.campingandcaravanningclub.co.uk
Dir: On W side of A165, 1m N of Scarborough
★ 🚐 £16.20-£20.60 🚐 £16.20-£20.60 ▲ £16.20-£20.60
Open Apr-Oct Booking advisable bank hols & peak
period Last arrival 21.00hrs Last departure noon
*This spacious site has been completely upgraded
to a high standard. The majority of pitches are
hardstandings of plastic webbing which allow the
grass to grow through normally. This is an
excellent family-orientated park with its own shop
and takeaway, within easy reach of the resort of
Scarborough. Please see the advertisement on
page 11 for information on Club sites and
membership. A 20-acre site with 300 touring
pitches, 100 hardstandings.*

Leisure: ◖ ⅍   Facilities: ↖ ⊙ ᠌ ✳ ᠔ ᠘ ᠌ ☂
Services: 🔌 🖭 🛢 ⬚ ⊞ ⬚ → ∪ ▶ ᠌ ┛ ᠘
🔵 💳 💳 📇 🇩

▶ ▶ ▶ ▶ 83% **Jacobs Mount Caravan Park**
(TA021868)

Jacobs Mount, Stepney Rd YO12 5NL
☎ 01723 361178 📠 01723 361178
🅔 jacobsmount@yahoo.co.uk
🅦 www.jacobsmount.co.uk
Dir: Direct access from A170
★ 🚐 £10.50-£16 🚐 £10.50-£16 ▲ £10.50-£16
Open Mar-Nov (rs Mar-May & Oct limited hours at
shop/bar) Booking advisable bank hols & late Jun-
early Sep Last arrival 21.00hrs Last departure
noon
*An elevated family-run park surrounded by
woodland and open countryside, yet only 2m from*
                         contd.

Jacobs Mount Caravan Park

*the beach. Touring pitches are terraced gravel
stands with individual services. A licensed bar and
family room provide meals and snacks, and there is
an adjoining games room. An 18-acre site with 156
touring pitches, 131 hardstandings and 60 statics.
Food preparation area.*

Leisure: ◖ ⅍ ⊡
Facilities: ↪ ↖ ⊙ ᠌ ✳ ᠔ ᠘ ᠌ ☂
Services: 🔌 ⅏ 🖭 🛢 ⬚ ⊞ ⬚ ✕ ⬚ → ∪ ▶ ◎ ᠔ ⁺ ⛽ ┛
Notes: Pets must be kept on leads
🔵 💳 💳 📇 🇩

▶ ▶ ▶ ▶ 71% **Spring Willows
Touring Caravan Park** (TA026794)

Main Rd, Staxton Roundabout YO12 4SB   SILVER
☎ 01723 891505 📠 01723 892123
🅔 fun4all@springwillows.fsnet.co.uk
🅦 www.springwillows.co.uk
Dir: A64 to Scarborough, then take A1039 to Filey.
Entrance on right
🚐 🚐 ▲
Open Mar-Jan (rs Mar & Oct bar, pool, take-away,
restaurant restricted) Booking advisable bank hols,
Etr, Jul & Aug Last arrival 18.00hrs Last departure
11.00hrs
*A lively, popular family park, with a spacious club
providing free evening entertainment during
weekends and in high season. At these times, food
is served throughout the day, together with a
popular take-away service. The Sharky's Kids Club
entertains young children, while the swimming pool
and games room with its many video games are
popular with older children. The attractions of
Scarborough and Filey are a short drive away.
A 26-acre site with 181 touring pitches.*

Leisure: ↥ ◖ ⅍
Facilities: ↖ ⊙ ᠌ ✳ ᠔ ᠘ ᠌ ☂
Services: 🔌 🖭 🛢 ⬚ ⊞ ⬚ ✕ ⬚ → ∪ ▶ ◎
Notes: No gazebos 🔵 💳 📇 🇩

▶ ▶ ▶ 74% **Arosa Caravan & Camping Park Ltd**
(TA011830)

Ratten Row, Seamer YO12 4QB
☎ 01723 862166 📠 01723 862166
🅔 info@arosacamping.co.uk
🅦 www.arosacamping.co.uk
Dir: 4m from Scarborough. From junct with unclass
road & A64 S of Seamer, N into village. Site 250yds
along Ratten Row
★ 🚐 £9.50-£20 🚐 £8.50-£19 ▲ £6.50-£19
                         contd.

Facilities: ↪ Bath ↖ Shower ⊙ Electric Shaver ᠌ Hairdryer ✳ Ice Pack Facility ᠔ Disabled Facilities ᠘ Public Telephone
᠌ Shop on Site or within 200yds ⬚ Mobile Shop (calls at least 5 days a week) ᠌ BBQ Area ☂ Picnic Area ☂ Dog Exercise Area

England

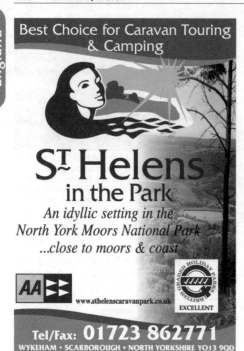
Open Mar-4 Jan Booking advisable bank hols, Jul-Aug, Xmas & New Year Last arrival 21.00hrs Last departure 11.00hrs
A compact family-owned park with pitches in small groups screened by trees. There is a popular family clubhouse with café and covered barbecue patio, a breakfast takeaway, and occasional entertainment at peak times. A 3.5-acre site with 105 touring pitches, 4 hardstandings.
Leisure: ◄ /M
Facilities: ⋔ ⊙ ℚ ✻ ᕹ ╲ ⚑ 㒼 ⊓ ⚲
Services: ⊟ ⊡ ⊻ ⓘ ⌀ ⊞ ⊤ ✕ ᚐ → ∪ ▸ ⌂ ⌴ ⚌ ⚲
⊞ ▦ ⊞ ▧ ⑨

► ► ► 76% Killerby Old Hall (TA063829)
Killerby YO11 3TW ☎ 01723 583799
◔ 01723 583799
Dir: Direct access via B1261 at Killerby, near Cayton
★ ⚑ £11.50-£14.50 ⚑ £11.50-£14.50
Open Mar-Oct Booking advisable BH's & school holidays Last departure noon
A small secluded park, well sheltered by mature trees and shrubs, located at the rear of the old hall. Use of the small indoor swimming pool is shared by visitors to the hall's holiday accommodation. A 2-acre site with 20 touring pitches, 20 hardstandings.
Grassed play area
Leisure: ᚐ ◄
Facilities: ⋔ ⊙ ℚ 㒼 ⊓
Services: ⊟ ⊡ → ∪ ▸ ⊙ ⌂ ⚲ ╲ ⊞ ⊞ ⑨

► ► ► 78% Scalby Close Park (TA020925)
Burniston Rd YO13 0DA
☎ 01723 365908
⊜ info@scalbyclosepark.co.uk
ⓦ www.scalbyclosepark.co.uk
Dir: 2m N of Scarborough on A615 coast road, 1m from junct with A171
★ ⚑ £10-£16 ⚑ £10-£16 ▲ £10-£16

SILVER

Open Mar-Oct Booking advisable bank hols & high season Last arrival 22.00hrs Last departure noon
An attractive park with enthusiastic owners who have carried out many improvements. A newly refurbished shower block, laundry and fully-serviced pitches are welcome additions, and the landscaping is also very good. An ideal base from which to explore the nearby coast and countryside. A 3-acre site with 42 touring pitches, 40 hardstandings and 5 statics.
Facilities: ⋔ ⊙ ✻ ╲ ᕹ
Services: ⊟ ⊡ ⓘ ⌀ ⊞ ⊤ → ∪ ▸ ⌴ ⚌ ⚲

SCOTCH CORNER   **Map 19 NZ20**

► ► ► 72% Scotch Corner Caravan Park (NZ210054)
DL10 6NS ☎ 01748 822530
◔ 01748 822530
⊜ marshallleisure@aol.com
ⓦ www.scotchcornercaravanpark.co.uk
Dir: From Scotch Corner junct of A1 & A66 take A6108 towards Richmond. 250mtrs then cross central reservation and return 200mtrs to site entrance
★ ⚑ £10-£14 ⚑ £10-£14 ▲ £10-£14
Open Etr-Oct Booking advisable public hols & Jul-Aug Last arrival 22.30hrs Last departure noon
A well-maintained site with good facilities, ideally situated as a stopover, and an equally good location for touring. The Vintage Hotel which serves food can be accessed from the rear of the site. A 7-acre site with 96 touring pitches, 4 hardstandings. Recreation area for children
Facilities: ⋔ ⊙ ℚ ✻ ╲ ᕹ ⊓
Services: ⊟ ⱳ ⊡ ⓘ ⌀ ⊞ ⊤ → ∪ ▸ ⚲
⊞ ▦ ⊞ Ⓞ ▧ ▨ ⑨

Services: ⊤ Toilet Fluid ✕ Café/ Restaurant ᚐ Fast Food/Takeaway ᚐ Baby Care ⊟ Electric Hook Up
ⱳ Motorvan Service Point ⊡ Launderette ⚌ Licensed Bar ⓘ Calor Gaz ⌀ Camping Gaz ⊞ Battery Charging

SELBY   Map 16 SE63

▶ ▶ ▶ 79% **The Ranch Caravan Park (SE664337)**
Cliffe Common YO8 6EF
☎ 01757 638984 📠 01757 638984
✉ ltbrownridge@aol.com
🌐 www.ranchcaravanpark.F9.co.uk
Dir: Exit A63 at Cliffe signed Skipwith. Site 1m N on left
★ 🚐 fr £10 🚐 fr £10 ▲ fr £8
Open all year Booking advisable bank holidays Last
arrival 22.00hrs Last departure noon
*A delightful sheltered park in open countryside
offering first class amenities. The enthusiastic and
welcoming family owners have created a country
club feel, with a tasteful bar, plus a sauna and
jacuzzi in a wooden chalet. A 7-acre site with 50
touring pitches, 50 hardstandings.*
Leisure: 🎠 Facilities: 🛁⊙🔗❄️🔥⅃⅂🏵🐾
Services: 🔌🛒🍴🔥🅿🗓🍺→🍴🚽🍴 💳 💳 💳 📶 📶

SHERIFF HUTTON   Map 19 SE66

▶ ▶ ▶ 81% **Camping & Caravanning Club Site (SE638652)**
Bracken Hill YO60 6QG ☎ 01347 878660
🌐 www.campingandcaravanningclub.co.uk
*Dir: From York follow 'Earswick Strensall' signs. Keep
left at filling station & Ship Inn. Site 2nd on right*
★ 🚐 £13.60-£17.80 🚐 £13.60-£17.80 ▲ £13.60-£17.80
Open Mar-Oct Booking advisable bank hols & peak
period Last arrival 21.00hrs Last departure noon
*A quiet rural site in open meadowland within easy
reach of York. This well-established park is friendly
and welcoming, and the landscaping is attractive
and mature. Please see the advertisement on page
11 for information on Club sites and membership.
A 10-acre site with 90 touring pitches,
16 hardstandings.*
Leisure: 🎠 Facilities: 🛁⊙🔗❄️🔥⅃🏵🐾
Services: 🔌🛒🍴🔥🅿🗓→🍴🍴🚽🍺 💳 💳 💳 📶 📶

SLINGSBY   Map 19 SE67

▶ ▶ ▶ 82% **Camping & Caravanning Club Site (SE699755)**
Railway St YO62 4AA ☎ 01653 628335
🌐 www.campingandcaravanningclub.co.uk
Dir: 0.25m N of Slingsby
★ 🚐 £13.60-£17.80 🚐 £13.60-£17.80 ▲ £13.60-£17.80
Open Mar-Oct Booking advisable bank hols & peak
period Last arrival 21.00hrs Last departure noon
*A well cared for park in a traditional North
Yorkshire. Pitches are a mixture of grass and
hardstanding, and there is a well-appointed toilet
block with cubicled facilities. The village pub
serving food is a few minutes walk away. Caravans
are prohibited on the A170 at Sutton Bank between
Thirsk and Helmsley. Please see the advertisement
on page 11 for information on Club sites and
membership.
A 3-acre site with 60 touring pitches,
7 hardstandings.*
Facilities: 🛁⊙🔗❄️🔥⅃🏵
Services: 🔌🛒🍴🔥🅿🗓→🍴🚽🍺
💳 💳 💳 📶 📶

▶ ▶ ▶ 79% **Robin Hood Caravan & Camping Park (SE701748)**
Green Dyke Ln YO62 4AP
☎ 01653 628391 📠 01653 628391
✉ info@robinhoodcaravanpark.co.uk
🌐 www.robinhoodcaravanpark.co.uk
*Dir: On edge of Slingsby. Access off B1257 (Malton-
Helmsley road)*
★ 🚐 £10-£17 🚐 £10-£17 ▲ £10-£17
Open Mar-Oct Booking advisable bank hols & 15
Jul-1 Sep Last arrival 18.00hrs Last departure
noon
*A pleasant, well-maintained grassy park, in a good
position for touring North Yorkshire. Situated on
the edge of the village of Slingsby, the park has
hardstandings and electricity for every pitch. A 2-
acre site with 32 touring pitches, 22 hardstandings
and 35 statics.*
Caravan hire, off-licence
Leisure: 🎠
Facilities: 🛁⊙🔗❄️🔥⅃🏵🐾
Services: 🔌🍴🔥🅿🗓→🚽🍺
Notes: 💳 💳 📶

SNAINTON   Map 17 SE98

▶ ▶ ▶ ▶ 81% **Jasmine Caravan Park (SE928813)**
Cross Ln YO13 9BE
☎ 01723 859240 📠 01723 859240
✉ info@jasminepark.co.uk
🌐 www.jasminepark.co.uk
Dir: Turn S off A170 in Snainton, then follow signs
★ 🚐 £11.50-£17 🚐 £11.50-£17 ▲ £9.50-£17

Open Mar-Dec Booking advisable 5 wks in advance
for bank hols Last arrival 22.00hrs Last departure
noon
*A peaceful and beautifully presented park on the
edge of a pretty village, and sheltered by high
hedges. The toilet block with individual wash
cubicles is maintained to a very high standard.
This picturesque park lies midway between
Pickering and Scarborough on the southern edge
of the North Yorkshire Moors. A 5-acre site with
94 touring pitches, 1 hardstanding and 11 statics.*
Baby changing unit
Facilities: 🔌🛁⊙🔗❄️🔥⅃🍺🏵
Services: 🔌🛒🍴🔥🅿🗓→🚽🍴🍺
Notes: No dogs in hire fleet, dogs must be on leads
💳 💳 💳 📶 📶

England

STAINFORTH Map 18 SD86

▶ ▶ ▶ ▶ 75% **Knight Stainforth**
Hall Caravan & Campsite (SD816672)
BD24 0DP ☎ 01729 822200

🖷 01729 823387
🅴 info@knightstainforth.co.uk
🆆 www.knightstainforth.co.uk
Dir: From W: on A65 take B6480 for Settle, left before
swimming pool signed Little Stainforth. From E:
through Settle on B6480, over bridge to swimming
pool, then turn right.
⊞ ⊞ ⅄
Open May-Oct Booking advisable bank hols & Jul-
Aug Last arrival 22.00hrs Last departure noon
Located near Settle and the River Ribble in the
Yorkshire Dales National Park, this well-maintained
family site is sheltered by mature woodland. It is an
ideal base for walking or touring in the beautiful
surrounding areas. The toilet block is appointed to
a very high standard. A 6-acre site with 100 touring
pitches and 60 statics.
Fishing on site.
Leisure: ◈ ⅏ ▭
Facilities: ⋔ ⊙ ⚚ ✳ ⅋ ⚘ ⅄ ⛾ ⛬
Services: ⊞ ⊟ ⅄ ⋔ ⊞ ⊡ ⊤ ⋔ → ∪ ▶ ⅃
Notes: No groups of young people
💳 💳 💳 💳 🗿

STAXTON Map 17 TA07

▶ ▶ ▶ ▶ 71% **Spring Willows**
Touring Caravan Park (TA026794)
Main Rd, Staxton Roundabout
YO12 4SB ☎ 01723 891505

🖷 01723 892123
🅴 fun4all@springwillows.fsnet.co.uk
🆆 www.springwillows.co.uk
Dir: A64 to Scarborough, then take A1039 to Filey.
Entrance on right
⊞ ⊞ ⅄
Open Mar-Jan (rs Mar & Oct bar, pool, take-away,
restaurant restricted) Booking advisable bank hols,
Etr, Jul & Aug Last arrival 18.00hrs Last departure
11.00hrs
A lively, popular family park with a spacious club
providing free evening entertainment during
weekends and in high season. At these times, food
is served throughout the day, together with a
popular take-away service. The Sharky's Kids Club
entertains young children, while the swimming pool
and games room with its many video games are
popular with older children. The attractions of
Scarborough and Filey are a short drive away.
A 26-acre site with 181 touring pitches.
Leisure: ⌇ ◈ ⅏
Facilities: ⋔ ⊙ ⚚ ✳ ⅋ ⚘ ⅄ ⛬ ⛾ ⛬
Services: ⊞ ⊟ ⅄ ⅄ ⊞ ⊡ ⊤ ✕ ⅏ → ∪ ▶ ◎
Notes: No gazebos 💳 💳 💳 🗿

STILLINGFLEET Map 16 SE54

▶ ▶ ▶ 69% **Home Farm Caravan & Camping**
(SE595427)
Moreby YO19 6HN ☎ 01904 728263
🖷 01904 720059
🅴 home_farm@hotmail.co.uk
Dir: 6m from York on B1222, 1.5m N of Stillingfleet
★ ⊞ fr £10 ⊞ fr £10 ⅄ £5-£8
Open Feb-Dec Booking advisable bank hols Last
arrival 22.00hrs
A traditional meadowland site on a working farm
bordered by parkland on one side and the River
Ouse on another. Facilities are in converted farm
buildings, and the family owners extend a friendly
welcome to tourers. An excellent site for relaxing
and unwinding in, yet only a short distance from
the attractions of York. A 5-acre site with 25 touring
pitches and 2 statics.
Facilities: ⋔ ⊙ ⚚ ✳ ⛾ ⛬ ⛬
Services: ⊞ ⅄ ⅄ ⊞ ⊡ ⊤ → ∪ ⅃
Notes: Dogs must be kept on leads

SUTTON-ON-THE-FOREST Map 19 SE56

▶ ▶ ▶ ▶ 83% **Goosewood**
Caravan Park (SE595636)
YO61 1ET ☎ 01347 810829

🖷 01347 811498
🅴 edward@goosewood.co.uk
🆆 www.goosewood.co.uk
Dir: From A1237 take B1363. After 5m turn right. Take
right turn after 0.5m & site on right
★ ⊞ £14.50-£16.50 ⊞ £14.50-£16.50

Open Feb-14 Jan Booking advisable BH's,
Jul & Aug Last arrival 20.00hrs Last departure
noon
An immaculately maintained park with its own lake
and seasonal fishing, set in attractive woodland just
six miles north of York. The generous patio pitches
are randomly spaced throughout the site. This
popular family park has a first class play area for
younger children, and a recreation barn for
teenagers, plus a new health spa. A 20-acre site
with 75 touring pitches, 75 hardstandings and 35
statics.
Fishing lake.
Leisure: ◈ ⅏
Facilities: ⅏ ⋔ ⊙ ⚚ ✳ ⚘ ⅄ ⛾ ⛬ ⛬
Services: ⊞ ⊟ ⅄ ⊞ ⊡ ⊤ ⋔ → ∪ ▶ ⅊ ⅃ 💳 💳 🗿

THIRSK   Map 19 SE48

► ► ► 64% **Sowerby Caravan Park** (SE437801)
Sowerby YO7 3AG ☎ 01845 522753 ▤ 01845 574520
*Dir: From A19 approx 3m S of Thirsk, turn W for
Sowerby. Turn R at junct. Site 1m on left*
★ ⊞ £8.75-£10 ⊞ £8.75-£10
Open Mar-Oct Booking advisable bank hols Last
arrival 22.00hrs
*A grassy site beside a tree-lined river bank, with
basic but functional toilet facilities. Tourers enjoy a
separate grassed area with an open outlook, away
from the statics. A 1-acre site with 25 touring
pitches, 5 hardstandings and 85 statics.*
Leisure: ◈ ⚲ Facilities: ╓ ☉ ⚹ & ⌧ ⅗
Services: ⊞ ▤ ◳ ⌧ ▦ ▦ → ∪ ⚇ ⏚

► ► 72% *Thirkleby Hall Caravan Park (SE472794)*
Thirkleby YO7 3AR ☎ 01845 501360 & 07799 641815
▤ 01347 838313
❸ greenwood.parks@virgin.net
ⓦ www.greenwoodparks.com
*Dir: Park 3m S of Thirsk on A19. Turn E through arched
gatehouse into Park*
⊞ ⊞ Å

Open Mar-Oct Booking advisable BH's & Aug wknds
Last arrival 22.30hrs Last departure 16.30hrs
*A long-established site in the grounds of the old
hall, with statics in wooded areas around a fishing
lake and tourers based on slightly sloping grassy
pitches. Toilet facilities are basic but clean and
functional, and this well-screened park has superb
views of the Hambledon Hills. A 53-acre site with
50 touring pitches and 185 statics.*
Fishing lake
Leisure: ◈ ⚲ ⊟ Facilities: ╓ ☉ ⚹ ⌧ ⼌ ⅗
Services: ⊞ ⚇ ◳ ▦ → ⏚ ⏚ ⏚ ⅗
Notes: Dogs must be kept on lead

THRESHFIELD   Map 18 SD96

► ► ► 81% *Wood Nook Caravan Park*
(SD974641)
Skirethorns BD23 5NU
☎ 01756 752412 ▤ 01756 752946
❸ bookings@woodnook.net
ⓦ www.woodnook.net
*Dir: From Skipton take B6265 to Threshfield, then B6160
for 50yds. Left into Skirethorns Ln, follow signs to park*
⊞ ⊞ Å
Open Mar-Oct Booking advisable bank hols & peak
periods Last arrival 22.00hrs Last departure noon
Gently-sloping site in a rural setting, completely
contd.

*hidden by natural features of surrounding hills and
woodland. Toilet facilities are housed in converted
farm buildings within the farmhouse courtyard, and
pitches are all on firm, well-drained ground or
hardstandings. The park is well situated for
ramblers, while the market town of Skipton is only
nine miles away. A 2-acre site with 48 touring
pitches, 27 hardstandings and 11 statics.*
Leisure: ⚲ Facilities: ╓ ☉ ⚹ ⌧ ⅗ ⅗
Services: ⊞ ▤ ◳ ⊟ ⌧ → ∪ ⏚
Notes: No groups ▦ ▦ ▦ ▦ ▦

TOLLERTON   Map 19 SE56

► ► ► 69% **Tollerton Holiday Park** (SE513643)
Station Rd YO61 1RD
☎ 01347 838313 ▤ 01347 838313
*Dir: From York take A19 towards Thirsk. At Cross Lanes
turn left towards Tollerton. 1m to Chinese restaurant
just before rail bridge. Entrance to site through
restaurant car park.*
★ ⊞ £13-£14 ⊞ £13-£14 Å £10-£14
Open Mar-Oct Booking advisable bank hols Last
arrival 20.00hrs Last departure 16.00hrs
*A small park within a few minutes walk of Tollerton
village. It is set in open countryside a short drive
from the Park & Ride for York, and the railway line
is close by. 50 touring pitches and 25 statics.*
Leisure: ⚲ Facilities: ╓ ☉ ⌧ & ⌧ ⅗
Services: ⊞ ▤ ⚇ ◳ ⊟ ⼌ → ⏚ ⏚ ⅗

TOWTHORPE   Map 19 SE65

► ► ► ► 76% **York Touring Caravan Site**
(SE648584)
Greystones Farm, Towthorpe Moor Ln YO32 9ST
☎ 01904 499275 ▤ 01904 499271
❸ info@yorkcaravansite.co.uk
ⓦ www.yorkcaravansite.co.uk
Dir: Turn off A64 at exit for Strensall/Haxby, site 1.5m on left
⊞ £10-£18.50 ⊞ £10-£18.50 Å £10-£18.50

Open all year Booking advisable bank hols Last
arrival 20.00hrs Last departure noon
*A purpose-built, high quality site with a select
'country club' feel. It is part of a leisure complex
with a golf driving range and a 9-hole putting
course, as well as an intimate bar and tasteful
bistro. The generous pitches are set within well-
manicured grassland with a backdrop of trees and
shrubs. A 6-acre site with 44 touring pitches,
12 hardstandings.*
Golf range on site
Leisure: ⚲ ⊟ Facilities: ╓ ☉ ⌧ ⚹ & ⌧ ⅗ ⼌ ⅗ ⅗
Services: ⊞ ▤ ⚇ ⊟ ✕ → ∪ ⏚ ◉ ⚇ ⏚ ▦ ▦ ▦ ▦ ▦

England

WEST KNAPTON   Map 19 SE87

NEW ▶ ▶ ▶ 77% **Wolds Way Caravan and Camping (SE896743)**
West Farm YO17 8JE ☎ 01944 728463 & 728180
Dir: Signed between Rillington & West Heslerton on A64 (Malton to Scarborough road). Site 1.5m
⚑ Å

Open Mar-Oct
A newly developed park on a working farm in a peaceful, high position on the Yorkshire Wolds, with magnificent views over the Vale of Pickering. This is an excellent walking area, with the Wolds Way passing the entrance to the park. A pleasant 1.5 mile path leads to a lavender farm, with its first-class coffee shop. The park is ideally situated for all the attractions of the area including the coast at Scarborough. A 7.5-acre site with 50 touring pitches.

Facilities: ⇥ 🛉 🛂

WHITBY   Map 19 NZ81
See also **Robin Hood's Bay**

▶ ▶ ▶ 77% **Ladycross Plantation Caravan Park (NZ821080)**
Egton YO21 1UA ☎ 01947 895502
📧 enquiries@ladycrossplantation.co.uk
🌐 www.ladycrossplantation.co.uk
Dir: On unclass road (signed) off A171 Whitby-Teeside road, 6m from Whitby centre
★ ⚑ £12.50-£15.50 ⚑ £12.50-£15.50 Å £10.50-£15.50

Open end Mar-Oct Booking advisable bank hols & Aug Last arrival 20.30hrs Last departure noon
A delightful woodland setting with pitches sited in small groups in clearings around an amenities block. The site is well placed for Whitby and the Moors. Children will enjoy exploring the woodland around the site. A 12-acre site with 100 touring pitches, 18 hardstandings.

Facilities: 🛉 ⊙ ⊙ ✳ ⌑ ▣ 🛂
Services: 🔌 🔲 🛉 ⊘ 🔳 ⊤ → ⌑ 🍴 💷 ⬛ 📷 ⑨

▶ ▶ ▶ 75% *Rigg Farm Caravan Park (NZ915061)*
Stainsacre YO22 4LP
☎ 01947 880430 📠 01947 880430
Dir: From A171 Scarborough road left onto B1416 signed Ruswarp. Right in 3.25m onto unclass road signed Hawsker. Left in 1.25m. Site in 0.5m
⚑ ⚑ Å
Open Mar-Oct Booking advisable bank hols & Jul-Aug Last arrival 22.00hrs Last departure noon
A neat rural site with distant views of the coast and
contd.

Whitby Abbey, set in peaceful surroundings. The former farm buildings are used to house reception and a small games room. A 3-acre site with 14 touring pitches, 14 hardstandings and 15 statics.

Leisure: ♦ ⌓ **Facilities:** 🛉 ⊙ ✳ ⌑ 🜂 ⌑
Services: 🔌 🔲 🛉 ⊘ 🔳 ⊤ → ⌑ 🍴 📷 ⬛ ⚙ 🛂
Notes: No ball games, cycling, skateboards, roller skating or kite flying 💷 ⬛ ⬛ ⬛ 📷 ⑨

▶ ▶ ▶ 72% *York House Caravan Park (NZ926071)*
YO22 4LW ☎ 01947 880354 📠 01947 880354
Dir: 3.5m S of Whitby, off A171 at Hawsker
⚑ ⚑ Å
Open Mar-Oct Booking advisable Spring bank hol & mid Jul-Aug Last arrival 22.00hrs Last departure noon
A peaceful, family-run country site a short distance from Whitby. On the edge of the North Yorkshire Moors National Park, it is ideal for touring coast or moors by day, and relaxing in the local pub in the evening. A 4-acre site with 59 touring pitches, 14 hardstandings and 41 statics.
Open area for games.

Leisure: ⌓ **Facilities:** 🛉 ⊙ ⊙ ✳ ⌑ 🜂 ▣ ⌑ ⛏
Services: 🔌 🔲 🛉 ⊘ 🔳 ⊤ → ⌑ 🍴 💷 ⚙ ⬛ 🛂
Notes: No smoking in toilet block, dogs must be on leads

WINKSLEY   Map 19 SE27

▶ ▶ ▶ 78% **Woodhouse Farm & Country Park (SE241715)**
HG4 3PG ☎ 01765 658309
📧 woodhouse.farm@talk21.com
🌐 www.woodhousewinksley.com
Dir: 6m W of Ripon off B6265 Pateley Bridge road, 2.5m from Fountains Abbey, signed Grantley
⚑ £10-£15 ⚑ £10-£15 Å £10-£15
Open Mar-Oct Booking advisable bank hols & mid Jul-Aug Last arrival 21.00hrs Last departure noon
An attractive rural, family site on a former working farm, with several camping areas screened by hedges. Visitors have access to surrounding meadowland, lake and mature woods. A former farm building has been converted into a country-style pub serving food mainly at weekends. A 16-acre site with 140 touring pitches and 62 statics.
Coarse fishing lake.

Leisure: ♦ ⌓ ⏹ **Facilities:** 🛉 ⊙ ⊙ ✳ ⌓ ⌑ 🜂 ▣ ⌑ ⛏
Services: 🔌 🔲 🛉 ⊘ 🔳 ⊤ ✕ → ⌑ 🍴
Notes: No commercial vehicles 💷 ⬛ ⑨

WYKEHAM   Map 17 SE98

▶ ▶ ▶ ▶ 83% *St Helens Caravan Park (SE967836)*
St Helens in the Park YO13 9QD
☎ 01723 862771 📠 01723 866613
📧 caravans@wykeham.co.uk
🌐 www.wykeham.co.uk
Dir: On A170 in village, 150yds on left beyond Downe Arms Hotel towards Scarborough
⚑ ⚑ Å
Open Feb-Jan (rs Nov-Jan shop/laundry closed)
Booking advisable bank hols & Jul-Aug Last arrival 22.00hrs Last departure 17.00hrs
contd.

England

Set on the edge of the North York Moors National Park this delightfully landscaped park is well-maintained and thoughtfully laid out with top quality facilities. The site is divided into terraces with tree-screening creating smaller areas, including an adults' zone. A cycle route leads through the surrounding Wykeham estate, and there is a short pathway to the adjoining Downe Arms country pub. A 25-acre site with 250 touring pitches, 2 hardstandings.
Caravan storage.

Leisure: ♠ ⚲ **Facilities:** ➡ ⟲ ⊙ ⓣ ⚹ ⚙ ⚫ ⚑ ⊞ ⚏ ⟕ ⚓
Services: ⚙ ⚏ ⚏ ⊘ ⊟ ⊡ ✗ ⚙ ⚏ → ∪ ⏵ ⊙ ⚪ ⚸ ⚒
⊙ ⊞ ⚏ ⚏ ⚏

See advertisement under SCARBOROUGH

YORK   **Map 16 SE65**
See also **Acaster Malbis**

▶ ▶ ▶ 61% *Riverside Caravan & Camping Park (SE598477)*
Ferry Ln, Bishopthorpe YO23 2SB
☎ 01904 705812 & 704442 ▤ 01904 705824
ⓔ info@yorkmarine.co.uk
ⓦ www.yorkmarine.co.uk
Dir: From A64 take A1036. Right at lights signed Bishopthorpe, left into main street at T-junct. At end of road right into Ancaster Ln, left in 150yds
⚏ ⚏ ⚏
Open Apr-Oct Booking advisable Jul-Sep, bank hols Last arrival 22.00hrs Last departure noon
A small level grassy park in a hedged field on the banks of the River Ouse, on the outskirts of York. This is a popular site with those who enjoy messing about on the river. A 1-acre site with 25 touring pitches.
Boat hire, slipway, fishing
Leisure: ⚲ **Facilities:** ⟲ ⊙ ⚹ ⚫ ⚑ ⊞ ⟕ ⚓
Services: ⚙ ⚏ ⊘ ⊟ ⊡ ✗ → ∪ ⏵ ⚪ ⚸ ⚒ ⚒ ⚒ ⊙ ⚏
Notes: Dogs must be on leads ⚏ ⚏

▶ ▶ ▶ 80% *Willow House Caravan Park (SE595570)*
Wigginton rd, Wigginton YO32 2RH
☎ 01904 750060 ▤ 01904 767030
ⓔ info@willowhouseyork.co.uk
ⓦ www.willowhouseyork.co.uk
Dir: A1237 north onto B1363 signed Helmsley/Wigginton. Site on right in 1m
⚏ ⚏ ⚏
Open all year Booking advisable All season Last arrival 21.00hrs Last departure noon
A peaceful, exclusive park set within a large lawn screened by shrubs. Coarse fishing is popular on the on-site lake. The immaculate toilet facilities are 100 metres from the pitching area. This adults-only site is less than 0.5 miles from the Park and Ride to York, and the extensive Clifton Moor out-of-town shopping complex. A 10-acre site with 30 touring pitches.
Facilities: ⟲ ⊙ ⚹ ⚫ ⚫ ⚓
Services: ⚙ ⚏ ⚏ ⊟ ⊡ → ∪ ⏵ ⚒ ⚒ ⚒
Notes: Adults only

YORKSHIRE, SOUTH

HATFIELD   **Map 16 SE60**

▶ ▶ ▶ 68% *Hatfield Waterpark (SE670098)*
Old Thorne Rd DN7 6EQ
☎ 01302 841572 & 737343 ▤ 01302 846368
Dir: Signed from Hatfield off A18
⚏ ⚏ ⚲
Open Apr-Oct (rs Nov-Mar Reduced visitor centre opening Nov-Mar) Booking advisable bank hols Last arrival 17.30hrs Last departure noon
A parkland setting offering instruction in a variety of sports from kayaking to power boating. There is something for everyone here, from taking part to watching the action. A seasonal warden keeps the centre running well, and there is also bunkhouse accommodation for 36, handy for tenters in very wet weather. A 10-acre site with 48 touring pitches. Canoeing, rowing, sailing, windsurfing & fishing.
Leisure: ⚲
Facilities: ⟲ ⊙ ⚹ ⚫ ⚫ ⚑ ⊞ ⟕ ⚓
Services: ⚙ ⚏ → ∪ ⏵ ⚪ ⚸ ⚒ ⊟ ⚏ ⚏ ⊙ ⊞ ⚏ ⚏

WORSBROUGH   **Map 16 SE30**

▶ ▶ 74% *Greensprings Touring Park (SE330020)*
Rockley Abbey Farm, Rockley Ln S75 3DS
☎ 01226 288298 ▤ 01226 288298
Dir: From M1 junct 36 take A61 to Barnsley. Turn left after 0.25m onto road signed to Pilley. Site entrance 1m at bottom of hill
★ ⚏ fr £9.50 ⚏ fr £9.50 ⚲ fr £4.50
Open Apr-Oct Booking advisable when hook up is required Last arrival 21.00hrs Last departure noon
A secluded and attractive farm site set amidst woods and farmland, with access to the river and several good local walks. There are two touring areas, one gently sloping and each with its own toilet block. Although not far from the M1, there is almost no traffic noise, and this site is convenient for exploring the area's industrial heritage, as well as the Peak District. A 4-acre site with 65 touring pitches, 13 hardstandings.
TV hook up.
Facilities: ⟲ ⊙ ⚹ ⚹ ⚓
Services: ⚙ ⚏ ⊘ → ∪ ⏵ ⚒ ⚒ ⊟ ⚏ ⚏

YORKSHIRE, WEST

BARDSEY   **Map 16 SE34**

▶ ▶ ▶ 81% *Glenfield Caravan Park (SE351421)*
120 Blackmoor Ln LS17 9DZ
☎ 01937 574657 ▤ 01937 579529
ⓔ glenfieldcp@aol.com
ⓦ www.ukparks.co.uk/glenfieldcp
Dir: From A58 at Bardsey turn into Church Lane, past church, up hill. Continue 0.5m, site on right
★ ⚏ fr £12 ⚏ fr £12 ⚲ fr £10
Open all year Booking advisable Last arrival 23.00hrs Last departure noon
A quiet family-owned rural site in a well-screened,
contd.

Leisure: ⚷ Indoor swimming pool ⚷ Outdoor swimming pool ⚹ Tennis court ♠ Games room ⚲ Children's playground ∪ Stables
⏵ 9/18 hole golf course ⚸ Boats for hire ⚒ Cinema ⚒ Fishing ◎ Mini golf ⚪ Watersports ⚏ Separate TV room

England

Glenfield Caravan Park
tree-lined meadow. The site has an excellent toilet block complete with family room. A convenient touring base for Leeds and the surrounding area. Discounted golf and food are available at the local golf club. A 4-acre site with 30 touring pitches, 30 hardstandings and 1 static.

Facilities: ⚓ ⊙ ⚑ ✳ ⚒ & 🛒 ⤬ ☐

Services: 🔌 📶 🛈 ⊞ → ∪ ▶ 🚽 ⚒ 🛁

▶ ▶ ▶ **74% Moor Lodge Park** (SE352423)
Blackmoor Ln LS17 9DZ
☎ 01937 572424 📠 01937 572424
📧 rodatmlcp@aol.com
🌐 www.ukparks.co.uk/moorlodge
Dir: Turn right after Bracken Fox pub (Ling Lane) then right at x-rds, site 0.5m on right
★ 🚐 £10 🚙 £10
Open all year Booking advisable BH's Last arrival 23.00hrs Last departure 23.00hrs
A neat, well-kept site in a peaceful and pleasant rural location convenient to surrounding areas of interest as well as Leeds. The touring area is for adults only. A 7-acre site with 12 touring pitches and 60 statics.

Leisure: ⚓ Facilities: ⚓ ⊙ ⚑ ✳ ⚒ & 🛒 ☐ ⤬

Services: 🔌 📶 🛈 ⊞ → ∪ ▶ ⊚ ⚒ 🛁

Notes: Adults only 🍴 💳 💳 💳 🔇 🛢

HORSFORTH   Map 19 SE23

▶ ▶ ▶ **77% St Helena's Caravan Park**
(SE240421)
Otley Old Rd LS18 5HZ
☎ 0113 284 1142
Dir: From A658 follow signs for Leeds/Bradford Airport. Then follow site signs
🚐 🚙 👤
Open Apr-Oct Booking advisable Last arrival 19.30hrs Last departure 14.00hrs
A well-maintained parkland setting surrounded by woodland yet within easy reach of Leeds with its excellent shopping and cultural opportunities, Ilkley, and the attractive Wharfedale town of Otley. Others may just want to relax within this adults-only park's spacious, pleasant surroundings. A 12-acre site with 60 touring pitches and 40 statics.

Facilities: ➡ ⚓ ⊙ ⚑ ✳ ⚒ & ⚒ ⤬

Services: 🔌 📶 → ▶ ⚒ 🛁 Notes: Adults only

CHANNEL ISLANDS
GUERNSEY

CASTEL   Map 24

▶ ▶ ▶ **79% Fauxquets Valley Farm**
GY5 7QA ☎ 01481 255460 📠 01481 251797
📧 info@fauxquets.co.uk
🌐 www.fauxquets.co.uk
Dir: Off pier. 2nd exit off rdbt. Top of hill left onto Queens Rd. Continue for 2m. Turn right onto Candie Rd. Opposite sign for German Occupation Museum
👤 £10.40-£12.60
Open mid Jun-Aug (rs May-mid Jun & 1-15 Sep Haybarn restaurant and bar closed) Booking advisable last 2 wks Jul-1st 3 wks Aug
A beautiful, quiet farm site in a hidden valley close to the sea. Friendly helpful owners who understand campers' needs offer good quality facilities and amenities, including an outdoor swimming pool, bar/restaurant, nature trail and sports areas. A 3-acre site with 100 touring pitches. Nature trail & bird watching.

Leisure: ⚓ ⚑ ⚒ ☐ Facilities: ⚓ ⊙ ⚑ ✳ ⚒ & 🛒 ⤬ 🐾

Services: 🔌 📶 ⚑ 🍴 ✎ ⊞ ✕ ⚒ → ∪ ▶ ⊚ ⚒ ⚒

💳 💳 🛢

ST SAMPSON   Map 24

▶ ▶ ▶ **77% Le Vaugrat Camp Site**
Route de Vaugrat GY2 4TA
☎ 01481 257468 📠 01481 251841
📧 enquiries@vaugratcampsite.com
🌐 www.users.globalnet.co.uk/~adgould
Dir: From main coast road on NW of island, site is signed at Port Grat Bay into Route de Vaugrat, near Peninsula Hotel
★ 👤 £13-£33.60

Open May-mid Sep Booking advisable all year
Overlooking the sea and set within the grounds of a lovely 17th-century house, this level grassy park is backed by woodland, and close to lovely sandy beaches. A 6-acre site with 150 touring pitches.

Leisure: ⚓ ⚒ ☐ Facilities: ⚓ ⊙ ⚑ ✳ & ⚒ 🛒 ⤬

Services: 🛈 ✎ ⊞ → ∪ ▶ ⚒ 🛁 📶

Notes: 🐾 🍴 💳 💳 🛢

England

VALE   Map 24

▶ ▶ ▶ 77% **La Bailloterie Camping & Leisure**
Bailloterie Ln GY3 5HA ☎ 01481 243636 &
07781 103420 🖹 01481 243225
🖶 info@campinginguernsey.com
🌐 www.campinginguernsey.com
*Dir: 3m N of St Peter Port, take Vale road to Crossways,
turn right into Rue du Braye. Site 1st left at sign*
▲ £10-£12
Open 15 May-15 Sep Booking advisable all times
Last arrival 23.00hrs
*A pretty rural site with one large touring field and a
few small, well-screened paddocks. This delightful
site has been in the same family ownership for over
30 years, and offers super facilities in converted
outbuildings. A 12-acre site with 100 touring
pitches.*
Volleyball net & boules pitch.

Leisure: ◣ ⚠ ▢ **Facilities:** 🍴 ⊙ ◥ ✳ 🛎 🔥 🔥 🐾
Services: 🚐 🗑 🛢 ⌀ 🗓 ✕ 🖴 🛒 → ∪ ▶ ◎ 🔥 🛁 🎯 🖉
Notes: Dogs allowed in restricted areas 💳 💳 🖵

HERM

HERM   Map 24

▶ ▶ ▶ 76% *Seagull Campsite*
GY1 3HR ☎ 01481 722377 🖹 01481 700334
🖶 camping@herm-island.com
🌐 www.herm-island.com
▲

Open May-Sep Last arrival 17.00hrs Last departure
17.30hrs
*An away-from-it-all location on the idyllic tiny island
of Herm. The well-maintained grassy site offers
stunning views over the sea and surrounding
islands, and all pitches are level, with some in
individually-terraced bays. Herm is traffic free, so
parking must be arranged with Trident Travel at
St Peter Port, Guernsey, on 01481 721379, or ask
when booking. Campers should check in at the
information office on the quay. 50 touring pitches.
Groceries can be delivered*

Facilities: ✳ 🛎 → 🎯 🖉 **Notes:** 🐾 💳 💳 🖵

> Campsites in popular areas get very
> crowded at busy times – it is advisable
> to book well in advance.

JERSEY

ST MARTIN   Map 24

PREMIER PARK

▶ ▶ ▶ ▶ ▶ 80% *Beuvelande Camp Site*
Beuvelande JE3 6EZ
☎ 01534 853575 & 852223 🖹 01534 857788
*Dir: Take A6 from St Helier to St Martin & follow
signs to campsite before St Martins church.*
🚐 🚐 ▲

Open May-15 Sep Booking advisable Last arrival
anytime
*A well-established site with excellent toilet
facilities, accessed via narrow lanes in peaceful
countryside close to St Martin. An attractive
bar/restaurant is the focal point of the park,
especially in the evenings, and there is a small
swimming pool and playground. Motorhomes
and towed caravans will be met at the ferry and
escorted to the site if requested when booking.
A 6-acre site with 150 touring pitches.*

Leisure: ≈ ◣ ⚠ ▢
Facilities: 🍴 ⊙ ✳ & 📞 🛎
Services: 🚐 🗑 🍴 🛢 ⌀ 🗓 ✕ → ∪ ▶ 🔥 🎯
💳 💳 💳 📶 🖵

▶ ▶ ▶ ▶ 77% **Rozel Camping Park**
Summerville Farm JE3 6AX
☎ 01534 855200 🖹 01534 856127
🖶 rozelcampingpark@jerseymail.co.uk
🌐 www.rozelcamping.co.uk
*Dir: Take A6 from St Helier through Five Oaks to St
Martins Church, turn right onto A38 towards Rozel, site
on right*
🚐 £14.40-£17.20 🚐 £14.40-£17.20
▲ £14.40-£17.20

contd.

Facilities: 🛁 Bath 🍴 Shower ⊙ Electric Shaver 🗓 Hairdryer ✳ Ice Pack Facility & Disabled Facilities 📞 Public Telephone
🛎 Shop on Site or within 200yds 💳 Mobile Shop (calls at least 5 days a week) 🔥 BBQ Area 🔥 Picnic Area 🐾 Dog Exercise Area

England

Open May-mid Sep Booking advisable Jul-Aug Last departure noon
An attractive and well-maintained secluded holiday site offering excellent amenities in a lovely farm location. The site is divided into paddocks, with hedges for screening and shelter. It is only a short walk from the beautiful sandy beach and harbour at Rozel Bay. A 4-acre site with 100 touring pitches and 20 statics.

Leisure: 🔆 🔦 ⚲ ☐
Facilities: 🛈 ⊙ ☍ ✳ ☍ 🛒 🎣
Services: 🔌 ⚙ 🛢 🛒 ⌨ 🔋 ☐ 🚽 → ∪ ▶ ☓ ⚡ 🔧
Notes: 🐾 No pets 💳 ▭ 🎞 🎬 ⏏

ST OUEN   Map 24

▶ ▶ ▶ ▶ 68% **Bleu Soleil Campsite**
La Route de Vinchelez, Leoville JE3 2DB
☎ 01534 481007 🖹 01534 481525
🖂 info@bleusoleilcamping.com
🌐 www.bleusoleilcamping.com
Dir: From St Helier ferry port take A2 toward St Aubin then turn right onto A12 passing airport to Leoville. Site on right of La Route de Vinchelez
★ ⚑ £5-£22

Open 28 Apr-Sep Last departure 10.00hrs
A compact tent park set in the NW corner of the island and surrounded by beautiful countryside. Greve-de-Lacq beach is close by, and the golden beaches at St Ouen's Bay and St Brelade's Bay are only a short drive away. There are 45 ready-erected tents for hire. A 1.5-acre site with 55 touring pitches and 50 statics.

Leisure: 🔆 🔦 ⚲ ☐
Facilities: 🛈 ⊙ ☍ ✳ 🛒 🎣
Services: 🔌 ⚙ 🛢 ☓ ⌨ 🚽 → ∪ ▶ ⊙ ☓ ⚡
💳 ▭ 🎞 🎬 ⏏

Don't forget matches, a torch and spare batteries, and the means to make a drink. Packet soups are sustaining until the shops open.

ISLE OF MAN

KIRK MICHAEL   Map 24 SC39

▶ ▶ ▶ 76% **Glen Wyllin Campsite (SC302901)**
IM6 1AL ☎ 01624 878231 & 878836 🖹 01624 878836
🖂 michaelcommissioners@manx.net
🌐 www.michaelcommissioners.com
Dir: From Douglas take A1 to Ballacraine, right at lights onto A3 to Kirk Michael. Left onto A4 signed Peel. Site entrance 100yds on right
⚑ ⚑
Open Apr-mid Sep Booking advisable end May-mid Jun & August Last departure noon
Set in a beautiful wooded glen with bridges over a pretty stream dividing the camping areas. A gently-sloping tarmac road gives direct access to a good beach. Hire tents available. A 9-acre site with 90 touring pitches.

Leisure: ⚲ ☐
Facilities: 🛈 ⊙ ☍ ✳ ☍ ☍ 🛒 🎣 ⛱ 🐕
Services: 🔌 🛢 🛒 ⌨ 🔋 ☐ 🚽 → ∪ 🔧
Notes: No excess noise after midnight, dogs must be kept under control

LAXEY   Map 24 SC48

▶ ▶ 70% **Laxey Commissioners Campsite (SC438841)**
Quarry Rd, Minorca Hill IM7 4BG
☎ 01624 862623 🖹 01624 862623
🖂 laxeycommissioners@manx.net
🌐 www.laxey.org
Dir: Off main road at Fairy Cottage filling station. Down Old Laxey Hill, over bridge, up Minorca Hill, left before tram bridge, past school
★ ⚑ fr £11 ⚑ fr £11 ⚑ fr £11

Open May-Sep (rs Etr wknds open only Fri-Mon incl)
A level grass park with open views over Laxey Glen, with easy foot access to the village and trams to Douglas and Ramsey. A 2-acre site with 20 touring pitches.

Facilities: 🛈 ⊙ ✳
Services: 🔌 → ⚡ 🔧 ☐ 🛒
Notes: No unaccompanied children under 18yrs

Services: 🅣 Toilet Fluid ✗ Café/ Restaurant 🍟 Fast Food/Takeaway 🍼 Baby Care 🔌 Electric Hook Up
🅥 Motorvan Service Point 🅞 Launderette ⚏ Licensed Bar 🛢 Calor Gaz ⬢ Camping Gaz 🔋 Battery Charging

Scotland

Scotland

ABERDEENSHIRE

ABOYNE　　　　　　　　　　Map 23 NO59

▶ ▶ ▶ 68% **Aboyne Loch Caravan Park (NO538998)**
AB34 5BR
☎ 013398 86244 & 01330 811351
🖥 01330 811669

Dir: On A93, 1m E of Aboyne
★ 🚐 fr £12 🚐 fr £12 ▲ fr £9
Open 31 Mar-Oct Booking advisable Jul-Aug Last arrival 20.00hrs Last departure 11.00hrs
Attractively-sited caravan park set amidst woodland on the shores of the lovely Aboyne Loch in scenic Deeside. The facilities are modern and immaculately maintained, and amenities include boat-launching, boating and fishing. An ideally-situated park for touring Royal Deeside and the Aberdeenshire uplands. A 6-acre site with 35 touring pitches, 25 hardstandings and 80 statics.
Coarse & pike fishing, boats for hire

Leisure: ♦ ⚫ **Facilities:** ℕ ☉ ⚑ ⚹ ☀ ⅙ ⚻ ⚑ ⅂
Services: ⚙ ⚐ ⬡ ⬛ ⬛ ⬡ → ∪ ▶ ♨ ⬙ ↘ ✈

FORDOUN　　　　　　　　Map 23 NO77

▶ ▶ ▶ 73% **Brownmuir Caravan Park (NO740772)**
AB30 1SJ ☎ 01561 320786 🖥 01561 320786
✉ brownmuircaravanpark@talk21.com
🌐 www.brownmuircaravanpark.co.uk
Dir: From N on the A90 take B966 signed Fettercairn & site 1.5m on left. From S take A90, turn off 4m N of Laurencekirk signed Fordoun, site 1m on right.
★ 🚐 £9-£10.50 🚐 £9-£10.50 ▲ £7-£9

Open Apr-Oct Booking advisable Last arrival 23.00hrs Last departure noon
A mainly static site set in a rural location with level pitches and good touring facilities. A 7-acre site with 9 touring pitches and 51 statics.

Leisure: ⚫ **Facilities:** ℕ ☉ ⚑ ⚹ ☀ ⅙ ⚻ ⚑ ⅂ ⅂
Services: ⚙ ⬛ ⚑ → ▶ ✈ ⬙

HUNTLY　　　　　　　　　Map 23 NJ53

NEW ▶ ▶ ▶ ▶ 84% **Huntly Castle Caravan Park (NJ525405)**
The Meadow AB54 4UJ ☎ 01466 794999
✉ enquiries@huntlycastle.co.uk
🌐 www.huntlycastle.co.uk
Dir: from Aberdeen on A96 to Huntly. 0.75m after rdbt

contd.

on outskirts of Huntly turn right towards town centre, left into Riverside Drive
★ 🚐 £13.50-£17.50 🚐 £13.50-£17.50 ▲ £8.50-£15
Open Apr-Oct Booking advisable Last arrival 20.00hrs Last departure noon
A high quality parkland site within striking distance of the Speyside Malt Whisky Trail, the beautiful Moray coast, and the Cairngorm mountains. The park provides exceptional toilet facilities, and there are some fully serviced pitches. The Indoor Activity Centre provides a wide range of games, and the attractive town of Huntly with its ruined castle is only 5 minutes walk away, with a wide variety of restaurants and shops. A 15-acre site with 90 touring pitches, 46 hardstandings and 40 statics.
Indoor activity centre, badminton, table tennis

Leisure: ♦ ⚫ **Facilities:** ℕ ☉ ⚑ ⚹ ☀ ⅙ ⚻ ⅂
Services: ⚙ ⚐ ⬡ ⬛ ⬛ ⬡ ⬡ → ▶ ✈ ⬙ ⬤ ⬛ ⬙

KINTORE　　　　　　　　Map 23 NJ71

▶ ▶ ▶ 77% **Hillhead Caravan Park (NJ777163)**
AB51 0YX ☎ 01467 632809 & 08704 130870
🖥 01467 633173
✉ enquiries@hillheadcaravan.co.uk
🌐 www.hillheadcaravan.co.uk
Dir: 1m from village & A96 (Aberdeen-Inverness road). From A96 follow caravan signs to park on B994, taking unclass road to site
★ 🚐 £11.45-£12.95 🚐 £11.45-£12.95 ▲ £7.10-£9.20
Open all year Booking advisable at all times Last arrival 22.00hrs Last departure 13.00hrs
A peaceful site in the River Don Valley, with pitches well screened by shrubs and trees, and laid out around a small central area containing a children's play space. Enthusiastic owners are constantly improving the facilities, and the park is very well maintained. A 1.5-acre site with 24 touring pitches, 4 hardstandings and 5 statics.
Caravan storage, accessories shop

Leisure: ⚫ **Facilities:** ℕ ☉ ⚑ ⚹ ☀ ⅙ ⚻ ⚑ ⅂ ⅂
Services: ⚙ ⬛ ⚑ ⬛ ⬛ ⬡ → ▶ ✈ ⬙ ⬛ ⬛ ⬛ ⬛ ⬙

MACDUFF　　　　　　　Map 23 NJ76

▶ ▶ 68% **Wester Bonnyton Farm Site (NJ741638)**
Gamrie AB45 3EP ☎ 01261 832470
🖥 01261 831853
✉ taylor@westerbonnyton.freeserve.co.uk
Dir: From A98 1m S of Macduff take B9031 signed Rosehearty. Site 1.25m on right
★ 🚐 £10-£12 🚐 £10-£12 ▲ £7-£10
Open Mar-Oct Booking advisable Jul-Aug
A spacious farm site in a screened meadow, with level touring pitches enjoying views across Moray Firth. The site is continually improving, and offers some electric hook-ups and a laundry. A 4-acre site with 10 touring pitches, 5 hardstandings and 45 statics.
Children's play barn

Leisure: ♦ ⚫ **Facilities:** ℕ ☉ ⚑ ⚻ ⚑ ⅂ ⅂
Services: ⚙ ⬛ ⚑ ⬛ → ▶ ⬙ ↘ ✈

Scotland

NORTH WATER BRIDGE   Map 23 NO66

▶ ▶ ▶ 73% **Dovecot Caravan Park (NO648663)**
AB30 1QL ☎ 01674 840630 📠 01674 840630
🅴 dovecotcaravanpark@tinyworld.co.uk
🅦 www.dovecotcaravanpark.com
Dir: Take A90, 5m S of Laurencekirk. At Edzell Woods sign turn left. Site 500yds on left
🚐 £10-£11 🚎 £10-£11 ▲ £7-£8
Open Apr-Oct Booking advisable Jul & Aug for hook ups Last arrival 20.00hrs Last departure noon
A level grassy site in a country area close to the A90, with mature trees screening one side and the River North Esk on the other. The immaculate toilet facilities make this a handy overnight stop in a good touring area. A 6-acre site with 25 touring pitches, 8 hardstandings and 44 statics.
Leisure: 🐟 ⚲ **Facilities:** 🅿⊙🔧✳🅱🐕
Services: 🚱🅸📋

ST CYRUS   Map 23 NO76

▶ ▶ ▶ ▶ 78% **East Bowstrips Caravan Park (NO745654)**
DD10 0DE ☎ 01674 850328 📠 01674 850328
🅴 tully@bowstrips.freeserve.co.uk
🅦 www.caravancampingsites.co.uk/ aberdeenshire/eastbowstrips.htm
Dir: From S on A92 (coast road) into St Cyrus. Pass hotel on left. 1st left then 2nd right signed
★ 🚐 £11-£12 🚎 £11-£12 ▲ £8-£12
Open Etr or Apr-Oct Booking advisable Jun-Aug Last arrival 22.00hrs Last departure noon
A quiet, rural site close to a seaside village, with modernised facilities and a particular welcome for the disabled. The park is surrounded by farmland on the edge of a village, with extensive views. Touring pitches are sited on rising ground amongst attractive landscaping. A 4-acre site with 33 touring pitches, 21 hardstandings and 18 statics. Separate garden with boule pitch
Leisure: ⚲ **Facilities:** 🅿⊙🔧✳🅱🐕
Services: 🚱🅸📋→ 🅹
Notes: If camping - no dogs allowed, if touring - dogs must be kept on lead at all times

TARLAND   Map 23 NJ40

▶ ▶ ▶ 77% **Camping & Caravanning Club Site (NJ477044)**
AB34 4UP ☎ 013398 81388
🅦 www.campingandcaravanningclub.co.uk
Dir: A93 from Aberdeen turn right in Aboyne at Struan Hotel onto B9094. After 6m take next right, then fork left before bridge, 600yds site on left
★ 🚐 £12.40-£16.70 🚎 £12.40-£16.70 ▲ £12.40-£16.70
Open Apr-Oct Booking advisable bank hols & peak period Last arrival 21.00hrs Last departure noon
A pretty park on the edge of the village, laid out on two levels. The upper area has hardstandings and electric hook-ups, and views over hills and moorland, while the lower level is well screened with mature trees and grassy. Please see

contd.

advertisement on page 11 for information on Club sites and membership. An 8-acre site with 90 touring pitches, 32 hardstandings.
Leisure: 🐟 ⚲ **Facilities:** 🅿⊙🔧✳🅱🐕
Services: 🚱🅸📋→ 🅿🅹🅻

ANGUS

EDZELL   Map 23 NO66

▶ ▶ ▶ 65% *Glenesk Caravan Park (NO602717)*
DD9 7YP ☎ 01356 648565 & 648523
Dir: on unclass road to Glen Esk, 1m N of B966
🚐🚎▲
Open Apr-Oct Booking advisable public hols & mid Jun-Aug Last arrival 22.00hrs Last departure 16.00hrs
A carefully maintained woodland site with caravans spread amongst the trees around a fishing lake, and tents located in a separate area. The pleasant owner and warden create a friendly atmosphere. An 8-acre site with 45 touring pitches and 10 statics.
Leisure: 🐟⚲🎣 **Facilities:** 🅿⊙🔧✳🅱🐕
Services: 🚱🅸📋→ 🅿🅹🅻

KIRRIEMUIR   Map 23 NO35

▶ ▶ ▶ ▶ 77% **Drumshademuir Caravan Park (NO381509)**
Roundyhill DD8 1QT
☎ 01575 573284 📠 01575 570130
🅴 easson@uku.co.uk
🅦 www.drumshademuir.com
Dir: Take A928 from A90 or A94 to Kirriemuir, park lies 3m N of Glamis Castle
🚐 £12.50-£14.25 🚎 £12.50-£14.25 ▲ £8-£10
Open all year Booking advisable public hols & Jun-Aug Last arrival 22.00hrs Last departure 16.00hrs
Set amidst farmland with lovely views across the Strathmore Valley. The park offers first class toilet facilities with heating in winter. All pitches have wheel runs or hardstandings so that caravans are always level on the slightly sloping site. Some separately sited larger pitches are also available. A 15-acre site with 80 touring pitches, 17 hardstandings and 47 statics.
Bar food, putting, woodland walk & caravan storage
Leisure: ⚲ **Facilities:** 🅿⊙🔧✳🅱🐕
Services: 🚱🅸📋✗→ 🅿🅹
Notes: Adults only in tents

Practise setting up your tent at home before you take it on holiday, and check that all guy ropes, pegs and poles are present and intact.

Facilities: ➡ Bath 🅿 Shower ⊙ Electric Shaver 🔧 Hairdryer ✳ Ice Pack Facility 🅱 Disabled Facilities ☎ Public Telephone 🐕 Shop on Site or within 200yds 🖅 Mobile Shop (calls at least 5 days a week) 🅱 BBQ Area 🅰 Picnic Area 🐕 Dog Exercise Area

MONIFIETH   Map 21 NO43

▶ ▶ ▶ ▶ **77% Riverview Caravan Park (NO502322)**
Marine Rd DD5 4NN ☎ 01382 535471
🖹 01382 535375

Best of British TOURING AND HOLIDAY PARKS

🅴 riverviewcaravan@btinternet.com
🅦 www.ukparks.co.uk/riverview
Dir: Signed in both directions from A930 in centre of Monifieth
🚐 🚍 Å

Open Apr-Oct (rs Nov-Mar Holiday homes open)
Booking advisable Jul-Aug Last arrival 22.00hrs Last departure 12.30hrs
A well-landscaped seaside site with individual hedged pitches, and direct access to the beach. The modernised toilet block has first class facilities which are immaculately maintained. Amenities include a multi-gym, sauna and steam rooms. A 5.5-acre site with 60 touring pitches, 40 hardstandings and 25 statics.
Multi-gym, sauna, steam bath

Leisure: ♦ ⚓ Facilities: ☜⊙☜✳☝☝☝☝☝
Services: ☝☝☝☝☝☝→☝☝☝☝☝☝
☝ ☝ ☝ ☝ ☝ ☝ ☝

ARGYLL & BUTE

BARCALDINE   Map 20 NM94

▶ ▶ ▶ **76% Camping & Caravanning Club Site (NM966420)**
PA37 1SG ☎ 01631 720348
🅦 www.campingandcaravanningclub.co.uk
Dir: N on A828, 7m from Connel Bridge, turn into site at Club sign on right (opp Marine Resource Centre)
★ 🚐 £12.40-£16.70 🚍 £12.40-£16.70 Å £12.40-£16.70
Open Apr-Oct Booking advisable bank hols & peak period Last arrival 21.00hrs Last departure noon
A sheltered site within a walled garden, bordered by Barcaldine Forest, close to Loch Creran. Tourers are arranged against the old garden walls, with some located outside in quiet grassed areas. There are pleasant woodland walks from the park, including the Sutherland memorial woods close by. Please see the advertisement on page 11 for information on Club sites and membership. A 4.5-acre site with 75 touring pitches, 27 hardstandings.
Leisure: ⚓ Facilities: ☜⊙☜✳☝☝☝☝
Services: ☝☝☝☝☝☝☝☝☝✗→☝☝
☝ ☝ ☝ ☝ ☝

CARRADALE   Map 20 NR83

▶ ▶ ▶ **78% Carradale Bay Caravan Park (NR815385)**
PA28 6QG ☎ 01583 431665
🅴 info@carradalebay.com
🅦 www.carradalebay.com
Dir: From Tarbert, A83 towards Campbeltown, left onto B842 Carradale road, right onto B879 site in 0.5m
🚐 🚍 Å
Open Apr-Sep Booking advisable bank hols & Jul-Aug Last arrival 22.00hrs Last departure noon
contd.

A beautiful, natural site on the sea's edge with superb views over Kilbrannan Sound to the Isle of Arran. Pitches are landscaped into small bays broken up by shrubs and bushes, and backed by dunes close to the long sandy beach. An 8-acre site with 75 touring pitches and 12 statics.
Facilities: ☜⊙☜✳☝☝☝
Services: ☝☝☝→☝☝☝☝☝☝ ☝ ☝ ☝ ☝ ☝

GLENDARUEL   Map 20 NR98

▶ ▶ ▶ **76% Glendaruel Caravan Park (NR005865)**
PA22 3AB ☎ 01369 820267 🖹 01369 820367
🅴 mail@glendaruelcaravanpark.co.uk
🅦 www.glendaruelcaravanpark.co.uk
Dir: From A83 take A815 to Strathur, then 13m to park on A886. By ferry from Gourock to Dunoon then B836, then A886 for approx 4m N. (This route not recommended for towing vehicles - 1:5 uphill gradient on B836)
★ 🚐 £13 🚍 £12-£14 Å £11-£13
Open Apr-Oct Booking advisable Spring bank hol & mid Jul-Aug Last arrival 22.00hrs Last departure noon
A very pleasant, well-established site in the beautiful Victorian gardens of Glendaruel House. The level grass and hardstanding pitches are set in 23 acres of wooded parkland in a valley surrounded by mountains, with many rare specimen trees. Facilities are immaculately maintained, and the owners are hospitable and friendly. A 3-acre site with 35 touring pitches, 24 hardstandings and 30 statics.
Sea trout & salmon fishing.

Leisure: ♦ ⚓ Facilities: ☜⊙☜✳☝☝☝☝☝
Services: ☝☝☝☝☝☝→☝ Notes: Dogs must be kept on lead at all times ☝ ☝ ☝

INVERUGLAS   Map 20 NN30

▶ ▶ ▶ **78% Loch Lomond Holiday Park (NN320092)**
G83 7DW ☎ 01301 704224 🖹 01301 704206
🅴 enquiries@lochlomond-caravans.co.uk
🅦 www.lochlomond-lodges.co.uk
Dir: On A82 3.5m N of Tarbet
★ 🚐 £15-£17 🚍 £15-£17
Open Mar-Oct (rs Dec-Jan main amenity building restricted hours) Booking advisable May-Aug Last arrival 20.00hrs Last departure 11.45hrs
A lovely setting on the shores of Loch Lomond with views of forests and mountains, and boat hire available. The small touring area is beautifully situated overlooking the loch, and handily placed for the toilets and clubhouse. A 6-acre site with 18 touring pitches and 72 statics.
Satellite TV, pool tables, boat hire.

Leisure: ♦ ⚓ ☐ Facilities: ☜⊙☜✳☝☝☝☝☝
Services: ☝☝☝☝☝→☝☝☝☝☝ ☝ ☝ ☝

> Never set up or dismantle a tent in high winds. Double-peg the main guy ropes by driving pegs in at different angles.

Scotland

LUSS   Map 20 NS39

▶ ▶ ▶ **79% Camping & Caravanning Club Site (NS360936)**
G83 8NT ☎ 01436 860658
ⓦ www.campingandcaravanningclub.co.uk
Dir: From Erkside bridge take A82 N towards Tarbet. (Ignore 1st sign for Luss). After workshops take next right at Lodge of Loch Lomond & International Camping sign. Site 200yds
★ 🚐 £13.60-£17.80 🚐 £13.60-£17.80 ▲ £13.60-£17.80
Open Mar-Oct Booking advisable bank hols & peak period Last arrival 21.00hrs Last departure noon
A lovely tenting site on the grassy western shore of Loch Lomond. The site has two superbly equipped toilet blocks, including a parent and child facility, and a good laundry. Club members' caravans and motorvans only permitted. Please see advertisement on page 11 for information on Club sites and membership. A 12-acre site with 90 touring pitches, 30 hardstandings.
Leisure: Ⓐ **Facilities:** 𝆕 ⊙ ♤ ⋇ ⅃ ⌵ ⌀ ⊟ 🏲
Services: 🚱 🖫 🖩 ⌀ ⊞ ⊡ → ▶ △ ⌡ 🐾
Notes: Caravan pitches for members only
💳 🚍 💳 📶 🔊

OBAN   Map 20 NM82
See also **Barcaldine**

▶ ▶ ▶ **76% *Oban Caravan & Camping Park (NM831277)***
Gallanachmore Farm, Gallanach Rd PA34 4QH
☎ 01631 562425 ▤ 01631 566624
ⓔ info@obancaravanpark.com
ⓦ www.obancaravanpark.co.uk
Dir: From Oban follow signs for Mull Ferry, then take turning past terminal signed Gallanach, for 2m to site
🚐 🚐 ▲

Open Etr/Apr-Oct Booking advisable Last arrival 23.00hrs Last departure noon
A well-equipped tourist park in an attractive location close to sea and ferries. This family park is an ideal boating centre, and offers two large rally areas in addition to the touring pitches, one with hardstandings and some electrics. A 15-acre site with 150 touring pitches, 35 hardstandings and 12 statics.
Indoor kitchen for tent campers
Leisure: ⚛ Ⓐ **Facilities:** 𝆕 ⊙ ♤ ⋇ ⌵ ⊟ 🏲
Services: 🚱 ⚘ 🖫 🖩 ⌀ ⊟ ⊡ → ∪ ▶ △ ⌖ 🐾 ⌡
💳 🚍 💳 📶 🔊

DRUM MOHR CARAVAN PARK
Near Edinburgh

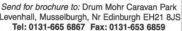

CITY OF EDINBURGH

EDINBURGH   Map 21 NT27

▶ ▶ ▶ ▶ **76% Meadowheads Mortonhall Caravan & Camping Park (NT265680)**
38 Mortonhall Gate, Frogston Rd East EH16 6TJ
☎ 0131 664 1533 ▤ 0131 664 5387
ⓔ mortonhall@meadowhead.co.uk
ⓦ www.meadowhead.co.uk
Dir: Take city by-pass to junct with A702 & follow signs to Mortonhall
🚐 £10-£23 🚐 £10-£23 ▲ £8-£19
Open 11 Mar-5 Jan (rs Nov-Jan shop closed)
Booking advisable Jul-Aug & New Year Last arrival 22.00hrs Last departure noon
This park is set in the 200-acre Mortonhall country estate to the south of Edinburgh, and provides a spacious camping area with grass-based and hard pitches, some with full service, bordered by mature trees. The excellent facilities are kept spotlessly cleaned and well cared for. A 22-acre site with 250 touring pitches, 43 hardstandings and 19 statics.
Leisure: ⚘ Ⓐ ☐ **Facilities:** 𝆕 ⊙ ♤ ⋇ ⌵ ⌀ 🐾 ⊟ 🏲
Services: 🚱 ⚘ 🖫 ⓨ 🖩 ⌀ ⊟ ⊡ ✕ → ∪ ▶ 🐾
💳 🚍 💳 📶 🔊

Leisure: ⚓ Indoor swimming pool ⚓ Outdoor swimming pool ⚬ Tennis court ⚘ Games room Ⓐ Children's playground ∪ Stables
▶ 9/18 hole golf course ⌖ Boats for hire 🎬 Cinema ⌡ Fishing ◎ Mini golf △ Watersports ☐ Separate TV room

Scotland

DUMFRIES & GALLOWAY

ANNAN   Map 21 NY16

▶ 67% Galabank Caravan & Camping Group
(NY192676)
North St DG12 5DQ ☎ 01461 203539 & 204108
Dir: Enter site via North Street
★ ♚ fr £10 ♚ fr £10 ▲ fr £8
Open Apr-early Sep Booking advisable Last
departure noon
*A tidy, well-maintained grassy little park close to
the centre of town but with pleasant rural views,
and skirted by River Annan. A 1-acre site with 30
touring pitches.*

Facilities: ⚹⚹⚹⚹⚹
Services: ⚹→⚹⚹⚹ Notes: Dogs must be on leads

BALMINNOCH   Map 20 NX26

▶ ▶ ▶ ▶ 72% Three Lochs Holiday Park
(NX272655)
DG8 0EP ☎ 01671 830304 🖷 01671 830335
🅴 info@3lochs.co.uk
🆆 www.3lochs.co.uk
*Dir: Follow A75 W towards Stranraer. Approx 10km
from Newton Stewart rdbt turn right at small x-roads,
follow signs to site, park 4m on right.*
★ ♚ £11-£12 ♚ £11-£12 ▲ £6.50-£11
Open Mar-Oct Booking advisable bank hols & Jul-
Aug Last arrival 22.00hrs Last departure 11.00hrs
*A remote and very peaceful park set in beautiful
moorland on the banks of Loch Heron, with further
lochs and woodland nearby. This spacious grass
park offers some fully-serviced pitches in a stunning
location, and as well as being an ideal holiday spot
for walkers and anglers, it provides a heated indoor
swimming pool and well-equipped games room.
A 22.5-acre site with 45 touring pitches,
20 hardstandings and 90 statics.*
Games room & snooker

Leisure: ⚹ ⚹ ⚹ Facilities: ⚹⚹⚹⚹⚹⚹⚹⚹⚹⚹
Services: ⚹⚹⚹⚹⚹⚹→⚹⚹

THE PERCENTAGE RATING
FOR ALL PARKS RANGES FROM
50% - 100%.

All of the campsites in this directory
are inspected annually by a team of
experienced inspectors

BEATTOCK   Map 21 NT00

NEW ▶ ▶ ▶ 77% Craigielands Country Park
(NY079023)
DG10 9RB ☎ 01683 300591 🖷 01683 300105
🅴 admin@craigielandsleisure.com
🆆 www.craigielandsleisure.com
★ ♚ £12-£18 ♚ £12-£18 ▲ £10-£18

Open Mar-6 Jan Pub open wknds only Booking
advisable Last arrival 23.00hrs Last departure noon
*A relaxed park in part of a former country estate on
the edge of the village of Beattock. A very large
coarse fishing lake is available free to campers,
stocked with trout, tench and carp. A bar and
restaurant serve home cooking, and there is some
entertainment at weekends during the high season.
A 56-acre site with 125 touring pitches,
10 hardstandings and 70 statics.*
Fishing lake

Leisure: ⚹ ⚹
Facilities: ⚹⚹⚹⚹⚹⚹⚹⚹
Services: ⚹⚹⚹⚹⚹⚹⚹⚹⚹→⚹⚹⚹⚹⚹⚹
Notes: Dogs must be kept on leads
⚹ ⚹ ⚹ ⚹ ⚹

BRIGHOUSE BAY   Map 20 NX64

PREMIER PARK

▶ ▶ ▶ ▶ ▶ 93% Brighouse Bay
Holiday Park (NX628453)
DG6 4TS ☎ 01557 870267
🖷 01557 870319
🅴 aa@brighouse-bay.co.uk
🆆 www.gillespie-leisure.co.uk
*Dir: Off B727 (Kirkcudbright to Borgu) or take A755
(Kirkcudbright) off A75 2m W of Twynholm. Signed*
♚ £11.90-£16.75 ♚ £11.90-£16.75
▲ £11.90-£16.75
Open all year (rs Nov-Mar Leisure Club closed
2 days a wk) Booking advisable Etr, Spring bank
hol & Jul-Aug Last arrival 21.30hrs Last
departure 11.30hrs
*This grassy site enjoys a marvellous coastal
setting adjacent to the beach and with superb
sea views. Pitches have been imaginatively
sculpted into the meadowland, with stone walls
and hedges blending in with the site's mature
trees. These features together with the large
range of leisure activities make this an excellent
holiday centre. A 30-acre site with 190 touring
pitches and 120 statics.*

contd.

Mini golf, riding, fishing, quad bikes, 18-hole golf.

Leisure: ⟨ symbols ⟩
Facilities: ⟨ symbols ⟩
Services: ⟨ symbols ⟩
⟨ symbols ⟩
See advertisement under KIRKCUDBRIGHT

CASTLE DOUGLAS   Map 21 NX76

► ► ► 77% **Lochside Caravan & Camping Site** (NX766618)
Lochside Park DG7 1EZ ☎ 01556 502949 & 503806
▤ 01556 503806
🅔 scottg2@dumgal.gov.uk
🆆 www.dumgal.gov.uk/services/depts/comres/campsites/lochside.htm
Dir: Off A75 towards Castle Douglas by Carlingwark Loch
★ 🚐 £9.30-£11.10 🚙 £9.30-£11.10 🛆 £9.30-£11.10
Open Etr-Oct Last arrival 19.30hrs Last departure noon
Well-managed municipal touring site in a pleasant location adjacent to Carlingwark Loch and parkland but close to the town. A 5.5-acre site with 161 touring pitches.
Putting & rowing boats (wknds & high season)
Leisure: ⟨ symbols ⟩
Facilities: ⟨ symbols ⟩
Services: ⟨ symbols ⟩
Notes: Dogs must be kept on leads

CREETOWN   Map 20 NX46

PREMIER PARK

► ► ► ► ► 83% *Castle Cary Holiday Park* (NX475576)
DG8 7DQ ☎ 01671 820264 ▤ 01671 820670
Dir: Signed with direct access off A75, 0.5m S of village
🚐 🚙 🛆
Open all year (rs Oct-Mar reception/shop, no heated outdoor pool) Booking advisable BH's & Jul-Aug Last arrival anytime Last departure noon
This attractive site in the grounds of Cassencarie House is sheltered by woodlands, and faces south towards Wigtown Bay. The park is in a secluded location with beautiful landscaping and excellent facilities. The bar/restaurant is housed in part of an old castle, and enjoys extensive views over the River Cree estuary. A 6-acre site with 50 touring pitches, 50 hardstandings and 26 statics.
Mountain bike hire, crazy golf, coarse fishing
Leisure: ⟨ symbols ⟩
Facilities: ⟨ symbols ⟩
Services: ⟨ symbols ⟩
Notes: Dogs must be kept on leads at all times
⟨ symbols ⟩
See advertisement under Preliminary Section

► ► ► 77% **Creetown Caravan Park (NX474586)**
Silver St DG8 7HU ☎ 01671 820377 ▤ 01671 820377
🅔 creetowncaravan@btconnect.com
🆆 www.creetown-caravans.co.uk
Dir: Off A75 into Creetown, turn between clock tower & hotel, then left along Silver St
★ 🚐 £10-£12.50 🚙 £10-£12.50 🛆 £7-£12.50
Open Mar-Oct Booking advisable Jul & Aug Last arrival 22.30hrs Last departure 14.00hrs
A neat and well-maintained park set in the village centre with views across the estuary on the coast of Wigtown Bay. Its attractive setting is beside the Moneypool Burn on the River Cree. Plenty of good amenities, including a heated outdoor swimming pool. A 3-acre site with 20 touring pitches and 54 statics. Games room, indoor hot tub
Leisure: ⟨ symbols ⟩ **Facilities:** ⟨ symbols ⟩
Services: ⟨ symbols ⟩

CROCKETFORD   Map 21 NX87

► ► ► ► 83% **Park of Brandedleys** (NX830725)
DG2 8RG ☎ 0845 4561760 ▤ 01556 690681
🅔 brandedleys@holgates.com
🆆 www.holgates.com
Dir: In village on A75, from Dumfries towards Stranraer site on left up minor road, entrance 200yds on right
🚐 🚙 🛆
Open all year (rs Nov-Mar bar/restaurant open Fri-Sun afternoon) Booking advisable public hols &
contd.

Facilities: 🛁 Bath 🚿 Shower ⊙ Electric Shaver 🔌 Hairdryer ✳ Ice Pack Facility ♿ Disabled Facilities 📞 Public Telephone 🛒 Shop on Site or within 200yds 📦 Mobile Shop (calls at least 5 days a week) 🔥 BBQ Area 🌲 Picnic Area 🐕 Dog Exercise Area

Scotland

Jul-Aug Last arrival 22.00hrs Last departure noon
*A well-maintained site in an elevated position off
the A75, with fine views of Auchenreoch Loch and
beyond. This comfortable park offers a wide range
of amenities, including a fine games room and a
tastefully-designed bar with adjoining bistro. Well
placed for enjoying walking, fishing, sailing and
golf. A 24-acre site with 80 touring pitches,
20 hardstandings and 63 statics.
Badminton court & outdoor draughts.*

Leisure: 🐟 ⚡ 🎱 🎮 🎾

Facilities: 🚿 🛁 ⊙ 🍳 ✳ 🛒 🚻 🏪 🖾 ⛽

Notes: Guidelines issued on arrival ● 🔌 📶 🔋

See advertisement on page 255

See advertisement on page 255

DALBEATTIE — Map 21 NX86

▶ ▶ ▶ ▶ **77% Glenearly Caravan Park
(NX838628)**
DG5 4NE ☎ 01556 611393 📠 01556 612058
*Dir: From Dumfries take A711 towards Dalbeattie. Park
entrance is past Edingham Farm on right, 200yds before
boundary sign*
★ 🏕 £9-£10.50 🚐 £9-£10.50 ▲ £9-£10.50

Open all year Booking advisable Jun-Aug Last
arrival 19.00hrs Last departure noon
*An excellent small park set in open countryside with
panoramic views of Long Fell, Maidenpap and
Dalbeattie Forest. The park is located in 84 beautiful
acres of farmland which visitors are invited to enjoy.
Luxury extras are provided in the laundry and toilets,
including washing powder and conditioner, sachets
of shampoo and shower gel, pegs and washing lines,
washing up liquid, brushes and cloths in the dish
washing area. A 10-acre site with 39 touring pitches,
17 hardstandings and 57 statics.*

Leisure: ⚡ 🎮 Facilities: 🛁 ⊙ ✳ 🛒 🚻 🏪
Services: 🔌 🔋 🔋 🖾 → ∪ ▶ ⚡ 🍴 🔋 Notes: No
commercial vehicles, dogs must be kept on leads

▶ ▶ **72% Islecroft Caravan & Camping Site
(NX837615)**
Colliston Park, Mill St DG5 4HE
☎ 01556 612236 & 612446
🌐 ianrobertson11@supanet.com
*Dir: From A710 in town centre. Access via Mill St.
Adjacent to Colliston Park*
★ 🏕 fr £8 🚐 fr £8 ▲ fr £8
Open Etr-Sep Booking advisable Last departure noon
A neat site close to the town shops. The park

contd.

*overlooks the well-landscaped town park, where there
is a variety of activities, and a river running through.
The facilities are clean and freshly painted. A 1.5-acre
site with 30 touring pitches, 6 hardstandings.*

Leisure: 🎮 Facilities: 🛁 ⊙ ✳ 🛒 🚻 🖾
Services: 🔌 → ▶ ⚡ 🍴 🔋 Notes: For holiday
purposes only, dogs must be on leads

DUMFRIES — Map 21 NX97
See **Shawhead**

ECCLEFECHAN — Map 21 NY17

▶ ▶ ▶ ▶ ▶ **76% Hoddom Castle Caravan
Park (NY154729)**
Hoddom DG11 1AS
☎ 01576 300251 📠 01576 300757
🌐 hoddomcastle@aol.com
🌐 www.hoddomcastle.co.uk
*Dir: From M74 junct 19, follow signs to site. From
A75 W of Annan take B723 for 5m to signs*
★ 🏕 £7-£13.50 🚐 £7-£13.50 ▲ £7-£13.50

Open Etr or Apr-Oct (rs early season cafeteria
closed) Booking advisable bank hols & Jul-Aug
Last arrival 21.00hrs Last departure 14.00hrs
*The peaceful, well-equipped park can be found
on the banks of the River Annan, and offers a
good mix of grassy and hard pitches, beautifully
landscaped and blending into the surroundings.
There are signed nature trails, maintained by the
park's countryside ranger, a 9-hole golf course,
trout and salmon fishing, and plenty of activity
ideas for children. A 28-acre site with 200 touring
pitches, 150 hardstandings and 44 statics.*
Nature trails, visitor centre & 9-hole golf course

Leisure: ⚡ ⚡ 🎮
Facilities: 🚿 🛁 ⊙ 🍳 ✳ 🛒 🚻 🏪 🖾 ⛽
Services: 🔌 🚽 🔋 🔋 🔋 🖾 🖾 🖾 ✕ 🖾 🖾 → ▶ ⊙ 🍴
● 🔌 📶 🔋

Scotland

GATEHOUSE OF FLEET   Map 20 NX55

76% **Auchenlarie Holiday Park (NX536522)**
DG7 2EX
☎ 01557 840251 📄 01557 840333
🖃 enquiries@auchenlarie.co.uk
🕲 www.auchenlarie.co.uk
Dir: Direct access off A75, 5m W of Gatehouse of Fleet
🚐 🚐 ⚠
Open Mar-Oct Booking advisable all year Last arrival 20.00hrs Last departure noon
A well-organised family park set on cliffs overlooking Wigtown Bay, with its own sandy beach. The tenting area, in sloping grass surrounded by mature trees, has its own sanitary facilities, while the marked caravan pitches are in paddocks with open views, and enjoy high quality toilets. The leisure centre includes swimming pool, gym, solarium and sports hall. A 32-acre site with 49 touring pitches, 49 hardstandings and 350 statics. Baby changing facilities

Leisure: ⚡ ⚡ ⚡ ⅍

Facilities: ⟋ ⟋ ⊙ ⚡ ✳ ⟋ ⚡ ⚡ ⚡ ⚡ ⚡

Services: ⚡ ⚡ ⚡ ⚡ ⚡ ⚡ ⚡ ⚡ × ⚡ → ⚡ ⊙ ⚡
⚡ ⚡ ⚡ ⚡ ⚡ ⚡

For full details of the AA pennant ratings scheme see pages 7-8

▶ ▶ ▶ 81% **Anwoth Caravan Site (NX595563)**
DG7 2JU ☎ 01557 814333 & 840251
📄 01557 814333
🖃 enquiries@auchenlarie.co.uk
🕲 www.ukparks.co.uk/anworth
Dir: From A75 into Gatehouse-of-Fleet, park on right towards Stranraer. Signed from town centre
🚐 🚐 ⚠
Open Mar-Oct Booking advisable Jul-Aug Last arrival 20.00hrs Last departure noon
A peaceful sheltered park within easy walking distance of the village, ideally placed for exploring the scenic hills, valleys and coastline. Guests may use the leisure facilities at the sister park, Auchenlarie Holiday Park. A 2-acre site with 28 touring pitches and 44 statics.

Facilities: ⟋ ⟋ ⊙ ⚡ ✳ ⚡ ⚡ ⚡ ⚡ ⚡

Services: ⚡ ⚡ ⚡ → ⚡ ⚡ ⚡ ⚡ ⚡ ⚡ ⚡

See advertisement on page 258

▶ ▶ ▶ 79% **Mossyard Caravan & Camping Park (NX546518)**
Mossyard DG7 2ET ☎ 01557 840226
📄 01557 840226
🖃 enquiry@mossyard.co.uk
🕲 www.mossyard.co.uk
Dir: 0.75m off A75 on private tarmaced farm road, 4.5m W of Gatehouse of Fleet
🚐 £9-£13 🚐 £8-£11 ⚠ £8-£10
Open Etr/Apr-Oct Booking advisable Spring BH, Jul-Aug, wknds

contd.

Auchenlarie Holiday Park

Gatehouse of Fleet, Dumfries & Galloway DG7 2EX

- On the A75 five miles from Gatehouse of Fleet
- Serviced pitches on hard-standing for all tourers, tents welcome
- Nightly entertainment & regular cabarets
- Indoor swimming pool, sauna, solarium & games hall
- Three bars, restaurant, shop & laundry

Caravans: £16-£21
Tents: £9.50-£13.50

Open March-October, booking always advisable.
Last arrival 20.00 hrs, last departure noon.

A family-run park set on cliffs overlooking Wigtown Bay, with its own sandy cove. The tenting area is set on terraces beside a burn, and there are also pitches for tents requiring electric hook-ups.

Most touring pitches have hard-standing and are serviced with water, electric & tv points.

Leisure: ⚡ ⚡ ⅍
Facilities: ⚡ ⊙ ⚡ ✳ ⚡ ⚡ ⚡ ⚡ ⚡ ⚡
Services: ⚡ ⚡ ⚡ ⚡ ⚡ ⚡ ⚡ × → ⚡ ⊙ ⚡ ⚡ ⚡ ⚡ ⚡ ⚡ ⚡

Telephone: 01557 840251   Fax: 01557 840333
Email: enquiries@auchenlarie.co.uk   www.auchenlarie.co.uk

Leisure: ⚡ Indoor swimming pool   ⚡ Outdoor swimming pool   ⚡ Tennis court   ⚡ Games room   ⅍ Children's playground   ⚡ Stables
▶ 9/18 hole golf course   ⚡ Boats for hire   ⚡ Cinema   ⚡ Fishing   ⊙ Mini golf   ⚡ Watersports   ⚡ Separate TV room

Scotland

Anwoth
Holiday Park
Gatehouse of Fleet,
Dumfries & Galloway DG7 2JU

**Open March-October, booking always advisable.
Last arrival 20.00 hrs, last departure noon.**

*Dir: From A75 into Gatehouse-of-Fleet, park on
right towards Stranraer. Signed from town centre*

*A peaceful sheltered park within easy walking
distance of the village, ideally placed for
exploring the scenic hills, valleys and coastline.
Guests may use the leisure facilities at the sister
park, Auchenlarie Holiday Park. A 2-acre site with
28 all inclusive touring pitches and 44 statics.*

Facilities: ➕ ⟨⟩ ☉ ☕ ✳ ☼ ⟨⟩
Services: 🔌 🅿 🛈 → ⟨⟩ 🗑 ⬚ 🔲 🔳

Telephone: 01557 814333
Fax: 01557 814333

*A grassy park with its own beach, located on a
working farm, and offering an air of peace and
tranquillity. Stunning sea and coastal views from
touring pitches, and the tenting field is almost on
the beach. A 6.5-acre site with 35 touring pitches
and 15 statics.*

Facilities: ⟨⟩ ☉ ☕ ⟨⟩   **Services:** 🔌 🅿 🛈 ⟨⟩ ⬚ → ∪ 🗑 🕿

GLENLUCE   Map 20 NX15

NEW ▶ ▶ ▶ **72% Glenluce Caravan & Camping
Park (NX198574)**
DG8 0QR ☎ 01581 300412 ☝ 01581 300754
🅴 enquiries@glenlucecaravans.co.uk
🌐 www.glenlucecaravans.co.uk
★ 🚐 £12-£17 🚍 £12-£17 ▲ £12-£17
Open Mar-Oct Booking advisable
*Set in the grounds of a former mansion, close to the
village of Glenluce with its shops and eating places.
Pitches are in the park or walled garden, there is a
heated indoor pool and spa. A 5-acre site with 20
touring pitches, 4 hardstandings and 30 statics.*
Leisure: ☔ **Facilities:** ⟨⟩ ☉ ☕ ✳ ☼ ⟨⟩ 🕿
Services: 🔌 🅿 🛈 → ∪ 🗑 🕿 ⬚ 🔳

▶ ▶ ▶ **72% Whitecairn Farm Caravan Park
(NX300434)**
DG8 0NZ ☎ 01581 300267 ☝ 01581 300434
🅴 enquiries@whitecairncaravans.co.uk
🌐 www.whitecairncaravans.co.uk
*Dir: Turn off A75 at Glenluce. Park signed from main street
onto unclassified road to Glassnock Bridge. Park 1.5m N*

🚐 £12-£17 🚍 £12-£17 ▲ £12-£17
Open all year Booking advisable Last arrival
22.00hrs Last departure 11.00hrs
*A well-maintained farmland site, in open
countryside with extensive views of Luce Bay. The
park is next to the owner's working farm along a
quiet country road. The toilets are centrally heated,
and the laundry is well equipped. A 12-acre site
with 10 touring pitches and 40 statics.*
Leisure: ☔ **Facilities:** ⟨⟩ ☉ ☕ ✳ ☼ ⟨⟩ 🕿
Services: 🔌 🅿 🛈 → ∪ 🗑 🕿 ⬚ 🔳 🔲

GLENTROOL VILLAGE   Map 20 NX37

▶ ▶ ▶ **77% Glentrool Holiday Park (NX400790)**
Bargrennan DG8 6RN
☎ 01671 840280 ☝ 01671 840342
🅴 enquiries@glentroolholidaypark.co.uk
🌐 www.glentroolholidaypark.co.uk
*Dir: Leave Newton Stewart on A714 towards Girvan,
right at Bargrennan towards Glentrool. Park on left
before village.*
★ 🚐 £8.50-£9.50 🚍 £8.50-£9.50 ▲ £8.50-£9.50
Open Mar-Oct Booking advisable Jul-Aug & BH's
Last arrival 21.00hrs Last departure noon
*A small park close to the village of Glentrool, and
bordered by the Galloway National Park. The keen
owners are experienced caravanners, and keep their
site neat, clean and freshly painted. The
on-site shop is well stocked. A 6.75-acre site with
14 touring pitches, 12 hardstandings and 26 statics.*
Leisure: ☔ **Facilities:** ⟨⟩ ☉ ☕ ✳ ☼ ⟨⟩ 🕿
Services: 🔌 🅿 🛈 ⬚ ⟨⟩ → 🗑 **Notes:** No cars by tents

GRETNA   Map 21 NY36

▶ ▶ ▶ ▶ **73% Braids Caravan Park (NY313674)**
Annan Rd DG16 5DQ ☎ 01461 337409
☝ 01461 337409
🅴 enquiries@thebraidscaravanpark.co.uk
🌐 www.thebraidscaravanpark.co.uk
*Dir: On B721, 0.5m from village on right, towards
Annan*
★ 🚐 £11.50-£13.50 🚍 £11.50-£13.50 ▲ £8-£15
Open all year Booking advisable Jul-Sep Last arrival
20.00hrs Last departure noon
*A well-maintained grassy site in the centre of the
village just inside Scotland. A good toilet block
provides a high standard of facilities, and several
hard pitches further enhance this busy and popular
park. A 6-acre site with 74 touring pitches, 29
hardstandings.*
Leisure: ☔ **Facilities:** ⟨⟩ ☉ ☕ ✳ ☼ ⟨⟩ 🕿
Services: 🔌 🅿 🛈 🛈 ⬚ ⟨⟩ → 🗑 🕿 ⬚ 🔳 🔲

▶ ▶ ▶ **78% Bruce's Cave Caravan & Camping
Park (NY266705)**
Cove Estate, Kirkpatrick Fleming DG11 3AT
☎ 01461 800285 ☝ 01461 800269
🅴 enquiries@brucescave.co.uk
🌐 www.brucescave.co.uk
*Dir: Exit A74(M) junct 21 for Kirkpatrick Fleming follow
N through village, pass Station Inn, at Bruce's Park turn
left. Over rail crossing to site entrance.*
★ 🚐 £8.50-£10.50 🚍 £8.50-£10.50 ▲ £5-£16.50

contd.

contd.

Abbreviations: BH/bank hols-bank holidays   Etr-Easter   Whit-Whitsun   dep-departure   fr-from   hrs-hours   m-mile   mdnt-midnight
rdbt-roundabout   rs-restricted service   wk-week   wknd-weekend   ✂-no dogs

Bruce's Cave Caravan & Camping Park
Open all year (rs Nov-Mar Shop closed, water
restriction) Booking advisable Last arrival 23.00hrs
Last departure 19.00hrs
*The lovely wooded grounds of an old castle and
mansion are the setting for this pleasant park. The
mature woodland is a haven for wildlife, and there
is a riverside walk to Robert the Bruce's Cave. A
toilet block with en suite facilities is of special
appeal to families. An 80-acre site with 75 touring
pitches, 60 hardstandings and 35 statics.*
BMX bike hire, coarse fishing, buggy, travelcot
Leisure: ⚙ Facilities: ➡ ⬆ ☉ ☜ ✳ ⬇ ⬆ ⬆ ⬆ ⬆
Services: ⬆ ⬆ ⬆ ⬆ ⬆ ⬆ ✕ → ∪ ⬆ ⬆ ⬆ ⬆
Notes: Dogs must be kept on lead

▶ ▶ ▶ 66% *The Old Toll Bar Caravan Park*
(NY325670)
Old Toll Bar, Sarkbridge DG16 5JD ☎ 01461 337439
✉ oldtollbar@sarkbridge.freeserve.co.uk
🌐 www.oldtollbar.co.uk
*Dir: From S: M6/A74 take 1st exit for Gretna. Right at
T-junct, site 200yds on right past Gretna Chase Hotel.
From N: exit A74(M) junct 22 (Gretna), follow Gateway
Outlet Village signs. Site on left after rdbt*
⬆ ⬆ ⬆

Open all year Booking advisable end June-early Oct
Last arrival 21.30hrs Last departure 11.00hrs
*A grassy park on the England/Scotland border
beside the River Sark bridge. This is the first house
in Scotland, and the park has its own licensed
marriage room. The touring area is behind the Old
Toll Bar café/restaurant, and this is an ideal stopover
when travelling to or from Scotland. A 5-acre site
with 70 touring pitches, 7 hardstandings.*
Facilities: ⬆ ☉ ⬆ ⬆ ⬆ ⬆ ⬆ ⬆
Services: ⬆ ⬆ ⬆ ⬆ ✕ → ⬆ ⬆ ⬆
Notes: Dogs on a lead at all times
⬆ ⬆ ⬆ ⬆ ⬆ ⬆

KIPPFORD   **Map 21 NX85**

▶ ▶ ▶ 78% **Kippford Holiday Park**
(NX844564)
DG5 4LF ☎ 01556 620636 🖷 01556 620607
✉ info@kippfordholidaypark.co.uk
🌐 www.kippfordholidaypark.co.uk
*Dir: From Dalbeattie S on A710, site 3.5m on right,
300yds past junct for Kippford*
★ ⬆ £12-£18 ⬆ £12-£18 ⬆ £9-£18

Open all year (rs Nov-Feb Booking required, no
shop) Booking advisable at all times Last arrival
21.30hrs Last departure noon
*An attractively landscaped park set in hilly
countryside close to the Urr Water estuary and a
sand/shingle beach, and with spectacular views.
The level touring pitches are on grassed hardstands
with private garden areas, and many are fully
serviced. The Doon Hill and woodland walks
separate the park from the lovely Kippford village.
An 18-acre site with 45 touring pitches, 22
hardstandings and 119 statics.*
Golf, fly fishing, nature walk, cycle hire
Leisure: ⚙ Facilities: ⬆ ☉ ⬆ ✳ ⬆ ⬆ ⬆ ⬆ ⬆
Services: ⬆ ⬆ ⬆ ⬆ ⬆ → ∪ ⬆ ⬆ ⬆ ⬆ ⬆ ⬆

KIRKCUDBRIGHT   **Map 20 NX65**

▶ ▶ ▶ ▶ 81% **Seaward Caravan Park**
(NX662494)
Dhoon Bay DG6 4TJ ☎ 01557 870267 & 331079
🖷 01557 870319
✉ aa@seaward-park.co.uk
🌐 www.gillespie-leisure.co.uk
Dir: 2m SW off B727 (Borgue road)
⬆ £10.25-£14.60 ⬆ £10.25-£14.60 ⬆ £10.25-£14.60
Open Mar-Oct (rs Mar-mid May & mid Sep-Oct
swimming pool closed) Booking advisable Spring
bank hols & Jul-Aug Last arrival 21.30hrs Last
departure 11.30hrs   *contd.*

Scotland

Services: 🅣 Toilet Fluid ✕ Café/ Restaurant 🏛 Fast Food/Takeaway 🐦 Baby Care ⚡ Electric Hook Up 🚐 Motorvan Service Point 🗐 Launderette ⚲ Licensed Bar 🔋 Calor Gaz ⌀ Camping Gaz ⊞ Battery Charging

A very attractive elevated park with outstanding views over Kirkcudbright Bay which forms part of the Dee Estuary. Access to a sandy cove with rock pools is just across the road. Facilities are well organised and neatly kept, and the park offers a very peaceful atmosphere. The leisure facilities of the other Gillespie parks are available to guests. An 8-acre site with 26 touring pitches and 30 statics. Pitch & putt

Leisure: ੧ ♦ ⚲ ⚞ Facilities: ➡ ⋒ ⊙ ⚲ ✳ ⚿ ௳ ⚎ ㄇ ㅏ
Services: ⬙ ⊡ ⓘ ⌔ → ∪ ⓣ ⓞ ⚄ ⚊ ▥ ▧ ▦

See advertisement on opposite page

▶ ▶ ▶ 75% **Silvercraigs Caravan & Camping Site (NX686508)**
Silvercraigs Rd DG6 4BT ☎ 01557 330123 & 01556 503806 ▤ 01557 330123
🅮 scottg2@dumgal.gov.uk
🅦 www.dgcommunity.net
Dir: In Kirkcudbright off Silvercraigs Rd. Access via A711, follow signs to site
★ ⊞ £9.30-£11.10 ⊟ £9.30-£11.10 ▲ £9.30-£11.10
Open Etr-Oct Last departure noon
A well-maintained municipal park in an elevated position with extensive views overlooking the picturesque, unspoilt town and harbour to the countryside beyond. Toilet facilities are of a very good standard, and the town centre is just a short stroll away. A 6-acre site with 50 touring pitches.
Leisure: ⚞ Facilities: ⋒ ⊙ ✳ ௳ ⚿ ௳ ㄇ
Services: ⬙ ⊡ → ∪ ⓣ ⌡ Notes: Dogs must be on leads

KIRKGUNZEON   Map 21 NX86

▶ ▶ ▶ 66% *Mossband Caravan Park (NX872665)*
DG2 8JP ☎ 01387 760208 ▤ 01387 760628
Dir: Adjacent to A711 to Dalbeattie, 1.5m E of Kirkgunzeon
⊞ ⊟ ▲
Open Etr-Oct Booking advisable mid Jul-mid Aug
Level park on the site of an old railway station, set in a peaceful rural location. This family-run park has good views of the countryside, and comfortable facilities. A 3-acre site with 25 touring pitches and 12 statics.
Leisure: ⚲ ♦ Facilities: ⋒ ⊙
Services: ⬙ ⓘ ⌔ ⊞ → ∪ ⓣ ⌡ ⚿

LANGHOLM   Map 21 NY38

▶ ▶ ▶ 76% **Ewes Water Caravan & Camping Park (NY365855)**
Milntown DG13 0DH ☎ 013873 80386 & 80358
▤ 013873 81670
🅮 aeneasmn@aol.com
Dir: Directly off A7 approx 0.5m N of Langholm. Situated within Langholm Rugby Club
⊞ ⊟ ▲
Open Apr-Sep Booking advisable last week in Jul Last departure noon
On the banks of the River Esk, this is a very attractive park in a sheltered wooded valley close to an unspoilt Borders town. A 2-acre site with 24 touring pitches.
Large playing area Facilities: ⋒ ⊙ ✳ ௳ ⚿ ௳ ㄇ ㅏ
Services: ⬙ ⓘ ⌔ ⊞ → ⓣ ⌡ ⚿

LOCHMABEN   Map 21 NY08

▶ ▶ ▶ 77% **Halleaths Caravan Site (NY098818)**
DG11 1NA ☎ 01387 810630 ▤ 01387 810005
🅮 halleathscaravanpark@btopenworld.com
🅦 www.caravan-sitefinder.co.uk/sites/2436/
Dir: From M74 take A709 to Dumfries. 3m from Lockerbie turn right. Signed to site
★ ⊞ £12 ⊟ £12 ▲ £7-£12
Open Mar-Nov Booking advisable bank hols & Jul-Aug Last arrival 23.30hrs Last departure noon
An open, gently sloping site with small trees and shrubs and attractive flower beds. A two-acre wood on one side provides an excellent dog walk, and the whole site is bordered by mature trees. Close to the three lochs around this historic little town, and the River Annan. An 8-acre site with 38 touring pitches and 50 statics.
Fishing (charged)
Leisure: ⚞ Facilities: ⋒ ⊙ ⚲ ✳ ⚿ ௳ ௳ ㄇ ㅏ
Services: ⬙ ⊡ ⓘ ⌔ ⊞ → ⓣ ⚁ ⚿ ⌡
Notes: Dogs must be kept on leads

▶ ▶ 78% **Kirkloch Caravan & Camping Site (NY082825)**
DG11 1PZ ☎ 01556 503806 ▤ 01556 503806
🅮 scottg2@dumgal.gov.uk
🅦 www.dgcommunity.net
Dir: In Lochmaben enter via Kirkloch Brae
★ ⊞ £7.50-£8.70 ⊟ £7.50-£8.70 ▲ £7.50-£8.70
Open Etr-Oct Last departure noon
A grassy lochside site with superb views and well-maintained facilities. Some hard pitches are available at this municipal park, which is adjacent to a golf club, and close to three lochs. A 1.5-acre site with 30 touring pitches.
Leisure: ⚞ Facilities: ⋒ ⊙ ⚲ ௳ ㄇ
Services: ⬙ → ⓣ ⌡ Notes: Dogs to be kept on lead

LOCKERBIE
See Ecclefechan

MOFFAT   Map 21 NT00

▶ ▶ ▶ 79% **Camping & Caravanning Club Site (NT085050)**
Hammerlands Farm DG10 9QL ☎ 01683 220436
🅦 www.campingandcaravanningclub.co.uk
Dir: From A74 follow Moffat sign. After 1m turn right by Bank of Scotland, right again in 200yds. Sign for site on right
★ ⊞ £13.60-£17.80 ⊟ £13.60-£17.80 ▲ £13.60-£17.80
Open Mar-Oct Booking advisable bank hols & peak period Last arrival 21.00hrs Last departure noon
Well-maintained level grass touring site, with extensive views of the surrounding hilly countryside from many parts of the park. This busy stopover site is always well maintained, and looks bright and cheerful thanks to meticulous wardens. Please see the advertisement on page 11 for information on Club sites and membership. A 10-acre site with 180 touring pitches, 42 hardstandings.
Leisure: ⚞ Facilities: ⋒ ⊙ ⚲ ✳ ௳ ⚿ ௳ ㅏ
Services: ⬙ ⅃ ⊡ ⓘ ⌔ ⊞ ⊡ → ∪ ⓣ ⛁ ⌡ ⚿
⚄ ⚊ ▤ ▧ ▦

Scotland

NEWTON STEWART   Map 20 NX46

▶ ▶ ▶ 66% **Creebridge Caravan Park (NX415656)**
Minnigaff DG8 6AJ ☎ 01671 402324 & 402432
🖹 01671 402324
✉ johnsharples1@btopenworld.co.uk
⊕ www.creebridgecaravanpark.com
Dir: 0.25m E of Newton Stewart at Minnigaff on bypass, signed off A75
🚐 fr £12 🚐 fr £12 ⚊ fr £12
Open all year (rs Mar only one toilet block open)
Booking advisable Jul-Aug Last arrival 20.00hrs Last departure 10.00hrs
A small family-owned site a short walk from the town's amenities. The site is surrounded by mature trees, and offers good facilities including an indoor games room and outdoor draughts. A 5.5-acre site with 36 touring pitches, 12 hardstandings and 50 statics.
Security street lighting

Leisure: ⚓ ⚙ Facilities: ╔⊙╗☀╚╚╥╗╥
Services: ⊞◷◉⌀⊞⊡→◐▶♨╯

PALNACKIE   Map 21 NX85

▶ ▶ ▶ 76% **Barlochan Caravan Park (NX819572)**
DG7 1PF ☎ 01556 600256 & 01557 870267
🖹 01557 870319
✉ aa@barlochan.co.uk
⊕ www.gillespie-leisure.co.uk
Dir: On A711, N of Palnackie, signed
🚐 £9.75-£14 🚐 £9.75-£14 ⚊ £9.75-£14
Open Apr-Oct Booking advisable Spring bank hol & Jul-Aug Last arrival 21.30hrs Last dep 11.30hrs
A small terraced park with quiet landscaped pitches in a level area backed by rhododendron bushes. There are spectacular views over the River Urr estuary, and the park has its own coarse fishing loch nearby. A 9-acre site with 20 touring pitches and 40 statics.
Fishing, pitch & putt

Leisure: ⚓ ⚙ ⊡ Facilities: ╔⊙╗☀╚╚╥╗╥
Services: ⊞◷◉⌀⊞⊡→▶╯🍽 ▦ ▧ 🔊
See advertisement under KIRKCUDBRIGHT

PARTON   Map 20 NX67

▶ ▶ ▶ 70% **Loch Ken Holiday Park (NX687702)**
DG7 3NE ☎ 01644 470282 🖹 01644 470297
✉ office@lochkenholidaypark.freeserve.co.uk
⊕ www.lochkenholidaypark.freeserve.co.uk
Dir: On A713, N of Parton
★ 🚐 £14-£16 🚐 £14-£16 ⚊ £10-£14

GOLD

contd.

Open mid Mar-mid Nov (rs Mar/Apr (ex Etr) & late Sep-Nov restricted shop hours) Booking advisable Etr, Spring bank hol & Jun-Aug Last arrival 20.00hrs Last departure noon
A busy and popular park with a natural water-borne emphasis, on the eastern shores of Loch Ken, with superb views. Family owned and run, it is in a peaceful and beautiful spot opposite the RSPB reserve, with direct access to the loch for boat launching. The park offers a variety of water sports, as well as farm visits and nature trails. Showers are charged for at £1 a time. A 7-acre site with 52 touring pitches, 4 hardstandings and 33 statics.
Bike, boat & canoe hire, fishing on loch.

Leisure: ⚙ Facilities: ╔⊙╗☀╚╚╥╗╥
Services: ⊞◷◉⌀⊞⊡→◐♨╯

PENPONT   Map 21 NX89

▶ ▶ ▶ 65% **Penpont Caravan and Camping Park (NX852947)**
DG3 4BH ☎ 01848 330470
✉ penpont.caravan.park@ukgateway.net
⊕ www.penpontcaravanandcamping.co.uk
Dir: From Thornhill on A702, site on left 0.5m before Penpont
🚐 🚐 ⚊
Open Etr or Apr-Oct Booking advisable Jul-Aug Last arrival 22.00hrs Last departure 14.00hrs
A slightly sloping site with good facilities, in a rural area on the edge of the village with extensive views across the surrounding countryside. The spacious camping area connects with a sports and recreation field beside the Scaur Water. A 1.5-acre site with 20 touring pitches and 20 statics.

Facilities: ╔⊙☀╥
Services: ⊞◷◉⌀⊡→◐▶╯╚

PORT WILLIAM   Map 20 NX34

▶ ▶ ▶ 73% **Kings Green Caravan Site (NX340430)**
32 South St DG8 9SG ☎ 01988 700880
Dir: Direct access from A747 at junct with B7085, towards Whithorn
★ 🚐 £7-£10 🚐 £7-£10 ⚊ £7-£10

Open Etr-Oct Booking advisable
Set beside the unspoilt village with all its amenities and the attractive harbour, this level grassy park is community owned and run. Approached via the coast road, the park has views reaching as far as the Isle of Man. A 3-acre site with 30 touring pitches.

Facilities: ╔⊙╗╚╚╥╗╥
Services: ⊞→▶◴╯

ROCKCLIFFE · Map 21 NX85

▶ ▶ ▶ 75% **Castle Point Caravan Park (NX851539)**
DG5 4QL ☎ 01556 630248
🅴 kce22@dial.pipex.com
Dir: From Dalbeattie take A710. After approx 5m take road signed to Rockcliffe. On entering the village site is signed
★ 🚐 £12-£15 🚐 £12-£15 ▲ £12-£15

Open Etr-mid Oct (rs Mar-Etr & late Oct limited supervision) Booking advisable Whit wk & Jul-Aug Last arrival 23.00hrs Last departure 11.00hrs
Set in an Area of Outstanding Natural Beauty, this level grass park is adjacent to a rocky shore, and has stunning views across the estuary and the surrounding hilly countryside. The park is noted for its flora and fauna, and has direct access to coastal walks and the attractive sandy beach. A 5-acre site with 22 touring pitches and 33 statics.
Facilities: ﮨ ⊙ ❋ ◬ ⴲ
Services: ⵗ 🆎 ⅄ ⌀ ⤵ → ∪ ▶ ⵗ ⅃ ⵉ

SANDHEAD · Map 20 NX04

▶ ▶ ▶ ▶ 75% **Sands of Luce Holiday Park (NX103510)**
Sands of Luce DG9 9JN ☎ 01776 830456
📠 01776 830477
🅴 info@sandsofluceholidaypark.co.uk
🅦 www.sandsofluceholidaypark.co.uk
Dir: From S & E - left off A75 onto B7084 signed Drummore. Site signed at junct with A716. From N - A77 through Stranraer towards Portpatrick, 2m & follow A716 signed Drummore, site signed in 5m
★ 🚐 fr £15 🚐 fr £15 ▲ fr £15
Open Mar-Oct Booking advisable Jul-Aug Last arrival 20.00hrs Last departure noon
A friendly site on the grassy banks on the edge of a beautiful sandy beach, with lovely views across Luce Bay. Facilities are well maintained and clean, and the area around the park is protected by the Nature Conservancy Council. A 30-acre site with 100 touring pitches and 190 statics.
Boat launching
Leisure: ◄ ⴲ **Facilities:** ﮨ ⊙ ⅄ ❋ ◬ ⵗ ⴲ ⴲ
Services: ⵗ 🆎 ⵉ ⌀ ⴲ → ⅃ ⵉ 🅹

Not all campsites accept pets.
It is advisable to check at the time of booking.

SANDYHILLS · Map 21 NX85

▶ ▶ ▶ 77% **Sandyhills Bay Leisure Park (NX892552)**
DG5 4NY ☎ 01557 870267 & 01387 780257
📠 01557 870319
🅴 info@sandyhills-bay.co.uk
🅦 www.gillespie-leisure.co.uk
Dir: On A710 coast road, 7m from Dalbeattie, 6.5m from Kirkbean
🚐 £9.75-£14 🚐 £9.75-£14 ▲ £9.75-£14
Open Apr-Oct Booking advisable Spring bank hol & Jun-Aug Last arrival 21.30hrs Last dep 11.30hrs
A well-maintained park in a superb location beside a 'blue-flag' beach, and close to many attractive villages. The flat, grassy site offers access to south-facing Sandyhills Bay and beach, and is sheltered by woods and hills. A 6-acre site with 26 touring pitches and 34 statics.
Leisure: ⴲ **Facilities:** ﮨ ⊙ ⅄ ❋ ⵗ ⴲ ⴲ ⴲ
Services: ⵗ ⅄ 🆎 ⵉ ⌀ ⴲ ⴲ → ∪ ▶ ⅃ ⵉ 🅹

See advertisement under KIRKCUDBRIGHT

SHAWHEAD · Map 21 NX87

▶ ▶ ▶ 75% **Barnsoul Farm (NX876778)**
DG2 9SQ
☎ 01387 730249 & 730453 📠 01387 730453
🅴 barnsouldg@aol.com
🅦 www.barnsoulfarm.co.uk
Dir: Leave A75 between Dumfries & Crocketford at site sign onto unclass road signed Shawhead. At T-junct turn right & immediate left. Site 1m on left, follow Barnsoul signs.
★ 🚐 £10-£15 🚐 £10-£15 ▲ £10-£12
Open Apr-Oct (rs Feb-Mar Chalets & bothies by appointment only) Booking advisable Jul & Aug Last arrival 23.00hrs Last departure noon
A very spacious, peaceful and scenic farm site with views across open countryside in all directions. Set in 250 acres of woodland, parkland and farmland, and an ideal centre for touring the surrounding unspoilt countryside. It offers excellent kitchen facilities and a dining area for lightweight campers. A 10-acre site with 30 touring pitches, 8 hardstandings and 6 statics.
Leisure: ⴲ **Facilities:** ﮨ ⊙ ⅄ ❋ ◬ ⵗ ⴲ ⴲ ⴲ
Services: ⵗ ⅄ 🆎 ⴲ → ∪ ◬ ⅃ ⵉ **Notes:** No unbooked groups, no loud noise after 23.00hrs

SOUTHERNESS · Map 21 NX95

 77% **Southerness Holiday Village (NX976545)**
DG2 8AZ
☎ 01387 880256 & 0870 420 2991
📠 01387 880429
🅴 enquiries@parkdeanholidays.co.uk
🅦 www.parkdeanholidays.co.uk
Dir: From S take A75 from Gretna to Dumfries. From N take A74, exit at A701 to Dumfries. Take A710 coast road. Approx 16m, site easily seen
★ 🚐 £8-£20 🚐 £10-£23.50 ▲ £8-£20
Open Mar-Oct Booking advisable Jul-Aug & bank hols Last arrival 21.00hrs Last departure 10.00hrs   *contd.*

Facilities: ➦ Bath ﮨ Shower ⊙ Electric Shaver ⅄ Hairdryer ❋ Ice Pack Facility ◬ Disabled Facilities ⵃ Public Telephone
ⵉ Shop on Site or within 200yds ⴲ Mobile Shop (calls at least 5 days a week) ⴲ BBQ Area ⴲ Picnic Area ⴲ Dog Exercise Area

Scotland

A continually improving holiday centre with the emphasis on family entertainment. On-site facilities include all-weather pitches, a supermarket, large laundry and a leisure centre. A sandy beach on the Solway Firth is close by. A 50-acre site with 90 touring pitches, 45 hardstandings and 485 statics. Amusement centre, live entertainment, kids' clubs

Leisure: ⚞ ⚱ ⚲
Facilities: ⚲⊙⚑✳⚓⚡⚟⚏⚡
Services: ⚡⚟⚟⚡⚡⚏⚡✕⚡→▸⊙⚡
⚏ ⚏ ⚏ ⚏ ⚏

STRANRAER   Map 20 NX06

▶ ▶ ▶ ▶ 74% **Aird Donald Caravan Park (NX075605)**
London Rd DG9 8RN ☎ 01776 702025
📧 enquiries@aird-donald.co.uk
🌐 www.aird-donald.co.uk
Dir: Turn left off A75 on entering Stranraer, (signed). Opposite school, site 300yds
★ ⚟ £11-£12 ⚟ £11-£12 ⚐ £6-£10
Open all year Booking advisable Last departure 16.00hrs
A spacious touring site, mainly grass but with tarmac hard-standing area, with pitches large enough to accommodate a car and caravan overnight without unhitching. On the fringe of town screened by mature shrubs and trees. Ideal stopover en route to Northern Irish ferry ports. A 12-acre site with 100 touring pitches.
Leisure: ⚲ **Facilities:** ⚲⊙⚑✳⚓⚡
Services: ⚡⚡⚏⚏→⚡▸⚡✳⚡⚡⚟⚏

WIGTOWN   Map 20 NX45

NEW ▶ ▶ ▶ 82% **Drumroamin Farm Camping & Touring Site (NX445507)**
1 South Balfern DG8 9DB ☎ 01988 840613
📧 enquiry@drumroamin.co.uk
🌐 www.drumroamin.co.uk
Dir: A75 towards Newton Stewart, turn onto A714 for Wigtown. Left on B7005 through Bladnock, A746 through Kirkinner. Take B7004 Garlieston, 2nd left opposite Kilsture Forest, site 0.75m at end of lane
★ ⚟ fr £5 ⚟ fr £5 ⚐ fr £5
Open all year Booking advisable Last arrival 21.00hrs Last departure noon
A open, spacious park in a quiet spot a mile from the main road, and close to Wigton Bay. A superb toilet block offers spacious showers, and there's a lounge/games room and plenty of room for children to play. A 5-acre site with 48 touring pitches and 2 statics.
Ball games area
Leisure: ⚱ ⚲ **Facilities:** ⚲⊙⚑✳⚓⚡⚟⚏
Services: ⚡⚟⚏→▸⚡⚟ **Notes:** No fires

> An increasing number of parks do not accept children. There is a list of adult-only sites on page 19.

EAST LOTHIAN

ABERLADY   Map 21 NT47

▶ ▶ 72% **Aberlady Caravan Park (NT482797)**
Haddington Rd EH32 0PZ ☎ 01875 870666
📄 01875 870666
Dir: off A6137
★ ⚟ fr £14 ⚟ fr £12 ⚐ fr £8

Open Mar-Oct Booking advisable Last arrival 22.00hrs Last departure noon
A small, simple campsite in pleasantly wooded surroundings, with a delightful outlook towards the Lammermuir Hills. It offers level pitches in a well-maintained meadow with electric hook-ups, and is within easy reach of Edinburgh and the East Lothian coast. A 4.5-acre site .
Shop with off-licence
Leisure: ⚲ **Facilities:** ⚲⊙⚑✳⚓⚡⚟⚏
Services: ⚡⚟⚡⚏⚏⚡→⚡▸⊙⚡⚡⚟
Notes: No ball games, no loud music

DUNBAR   Map 21 NT67

PREMIER PARK

▶ ▶ ▶ ▶ ▶ 84% **Thurston Manor Holiday Home Park (NT712745)**
Innerwick EH42 1SA
☎ 01368 840643 📄 01368 840261
📧 mail@thurstonmanor.co.uk
🌐 www.thurstonmanor.co.uk
Dir: 4m S of Dunbar, signed off A1
★ ⚟ £15-£25 ⚟ £15-£25 ⚐ £13-£20
Open Mar-8 Jan (rs 1-23 Dec wknds only)
Booking advisable Etr, bank hols & high season
Last arrival 23.00hrs Last departure noon
A pleasant park set in 250 acres of unspoilt countryside. The touring and static areas of this large park are in separate areas. The main touring area occupies an open, level position, and the toilet facilities are modern and exceptionally well maintained. The park boasts a well-stocked fishing loch, a heated indoor swimming pool, steam room, sauna, jacuzzi, mini-gym and fitness room and seasonal entertainment. A 250-acre site with 100 touring pitches, 45 hardstandings and 420 statics.
Private lake, fitness room, sauna/steam
Leisure: ⚞ ⚱ ⚲ ⚟ **Facilities:** ⚲⊙⚑✳⚓⚡⚟⚏
Services: ⚡⚟⚡⚡⚏⚡⚏⚡✕ ⚏⚡→⚡
⚏ ⚏ ⚏ ⚏ ⚏

See advertisement on opposite page

Services: ⊤ Toilet Fluid ✕ Café/ Restaurant ⚟ Fast Food/Takeaway ⚟ Baby Care ⚡ Electric Hook Up
⚟ Motorvan Service Point ⚏ Launderette ⚟ Licensed Bar ⚟ Calor Gaz ⚟ Camping Gaz ⚏ Battery Charging

▶ ▶ ▶ 70% **Belhaven Bay Caravan & Camping Park (NT661781)**
Belhaven Bay EH42 1TU
☎ 01368 865956 🖷 01368 865022
ⓔ belhaven@meadowhead.co.uk
ⓦ www.meadowhead.co.uk
Dir: From A1 onto A1087 towards Dunbar. Site (1m) in John Muir Park

🚐🚙Å

Open Mar-Oct Booking advisable Last departure noon
Small, well-maintained park in a sheltered location and within walking distance of the beach. This is an excellent spot for seabird watching, and there is a good rail connection with Edinburgh from Dunbar. A 40-acre site with 52 touring pitches, 11 hardstandings and 64 statics.
Internet Café

Leisure: ⚠ **Facilities:** ⋒⊙🗟⋇👌📞🖳🖦🗚🛉
Services: 🖳🖵🗟🗊→∪🍴◎🛆🍺
Notes: Dogs on lead at all times 💳 💳 ⑤

▶ ▶ ▶ 72% **Camping & Caravanning Club Site (NT723773)**
Barns Ness EH42 1QP ☎ 01368 863536
ⓦ www.campingandcaravanningclub.co.uk
Dir: On A1, 6m S of Dunbar (near power station). Sign for Barns Ness & Skateraw 1m down road. Turn right at site sign towards lighthouse
★ 🚐 £11.30-£14.80 🚙 £11.30-£14.80
Å £11.30-£14.80
Open Mar-Oct Booking advisable bank hols & peak period Last arrival 21.00hrs Last departure noon
A grassy, landscaped site close to the foreshore and lighthouse on a coastline noted for its natural and geological history. Please see the advertisement on page 11 for information on Club sites and membership. A 10-acre site with 80 touring pitches.

Leisure: ⚠
Facilities: ⋒⊙🗟⋇📞🖳🛉
Services: 🖳🗟🗊🗊→∪🍴🛆🍺🖳
💳 💳 💳 ⑤

LONGNIDDRY   Map 21 NT47

68% **Seton Sands Holiday Village (NT420759)**
EH32 0QF
☎ 01875 813333 🖷 01875 813531
ⓦ www.havenholidays.com
Dir: Take A1 to A198 exit, then B6371 to Cockenzie & right onto B1348. Park 1m on right
★ 🚐 £11-£52 🚙 £11-£52 Å £8-£39
Open mid Mar-Oct (rs mid Mar-May & Sep-Oct Some facilities may be reduced) Booking advisable school hols Last departure 10.00hrs
A well-equipped holiday centre with plenty of organised entertainment, clubs and bars, restaurants, and sports and leisure facilities. A multi-sports court, heated swimming pool, and various play areas ensure that there is plenty to do, and there is plenty to see and do in and around nearby Edinburgh. The good touring facilities are separate from the large static areas.

A 1.75-acre site with 40 touring pitches and 648 statics.
Leisure: 🏊 ⚡ 🎾 ⚠ **Facilities:** ⋒⊙🗟👌📞🖳
Services: 🖳🗟🛒🗊∅✗→∪🍴🛆⚡🍺
Notes: Dogs not allowed during peak periods, max. of 2 dogs per pitch 💳 💳 💳 🖳 ⑤

MUSSELBURGH   Map 21 NT37

▶ ▶ ▶ ▶ 78% **Drum Mohr Caravan Park (NT373734)**
Levenhall EH21 8JS ☎ 0131 665 6867
🖷 0131 653 6859
ⓔ bookings@drummohr.org
ⓦ www.drummohr.org
Dir: Leave A1 at junct with A199 towards Musselburgh, at rdbt turn right onto B1361 signed Prestonpans, take 1st left & site 400yds
★ 🚐 £13-£16 🚙 £13-£16 Å £13-£16
Open Mar-Oct Booking advisable Jul-Aug Last arrival 20.00hrs Last departure noon
This attractive park is sheltered by mature trees on all sides, and carefully landscaped within. The park is divided into separate areas by mature hedging and planting of trees and ornamental shrubs. Pitches are generous in size, and there are a number of fully serviced pitches plus first-class amenities. A 9-acre site with 120 touring pitches, 50 hardstandings and 10 statics.
Leisure: ⚠ **Facilities:** ⋒⊙🗟⋇👌📞🖳🛉
Services: 🖳🗟🛒🗟∅🗊🗊→🍴⚡💳 💳 💳 🖳 ⑤

See advertisement under EDINBURGH

Scotland

NORTH BERWICK Map 21 NT58

▶ ▶ ▶ ▶ 77% *Meadowhead's Tantallon Caravan & Camping (NT570850)*
Dunbar Rd EH39 5NJ
☎ 01620 893348 🖷 01620 895623
📧 tantallon@meadowhead.co.uk
🌐 www.meadowhead.co.uk
Dir: Off A198 Dunbar road
🚐🚐👤
Open Mar-Oct Booking advisable Jul-Aug Last arrival 20.00hrs Last departure noon
A large and well-serviced grassland site with outstanding views across the water to the coast of Fife. The site is convenient for the town and Edinburgh, with direct access to the beach and many local attractions. A 10-acre site with 147 touring pitches, 10 hardstandings and 60 statics. Putting green
Leisure: 🌊 🎱 🖵 Facilities: 🏪⊙🍴✳🕹🛒🚾🛉🔥🐾
Services: 🔌🛒🗑🛢🖊🗑🔲→🗑▶◉🍴🍺 🚰 🚗 🚙 🗺

FIFE

LUNDIN LINKS Map 21 NO40

▶ ▶ ▶ 81% **Woodland Gardens Caravan & Camping Site (NO418031)**
Blindwell Rd KY8 5QG ☎ 01333 360319
📧 woodlandgardens@lineone.net
🌐 www.woodland-gardens.co.uk
Dir: Off A915 coast road at Largo. At E end of Lundin Links, turn N off A915, 0.5m signed   *contd.*

Scottish ★★★★★

Thistle

AA ▶▶▶▶▶

CRAIGTOUN MEADOWS HOLIDAY PARK

ADAC   *St Andrews*   ANWB

• Shop • Restaurant • Launderette •
• Games Room • Children's Play Areas •
• Tennis Court •

Craigtoun Meadows Holiday Park
Mount Melville, St Andrews Fife. KY16 8PQ.
Tel: +44 (0)1334 475959
Fax: +44 (0)1334 476424
email: craigtoun@aol.com
www.craigtounmeadows.co.uk

★ 🚐 £10-£12 🚐 £10-£12 👤 £8-£12
Open Apr-Oct Booking advisable Jul-Aug Last arrival 21.00hrs Last departure noon
A secluded and sheltered 'little jewel' of a site in a small orchard under the hill called Largo Law. This very attractive site is family owned and run to an immaculate standard, and pitches are grouped in twos and threes by low hedging and gorse. A 1-acre site with 20 touring pitches and 5 statics.
Leisure: 🌊 🖵 Facilities: 🏪⊙🍴✳🚾🔥🕹
Services: 🔌🛒🗑🔲→🗑▶🖊🛢
Notes: Children over 14 only

ST ANDREWS Map 21 NO51

▶ ▶ ▶ ▶ ▶ 90% **Craigtoun Meadows Holiday Park (NO482150)**
Mount Melville KY16 8PQ ☎ 01334 475959
🖷 01334 476424

GOLD

📧 craigtoun@aol.com
🌐 www.craigtounmeadows.co.uk
Dir: From M90 junct 8 onto A91 to St Andrews. Just after Guardbridge turn right for Strathkinness. At 2nd x-rds after Strathkinness turn left for Craigtoun
★ 🚐 £15.50-£22 🚐 £15.50-£22 👤 £15.50-£16.50
Open Mar-Oct (rs Mar-Etr & Sep-Oct shops and restaurant open shorter hrs) Booking advisable bank hols & Jun-Aug Last arrival 21.00hrs Last departure noon
An attractive site set unobtrusively in mature woodlands, with large pitches in hedged paddocks. All pitches are fully serviced, and there are also some patio pitches and a summerhouse containing picnic tables and chairs. The modern toilet block provides cubicled en suite facilities as well as spacious showers, baths, disabled facilities and baby changing areas. A licensed restaurant and coffee shop are popular, and there is a takeaway, a launderette and shop, and indoor and outdoor games areas. Located near the sea and sandy beaches. A 32-acre site with 58 touring pitches, 58 hardstandings and 157 statics.
Leisure: 🎾🌊🎱 Facilities: ⌨🏪⊙🍴✳🚾🛉🛒🔥🗑🔥
Services: 🔌🛒🗑🛢🔲→🗑▶🍺🖊
Notes: 🚫 No groups under 18yrs 🍴 🚰 🚗 🗺

THE PERCENTAGE RATING FOR ALL PARKS RANGES FROM 50% - 100%.

All of the campsites in this directory are inspected annually by a team of experienced inspectors

---

HIGHLAND

ARISAIG
Map 22 NM68

▶ ▶ ▶ ▶ **77% Camusdarach Campsite (NM664916)**
Camusdarach PH39 4NT ☎ 01687 450221
📄 01687 450394
✉ camdarach@aol.com
🌐 www.camusdarach.com
Dir: On B8008, 4m N of Arisaig. Turn off A830 at Arisaig and follow coastal route.
★ 🚐 £12-£14 🚐 £12-£14 ⛺ £10-£12

Open 15 Mar-15 Oct Booking advisable school holidays Last arrival 22.00hrs Last departure 18.00hrs
A very attractive, quiet and secluded park with direct access to a silver beach. The striking scenery and coastal setting are part of the appeal here, and the superbly designed and equipped toilet block is a pleasure to use. The site is 4m from the Arisaig ferry, and 6m from the Mallaig ferry to the Isle of Skye. A 2.75-acre site with 42 touring pitches, 2 hardstandings.
Baby changing facilities
Facilities: 📶⊙🕎✳️♿
Services: 🔌⚙️🛢🔥→❘➤✦🔥🕎●🚐🚮🔩

▶ ▶ ▶ **74% Gorten Sands Caravan Site (NM640879)**
Gorten Farm PH39 4NS ☎ 01687 450283
Dir: A830 to Point, 0.5m W of Arisaig, (follow coastal route). Left at sign 'Back of Keppoch'. Then 0.75m to road across cattle grid
★ 🚐 fr £12 🚐 £10-£12 ⛺ £9.50-£12.50
Open Etr-Sep Booking advisable Jul-Aug Last arrival 20.00hrs Last departure noon
A well-run site with mainly modern facilities, carefully maintained and peacefully located off the beaten track. The site has direct access to the beach and sands, with good views of Skye and islands. A 6-acre site with 45 touring pitches, 4 hardstandings.
Facilities: 📶⊙🕎✳️🔥🐕
Services: 🔌⚙️🛢🔩→❘➤✦🕎

> Sites that take dogs may not accept all breeds. Check at the time of booking that your dog will be welcome.

BALMACARA
Map 22 NG82

▶ ▶ ▶ **76% Reraig Caravan Site (NG815272)**
IV40 8DH ☎ 01599 566215
✉ warden@reraig.com
🌐 www.reraig.com
Dir: On A87 3.5m E of Kyle, 2m W of junct with A890
🚐🚐⛺
Open May-Sep Booking advisable Last arrival 22.00hrs Last departure noon
Set on level, grassy ground surrounded by trees, the site is located on the saltwater Sound of Sleet, and looks south towards Loch Alsh and Skye. Very nicely organised with a high standard of maintenance, and handy for the bridge crossing to the Isle of Skye. A 2-acre site with 45 touring pitches, 23 hardstandings.
Facilities: 📶⊙🕎🕎
Services: 🔌⚙️ **Notes:** Restrictions on awnings, no large or trailer tents ● 🚐 🔥 🔩

BOAT OF GARTEN
Map 23 NH91

▶ ▶ ▶ **76% Campgrounds of Scotland (NH939191)**
PH24 3BN ☎ 01479 831652 📄 01479 831450
✉ briangillies@totalise.co.uk
🌐 www.campgroundsofscotland.com
Dir: From A9 take A95 to Grantown-on-Spey, then follow signs for Boat of Garten. Park in village centre.
★ 🚐 £12.50-£17.50 🚐 £12.50-£17.50 ⛺ £8-£12

Open all year Booking advisable 26 Dec-2 Jan & 25 Jul-7 Aug Last arrival 22.00hrs Last departure 11.00hrs
A very attractive site in a beautiful location with outstanding views. Young trees and bushes enhance the park, which is set in mountainous woodland near the River Spey and Loch Garten. A 3.5-acre site with 37 touring pitches, 20 hardstandings and 60 statics.
Leisure: ⚠ **Facilities:** 📶⊙🕎✳️♿📞🕎
Services: 🔌🛢🛢🗑️➕🖥🍴✕→❘➤✦

See advertisement on page 268

> Don't forget matches, a torch and spare batteries, and the means to make a drink. Packet soups are sustaining until the shops open.

Facilities: 🛁 Bath 📶 Shower ⊙ Electric Shaver 🕎 Hairdryer ✳️ Ice Pack Facility ♿ Disabled Facilities 📞 Public Telephone 🕎 Shop on Site or within 200yds 🚐 Mobile Shop (calls at least 5 days a week) 🔥 BBQ Area 🍴 Picnic Area 🐕 Dog Exercise Area

Boat of Garten
Caravan & Camping Park

This Thistle Award winning Holiday Park is set in a traditional Highland Village. Nearby there is the Strathspey Steam Railway and the famous Ospreys. Fishing on the River Spey, an 18 hole golf course and tennis are all within walking distance. The Park offers an ideal base for exploring the Spey Valley and the Highlands.
**BOAT OF GARTEN,
INVERNESS-SHIRE PH24 3BN**
Tel: 01479 831 652 Fax: 01479 831 450
www.campgroundsofscotland.com

CANNICH   **Map 22 NH33**

▶ ▶ ▶ 71% **Cannich Caravan and Camping Park** (NH345317)
IV4 7LN ☎ 01456 415364 ▤ 01456 415364
✉ enquiries@highlandcamping.co.uk
ⓦ www.highlandcamping.co.uk
Dir: On A831, 200yds SE of Cannich Bridge
★ ⊕ fr £9 ⊕ fr £9 ▲ fr £9

Open Mar-Oct (rs Dec-Feb Winter opening by arrangement) Booking advisable Jul & Aug Last arrival 23.00hrs Last departure noon
Quietly situated in Strath Glass, close to the River Glass and Cannich village. This family-run park has attractive mountain views, and is set in ideal walking and naturalist country. A 6-acre site with 43 touring pitches, 15 hardstandings and 15 statics. Mountain bike hire
Leisure: ◆ ⚑ ☐ Facilities: ↖ ⊙ ℝ ✳ ⅃ ⅃ ⚏ ☴
Services: ⊕ ⅃ ▦ ▯ ⌀ ⊞ ▯ ↝ → ↘ ♪ ⅃
Notes: Dogs must be kept on lead 💳 ▦ ▦ Ⓢ

CORPACH   **Map 22 NN07**

▶ ▶ ▶ ▶ ▶ 83% **Linnhe Lochside Holidays** (NN074771)
PH33 7NL
☎ 01397 772376 ▤ 01397 772007
✉ relax@linnhe-lochside-holidays.co.uk
ⓦ www.linnhe-lochside-holidays.co.uk
Dir: On A830, 1m W of Corpach, 5m from Fort William
⊕ £15-£17 ⊕ £15-£17 ▲ £11-£13
Open Etr-Oct (rs 15 Dec-Etr shop/main wc block closed, no tourers) Booking advisable school hols & peak periods Last arrival 21.00hrs Last departure 11.00hrs
An excellently maintained site in a beautiful setting on the shores of Loch Eil, with Ben Nevis to the east and the mountains and Sunart to the west. The owners have worked in harmony with nature to produce an idyllic environment, where they offer the highest standards of design and maintenance. A 5.5-acre site with 85 touring pitches, 63 hardstandings and 100 statics. Launching slipway, free fishing.
Leisure: ⚑ Facilities: ↝ ↖ ⊙ ℝ ✳ ⅃ ⅃ ⚏ ☴ ⅃ ☴ ☴
Services: ⊕ ⅃ ▦ ▯ ⌀ ⊞ ▯ → ▶ ⊙ ♪
Notes: No cars by tents, no overnight touring pitches available 💳 ▦ ▦ ▦ Ⓢ

Tel: **Fax:**
01397   01397
772376   772007

Linnhe
LOCHSIDE HOLIDAYS

Corpach, Fort William, Highlands PH33 7NL
www.linnhe-lochside-holidays.co.uk
relax@linnhe-lochside-holidays.co.uk

Almost a botanical garden, Linnhe is recognised as one of the best and most beautiful lochside parks in Britain. Magnificent scenery, wonderful views, peace and tranquility. Hard standings and hook-ups to all touring pitches. Tent pitches. Superb amenities, launderette, shop and bakery, private beach and free fishing. Holiday caravans and luxury pine chalets for hire. Pets accepted. Colour brochure sent with pleasure.

DAVIOT   Map 23 NH73

▶ ▶ ▶ 76% **Auchnahillin Caravan and Camping Centre (NH742386)**
IV2 5XQ ☎ 01463 772286 📠 01463 772282
📧 info@auchnahillin.co.uk
🌐 www.auchnahillin.co.uk
Dir: 7m S of Inverness, just off A9 on B9154, Daviot-East & Moy road
🚐 £8-£10 🚎 £8-£10 ▲ £8-£10
Open 15 Mar-Oct Booking advisable Jun-Aug Last departure 17.00hrs
Surrounded by hills and forests, this level, grassy site offers clean and spacious facilities. The owner lives in a bungalow on the site. A 10-acre site with 75 touring pitches, 4 hardstandings and 35 statics. Limited facilities for disabled

Leisure: ⚠ **Facilities:** ⬧⊙🔍✳🔧⬧⬧🐕
Services: 🔌💡🔧🔥🧺✕ ⬧→🪒
Notes: No noise after midnight 💳 💳 💳 💳 💳

DINGWALL   Map 23 NH55

▶ ▶ ▶ ▶ 73% **Camping & Caravanning Club Site (NH555588)**
Jubilee Park Rd IV15 9QZ ☎ 01349 862236
🌐 www.campingandcaravanningclub.co.uk
Dir: A862 to Dingwall, turn right onto Hill St, past filling station. Right onto High St, 1st left after railway bridge. Site ahead
★ 🚐 £13.60-£17.80 🚎 £13.60-£17.80 ▲ £13.60-£17.80
Open Apr-Oct Booking advisable bank hols & peak period Last arrival 21.00hrs Last departure noon
A quiet park with attractive landscaping and very good facilities maintained to a high standard. A convenient touring centre, close to the historic market town of Dingwall. Please see the advertisement on page 11 for information on Club sites and membership. A 6.5-acre site with 83 touring pitches.

Facilities: ⬧⊙🔍✳🔧⬧🐕
Services: 🔌♿💡🔧🔥🧺→◡⬧🪒💳 💳 💳 💳 💳

DORNOCH   Map 23 NH78

73% **Grannie's Heilan Hame Holiday Park (NH818924)**
Embo IV25 3QD
☎ 01862 810383/810753 & 0191 275 9098
📠 01862 810368
📧 enquiries@parkdeanholidays.co.uk
🌐 www.parkdeanholidays.co.uk
Dir: A949 to Dornoch, turn left in square & follow signs for Embo
★ 🚐 £8-£20 🚎 £10-£23.50 ▲ £8-£20
Open Mar-Oct Booking advisable Jul-Aug & bank hols Last arrival 21.00hrs Last dep 10.00hrs
A holiday centre with a wide range of leisure facilities, including indoor swimming pool with sauna and solarium, separate play areas for under and over fives, putting green, tennis courts and very much more. The sanitary facilities are clean and well maintained, and the park is set on the beach yet handy for the

contd.

Highlands. A 60-acre site with 220 touring pitches and 186 statics.
Spa bath, sauna, solarium, family entertainment

Leisure: 🔍🔍🔍⚠ **Facilities:** ⬧⊙🔍✳⬧🐕
Services: 🔌💡🔧⬧🔥🧺✕ ⬧→🪒◎🪒
💳 💳 💳 💳 💳

▶ ▶ ▶ ▶ 78% **Pitgrudy Caravan Park (NH795911)**
Poles Rd IV25 3HY ☎ 01862 810001 📠 01862 821382
Dir: On B9168, between A9 and A949
🚐🚎
Open May-Sep Booking advisable Jul-Aug Last arrival 20.00hrs Last departure noon
An immaculate park in a lovely environment. Many of the pitches are fully serviced, and all have their own water supply. This very quiet park is close to the historic town of Dornoch in rural surroundings, and convenient for beaches, mountains and lochs. A 3.5-acre site with 50 touring pitches, 10 hardstandings and 38 statics.

Facilities: ⬧⊙🔍⬧🔥🐕 **Services:** 🔌💡⬧→▶🪒⬧

FORT WILLIAM   Map 22 NN17
See also **Corpach**

AA Campsite of the Year for Scotland 2006

▶ ▶ ▶ ▶ 85% **Glen Nevis Caravan & Camping Park (NN124722)**
Glen Nevis PH33 6SX
☎ 01397 702191 📠 01397 703904
📧 holidays@glen-nevis.co.uk
🌐 www.glen-nevis.co.uk
Dir: In northern outskirts of Fort William follow A82 to mini-rdbt. Exit for Glen Nevis. Site 2.5m on right
★ 🚐 £9.50-£14 🚎 £9.20-£13.60 ▲ £8.90-£13.60

GOLD

Open 15 Mar-Oct (rs Mar & mid-end Oct limited shop & restaurant facilities) Booking advisable Jul-Aug Last arrival 22.00hrs Last departure noon
A tasteful site with well-screened enclosures, at the foot of Ben Nevis in the midst of some of the Highlands' most spectacular scenery; an ideal area for walking and touring. The park boasts a restaurant which offers a high standard of cooking and provides good value for money. A 30-acre site with 380 touring pitches, 150 hardstandings and 30 statics.

Leisure: ⚠ **Facilities:** ⬧⊙🔍✳🔧⬧⬧🐕
Services: 🔌♿💡🔧⬧🔥🧺✕ ⬧→▶🎬🪒
Notes: Closed to vehicle entry 23.00. Quiet 23.00-08.00 💳 💳 💳 💳

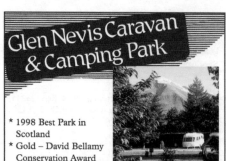
GAIRLOCH   Map 22 NG87

▶ ▶ ▶ 76% **Gairloch Caravan & Camping Park** (NG798773)
Strath IV21 2BX ☎ 01445 712373
🌐 info@gairlochcaravanpark.com
🌐 www.gairlochcaravanpark.com
Dir: From A832 take B8021 signed Melvaig, towards Strath. After 0.5m turn right, just after Millcroft Hotel. Immediately right again
🚐 🚐 ▲
Open Etr-Oct Booking advisable Last arrival 20.00hrs Last departure noon
A clean, well-maintained site on flat coastal grassland close to Loch Gairloch. The facilities were refurbished a couple of years ago; and the wardens are hard working and well organised. A 6-acre site with 70 touring pitches, 1 hardstanding and 8 statics.
Facilities: 🌂 ⊙ ⚲ ✳ ⚫ 🛁
Services: 🚐 🚿 ⊞ �� → ∪ ▶ ↳ ✦
Notes: Dogs must be kept on leads at all times 🍽 🚫

▶ ▶ ▶ 75% **Sands Holiday Centre** (NG758784)
IV21 2DL ☎ 01445 712152 📠 01445 712518
🌐 litsands@aol.co.uk
🌐 www.highlandcaravancamping.co.uk
Dir: 3m W of Gairloch on B8021
★ 🚐 £8.50-£14 🚐 £8.50-£14 ▲ £8.50-£11
Open 20 May-10 Sep (rs Apr-19 May & 11 Sep-mid Oct shop & some toilets closed) Booking advisable Jul-Aug Last arrival 22.00hrs Last departure noon
Close to a sandy beach with a panoramic outlook towards Skye, a well-maintained park with very good facilities. The large laundry makes this an ideal family site. A 51-acre site with 360 touring pitches and 20 statics.
Boat slipway
Leisure: ⚫ 🖾 Facilities: 🌂 ⊙ ⚲ ✳ ⚫ 🛁 ⚫ ⚫ 🛁 🌂
Services: 🚐 🚿 ⊞ 🖉 ⊞ 🔲 → ∪ ▶ ✦ 🍽 ▬ ▬ ▬ 🚫

GLENCOE   Map 22 NN15

▶ ▶ ▶ ▶ 76% **Invercoe Caravan & Camping Park** (NN098594)
PH49 4HP ☎ 01855 811210 📠 01855 811210
🌐 invercoe@sol.co.uk
🌐 www.invercoe.co.uk
Dir: Right off A82 at Glencoe Hotel onto B863 for 0.25m
★ 🚐 £16-£20 🚐 £16-£20 ▲ £15-£20

Open all year Booking advisable Jul-Aug for electric hook ups Last departure noon
Level grass site set on the shore of Loch Leven, with excellent mountain views. The area is ideal for both walking and climbing, and also offers a choice of several freshwater and saltwater lochs. Convenient for the good shopping at Fort William. A 5-acre site with 60 touring pitches and 5 statics.
Leisure: 🖾 Facilities: 🌂 ⊙ ⚲ ✳ ⚫ 🛁 🌂
Services: 🚐 🚾 🚿 🖉 ⊞ 🔲 → ▶ ✦ ✦ Notes: No large group bookings 🍽 ▬ 🚫

▶ ▶ ▶ 79% **Camping & Caravanning Club Site** (NN111578)
PH49 4LA ☎ 01855 811397
🌐 www.campingandcaravanningclub.co.uk
Dir: 1m SE from Glencoe village on A82
★ 🚐 £13.60-£17.80 🚐 £13.60-£17.80 ▲ £13.60-£17.80
Open Apr-Oct Booking advisable bank hols & peak period Last arrival 21.00hrs Last departure noon
A partly sloping site with separate areas of grass and gravel hardstands. Set in mountainous woodland one mile from the village, and adjacent to the visitors' centre. Please see the advertisement on

contd.

Scotland

page 11 for information on Club sites and membership. A 40-acre site with 120 touring pitches, 55 hardstandings.

Facilities: ⬤⊙🚻✳️♿📞⛽🏧🐕

Services: 🔌🛒🔋🚮🚿🗑️→∪▶🛢♨🎣

GRANTOWN-ON-SPEY Map 23 NJ02

▶ ▶ ▶ ▶ 83% **Grantown on Spey Caravan Park** (NJ028283)
Seafield Av PH26 3JQ
☎ 01479 872474 📠 01479 873696
📧 warden@caravanscotland.com
🌐 www.caravanscotland.com

GOLD

Dir: From town turn N at Bank of Scotland, park straight ahead for 0.25m

🚐 £13-£22 🚐 £13-£22 ▲ £8-£15

Open 15 Dec-Oct Booking advisable Etr, May day, Spring BH & Jul-Aug Last arrival 22.00hrs Last departure noon

A scenic park in a mature setting near the river, surrounded by hills, mountains, moors and woodland. The park is very well landscaped, and is in a good location for golf, fishing, mountaineering, walking, sailing and canoeing. Fully-serviced pitches are sought after, and there is a luxury toilet block. A 29-acre site with 120 touring pitches, 60 hardstandings and 45 statics.
Freezer facility

Leisure: ⬤ /🏠

Facilities: ⬤⊙🚻✳️♿📞⛽🏧🪑🐕

Services: 🔌🛒🔋🚮🚿🗑️🚽→∪▶⊙🛢🎣

INVERGARRY Map 22 NH30

▶ ▶ ▶ 77% **Faichemard Farm Camping & Caravan Site** (NH288016)
Faichemard Farm PH35 4HG ☎ 01809 501314
📧 dgrant@fsbdial.co.uk

Dir: 1m W of Invergarry off A87, past Ardgarry Farm and Faichem Park site

★ 🚐 £7.50 🚐 £7.50 ▲ £7.50

Open Apr-Oct Booking advisable Jul & Aug Last arrival 22.00hrs Last departure 11.30hrs

A beautiful location in mountainous country with outstanding views. The park has units spread widely in individual pitches amongst bracken-clad hills, but all pitches are level. A 10-acre site with 35 touring pitches, 10 hardstandings.
Every pitch has own picnic table

Facilities: ⬤⊙🚻✳️📞🪑🐕

Services: 🔌🔋🗑️→🛢♨🎣🏧 **Notes:** Adults only

INVERNESS Map 23 NH64

PREMIER PARK

▶ ▶ ▶ ▶ ▶ 80% **Torvean Caravan Park** (NH654438)
Glenurquhart Rd IV3 8JL ☎ 01463 220582
📠 01862 821382

Dir: 1m W of Inverness on A82 at Tomnahuich Canal bridge

🚐 🚐

Open Apr-Oct Booking advisable Jun-Aug Last arrival 20.00hrs Last departure noon

Located on the Caledonian Canal, this park is quiet and well secluded yet close to Inverness town centre. Every feature of the park has been planned, constructed and maintained to the highest standard, The landscaped grounds are immaculate, and there is a good quality children's play area. A 3-acre site with 50 touring pitches and 10 statics.

Leisure: /🏠

Facilities: ⬤⊙🚻♿📞🏧🖥️

Services: 🔌🛒🔋🚮🚿🗑️→∪▶⊙🎣🚽🏧🎣

Notes: No motorcycles, no traders, 1 small pet allowed per group

---

Never set up or dismantle a tent in high winds. Double-peg the main guy ropes by driving pegs in at different angles.

Facilities: ➡️ Bath 🚿 Shower ⊙ Electric Shaver 🔋 Hairdryer ✳️ Ice Pack Facility ♿ Disabled Facilities 📞 Public Telephone 🏧 Shop on Site or within 200yds 🖥️ Mobile Shop (calls at least 5 days a week) 🍴 BBQ Area 🪑 Picnic Area 🐕 Dog Exercise Area

JOHN O'GROATS Map 23 ND37

▶ ▶ ▶ 74% **John O'Groats Caravan Site (ND382733)**
KW1 4YR ☎ 01955 611329 & 077 6233 6359
🖹 01955 611329
🟢 info@johnogroatscampsite.co.uk
ⓦ www.johnogroatscampsite.co.uk
Dir: At end of A99
🚐 £9 🚘 £9 Å £9

Open Apr-Sep Booking advisable Last arrival
22.00hrs Last departure noon
*An attractive site in an open position above the
seashore and looking out towards the Orkney
Islands. The passenger ferry which does day trips
to the Orkneys is nearby, and there are grey seals to
watch, and sea angling organised by the site
owners. A 4-acre site with 90 touring pitches,
20 hardstandings.*
Facilities: 🅿️⊙🢱✳�🌡🧺
Services: 🔌⛽️📦🛒🧺📧🔋➔ 🍴

LAIDE Map 22 NG99

▶ ▶ 64% **Gruinard Bay Caravan Park (NG903918)**
Laide IV22 2ND ☎ 01445 731225
🟢 gruinard@ecosse.net
ⓦ www.highlandbreaks.com
Dir: On A832, 100yds N of village
★ 🚐 £10 🚘 £10 Å £10

Open Apr-Oct Booking advisable Jul-Aug Last
arrival 22.00hrs Last departure 11.00hrs
*Pitches are right next to the water's edge only six
feet above the beach at this well-placed site on the
outskirts of Laide. Tents are set further back on
grass pitches, but enjoy the same views across the
bay to Gruinard Island. A 3.25-acre site with 43
touring pitches and 14 statics.*
Free hot water
Facilities: 🅿️⊙🢱✳🧺🎣
Services: 🔌📦🛒🧺📧➔ 🔋 🍴
Notes: No pets in rental units 📷 📠 🦢

> Remember that prices and opening times
> are liable to change within the currency
> of this guide. It is always best
> to telephone in advance.

LAIRG Map 23 NC50

▶ ▶ ▶ 70% **Dunroamin Caravan Park (NC585062)**
Main St IV27 4AR ☎ 01549 402447 🖹 01549 402784
🟢 enquiries@lairgcaravanpark.co.uk
ⓦ www.lairgcaravanpark.co.uk
Dir: 300mtrs from centre of Lairg on S side of A839
★ 🚐 £9-£11 🚘 £8.50-£11 Å £4.50-£11

Open Apr-Oct Booking advisable anytime Last
arrival 22.00hrs Last departure noon
*An attractive little park with clean and functional
facilities, adjacent to a licensed restaurant. The park
is close to the lower end of Loch Shin, and a short
distance from the town. A 4-acre site with 40
touring pitches, 8 hardstandings and 9 statics.*
Facilities: 🅿️⊙🢱✳🧺🔋
Services: 🔌📦🛒🧺📧✕ 🍴➔🔋🍴
Notes: No vehicles to be driven on site between
23.00-07.00 📷 📠 📺 🦢

▶ ▶ ▶ 63% **Woodend Caravan & Camping Site (NC551127)**
Achnairn IV27 4DN ☎ 01549 402248 🖹 01549 402248
*Dir: 4m N of Lairg off A836 onto A838, signed at
Achnairn.*
🚐 🚘 Å
Open Apr-Sep Booking advisable Last arrival
23.00hrs
*A clean, fresh site set in hilly moors and woodland
with access to Loch Shin. The area is popular with
fishing and boating enthusiasts, and there is a
choice of golf courses within 30 miles. A spacious
camper's kitchen is a useful amenity. A 4-acre site
with 55 touring pitches and 5 statics.*
Leisure: 🅰
Facilities: 🅿️⊙🢱✳🔋
Services: 🔌📦🛒🧺📧➔🔋 🍴🔋

NAIRN Map 23 NH85

▶ ▶ ▶ 75% **Camping & Caravanning Club Site (NH852552)**
Delnies Wood IV12 5NX ☎ 01667 455281
ⓦ www.campingandcaravanningclub.co.uk
*Dir: Off A96 (Inverness to Aberdeen road). 2m W of
Nairn*
★ 🚐 £11.30-£14.80 🚘 £11.30-£14.80 Å £11.30-£14.80
Open Apr-Oct Booking advisable BH's & peak
period Last arrival 21.00hrs Last departure noon
*An attractive site set amongst pine trees, with
facilities maintained to a good standard. The park is*

contd.

Services: 🅣 Toilet Fluid ✕ Café/ Restaurant 🍔 Fast Food/Takeaway 🍼 Baby Care 🔌 Electric Hook Up
🚐 Motorvan Service Point 🔲 Launderette 🍷 Licensed Bar 🛢 Calor Gaz 🔥 Camping Gaz 🔋 Battery Charging

close to Nairn with its beaches, shopping, golf and leisure activities. See advertisement on page 11 for information on Club sites and membership. A 14-acre site with 75 touring pitches.

Leisure: ♣ 瓜 Facilities: ♠☉❀✳✿❦❧☀
Services: ▣❶❷⌂⊟⊡➔∪▶⚠♪☎
🚐 ▦ ▦ 🔲 🔲

POOLEWE   Map 22 NG88

▶ ▶ ▶ 77% Camping & Caravanning Club Site (NG862812)
Inverewe Gardens IV22 2LF ☎ 01445 781249
🌐 www.campingandcaravanningclub.co.uk
Dir: On A832, N of Poolewe village
★ 🚐 £13.60-£17.80 🚍 £13.60-£17.80 ▲ £13.60-£17.80
Open Apr-Oct Booking advisable bank hols & peak period Last arrival 21.00hrs Last departure noon
A well-run site located in Loch Ewe Bay, not far from Inverewe Gardens. The Club has improved this site in the past few years, and continues to upgrade the facilities. The warm waters of the Gulf Stream attract otters and seals. Please see the advertisement on page 11 for full details of Club members' benefits. A 3-acre site with 55 touring pitches, 8 hardstandings.

Facilities: ♠☉❀✳✿❦☀
Services: ▣❶❷⌂⊟⊡➔∪♪☎🚐 ▦ ▦ 🔲 🔲

RESIPOLE (LOCH SUNART)   Map 22 NM76

▶ ▶ ▶ ▶ 77% Resipole Farm (NM725639)
PH36 4HX ☎ 01967 431235 🖷 01967 431777
🅔 info@resipole.co.uk
🌐 www.resipole.co.uk
Dir: From Corran Ferry take A861. Park 8m W of Strontian
★ 🚐 £11-£12.50 🚍 £11-£12 ▲ £10-£12
Open Apr-Oct Booking advisable bookings only for elec hook ups Last arrival 22.00hrs Last departure 11.00hrs
A quiet, relaxing park in beautiful surroundings, with deer frequently sighted, and of great interest to naturalists. Situated on the saltwater Loch Sunart in the Ardnamurchan Peninsula, and offering a great deal of space and privacy. Hidden away within the park's woodland is a 9-hole golf course, and a restaurant and lounge bar. An 8-acre site with 85 touring pitches, 25 hardstandings and 9 statics. Private slipway, art gallery

Facilities: ♠☉❀✳✿❦❧☀
Services: ▣♆❶❷♪❶⌂⊟⊡✗➔✈♪
Notes: Dogs must be kept on leads 🚐 ▦ 🔲 🔲

ROSEMARKIE   Map 23 NH75

▶ ▶ ▶ 77% Camping & Caravanning Club Site (NH739569)
Ness Rd East IV10 8SE ☎ 01381 621117
🌐 www.campingandcaravanningclub.co.uk
Dir: Take A832. A9 at Tore rdbt. Through Avoch, Fortrose then right at police house. Down Ness Rd. 1st left, small turn signed Golf & Caravan site
★ 🚐 £16.10-£17.80 🚍 £16.10-£17.80 ▲ £16.10-£17.80
Open Apr-Oct Booking advisable bank hols & peak period Last arrival 21.00hrs Last departure noon
contd.

A superb club site set along the water's edge, with beautiful views over the bay where resident dolphins swim. Two excellent toilet blocks, including a disabled room, and a family room with en suite facilities, have greatly enhanced the facilities here. A smart reception area sets the standard for this very clean and well-maintained site. Please see the advertisement on page 11 for information on Club sites and membership. A 4-acre site with 60 touring pitches.

Facilities: ♠☉❀✳✿❦❧☀
Services: ▣❶❷⌂⊟⊡➔∪▶⚠♪☎
🚐 ▦ ▦ 🔲 🔲

TAIN   Map 23 NH78

▶ ▶ ▶ 73% Dornoch Firth Caravan Park (NH748844)
Meikle Ferry South IV19 1JX ☎ 01862 892292
🖷 01862 892292
🅔 will@dornochfirth.co.uk
🌐 www.dornochfirth.co.uk
Dir: Follow A9 N past Tain to Meikle ferry rdbt, straight across onto A836 then immediate 1st right
★ 🚐 £12-£15 🚍 £12-£15 ▲ £7.75-£9.50
Open all year (rs Nov-Mar Static caravans closed) Booking advisable Jul-Aug Last arrival 22.00hrs Last departure noon
A pleasant family site with open views of Dornoch Firth and the lovely coastal and country scenery. The immaculately maintained facilities and lovely flower beds make this a delightful base for touring the immediate vicinity with its many places of interest. A 2-acre site with 30 touring pitches, 10 hardstandings and 20 statics.
Bar/Restaurant adjacent to site

Leisure: 瓜
Facilities: ♠☉❀✳✿❦☀
Services: ▣❶❷⌂⊟➔∪▶◎⚠♣♪☎
🚐 ▦ ▦ 🔲 🔲

THURSO   Map 23 ND16

▶ ▶ ▶ 65% Thurso Caravan & Camping Site (ND111688)
Smith Ter, Scrabster Rd KW14 7JY
☎ 01847 895782 & 894631 🖷 01847 893156
Dir: Signed on A836 W of town
★ 🚐 £9.60-£10.80 🚍 £9.60-£10.80 ▲ £6.90-£9.90
Open May-Sep Booking advisable
A large grassy site set high above the coast on the west side of town, with panoramic views out to sea and the Orkney island of Hoy. Convenient for ferries to the islands, and all the town's facilities. A 4.5-acre site with 95 touring pitches and 10 statics.

Leisure: 瓜
Facilities: ♠☉❦❧☀
Services: ▣❶➔▶⚠♣♨♪

> The number of touring pitches listed for each site includes tents, caravans and motorvans.

Scotland

ULLAPOOL   Map 22 NH19

► ► ► 77% **Ardmair Point Camping & Caravan Park (NH108983)**
IV26 2TN ☎ 01854 612054 🖷 01854 612757
🅴 sales@ardmair.com
ⓦ www.ardmair.com
Dir: 3m N of Ullapool on A835, turn at phone box at beach at Ardmair
★ ⚏ fr £12 ⚏ fr £11 ▲ fr £11
Open May-Sep Booking advisable Jul-Aug Last arrival 21.00hrs Last departure noon
An excellent touring site on small peninsula, with superb views of surrounding mountains and sea lochs, and an interesting children's play area. Pitches adjoin and overlook the beaches, and there is a shop. A 7-acre site with 137 touring pitches, 14 hardstandings.
Boats, canoes for hire.
Leisure: ⚒ Facilities: ⌀⊙ℚ⚹⚅℄⚍⛾
Services: ⚙⛛🛢🔋⏁→▶⚊🗑💷🔌🔌🔌 ⑊

► ► ► 70% **Broomfield Holiday Park (NH123939)**
West Shore St IV26 2UT ☎ 01854 612020 & 612664
🖷 01854 613151
🅴 sross@broomfieldhp.com
ⓦ www.broomfieldhp.com
Dir: Take 2nd right past harbour
⚏ fr £13 ⚏ fr £12 ▲ £8-£13

Open Etr/Apr-Sep Booking advisable for group bookings only Last departure noon
Set right on the water's edge of Loch Broom and the open sea, with lovely views of the Summer Isles. The park is close to the harbour and town centre with their restaurants, bars and shops. A 12-acre site with 140 touring pitches.
Leisure: ⚒ Facilities: ⌀⊙⚹℄⚍🖵🏛
Services: ⚙⛛🛢⏁→▶⊙⚊🗑💷 🔌🔌 ⑊

MIDLOTHIAN

ROSLIN   Map 21 NT26

► ► ► ► 77% **Slatebarns Caravan Club Site (NT277632)**
EH25 9PU ☎ 0131 440 2192
Dir: From A720 by-pass take A701, signed Penicuik & Peebles. S to B7006, turn left signed Roslin Chapel. Follow unclass road at end of village
★ ⚏ £12.50-£16 ⚏ £12.50-£16 ▲ £10-£12
Open Etr-Oct Booking advisable Jul & Aug Last arrival 20.00hrs Last departure noon

contd.

A good modern site with marked pitches, set in a rural landscape near to Roslin Glen and the historic 15th-century Rosslyn Chapel yet within easy access of Edinburgh. The site offers excellent amenities, and has been planted liberally with trees and shrubs to make for a pleasant and peaceful environment. A 2.5-acre site with 30 touring pitches, 21 hardstandings.
Facilities: ⌀⊙⚹⚹℄⚍🖵⛾
Services: ⚙⛛🛢🔋→⊙▶⚊🗑🔌

MORAY

ALVES   Map 23 NJ16

► ► ► 67% *North Alves Caravan Park (NJ122633)*
IV30 8XD ☎ 01343 850223
Dir: 1m W of A96, halfway between Elgin & Forres. Site signed on right
⚏⚏▲
Open Apr-Oct Booking advisable peak periods Last arrival 23.00hrs Last departure noon
A quiet rural site in attractive rolling countryside within three miles of a good beach. The site is on a former farm, and the stone buildings are quite unspoilt. A 10-acre site with 45 touring pitches and 45 statics.
Leisure: ⚓⚒🖵 Facilities: ⌀⊙ℚ⚹℄⚍⛾
Services: ⚙🛢🔋⏁→⊙▶⚊🍴🗑⚊

CRAIGELLACHIE   Map 23 NJ24

► ► ► 76% **Camping & Caravanning Club Site (NJ257449)**
AB38 9SD ☎ 01340 810414
ⓦ www.campingandcaravanningclub.co.uk
Dir: From S leave A9 at Carrbridge, A95 to Grantown-on-Spey, leaving Aberlour on A941. Take next left onto B9102 signed Archiestown. Site 3m on left
★ ⚏ £13.60-£17.80 ⚏ £13.60-£17.80 ▲ £13.60-£17.80
Open Apr-Oct Booking advisable bank hols & peak period Last arrival 21.00hrs Last departure noon
A very nice rural site with views across meadowland towards Speyside, and the usual high Club standards. Hardstandings are well screened on an upper level, and grass pitches with more open views are sited lower down. Please see the advertisement on page 11 for information on Club sites and membership. A 7-acre site with 75 touring pitches, 17 hardstandings.
Leisure: ⚒ Facilities: ⌀⊙ℚ⚹℄⚍⛾
Services: ⚙⛛🛢🔋⏁→🗑⚊💷🔌🔌 ⑊

CULLEN   Map 23 NJ56

NEW ► ► ► 82% **Cullen Bay Holiday Park (NJ516674)**
Logie Head AB56 4TW ☎ 01542 840766
🅴 enquiries@cullenbay.co.uk
ⓦ www.cullenbayholidaypark.co.uk
Dir: From Portsoy on A98 into Cullen, 1st right into Seafield Street, site at end of road
★ ⚏ £11.75-£14.50 ⚏ £11.75-£14.50 ▲ £9-£12.50
Open Apr-Oct Booking advisable Last arrival 21.30hrs Last departure noon

contd.

A cliff top site with fine views over the small Scottish fishing port of Cullen. The site is well maintained, and offers a modern and well appointed toilet block with full disabled facilities and a new laundry. It is well placed for accessing the north east coastline with its small and picturesque fishing ports and dolphin colonies offshore and is but a short distance from the Speyside Malt Whisky Trail. A 4-acre site with 22 touring pitches, 7 hardstandings and 35 statics.

Facilities: ⬚⊙⬚⬚⬚⬚

Services: ⬚⬚⬚⬚⬚→⬚⬚⬚⬚

FINDHORN   Map 23 NJ06

NEW ► ► ► 72% **Findhorn Bay Holiday Park (NJ058623)**
Findhorn IV36 3TY ☎ 01309 690203 🖨 01309 690933
🅔 info@findhornbayholidaypark.com
🅦 www.findhornbayholidaypark.com
Dir: Turn off A96, follow Findhorn signs. Site 1m from Findhorn
★ ⬚ £11.50-£14 ⬚ £11.50-£14 ⬚ £8.50-£12
Open Apr-Oct (rs Dec-Mar No tents, 3 night min. stay) Booking advisable Jul-Aug Last arrival 21.00hrs Last departure noon
A meadowland site owned by and next to the Findhorn Foundation in the stunningly attractive bay, popular with watersports enthusiasts and nature lovers. Facilities include a café serving snacks in landscaped gardens, and a well-stocked shop. A 5-acre site with 75 touring pitches and 19 statics. Organic food shop, arts centre

Leisure: ⬚ **Facilities:** ⬚⊙⬚⬚⬚
Services: ⬚⬚⬚→⬚⬚⬚⬚
Notes: Dogs allowed by agreement ⬚ ⬚ ⬚ ⬚

FOCHABERS   Map 23 NJ35

► ► ► 72% **Burnside Caravan Park (NJ350580)**
IV32 7ET ☎ 01343 820511 & 820362 🖨 01343 821291
Dir: Located 0.5m E of town off A96
★ ⬚ £9-£14 ⬚ £9-£14 ⬚ £7.50-£12

Open Apr-Oct Booking advisable Jul-Aug Last departure noon
Attractive site in a tree-lined, sheltered valley with a footpath to the village. Owned by the garden centre on the opposite side of the A96. A 5-acre site with 51 touring pitches, 30 hardstandings and 101 statics. Jacuzzi & sauna

Leisure: ⬚⬚⬚⬚ **Facilities:** ⬚⊙⬚⬚⬚⬚⬚
Services: ⬚⬚⬚⬚⬚→⬚⬚⬚⬚ ⬚ ⬚ ⬚ ⬚

LOSSIEMOUTH   Map 23 NJ27

► ► ► ► 72% *Silver Sands Leisure Park (NJ205710)*
Covesea, West Beach IV31 6SP ☎ 01343 813262
🖨 01343 815205
🅔 holidays@silversands.freeserve.co.uk
🅦 www.travel.to/silversands
Dir: From Lossiemouth follow B9040, 2m W to site
⬚ ⬚ ⬚
Open Apr-Oct (rs Apr, May & Oct shops & entertainment restricted) Booking advisable Jul-Aug Last arrival 22.00hrs Last departure noon
A large holiday park with entertainment during the peak season, set on the links beside the shore of the Moray Firth. Touring campers and caravans are catered for in three areas: one offers de-luxe fully-serviced facilities, while the others are either unserviced or include electric hook-ups and water. There's a well-stocked shop, a clubroom and bar, and takeaway food outlet. A 7-acre site with 140 touring pitches and 200 statics. Children's entertainment.

Leisure: ⬚ ⬚ ⬚ ⬚
Facilities: ⬚⬚⊙⬚⬚⬚⬚⬚⬚⬚⬚
Services: ⬚⬚⬚⬚⬚⬚⬚⬚✕⬚→⬚⬚⬚⬚⬚⬚
Notes: Over 14yrs only in bar ⬚ ⬚ ⬚ ⬚

NORTH LANARKSHIRE

MOTHERWELL   Map 21 NS75

► ► ► 75% **Strathclyde Country Park Caravan Site (NS717585)**
366 Hamilton Rd ML1 3ED ☎ 01698 266155
🖨 01698 252925
🅔 strathclydepark@northlan.gov.uk
Dir: From M74 junct 5, direct access to park
★ ⬚ £10-£15 ⬚ £10-£15 ⬚ £4.50-£8.50

Open Apr-Oct Booking advisable Jun-Aug Last arrival 22.30hrs Last departure noon
An attractive landscaped site situated in a country park amidst woodland and meadowland with lots of attractions. A large grass area caters for 150 tents, while 100 well-screened pitches, with electrics and some hardstandings, are also available. 250 touring pitches.

Leisure: ⬚ **Facilities:** ⬚⊙⬚⬚⬚⬚⬚⬚⬚
Services: ⬚⬚⬚⬚✕⬚→⬚⬚⬚⬚⬚⬚
Notes: Site rules available on request by post
⬚ ⬚ ⬚ ⬚ See advertisement on page 276

Scotland

Scotland

PERTH & KINROSS

ABERFELDY   Map 23 NN84

▶ ▶ ▶ 73% *Aberfeldy Caravan Park (NN858495)*
Dunkeld Rd PH15 2AQ ☎ 01887 820662 &
01738 475211 📠 01738 475210
Dir: Off A827, on E edge of town
🚐 🚐 ⚠

Open late Mar-late Oct Booking advisable Jun-Aug
Last arrival 20.00hrs Last departure noon
*A very well-run and well-maintained site, with good
facilities and some landscaping, at the eastern end
of the town and lying between main road and banks
of the River Tay. Good views from site of
surrounding hills. A 5-acre site with 92 touring
pitches and 42 statics.*

Leisure: 🄰 Facilities: 🄽⊙🄽🖳🄻🄻🄻🄻🄻🄻
Services: 🄽🖳🄽🄽🄽→🄻🄻🄻🄻🄻 🄻🄻🄻🄻 🄻

BLAIR ATHOLL   Map 23 NN86

PREMIER PARK

▶ ▶ ▶ ▶ ▶ 80% **Blair Castle
Caravan Park (NN874656)**
PH18 5SR ☎ 01796 481263
📠 01796 481587
📧 mail@blaircastlecaravanpark.co.uk
🌐 www.blaircastlecaravanpark.co.uk
*Dir: From A9 junct with B8079 at Aldclune, then NE
to Blair Atholl. Park on right after crossing bridge in
village*
★ 🚐 £11-£15 🚐 £11-£15 ⚠ £8-£15

Open Mar-Nov Booking advisable bank hols &
Jul-Aug Last arrival 21.30hrs Last departure
noon
*Attractive site set in impressive seclusion within
the Atholl estate, surrounded by mature
woodland and the River Tilt. Although a large
park, the various groups of pitches are located
throughout the extensive parkland, and each has
its own sanitary block with all-cubicled facilities
of a very high standard. There is a choice of
grass pitches, hard standings, or fully-serviced
pitches. This park is particularly suitable for the
larger type of motorhome. A 32-acre site with
280 touring pitches and 105 statics.*
Internet gallery

Leisure: ⚓🄰 Facilities: 🄽🄽⊙🄽☀🄻🄻🄻🄻🄻🄻
Services: 🄽🖳🄽🄽🄽🄽🄽→🄽🄻🄻🄻
🄻🄻🄻🄻🄻 🄻🄻 🄻

Scotland

PREMIER PARK

▶ ▶ ▶ ▶ ▶ 80% *River Tilt Caravan Park (NN875653)*
PH18 5TE ☎ 01796 481467 🖷 01796 481511
🅔 stuart@rivertilt.fsnet.co.uk
🅦 www.rivertilt.co.uk
Dir: 7m N of Pitlochry on A9, take B8079 to Blair Atholl & site at rear of Tilt Hotel
🏕🚐⚠
Open 17 Mar-7 Nov Booking advisable Jul-Aug Last arrival 21.00hrs Last departure 11.00hrs
An attractive park with magnificent views of the surrounding mountains, idyllically set in hilly woodland country on the banks of the River Tilt, next to the golf course. Fully-serviced pitches are available, and the park boasts its own bistro and restaurant. There is also a leisure complex with heated indoor swimming pool, sun lounge area, spa pool and gym, all available for an extra charge. Outdoors there is a short tennis court. The toilet facilities are very good. A 2-acre site with 37 touring pitches and 55 statics.
Multi-gym, sauna, solarium, steam room, spa pool.
Leisure: 🏊 🎾 **Facilities:** 🛁 ⊙ 🍴 ✳ 🐾 🏇
Services: 🚐 🔲 🍴 ⌀ ✕ → ∪ ▶ ⊙ 🎣
💳 💳 💳 🚉 📶 📷

DUNKELD
Map 21 NO04

▶ ▶ ▶ 76% **Inver Mill Farm Caravan Park (NO015422)**
Inver PH8 0JR ☎ 01350 727477 🖷 01350 727477
🅔 invermill@talk21.com
🅦 www.visitdunkeld.com/perthshire-caravan-park.htm
Dir: Turn off A9 onto B822 then immediately right to Inver
★ 🚐 £13-£14
Open end Mar-Oct Booking advisable Jul-Aug & wknds Last arrival 22.00hrs Last departure noon
A peaceful park on level former farmland, located on the banks of the River Braan and surrounded by mature trees and hills. The active resident owners keep the park in very good condition. A 5-acre site with 65 touring pitches.
Facilities: 🛁 ⊙ 🍴 ✳ ᗢ 🐾
Services: 🚐 🔲 ⌀ 🔲 → ▶ 🎣 🚉

KINLOCH RANNOCH
Map 23 NN65

▶ 67% **Kilvrecht Campsite (NN623567)**
PH8 0JR ☎ 01350 727284 🖷 01350 727811
🅔 hamish.murray@forestry.gsi.gov.uk
Dir: 3m along S shore of Loch Rannoch. Approach via unclass road along Loch, with Forestry Commission signs
★ 🚐 £6 🚐 £6 ⚠ £3-£6
Open Etr-Oct Last arrival 22.00hrs Last departure 10.00hrs
Set in a remote and beautiful spot in a large forest clearing, about 0.75m from Loch Rannoch shore. This small and basic campsite has no hot water, but the few facilities are very well maintained. A 17-acre site with 60 touring pitches.
Facilities: ᗢ 🏕 🏇
Services: → ✕ 🎣 **Notes:** No fires

PERTH
Map 21 NO12

▶ ▶ ▶ 73% **Camping & Caravanning Club Site (NO108274)**
Scone Palace, Scone PH2 6BB
☎ 01738 552323
🅦 www.campingandcaravanningclub.co.uk
Dir: Follow signs for Scone Palace, continue for 2m. Turn left, follow site signs. 1m left onto Racecourse Rd. Site entrance from car park
★ 🚐 £12.40-£16.70 🚐 £12.40-£16.70 ⚠ £12.40-£16.70
Open Mar-Oct Booking advisable bank hols & peak period Last arrival 21.00hrs Last departure noon
A delightful woodland site, sheltered and well screened from the adjacent Scone racecourse. The two amenity blocks are built of timber and blend in well with the surroundings of mature trees. Super pitches add to the park's appeal. Please see advertisement on page 11 for information on Club sites and membership. A 16-acre site with 150 touring pitches, 40 hardstandings.
Leisure: 🎣 🛝 **Facilities:** 🛁 ⊙ 🍴 ✳ ᗢ 🐾 🏇
Services: 🚐 ⚡ 🔲 ⌀ 🔲 🔲 → ∪ 🎣 🚉
💳 💳 💳 📶 📷

PITLOCHRY
Map 23 NN95

▶ ▶ ▶ ▶ 73% *Faskally Caravan Park (NN916603)*
PH16 5LA ☎ 01796 472007 🖷 01796 473896
🅔 ehay@easynet.co.uk
🅦 www.faskally.co.uk
Dir: 1.5m N of Pitlochry on B8019
🏕🚐⚠

Open 15 Mar-Oct Booking advisable Jul-Aug Last arrival 23.00hrs
A large park attractively divided into sections by mature trees, set in gently-sloping meadowland beside the tree-lined River Garry. The excellent amenities include a leisure complex with heated indoor swimming pool, sauna and steam room, bar, restaurant and indoor amusements. The park is close to but unaffected by the A9. A 27-acre site with 200 touring pitches and 130 statics.
Steam room, spa & sauna
Leisure: 🏊 🎣 🛝
Facilities: 🛁 ⊙ 🍴 ✳ ᗢ 🐾 🚉
Services: 🚐 🔲 🍴 ⌀ 🔲 ✕ → ∪ ▶ ✕ 🎣
💳 💳 📶 📷

See advertisement on page 278

Leisure: 🏊 Indoor swimming pool 🏊 Outdoor swimming pool 🎾 Tennis court 🔴 Games room 🛝 Children's playground ∪ Stables
▶ 9/18 hole golf course ✕ Boats for hire 🎬 Cinema 🎣 Fishing ◎ Mini golf 🛟 Watersports 🔲 Separate TV room

Scotland

▶▶▶▶

Faskally
Caravan Park

Pitlochry, Perthshire PH16 5LA
Tel: (01796) 472007 & 473202
Fax: (01796) 473896

This park is situated outside the town and on the banks of the River Garry, which is bordered on one side by the main road. It is on gently sloping grassland dotted with trees and with splendid views. Indoor Leisure Pool with Spa Bath, Sauna and Steam Room. New Chalets introduced in 2002.
Turn off A9 Pitlochry by-pass ½ mile north of town then proceed 1 mile north on B8019. Bar and Restaurant.

E-mail: ehay@easynet.co.uk
Web: www.faskally.co.uk

▶ ▶ ▶ ▶ **77% Milton of Fonab Caravan Site (NN945573)**
Bridge Rd PH16 5NA ☎ 01796 472882
▤ 01796 474363
🅴 info@fonab.co.uk
🅦 www.fonab.co.uk
Dir: 0.5m S of town off A924
★ 🚐 £12.50-£14.50 🚐 £12.50-£14.50
🅰 £12.50-£14.50
Open Apr-Oct Booking advisable Jul-Aug & bank hols Last arrival 21.00hrs Last departure 13.00hrs
Set on the banks of the River Tummel, with extensive views down the river valley to the mountains, this park is close to the centre of Pitlochry, adjacent to the Pitlochry Festival Theatre. The sanitary facilities are exceptionally good, with most contained in combined shower/wash basin and toilet cubicles. A 15-acre site with 154 touring pitches and 36 statics.
Mountain bike hire & free trout fishing
Facilities: ➔ ⋔ ⊙ ⍾ ✻ ᗱ ⵜ 🐾 ⵘ
Services: 🖵 🖃 ᗺ ⌀ → ⌾ ⊙ ↯ ᗺ
Notes: Couples & families only, no motor cycles.

TUMMEL BRIDGE   **Map 23 NN75**

🌳

70% Tummel Valley Holiday Park (NN764592)
PH16 5SA
☎ 01882 634221 & 0870 420 2991
▤ 01882 634302
🅴 enquiries@parkdeanholidays.co.uk
🅦 www.parkdeanholidays.co.uk
Dir: From Perth take A9 N to bypass Pitlochry. 3m after Pitlochry turn onto B8019 signed Tummel Bridge. Park 11m on left
★ 🚐 £8-£20 🚐 £10-£23.50
Open Mar-Oct Booking advisable at all times Last arrival 21.00hrs Last departure 10.00hrs
A well-developed site amongst mature forest in an attractive valley, beside the famous bridge. Play areas and the bar are sited alongside the river, and this is an ideal base in which to relax. A 55-acre site with 33 touring pitches and 159 statics.
Cycle hire, fishing rod hire, family entertainment
Leisure: ᗘ ⚉ ⋔
Facilities: ➔ ⋔ ⊙ ⍾ ✻ ᗱ ⵡ ᗺ ⵘ ⵜ
Services: 🖵 🖃 ᗺ ⌀ ⵙ ✗ ⵊ → ⌾
🖻 🖃 🅅🅸🆂🅰 🆇 🖻

SCOTTISH BORDERS

COLDINGHAM   **Map 21 NT96**

▶ ▶ ▶ ▶ **79% Scoutscroft Holiday Centre (NT906662)**
St Abbs Rd TD14 5NB ☎ 018907 71338
▤ 018907 71746
🅴 holidays@scoutscroft.co.uk
🅦 www.scoutscroft.co.uk
Dir: From A1 take B6438 signed Coldingham & Scoutscroft is on the right, on the edge of Coldingham village
★ 🚐 £14-£20 🚐 £14-£20
Open Mar-Nov (rs Mar-May, Sep, Oct Crofters Bar only, arcade wknds only) Booking advisable BH's, Jul-Aug, wknds Last arrival mdnt Last departure noon
A large family-run site with good facilities and plenty of amenities including bars, restaurant, and children's games rooms. Set on the edge of the village and close to the sea, with separate areas and toilet blocks for tourers. A 16-acre site with 60 touring pitches, 32 hardstandings and 120 statics.
Sub Aqua Centre, cash machine
Leisure: ⚉ ⋔ ☐
Facilities: ➔ ⋔ ⊙ ⍾ ✻ ᗱ ⵊ ᗺ ⵘ ⵜ
Services: 🖵 🖃 ᗺ ᗻ ⌀ ⍰ 🆃 ✗ ⵊ → ∪ ↯ ᗺ ᗺ
🖻 🖃 🅅🅸🆂🅰 🖻 🖻

Abbreviations: BH/bank hols-bank holidays Etr-Easter Whit-Whitsun dep-departure fr-from hrs-hours m-mile mdnt-midnight
rdbt-roundabout rs-restricted service wk-week wknd-weekend ⌀-no dogs

JEDBURGH   Map 21 NT62

▶ ▶ ▶ **75% Camping & Caravanning Club Site (NT658219)**
Elliot Park, Edinburgh Rd TD8 6EF ☎ 01835 863393
Ⓦ www.campingandcaravanningclub.co.uk
Dir: Site entrance opp Edinburgh & Jedburgh Woollen Mills. N of Jedburgh on A68 (Newcastle - Edinburgh road)
★ 🚐 £12.40-£16.70 🚐 £12.40-£16.70 ▲ £12.40-£16.70
Open Apr-Oct Booking advisable bank hols & peak period Last arrival 21.00hrs Last departure noon
A touring site on the northern edge of town, nestling at the foot of cliffs close to Jed Water. Hardstandings are a welcome feature for caravans. Please see the advertisement on page 11 for information on Club sites and membership. A 3-acre site with 60 touring pitches, 20 hardstandings.
Facilities: 🚿 ⊙ 🔌 ✹ ⚑ ⚐ ☎ 🏕
Services: 🔌 ⚖ 🛢 🔧 🚰 🗑 → ▶ ⚐ 🗑 🚙 ⚑ 💳 💳 🏧 💷

▶ ▶ ▶ **71% *Jedwater Caravan Park (NT665160)***
TD8 6PJ ☎ 01835 869595 & 07050 219219
🖨 01835 869595
✉ jedwater@clara.co.uk
Ⓦ www.jedwater.co.uk
Dir: 3.5m S of Jedburgh on A68
🚐 🚐 ▲
Open Etr-Oct Booking advisable high season Last arrival mdnt Last departure noon
A quiet riverside site in a beautiful valley, run by resident owners as a peaceful retreat. The touring area is separate from statics, and this site is an ideal touring base. A 10-acre site with 30 touring pitches and 75 statics.
Bike hire, trampoline, football field.
Leisure: ⚓ 🎣 ▢
Facilities: 🚿 ⊙ 🔌 ✹ ⚐ ☎ 🏕 🔺 🐕
Services: 🔌 🛢 🔧 🗑 🗑 → ⚐ ▶ ⚙

KELSO   Map 21 NT73

▶ ▶ ▶ ▶ **78% Springwood Caravan Park (NT720334)**
TD5 8LS ☎ 01573 224596
🖨 01573 224033
✉ tourers@springwood.biz
Ⓦ www.springwood.biz
Dir: On A699, signed Newton St Boswells
★ 🚐 fr £16 🚐 fr £16

GOLD

Open 31 Mar-9 Oct Booking advisable bank hols & Jul-Aug Last arrival 23.00hrs

contd.

Set in a secluded position on the banks of the tree-lined River Teviot, this well-maintained site enjoys a pleasant and spacious spot in which to relax. It offers a high standard of modern toilet facilities which are mainly contained in cubicled units. Floors Castle and the historic town of Kelso are close by. A 2-acre site with 17 touring pitches and 210 statics.
Leisure: ⚓ 🎣
Facilities: 🚿 ⊙ 🔌 ✹ ⚐ ☎ 🏕
Services: 🔌 🛢 🔧 🗑 → ⚐ ▶ ⚙ 🗑 🚙 ⚑ 💳 💳 🏧 💷

LAUDER   Map 21 NT54

▶ ▶ ▶ **77% Camping & Caravanning Club Site (NT508533)**
Carfraemill, Oxton TD2 6RA ☎ 01578 750697
Ⓦ www.campingandcaravanningclub.co.uk
Dir: From Lauder, right at rdbt onto A697, then left at Lodge Hotel (signed). Site on right behind Carfraemill Hotel
★ 🚐 £12.40-£16.70 🚐 £12.40-£16.70
▲ £12.40-£16.70
Open Mar-Oct Booking advisable BH's & peak period Last arrival 21.00hrs Last departure noon
A meadowland site with good facilities housed in pine lodge buildings, and pleasant surroundings. Ideal either as a touring base or transit site, it is extremely well maintained. Please see the advertisement on page 11 for information on Club sites and membership. A 5-acre site with 60 touring pitches, 9 hardstandings.
Facilities: 🚿 🔌 ✹ ⚐ ☎ 🏕 🐕
Services: 🔌 🛢 🔧 🚰 🗑 → ⚐ 🗑 ⚙ 🚙 💳 💳 🏧 💷

▶ ▶ ▶ **72% Thirlestane Castle Caravan & Camping Site (NT536473)**
Thirlestane Castle TD2 6RU
☎ 01578 718884 & 07976 231032
🖨 01578 718749
✉ thirlestanepark@btconnect.com
Ⓦ www.thirlestanecastlepark.co.uk
Dir: Signed off A68 & A697, just S of Lauder
★ 🚐 £12 🚐 £12 ▲ £11
Open Apr-1 Oct Booking advisable Jul-Aug Last arrival 22.00hrs Last departure noon
Set in the grounds of the impressive Thirlestane Castle, with mainly level grassy pitches. The park and facilities are kept in sparkling condition. A 5-acre site with 60 touring pitches and 15 statics.
Facilities: 🚿 ⊙ ✹ ☎ 🏕
Services: 🔌 🛢 → ▶ ⚙ 🚙

An increasing number of parks do not accept children. There is a list of adult-only sites on page 19.

Facilities: 🛁 Bath 🚿 Shower ⊙ Electric Shaver 🔌 Hairdryer ✹ Ice Pack Facility ⚐ Disabled Facilities ☎ Public Telephone 🚙 Shop on Site or within 200yds 🗑 Mobile Shop (calls at least 5 days a week) 🏕 BBQ Area 🔺 Picnic Area 🐕 Dog Exercise Area

Scotland

PEEBLES   Map 21 NT24

▶ ▶ ▶ ▶ 72% **Crossburn Caravan Park (NT248417)**
Edinburgh Rd EH45 8ED ☎ 01721 720501
📄 01721 720501
🅔 enquiries@crossburncaravans.co.uk
🅦 www.crossburncaravans.com
Dir: 0.5m N of Peebles on A703
★ 🚐 £10-£15 🚐 £10-£15 ▲ £10-£11

Open Apr-Oct Booking advisable Jul-Aug Last arrival 21.00hrs Last departure 14.00hrs
A peaceful site in a relatively quiet location, despite the proximity of the main road which partly borders the site, as does the Eddleston Water. There are lovely views, and the park is well stocked with trees, flowers and shrubs. Facilities are maintained to a high standard, and fully-serviced pitches are available. A large caravan dealership is on the same site. A 6-acre site with 45 touring pitches, 15 hardstandings and 85 statics.

Leisure: ⚓ ⚙

Facilities: ➡ ⚘ ☉ 🅣 🅛 🕂 🛒 🦮 ⚓

Services: 🔌 📖 🗄 ⚙ ⚙ 🅣 ➡ → ∪ ⌂ ⚒

Notes: Dogs must be kept on leads 🐾 ⬛ ⬛ 🔯

▶ ▶ ▶ 74% *Rosetta Caravan & Camping Park (NT245415)*
Rosetta Rd EH45 8PG ☎ 01721 720770
📄 01721 720623
Dir: Signed from all main roads from Peebles
🚐 🚐 ▲
Open Apr-Oct Booking advisable BH's, Jul & Aug
Last arrival 23.00hrs Last departure 15.00hrs
A pleasant site set in 40 acres of parkland around a late Georgian mansion and stable block. Some of the stable buildings house the toilet facilities and bar. A 25-acre site with 160 touring pitches and 48 statics.

Leisure: ⚓ ⚙ ⚏

Facilities: ⚘ ☉ 🕂 ☀ 🅛 🛒 🦮 ⚓

Services: 🔌 📖 🍺 🗄 ⚙ 🅣 → ∪ ⌂ ⚒ ⚒

ROSETTA CARAVAN PARK
Peebles, Borders – Scotland
Tel: 01721 720770 Fax: 01721 720623

Family owned Park, Georgian Mansion with wooded estate. 45 acres. Lounge Bar in Courtyard, Shop, Childrens Bowling and Putting Green, Play Area, Electric hook-ups, adjacent to Golf Course. Fishing available on River Tweed. Quiet and peaceful Park. Write or phone for colour brochure.

SELKIRK   Map 21 NT42

▶ ▶ ▶ 70% *Victoria Park Caravan & Camping Park (NT465287)*
Victoria Park, Buccleuch Rd TD7 5DN
☎ 01750 20897 📄 01750 20897
Dir: From A707/A708 N of town, cross river bridge & take 1st left, then left again
🚐 🚐 ▲

Open Apr-Oct Booking advisable Jul-Aug Last arrival 20.00hrs Last departure 14.00hrs
A consistently well-maintained site with good basic facilities forming part of public park and swimming pool complex close to River Ettrick. A 3-acre site with 60 touring pitches.
Fitness room & sauna.

Leisure: ⚓ ⚙

Facilities: ⚘ ☉ 🕂 ☀ 🅛 🛒 🖳 🦮 ⚓

Services: 🔌 📖 ⚙ ✕ → ∪ ⌂ ⚒ ⬛ 🔯

SOUTH AYRSHIRE

AYR
Map 20 NS32

76% **Craig Tara** (NS300184)
KA7 4LB ☎ 01292 265141
🖹 01292 445206
ⓦ www.havenholidays.com
Dir: From Ayr take A77 towards Stranraer, then 2nd right after Bankfield Rdbt. Left at Doonholm Rd, then right into Greenfield Ave, left at next junct, then follow signs.
★ ⚘ £11-£53 ⚘ £11-£53
Open mid Mar-Oct (rs mid Mar-May & Sep-Oct Some services may be limited) Booking advisable School hols Last departure 10.00hrs
A large, well-maintained holiday centre with on-site entertainment and sporting facilities to suit all ages. The touring area is set apart from the main complex at the entrance to the park, and campers can use all the facilities, including water world, soft play areas, sports zone, show bars, and supermarket with in-house bakery. There is a bus service to Ayr. A 213-acre site with 29 touring pitches, 29 hardstandings and 608 statics.
Access to beach from park
Leisure: ₹ ९ ९ ⚔ ⚑
Facilities: ⚑ ⊙ ९ ₺ ⚑ ﹪ ⚑
Services: ⚑ ⚑ ९ ☕ ✗ ⚑ → ⌐ ⊙ ⚑
Notes: Max 2 dogs per pitch ⚑ ⚑ ⚑ ⚑ ⚑

BARRHILL
Map 20 NX28

NEW ▶ ▶ ▶ ▶ 77% **Windsor Holiday Park** (NX216835)
KA26 0PZ ☎ 01465 821355
Dir: On A714 (Newton Stewart to Girvan road). 1m N of Barrhill
⚘ ⚑

Open Mar-Nov
A small, friendly park in a tranquil rural location, screened from the A714 by trees. The park is terraced and well landscaped, and a high quality amenity block includes disabled facilities. A 6-acre site with 49 touring pitches.
Facilities: ⚑

COYLTON
Map 20 NS41

75% **Sundrum Castle Holiday Park** (NS405208)
KA6 5JH
☎ 01292 570057 & 0870 420 2991
🖹 01292 570065
ⓔ enquiries@parkdeanholidays.co.uk
ⓦ www.parkdeanholidays.co.uk
Dir: Just off A70, 4m E of Ayr near Coylton.
★ ⚘ £10-£22 ⚘ £12-£25.50 ⚑ £10-£22
Open Mar-Oct Booking advisable all times Last arrival 21.00hrs Last departure 10.00hrs
A large family holiday centre, with plenty of on-site entertainment, just a 10 min drive from the centre of Ayr. Leisure facilities include an indoor swimming pool, mini 10-pin bowling, clubs for teenies and teenagers, and the touring area is adequate and clean. A 30-acre site with 32 touring pitches and 245 statics.
Amusement arcade, live family entertainment.
Leisure: ₹ ९ ⚔ ⚑ **Facilities:** ⚑ ⊙ ९ ₺ ⚑
Services: ⚑ ⚑ ९ ☕ ∅ ✗ ⚑ ⚑ → ⌐ ⚑ ⚑ ⚑
Notes: No cars by tents ⚑ ⚑ ⚑ ⚑ ⚑

MAYBOLE
Map 20 NS20

▶ ▶ ▶ 75% **Camping & Caravanning Club Site** (NS247103)
Culzean Castle KA19 8JX ☎ 01655 760627
ⓦ www.campingandcaravanningclub.co.uk
Dir: From N on A77 in Maybole turn right onto B7023 (signed Culzean & Maidens) and 100yds turn left. Site 4m on right
★ ⚘ £13.60-£17.80 ⚘ £13.60-£17.80 ⚑ £13.60-£17.80
Open Mar-Oct Booking advisable bank hols & peak period Last arrival 21.00hrs Last departure noon
A mainly level grass park with some gently sloping pitches and hard stands along the bed of an old railway, situated at the entrance to the castle and country park. The park is surrounded by trees on three sides and has lovely views over Culzean Bay. Please see the advertisement on page 11 for information on Club sites and membership. A 10-acre site with 90 touring pitches, 25 hardstandings.
Leisure: ⚑ **Facilities:** ⚑ ⊙ ९ ⚑ ₺ ⚑ ⚑
Services: ⚑ ⚑ ⚑ ∅ ⚑ ⚑ → ⌐ ▶ ⚑ ⚑ ⚑ ⚑ ⚑ ⚑ ⚑

The number of touring pitches listed for each site includes tents, caravans and motorvans.

Not all campsites accept pets. It is advisable to check at the time of booking.

Remember to check your tent or caravan thoroughly before leaving home to ensure everything is in good order.

Leisure: ₹ Indoor swimming pool ₹ Outdoor swimming pool ९ Tennis court ⚔ Games room ⚑ Children's playground ⌐ Stables
▶ 9/18 hole golf course ⚓ Boats for hire ⚑ Cinema ⚑ Fishing ⊙ Mini golf ⚑ Watersports ⚑ Separate TV room

Scotland

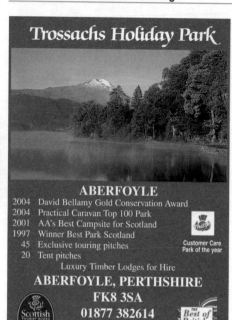

Trossachs Holiday Park

ABERFOYLE

2004	David Bellamy Gold Conservation Award
2004	Practical Caravan Top 100 Park
2001	AA's Best Campsite for Scotland
1997	Winner Best Park Scotland
45	Exclusive touring pitches
20	Tent pitches

Luxury Timber Lodges for Hire

ABERFOYLE, PERTHSHIRE
FK8 3SA
01877 382614
(anytime)

www.trossachsholidays.co.uk

Customer Care
Park of the year

SOUTH LANARKSHIRE

ABINGTON   Map 21 NS92

NEW ► ► ► **73% Mount View Caravan Park (NS935235)**
ML12 6RW ☎ 01864 502808 🖥 01864 502808
📧 info@mountviewcaravanpark.co.uk
🌐 www.mountviewcaravanpark.co.uk
Dir: M74 junct 13 onto A702 S into Abington. Left into Station Road, over river & railway. Park on right
🚐 £13.50 🚐 £13.50 ⚠ £8
Open Mar-Oct Booking advisable
A developing park, surrounded by the Southern Uplands and handily located between Carlisle and Glasgow. It is an excellent stopover site for those traveling between Scotland and the South. The West Coast railway passes beside the park. A 5.5-acre site with 50 touring pitches and 20 statics.
Facilities: 📶 ⊙ ℚ & 🗚 Services: 🚰 🔋 🛢 → 🚿 🛒
Notes: Dogs must be kept on leads 🐕 📺 📡 🅿

KIRKFIELDBANK   Map 21 NS84

► ► **72% *Clyde Valley Caravan Park (NS868441)***
ML11 9TS ☎ 01555 663951 & 01698 357684
🖥 01698 357684
Dir: From Glasgow on A72, cross river bridge at Kirkfieldbank & site on left. From Lanark on A72, right at bottom of steep hill before going over bridge
🚐 🚐 ⚠

contd.

Open Apr-Oct Booking advisable anytime Last arrival 23.00hrs Last departure noon
A long-established site with a central grassy touring area surrounded by trees and shrubs, set in hilly country with access to the river, and adjacent to the Clyde Walk. A 5-acre site with 50 touring pitches and 65 statics.
Leisure: 🅰 Facilities: 📶 ⊙ & 🚻 🛒
Services: 🚰 🔋 🛢 🍴 🗄 🚽 → 🚿 🛒 🐾 🍼 ⚡

STIRLING

ABERFOYLE   Map 20 NN50

► ► ► ► **78% Trossachs Holiday Park (NS544976)**
FK8 3SA ☎ 01877 382614
🖥 01877 382732
📧 info@trossachsholidays.co.uk
🌐 www.trossachsholidays.co.uk
Dir: Access on E side of A81 1m S of junct A821 & 3m S of Aberfoyle
★ 🚐 £12-£18 🚐 £12-£18 ⚠ £10-£16

Open Mar-Oct Booking advisable anytime Last arrival 21.00hrs Last departure noon
An imaginatively designed terraced site offering a high degree of quality all round, with fine views across Flanders Moss. All touring pitches are fully serviced with water, waste, electricity and TV aerial, and customer care is a main priority. Set in 20 acres of ground within the Queen Elizabeth Forest Park, with plenty of opportunities for cycling off-road on mountain bikes, which can be hired or bought on site. A 40-acre site with 65 touring pitches, 45 hardstandings and 70 statics. Cycle hire.
Leisure: 🎣 🅰 🎱 Facilities: 📶 ⊙ ℚ ✻ 🚻 🛒 🗚 🐾
Services: 🚰 🔋 🛢 🗄 🚽 → 🚿 🛒 ⚡
🐕 📺 📡 🅿 🍴

AUCHENBOWIE   Map 21 NS78

► ► ► **69% Auchenbowie Caravan & Camping Site (NS795880)**
FK7 8HE ☎ 01324 823999 🖥 01324 822950
Dir: 0.5m S of M9/M80 junct 9. Turn right off A872 for 0.5m, signed
🚐 £9-£10 🚐 £9-£10 ⚠ £9-£10
Open Apr-Oct Booking advisable mid Jul-mid Aug Last departure noon
A pleasant little site in a rural location, with mainly level grassy pitches. The friendly owner and warden

contd.

create a relaxed atmosphere, and given its position close to the junction of the M9 and M80 motorways, this is a handy stopover spot for tourers. A 3.5-acre site with 60 touring pitches and 12 statics.

Leisure: ⚑ Facilities: ⚘⊙⚑╚⌂
Services: ⚡🛢🖊→∪▶♨🗑🔋🎡 🚮 📷 🔲

BALMAHA Map 20 NS49

▶ ▶ ▶ ▶ 77% **Camping & Caravanning Club Site** (NN407927)
Milarrochy Bay G63 0AL ☎ 01360 870236
ⓦ www.campingandcaravanningclub.co.uk
Dir: A811 Balloch to Stirling Rd, take Drymen turning. In Drymen, take B837 for Balmaha. After 5m road turns sharp right up steep hill. Site 1.5m further on
★ 🚐 £13.60-£17.80 🚐 £13.60-£17.80 ⚑ £13.60-£17.80
Open Mar-Oct Booking advisable BH's & peak period Last arrival 21.00hrs Last departure noon
On the quieter side of Loch Lomond next to the 75,000-acre Queen Elizabeth Forest, this attractive site offers very good facilities. Disabled toilets and family rooms are to a high standard. Please see advertisement on page 11 for information on Club sites and membership. A 12-acre site with 150 touring pitches, 23 hardstandings.
Leisure: ⚑ Facilities: ⚘⊙⚑✳👤╚🐾🐕
Services: ⚡🌥🖊🛢🖊⚡🕐→⚓🍴🔋
🎡 🚮 📷 🔲

BLAIRLOGIE Map 21 NS89

▶ ▶ ▶ ▶ 83% **Witches Craig Caravan & Camping Park** (NS821968)
FK9 5PX
☎ 01786 474947 📠 01786 447286
🅴 info@witchescraig.co.uk
ⓦ www.witchescraig.co.uk
Dir: 3m NE of Stirling on A91 Hillfoots-St Andrews rd
★ 🚐 £12-£15 🚐 £12-£15 ⚑ £11-£15
Open Apr-Oct Booking advisable Jul-Aug Last arrival 21.00hrs Last departure 13.00hrs
In an attractive setting with direct access to the lower slopes of the dramatic Ochil Hills, this is a well-maintained family-run park. It is in the centre of Braveheart country, with easy access to historical sites and many popular attractions. A 5-acre site with 60 touring pitches, 26 hardstandings.
Food preparation, baby bath & changing area
Leisure: ⚑ Facilities: ⚘⊙⚑✳👤╚🔥⌂🐕
Services: ⚡🌥🖊🛢🖊⚡🕐→∪▶⊙♨🔋

CALLANDER Map 20 NN60

▶ ▶ ▶ 77% **Gart Caravan Park** (NN643070)
The Gart FK17 8LE
☎ 01877 330002 📠 01877 330002
🅴 enquiries@gart-caravan-park.co.uk
ⓦ www.gart-caravan-park.co.uk
Dir: 1m E of Callander on A84
★ 🚐 fr £17 🚐 fr £17
Open Etr or Apr-15 Oct Booking advisable BHs & Jul-Aug Last arrival 22.00hrs Last departure 11.30hrs
A well-screened caravan park bordered by trees and

contd.

shrubs, near to the Queen Elizabeth Park amidst ideal walking and climbing country. A feature of the park is the careful attention to detail in the maintenance of facilities, and the owners are very helpful and friendly. A 26-acre site with 128 touring pitches and 66 statics.
Fishing on site
Leisure: ⚑ Facilities: ⚘⊙⚑✳👤╚🔋🐕
Services: ⚡🌥🖊🛢→∪▶⚓🔋
Notes: No commercial vehicles 🎡 🚮 📷 🔲

LOCHEARNHEAD Map 20 NN52

NEW ▶ ▶ ▶ 73% **Balquhidder Braes Holiday Park** (NN572209)
Balquhidder Station FK19 8NX ☎ 01567 830293
Dir: On A84, approx 1m S of Lochearnhead
🚐 ⚑
Open all year
A compact family park with views of the Braes of Balquhidder, in an Area of Outstanding Natural Beauty. There is plenty to do nearby, including visit Rob Roy's grave and watch the wildlife. A 2-acre site with 50 touring pitches.
Facilities: ⚘

Facilities: 🛁 Bath ⚘ Shower ⊙ Electric Shaver ⚑ Hairdryer ✳ Ice Pack Facility 👤 Disabled Facilities ╚ Public Telephone 🔋 Shop on Site or within 200yds 📷 Mobile Shop (calls at least 5 days a week) 🔥 BBQ Area 🎡 Picnic Area 🐕 Dog Exercise Area

Scotland

LUIB   Map 20 NN42

NEW ► ► ► ► 79% **Glendochart Holiday Park**
(NN477278)
FK20 8QT ☎ 01567 820637 🖷 01567 820024
🕀 info@glendochart-caravanpark.co.uk
🌐 www.glendochart-caravanpark.co.uk
*Dir: On A85 (Oban to Stirling road), midway between
Killin & Crainlarich*
🖭 **Å**
Open Mar-Oct
*A small, well maintained park on a hillside in
Glendochart, with imaginative landscaping and
glorious mountain and hill views. The site is well
located for trout and salmon fishing, and ideal for
walking. A 7-acre site with 95 touring pitches.*
Facilities: 🖎

STIRLING
See **Auchenbowie**

STRATHYRE   Map 20 NN51

NEW ► ► ► 69% **Immervoulin Caravan and
Camping Park (NN560164)**
FK18 8NJ ☎ 01877 384285
Dir: Off A84, approx 1m S of Strathyre
🖭 **Å**
Open Mar-Oct
*A family run park on open meadowland next to the
River Balvaig, where fishing, canoeing and other
water sports can be enjoyed. A riverside walk leads
to Loch Lubnaig, and the village of Strathyre offers
restaurants. A relaxed park with lovely scenery.
A 5-acre site with 50 touring pitches.*
Facilities: 🖎

WEST DUNBARTONSHIRE

BALLOCH   Map 20 NS38

► ► ► ► 77% **Lomond Woods Holiday
Park (NS383816)**
Old Luss Rd G83 8QP ☎ 01389 755000
🖷 01389 755563   *GOLD*
🕀 lomondwoods@holiday-parks.co.uk
🌐 www.holiday-parks.co.uk
*Dir: From A82, 17m N of Glasgow, take A811 (Stirling to
Balloch road). Left at 1st rdbt, follow signs for holiday
park, 150yds on left*
★ 🖭 £15-£20 🖭 £15-£20
Open all year *Booking advisable all dates Last
arrival 21.00hrs Last departure noon*
*A mature park with well-laid out pitches screened
by trees and shrubs, surrounded by woodland and
hills. The park is within walking distance of 'Loch
Lomond Shores', a complex of leisure and retailing
experiences which is the main gateway to
Scotland's first National Park. Amenities include an
inspiring audio-visual show, open-top bus tours,
and loch cruises. A 13-acre site with 110 touring
pitches and 35 statics.*
Leisure: 🟊 ⚲ 🎠 **Facilities:** 🛏🖎⊙🏋☀☖🕭🛒🍴🐾
Services: 🚰⛽🚻🅿✎🖃🔲🛒🔌→∪🅿☖✕🥄
🍴 🔲 🔲 🔲

EAST CALDER   Map 21 NT06

► ► ► 83% **Linwater Caravan Park
(NT104696)**
West Clifton EH53 0HT   *GOLD*
☎ 0131 333 3326 🖷 0131 333 1952
🕀 linwater@supanet.com
🌐 www.linwater.co.uk
*Dir: Signed along B7030 off M9 junct 1 or from
Wilkieston on A71*
🖭 £11-£14 🖭 £11-£14 Å £9-£12
Open late Mar-late Oct *Booking advisable BH's &
Aug Last arrival 21.00hrs Last departure noon*
*A farmland park in a peaceful rural area within easy
reach of Edinburgh. The very good facilities are
housed in a Scandinavian-style building, and are
well maintained by resident owners. Nearby are
plenty of pleasant woodland walks. A 5-acre site
with 60 touring pitches, 11 hardstandings.*
Leisure: ⚲ **Facilities:** 🛏⊙🏋☀☖🕭🐾
Services: 🚰⛽🚻✎🖃→∪🅿🥄🔲🔲 🔲 🔲

LINLITHGOW   Map 21 NS97

► ► ► 68% **Beecraigs Caravan & Camping Site
(NT006746)**
Beecraigs Country Park, The Park Centre EH49 6PL
☎ 01506 844516 🖷 01506 846256
🕀 mail@beecraigs.com
🌐 www.beecraigs.com
*Dir: From Linlithgow on A803 or from Bathgate on
B792, follow signs to country park. Reception either at
restaurant or park centre.*
★ 🖭 £11-£16 🖭 £11-£16 Å £10-£12
Open all year *Booking advisable all year Last arrival
22.30hrs Last departure noon*
*A wildlife enthusiast's paradise where even the
timber facility buildings are in keeping with the
environment. Beecraigs is situated peacefully in the
open countryside of the Bathgate Hills. Small bays
with natural shading offer intimate pitches, and
there's a restaurant serving lunch and evening
meals. A 6-acre site with 36 touring pitches,
36 hardstandings.*
Children's bath, country park facilities
Leisure: ⚲ **Facilities:** 🛏⊙🏋☀☖🕭🛒🍴🐾
Services: 🚰⛽🚻✕🔌→∪🅿🥄🔲 **Notes:** No cars
by tents, no ball games near caravans, no noise
after 22.00 🔲 🔲 🔲

SCOTTISH ISLANDS

ARRAN, ISLE OF

LOCHRANZA   Map 20 NR95

▶ ▶ ▶ 76% *Lochranza Caravan & Camping Site (NR942500)*
KA27 8HL ☎ 01770 830273 ▤ 01770 830600
🄴 office@lochgolf.demon.co.uk
🅦 www.arran.net
Dir: On A84 at N tip of island, beside Kintyre ferry and 14m M of Brodick for ferry to Ardrossan
🚐🚐 Å
Open mid Mar-Oct Booking advisable Whit & Aug Last arrival 22.00hrs Last departure 13.00hrs
Attractive park in a beautiful location, run by friendly family owners. The park is adjacent to an 18-hole golf course, opposite the famous Arran Distillery, between tree-lined hills on the edge of the village. Golf and ferry packages can be arranged. A 2.5-acre site with 60 touring pitches, 10 hardstandings.
18-hole golf course
Facilities: 🏠⊙🏴✳🅑&🗻📯📮🐴
Services: 🚻🗑🔋💧🚽🅣→U▶🎣 **Notes:** No fires

MULL, ISLE OF

CRAIGNURE   Map 20 NM73

▶ ▶ ▶ 81% **Shieling Holidays (NM724369)**
PA65 6AY ☎ 01680 812496
🅦 www.shielingholidays.co.uk
Dir: From ferry left onto A849 to Iona. 400mtrs left at church, follow site signs towards sea
🚐 £13-£14.50 🚐 £13-£14.50 Å £13-£14.50
Open Apr-Oct Booking advisable Spring bank hol & Jul-Aug Last arrival 22.00hrs Last departure noon
A lovely site on the water's edge with spectacular views, and less than 1m from ferry landing. There is a camper's shelter in a disused byre which is especially popular in poor weather. Hardstandings and service points are provided for motorhomes, and there are astro-turf pitches for tents. The park offers bunkhouse accommodation for families. A 6-acre site with 90 touring pitches, 27 hardstandings and 15 statics.
Adventure playground, bikes
Leisure: ◣⚒🏓 **Facilities:** ↔🏠⊙🏴✳&🗻📯📮🐴
Services: 🚻⛽🔋💧🗑🅣→▶🎣🍴🔲🔳🔈🥤

SKYE, ISLE OF

EDINBANE   Map 22 NG35

▶ ▶ ▶ 76% **Loch Greshornish Caravan Site (NG343524)**
Borve, Arnisort IV51 9PS ☎ 01470 582230
🄴 info@skyecamp.com
🅦 www.skyecamp.com
Dir: By loch shore. Approx 12m from Portree on A850 Dunvegan road
★ 🚐 £8.75-£10.50 🚐 £8.75-£10.50 Å £8-£8.50
Open Apr-Oct Booking advisable Jul-Aug Last arrival 22.00hrs Last departure noon
A pleasant open site, mostly level and with a high standard of maintenance. There is a campers' shelter in a disused byre which is popular in poor weather, and a licensed shop. A 5-acre site with 130 touring pitches.
Bike hire, canoe hire
Facilities: 🏠⊙🏴✳🅑&🗻📯📮🐴
Services: 🚻🅣→U🎣 **Notes:** Dogs must be kept under control and exercised off site

STAFFIN   Map 22 NG46

▶ ▶ 70% **Staffin Camping & Caravanning (NG492670)**
IV51 9JX ☎ 01470 562213 ▤ 01470 562705
🄴 staffin@namacleod.freeserve.co.uk
🅦 www.staffincampsite.co.uk
Dir: On A855, 16m N of Portree
★ 🚐 fr £10 🚐 fr £10 Å fr £10
Open Apr-Oct Booking advisable Jul-Aug Last arrival 22.00hrs Last departure 11.00hrs
A large sloping grassy site with level hardstandings for motor homes and caravans, close to the village of Staffin. The toilet block is to a very good standard. A 2.5-acre site with 50 touring pitches, 18 hardstandings.
Picnic tables
Facilities: 🏠⊙🏴✳&🗻🐴
Services: 🚻🔋💧🗑→🦽🎣🥤
Notes: No music after 23.00

Scotland

Wales

ANGLESEY, ISLE OF

BRYNTEG   Map 14 SH48

NEW ▶ ▶ ▶ **70% Garnedd Touring Park** (SH495818)
Lùn Bryn Mair LL78 8QA ☎ 01248 853240
℮ mmpicomac@aol.com
★ ⊕ £12-£14 ⊕ £12-£14 ▲ £8-£10
Open Mar-Oct Booking advisable public & school hols Last arrival 21.00hrs Last departure 11.00hrs
Friendly owners offer a warm welcome to this secluded, peaceful park which enjoys impressive views of the Snowdonia mountain range.The owners are still improving the park facilities which are clean and well maintained. The spacious pitches are attractively laid out with central grass play areas for children. An ideal family holiday location with beaches and shops within easy reach. A 5-acre site with 40 touring pitches and 1 static.
Facilities: ℕ☉⚒✱🍴🎋
Services: 🔌🍴🛢️🚿→∪▶🔥🚮🔦

DULAS   Map 14 SH48

▶ ▶ ▶ ▶ **74% Tyddyn Isaf Caravan Park** (SH486873)
Lligwy Bay LL70 9PQ
☎ 01248 410203 📠 01248 410667
℮ enquiries@tyddynisaf.demon.co.uk
ⓦ www.tyddynisaf.demon.co.uk
GOLD
Dir: Take A5025 through Benllech to Moelfre rdbt, left towards Amlwch to Brynrefail village. Turn right opposite craft shop. Park 0.5m down lane on right
⊕ £18-£26 ⊕ £18-£26 ▲ £15-£26

Open Mar-Oct (rs Mar-Jul & Sep-Oct Bar & shop opening limited) Booking advisable May bank hol & Jun-Aug Last arrival 22.00hrs Last departure 11.00hrs
A beautifully situated, very large family park on quite steeply rising ground adjacent to a sandy beach, with magnificent views overlooking Lligwy Bay. Access to the beach is by private footpath (lengthy from some pitches), or by car for the less energetic. The park has very good toilet facilities, a well-stocked shop, and a clubhouse serving meals and takeaway food. Reception is a long, steep walk from the entrance and many pitches. A 16-acre site with 80 touring pitches, 20 hardstandings and 56 statics.
Baby changing unit
Leisure: ⚙🏓 **Facilities:** ℕ☉🍴✱&🔦🛒🎋🐕
Services: 🔌🍴🛢️🚿→∪🔥🚮🔦
Notes: Dogs must be kept on leads

▶ ▶ ▶

ty newydd
LEISURE PARK
Proprietors: Mike & Cathi
Llanbedrgoch, Isle of Anglesey LL76 8TZ
Tel: 01248 450677 / 07712 676505
Fax: 01248 450711

This small, select, family-run park is ideally situated for Benllech Bay with extensive views of Snowdonia. Facilities include licensed country club and restaurant serving meals for the family, well-equipped shop, excellent toilet facilities, free showers, disabled toilet, baby changing room, laundry room, children's playground and games room, heated outdoor swimming pool, health centre with spa, sauna, pool, electric hook-ups and luxury fully-equipped caravans for hire.
Dogs on leads are welcomed.
Sailing, water skiing, fishing, climbing, walking, golf, pony trekking and safe sandy beaches are available on the island. 9 hole golf course within ½ mile.

LLANBEDRGOCH   Map 14 SH58

▶ ▶ ▶ **66% Ty Newydd Leisure Park** (SH508813)
LL76 8TZ ☎ 01248 450677 📠 01248 450711
℮ mike@tynewydd.com
ⓦ www.tynewydd.com
Dir: A5025 from Brittania Bridge. Through Pentraeth village, bear left at layby. Site 0.75m on right
★ ⊕ £10-£27 ⊕ £10-£27 ▲ £10-£27

Open Whit-mid Sep (rs Mar-Whit & mid Sep-Oct club/shop wknds only, outdoor pool closed) Booking advisable Etr, Whit & Jul-Aug Last arrival 23.30hrs Last departure 10.00hrs
A low-density park with many facilities including a heated outdoor pool, a club with restaurant, a good playground, and a fitness centre with pool and gym for which an extra charge is made. A 4-acre site with 48 touring pitches, 15 hardstandings and 62 statics.
Sauna & Jacuzzi
Leisure: 🏊🎣🏓⚙ **Facilities:** ℕ☉🍴✱&🔦🛒🎋🐕
Services: 🔌🍴🛢️🛢️🚿→∪▶🔥🚮🔦

Wales

Wales

MARIAN-GLAS   Map 14 SH58

▶ ▶ ▶ ▶ 92% **Home Farm Caravan Park (SH498850)**
LL73 8PH ☎ 01248 410614
🖹 01248 410900
🌐 enq@homefarm-anglesey.co.uk
🌐 www.homefarm-anglesey.co.uk
Dir: On A5025, 2m N of Benllech; park entrance 300mtrs beyond church
★ ⊞ £10.50-£22.50 ⊞ £10.50-£22.50 ⚊ £10.50-£18.25

Open Apr-Oct Booking advisable bank hols Last arrival 21.00hrs Last departure noon
A first class park in an elevated and secluded position sheltered by trees. The peaceful rural setting affords views of farmland, the sea, and the mountains of Snowdonia. The modern toilet block has helped to win numerous awards, and there are excellent play facilities for children both indoors and out. The area is blessed with sandy beaches, and local pubs and shops cater for everyday needs. A 6-acre site with 98 touring pitches, 21 hardstandings and 84 statics.
Indoor adventure playground
Leisure: ↺ ⚊ ⚐ ▱
Facilities: ⇥ ☈ ⊙ ⚑ ⚹ ⚙ ☊ ⚙ ⚔ ☈
Services: ☎ ⚒ ⚙ ⚙ ⚘ 🔋 Ⅱ → ∪ ▶ ⚙ ⚙
⚙ ⚙ ⓓ ⚙ 🗑

PENTRAETH   Map 14 SH57

▶ ▶ ▶ 77% **Rhos Caravan Park (SH517794)**
Rhos Farm LL75 8DZ ☎ 01248 450214
🖹 01248 450214
Dir: Site on left of A5025, 1m N of Pentraeth
★ ⊞ £10-£12 ⊞ £10-£12 ⚊ £10-£12

Open Etr-Oct (rs Mar shop restricted) Booking advisable Spring bank hol & Jul-Aug Last arrival 22.00hrs Last departure 16.00hrs

A warm welcome awaits families at this spacious park on level, grassy ground with easy access to the main road to Amlwch. This 200-acre working farm has a games room, two play areas and farm animals to keep children amused, with good beaches, pubs, restaurants and shops nearby. The two toilet blocks are kept to a good standard by enthusiastic owners who are constantly improving the facilities. A 15-acre site with 98 touring pitches and 66 statics.
Leisure: ⚐ Facilities: ☈ ⊙ ⚹ ⚙ ⚔ ☈
Services: ☎ ⚙ ⚙ ⚘ 🔋 Ⅱ → ∪ ▶ ⚙ ⚙ ⚙
⚙ ⚙ ⚙ ⚙ 🗑

RHOS LLIGWY   Map 14 SH48

▶ ▶ ▶ 73% **Ty'n Rhos Caravan Park (SH497868)**
LL72 8NL ☎ 01248 852417 🖹 01248 853417
🌐 robert@bodafonpark.fsnet.co.uk
🌐 www.bodafonpark.co.uk
Dir: Take A5025 from Benllech to Moelfre rdbt, turn right to T-junct in Moelfre. Left, then approx 2m to site on right
★ ⊞ £14-£18 ⊞ £14-£18 ⚊ £8-£18

Open Mar-Oct Booking advisable BH's & Aug Last arrival 21.00hrs Last departure noon
A well-established family park set in quiet countryside, close to the beautiful beach at Lligwy Bay, and cliff walks along the Heritage Coast. It makes a popular base for visiting historic Din Lligwy, and the shops at picturesque Moelfre, with sea and offshore fishing, boating and village inns all adding to its attractions. A 10-acre site with 50 touring pitches, 50 hardstandings and 80 statics.
Facilities: ☈ ⚹ ⚙ ⚙ ☈
Services: ☎ ⚙ ⚙ ⚘ → ⚙ ⚙ ⚙

RHOSNEIGR   Map 14 SH37

▶ ▶ ▶ 77% **Ty Hen (SH323737)**
Station Rd LL64 5QZ
☎ 01407 810331 🖹 01407 810331
🌐 bernardtyhen@hotmail.com
🌐 www.tyhen.com
Dir: A55 across Anglesey. At exit 5 follow signs to Rhosneigr, at clock turn right. Entrance adjacent to Rhosneigr railway station.
★ ⊞ £15-£17 ⊞ £15-£17 ⚊ £10

Open mid Mar-Oct Booking advisable All year Last arrival 21.00hrs Last departure noon
Attractive seaside position near a large fishing lake and riding stables, in lovely countryside. A smart toilet block offers a welcome amenity at this popular family park, where friendly owners are always on hand. A 7.5-acre site with 38 touring pitches, 5 hardstandings and 42 statics.
Fishing, family room
Leisure: ↺ ⚊ ⚐
Facilities: ☈ ⊙ ⚑ ⚹ ⚙ ☊ ☈
Services: ☎ ⚙ Ⅱ → ∪ ▶ ⚙ ⚙
Notes: 1 motor vehicle per pitch, dogs on leads, children in tents/tourers/statics by 22.00hrs
⚙ ⚙ 🗑

contd.

Services: Ⅱ Toilet Fluid ✕ Café/ Restaurant 🍟 Fast Food/Takeaway 🚼 Baby Care 🔌 Electric Hook Up
🔧 Motorvan Service Point ⓢ Launderette ♀ Licensed Bar 🛢 Calor Gaz ⚗ Camping Gaz 🔋 Battery Charging

CAERPHILLY

CWMCARN   Map 09 ST29

► ► ► 71% *Cwmcarn Forest Drive Campsite*
(ST230935)
Visitor Centre & Campsite NP11 7FA
☎ 01495 272001 🖹 01495 271403
✉ cwmcarn-vc@caerphilly.gov.uk
🌐 www.caerphilly.gov.uk/visiting
*Dir: From M4 junct 28 follow signs for Risca, 7m on
A467. Site well signed*
🚐 🚙 Å

Open Jan-24 Dec Booking advisable All year Last
arrival 17.00hrs Last departure 12.00hrs
*Set behind the visitor centre and nestling alongside
the banks of the Nantcarn stream, this small park is
set in a stunningly scenic spot. It can be found at
the start of a seven-mile drive through forest and
rolling hills, with strategic parking spots containing
picnic tables and barbecues. An idyllic spot for
cyclist, mountain bikers and walkers. A 2.5-acre site
with 37 touring pitches, 3 hardstandings.*
Forest drive, fishing
Facilities: 🅿 ⊙ 🔥 ⌇ 🍴
Services: 🚐 🛢 ✕ → 🌀 🛒
Notes: No youth groups, no open fires, dogs must
be on leads 💳 💳 💳 📶 🔲

CARDIFF

CARDIFF   Map 09 ST17

► ► ► 77% *Cardiff Caravan Park (ST171773)*
Pontcanna Fields CF11 9LB
☎ 029 2039 8362 & 2044 5900 🖹 029 2039 8362
✉ p.owens@cardiff.gov.uk
*Dir: Turn off M4 onto A48 towards Cardiff. Pass Tesco
Extra on left, under footbridge, left past Llandaff
Llandaff /City Centre. Follow signs to Sophia Gardens/
Welsh Institute of Sport. Site in park just past
Glamorgan County Cricket ground*
🚐 🚙 Å
Open all year Booking advisable All year Last
departure noon
*A popular municipal park within easy walking
distance of the city centre, Cardiff Castle, and the
Millennium Stadium. This busy park is often full,
and the facilities are well kept by a keen and*

contd.

*friendly warden. A 2-acre site with 95 touring
pitches, 45 hardstandings.*
Cycle hire & baby changing facilities
Facilities: 🅿 ⊙ 🔥 ✳ 🔥 ⌇ 🍴
Services: 🚐 🛢 🛢 🗐 → 🌀 🌀 🛒 🍴 ♨ 🛒
💳 💳 💳 🅾 💳 📶 🔲

CARMARTHENSHIRE

CROSS HANDS   Map 08 SN51

► ► ► 77% **Black Lion Caravan &
Camping Park (SN572129)**
78 Black Lion Rd, Gorslas SA14 6RU
☎ 01269 845365
✉ blacklionsite@aol.com
🌐 www.caravansite.com
*Dir: M4 junct 49 onto A48 to Cross Hands rdbt, right
onto A476 (Llandeilo). 0.5m at Gorslas sharp right into
Black Lion Rd. Site 0.5m on right, (follow brown tourist
signs from Cross Hands rdbt)*
★ 🚐 £10-£12 🚙 £10-£12 Å £8-£10
Open Apr-Oct (rs Oct-Mar Main toilet block closed)
Booking advisable all times Last arrival 22.00hrs
Last departure 11.00hrs
*Cheerful and friendly owners keep this improving
park clean and well maintained. New toilet and
shower facilities include a separate room for
disabled guests, and this is a popular overnight
stop for people travelling on the Irish ferries. The
National Botanic Garden of Wales is about
10 minutes drive away. A 12-acre site with
45 touring pitches, 10 hardstandings.*
Caravan storage, spa hot tub
Leisure: 🄰 **Facilities:** 🅿 ⊙ 🔥 ✳ 🔥 ⌇ 🍴 🛒 📺 🍴 🍴
Services: 🚐 🛢 🛢 🗐 🗐 → 🌀 ♨ 🛒

HARFORD   Map 08 SN64

► ► ► 78% **Springwater Lakes (SN637430)**
SA19 8DT ☎ 01558 650788 🖹 01558 650788
*Dir: 4m E of Lampeter on A482, entrance well signed on
right*
★ 🚐 fr £12 🚙 fr £12 Å fr £12
Open Mar-Oct Booking advisable Jun-Aug Last
arrival 21.00hrs Last departure 11.00hrs
*In a rural setting overlooked by the Cambrian
Mountains, this park is adjoined on each side by
four spring-fed and well-stocked fishing lakes. All
pitches have hardstandings, electricity and TV hook-
ups, and there is a small and very clean toilet block
and a shop. A 20-acre site with 20 touring pitches,
12 hardstandings.*
TV hook ups, 4 fishing lakes
Facilities: 🅿 ⊙ ✳ 🔥 ⌇ 🍴
Services: 🚐 → 🌀 🛒 🛒
Notes: Dogs must be kept on leads at all times,
children must be supervised around lakes

> THE PERCENTAGE RATING
> FOR ALL PARKS RANGES FROM
> 50% - 100%.

Wales

Leisure: 🏊 Indoor swimming pool 🏊 Outdoor swimming pool 🎾 Tennis court 🎯 Games room 🄰 Children's playground ♨ Stables
▶ 9/18 hole golf course ⛵ Boats for hire 🎬 Cinema 🎣 Fishing ⦿ Mini golf 🌊 Watersports 🔲 Separate TV room

LLANDOVERY   Map 09 SN73

▶ ▶ ▶ 79% **Erwlon Caravan & Camping Park**
(SN776343)
Brecon Rd SA20 0RD ☎ 01550 720332
🌐 peter@erwlon.fsnet.co.uk
Dir: 1m E of Llandovery on A40
★ 🚐 fr £10 🚐 fr £10 Å fr £10

Open all year Booking advisable BH's Last arrival
anytime Last departure noon
*Long-established family-run site set beside a brook
in the Brecon Beacons foothills. The town of
Llandovery and the hills overlooking the Towy
valley are a short walk away. A superb facilities
block with cubicled washrooms, family and
disabled rooms is part of ongoing improvements.
An 8-acre site with 75 touring pitches,
15 hardstandings.*
Leisure: ⚲
Facilities: 🅁⊙🚻✻💧👌🏖️🅣🛒🐾
Services: 🚿🖤🅑🚽🔌⊞→🗑️🚱🍴

LLANGADOG   Map 09 SN72

▶ ▶ ▶ 76% **Abermarlais Caravan Park**
(SN695298)
SA19 9NG ☎ 01550 777868 & 777797
🌐 www.ukparks.co.uk/abermarlais
*Dir: On A40 midway between Llandovery and Llandeilo,
1.5m NW of Llangadog*
★ 🚐 £8.50-£10.50 🚐 £8.50-£10.50 Å £8.50-£10.50
Open 15 Mar-15 Nov (rs Nov, Dec & Mar 1 toilet
block, water point no hot water) Booking advisable
bank hols & 15 Jul-Aug Last arrival 23.00hrs Last
departure noon
*An attractive, well-run site with a welcoming
atmosphere. This part-level, part-sloping park is in a
wooded valley on the edge of the Brecon Beacons
National Park, beside the River Marlais. A 17-acre*
contd.

site with 88 touring pitches, 2 hardstandings.
Volleyball, badminton court & softball tennis net
Leisure: ⚲
Facilities: 🅁⊙✻💧👌🏖️🐾🛒
Services: 🚿🖤🅑🅓⊞🔌→🗑️🚱🍴
Notes: Dogs must be kept on leads, no open fires,
silence from 23.00-08.00hrs 💳 ▦ ⓪ 🚫 🔟

LLANWRDA
See **Harford**

NEWCASTLE EMLYN   Map 08 SN34
See also **Cenarth (Ceredigion)**

▶ ▶ ▶ ▶ ▶ 84% **Cenarth Falls
Holiday Park (SN265421)**
Cenarth SA38 9JS ☎ 01239 710345
📠 01239 710344
🌐 enquiries@cenarth-holipark.co.uk
🌐 www.cenarth-holipark.co.uk
*Dir: Off A484 on outskirts of Cenarth towards
Cardigan*
★ 🚐 £13-£22 🚐 £13-£22 Å £13-£22

Best of British
TOURING AND HOLIDAY PARKS

Open Mar-18 Dec Booking advisable bank hols &
Jul-Aug Last arrival 20.00hrs Last departure 11.00hrs
*A high quality park with excellent facilities, close
to the village of Cenarth where the famous
salmon and sea trout River Teifi cascades
through the Cenarth Falls Gorge. A well-
landscaped park with an indoor heated swimming
pool and fitness suite, and a restaurant and bar.
A 2-acre site with 30 touring pitches,
30 hardstandings and 89 statics.*
Pool table, health & leisure complex
Leisure: ≋ ⚲
Facilities: 🅁⊙🚻✻👌💧
Services: 🚿🖤🅑🚽🅑🅓⊞✕→🍴🍴🐾
Notes: No dogs 14 Jul-3 Sep 💳 ▦ 🚫 🔟

▶ ▶ ▶ 74% **Afon Teifi Caravan & Camping Park**
(SN338405)
Pentrecagal SA38 9HT ☎ 01559 370532
🌐 afon.teifi@virgin.net
🌐 www.afonteifi.co.uk
Dir: Signed off A484, 2m E of Newcastle Emlyn
★ 🚐 £12-£13 🚐 £12-£13 Å £8-£13
Open Apr-Oct (rs Nov-Mar when facilities limited,
no toilet block) Booking advisable peak periods Last
arrival 23.00hrs
contd.

Afon Teifi Caravan & Camping Park

Set on the banks of the River Teifi, a famous salmon and sea trout river, this park is secluded with good views. Family owned and run, and only 2 miles from the market town of Newcastle Emlyn. A 6-acre site with 110 touring pitches, 10 hardstandings and 10 statics.
15 acres of woodland, fields & walks

Leisure: ◣ ⚠ **Facilities:** �));⬤🦐✳&℣🛒🍴🌲🐕
Services: 🖃🖳🛢🍽⑂🔌🚽→🅿◭💢🧴

NEW ► ► ► 78% **Dolbryn Camping & Caravanning** (SN298382)
Capel Iwan Rd SA38 9LP ☎ 01239 710683
Dir: On A484 (Carmarthan to Cardigan road). 2m from Newcastle Emlyn (signed)
🖳Å
Open Mar-Nov
A secluded park set in a peaceful valley with a stream, ponds, mature trees and an abundance of wildlife in 13 acres, that include a vineyard and plenty of nature walks. Enthusiastic new owners are making substantial improvements to the park, and have tastefully refurbished the toilets and showers which are located in rustic farm outbuildings. The cosy bar offers a chance to get together with fellow campers, or take part in family activities. A 6-acre site with 41 touring pitches.
Facilities: 🦐

► ► ► 72% **Moelfryn Caravan & Camping Site** (SN321370)
Ty-Cefn, Pant-y-Bwlch SA38 9JE ☎ 01559 371231
🖷 01559 371231
🄴 moelfryn@tinyonline.co.uk
Dir: Take A484 from Carmarthen towards Cynwyl Elfed. Pass Blue Bell Inn on right and after 200yds take left fork on to B4333 towards Hermon. After 7m brown sign on left. Turn left, site on right
★ 🖳£7-£11 🚗£7-£11 Å£6-£10
Open Mar-10 Jan Booking advisable Jul/Aug Last arrival 22.00hrs Last departure noon
A small family-run park in an elevated location overlooking the valley of the River Teifi. Pitches are level and spacious, and well screened by hedging and mature trees. Facilities are well maintained, clean and tidy, and the playing field is well away from the touring area. A 3-acre site with 25 touring pitches, 13 hardstandings.
Caravan storage
Leisure: ⚠ **Facilities:** 🦐⬤🐟✳🛒🛒
Services: 🖃→🔌🅿◭⌁🧴🖳

► ► ► 77% **Camping & Caravanning Club Site** (SN779435)
SA20 0NT ☎ 01550 760257
🖾 www.campingandcaravanningclub.co.uk
Dir: From Llandovery take A483, turn left signed Rhandirmwyn for 7m, left at post office, site on left before river
★ 🖳£13.60-£17.80 🚗£13.60-£17.80 Å£13.60-£17.80
Open Mar-Oct Booking advisable bank hols & peak period Last arrival 21.00hrs Last departure noon
On the banks of the Afon Tywi near Towy Forest and the Llyn Brianne reservoir, this secluded park has superb views from all pitches. The park is divided into paddocks by mature hedging, and facilities and grounds are very well tended. Please see advertisement on page 11 for information on Club sites and membership. An 11-acre site with 90 touring pitches, 12 hardstandings.
Leisure: ⚠ **Facilities:** 🦐⬤🐟✳&℣🛒🐕
Services: 🖃⑂🛢⌁🔌🚽→◭⌁🧴🖳
🖸 🔲🔲🔲 🔳 🄾

CEREDIGION

► ► ► 77% **Aeron Coast Caravan Park** (SN462633)
North Rd SA46 0JF ☎ 01545 570349
🄴 aeroncoastcaravanpark@
aberaeron.freeserve.co.uk
🖾 www.aberaeron.co.uk/aeron_coast/acoast2.htm
Dir: On A487 (coast road) on N edge of Aberaeron, signed. Filling station at entrance
🖳£12-£16 🚗£12-£16 Å£12-£16
Open Mar-Oct Booking advisable bank & school hols Last arrival 23.00hrs Last departure 11.00hrs
Set in a spacious 22 acres of coastal parkland, with direct entry onto the beach and only 200yds from the attractive small town and harbour. This park has a wide range of indoor and outdoor activities, and caters well for the whole family. A 22-acre site with 100 touring pitches, 23 hardstandings and 200 statics.
Indoor leisure rooms & entertainment hall
Leisure: ⚞🏊◣⚠🖵 **Facilities:** 🦐⬤✳&℣🛒
Services: 🖃⑂🖳🛢🍽⌁🚽→◉◭🧴
Notes: Families only, no motorcycles, no letting static caravans 🖸 🔲🔲🔲 🔳 🄾

► ► ► 76% **Ocean View Caravan Park** (SN592842)
North Beach, Clarach Bay SY23 3DT
☎ 01970 828425 & 623361
🄴 alan@grover10.freeserve.co.uk
🖾 www.oceanviewholidays.com
Dir: Turn off A487 in Bow Street. Straight on at next x-roads. Site 2nd on right
★ 🖳£11-£14 🚗£11-£14
Open Mar-Oct Booking advisable bank hols & high season Last arrival 20.00hrs Last departure noon

contd.

Wales

In a sheltered valley on gently sloping ground, with wonderful views of both the sea and the countryside. The beach of Clarach Bay is just 200 yards away, and this welcoming park is ideal for all the family. A 9-acre site with 24 touring pitches, 15 hardstandings and 56 statics.

Facilities: 🅰️☉🔁✳️🚿🍽️🏪🎯🐕
Services: 🔌🚱🗓️→🚰🏪🅿️🅾️💧🔋🔧🗑️

BETTWS EVAN   Map 08 SN34

▶ ▶ ▶ **72% Pilbach Holiday Park (SN306476)**
SA44 5RT ☎ 01239 851434 📠 01239 851969
🅰️ info@pilbach.com
🅦 www.pilbach.com
Dir: S on A487, turn left onto B4333
🚐 £12-£22 🚐 £12-£22 🅰️ fr £12
Open Mar-Oct (rs Mar-Spring BH & Oct swimming pool closed) Booking advisable Spring BH & Jul-Aug Last arrival 22.00hrs Last departure noon
Set in secluded countryside, with two separate paddocks and pitches clearly marked in the grass. This park makes a good base for visiting this very scenic area and nearby seaside resorts. It has a heated outdoor swimming pool, and entertainment in the club two or three times a week in high season. A 15-acre site with 65 touring pitches, 10 hardstandings and 70 statics.
Bike/skateboard parks

Leisure: 🏊♨️⛏️♨️ **Facilities:** 🅰️☉🔁🚿🏪🎯🐕
Services: 🔌🚱🍽️🅾️✖️→🚰🅿️🏪🔋🔧
🔋 📧 📱 🔋

BORTH   Map 14 SN69

66% **Brynowen Holiday Park (SN613885)**
SY24 5LS
☎ 01970 871366 & 871125
🅰️ gmbrynowen@park-resorts.com
🅦 www.park-resorts.com
Dir: Signed off B4353, S of Borth
🚐🚐
Open Mar-14 Jan Booking advisable Last departure 10.00hrs
Enjoying spectacular views across Cardigan Bay and the Cambrian mountains, a small touring park in a large and well-equipped holiday centre. The well-run park offers a wide range of organised activities and entertainment for all the family from morning until late in the evening. A long sandy beach is a few minutes drive away. A 52-acre site with 16 touring pitches and 480 statics.

Leisure: ♨️⛏️ **Facilities:** 🅰️🔁♿🍽️🏪🐕
Services: 🔌🚱🍽️✖️♿→🏪
Notes: No cars by caravans 🔋 📧 📱 🔋

CENARTH   Map 08 SN24

NEW ▶ ▶ ▶ 80% **Argoed Meadow Caravan and Camping Site (SN268415)**
Argoed Farm SA38 9JL ☎ 01239 710690
🅦 www.cenarthcamping.co.uk
🚐🚐🅰️
Open all year Booking advisable
Pleasant open meadowland on the banks of the River Teifi, very close to Cenarth Falls gorge. This newly developed site has a new toilet block. A 3-acre site with 30 touring pitches, 5 hardstandings.

Facilities: 🅰️☉🔁♿🍽️🏪🎯🐕
Services: 🔌🚱🚿🔧🗓️✖️→🅾️🏪🔋
Notes: Dogs must be kept on leads

CROSS INN   Map 08 SN35

▶ ▶ ▶ 77% **Camping & Caravanning Club Site (SN383566)**
Llwynhelyg SA44 6LW ☎ 01545 560029
🅦 www.campingandcaravanningclub.co.uk
Dir: Left from A487 (Cardigan-Aberystwyth) at Synod Inn.Take A486 signed New Quay. In village of Cross Inn, left after Penrhiwgaled Arms Pub. Site 0.75m on right
★ 🚐 £12.40-£16.70 🚐 £12.40-£16.70 🅰️ £12.40-£16.70
Open Mar-Oct Booking advisable bank hols & peak period Last arrival 21.00hrs Last departure noon
An excellent, attractive touring site in an elevated rural position with extensive country views. A footpath from the site joins the coastal walk, and the pretty village of New Quay is only a short drive away. Please see advertisement on page 11 for information on Club sites and membership. A 14-acre site with 90 touring pitches, 6 hardstandings.

Leisure: ⛏️ **Facilities:** 🅰️☉🔁✳️♿🍽️🏪🎯🐕
Services: 🔌🛢️🚱🔧🗓️🕐→🅾️🔧🏪
🔋 📧 📱 🔋

LLANON   Map 08 SN56

▶ ▶ ▶ 74% Woodlands Caravan Park
(SN511668)
SY23 5LX ☎ 01974 202342 & 202454
▤ 01974 202342
Dir: Through Llanon exit A487 at international sign, park 280yds right
★ ⊞ £9-£21 ⊞ £9-£21 ▲ £9-£21

Open Apr-Oct (rs Mar toilet block closed) Booking advisable school hols Last arrival 21.30hrs Last departure noon
A well-maintained mainly grass site surrounded by mature trees and shrubs near woods and meadowland, adjacent to the sea and a stony beach. Shower facilities have now been upgraded. The park is half a mile from the village. A 4-acre site with 40 touring pitches, 10 hardstandings and 54 statics.
Facilities: ⋔ ⊙ ⏴ ✳ ⌷ ⋔
Services: ⊞ ⊟ ⅃ ⌀ ⊞ ⊡ → ∪ ▶ ◎ ♪

YSTRAD AERON   Map 08 SN55

▶ ▶ ▶ 71% Hafod Brynog (SN525563)
SA48 8AE ☎ 01570 470084
✉ amies@hafodbrynog.fsnet.co.uk
Dir: On A482 (Lampeter - Aberaeron road) in village of Ystrad Aeron, entrance to Brynog Arms pub
★ ⊞ £8-£10 ⊞ £8-£10 ▲ £7-£10
Open Apr-Oct Booking advisable bank hols Last arrival 21.00hrs Last departure noon
This peaceful park with fine open views over the countryside is a perfect place to unwind, yet it is within easy reach of the coastal resort of Aberaeron. The village pubs which serve meals are a few minutes walk from the park.
A 7-acre site with 25 touring pitches, 2 hardstandings and 30 statics.
Facilities: ⋔ ⊙ ⏴ ✳ ⌷ ⏴
Services: ⊞ ⊟ ⅃ ⌀ → ♪

CONWY

ABERGELE
See also **Betws-Yn-Rhos**

NEW ▶ ▶ ▶ 82% Roberts Caravan Park
(SH937740)
Waterloo Service Station, Penrefail Crossroads
LL22 8PN ☎ 01745 833265
✉ gailyroberts@btinternet.com
Dir: Turn off A548 onto B5381 signed St Asaph, park 100yds on left
★ ⊞ fr £14 ⊞ fr £14
Open Apr-Oct Booking advisable bank hols
A pretty hillside park with countryside views towards the coast. The spacious serviced pitches and excellent toilet facilities enhance this beautifully landscaped park, and will appeal to those seeking peace and relaxation. The friendly owners are always on hand. A filling station and shop are handily placed at the entrance. A 3-acre site with 50 touring pitches.
Facilities: ⋔ ⊙ ⏴ ⋔
Services: ⊞ ⌀ → ▶ ⅃ ⌷ ⊞ ⊛ ⊡ ⊞ ⊠ ⑤

BETWS-YN-RHOS   Map 14 SH97

▶ ▶ ▶ 77% Hunters Hamlet Caravan Park
(SH928736)
Sirior Goch Farm LL22 8PL ☎ 01745 832237 &
07721 552106 ▤ 01745 833978
✉ huntershamlet@aol.com
Ⓦ www.caravancampingsites.co.uk/conwy/huntershamlet.htm
Dir: From A55 Wbound, A547 into Abergele. Straight through lights, 1st left by George & Dragon pub, onto A548. 2.75m right at x-rds onto B5381. Site 0.5m on left
★ ⊞ £12-£15 ⊞ £12-£15
Open 21 Mar-Oct Booking advisable bank hols & Jul-Aug Last arrival 22.00hrs Last departure noon
A quiet working farm park next to the owners' Georgian farmhouse. Pitches are in two grassy paddocks with pleasant views, and the beach is 3 miles away. The very good toilets include unisex bathrooms, and are kept spotless. A 2-acre site with 23 touring pitches, 23 hardstandings.
Baby bath & changing facilities
Leisure: ⚙ Facilities: ⇴ ⋔ ⊙ ⏴ ✳ ⅋ ⊓
Services: ⊞ ⅃ ⊡ → ▶ ♪ ⏴
Notes: No tents, dogs must not be left unattended.
No ball games on central grass areas
⊛ ⊡ ⊞ ⊠ ⑤

Wales

Leisure: ⚲ Indoor swimming pool   ⚳ Outdoor swimming pool   ⚴ Tennis court   ⚙ Games room   ⚒ Children's playground   ∪ Stables
▶ 9/18 hole golf course   ⚓ Boats for hire   ⚏ Cinema   ♪ Fishing   ◎ Mini golf   ⚆ Watersports   ⊡ Separate TV room

CERRIGYDRUDION   Map 14 SH94

▶ ▶ ▶ 77% **Glan Ceirw Caravan
Park (SH963461)**
Ty Nant LL21 0RF ☎ 01490 420346
🖷 01490 420346
🅱 glanceirwcaravanpark@tinyworld.co.uk
Ⓦ www.ukparks.co.uk/glanceirw

Dir: From A5 Betws-y-Coed onto unclass road 1m after
Cerrig-y-Drudion, park 0.25m on left. From Corwen for
8m, then 2nd left onto unclass road after Country Cooks
★ 🛖 £10-£18 🚐 £10-£18 ▲ £6-£12
Open Mar-Oct Booking advisable bank hols & Jul-
Sep Last arrival 22.00hrs Last departure noon
*A small riverside site in a rural location, with
pleasant owners. Guests can enjoy the use of two
games rooms, a bar lounge and a jacuzzi, and an
amenity block. An ideal touring point for
Snowdonia and North Wales. A 4.5-acre site with
15 touring pitches, 9 hardstandings and 29 statics.*
Leisure: 🏊 ⚲ 🎱
Facilities: 🅿 ⊙ ✳ 🛏 🛒 🛒 ☂
Services: 🔌 🛒 🍴 → 🍴 🛒
Notes: No cars by tents

> Practise setting up your tent at home
> before you take it on holiday, and check
> that all guy ropes, pegs and poles are
> present and intact.

LLANDDULAS   Map 14 SH97

▶ ▶ ▶ ▶ 83% **Bron-Y-Wendon Caravan Park
(SH785903)**
Wern Rd LL22 8HG ☎ 01492 512903
🖷 01492 512903
🅱 bron-y-wendon@northwales-holidays.co.uk
Ⓦ www.northwales-holidays.co.uk

Dir: Take A55 W. Turn right at sign for Llanddulas A547
junct 23, then sharp right. 200yds, under A55 bridge.
Park on left
★ 🛖 £13-£16 🚐 £13-£16
Open all year Booking advisable bank hols Last
arrival anytime Last departure 11.00hrs
*A good quality site with sea views from every pitch,
and excellent purpose-built toilet facilities. Staff are
helpful and friendly, and everything from
landscaping to maintenance has a stamp of
excellence. An ideal seaside base for touring
Snowdonia, with lots of activities available nearby.
An 8-acre site with 130 touring pitches, 85
hardstandings.*
Tourist info, heated shower blocks
Leisure: 🎣 **Facilities:** 🅿 ⊙ ⚲ ✳ 🛒 🛒 ☂
Services: 🔌 🚰 🍴 → 🍴 🛒 🍴
🍴 🛒 🍴

LLANRWST   Map 14 SH86

▶ ▶ ▶ 78% **Bodnant Caravan Park (SH805609)**
Nebo Rd LL26 0SD ☎ 01492 640248 🖷 01492 640248
🅱 ermin@bodnant-caravan-park.co.uk
Ⓦ www.bodnant-caravan-park.co.uk

Dir: S in Llanrwst, turn off A470 opposite Birmingham
garage onto B5427 signed Nebo. Site 300yds on right,
opposite leisure centre
🛖 £9.25-£14.50 🚐 £9.25-£14.50 ▲ £9.25-£11.50
Open Mar-end Oct (rs Mar 1 toilet block open if
weather very bad in the spring) Booking advisable
Etr, May Day, Spring bank hol & Jul-Aug Last arrival
21.00hrs Last departure 11.00hrs
*This stunningly attractive park is filled with flower
beds (many times winner of Wales in Bloom
competition for the best kept touring caravan park),
and the landscape includes shrubberies and trees.
The statics are unobtrusively sited, and the toilet
blocks are very well kept. There is a separate
playing field and rally field. A 5-acre site with 54
touring pitches and 2 statics.*
8 multi-service caravan pitches
Facilities: 🅿 ⊙ ⚲ ✳ 🛒 🛒 ☂
Services: 🔌 🍴 🍴 → 🍴 🛒 🛒
Notes: Main gates locked 23.00-08.00hrs No noise
after 23.00hrs 🍴 🛒 🍴

TAL-Y-BONT (NEAR CONWY)   Map 14 SH76

▶ 88% **Tynterfyn Touring Caravan Park (SH768692)**
LL32 8YX ☎ 01492 660525
🅱 glentynterfyn@tinyworld.co.uk
Dir: 5m S of Conwy on B5106, road sign Tal-y-Bont, 1st
on left
★ 🛖 £7-£7.50 🚐 £7.50 ▲ £5-£15
Open Mar-Oct Tent pitches only for 28 days in year.
Booking advisable bank hols & Jul-Aug Last arrival
22.00hrs Last departure noon

contd.

A quiet, secluded little park set in the beautiful Conwy Valley, and run by family owners. The grounds are tended with care, and the older-style toilet facilities sparkle. There is lots of room for children and dogs to run around. A 2-acre site with 15 touring pitches, 4 hardstandings.

Leisure: ⚄

Facilities: ⌕ ⊙ ⚲ ✳ ♞

Services: ⚙ ▯ ⌀ ⊞ → ∪ ⌣ ⤵ ⚖

TOWYN (NEAR ABERGELE)   Map 14 SH97

65% Ty Mawr Holiday Park (SH965792)
Towyn Rd LL22 9HG
☎ 01745 832079 ▤ 01745 827454
🅴 admin.tymawr@parkresorts.com
🆆 www.park-resorts.com
Dir: On A548, 0.25m W of Towyn
⚐⚑🅰

Open Etr-Oct (rs Apr (excluding Etr)) Booking advisable at all times Last arrival midnight Last departure 10.00hrs
A very large coastal holiday park with extensive leisure facilities including sports and recreational amenities, and club and eating outlets. The touring facilities are rather dated but clean. An 18-acre site with 282 touring pitches and 470 statics.
Free evening entertainment

Leisure: ⚲ ⚄ ⚄

Facilities: ⌕ ⊙ ⚲ ✳ ♿ ⌕ ⚖ ♞

Services: ⚙ ▯ ⵙ ⌀ ⚄ ✕ ♨ → ∪ ▶ ◎
🚐 🍴 🚮 🎣 🔟

See advertisement on opposite page

DENBIGHSHIRE

CORWEN   Map 15 SJ04
See also **Llandrillo**

▶ ▶ **70% Llawr-Betws Farm Caravan Park (SJ016424)**
LL21 0HD ☎ 01490 460224 & 460296
🆆 www.ukparks.co.uk/llawrbetws
Dir: 3m W of Corwen off A494 (Bala road)
⚐⚑🅰

Open Mar-Oct Booking advisable bank hols & Jul-Aug Last arrival 23.00hrs Last departure noon
A quiet grassy park with mature trees and mainly level pitches. The friendly owners keep the facilities in good condition. A 2.5-acre site with 35 touring pitches and 72 statics.
Fishing

Leisure: ⚲ ⚄

Facilities: ⌕ ⊙ ✳ ⌕ 🗖 ♞

Services: ⚙ ▯ ⌀ ⌀ ⊞ ⟶ 🚮 ⤵ ⚖

LLANDRILLO   Map 15 SJ03

▶ ▶ ▶ **74% Hendwr Country Park (SJ035386)**
LL21 0SN ☎ 01490 440210 ▤ 01490 440730
🆆 www.hendwrcaravanpark.freeserve.co.uk
Dir: From Corwen (A5) take B4401 for 4m. Turn right at Hendwr sign. Site 0.5m on right down wooded driveway
★ 🚐 £14-£16 🚑 £14-£16 🅰 £14-£16
Open all year (rs Nov-Mar no toilet facilities during this period) Booking advisable BH's & school hols Last arrival 22.00hrs Last departure 16.00hrs
Set in parkland at the end of a tree-lined lane, Hendwr (it means 'old tower') has a stream meandering through its grounds. All around is the stunning mountain range of Snowdonia, and the toilet facilities are good. A 10-acre site with 40 touring pitches, 2 hardstandings and 80 statics.
Wet weather camping facilities

Facilities: ⌕ ⊙ ⚲ ✳ ⌕ ⚖

Services: ⚙ ▯ ⌀ ⊞ ⌟ → ⤵

Notes: Dogs must be kept on leads at all times

LLANGOLLEN   Map 15 SJ24

▶ ▶ **78% Penddol Caravan Park (SJ209427)**
Abbey Rd LL20 8SS ☎ 01978 861851
Dir: From Llangollen on A542, Abbey Rd, turn into Eisteddfodd Pavilion, then over hump back bridge. Site on left
🚑 £10-£12 🚑 £10-£12 🅰 £8-£10
Open Mar-Oct Booking advisable Last departure 16.00hrs
An elevated adults-only park enjoying panoramic views across the beautiful Vale of Llangollen. The Llangollen canal runs alongside this tidy park, offering scenic walks and horse drawn barge trips. Nearby is the Eisteddfod Pavilion, and the Llangollen steam railway. A 2.25-acre site with 30 touring pitches and 1 static.

Facilities: ⌕ ♿

Services: ⚙ ⮡ → ▶ ⤵ ⤵ ▯ ⚖

Notes: Adults only

▶ ▶ **78% Ty-Ucha Caravan Park (SJ232415)**
Maesmawr Rd LL20 7PP ☎ 01978 860677
Dir: 1m E of Llangollen. Signed 250yds off A5
🚑 fr £9 🚑 fr £8
Open Etr-Oct (rs Mar toilet block closed) Booking advisable BH's Last arrival 22.00hrs Last departure 13.00hrs
A very tranquil site in beautiful surroundings, with a small stream on site, and superb views. Ideal for country and mountain walking, and handily placed near the A5. There is a new games room with table tennis. A 4-acre site with 40 touring pitches.

Leisure: ⚲

Facilities: ⌕ ⊙

Services: ⚙ ⌀ ⌀ ⊞ → ∪ ▶ ⚌ ⤵ ⚌ ⤵ ▯ ⚖

Notes: No tents

For full details of the AA pennant ratings scheme see pages 7-8

Facilities: ⮢ Bath ⌕ Shower ⊙ Electric Shaver ⚲ Hairdryer ✳ Ice Pack Facility ♿ Disabled Facilities ⌕ Public Telephone
⚖ Shop on Site or within 200yds 🚐 Mobile Shop (calls at least 5 days a week) 🎇 BBQ Area 🗖 Picnic Area ♞ Dog Exercise Area

Wales

Wales

PRESTATYN   Map 15 SJ08

 72% **Presthaven Sands (SJ091842)**
Gronant LL19 9TT
☎ 01745 856471 🖹 01745 886646
Ⓦ www.havenholidays.com
Dir: A548 from Prestatyn towards Gronant. Park signed
🚐

Open mid Mar-Oct (rs mid Mar-May & Sep-Oct
Facilities may be reduced) Booking advisable
School hols Last arrival 22.00hrs Last departure
noon
*Set beside two miles of superb sandy beaches
and dunes, this large holiday centre offers
extensive leisure and sports facilities and lively
entertainment for all the family. The leisure
complex houses clubs, swimming pools,
restaurants, shops, a hair salon, launderette and
pub, and the touring area is separate from the
much larger static section. A 130-acre site with
220 touring pitches and 672 statics.*
Leisure: ⚑ ⚘ ⚘ ⚘ /Ⓜ 🖵 Facilities: 🖳
Services: 🗗 ♇ ✗ 🏭 🖤 🞇 📧 🝙 🝙 🖃 🝙 🝙

RHUALLT   Map 15 SJ07

► ► ► 85% **Penisar Mynydd Caravan Park
(SJ093770)**
Caerwys Rd LL17 0TY ☎ 01745 582227
🖹 01745 582227
Ⓔ penisarmynydd@btinternet.com
*Dir: From Llandudno take 1st left at top of Rhuallt Hill
(junct 29). From Chester take junct 29, follow signs for
Dyserth, park 500yds on right*
★ 🚐 £12-£14 ⚏ £12-£14
Open Mar-Jan Booking advisable bank hols Last
arrival 22.00hrs
*A very tranquil, attractively laid-out park set in three
grassy paddocks with a superb facilities block
including a disabled room and dishwashing
area.The majority of pitches are super pitches.
Everything is immaculately maintained, and the
amenities of the seaside resort of Rhyll are close by.
A 6.75-acre site with 75 touring pitches,
75 hardstandings.*
Facilities: 🖍 ⊙ ✳ ♿ ⓛ 🖃 🐾
Services: 🗗 🖴 🛢 🖃 → ∪ ▶ ⓪ ✈ 🖳

RUABON   Map 15 SJ34

► ► ► 72% **James' Caravan Park (SJ300434)**
LL14 6DW ☎ 01978 820148 🖹 01978 820148
Ⓔ ray@carastay.demon.co.uk
Dir: 0.5m W of the A483/A539 junct to Llangollen
★ 🚐 £10-£12 ⚏ £10-£15 Å fr £10
Open all year Booking advisable BH's Last arrival
21.00hrs Last departure 11.00hrs
*A well-landscaped park on a former farm, with
modern heated toilet facilities. Old farm buildings
house a collection of restored original farm
machinery, and the village shop, four pubs, take
away and launderette are a ten-minute walk away.
A 6-acre site with 40 touring pitches, 4 hardstandings.*
Freezer chest
Facilities: 🖍 ⊙ ⚜ ✳ ♿ ⓛ 🐾
Services: 🗗 🛢 ⌀ 🖃 → ▶ 🖃 🖳

GWYNEDD

ABERSOCH   Map 14 SH32

► ► ► 77% **Beach View Caravan Park (SH316262)**
Bwlchtocyn LL53 7BT ☎ 01758 712956
*Dir: Through Abersoch & Sarn Bach. Over x-rds then
next left signed Porthtocyn Hotel. Continue past chapel
until you find another sign to Porthtocyn Hotel. Turn left
and park on left.*
★ 🚐 £12-£15 ⚏ £12-£15 Å £9-£15.50
Open mid Mar-mid Oct Booking advisable Jul, Aug
& BH's Last arrival 21.00hrs Last departure 11.00hrs
*A compact family park with very enthusiastic
owners who make continual improvements.
Immaculately maintained grounds and excellent
facilities are matched by great sea and country
views. Six minutes walk from the beach. A 4-acre
site with 47 touring pitches.*
Facilities: 🖍 ⊙ ⚗ ✳ 🐾
Services: 🗗 🛢 🛢 ⌀ 🖃 → ∪ ▶ ⚘ ✈ ✈ 🖳

► ► ► 77% **Bryn Bach Caravan & Camping Site
(SH315258)**
Tyddyn Talgoch Uchaf, Bwlchtocyn LL53 7BT
☎ 01758 712285
Ⓔ brynbach@abersochcamping.co.uk
Ⓦ www.abersochcamping.co.uk
*Dir: From Abersoch take Sarn Bach road for approx 1m,
left at sign for Bwlchtocyn. Site approx 1m on left*
★ 🚐 £14-£17 ⚏ £13-£17 Å £12-£17
Open Mar-Oct Booking advisable at all times Last
arrival 22.00hrs Last departure 11.00hrs
*This well-run, elevated park overlooks Abersoch
Bay, with lovely sea views towards the Snowdonia
mountain range. Pitches are well laid out in
sheltered paddocks, with well-placed modern
facilities. Fishing, watersports, golf and beach
access are all nearby. A 4-acre site with 30 touring
pitches and 2 statics.*
Private shortcut to beach, boat storage
Leisure: /Ⓜ Facilities: 🖍 ⊙ ⚗ ♿ ♨ 🖃 🗚
Services: 🗗 🖴 🖃 → ∪ ▶ ⚘ ✈ ✈ 🖳
Notes: Families & couples only

► ► ► 76% **Deucoch Touring Park (SH303269)**
Sarn Bach LL53 7LD ☎ 01758 713293
*Dir: From Abersoch take Sarn Bach road, at x-rds turn
right, site on right in 800yds*
★ 🚐 £16 ⚏ £14 Å £13
Open Mar-Oct Booking advisable school hols Last
arrival 22.00hrs Last departure 11.00hrs
*A sheltered site with sweeping views of Cardigan
Bay and the mountains, just a mile from Abersoch
and a long sandy beach. The facilities block is well
maintained, and this site is of special interest to
watersports enthusiasts and those touring the Llyn
Peninsula. A 5-acre site with 68 touring pitches,
10 hardstandings.*
Leisure: /Ⓜ Facilities: 🖍 ⊙ ⚗ ✳ ♿ ⓛ 🖃 ♨
Services: 🗗 🖃 → ∪ ▶ ⚘ ✈ ✈ 🖳
Notes: Families only

Services: Ⓣ Toilet Fluid ✗ Café/ Restaurant 🍟 Fast Food/Takeaway 🍼 Baby Care 🔌 Electric Hook Up
🚐 Motorvan Service Point 🖃 Launderette ⚘ Licensed Bar 🛢 Calor Gaz ⌀ Camping Gaz 🖽 Battery Charging

► ► ► 66% **Rhydolion** (SH284275)
Rhydolion, LLangian LL53 7LR ☎ 01758 712342
🅴 enquiries@rhydolion.co.uk
🆆 www.rhydolion.co.uk/caravan_camping.htm
*Dir: From A499 take unclassified road to Llangian for
1m, turn left into and through Llangian. Site 1.5m after
road fork towards Hell's Mouth/Porth Neigwl*
🏕 ⚠

Open Mar-Oct Booking advisable Last arrival
22.00hrs Last departure noon
*A peaceful park with good views, on a working farm
close to the long sandy surfers beach at Hell's
Mouth. The toilet block is kept to a high standard by
the friendly owners, and nearby Abersoch is a
Mecca for boat owners and water sports
enthusiasts. A 1.5-acre site.*
3 fridge freezers

Leisure: ⚠ **Facilities:** ⋔⊙✳⌁
Services: 🔌🚽🗑→∪🍴♨✂🔧🔥

Notes: Families and couples only

BALA   **Map 14 SH93**

► ► ► ► 76% **Pen Y Bont Touring & Camping
Park** (SH932350)
Llangynog Rd LL23 7PH ☎ 01678 520549
🖨 01678 520006
🅴 information@penybont-bala.co.uk
🆆 www.penybont-bala.co.uk
Dir: From A494 take B4391. Site 0.75m on right
★ 🏕 £11.50-£14 🚐 £11.50-£14 ⚠ £6.50-£11.50
Open Apr-Oct Booking advisable BH's & school hols
Last arrival 21.00hrs Last departure 13.00hrs
*A very attractively landscaped park in a woodland
country setting, very close to the River Dee and Bala
Lake. The park offers excellent facilities, and most
pitches have water and electricity. Lake Bala is
famous for its water sports, with River Tryweryn
catering for enthusiasts of canoe slalom and white-
water rafting. A 7-acre site with 95 touring pitches,
59 hardstandings.*

Facilities: ⋔⊙🍴✳♿🔔🛒🏧⌂⌁
Services: 🔌🚾🗑🧼🚽🅣📞→🍴🧺🎱✂
💳 💳 💳 💳 🔌 💷

PEN Y BONT TOURING & CAMPING PARK

Bala LL23 7PH
Tel: 01678 520549
www.penybont-bala.co.uk

AA

To Betws-y-coed, Snowdon, Portmeirion
To Corwen, Llangollen, Chester
A4212   A494

WHITE WATER RAFTING CENTRE

N

BALA TOWN

WATER SPORTS CENTRE   B4391

SAILING CLUB

To Barmouth, Harlech
To Llangynog, Oswestry

A494   BALA LAKE   B4391

B4403

PENYBONT TOURING & CAMPING PARK

Closest park to Bala's shops, pubs, restaurants;
free clean hot showers; private vanity cubicles;
disabled/baby changing room; laundry; undercover dishwashing area; shop, calor gas;
dogs welcome; all electric pitches with hard
standing strips.

An Excellent Four Star Graded Park   ★★★★

► ► ► 74% **Camping & Caravanning Club Site**
(SH962391)
Crynierth Caravan Park, Cefn-Ddwysarn LL23 7LN
☎ 01678 530324
🆆 www.campingandcaravanningclub.co.uk
*Dir: A5 onto A494 to Bala. Through Bethal and Sarnau.
Right at sign onto unclassified road, site 400yds on left*
★ 🏕 £13.60-£17.80 🚐 £13.60-£17.80
⚠ £13.60-£17.80
Open Mar-Oct Booking advisable bank hols & peak
period Last arrival 21.00hrs Last departure noon
*A quiet pleasant park with interesting views and
high class facilities, set back from the main road in
a very secluded position. Lake Bala offers great
appeal for the water sports enthusiast, as does the
nearby River Tryweryn, a leading slalom course in
white-water rafting. Please see the advertisement
on page 11 for information on Club sites and
membership. A 4-acre site with 50 touring pitches,
8 hardstandings.*

Leisure: ⚠
Facilities: ⋔⊙🍴✳♿🔔🏧⌁
Services: 🔌🚾🗑🧼🚽🅣→🛒
💳 💳 💳 🔌 💷

Wales

Leisure: 🏊 Indoor swimming pool   🏊 Outdoor swimming pool   🎾 Tennis court   🎱 Games room   ⚠ Children's playground   ∪ Stables
🏌 9/18 hole golf course   ⛵ Boats for hire   🎬 Cinema   🎣 Fishing   ◎ Mini golf   ⛵ Watersports   📺 Separate TV room

▶ ▶ ▶ 91% **Glanllyn Lakeside Caravan & Camping Park (SH891322)**
Llanuwchllyn LL23 7ST ☎ 01678 540227 & 540441
✉ info@glanllyn.com
ⓦ www.glanllyn.com
Dir: 2.5m SW of Bala on A494
🚐 fr £12 🚐 fr £12 ▲ fr £12
Open mid Mar-mid Oct Booking advisable Bank hols Last arrival 22.00hrs Last departure 14.00hrs
A spacious picturesque park set in 16 acres of mature parkland bordering the south shore of Bala Lake, with wonderful mountain views. It is an ideal holiday base for walking, or enjoying watersports on the lake, as the park offers direct access from the private shingle beach, and equipment can be hired nearby. The modern toilet facilities are excellent. A 16-acre site with 100 touring pitches, 10 hardstandings.
Baby changing area
Leisure: ⚕ Facilities: 🅿 ⊙ ⚑ ✳ ⚓ ℂ ☂ ⛺
Services: 🖭 ↯ 🗄 🛢 ⌀ 🗓 ➹ → ▶ ♨ ⚴ 🐾 🎵
Notes: No fires or disposable BBQs 💳 💳 💳 📷 🖥 🔊

NEW ▶ ▶ ▶ 82% **Tyn Cornel Camping & Caravan Park (SH895400)**
Frongoch LL23 7NU ☎ 01678 520759
📠 01678 520759
✉ peter.tooth@talk21.com
ⓦ www.tyncornel.co.uk
Dir: From Bala take A4212 (Porthmadog road) for 4m. Site on left before National Whitewater Centre
🚐 £10-£13 🚐 £10-£13 ▲ £10-£13
Open Mar-Oct Booking advisable At all times Last arrival 21.00hrs Last departure noon
A delightful riverside park with mountain views, popular with those seeking a base for river kayaks and canoes, with access to the nearby White Water Centre and riverside walk with tearoom. The helpful, resident owners keep the modern facilities spotlessly clean. A 3-acre site with 37 touring pitches.
Facilities: 🅿 ⊙ ⚑ ✳ ⚓ ℂ ☂ ⛺
Services: 🖭 🛢 ⌀ ➹ → ▶ ♨ ⚴ 🐾 🎵

▶ ▶ ▶ 73% *Tytandderwen Caravan Park (SH955364)*
LL23 7EP ☎ 01678 520273 📠 01678 521393
Dir: From B4401 take B4391 then unclass rd signed Tytandderwen
🚐 🚐 ▲

Open Mar-Oct Booking advisable peak periods
A secluded family park with superb views, and
contd.

fishing on site in the River Dee. A large modern facilities block includes laundry, dishwashing and disabled unit, and this is an ideal base for watersports, walking and climbing. An 8-acre site with 55 touring pitches and 60 statics.
Leisure: ◆ ⚕ Facilities: 🅿 ⊙ ⚑ ✳ ⚓ ℂ ☂
Services: 🖭 🗄 🛢 ⌀ 🗓 ➹ → ▶ ♨ ⚴ 🐾 🎵 ⚘

▶ ▶ ▶ ▶ 79% **Hendre Mynach Touring Caravan & Camping Park (SH605170)**
Llanaber Rd LL42 1YR ☎ 01341 280262
📠 01341 280586
✉ mynach@lineone.net
ⓦ www.hendremynach.co.uk
★ 🚐 £10-£22 🚐 £10-£20 ▲ £8-£19

Open Mar-9 Jan (rs Nov-8 Jan shop closed) Booking advisable bank hols & Jul-Aug Last arrival 22.00hrs Last departure noon
A lovely site with immaculate facilities, situated off the A496 on the northern outskirts of Barmouth, and near to the railway, with almost direct access to promenade and beach. Caravanners should not be put off by the steep descent, as park staff are always on hand if needed. The toilet facilities are modern and excellent, and pitches have TV and satellite hook-up as well as water and electricity. A small café serves light meals and take-aways. A 10-acre site with 240 touring pitches, 50 hardstandings. 50 TV hook ups.
Leisure: ⚕ Facilities: 🅿 ⊙ ⚑ ✳ ⚓ ℂ ☂ ⛺
Services: 🖭 ↯ 🗄 🛢 ⌀ 🗓 ✗ 🧹 → ∪ ⚴ 🎵
💳 💳 💳 🖥 🔊

▶ ▶ ▶ 83% **Trawsdir Touring & Camping Park (SH596198)**
Caerddaniel Caravan Park, Llanaber LL42 1RR
☎ 01341 280999 & 280611 📠 01341 280740
✉ enquiries@barmouthholidays.co.uk
ⓦ www.barmouthholidays.co.uk
Dir: 3m N of Barmouth on A496, just past Wayside pub on right
★ 🚐 £18-£23 🚐 £18-£23 ▲ £10-£18
Open Mar-Oct Booking advisable Etr, Whitsun & Jul-Aug Last arrival 21.00hrs Last departure noon
A good quality park on a working sheep farm with views to the sea and hills, and very accessible to motor traffic. The modern facilities are very clean and well maintained, and tents and caravans have their own designated areas divided by dry-stone
contd.

walls. A 15-acre site with 50 touring pitches, 23 hardstandings.
Milk/bread etc available from reception

Leisure: ⚫

Facilities: 🐾⊙🍴☀️&℄👥🐕

Services: 🔌⛽🛢️⌿🔀→∪🡒

Notes: Families & couples only

BETWS GARMON — Map 14 SH55

▶ ▶ ▶ ▶ **76% Bryn Gloch Caravan & Camping Park (SH534574)**
LL54 7YY ☎ 01286 650216 🖷 01286 650591
🅱 eurig@bryngloch.co.uk
🆆 www.bryngloch.co.uk
Dir: On A4085 7m SE of Caernarfon
★ 🚐 £13-£15 🚎 £13-£15 ⚫ £13-£15
Open all year Booking advisable school & bank hols
Last arrival 23.00hrs Last departure 17.00hrs
An excellent family-run site with immaculate modern facilities, and all level pitches in beautiful surroundings. The park offers the best of two worlds, with its bustling holiday atmosphere and the peaceful natural surroundings. The 25 acres of level fields are separated by mature hedges and trees, guaranteeing sufficient space for families wishing to spread themselves out. There are plenty of walks in the area, and a constant source of interest is the babbling stream, Gwyrfai. A 12-acre site with 160 touring pitches, 40 hardstandings and 40 statics.
Family bathroom, mother & baby room.

Leisure: ⚫ ⚫ ▢

Facilities: ⇥🐾⊙🍴☀️&℄👥🌳🎖️🐕

Services: 🔌⛽🛢️⌿🔀🖩🔀→∪🡒⊙♨🡒

🔲 🔲 🔲 🔲 🔲

CAERNARFON — Map 14 SH46
See also **Dinas Dinlle & Llandwrog**

▶ ▶ ▶ **77% Plas Gwyn Caravan Park (SH523632)**
Llanrug LL55 2AQ ☎ 01286 672619
🅱 info@plasgwyn.co.uk
🆆 www.plasgwyn.co.uk
Dir: A4086, 3m E of Caernarfon
★ 🚐 £10.50-£14 🚎 £10.50-£14 ⚫ £6-£9
Open Mar-Oct Booking advisable BH's Last arrival 22.00hrs
A secluded park handy for beaches, historic Caernarfon, and walking. The site is set within the grounds of Plas Gwyn House, a Georgian property with colonial additions, and the friendly owners are constantly improving the facilities. A 1.5-acre site with 27 touring pitches, 4 hardstandings and 18 statics.

Facilities: 🐾⊙🍴☀️🎖️🐕

Services: 🔌⛽🛢️⌿🖩🔀→∪🡒♨🡒

🔲 🔲 🔲 🔲 🔲

> The number of touring pitches listed for each site includes tents, caravans and motorvans.

▶ ▶ ▶ **77% Riverside Camping (SH505630)**
Seiont Nurseries, Pont Rug LL55 2BB
☎ 01286 678781 🖷 01286 677223
🅱 brenda@riversidecamping.freeserve.co.uk
🆆 www.riversidecamping.co.uk
Dir: 2m from Caernarfon on right of A4086 towards Llanberis, also signed Seiont Nurseries.
★ 🚐 £10-£16 🚎 £10-£16 ⚫ £10-£13
Open Etr-end Oct Booking advisable Jul-Aug & BH's
Last arrival anytime Last departure 20.00hrs
Set in the grounds of a large garden centre beside the small River Seiont, this park is approached by an impressive tree-lined drive. Facilities are very good, and include a café/restaurant and laundry. A 4.5-acre site with 60 touring pitches, 2 hardstandings.
Family shower room & baby changing facilities

Leisure: ⚫ **Facilities:** 🐾⊙🍴☀️&🐕

Services: 🔌🛢️✕♨🡒∪🡒♨🡒🖩🡒

Notes: No fires, no loud music, dogs must be kept on leads

▶ ▶ ▶ **71% Ty'n yr Onnen Mountain Farm Caravan & Camping (SH534588)**
Waunfawr LL55 4AX ☎ 01286 650281
🖷 01286 650043
Dir: At Waunfawr on A4085, into unclass road opposite church. Site signed
🚐 🚎 ⚫
Open Spring bank hol-Oct (rs Etr & Mayday bank hol open if weather permitting) Booking advisable Spring bank hol & Jul-Aug Last arrival 21.00hrs Last departure 10.00hrs

contd.

Wales

Ty'n yr Onnen Mountain Farm Caravan & Camping
A gently-sloping site on a 200-acre sheep farm, set in magnificent surroundings with mountain views. This secluded park is well equipped, with quality toilet facilities. Access is by single track unclassified road. A 4-acre site with 20 touring pitches and 4 statics.
Fishing & nature park

Leisure: ♦ ⚘ ▱

Facilities: ➜ ♟ ⊙ ♋ ✻ ᗒ ᑐ ♨ ⚞ ⇞

Services: ▭ ⊠ ⬦ ⬦ ⊞ ▯ → ∪ ▸ ◬ ↘ ☲ ♩ ⚞
⬤ ▭ ▱ ▨ ⚲

► ► **76% Cwm Cadnant Valley (SH487628)**
Cwm Cadnant Valley, Llanberis Rd LL55 2DF
☎ 01286 673196 🖷 01286 675941
🅰 aa@cadnantvalley.co.uk
🆆 www.cadnantvalley.co.uk
Dir: On outskirts of Caernarfon on A4086 towards Llanberis
▭ ▭ ▲

Open 14 Mar-3 Nov Booking advisable bank hols & Jul-Aug Last arrival 22.00hrs Last departure 11.00hrs
Set in an attractive wooded valley with a stream is this terraced site with secluded pitches. It is located on the outskirts of Caernarfon, close to the main Caernarfon-Llanberis road. A 4.5-acre site with 60 touring pitches.
Family room with baby changing facilities

Leisure: ⚘

Facilities: ♟ ⊙ ♋ ✻ ᗒ ᑐ ♨ ⚞ ⇞

Services: ▭ ⊠ ⬦ ⬦ ⊞ ▯ → ∪ ▸ ◬ ↘ ♩
⬤ ▭ ▱ ▨ ⚲

CRICCIETH   **Map 14 SH43**

NEW ► ► ► ► 78% **Eisteddfa (SH518394)**
Eisteddfa Lodge, Pentrefelin LL52 0PT
☎ 01766 522696
🅰 eisteddfa@criccieth.co.uk
🆆 www.eisteddfapark.co.uk
▭ £10.60-£14.80 ▭ £10.60-£14.80 ▲ £8.80-£12.95
Open Mar-Oct Booking advisable Bank & school hols Last arrival 22.30hrs Last departure 11.00hrs
A quiet, secluded park on elevated ground, sheltered by the Snowdonia Mountains and with lovely views of Cardigan Bay. The owners are carefully improving the park whilst preserving its unspoilt beauty, and are keen to welcome families, who will appreciate the cubicled facilities. There's a field and play area, and woodland walks, with Criccieth nearby. An 11-acre site with 100 touring pitches, 17 hardstandings.
Football pitch, baby bath

Leisure: ♦ ⚘ Facilities: ♟ ⊙ ♋ ✻ ᗒ ♨ ⚞ ⇞
Services: ▭ ⬦ ⬦ ⊞ → ∪ ▸ ◎ ◬ ↘ ☲ ♩ ⬚

► ► 81% **Llwyn-Bugeilydd Caravan & Camping Site (SH498398)**
LL52 0PN ☎ 01766 522235 & 07854 063192
Dir: From Porthmadog on A497, 1m N of Criccieth on B4411. Site 1st on right. From A55 take A487 through Caernarfon; after Bryncir turn right on to B4411, site on left after 3.5m.
★ ▭ £7.50-£10 ▭ £7.50-£10 ▲ £7.50-£10
Open Mar-Oct Booking advisable Etr, Whit & Jul-Aug Last arrival anytime Last departure 11.00hrs
A quiet rural site with sea and mountain views, and well-tended grass pitches. The toilets are kept very clean, and the resident owners are always on hand. A 6-acre site with 45 touring pitches.

Facilities: ♟ ⊙ ♋ ✻ ᗒ ♨ ⚞ ⇞
Services: ▭ ⊠ ⬦ ⬦ ⊞ → ∪ ▸ ◎ ☲ ♩ ⬚

► ► 76% **Tyddyn Cethin Caravan Park (SH492404)**
LL52 0NF ☎ 01766 522149
Dir: N from Criccieth on B4411. Tyddyn Cethin 4th site on right
★ ▭ £10-£12 ▭ £10-£12 ▲ £9-£10
Open Mar-Oct Booking advisable Feb-Mar Last arrival 22.00hrs Last departure noon
A very high quality little park in a pretty setting on the banks of the River Dwyfor. The enthusiastic owners maintain the grounds and sanitary facilities to an excellent standard. An 8-acre site with 60 touring pitches and 40 statics.
Fishing on site.

Facilities: ➜ ♟ ⊙ ♋ ✻ ⚞ ⇞
Services: ▭ ⬦ ⊞ → ∪ ▸ ◎ ◬ ☲ ♩ ⬚
Notes: Dogs must be kept on leads

► 68% **Tyddyn Morthwyl Camping & Caravan Site**
(SH488402)
LL52 ONF ☎ 01766 522115
✉ trumper@henstabl147freeserve.co.uk
Dir: 1.5m N of Criccieth on B4411
★ ⊞ fr £6 ⊞ fr £6 ▲ fr £6
Open Etr-Oct (rs Mar & Oct) Booking advisable
Spring bank hol & Jul-Aug Last departure 14.00hrs
*A quiet sheltered site with level grass pitches in
three fields. The simple facilities include some
electric hook-ups, and the sea is close by. A 10-acre
site with 60 touring pitches and 22 statics.*

Facilities: ⬤ ☉ ✻ ♨

Services: ⊡ ⊞ → ∪ ▶ ↳ ♪ ⏗

Notes: Dogs must be kept on leads at all times

DINAS DINLLE   **Map 14 SH45**

► ► ► ► 77% **Dinlle Caravan Park**
(SH443568)
LL54 5TW ☎ 01286 830324 🖷 01286 831526
✉ enq@thornleyleisure.co.uk
🌐 www.thornleyleisure.co.uk
*Dir: Turn right off A499 at sign for Caernarfon Airport.
2m W of Dinas Dinlle coast*
⊞ £6.50-£17 ⊞ £6.50-£17 ▲ £6.50-£17

Open May-Aug (rs Mar-Apr & Sep-Nov club, shop,
swimming pool restricted hours) Booking advisable
Spring bank hol & Jul-Aug Last arrival 23.00hrs Last
departure noon
*A very accessible, well-kept grassy site, adjacent to
sandy beach, with good views to Snowdonia. The
park is situated in acres of flat grassland, with
plenty of room for even the largest groups. A
lounge bar and family room are comfortable places
in which to relax, and children are well provided for
with an exciting adventure playground. The beach
road gives access to the golf club, a nature reserve,
and to Air World at Caernarfon Airport. A 20-acre
site with 175 touring pitches and 167 statics.*

Leisure: ⚡ ♣ ⋔

Facilities: ⬤ ☉ ☜ ✻ ♨ ☏

Services: ⊡ 👙 ⊡ ♀ ⌀ ∅ ⊡ → ∪ ♪ ⏗
🔲 🔲 🔲 🔲 🔲

DYFFRYN ARDUDWY   **Map 14 SH52**

► ► ► 77% **Murmur-yr-Afon Touring Park**
(SH586236)
LL44 2BE ☎ 01341 247353 🖷 01341 247353
✉ mills@murmuryrafon25.freeserve.co.uk
🌐 www.murmuryrafon.co.uk
Dir: On A496 N of village
★ ⊞ £8.50-£18.25 ⊞ £8.50-£18.25 ▲ £6.50-£16

Open Mar-Oct Booking advisable bank hols Last
arrival 22.00hrs Last departure 11.30hrs
*A pleasant family-run park alongside a wooded
stream on the edge of the village, and handy for
large sandy beaches. Expect good, clean facilities,
and lovely views of rolling hills and mountains.
A 4-acre site with 67 touring pitches,
30 hardstandings.*

Leisure: ⋔

Facilities: ⬤ ☉ ☜ ✻ ♨ ⚲ ⏗ ♨ ☏

Services: ⊡ ⊡ ⊞ → ∪ ♨ ♪

Leisure: ⚡ Indoor swimming pool ⚡ Outdoor swimming pool ⚬ Tennis court ♣ Games room ⋔ Children's playground ∪ Stables
▶ 9/18 hole golf course ↳ Boats for hire 🎬 Cinema ♪ Fishing ◎ Mini golf ⚠ Watersports ⬜ Separate TV room

LLANDWROG   Map 14 SH45

▶ ▶ ▶ ▶ 76% **White Tower Caravan Park**
(SH453582)
LL54 5UH ☎ 01286 830649 & 07802 562785
🖷 01286 830649
🅴 whitetower@supanet.com
🅦 www.whitetower.supanet.com
*Dir: 1.5m from village along Tai'r Eglwys road. From
Caernarfon take A487 Porthmadog road. Cross rdbt,
take 1st right. Park 3m on right*
★ 🚐 £10-£16 🚐 £10-£16 ▲ £10-£16
Open Mar-15 Jan (rs Mar-mid May & Sep-Oct bar
open wknds only) Booking advisable bank hols &
Jul-Aug Last arrival 23.00hrs Last departure noon
*There are lovely views of Snowdonia from this park
located just 2 miles from the nearest beach at Dinas
Dinlle. A well-maintained toilet block has key access,
and the hard pitches have water and electricity.
Popular amenities include an outdoor heated
swimming pool, a lounge bar with family room, and
a games and TV room. A 6-acre site with 104 touring
pitches, 80 hardstandings and 54 statics.*
Leisure: ⚡ ⚓ ⚠ 🏳 Facilities: 🅿 ⊙ 🍽 ✳ & 🗘
Services: 🖭 🎬 🍴 🖉 🖶 🚰 → ∪ ▶ ♨ ⚓ ✗ 🎍 🖲
🌐 🚏 🚋 🍺 🏧

LLANRUG   Map 14 SH56

▶ ▶ ▶ 77% **Llys Derwen Caravan & Camping Site**
(SH539629)
Ffordd Bryngwyn LL55 4RD ☎ 01286 673322
🅴 llysderwen@aol.com
🅦 www.llysderwen.co.uk
*Dir: From A55 junct 13 (Caernarfon) take A4086 to
Llanberis, through Llanrug, turn right at pub, site 60yds
on right*
★ 🚐 £10-£12 🚐 £10-£12 ▲ fr £8
Open Mar-Oct Booking advisable Last arrival
10.30hrs Last departure noon
*A pleasant site set in woodland within easy reach of
Caernarfon, Snowdon, Anglesey and the Lleyn
Peninsula. The keen owners are planning several
improvements. A 5-acre site with 30 touring pitches
and 2 statics.*
Facilities: 🅿 ⊙ ✳ 🚲 🏘
Services: 🖭 🖶 → ∪ ▶ ♨ ✗ 🎍 🖲

LLANYSTUMDWY   Map 14 SH43

▶ ▶ ▶ 73% **Camping & Caravanning Club Site**
(SH469384)
Tyddyn Sianel LL52 0LS ☎ 01766 522855
🅦 www.campingandcaravanningclub.co.uk
*Dir: From Criccieth take A497 W, 2nd right to
Llanystumdwy, site on right*
★ 🚐 £13.60-£17.80 🚐 £13.60-£17.80 ▲ £13.60-£17.80
Open Mar-Oct Booking advisable bank hols & peak
period Last arrival 21.00hrs Last departure noon
*An attractive site close to one of many beaches in
the area, and with lovely mountain and sea views.
There is a good range of well-maintained facilities,
and the mainly sloping site is handy for walking in
the Snowdonia National Park or on the local
network of quiet country lanes. Please see the*

contd.

*advertisement on page 11 for information on Club
sites and membership. A 4-acre site with 70 touring
pitches, 4 hardstandings.*
Facilities: 🅿 ⊙ 🍽 ✳ & 🗘 🏘 🏕
Services: 🖭 🎬 🍴 🖉 🖶 🖵 → ∪ ▶ 🎍 🚲 🔚 🚏 🚋 🕱 🏧

PONTLLYFNI   Map 14 SH45

▶ ▶ ▶ 77% **St Ives Touring Caravan Park**
(SH432524)
Lon-Y-Wig LL54 5EG ☎ 01286 660347
🖷 01286 660542
🅴 st.ivestouringpark@btopenworld.com
🅦 www.stivestouringcaravans.co.uk
Dir: Off A499 along lane towards beach from village centre
★ 🚐 £10-£12 🚐 £10-£12 ▲ £8-£12
Open Mar-Oct Booking advisable all times Last
arrival 21.00hrs Last departure 11.00hrs
*An immaculate little site with good facilities, within
easy walking distance of the beach. Improvements
made over the years include a small shop selling
necessities, plus hardstandings and external
lighting. Fishing tackle, bait and rod hire is
available, and the beach is 150mtrs away.
A 1.25-acre site with 20 touring pitches,
19 hardstandings.*
Facilities: 🅿 ⊙ ✳ 🚲 🖵 🏕
Services: 🖭 🎬 🍴 🖶 🖵 → ∪ ▶ 🎍

▶ ▶ 71% **Llyn-y-Gele Farm & Caravan Park**
(SH432523)
LL54 5EG ☎ 01286 660289 & 660283
*Dir: Off A499, 7m S of Caernarfon. Right in Pontllyfni by
shop & garage*
★ 🚐 £7-£10 🚐 £7-£10 ▲ fr £7
Open Etr-Oct Booking advisable Jul-Aug Last arrival
22.00hrs Last departure 13.00hrs
*A quiet, well-kept farm site with its own path to the
beach 5-7 minutes walk away. This small park is in
the centre of the village, and is well located for
touring the Lleyn Peninsula, Anglesey and
Snowdonia. A 4-acre site with 6 touring pitches and
24 statics.*
Leisure: ⚠ Facilities: 🅿 ⊙ ✳ 🏘
Services: 🖭 🍴 → 🎍 🚲

PONT-RUG
See **Caernarfon**

PORTHMADOG   Map 14 SH53

🏖 77% **Greenacres** (SH560381)
Black Rock Sands, Morfa Bychan
LL49 9YB
☎ 01766 512781 🖷 01766 512084
🅦 www.havenholidays.com
*Dir: After high street, turn between Woolworths &
post office towards Black Rock Sands. 2m park
entrance on left*
★ 🚐 £14-£73 🚐 £14-£73
Open mid Mar-Oct (rs mid Mar-May & Sep-Oct
Some facilities may be reduced) Booking
advisable school hols Last arrival 18.00hrs Last
departure 10.00hrs
A quality holiday park on level ground just a contd.

Wales

short walk from Black Rock Sands, and set against a backdrop of Snowdonia National Park. All touring pitches are on hardstandings surrounded by closely-mown grass, and near the entertainment complex. A full programme of entertainment, organised clubs, indoor and outdoor sports and leisure including a high-level 'ropeworks' adventure course, pubs, shows and cabarets all add to a holiday here. A 121-acre site with 48 touring pitches and 370 statics.

Leisure: ॰ ৹ ৎ ⚁ **Facilities:** ⌂ ☉ ৎ ঌ ৻ ⅀

Services: ₪ ⊟ ⍟ ℹ ⌀ ✕ ⬚ → ♪ ◎ ⚄ ♫ ♪

Notes: Dogs not allowed in school holidays

⬤ ▦ ▦ ▦ ◙

PWLLHELI   Map 14 SH33

▶ ▶ ▶ 69% **Abererch Sands Holiday Centre (SH403359)**
LL53 6PJ ☎ 01758 612327 ▤ 01758 701556
✉ enquiries@abererch-sands.co.uk
ⓦ www.abererch-sands.co.uk
Dir: On A497 (Porthmadog-Pwllheli road), 1m from Pwllheli
★ ⊞ £15-£17 ⊞ £13.50-£15.50 ▲ £14.50-£16.50

Open Mar-Oct Booking advisable school & bank holidays Last arrival 21.00hrs Last departure 21.00hrs
Glorious views of Snowdonia and Cardigan Bay can be enjoyed from this very secure, family-run site adjacent to a railway station and a 4-mile stretch of sandy beach. A large heated indoor swimming pool, snooker room, pool room, fitness centre and children's play area make this an ideal holiday venue. An 85-acre site with 70 touring pitches, 70 hardstandings and 90 statics.
Snooker room, fitness room

Leisure: ॰ ৎ ⚁ **Facilities:** ⌂ ☉ ৎ ✳ ঌ ৻ ⅀ ☂

Services: ₪ ⤵ ⊟ ℹ ⌀ ⊟ ⊡ → ∪ ♪ ♨ ✚ ⚄ ♪

⬤ ▦ ▦ ▦ ◙

TALSARNAU   Map 14 SH63

▶ ▶ ▶ ▶ 78% **Barcdy Touring Caravan & Camping Park (SH623368)**
LL47 6YG ☎ 01766 770736
✉ anwen@barcdy.co.uk
ⓦ www.barcdy.co.uk
Dir: From Maentwrog take left turn for Harlech, on A496. Barcdy 4m on the left
★ ⊞ £10.50-£13 ⊞ £10.50-£13 ▲ £10.50-£13
Open Apr-Sep (rs Etr-Spring bank hol & mid-end Sep only two fields open, food shop closed) Booking advisable BH's
contd.

Barcdy Touring Caravan & Camping Park
A quiet picturesque park on the edge of the Vale of Ffestiniog near the Dwryd estuary. Two touring areas serve the park, one near the park entrance, and the other with more secluded terraced pitches beside a narrow valley. Footpaths through adjacent woodland lead to small lakes and an established nature trail. No dogs allowed. A 12-acre site with 68 touring pitches, 2 hardstandings and 30 statics.

Facilities: ⌂ ☉ ৎ ✳ ☂

Services: ₪ ⊟ ℹ ⌀ ⊟ → ∪ ♪ ⅀

Notes: ✇ ⬤ ▦ ▦ ◙

TAL-Y-BONT   Map 14 SH52

▶ ▶ 68% *Benar Beach Camping & Touring Park (SH573226)*
LL43 2AR ☎ 01341 247571 & 247001
Dir: 1m from A496, halfway between Harlech & Barmouth
⊞ ⊞ ▲
Open Mar-3 Oct Booking advisable peak periods
A spacious level park sheltered by sand dunes and close to the beach, with lovely mountain views. The simple facilities are housed in two portaloos and a main block. A 5-acre site with 45 touring pitches. Satellite & TV hook-ups.

Facilities: ⌂ ☉ ✳ ৻ ⅀ ☂

Services: ₪ → ∪ ♪

TYWYN   Map 14 SH50

▶ ▶ ▶ 76% *Ynysymaengwyn Caravan Park (SH602021)*
LL36 9RY ☎ 01654 710684 ▤ 01654 710684
✉ rita@ynysy.co.uk
ⓦ www.ynysmaengwyn.co.uk
Dir: On A493, 1m N of Tywyn, towards Dolgellau
⊞ ▲
Open Etr or Apr-Oct Booking advisable Jul-Aug Last arrival 23.00hrs Last departure noon
A lovely park set in the wooded grounds of a former manor house, with woodland and river walks, fishing and a sandy beach nearby. The attractive stone amenity block is clean and well kept, and this smart municipal park is ideal for families. A 4-acre site with 80 touring pitches and 115 statics.

Leisure: ⚁

Facilities: ⌂ ☉ ৎ ✳ ঌ ৻ ⅀ ☂ ☂

Services: ₪ ⊟ ℹ ⌀ ⊟ → ∪ ♪ ◎ ♨ ⚄ ♪ ⅀

Notes: Dogs must be kept on leads at all times

MONMOUTHSHIRE

ABERGAVENNY   Map 09 SO21

► ► ► 69% **Pyscodlyn Farm Caravan & Camping Site (SO266155)**
Llanwenarth Citra NP7 7ER ☎ 01873 853271
▤ 01873 853271
➋ pyscodlyn.farm@virgin.net
Ⓦ www.pyscodlyncaravanpark.com
Dir: From Abergavenny take A40 (Brecon road), site 1.5m from entrance of Nevill Hall Hospital, on left 50yds past phone box
★ ➔ £9-£10 ➔ £9-£10 ▲ £8-£10
Open Apr-Oct Booking advisable bank hols
With its outstanding views of the Brecon Beacons, this quiet park in the Brecon National Park makes a pleasant venue for country lovers. The Sugarloaf Mountain and the River Usk are within easy walking distance, and despite being a working farm, dogs are welcome. A 4.5-acre site with 60 touring pitches, 60 hardstandings and 6 statics.
Facilities: ⚐☉✳ ⌂
Services: ⚑⭑∅→∪▶☺♩⚡

DINGESTOW   Map 09 SO41

► ► ► 79% *Bridge Caravan Park & Camping Site (SO459104)*
Bridge Farm NP25 4DY ☎ 01600 740241
▤ 01600 740241
➋ info@bridgecaravanpark.co.uk
Dir: Signed from Raglan. Off A449 (South Wales-Midlands road)
➔ ➔ ▲
Open Etr-Oct Booking advisable bank hols Last arrival 22.00hrs Last departure 16.00hrs
The River Trothy runs along the edge of this quiet village park, which has been owned by the same family for many years. Touring pitches are both grass and hardstanding, and there is a backdrop of woodland. The refurbished toilet block and new laundry equipment have considerably enhanced the facilities here. A 4-acre site with 94 touring pitches, 15 hardstandings.
Fishing.
Facilities: ⚐☉⚁✳⭑⚡⚡⌂
Services: ⚑⚐⊡∅⊞⊤→∪▶✛⚌♩

If a park's amenities/facilities are important to you, please check their availability at the time of booking.

An increasing number of parks do not accept children. There is a list of adult-only sites on page 19.

MITCHEL TROY   Map 09 SO41

► ► ► 68% **Glen Trothy Caravan & Camping Park (SO496105)**
NP25 4BD ☎ 01600 712295
➋ enquiries@glentrothy.co.uk
Ⓦ www.glentrothy.co.uk
Dir: Approx midway between Monmouth & Raglan, signed off B4293. Site at entrance to village
★ ➔ fr £10 ➔ fr £10 ▲ fr £7
Open Mar-Oct Booking advisable BH's & high season Last arrival 21.00hrs Last departure noon
A very pretty park in a well-wooded area beside the River Trothy, where free fishing by licence is available. Three large fields are neatly cut, and the friendly owners keep the facilities to a good standard. A 6.5-acre site with 84 touring pitches, 64 hardstandings.
Leisure: ⚘ **Facilities:** ⚐☉⚁✳⭑⚡
Services: ⚑⊡∅⊞→▶⚘✛⚌♩⚡
Notes: ⚠ No camp fires, BBQ's must be purpose built & 18in off ground

MONMOUTH   Map 10 SO51

► ► ► 77% **Monmouth Caravan Park (SO498135)**
Rockfield Rd NP5 3BA ☎ 01600 714745
▤ 01600 716690
➋ mail@monmouthcaravanpark.co.uk
Dir: From A40 take B4233 S of Monmouth, leading into Rockfield Road & site is opposite fire station
★ ➔ £13.50-£15.50 ➔ £13.50-£15.50 ▲ £10-£15.50
Open Mar-4 Jan Booking advisable Jun-Sep Last arrival 20.00hrs Last departure 13.00hrs
A neat, attractive, level park offering clean and bright toilet facilities. There is a small licensed bar serving bar meals with occasional entertainment at weekends. Offa's Dyke footpath is only a few yards away, and the town is within easy walking distance. A 3-acre site with 60 touring pitches, 12 hardstandings and 15 statics.
Facilities: ⚐☉⚁✳⚡⭑⚡⌂⊞⌂
Services: ⚑⚑⭑∅⊞⊤✕⚒→∪▶⚘✛⚌♩⊡⚡
💳 💳 💳💳 💳 🔲

USK   Map 09 SO30

► ► ► ► 79% **Pont Kemys Caravan & Camping Park (SO348058)**
Chainbridge NP7 9DS ☎ 01873 880688
▤ 01873 880270
➋ info@pontkemys.com
Ⓦ www.pontkemys.com

contd.

Dir: On B4598 (Usk - Abergavenny road), 300yds N of Chainbridge, 4m from Usk
★ ⚌ £12-£14 ⚌ £12-£14 ▲ £12-£14
Open Mar-Oct Booking advisable BH's & Jul-Aug Last arrival 22.00hrs Last departure noon
A peaceful park next to the River Usk, offering a good standard of facilities. The park is in a rural area with mature trees and country views, and attracts quiet visitors who enjoy the many attractions of this area. An 8-acre site with 65 touring pitches, 8 hardstandings.
Mother & baby room, kitchen facilities for groups
Leisure: ▭
Facilities: �🛉⊙🍴✳⚅⚬⚍🆑♞
Services: ⚡🕁🖳🛢⌀🖵🅃➔🍴⚒🔧
Notes: Dogs must be kept on leads at all times
⬤ ▦ ▦ ▨ ◲

PEMBROKESHIRE

▶ ▶ ▶ **82% Creampots Touring Caravan & Camping Park (SM882131)**
Broadway SA62 3TU ☎ 01437 781776
Ⓦ www.creampots.co.uk
Dir: From Haverfordwest take B4341 to Broadway. Turn left signed Milford Haven. Park 2nd entrance, 500yds on right
★ ⚌ £10.50-£12.50 ⚌ £10.50-£12.50 ▲ £10-£12
Open Apr-Oct Booking advisable Jul-Aug & bank hols Last arrival 21.00hrs Last departure noon
Set just outside the Pembrokeshire National Park, this quiet site is just 1.5m from a safe sandy beach at Broad Haven, and the coastal footpath. The park is well laid out and carefully maintained, and the toilet block offers a good standard of facilities. An 8-acre site with 71 touring pitches, 14 hardstandings and 1 static.
Facilities: ⛤⊙🍴✳⚅
Services: ⚡🖳🛢➔⚬⚔⚒🔧⚒⬤ ▦ ▨ ▨ ◲

▶ ▶ ▶ **74% South Cockett Caravan & Camping Park (SM879135)**
South Cockett SA62 3TU
☎ 01437 781296 & 781760 🖷 01437 781296
ⓔ esmejames@hotmail.co.uk
Ⓦ www.southcockett.co.uk
Dir: From Haverfordwest take B4341 to Broadhaven, at Broadway turn left, site is 300yds.
★ ⚌ £10.50-£12.50 ⚌ £10.50-£12.50 ▲ £9-£10.50
Open Etr-Oct Booking advisable Jul-Aug Last arrival 23.30hrs
A small park on a working farm, with touring areas divided into neat paddocks by high, well-trimmed hedges. Good toilet facilities, and in a convenient location for the lovely beach at nearby Broad Haven. A 6-acre site with 73 touring pitches.
Facilities: ⛤⊙✳⚬
Services: ⚡🖳🛢⌀🖵➔⚬⚔⚒🔧

▶ ▶ ▶ **69% Masterland Farm Touring Caravan Park (SN095060)**
Broadmoor SA68 0RH ☎ 01834 813298
🖷 01834 814408
ⓔ bonsermasterland@aol.com
Ⓦ www.ukparks.co.uk/masterland
Dir: Exit A4777 at Broadmoor onto B4586. Site 400yds on right
⚌ £8-£16 ⚌ £8-£16 ▲ £8-£16
(rs off season bar & restaurant open at weekends only) Booking advisable Last arrival 21.00hrs Last departure 10.30hrs
A small site on a working farm set on the edge of the Pembrokeshire Coast National Park. It makes an ideal centre for touring the many places of interest in the area, and is only four miles from the beaches at Tenby. The Piggy Wiggy restaurant and Stable Bar are open during high season (evenings only) and most weekends. A 2.5-acre site with 38 touring pitches, 23 hardstandings.
Library
Leisure: ⚭ ⚘ Facilities: ⛤⊙🍴✳⚬⚅♞
Services: ⚡🖳⚓🛢⌀🖵🅇➔⚬⚔🔧
Notes: No bicycles

▶ ▶ ▶ **77% Fishguard Bay Caravan & Camping Park (SM984383)**
Garn Gelli SA65 9ET
☎ 01348 811415 🖷 01348 811425
ⓔ enquiries@fishguardbay.com
Ⓦ www.fishguardbay.com
Dir: Take A487 (Fishguard-Cardigan road). Park (signed) 3m from Fishguard, on left
★ ⚌ £11.50-£13.50 ⚌ £11.50-£13.50 ▲ £10.50-£12.50

Open Mar-9 Jan Booking advisable Jul-Aug Last departure noon
Set high up on cliffs with outstanding views of Fishguard Bay, and the Pembrokeshire Coastal Path running right through the centre. The park is extremely well kept, with three good toilet blocks, a common room with TV, a lounge/library, decent laundry, and well-stocked shop. A 5-acre site with 50 touring pitches and 50 statics.
View point.
Leisure: ⚭ ⚘ ▭
Facilities: ⛤⊙🍴✳⚬⚅
Services: ⚡🖳🛢⌀🖵🅃➔⚬⚔⚒🔧
⬤ ▦ ◉ ▨ ◲

Wales

Wales

▶ ▶ ▶ 72% **Gwaun Vale Touring Park (SM977356)**
Llanychaer SA65 9TA ☎ 01348 874698
🄴 margaret.harries@talk21.com
Dir: From Fishguard take B4313. Site 1.5m on right
★ 🏕 £10-£11.50 🚐 £10-£11.50 ▲ £8.50-£10
Open Apr-Oct Booking advisable Jul-Aug Last
arrival anytime Last departure noon
*Located at the opening of the beautiful Gwaun
Valley, this well-kept park is set on the hillside with
pitches tiered on two levels. There are lovely views
of the surrounding countryside, and good facilities.
A 1.75-acre site with 29 touring pitches, 5
hardstandings.*
Guide books available
Leisure: ⅍
Facilities: ⎕⊙⅃⋇⅃⅃⅃⎕⅃ 🐾
Services: ⎕⅃⅃⅃⅃→∪⅃⅃⅃⅃
Notes: Dogs must be kept on leads

HASGUARD CROSS   Map 08 SM80

▶ ▶ ▶ 77% **Hasguard Cross Caravan Park
(SM850108)**
SA62 3SL ☎ 01437 781443 🖷 01437 781443
🄴 enquiries@hasguardcross.co.uk
🅦 www.hasguardcross.co.uk
*Dir: From Haverfordwest take B4327 towards Dale. After
7m turn right at x-rds & site is 1st entrance on right*
★ 🚐 £15-£18 🚐 £15-£18
Open all year Booking advisable Spring bank hol &
Jun-Aug Last arrival 21.00hrs Last departure
10.00hrs
*A very clean, efficient and well-run site in
Pembrokeshire National Park with views of
surrounding hills just 1.5m from sea and beach at
Little Haven. The toilet and shower facilities are
immaculately clean, and there is a licensed bar
(evenings only) serving a good choice of food. A
4.5-acre site with 12 touring pitches and 42 statics.*
Facilities: ⎕⊙⋇⅃⅃⅃⅃⎕ 🐾
Services: ⎕⅃⅃⅃⅃✕⅃⅃→∪⅃⅃⅃⅃

▶ ▶ ▶ 80% **Redlands Caravan & Camping Park
(SM853109)**
SA62 3SJ ☎ 01437 781300 🖷 01437 781300
🄴 info@redlandscamping.co.uk
🅦 www.redlandstouring.co.uk
*Dir: From Haverfordwest take B4327 towards Dale. Site
7m on right*
★ 🚐 £11.75-£14 🚐 £11.75-£14 ▲ £10-£14
Open Mar-Dec (rs off peak Shop only open in peak
season) Booking advisable BHs & Jul-Aug Last
arrival 22.00hrs Last departure noon
*A family owned and run park set in five acres of
level grassland with tree-lined borders, close to
many sandy beaches and the famous coastal
footpath. Ideal for exploring the Pembrokeshire
National Park. A 5-acre site with 64 touring pitches,
11 hardstandings.*
Use of deep freezers
Facilities: ⎕⊙⅃⋇⅃⅃⅃ 🐾
Services: ⎕⅃⅃⅃⅃⅃⅃→∪⅃⅃⅃⅃

HAVERFORDWEST   Map 08 SM91

▶ ▶ 73% **Nolton Cross Caravan Park (SM879177)**
Nolton SA62 3NP ☎ 01437 710701 🖷 01437 710329
🄴 noltoncross@nolton.fsnet.co.uk
🅦 www.noltoncross-holidays.co.uk
*Dir: 1m off A487 (Haverfordwest - St David's road) at
Simpson Cross*
★ 🚐 £6.50-£9.50 🚐 £6.50-£9.50
Open Mar-Dec Booking advisable High season Last
arrival 22.00hrs Last departure noon
*High grassy banks surround the touring area of this
park next to the owners' working farm. It is located
on open ground above the sea and St Bride's Bay
which are both 1.5m away, and there is a coarse
fishing lake close by. A 4-acre site with 15 touring
pitches and 30 statics.*
Leisure: ⅍
Facilities: ⎕⊙⋇⅃⅃⅃⎕
Services: ⎕⅃⅃⅃⅃⅃→∪⅃⅃ 🔌 📺 🄰

LANDSHIPPING   Map 08 SN01

▶ ▶ 73% *New Park Farm (SN026111)*
SA67 8BG ☎ 01834 891284 🖷 01834 891284
Dir: 7m W of Narberth, along unclass road off A4075
🚐🚐 ▲
Open Etr-Oct Booking advisable peak periods Last
arrival 20.00hrs Last departure noon
*A very pleasant, quiet farm site which has
undergone much upgrading. The touring
area is well landscaped and terraced, and the basic
facilities are adequate and very clean. A 2-acre site
with 30 touring pitches, 20 hardstandings and
30 statics.*
Facilities: ⎕⊙⋇⅃⎕
Services: ⎕⅃⅃⅃⅃→∪⅃⅃

LITTLE HAVEN
See **Hasguard Cross**

ROSEBUSH   Map 08 SN02

▶ ▶ 73% **Rosebush Caravan Park
(SN073293)**
Rhoslwyn SA66 7QT
☎ 01437 532206 & 0831 223166
🖷 01437 532206
*Dir: From Fishguard take B4313 towards Narberth. Site
signed left*
★ 🚐 £10-£12 🚐 £9.50 ▲ £7.50
Open 14 Mar-Oct Booking advisable peak season
Last arrival 23.00hrs Last departure noon
*A most attractive park with a large ornamental lake
at its centre and good landscaping. Set off the main
tourist track, it offers lovely views of the Presely
Hills which can be reached by a scenic walk.
Rosebush is a quiet village with a handy pub, and
the park owner also runs the village shop. Due to
the deep lake on site, children are not accepted. A
12-acre site with 65 touring pitches and 15 statics.*
Facilities: ⎕⊙⅃⋇⅃⅃⅃ 🐾
Services: ⎕⅃⎕→◎⅃
Notes: Adults only

ST DAVID'S   Map 08 SM72

▶ ▶ ▶ 85% **Caerfai Bay Caravan & Tent Park**
(SM759244)
Caerfai Bay SA62 6QT ☎ 01437 720274 ▤ 01437 720577
📧 info@caerfaibay.co.uk
🌐 www.caerfaibay.co.uk
Dir: At St David's turn off A487 at Visitor Centre/Grove
Hotel. Follow signs for Caerfai Bay. Right at end of road
★ ⊞ £10-£14 ⊞ £8-£14 ⚑ £8-£10

Open Mar-mid Nov Booking advisable school hols
Last arrival 21.00hrs Last departure 11.00hrs
Magnificent coastal scenery and an outlook over St
Bride's Bay can be enjoyed from this delightful site,
located just 300yds from a bathing beach. The
facilities include four en suite family rooms which
are an asset to the park. There is a farm shop very
close by. A 10-acre site with 117 touring pitches,
9 hardstandings and 32 statics.
Family washrooms
Facilities: ⋒ ⊙ ⊒ ⋇ ⚵ ℓ ♨
Services: ▯ ⅏ ▤ ⅋ ⌘ ⊞ → ▸ ⚶ ⅃ ● ▦ ▨ ⑤

▶ ▶ ▶ 77% *Hendre Eynon Camping & Caravan*
Site **(SM773280)**
SA62 6DB ☎ 01437 720474 ▤ 01437 720474
Dir: Take A487 (Fishguard road) from St David's, fork
left at rugby club signed Llanrhian. Site 2m on right (do
no take turn to Whitesands)
⊞ ⊞ ⚑

Open May-Sep (rs 27 Mar-Apr one toilet block &
showers rooms only) Booking advisable school hols
Last arrival 21.00hrs Last departure noon
A peaceful country site on a working farm, with a
modern toilet block including family rooms. Within
easy reach of many lovely sandy beaches, and 2
miles to the cathedral city of St David's. A 7-acre
site with 48 touring pitches and 2 statics.
Facilities: ⋒ ⊙ ⋇ ⚵ ℓ ♈
Services: ▯ ▤ ⅋ ⊞ → ▸ ⚶ ⅃ ⅃ ℞
Notes: No more then two dogs per unit

▶ ▶ 75% **Camping & Caravanning Club Site**
(SM805305)
Dwr Cwmdig, Berea SA62 6DW
☎ 01348 831376
🌐 www.campingandcaravanningclub.co.uk
Dir: S on A487, right at Glyncheryn Farmers Stores in
Croesgoch. After 1m turn right follow signs to
Abereiddy. At x-roads left. Site 75yds on left
★ ⊞ £12.40-£16.70 ⊞ £12.40-£16.70 ⚑ £12.40-£16.70
Open Apr-Oct Booking advisable bank hols & peak
period Last arrival 21.00hrs Last departure noon
An immaculately kept small site in open country
near the Pembrokeshire Coastal Path. The slightly
sloping grass has a few hardstandings for motor
homes, and plenty of electric hook-ups. Please see
advertisement on page 11 for information on Club
sites and membership. A 4-acre site with 40 touring
pitches, 4 hardstandings.
Facilities: ⋒ ⊙ ⊒ ⋇ ℓ ♨
Services: ▯ ▤ ⅃ ⅋ ⊞ ⊞ → ⚶ ⅃ ● ▦ ▨ ⑤

▶ ▶ 78% **Tretio Caravan & Camping Park**
(SM787292)
SA62 6DE ☎ 01437 781600 ▤ 01437 781594
📧 info@tretio.com
🌐 www.tretio.com
Dir: Leaving St David's keep left at Rugby Football Club,
straight on 3m. Site signed on right
★ ⊞ £6-£14 ⊞ £6-£14 ⚑ £6-£14
Open 14 Mar-14 Oct Booking advisable bank hols &
mid Jul-Aug Last arrival 20.00hrs Last departure
10.00hrs
An attractive site in a very rural spot with distant
country views, and beautiful local beaches. A
mobile shop calls daily at peak periods, and the tiny
cathedral city of St David's is only 3 miles away. A
6.5-acre site with 40 touring pitches and 30 statics.
Pitch & putt, bike rental, ball games area
Leisure: ⚠ **Facilities:** ⋒ ⊙ ⊒ ⋇ ⚵ ♉ ♈
Services: ▯ ▤ ⊞ ⊞ ⅋ → ▸ ⊙ ⚶ ⅃ ▨ ℞
Notes: Dogs kept on leads at all time ● ▦ ▨ ⑤

TAVERNSPITE   Map 08 SN11

▶ ▶ ▶ 76% **Pantglas Farm Caravan Park**
(SN175122)
SA34 0NS ☎ 01834 831618 ▤ 01834 831193
📧 neil.brook@btinternet.com
🌐 www.pantglasfarm.com
Dir: Leave A477 to Tenby at Red Roses x-roads onto
B4314 to Tavernspite. Take middle road at village
pumps. Site 0.5m on left
★ ⊞ £10.25-£12.50 ⊞ £10.25-£12.50 ⚑ £6-£11
Open Etr-17 Oct Booking advisable Spring bank hol
& Jul-Aug Last arrival 23.00hrs Last departure
10.30hrs
A quiet site in a rural location with pitches located
in three enclosures, and views across the rolling
countryside towards Carmarthen Bay. There is a
large activity play area for children, an indoor
games room, and a licensed bar, and the toilet
facilities are well maintained. The park is well
situated for exploring the beautiful surrounding
area and the coastline. A 10-acre site with
contd.

Wales

Facilities: ⊯ Bath ⋒ Shower ⊙ Electric Shaver ⊒ Hairdryer ⋇ Ice Pack Facility ⚵ Disabled Facilities ℓ Public Telephone
℞ Shop on Site or within 200yds ● Mobile Shop (calls at least 5 days a week) ▦ BBQ Area ⊼ Picnic Area ♈ Dog Exercise Area

86 touring pitches, 3 hardstandings.
Year round caravan weekly storage
Leisure: ❤ ⚠ **Facilities:** 🅿 ⊙ ✳ & 🛁 🌂 🐾
Services: 🔌 🗑 ♀ 🛍 ⊘ 🎁 → ∪ 🔧 🔋
Notes: Children must be supervised/controlled at all times

TENBY	Map 08 SN10

77% Kiln Park Holiday Centre (SN119002)
Marsh Rd SA70 7RB
☎ 01834 844121 📠 01834 845387
✉ gary.turner@bourneleisuregroup.co.uk
🌐 www.havenholidays.com
Dir: Follow A477/A478 to Tenby for 6m, then follow signs to Penally, park is 0.5m on left.
🚐 🚍 Å
Open mid Mar-Oct (rs mid Mar-May & Sep-Oct Some facilities may be reduced) Booking advisable school hols Last arrival 22.00hrs Last departure 10.00hrs
A large holiday complex complete with leisure and sports facilities, and plenty of entertainment for all the family. There are bars and cafés, and plenty of security. This touring, camping and static site is on the outskirts of town, with a short walk through dunes to the sandy beach. The well-equipped toilet block is very clean. A 103-acre site with 240 touring pitches and 620 statics.

contd.

Wales

Entertainment complex, bowling & putting green
Leisure: ⬨ ⬨ ⬨ ⬨ ⬨
Facilities: ⬨ ⬨ ⬨ ⬨ ⬨ ⬨ ⬨ ⬨
Services: ⬨ ⬨ ⬨ ⬨ ⬨ ⬨ → ⬨ ⬨ ⬨ ⬨ ⬨ ⬨ ⬨
Notes: No dogs in Jul & Aug ⬨ ⬨ ⬨ ⬨ ⬨

▶ ▶ ▶ ▶ **77% Trefalun (SN093027)**
Devonshire Dr, St Florence SA70 8RD
☎ 01646 651514 & 0500 655314 🖷 01646 651746
✉ trefalun@aol.com
🌐 www.trefalunpark.co.uk
Dir: 1.5m NW of St Florence & 0.5m N of B4318
★ ⬨ £10.50-£18 ⬨ £10.50-£18 ⬨ £9-£15.50
Open Etr-Oct Booking advisable bank hols & Jul-Aug Last arrival 20.00hrs Last departure noon
Set within 12 acres of sheltered, well-kept grounds, this park nestles among some of Pembrokeshire's finest scenery. This quiet country park offers well-maintained level grass pitches separated by bushes and trees, with plenty of space to relax in. Children will enjoy the enclosed play area, and can feed the park's friendly pets. Plenty of activities are available at the nearby Heatherton Country Sports Park, including go-karting, indoor bowls, golf and bumper boating. A 7-acre site with 90 touring pitches, 29 hardstandings and 10 statics.
Leisure: ⬨ **Facilities:** ⬨ ⬨ ⬨ ⬨ ⬨ ⬨ ⬨ ⬨
Services: ⬨ ⬨ ⬨ ⬨ ⬨ → ⬨ ⬨ ⬨ ⬨ ⬨ ⬨ ⬨ ⬨
⬨ ⬨ ⬨ ⬨

See advertisement on opposite page

▶ ▶ ▶ ▶ **76% Well Park Caravan & Camping Site (SN128028)**
SA70 8TL ☎ 01834 842179 🖷 01834 842179
✉ enquiries@wellparkcaravans.co.uk
🌐 www.wellparkcaravans.co.uk
Dir: Off A478 on right approx 1.5m before Tenby
★ ⬨ £10-£20 ⬨ £10-£20 ⬨ £10-£20
Open Mar-Oct (rs Mar-mid Jun & mid Sep-Oct bar, launderette, baby room may be closed) Booking advisable Spring BH & Jul-Aug Last arrival 22.00hrs Last departure 11.00hrs
A very well-run park with good landscaping from trees, ornamental shrubs, and attractive flower borders. The friendly resident owners keep the upmarket toilets clean and sparkling, and amenities include a launderette and indoor dishwashing, games room with table tennis, and an enclosed and well-equipped play area. A 10-acre site with 100 touring pitches, 14 hardstandings and 42 statics. TV hookups
Leisure: ⬨ ⬨ ⬨
Facilities: ⬨ ⬨ ⬨ ⬨ ⬨ ⬨ ⬨ ⬨
Services: ⬨ ⬨ ⬨ ⬨ ⬨ ⬨ ⬨ → ⬨ ⬨ ⬨ ⬨ ⬨ ⬨
Notes: Family parties only

Sites that take dogs may not accept all breeds. Check at the time of booking that your dog will be welcome.

▶ ▶ ▶ **74% Wood Park Caravans (SN128025)**
New Hedges SA70 8TL ☎ 0845 129 8314
✉ info@woodpark.co.uk
🌐 www.woodpark.co.uk
Dir: At rdbt 2m N of Tenby follow A478 towards Tenby, then take 2nd right & right again
★ ⬨ £9-£18 ⬨ £9-£18 ⬨ £9-£14
Open Spring BH-Sep (rs Etr-Spring BH & Sep-Oct bar & launderette may not open) Booking advisable Spring BH & Jul-Aug Last arrival 22.00hrs Last departure 10.00hrs
Nestling in beautiful countryside between the popular seaside resorts of Tenby and Saundersfoot, and with Waterwynch Bay just a 15-minute walk away. This peaceful site provides a spacious and relaxing atmosphere for holidays. The slightly sloping touring area is partly divided by shrubs into three paddocks. A 10-acre site with 60 touring pitches and 90 statics.
Leisure: ⬨ ⬨
Facilities: ⬨ ⬨ ⬨ ⬨ ⬨ ⬨ ⬨
Services: ⬨ ⬨ ⬨ ⬨ ⬨ ⬨ ⬨ → ⬨ ⬨ ⬨ ⬨ ⬨ ⬨
Notes: 1 car per unit only, only small dogs accepted, no dogs Jul-Aug & Bank Hols

POWYS

BRECON   Map 09 SO02

▶ ▶ ▶ ▶ **83% Brynich Caravan Park (SO069278)**
Brynich LD3 7SH ☎ 01874 623325
🖷 01874 623325
✉ holidays@brynich.co.uk
🌐 www.brynich.co.uk
Dir: 2km E of Brecon on A470, 200mtrs from junct with A40
★ ⬨ £13-£18 ⬨ £13-£18 ⬨ £4-£13
Open 20 Mar-29 Oct Booking advisable bank & school hols Last arrival 20.00hrs Last departure noon
A very attractive and well-appointed site with commanding views of the Brecon Beacons. Colourful flower beds create a lovely display in the grounds, and a well-stocked shop is very popular. A superb restaurant/bar in a 17th-century barn, and a large soft indoor play area and outdoor boules pitch have considerably enhanced the facilities. A 20-minute walk along the canal towpath leads into the charming market town of Brecon. A 20-acre site with 130 touring pitches, 35 hardstandings. Adventure playground, indoor play area, off-licence
Leisure: ⬨
Facilities: ⬨ ⬨ ⬨ ⬨ ⬨ ⬨ ⬨ ⬨ ⬨ ⬨
Services: ⬨ ⬨ ⬨ ⬨ ⬨ ⬨ ⬨ ⬨ ⬨ → ⬨ ⬨ ⬨ ⬨ ⬨
Notes: No rollerskates, skateboards, or motorized scooters. Only environmentally friendly ground sheets
⬨ ⬨ ⬨ ⬨ ⬨

Wales

The Best of British TOURING AND HOLIDAY PARKS

Pencelli Castle Caravan & Camping Park

Peacefully set at the foothills of the Brecon Beacons and within walking distance of the highest peaks. Adjoining Brecon Canal and the Taff Cycle Trail. Village pub 150 yards. Shop, drying room, hardstandings, serviced pitches, and luxurious shower block. Also red deer, ducks, vintage farm machinery & children's playarea. On bus route. Open all year. Assistance dogs only.

- 2006 AA - Best Campsite in Wales
- 2005, 03 & 02 Loo of the Year - Winner Best Caravan Park in Wales
- 2005, 04, 03 & 02 Practical Caravan - The Top 100 Family Park in Wales
- 2004 Wales in Bloom - Winner Caravan & Holiday Parks
- 2003 National Tourism Awards - Best Place to Stay in Wales, self catering
- 2003 Loo of the Year - Overall National Winner Wales
- 2005, 04, 03 , 02 & 01 Gold - David Bellamy Conservation Award
- 2002 AA - Best Campsite in Wales
- 2001 Calor Gas - Best Park in Wales

Pencelli • Brecon • Powys Wales • LD3 7LX • Tel: 01874 665 451
Email: AA@pencelli-castle.co.uk   www.pencelli-castle.co.uk

AA Campsite of the Year for Wales 2006

▶ ▶ ▶ ▶ **92%** *Pencelli Castle*
Caravan & Camping Park (SO096248)
Pencelli LD3 7LX ☎ 01874 665451
🖷 01874 665452
🌐 aa@pencelli-castle.co.uk
🌐 www.pencelli-castle.co.uk
Dir: Turn off A40 2m E of Brecon onto B4558, follow signs to Pencelli
🚐 🚐 Å

Open all year Booking advisable bank & school hols
Last arrival 22.00hrs Last departure noon
Lying in the heart of the Brecon Beacons National Park, this charming park offers peace, beautiful scenery and high quality facilities. The park is bordered by the Brecon and Monmouth Canal. Attention to detail is superb, and the well-equipped heated toilets with en suite cubicles are matched by a drying room for clothes and boots, full laundry, and shop. A 10-acre site with 80 touring pitches, 40 hardstandings.
Bike hire
Leisure: ∆ Facilities: 🌂⊙🔧✳&📞🔥
Services: 🖂🔌🍴🍷⏢🎱→∪🔫 ♪ Notes: ❀ No radios or music 💳 💳 💳 💳 💳

▶ ▶ ▶ **74%** *Bishops Meadow Caravan Park*
(SO060300)
Bishops Meadow, Hay Rd LD3 9SW
☎ 01874 610000 🖷 01874 614922
🌐 enquiries@bishops-meadow.co.uk
Dir: From A470 take B4602. Site on right
🚐 🚐 Å

Bishops Meadow Caravan Park
Open Mar-Oct Booking advisable BH's
A rural park close to the Brecon Beacons and with spectacular views. The family-owned and run park offers a heated outdoor swimming pool, an adjacent all-day restaurant, and a lounge bar open in the evenings. Facilities are very well kept, and the town is about one mile away. A new amenity block was completed in 2005. A 3.5-acre site with 82 touring pitches, 24 hardstandings.
Leisure: 🏊 🎱 ∆ Facilities: 🌂🌂⊙✳&📞🔥
Services: 🖂🔌🍴🍷⏢🎱✕🍷→∪▶🔫🎱♪🎱
💳 💳 💳 💳 💳 💳

BRONLLYS   **Map 09 SO13**

▶ ▶ ▶ **75% Anchorage Caravan Park (SO142351)**
LD3 0LD ☎ 01874 711246 & 711230 🖷 01874 711711
🌐 www.ukparks.co.uk/anchorage
Dir: 8m NE of Brecon on A438, in Bronllys
★ 🚐 fr £10 🚐 fr £10 Å fr £10
Open all year (rs Nov-Mar TV room closed) Booking advisable BH's & Aug Last arrival 23.00hrs Last departure 18.00hrs
A well-maintained site with a choice of south-facing, sloping grass pitches and superb views of the Black Mountains, or a more sheltered lower area with a number of excellent super pitches. The site is a short distance from the water sports centre at Llangorse Lake. An 8-acre site with 110 touring pitches, 8 hardstandings and 101 statics.
Baby bath room, post office & hairdressers
Leisure: 🏊🎱 Facilities: 🌂🌂⊙🔧✳&📞🔥🌂
Services: 🖂⏢🍴🍷⏢→∪🔫

BUILTH WELLS   **Map 09 SO05**

▶ ▶ ▶ **73% Fforest Fields Caravan & Camping Park (SO100535)**
Hundred House LD1 5RT ☎ 01982 570406
🌐 office@fforestfields.co.uk
🌐 www.fforestfields.co.uk
Dir: From town follow New Radnor signs on A481. 4m signed entrance on right, 0.5m before Hundred House village
🚐 🚐 Å

Open Etr & Apr-Oct (rs Nov-Mar toilets & showers closed) Booking advisable BH's & Jul-Aug Last arrival 21.00hrs Last departure 18.00hrs
A sheltered park in a hidden valley with wonderful views and plenty of wildlife. Set in unspoilt countryside, this is a peaceful park with delightful

contd.

contd.

Fforest Fields Caravan & Camping Park
hill walks beginning on site. The historic town of Builth Wells and the Royal Welsh Showground are only 4 miles away, and there are plenty of outdoor activities in the vicinity. A 7-acre site with 60 touring pitches, 15 hardstandings.
Woodland, streams and ponds

Facilities: ⚘ ⊙ ◲ ✳ ⌂ 🛒 ♈

Services: 🖥 🖩 🅰 🖉 🗉 ⌨ ↦ ▸ ♨ ◢ ✎

CHURCHSTOKE   Map 15 SO29

▶ ▶ ▶ **77% Mellington Hall Caravan Park (SO257920)**
Mellington SY15 6HX ☎ 01588 620011
🖷 01588 620853
🅴 info@mellingtonhallcaravanpark.co.uk
🅦 www.mellingtonhallcaravanpark.co.uk
Dir: Leave A489 1.5m W of Churchstoke turn onto B4385 to Mellington
★ 🚐 fr £15 🚙 fr £15 ⛺ fr £5

Open all year Booking advisable BH's Last arrival 20.00hrs
A small touring park set a mile down a wooded private drive in the grounds of Mellington Hall Hotel, with its attractive bistro. The 270 acres of

park and farmland guarantee peace and seclusion, and there is plenty of wildlife and thousands of rare trees. Offa's Dyke footpath runs through the grounds, and this park is ideal for walking, cycling and fishing. A 4-acre site with 40 touring pitches, 40 hardstandings and 95 statics.
Fishing pool, hiking maps

Leisure: ⚿   **Facilities:** ⚘ ⊙ ◲ ⅃ ↄ ♈ ⌂ ♈
Services: 🖥 🖩 ⚲ 🅰 ✕ ↦ ⌨ ◢ ✎
Notes: No cars by caravans or tents

▶ ▶ **74% Bacheldre Watermill Touring & Camping Park (SO243928)**
Bacheldre Watermill SY15 6TE ☎ 01588 620489
🖷 01588 620105
🅴 info@bacheldremill.co.uk
🅦 www.bacheldremill.co.uk
Dir: Turn S off A489, 2m W of Churchstoke, site on right
🚐 🚙 ⛺
Open all year Booking advisable bank hols/summer Last departure noon
A secluded little park in the grounds of an 18th-century working watermill on the border of Wales and Shropshire. Tours of the mill can be arranged. A 2-acre site with 25 touring pitches.

Facilities: ⚘ ⊙ ✳ ✎
Services: 🖥 ↦ ⌨ ◢ 🖩

CRICKHOWELL   Map 09 SO21

▶ ▶ ▶ **73% Riverside Caravan & Camping Park (SO215184)**
New Rd NP8 1AY ☎ 01873 810397
Dir: On A4077, well signed from A40
★ 🚐 fr £12 🚙 fr £12 ⛺ fr £9
Open Mar-Oct Booking advisable for stays over 1 wk Last arrival 22.00hrs
A very well tended adults-only park in delightful countryside on the edge of the small country town of Crickhowell. The adjacent riverside park is an excellent facility for all, including dog-walkers. Crickhowell has numerous specialist shops including a first-class delicatessen. Within a few minutes walk from the park are several friendly pubs with good restaurants. A 3.5-acre site with 35 touring pitches and 20 statics.

Facilities: ⚘ ⊙ ✳ ↄ ✎
Services: 🖥 🅰 🖉 🗉 ↦ ⌨ ▸ ✕
Notes: Adults only, no hangliders or paragliders

LLANBRYNMAIR   Map 14 SH80

▶ ▶ ▶ **79% Cringoed Caravan Park (SO887015)**
The Birches SY19 7DR
☎ 01650 521237 🖷 01650 521237
🅴 cringoedcaravan.park@virgin.net
Dir: Off A470 onto B4518, park 1.25m on right
★ 🚐 £10-£16 🚙 £10-£16 ⛺ £8-£12
Open 7 Mar-7 Jan Booking advisable BH's Last arrival 22.00hrs Last departure noon
On the banks of the River Twymyn, a family-run park set amongst beautiful hillside and open scenery just 30 minutes drive from the coastal

contd.   *contd.*

Wales

Facilities: ↔ Bath ⚘ Shower ⊙ Electric Shaver ◲ Hairdryer ✳ Ice Pack Facility ↄ Disabled Facilities ☎ Public Telephone
✎ Shop on Site or within 200yds 🗉 Mobile Shop (calls at least 5 days a week) ⌂ BBQ Area ♈ Picnic Area 🐾 Dog Exercise Area

resort of Aberdovey. An ideal location for touring the many local attractions, and with bright, well-maintained toilet facilities. A 20-acre site with 35 touring pitches, 4 hardstandings and 31 statics.

Leisure: ◣ /瓜 Facilities: 🀄🀄✲🀄🀄
Services: 🀄🀄🀄🀄→🀄🀄🀄🀄

LLANDRINDOD WELLS   Map 09 SO06

▶ ▶ ▶ 76% **Disserth Caravan & Camping Park (SO035583)**
Disserth, Howey LD1 6NL
☎ 01597 860277 🗎 01597 860147
🅔 m.hobbs@virgin.net
🅦 www.disserth.com
Dir: 1m off A483, between Howey & Newbridge on Wye, by 13th-century church
★ 🀄 £8.50-£13 🀄 £8.50-£13 ▲ £8.50-£13
Open Mar-Oct Booking advisable BH's & Royal Welsh Show Last arrival 22.00hrs Last departure noon
A delightful, secluded little park nestling in a beautiful valley on the banks of the River Ithon, a tributary of the River Wye. The park is next to a 13th-century church, and has a small bar and bistro. The chalet toilet block offers spacious cubicles containing shower, wash-hand basin and WC. A 4-acre site with 35 touring pitches and 20 statics. Private trout fishing.

Facilities: 🀄☉🀄✲🀄🀄🀄🀄
Services: 🀄🀄🀄🀄🀄🀄→🀄▶🀄🀄

▶ ▶ 81% **Dalmore Camping & Caravanning Park (SO045568)**
Howey LD1 5RG ☎ 01597 822483 🗎 01597 822483
Dir: 3m S of Llandrindod Wells off A483. 4m N of Builth Wells, at top of the hill.
★ 🀄 £7-£10 🀄 £7-£10 ▲ £7-£10
Open Mar-Oct Booking advisable Jun-Aug Last arrival 22.00hrs Last departure noon
An intimate, and well laid out adults-only park. Pitches are attractively terraced to ensure that all enjoy the wonderful views from this splendidly landscaped little park. Dogs are not allowed. A 3-acre site with 20 touring pitches, 9 hardstandings and 20 statics.

Facilities: 🀄☉🀄✲🀄🀄🀄
Services: 🀄🀄🀄🀄→▶☉🀄🀄🀄🀄🀄
Notes: ⚘ Adults only

LLANGORS   Map 09 SO12

▶ ▶ ▶ 71% **Lakeside Caravan Park (SO128272)**
LD3 7TR ☎ 01874 658226 🗎 01874 658430
🅔 holidays@lakeside.zx3.net
🅦 www.lakeside-holidays.net
Dir: Leave A40 at Bwlch onto B4560 towards Talgarth. Site signed towards lake in Llangors centre
★ 🀄 £8-£10 🀄 £8-£10 ▲ £8-£10
Open Jun-Sep (rs Mar-May & Oct Clubhouse, restaurant, shop limited) Booking advisable Etr, May wk, summer school hols Last arrival 21.30hrs Last departure 10.00hrs

contd.

Next to Llangorse common and lake, this attractive park has launching and mooring facilities and is an ideal centre for water sports enthusiasts. Popular with families, and offering a clubhouse/bar, with a well-stocked shop and café/takeaway next door. Boats and windsurf equipment can be hired on site. A 2-acre site with 40 touring pitches and 72 statics. Boat & bike hire, windsurfing & fishing from boats

Leisure: ◣ /瓜
Facilities: 🀄☉🀄✲🀄🀄🀄🀄🀄
Services: 🀄🀄🀄🀄🀄🀄🀄✕🀄→🀄🀄🀄🀄
🀄 🀄 🀄 🀄 🀄

MIDDLETOWN   Map 15 SJ31

▶ ▶ ▶ 76% **Bank Farm Caravan Park (SJ293123)**
SY21 8EJ ☎ 01938 570526
🅔 gill@bankfarmcaravans.fsnet.co.uk
🅦 www.bankfarmcaravans.co.uk
Dir: 13m W of Shrewsbury, 5m E of Welshpool on A458
★ 🀄 fr £10 🀄 fr £10 ▲ fr £8
Open Mar-Oct Booking advisable BH's Last arrival 20.00hrs
An attractive park on a small farm, maintained to a high standard. There are two touring areas, one on either side of the A458, and each with its own amenity block, and immediate access to hills, mountains and woodland. A pub serving good food, and a large play area are nearby. A 2-acre site with 35 touring pitches and 33 statics. Coarse fishing pool, jacuzzi

Leisure: ◣ /瓜
Facilities: 🀄☉✲🀄🀄🀄
Services: 🀄🀄🀄→▶🀄🀄

PRESTEIGNE   Map 09 SO36

▶ ▶ ▶ 72% **Rockbridge Park (SO294654)**
LD8 2NF ☎ 01547 560300 🗎 01547 560300
🅔 dustinrockbridge@hotmail.com
Dir: 1m W of Presteigne off B4356
★ 🀄 £10-£12 🀄 £10-£11 ▲ £8-£10
Open Apr-Oct Booking advisable public & school hols Last arrival 21.30hrs Last departure noon
A pretty little park set in meadowland with trees and shrubs along the banks of the River Lugg. A bridge across the stream gives good access to nearby footpaths. Facilities are very well maintained, and the owner is friendly and helpful. Dogs are not allowed on site. A 3-acre site with 35 touring pitches and 30 statics.

Facilities: 🀄☉✲🀄🀄
Services: 🀄🀄🀄🀄→▶🀄🀄
Notes: ⚘

Always take your wellies, no matter how dry the weather seems. Early morning grass is soaking wet!

Wales

RHAYADER   Map 09 SN96

▶ ▶ ▶ 75% **Wyeside Caravan & Camping Park**
(SO967686)
Llangurig Rd LD6 5LB ☎ 01597 810183
🄴 info@wyesidecamping.co.uk
🅆 www.wyesidecamping.cu.uk
Dir: 400mtrs N of Rhayader town centre on A470
★ 🚐 £10-£12 🚍 £10-£12 ▲ £10
Open Mar-Oct Booking advisable Bank & school
hols Last arrival 22.30hrs Last departure noon
*With direct access from the A470, the park nestles
on the banks of the River Wye. Just 400 metres
away is the centre of this market town, and the site
is next to a recreation park with tennis courts,
bowling green and children's playground. There are
good riverside walks from here. A 6-acre site with
140 touring pitches and 39 statics.*

Facilities: 🅟 🏧 🤸 🍴 🦮 🍺
Services: 🔌 🍴 🛄 🖨 🍦 ⊕ ◎ 🛢 🍴 🛒
💳 💳 💳 💳

SWANSEA

PONTARDDULAIS   Map 08 SN50

▶ ▶ ▶ 77% **River View Touring Park**
(SN578086)
The Dingle, Llanedi SA4 1FH
☎ 01269 844876 📠 01269 832076
🄴 info@riverviewtouringpark.com
🅆 www.riverviewtouringpark.com
*Dir: From M4 junct 49 take A483 signed Llandeilo. 0.5m,
1st left after lay-by, follow lane to site*
★ 🚐 £10-£13 🚍 £10-£13 ▲ £10-£13
Open Mar-3 Jan Booking advisable at all times Last
arrival 20.00hrs Last departure noon
*This peaceful park is set on two levels in a sheltered
valley with an abundance of wild flowers and
wildlife. The River Gwli flows around the bottom of
the park in which fishing for brown trout is possible.
A new facility block was built in 2005, and the top
level of the park has also been developed. It is
ideally situated for visiting the beaches of South
Wales, The Black Mountains and the Brecon
Beacons. A 6-acre site with 60 touring pitches,
20 hardstandings.*
Outdoor activities organised, tourist info

Facilities: 🅟 ☉ 🏧 ✳ 🦮 🍺
Services: 🔌 → ⊕ ▶ 🛒 🛢 🔘
Notes: Dogs must be kept on leads

PORT EINON   Map 08 SS48

▶ ▶ ▶ 71% **Carreglwyd Camping & Caravan Park**
(SS465863)
SA3 1NN ☎ 01792 390795 📠 01792 390796
Dir: Follow A4118 to Port Einon, site adjacent to beach
🚐 🚍 ▲
Open Mar-Dec Booking advisable Jul/Aug, Etr, BH's
Last arrival 18.00hrs Last departure 16.00hrs
*Set in an unrivalled location alongside the safe
sandy beach of Port Einon on the Gower Peninsula,
this popular park is an ideal family holiday spot.*
contd.

*Close to an attractive village with pubs and shops,
most pitches offer sea views. The sloping ground
has been partly terraced, and facilities are provided
by two toilet blocks which might be stretched
during busy periods. A 12-acre site with 150 touring
pitches.*

Facilities: 🅟 ☉ 🤸 🛒 🍺
Services: 🔌 🍴 🛢 🛄 🍦 🖨 → ⊕ 🛢 🛒
Notes: Dogs must be kept on leads at all times
💳 💳 💳 💳 💳 💳 💳

RHOSSILI   Map 08 SS48

▶ ▶ ▶ 72% **Pitton Cross Caravan & Camping Park**
(SS434877)
SA3 1PH ☎ 01792 390593 📠 01792 391010
🄴 enquiries@pittoncross.co.uk
🅆 www.pittoncross.co.uk
Dir: 2m W of Scurlage on B4247
★ 🚐 £10-£17.95 🚍 £10-£17.95 ▲ £10-£17.95

Open Feb-Nov Booking advisable Spring BH & Jul-
Aug Last arrival 20.00hrs Last departure 11.00hrs
*Surrounded by farmland close to sandy Menslade
Bay, which is within walking distance across the
fields. This grassy park is divided by hedging into
paddocks. Nearby Rhossili Beach is popular with
surfers. A 6-acre site with 100 touring pitches,
16 hardstandings.*
Motor caravan service bay & baby bath

Leisure: 🎢 **Facilities:** 🅟 ☉ 🏧 ✳ 🤸 🦮 🛒 🍺
Services: 🔌 🍴 🛢 🛄 🍦 🖨 🖊 → ⊕ ▶ 🛢
Notes: Dogs must be kept on leads, quiet at all
times. 💳 💳 💳 💳 💳

SWANSEA   Map 09 SS69

66% **Riverside Caravan Park**
(SS679991)
Ynys Forgan Farm, Morriston SA6 6QL
☎ 01792 775587 📠 01792 775587
🅆 www.riversideswansea.com
*Dir: Leave M4 junct 45 towards Swansea, and turn
left into private road signed to park*
🚐 🚍 ▲
Open all year (rs winter months pool & club
closed) Booking advisable bank & main school
hols Last arrival mdnt Last departure noon
*A large and busy park close to the M4 but in a
quiet location beside the River Taw. This friendly
family orientated park has a licensed club and
bar with a full high-season entertainment
programme. There is a choice of eating outlets*
contd.

Wales

Wales

with the clubhouse restaurant, takeaway or chip shop. The park has a good indoor pool. It makes a good base for touring Mumbles and Gower beaches. A 5-acre site with 90 touring pitches and 256 statics.
Fishing on site by arrangement.
Leisure: ⚲ ⚓ ⚏ ☐
Facilities: ⚑⊙⚲⚒⚹⚖⚘⚌⚊⚏
Services: ⚑⚏⚐⚲⚹⚘⚏⚐ ⚌→∪⚐⚌⚙⚏⚍
Notes: Dogs by arrangement only (no aggressive dog breeds permitted) ⚏ ⚏ ⚏ ⚏ ⚏

VALE OF GLAMORGAN

LLANTWIT MAJOR   Map 09 SS96

▶ ▶ ▶ 78% **Acorn Camping & Caravan Site** (SS973678)
Ham Ln South CF61 1RP
☎ 01446 794024 📠 01446 794024
🅔 info@acorncamping.co.uk
🆆 www.acorncamping.co.uk
Dir: B4265 to Llantwit Major following camping signs. Approach site through Ham Manor residential park
★ ⚏ £7.50-£8.50 ⚏ £7.50-£8.50 ⚏ £7.50-£8.50
Open Feb-8 Dec Booking advisable BH's, school holidays Last arrival 22.00hrs Last departure noon
A peaceful country site in level meadowland, with some individual pitches divided by hedges and shrubs. About 1 mile from the beach, which can be approached by a clifftop walk, and the same distance from the historic town of Llantwit Major. A new internet station provide 20minutes' use for £1, and there's an excellent full size snooker table in a separate room. A 4.5-acre site with 90 touring pitches, 10 hardstandings and 15 statics.
Internet access
Leisure: ⚓ ⚏ **Facilities:** ⚑⊙⚲⚹⚖⚘⚊
Services: ⚑⚲⚹⚏⚐ ⚌→∪⚍
Notes: No noise 23.00-07.00hrs
⚏ ⚏ ⚏ ⚏ ⚏

▶ ▶ ▶ 77% *Llandow Touring Caravan Park* (SS956713)
CF7 7PB ☎ 01446 794527
🅔 enquiries@llandow.co.uk
🆆 www.llandowcaravanpark.com
Dir: Signed off B4270
⚏ ⚏ ⚏
Open Feb-Nov Booking advisable bank hols & end Jun-Aug Last arrival 10.00hrs Last departure noon
An open park surrounded by high shrubbed banks and trees, located midway between the historic town of Llantwit Major and the quaint market town of Cowbridge. Glamorgan's Heritage Coast is just three miles away. A 6-acre site with 100 touring pitches, 30 hardstandings.
Caravan storage
Leisure: ⚏
Facilities: ⚑⊙⚲⚹⚘⚊⚏⚍
Services: ⚑⚐⚲⚹⚏⚐→∪⚍
⚏ ⚏ ⚏ ⚏ ⚏

WREXHAM

EYTON   Map 15 SJ34

PREMIER PARK

▶ ▶ ▶ ▶ ▶ 86% **The Plassey Leisure Park** (SJ353452)
The Plassey LL13 0SP
☎ 01978 780277 📠 01978 780019
🅔 enquiries@theplassey.co.uk
🆆 www.theplassey.co.uk
Dir: Leave A483 at Bangor-on-Dee exit, onto B5426 for 2.5m. Park entrance signed on left
⚏ £11-£19.50 ⚏ £11-£19.50 ⚏ £11-£19.50

Open Mar-Oct Booking advisable wknds, bank & school hols Last arrival 21.00hrs Last departure 18.00hrs
A lovely park set in several hundred acres of quiet farm and meadowland in the Dee Valley. The superb toilet facilities include individual cubicles for total privacy and security, while the Edwardian farm buildings have been converted into a restaurant, coffee shop, beauty studio, and various craft outlets. There is plenty here to entertain the whole family, from scenic walks and swimming pool to free fishing, and use of the 9-hole golf course. A 10-acre site with 110 touring pitches, 45 hardstandings.
Sauna, badminton, fishing & 9-hole golf
Leisure: ⚲ ⚓ ⚏
Facilities: ⚑⊙⚲⚹⚖⚘⚊⚏⚌⚍
Services: ⚑⚏⚐⚲⚹⚘⚏⚐✕ ⚌→∪⚐◎⚙⚍
Notes: No footballs, bikes or skateboards, dogs must be kept on leads ⚏ ⚏ ⚏ ⚏ ⚏

See advertisement on opposite page

All of the campsites in this directory are inspected annually by a team of experienced inspectors

Remember that prices and opening times are liable to change within the currency of this guide. It is always best to telephone in advance.

THE PERCENTAGE RATING
FOR ALL PARKS RANGES FROM
50% - 100%.

An increasing number of parks do
not accept children. There is a list of
adult-only sites on page 19.

Campsites in popular areas get very
crowded at busy times – it is advisable
to book well in advance.

Don't forget matches, a torch and
spare batteries, and the means to make
a drink. Packet soups are sustaining until
the shops open.

**For full details of the AA pennant
ratings scheme see pages 7-8**

Wales

Facilities: ➥ Bath 🚿 Shower ☺ Electric Shaver ✄ Hairdryer ✳ Ice Pack Facility ♿ Disabled Facilities 📞 Public Telephone
🛒 Shop on Site or within 200yds 📧 Mobile Shop (calls at least 5 days a week) ⊞ BBQ Area 🎋 Picnic Area 🐕 Dog Exercise Area

Ireland

NORTHERN IRELAND
CO ANTRIM

ANTRIM   Map 01 D5

▶ ▶ ▶ 68% **Sixmilewater Caravan Park**
Lough Rd BT41 4DQ ☎ 028 9446 4963
🖥 028 9446 2968
🌐 info@antrim.gov.uk
*Dir: 1m from town centre, follow signs for Antrim
Forum/Loughshore Park. On Dublin road take turn for
Lough road, passing Antrim Forum on right. Park at end
of Lough Rd*
★ ⚘ £11.50-£13 ⚘ £11.50-£13 ▲ £8-£10
Open Etr-Sep Booking advisable all dates Last
arrival 21.00hrs Last departure noon
*A pretty tree-lined site in a large municipal park,
within walking distance of Antrim and the Antrim
Forum leisure complex yet very much in the
countryside. The modern toilet block is well
equipped, and other facilities include a laundry and
electric hook-ups. A 9.75-acre site with 42 touring
pitches, 18 hardstandings.*
Watersport, angling stands & launching facilities
Leisure: ◖ 🖵
Facilities: �🖿 ⊙ ⦦ ὣ ⅃ 盫 ☵
Services: ⦿ 🖥 ✕ ᵜ → ▶ 🛆 ❤ ⅃ 🛢
Notes: Max stay 7 nights, no noise between 22.00 -
08.00hrs, dogs must be kept under control and on a
lead

BALLYMONEY   Map 01 C6

▶ ▶ ▶ ▶ 70% **Drumaheglis Marina &
Caravan Park**
36 Glenstall Rd BT53 7QN ☎ 028 2766 6466
& 2766 0227 🖥 028 2766 7659
🌐 helen.neill@ballymoney.gov.uk
🌐 www.ballymoney.gov.uk
*Dir: Signed off A26, approx 1.5m outside Ballymoney
towards Coleraine, off B66 S of Ballymoney*
★ ⚘ fr £14.50 ⚘ fr £14.50 ▲ fr £10.50
Open 17 Mar-Oct Booking advisable BH's &
summer months Last arrival 20.00hrs Last
departure 13.00hrs
*Exceptionally well-designed and laid out park
beside the Lower Bann River, with very spacious
pitches and two quality toilet blocks. Ideal base for
touring Antrim or for water sports enthusiasts.
A 16-acre site with 55 touring pitches, 55
hardstandings.*
Marina berthing, table tennis
Leisure: ⚠
Facilities: �🖿 ⊙ ⦦ ✳ ᵜ ὣ 盫 ⅃ ☵
Services: ⦿ ᵜ → ▶ 🛆 ⅃ 🖥 🛢
Notes: Dogs must be kept on lead 🖼 🖼

BUSHMILLS   Map 01 C6

▶ ▶ ▶ ▶ 88% **Ballyness Caravan Park**
40 Castlecatt Rd BT57 8TN
☎ 028 2073 2393 🖥 028 2073 2713
🌐 info@ballynesscaravanpark.com
🌐 www.ballynesscaravanpark.com
Dir: 0.5m S of Bushmills on B66, follow signs.
★ ⚘ fr £15 ⚘ fr £15 ▲ fr £10
Open 17 Mar-Oct Booking advisable Jun-Aug & Etr
Last arrival 21.00hrs Last departure noon
*A quality park with superb toilet and other facilities,
on farmland beside St Columb's Rill, the stream
that supplies the famous nearby Bushmills
distillery. The friendly owners built this park with
the discerning camper in mind. There is a pleasant
walk around several ponds, and the park is
peacefully located close to the beautiful north
Antrim coast. A 16-acre site with 36 touring pitches,
30 hardstandings and 50 statics.*
Leisure: ⚠
Facilities: ᵜ 🖿 ⊙ ⦦ ✳ 🛆 ◖ ☵
Services: ⦿ ⅃ 🖥 🖙 ⌀ 🖥 🖽 ᵜ → ▶ ⅃ 🛢 🖼 🖼 🖼 🖼 🖼

CUSHENDALL   Map 01 D6

▶ ▶ 72% *Cushendall Caravan Camp*
62 Coast Rd BT44 0QW ☎ 028 2177 1699
*Dir: On A2, 1m S of town, start of main coast road by
lifeboat station*
⚘ ⚘ ▲
Open mid Mar-mid Oct Booking advisable peak
periods Last arrival 21.00hrs Last departure
14.00hrs
*A pleasant site next to the beach and sailing club,
on a spectacular stretch of the north Antrim coast.
All touring pitches are fully serviced on
hardstandings. A 1-acre site with 26 touring pitches,
5 hardstandings and 64 statics.*
Facilities: 🖿 ⊙ ⦦ ◖ ☵ 盫 ⅃
Services: 🖥 → ∪ ▶ ⊚ 🛆 ✕ ⅃ **Notes:** Dogs must be
kept on a lead

CUSHENDUN   Map 01 D6

▶ ▶ ▶ 74% **Cushendun Caravan Park**
14 Glendun Rd BT44 0PX ☎ 028 2176 1254
*Dir: From A2 take B92 for 1m towards Glenarm, clearly
signed*
★ ⚘ £15.50-£17.50 ⚘ £15.50-£17.50 ▲ £7.50-£11.50
Open Etr-Sep Booking advisable Jul-Aug Last
arrival 22.00hrs Last departure 12.30hrs
*A pretty little grassy park surrounded by trees, with
separate secluded areas offering some privacy, and
static vans discreetly interspersed with tourers. The
beautiful north Antrim coast is a short drive away
through scenic countryside. A 3-acre site with
12 touring pitches and 64 statics.*
Leisure: ◖ 🖵
Facilities: ᵜ 🖿 ⊙ ⦦ ◖ ☵
Services: ⦿ 🖥 → ∪ ▶ ⊚ ✕ ⅃ 🖼 🖼 🖼 🖼 🖼

(vertical text) Ireland

LARNE   Map 01 D5

▶ ▶ ▶ **60% Curran Court Caravan Park**
131 Curran Rd BT40 1BD ☎ 028 2827 3797
🗎 028 2826 0096
*Dir: Site on A2, 0.25m from ferry. From town centre
follow signs for Leisure Centre, opposite Curran Court
Hotel*
★ 🚐 £11-£12 🚍 £11-£12 Å £5-£6
Open Apr-Sep Booking advisable main season
*A handy site for the ferry. When the reception is
closed, the owners can be contacted at the Curran
Court Hotel across the road. A 3-acre site with 30
touring pitches.*
Bowling & putting greens
Leisure: 🅰 Facilities: 🖪 🕭 🕻 🖳 🖬 🕱 🚡
Services: 🖭 🗟 🖉 ✕ → 🕨 ◉ ↳ 🛒 🗡
🖭 💳 🖼 ⓓ 🖲 🖼 🗟

CO BELFAST

DUNDONALD   Map 01 D5

▶ ▶ ▶ **71% Dundonald Touring Caravan Park**
111 Old Dundonald Rd BT16 1XT ☎ 028 9080 9100
& 9080 9101 🗎 028 9048 9604
🅔 sales@castlereagh.gov.uk
🕸 www.theicebowl.com
*Dir: From Belfast city centre follow M3 & A20 to City
Airport. Then A20 to Newtownards & follow signs to
Dundonald & Ulster Hospital. At hospital turn right at
sign for Dundonald Ice Bowl. Follow road to end, then
turn right, Ice Bowl on left*
★ 🚐 fr £16 🚍 fr £16 Å fr £9
Open Apr-Sep (rs Oct-Mar Open on request)

Booking advisable Jul-Aug Last arrival 23.00hrs Last
departure noon
*A purpose-built park in a quiet corner of Dundonald
Leisure Park on the outskirts of Belfast. This
peaceful park is ideally located for touring County
Down, and exploring the capital. A 1.5-acre site with
22 touring pitches, 22 hardstandings.*
Discount at ice rink, bowling, indoor play area
Leisure: 🅰 Facilities: 🖪 ◉ 🕽 ✳ 🕭 🕻 🖳 🖬 🖾
Services: 🖭 🍴 🖮 🛒 → 🕨 🕨 ◉ 🛒 🗡 🗟
Notes: Dogs must be kept on a lead 🖭 🖼 🖾 🗟

CO DOWN

CASTLEWELLAN   Map 01 D5

▶ ▶ ▶ **78% Castlewellan Forest Park**
BT31 9BU ☎ 028 4377 8664 🗎 028 4377 1762
🕸 www.forestserviceni.gov.uk
*Dir: Off A25, in Castlewellan turn right at Upper Square,
turn into Forest Park, signed*
★ 🚐 £9-£14.50 🚍 £9-£14.50 Å £9-£14.50
Open Etr-Oct Booking advisable Etr-Oct Last arrival
20.00hrs Last departure 15.00hrs
*Attractive forest park site, situated down a long
drive with views of the castle. The site is broken up
into smaller areas by mature trees and shrubs. A 5-
acre site with 140 touring pitches, 45 hardstandings.*
Facilities: 🖪 ◉ 🕭 🕻 🖳 🖬 🖾
Services: 🖭 ✕ → 🕨 🕨 ◉ 🛒 🗡 🗟
Notes: No open fires, dogs must be on leads

KILLYLEAGH   Map 01 D5

▶ ▶ ▶ **85% Camping & Caravanning
Club Site**
Delamont Country Park,
Downpatrick Rd BT30 9TZ ☎ 028 4482 1833
🕸 www.campingandcaravanningclub.co.uk
*Dir: From Belfast take A22. Site 1m S of Killyleagh and
4m N of Downpatrick*
★ 🚐 £13.60-£17.80 🚍 £13.60-£17.80 Å £13.60-£17.80
Open Mar-Oct Booking advisable BH's & peak
period Last arrival 21.00hrs Last departure noon
*A spacious park enjoying superb views and walks,
in a lovely and interesting part of the province. The
facilities are of a very high order, and include fully-
serviced pitches and excellent toilets. The site is
close to Strangford Loch Marine Water reserve, a
medieval fairy fort, and a blue flag beach. Please
see the advertisement on page 11 for information
on Club sites and membership. A 4.5-acre site with
63 touring pitches, 63 hardstandings.*
Facilities: 🖪 ◉ 🕽 ✳ 🕭 🕻 🖬
Services: 🖭 🗟 🛢 🖉 🖽 🕠 → 🕨 🛒 🗡 🖳
🖭 🖼 🖾 🗟

NEWCASTLE   Map 01 D5

▶ ▶ ▶ **82% Tollymore Forest Park**
Bryansford Rd BT33 0PW ☎ 028 4372 2428
🗎 028 4377 1762
🕸 www.forestserviceni.gov.uk
*Dir: From A2 at Newcastle take B180, site signed on
right*
★ 🚐 £9-£14.50 🚍 £9-£14.50 Å £9-£14.50
Open all year Booking advisable all year Last arrival
20.00hrs Last departure 15.00hrs
*Popular site with a family field and a large tent area,
set in a beautiful, extensive forest park. There are
plenty of walks to be enjoyed, and the coast is a
short drive away. A 7.5-acre site with 152 touring
pitches, 80 hardstandings.*
Facilities: 🖪 ◉ 🕻 🖳 🖬 🖾
Services: 🖭 → 🕨 🕨 ◉ 🛒 🗡 🗟 Notes: Families only,
no open fires, dogs must be on leads

CO FERMANAGH

IRVINESTOWN

NEW ▶ ▶ ▶ 75% **Castle Archdale Caravan Park & Camping Site**
Lisnarick BT94 1PP ☎ 028 6862 1333 & 6863 2159
Dir: site off B82 (Enniskillen to Kesh road). 10m from Enniskillen
🚐 Å
Open Apr-Oct
On the shores of Lower Loch Erne amidst very scenic countryside, this site is ideal for water sports enthusiasts with its marina and launching facilities. Other amenities available on the site include pony trekking, pedal go-karting, cycle hire and coarse fishing. An 11-acre site with 298 touring pitches.
Facilities: ↑

KESH   Map 01 C5

▶ ▶ ▶ 70% *Lakeland Caravan Park*
Drumrush, Boa Island Rd BT93 1AD
☎ 028 6863 1578
Dir: 2.5m outside Kesh on Boa Island road
🚐 🚐 Å
A busy site focusing on watersports, ideally located on the edge of Lower Lough Erne, and enjoying elevated views and loughside walks. Facilities include marina berths, a sauna, a fully-licensed bar and restaurant, and a private beach and bathing area. A 30-acre site with 50 touring pitches and 140 statics.
Facilities: ↑ ⊙ ⏧ ℓ
Services: 🔲 🔳 ♀ ✕

NEW ▶ ▶ ▶ 79% **Loaneden Caravan Park**
Highgrove, Muckross Bay BT93 1TZ
☎ 028 6863 1603
Dir: From Enniskillin on entering Kesh follow site sign on left over bridge
🚐
Open Feb-Nov
A purpose built caravan park with good facilities and friendly owners. The touring area is part of a much bigger static park. It lies within a few minutes of the marina and beach, and fishing, boating and windsurfing are all available nearby. A 35-acre site with 298 touring pitches.
Facilities: ↑

LISNASKEA   Map 01 C5

▶ ▶ ▶ 81% *Lisnaskea Caravan Park*
BT92 0NZ ☎ 028 6772 1040
Dir: Exit Lisnaskea on B514 to Carrybridge, site signed at fork in road.
🚐 🚐 Å
Open Mar-Nov Booking advisable Jul-Aug Last arrival 21.00hrs Last departure noon
A pretty riverside site set in peaceful countryside, with well-kept facilities and friendly owners. Fishing is available on the river, and this quiet area is an

contd.

ideal location for touring the lakes of Fermanagh. A 6-acre site with 43 touring pitches, 43 hardstandings and 8 statics.
Leisure: ⚠
Facilities: ↑ ⊙ ✳ ⅄ ℓ ↑
Services: 🔲 ℓ ⌀ → ∪ ▶ 🕂 🍴 ✂ 🔲 🐾

CO LONDONDERRY

COLERAINE   Map 01 C6

▶ ▶ ▶ 62% **Tullans Farm Caravan Park**
46 Newmills Rd BT52 2JB ☎ 028 7034 2309
📠 028 7034 2309
🅰 tullansfarm@hotmail.com
🆆 www.tullansfarmcaravanpark.co.uk
Dir: exit A29 (ring road) at rdbt between Lodge Rd rdbt & Ballycastle Rd. Then follow sign for Windyhall
★ 🚐 £13-£15 🚐 £13-£15 Å £8-£12
Open 18 Mar-Sep Booking advisable BH's & wknds
Last arrival 21.30hrs Last departure 13.00hrs
A lovely rural site off the beaten track in quiet farmland, but only one mile away from Coleraine, and handy for the beaches at Portrush and Portstewart. Good clean facilities are maintained by the friendly family owners. A 4-acre site with 35 touring pitches, 35 hardstandings and 20 statics.
Snooker
Leisure: ◀ ⚠ ☐
Facilities: ↑ ⊙ ✳ ⅄ ℓ 🏕 ↑
Services: 🔲 🔳 ℓ ⌀ 🔲 → ∪ 🕂 🍴 ✂ 🐾
Notes: Dogs must be kept on a lead

CO TYRONE

DUNGANNON   Map 01 C5

▶ ▶ ▶ 81% **Dungannon Park**
Moy Rd BT71 6DY ☎ 028 8772 7327
📠 028 8772 9169
🅰 dungannonpark@utvinternet.com
Dir: M1 junct 15, then A29, left at 2nd traffic lights
★ 🚐 £12 🚐 £12 Å £8
Open Mar-Oct Booking advisable all wknds & BH's
Last arrival 20.30hrs Last departure noon
Modern caravan park in a quiet area of a public park with fishing lake and excellent facilities, especially for disabled. A 2-acre site with 20 touring pitches, 12 hardstandings.
Vending machine
Leisure: ◀ ⚠ ☐
Facilities: ↑ ⊙ ⏧ ℓ ⅄ 🔲 🏕 🅿 ↑
Services: 🔲 🔳 → ∪ 🕂 🍴 🍴 ✂ 🔲 🔳 🔲 🌀

Sites that take dogs may not accept all breeds. Check at the time of booking that your dog will be welcome.

Facilities: 🛁 Bath 🔆 Shower ⊙ Electric Shaver ⅄ Hairdryer ✳ Ice Pack Facility ⅂ Disabled Facilities ℓ Public Telephone 🔲 Shop on Site or within 200yds 🔳 Mobile Shop (calls at least 5 days a week) 🏕 BBQ Area 🅿 Picnic Area ↑ Dog Exercise Area

Ireland

REPUBLIC OF IRELAND

CO CLARE

KILRUSH   Map 01 B3

▶ ▶ ▶ 57% *Aylevarroo Caravan and Camping Park*
☎ 065 9051102
🌐 aylevarroo@njogorman.ie
Dir: 1.5m before Kilrush on N67 close to Tarbert car ferry
🏕 🚐 🅰
Open 24 May-13 Sep Booking advisable Last arrival 22.00hrs Last departure noon
A peaceful park in rolling countryside right on the edge of the Shannon Estuary. A 7.5-acre site with 36 touring pitches and 10 statics.
Basketball court.
Leisure: ♒ ♣ ⚲ 🗔 Facilities: ⋔ ⊙ ✳ 🔧
Services: 🔌 🛢 ⟿ ∪ ▶ ◉ ♨ ⊁ ♩ 🔋 🔋 Notes: ⊗

CO CORK

BALLINSPITTLE   Map 01 B2

▶ ▶ ▶ ▶ 74% **Garrettstown House Holiday Park**
☎ 021 4778156 & 4775286 📠 021 4778156
🌐 reception@garrettstownhouse.com
Dir: 6m from Kinsale, through Ballinspittle, past school & football pitch on main road to beach. Beside stone estate entrance
★ 🚐 €16-€19 🚐 €16-€19 🅰 €14.50-€17
Open May-Sep (rs Etr-1 Jun No shop) Last arrival 22.00hrs Last departure noon
Elevated holiday park with tiered camping areas and superb panoramic views. Plenty of on-site amenities, and close to beach and forest park. A 7-acre site with 60 touring pitches and 80 statics.
Childrens club, crazy golf, video shows
Leisure: ♒ ♣ ⚲ 🗔 Facilities: ⋔ ⊙ 🗙 ✳ ⚲ 🔧 🔋 🅃
Services: 🔌 🛢 🥫 ⌀ 🖳 🅃 ✗ 🍴 🚩 ⟿ ∪ ▶ ◉ ♨ ⊁ ♩

BALLYLICKEY   Map 01 B2

▶ ▶ ▶ ▶ 75% **Eagle Point Caravan and Camping Park**
☎ 027 50630
🌐 eaglepointcamping@eircom.net
🌐 www.eaglepointcamping.com
Dir: N71 to Bandon, then R586 to Bantry, then N71 4m to Glengarriff, opp petrol station
🚐 €21-€22 🚐 €21-€22 🅰 €21-€22
Open 21 Apr-Sep Booking advisable Last arrival 22.00hrs Last departure noon
An immaculate park set in an idyllic position overlooking the rugged bays and mountains of West Cork. Boat launching facilities and small pebble beaches, in an Area of Outstanding Natural Beauty. A 20-acre site with 125 touring pitches.
Leisure: ♒ ⚲ 🗔 Facilities: ⋔ ⊙ ✳ 🔧 🔋
Services: 🔌 🚲 🖳 🅃 ⟿ ▶ ♨ ♩ Notes: ⊗ 💳 💳

GARRETTSTOWN HOUSE HOLIDAY PARK ▶ ▶ ▶ ▶

Garrettstown, Kinsale, Co Cork
Tel: 00 353 21 4778156/4775286

Top class spacious park in old world setting of Garrettstown estate near beach and forest. Ideally located for touring, scenic, historic and amenity areas of the south. Kinsale, gourmet centre of Ireland is 6 miles. Cork/Ringaskiddy ferryport 25 miles. Numerous facilities and activities on site or within 16 km.
Recommended by all main camping clubs including BFE 4 star

CO DONEGAL

PORTNOO   Map 01 B5

▶ ▶ 62% **Boyle's Caravan Park**
☎ 074 9545131 & 086 8523131
Dir: Turn off N56 at Ardra onto R261 for 6m. Follow signs for Santaann Drive
🏕 🚐 🅰
Open 18 Mar-Oct Booking advisable Last arrival 23.00hrs Last departure 11.00hrs
Set at Banna Beach and close to a huge selection of water activities on a magnificent stretch of the Atlantic. This open park nestles among the sand dunes, and offers well-maintained facilities. A 1.5-acre site with 20 touring pitches and 10 statics.
Facilities: ⋔ ⊙ ✳ 🔧 🔋 🅃
Services: 🔌 ⚲ 🛢 ⌀ ⟿ ∪ ▶ ♨ ⊁ ♩ 🖳

CO DUBLIN

CLONDALKIN   Map 01 D4

▶ ▶ ▶ ▶ 72% *Camac Valley Tourist Caravan & Camping Park*
Naas Rd ☎ 01 4640644 📠 01 4640643
🌐 info@camacvalley.com
🌐 www.camacvalley.com
Dir: Directly off N7, near Clondalkin, follow signs after Red Cow rdbt on N7
🏕 🚐 🅰
Open all year Booking advisable Jul & Aug Last arrival anytime Last departure noon

contd.

Services: 🅃 Toilet Fluid ✗ Café/ Restaurant 🖳 Fast Food/Takeaway 🚩 Baby Care 🔌 Electric Hook Up
🚲 Motorvan Service Point 🖳 Launderette ⚲ Licensed Bar 🛢 Calor Gaz ⌀ Camping Gaz 🔋 Battery Charging

A pleasant lightly wooded park with good layout, facilities and security, within an hour's drive or bus ride of city centre. A 15-acre site with 163 touring pitches, 113 hardstandings.

Leisure: 🄰 ▫️ Facilities: ⌀⊙🔾⚃⛐🌡️🪣🎋🏄

Services: 🔌🔲⌀🅴→⋃🅿️◎♨️🍴⚓🚰🔳

CO KERRY

CAHERDANIEL   Map 01 A2

▶ ▶ ▶ ▶ 70% *Wave Crest Caravan and Camping Park*

☎ 066 9475188 ▤ 066 9475188

🌐 wavecrest@eircom.net

🅦 www.wavecrestcamping.com

Dir: From Sneem on N70 (Ring of Kerry road), 1m before Caherdaniel on left

🚐🚍🅰

Open 15 Mar-15 Oct (rs 15 Mar-1 May & Sep-15 Oct Shop closed) Last arrival 22.00hrs Last departure noon

Seaside site, with pitches tucked away in the natural contours of the hillside, and offering plenty of privacy. Very good facilities, and an excellent shop. A 5.5-acre site with 120 touring pitches, 65 hardstandings and 2 statics.

Boat anchorage, fishing, pool, foreign exchange

Leisure: ⚓ 🄰 ▫️ Facilities: ⌀⊙🔾✳⚃⛐🌡️🪣🎋🏄

Services: 🔌🔲🅰⌀🅴🅃✕ 🧺→⋃🅿️♦✂🔧

Notes: Dogs must be kept on a lead 🔳

KILLORGLIN   Map 01 A2

▶ ▶ 56% *West's Caravan Park & Static Hire*

Killarney Rd

☎ 066 9761240 ▤ 066 9761833

🌐 enquiries@westcaravans.com

Dir: 1m on Killorglin road from Killorglin town

🚐🚍🅰

Open Apr-Oct Booking advisable Last arrival 21.00hrs Last departure noon

Pretty little site on banks of, but safely fenced off from, River Laune, offering trout and salmon fishing, and good facilities for families. A 3.5-acre site with 10 touring pitches, 3 hardstandings and 50 statics.

Salmon & trout fishing, static caravan hire

Leisure: ⚃ ⚓ 🄰 ▫️ Facilities: ⌀⊙🔾✳⛐🎋

Services: 🔌🔲🅴🧺→⋃🅿️🚰

Notes: Dogs must be on leads and are charged for
🔳 🔳

CO MAYO

CASTLEBAR

NEW ▶ ▶ ▶ ▶ 70% *Lough Lannagh Caravan Park*

Westport Rd☎ 094 9027111 ▤ 094 9027295

🌐 llv@eircom.net

🅦 www.loughlannagh.ie

Dir: N5, N60, N84 to Castlebar, then ring road towards Westport. Signed on all approach roads to Westport rdbt on Castlebar ring road.

🚐 €20-€26 🚍 €20-€26 🅰 €20-€26

Open 10 Jan-14 Dec Booking advisable Etr hols & Jun-
contd.

Camac Valley
Dublin
Tourist Caravan & Camping Park

Dublin's premier tourist Caravan & Camping Park
The only campsite close to Dublin City Centre
(approx. 8km away)
We have 113 hard stand, fully powered (10 amp)
pitches & room for 70+ tents

Our excellent facilities include showers, toilets, laundry rooms, chemical toilet disposal areas, baby changing room, wet weather room/campers' kitchen, library, a fabulous children's playground and a high-speed broadband internet café.

Each fully powered pitch is hard standing with a water tap & an outlet for gray water.

Our reception area has plenty of tourist information available and we sell Camping Gaz, maps of Dublin and Ireland, postcards and postage stamps. Hot and cold drinks, snacks and ice cream are all available from our vending machines.

The campsite has *24 hour security* and entrance & exit to the site is strictly controlled ensuring a safe and pleasant stay for all.

Camac Valley Tourist Caravan & Camping Park
Boot Road, Clondalkin Dublin 22
Tel: +353 1 464 0644 Fax: +353 1 464 0643
email: info@camacvalley.com www.camacvalley.com

Aug Last arrival 20.00hrs Last departure 10.00hrs

This park is part of the Lough Lannagh Village which is situated in a wooded area a short walk form Castlebar town. Leisure facilities include a purpose built fitness and relaxation centre, tennis courts, kids play area and café. A 2.5-acre site with 20 touring pitches.

Leisure: ⚓ → ⋃ 🅿️18 ◎ ♨️♨️ 🔧

Facilities: ⌀🛒⊙✳🏔🎋⚃→🪣

Services: 🔲⚓🔳🔳🔳🔳

Notes: No noise after 22.00hrs, no dogs Jul-Aug (ex guide dogs)

KNOCK   Map 01 B4

▶ ▶ ▶ 70% *Knock Caravan and Camping Park*

Claremorris Rd ☎ 094 9388100 ▤ 094 9388295

🌐 info@knock-shrine.ie

🅦 www.knock-shrine.ie/accommodation

Dir: From rdbt in Knock, through town. Park entrance on left 1km, opposite petrol station

🚐 €18.50-€20.50 🚍 €18.50-€20.50 🅰 €18.50-€20.50

Open Mar-Nov Booking advisable Aug Last arrival 22.00hrs Last departure noon

A pleasant, very well maintained caravan park within the grounds of Knock Shrine, offering spacious terraced pitches and excellent facilities. A 10-acre site with 88 touring pitches, 88 hardstandings and 17 statics.

Leisure: ⚓ 🄰 ▫️

Facilities: ⌀⊙🔾✳⚃⛐🎋🏄

Services: 🔌🛒🔲🅰⌀🅴🅃→⋃🅿️🔧🚰

Notes: Dogs must be kept on leads 🔳

Leisure: 🏊 Indoor swimming pool 🏊 Outdoor swimming pool 🎾 Tennis court ⚓ Games room 🄰 Children's playground ⋃ Stables
🅿️ 9/18 hole golf course ⚓ Boats for hire 🎬 Cinema 🎣 Fishing ◎ Mini golf ♦ Watersports ▫️ Separate TV room

CO ROSCOMMON

BOYLE   Map 01 B4

▶ ▶ ▶ ▶ **70% Lough Key Forest Park**
☎ 071 9662363 & 9662212 🗐 071 9663266
🇪 seamus.duignan@coillte.ie
🇼 www.coillte.ie/tourism_and_recreation
Dir: Follow Lough Key Forest Park signs, site within grounds. Approx 0.5m from entrance. Park 3km E of Boyle on N4
🚐 €14-€16 🚐 €14-€16 🅰 €11-€14
Open 14 Apr-10 Sep Pre-booking essential Booking advisable 3 wks before arrival Last arrival 22.00hrs Last departure noon
Peaceful and very secluded site within the extensive grounds of a beautiful forest park. Lough Key offers boat trips and waterside walks, and there is a viewing tower. A 15-acre site with 72 touring pitches, 52 hardstandings.

Leisure: 🛝 ▢
Facilities: 🇷 ⊙ ᴊ ᴌ ⩚ 🐾
Services: 🖼 🖃 → ▶ ᴧ ⌁ 🍴
Notes: No cars by tents

CO WATERFORD

CLONEA   Map 01 C2

▶ ▶ ▶ **70% Casey's Caravan Park**
☎ 058 41919
Dir: From R675 (Dungarvan road), follow signs to Clonea Bay. Site at end of road
🚐 🚐 🅰

Open May-6 Sep Booking advisable May-Jun Last arrival 22.00hrs Last departure noon
Spacious, well-kept park with excellent toilet facilities, next to beach. A 4.5-acre site with 108 touring pitches and 170 statics.
Crazy golf & games room.

Leisure: 🏊 🛝 ▢
Facilities: 🇷 ⊙ ᴊ ⋇ ᴌ ⩌ ᴌ
Services: 🖼 🗐 🖉 🚿 → ▶ ⌁ 🍴

CO WEXFORD

WEXFORD   Map 01 D3

▶ ▶ ▶ **56% Ferrybank Caravan Park**
Ferrybank☎ 053 44378 & 43274 🗐 053 45947
Dir: Beside bridge, NW of Wexford harbour, off R741
🚐 🚐 🅰
Open Apr-Sep (rs Etr & Sep) Booking advisable Whit wknd & Aug bank hol Last arrival 22.00hrs Last departure 16.00hrs
An open site beside the sea and on the edge of Wexford, with level grassy pitches. A 4.5-acre site with 110 touring pitches.

Leisure: 🏊 🏌 🛝 ▢
Facilities: 🇷 ⊙ ⋇ ᴊ ᴌ 🛒 ⩚
Services: 🖼 🗐 ✕ 🚿 → ∪ ▶ ⊙ ᴧ ⌁ 🍴 🍴

CO WICKLOW

DONARD   Map 01 D3

▶ ▶ ▶ **68% Moat Farm Caravan & Camping Park**
☎ 045 404727 🗐 045 404727
🇪 moatfarm@ireland.com
Dir: 15km S of Blessington on N81, then left at Old Toll House Pub. Follow signs to Donard, park is 4km.
🚐 €18 🚐 €18 🅰 €18
Open 15 Mar-Sep Booking advisable BH's & Jun-Aug Last arrival 21.00hrs Last departure noon
Quiet open parkland on an organic farm in the foothills of the Wicklow Mountains. Plenty of grassy space and a good area with hardstandings for vans. Very attractive facilities. A 2.75-acre site with 40 touring pitches.
Campers' kitchen

Leisure: ▢
Facilities: 🇷 ⊙ 🏌 ⋇ ᴊ ᴌ 🛒 ⩌ ⩚ 🐾
Services: 🖼 🗐 🖉 🚿 → 🍴
Notes: Dogs must be kept on leads at all times

INDEX

Entries are alphabetically arranged by town name, then by campsite name. The following abbreviations have been used: C&C=Caravan & Camping/Caravan & Campsite, HP=Holiday Park, CP=Caravan Park, C&C Club=Camping & Caravanning Club Site

The Automobile Association would like to thank the following for supplying photographs for this book:
Waterside Holiday Park 4; South West Lakes Trust 5, 6;
Oxon Hall Touring Park 14; Glen Nevis Caravan & Camping Park 15;
Pencelli Castle Caravan & Camping Park 15
The following photographs are held in the Automobile Association's own photo library (AA World Travel Library) and were taken by these photographers:
Sue Anderson 13; Adrian Baker 9; Ian Burgum 3r; Steve Day 1, 2, 31, 21; Steve Gregory 17; Caroline Jones 16; Ken Paterson 7

County Maps

The county map shown here will help you identify the counties within each county. You can look up each county in the guide using the county names at the top of each page. To find towns featured in the guide use the atlas and the index.

England

1 Bedfordshire
2 Berkshire
3 Bristol
4 Buckinghamshire
5 Cambridgeshire
6 Greater Manchester
7 Herefordshire
8 Hertfordshire
9 Leicestershire
10 Northamptonshire
11 Nottinghamshire
12 Rutland
13 Staffordshire
14 Warwickshire
15 West Midlands
16 Worcestershire

Scotland

17 City of Glasgow
18 Clackmannanshire
19 East Ayrshire
20 East Dunbartonshire
21 East Renfrewshire
22 Perth & Kinross
23 Renfrewshire
24 South Lanarkshire
25 West Dunbartonshire

Wales

26 Blaenau Gwent
27 Bridgend
28 Caerphilly
29 Denbighshire
30 Flintshire
31 Merthyr Tydfil
32 Monmouthshire
33 Neath Port Talbot
34 Newport
35 Rhondda Cynon Taff
36 Torfaen
37 Vale of Glamorgan
38 Wrexham

Western
Isles

Orkney Islands

Shetland Islands

Highland

Moray

Aberdeen City

Aberdeenshire

SCOTLAND

Angus

Perth &
Kinross

Dundee City

Argyll
& Bute

Stirling

Fife

East
Lothian

Argyll
& Bute

Stirling

18

22

Fife

25

20

Falkirk

Inverclyde

23

17

North
Lanarkshire

West
Lothian

City of
Edinburgh

North
Ayrshire

21

Midlothian

19

South Lanarkshire

Borders
(Scottish)

North
Ayrshire

24

South
Ayrshire

19

Borders
(Scottish)

Dumfries &
Galloway

Northumberland

Tyne & Wear

Isle
of Man

Cumbria

Durham

North
Yorkshire

Isle of
Anglesey

Lancashire

West
Yorkshire

East Riding
of Yorkshire

Merseyside

6

South
Yorkshire

Conwy

30

Cheshire

Derbyshire

Lincolnshire

29

38

11

Gwynedd

ENGLAND

13

Shropshire

9

12

Norfolk

WALES

15

Ceredigion

Powys

16

14

10

5

Suffolk

Pembrokeshire

7

1

Carmarthenshire

Gloucestershire

4

8

Essex

Swansea

3

Oxfordshire

Greater
London

31

26

32

2

Surrey

Kent

33

35

36

Wiltshire

Hampshire

West
Sussex

East
Sussex

27

28

34

Somerset

Cardiff

37

Dorset

Devon

Isle of
Wight

Cornwall

Isles of
Scilly

Guernsey

Jersey

0   20   40   60   80   100 miles

0 20 40 60 80 100 120 140 160 kilometres

KEY TO ATLAS

Shetland Islands

24

Orkney Islands

- ● **Caravan and Camping**
- ○ Town/Village name
- ⊕ Motorway junction
- ⊕ Restricted motorway junction
- ⊕ Vehicle ferry
- ⊕ Vehicle ferry-fast catamaran

22

23

Inverness

Aberdeen

Fort William

Perth

20

Glasgow

Edinburgh

21

Londonderry

Larne

Belfast

Stranraer

Newcastle upon Tyne

Carlisle

Isle of Man

Kendal

24

18

Middlesbrough

19

1

Leeds

York

Kingston upon Hull

17

Galway

Dublin

Holyhead

Liverpool

Manchester

16

Sheffield

Lincoln

Limerick

Rosslare

Cork

Aberystwyth

14

15

Nottingham

Birmingham

10

11

Norwich

12

13

Cambridge

Colchester

8

9

Carmarthen

Gloucester

Oxford

LONDON

Cardiff

Bristol

Guildford

6

7

Barnstaple

4

5

Maidstone

Dover

2

3

Taunton

Southampton

Bournemouth

Brighton

Plymouth

Exeter

Penzance

Isles of Scilly

Channel Islands

24

TM

TR

KENT

STRAIT OF DOVER

• Caravan and Camping
○ Town/Village name

0   10 miles

0   10   20 kilometres

8

CARDIGAN BAY

Legend:
- Caravan and Camping
- Town/Village name

0 ——— 10 miles
0 ——— 10 ——— 20 kilometres

For continuation pages refer to numbered arrows

14

0 1 2 3 4 5 6 7 8 9 0

2

1

0

9 Cemaes
Amlwch
Dulas
ISLE OF
ANGLESEY Rhos Lligwy
Holyhead Llanerchymedd Marian-Glas
Benllech Llandudno Rhos-on-Sea Rhyl
8 Llanfachraeth Brynteg Red Wharf Bay Deganwy Colwyn Bay Towyn
Trearddur Bay A5 Llanbedrgoch Conwy Abergele
Holy Llangefni Llangoed Penmaenmawr Llandulas
Island Pentraeth Beaumaris Llansanffraid Betws-yn-Rhos
Llangefni Menai Llanfairfechan Glan Conwy
Rhosneigr Bangor Llannefydd
7 Llanfair Tal-y-Cafn Llanfair Henl
Aberffraw Llanllechid Talhaiarn Llansannan
Y Felinheli Bethesda Tal-y-Bont Llangernyw Bylchau
Newborough Trefriw
6 Caernarfon Llanrug CONWY
Bontnewydd Llanberis Llanrwst
Llwnda Betws Garmon Capel Curig
Dinas Dinlle Betws-y-Coed
5 Caernarfon Llandwrog Penmachno Pentrefoelas
Bay Pontllyfni Penygroes Rhyd Ddu Dolwyddelan Cerrigydrudion
Clynnog-fawr Y Maer
SH Beddgelert Penmachno
4 Llanaelhaearn Prenteg Blaenau Ffestiniog
Morfa Nefyn PENINSULA Tremadog Maentwrog Ffestiniog Bala
Nefyn Llanystumdwy Porthmadog Rhyd-yr-hyndeudraeth
Bodfuan Criccieth Talsarnau
3 Pwllheli Borth-y-Gest Trawsfynydd G W Y N E D D
Sarn Harlech Llanuwchllyn
Llanbedrog
Aberdaron Y Rhiw Abersoch Llanbedr Ganllwyd Lla
2 Dyffryn Ardudwy Per
Bardsey Tal-y-bont A470 A494
Island
Barmouth Dolgellau Dinas-Mawddwy
1 Fairbourne A470 Mallwyd Llangadfan
Llwyngwril Corris
Cemmaes Road
Bryncrug Llanbrynmair
0 Tywyn Pennal Machynlleth
Carno
Aberdyfi
9 Borth
Town/Village name
Caravan and Camping Tal-y-bont
0 10 miles Llanidloes
SN Aberystwyth Capel Pontarfynach
0 10 20 kilometres CARDIGAN BAY Bangor 9

For continuation pages refer to numbered arrows

20

C EDIN	City of Edinburgh
C GLAS	City of Glasgow
CLACKS	Clackmannanshire
DUND C	Dundee City
E DUNS	East Dunbartonshire
E RENS	East Renfrewshire
INVER	Inverclyde
MDLOTH	Midlothian
N LANS	North Lanarkshire
RENS	Renfrewshire
W DUNS	West Dunbartonshire
W LOTH	West Lothian

For continuation pages refer to numbered arrows

23

• Caravan and Camping
○ Town/Village name

24

(HP)

Hermo Ness
Haroldswick
Unst
Fetlar
Yell
Papa
Stour
Muckle
Roe
Whalsay
SHETLAND
ISLANDS
Sandness
(HU)
MAINLAND
LERWICK
Scalloway
Bressay
West
Burra

Sumburgh
Head
Aberdeen
Kirkwall

**Shetland
Islands**

0   10 miles
0   10   20 kilometres

Orkney
Islands

0   10 miles
0   10   20 kilometres

● Caravan and Camping
○ Town/Village name

Papa
Westray
North
Ronaldsay
Westray
Lerwick
Sanday
Eday
Rousay
Stronsay
Brough Head
MAINLAND
(HY)
ORKNEY
KIRKWALL
Shapinsay
Stromness
ISLANDS
Scapa
Flow
HOY
Burray
Aberdeen
Flotta
St Margaret's Hope
South
Ronaldsay
PENTLAND FIRTH
Dunnet
Head
Island of
Stroma
(ND)
Scrabster
Duncansby Head
Gills John o' Groats
Thurso
A836
A99

Isle of Man

0   5 miles
0   10 kilometres

(NX)
Point
of Ayre
A10
Bride
Jurby
Andreas
Ramsey
Bay
Sulby
Ramsey
Ballaugh
A3
Kirk Michael
ISLE
Maughold
(SC)
OF
Peel
MAN
Laxey
St John's
Dalby
Crosby
Onchan
Foxdale
DOUGLAS
St Marks
Ballasalla
Port Erin
ISLE OF MAN
(RONALDSWAY)
Port
St Mary
Castletown
Heysham
Liverpool
Calf of Man

0   1   2   3 miles
0   1   2   3   4 kilometres

L'Ancresse
Grandes
Rocques
Vale
Weymouth
Poole
(Summer Only)
St Sampson
Herm
L'Erée
Castel
King's
Mills
St Peter Port
St Saviour
St Andrew
Roquaine
Bay
St Peter's
St Martin
Jersey
Portsmouth
Jerbourg

Guernsey

Alderney
Herm
FRANCE
Sark
GUERNSEY
JERSEY

La Grève
de Lecq
St John
Bouley
Bay
L'Etacq
St Mary
Trinity
Rozel
St Ouen
St Peter
St Lawrence
St Martin
St Ouen's
Bay
Beaumont
Millbrook
Five Oaks
Gorey
St Brelade
St Aubin
Grouville
Corbière
St Helier
St Clement
Guernsey, Poole (Summer Only)
Weymouth via Guernsey
Guernsey, Portsmouth

Jersey

0   1   2   3 miles
0   1   2   3   4 kilometres

Readers' Report Form

Please send this form to:
  Caravan & Camping Britain & Ireland
  AA Lifestyle Guides
  14th Floor
  Fanum House
  Basingstoke RG21 4EA

  or fax: 01256 491647
  or e-mail: lifestyleguides@theAA.com

Readers' Report form

Please use this form to recommend any caravan and camping park where you have stayed, whether it is included in the guide or not. You can also help us to improve the guide by completing the short questionnaire on the reverse.

The AA does not undertake to arbitrate between guide readers and campsites, or to obtain compensation or engage in correspondence.

Date:

Your name (block capitals)

Your address (block capitals)

....

....

....

.... e-mail address:

Name of Park:

Comments

....

....

....

....

....

....

....

(please attach a separate sheet if necessary)

PTO

Readers' Report Form

How often do you visit a caravan park or camp site?

Once a year ☐   Twice a year ☐   3 times a year ☐ More than 3 times ☐

How long do you generally stay at a park or site?

One night ☐   Up to a week ☐   1 week ☐   2 weeks ☐   Over 2 weeks ☐

Do you have a: tent ☐   caravan ☐   motorhome ☐

Which of the following in most important when choosing a site?

☐ Location   ☐ Toilet/Washing facilities
☐ Personal Recommendation   ☐ Leisure facilities
☐ Other

Do you prefer self-contained, cubicled washrooms with WC, shower and washhand basin to open-plan separate facilities?

Yes   ☐   No   ☐   Don't Mind ☐

Do you buy any other camping guides? If so, which ones?

....

Have you read the introductory pages and features in this guide? ....

Do you use the location atlas in this guide? ....

Which of the following most influences your choice of park from this guide?

Gazetteer entry information and description ☐

Photograph ☐   Advertisement ☐

Do you have any suggestions to improve the guide?

....

....

....

....

....

Please send this form to:
    Caravan & Camping Britain & Ireland
    AA Lifestyle Guides
    14th Floor
    Fanum House
    Basingstoke RG21 4EA

**Readers'
Report form**

or fax: 01256 491647
or e-mail: lifestyleguides@theAA.com

Please use this form to recommend any caravan and camping park where you have stayed, whether it is included in the guide or not. You can also help us to improve the guide by completing the short questionnaire on the reverse.

The AA does not undertake to arbitrate between guide readers and campsites, or to obtain compensation or engage in correspondence.

Date:

Your name (block capitals)

Your address (block capitals)

....

....

....

.... e-mail address:

Name of Park:

Comments

....

....

....

....

....

....

....

(please attach a separate sheet if necessary)

PTO

Readers' Report Form

How often do you visit a caravan park or camp site?

Once a year ☐   Twice a year ☐   3 times a year ☐ More than 3 times ☐

How long do you generally stay at a park or site?

One night ☐   Up to a week ☐   1 week ☐   2 weeks ☐   Over 2 weeks ☐

Do you have a: tent ☐   caravan ☐   motorhome ☐

Which of the following in most important when choosing a site?

☐ Location   ☐ Toilet/Washing facilities
☐ Personal Recommendation   ☐ Leisure facilities
☐ Other

Do you prefer self-contained, cubicled washrooms with WC, shower and washhand basin to open-plan separate facilities?

Yes   ☐   No   ☐   Don't Mind ☐

Do you buy any other camping guides? If so, which ones?

....

Have you read the introductory pages and features in this guide? ....

Do you use the location atlas in this guide? ....

Which of the following most influences your choice of park from this guide?

Gazetteer entry information and description ☐

Photograph ☐   Advertisement ☐

Do you have any suggestions to improve the guide?

....

....

....

....

....

Please send this form to:
    Caravan & Camping Britain & Ireland
    AA Lifestyle Guides
    14th Floor
    Fanum House
    Basingstoke RG21 4EA

Readers' Report form

or fax: 01256 491647
or e-mail: lifestyleguides@theAA.com

Please use this form to recommend any caravan and camping park where you have stayed, whether it is included in the guide or not. You can also help us to improve the guide by completing the short questionnaire on the reverse.

The AA does not undertake to arbitrate between guide readers and campsites, or to obtain compensation or engage in correspondence.

Date:

Your name (block capitals)

Your address (block capitals)

....

....

....

.... e-mail address:

Name of Park:

Comments

....

....

....

....

....

....

....

(please attach a separate sheet if necessary)

Readers' Report Form

How often do you visit a caravan park or camp site?

Once a year ☐   Twice a year ☐   3 times a year ☐   More than 3 times ☐

How long do you generally stay at a park or site?

One night ☐   Up to a week ☐   1 week ☐   2 weeks ☐   Over 2 weeks ☐

Do you have a: tent ☐   caravan ☐   motorhome ☐

Which of the following in most important when choosing a site?

☐ Location   ☐ Toilet/Washing facilities
☐ Personal Recommendation   ☐ Leisure facilities
☐ Other

Do you prefer self-contained, cubicled washrooms with WC, shower and washhand basin to open-plan separate facilities?

Yes ☐   No ☐   Don't Mind ☐

Do you buy any other camping guides? If so, which ones?

....

Have you read the introductory pages and features in this guide? ....

Do you use the location atlas in this guide? ....

Which of the following most influences your choice of park from this guide?

Gazetteer entry information and description ☐

Photograph ☐   Advertisement ☐

Do you have any suggestions to improve the guide?

....

....

....

....

....

Please send this form to:
Caravan & Camping Britain & Ireland
AA Lifestyle Guides
14th Floor
Fanum House
Basingstoke RG21 4EA

Readers' Report form

or fax: 01256 491647
or e-mail: lifestyleguides@theAA.com

Please use this form to recommend any caravan and camping park where you have stayed, whether it is included in the guide or not. You can also help us to improve the guide by completing the short questionnaire on the reverse.

The AA does not undertake to arbitrate between guide readers and campsites, or to obtain compensation or engage in correspondence.

Date:

Your name (block capitals)

Your address (block capitals)

....

....

....

.... e-mail address:

Name of Park:

Comments

....

....

....

....

....

....

....

(please attach a separate sheet if necessary)

PTO

Readers' Report Form

How often do you visit a caravan park or camp site?

Once a year ☐   Twice a year ☐   3 times a year ☐   More than 3 times ☐

How long do you generally stay at a park or site?

One night ☐   Up to a week ☐   1 week ☐   2 weeks ☐   Over 2 weeks ☐

Do you have a: tent ☐   caravan ☐   motorhome ☐

Which of the following in most important when choosing a site?

☐ Location   ☐ Toilet/Washing facilities
☐ Personal Recommendation   ☐ Leisure facilities
☐ Other

Do you prefer self-contained, cubicled washrooms with WC, shower and washhand basin to open-plan separate facilities?

Yes ☐   No ☐   Don't Mind ☐

Do you buy any other camping guides? If so, which ones?

....

Have you read the introductory pages and features in this guide? ....

Do you use the location atlas in this guide? ....

Which of the following most influences your choice of park from this guide?

Gazetteer entry information and description ☐

Photograph ☐   Advertisement ☐

Do you have any suggestions to improve the guide?

....

....

....

....

....